Rhonda ni Back

Handbook of Research on Nonprofit Economics and Management

Edited by

Bruce A. Seaman

Associate Professor of Economics, Core Faculty member, Nonprofit Studies Program, and Affiliated Faculty member, Fiscal Research Center, Andrew Young School of Policy Studies, Georgia State University, USA

and

Dennis R. Young

Bernard B. and Eugenia A. Ramsey Professor of Private Enterprise and Director, Nonprofit Studies Program, Andrew Young School of Policy Studies, Georgia State University, USA

Edward Elgar
Cheltenham, UK • Northampton, MA, USA

Published by
Edward Elgar Publishing Limited
The Lypiatts
15 Lansdown Road
Cheltenham
Glos GL50 2JA
UK

Edward Elgar Publishing, Inc.
William Pratt House
9 Dewey Court
Northampton
Massachusetts 01060
USA

A catalogue record for this book
is available from the British Library

Library of Congress Control Number: 2009937756

Mixed Sources
Product group from well-managed
forests and other controlled sources
www.fsc.org Cert no. SA-COC-1565
© 1996 Forest Stewardship Council

ISBN 978 1 84720 358 8 (cased)

Printed and bound by MPG Books Group, UK

Contents

Contributors

Salvatore Alaimo, PhD, is Assistant Professor of Public and Nonprofit Administration at Grand Valley State University, Grand Rapids, Michigan and a consultant for nonprofit organizations.

James Alm, PhD, is Professor of Economics in the Andrew Young School of Policy Studies at Georgia State University. His research has focused on various issues in public economics, including tax compliance, the marriage tax, and taxpayer responses to taxes. He has also worked extensively on fiscal and decentralization reforms in numerous countries. Previously, he has served as Chair of the Department of Economics in the Andrew Young School of Policy Studies and as Dean of the School. He is currently editor of *Public Finance Review*.

Woods Bowman, PhD, is Professor of Public Service Management at DePaul University, Chicago. Before joining the DePaul faculty he served as Chief Financial Officer of Cook County and interim Executive Director of Goodwill Industries of Metropolitan Chicago.

Eleanor Brown, PhD, is James Irvine Professor of Economics at Pomona College, California, and editor of the *Nonprofit and Voluntary Sector Quarterly*. Her research interests include resource allocation in the absence of profit-maximizing behavior, through private philanthropy, volunteer labor, government, nonprofit organizations, and within the family.

Cyril F. Chang, PhD, is Suzanne Downs Palmer Professor of Economics at the Fogelman College of Business and Economics, University of Memphis, Tennessee, where he is also the Director of the Methodist Le Bonheur Center for Healthcare Economics.

Joseph J. Cordes, PhD, is Professor of Economics, Public Policy, and Public Administration in the Trachtenberg School of Public Policy and Public Administration at George Washington University, Washington, DC, and an Associate Scholar in the Center on Nonprofits and Philanthropy at the Urban Institute, Washington, DC.

Katherine Coventry is a PhD candidate at the Trachtenberg School of Public Policy and Public Administration at George Washington University.

Lewis Faulk is a PhD candidate in Public Policy at Georgia State University and the Georgia Institute of Technology in Atlanta, Georgia. He is a graduate research assistant in the Nonprofit Studies Program at the Andrew Young School of Policy Studies at Georgia State University.

Martin F. Grace, PhD, is the James S. Kemper Professor of Risk Management and Associate Director and Research Associate of the Center for Risk Management and Insurance Research at Georgia State University. He is a former President of The Risk Theory Society and is a current associate editor of the *Journal of Risk and Insurance*.

Femida Handy, PhD, is Professor of Social Policy and Practice at the University of Pennsylvania. Her research interests include nonprofit entrepreneurship and volunteerism, comparative and international aspects of the nonprofit and voluntary sector, and social accounting.

Patricia Hughes, PhD, is Professor of Economics at St Cloud State University, Minnesota. She is currently Director of the Graduate Program of Public and Nonprofit Institutions at SCSU. Her research interests focus on efficiency, funding, and management of nonprofit and government organizations.

Renée A. Irvin, PhD, is Associate Professor of Planning, Public Policy and Management at the University of Oregon, where she directs the university's Graduate Certificate in Nonprofit Management Program. Her research centers on nonprofit economics and management, philanthropy and wealth policy.

Laura Leete, PhD, is Assistant Professor and Director of the Undergraduate Program for the Department of Planning, Public Policy and Management at the University of Oregon. Her research interests include workforce development policy and labor market institutions; poverty and social policy; nonprofit economics and nonprofit labor markets.

William Luksetich, PhD, is Professor of Economics at St Cloud State University, Minnesota. He has done research in the areas of the economics of nonprofits, cultural economics, efficiency of fundraising activities, the determinants of the number of nonprofits across states, and the economics of crime. His current research involves the measurement of economic freedom and its relation to economic welfare, political and religious determinants of charitable contributions, and the efficiency of sports gaming markets.

Laurie Mook, PhD, is Director of the Social Economy Centre of the University of Toronto. His research focuses on social and environmental accounting, social economy organizations, and volunteerism.

Jan Myslivecek received his PhD in 2009 at CERGE-EI, an economic program in Prague, Czech Republic. His research focused on theoretical aspects of quality assurance methods, mainly certification and self-regulation. He is currently working for The Boston Consulting Group as a Senior Analyst.

Andreas Ortmann, PhD, is Professor of Experimental and Behavioural Economics in the Australian Business School at the University of New South Wales, Sydney. He is also a Research Associate at the Centre for Social Impact at the same school. He is interested in the origin and evolution of languages, moral sentiments, and organizations.

Sharon M. Oster, PhD, is Dean and Frederic D. Wolfe Professor of Management and Entrepreneurship at the Yale School of Management. A specialist in competitive strategy, microeconomic theory, industrial organization, the economics of regulation and antitrust, and nonprofit strategy, she has written extensively on the regulation of business and competitive strategy.

Anne E. Preston, PhD, is Department Chair and Professor of Economics at Haverford College, Philadelphia. Her research interests include labor economics, applied econometrics, macroeconomics, and experimental and behavioral economics.

Michael Rushton, PhD, is Director of Arts Administration Programs in the School of Public and Environmental Affairs at Indiana University, and co-editor of the *Journal of Cultural Economics*.

Daniel W. Sacks, is a PhD student in Applied Economics at the Wharton School of the University of Pennsylvania.

Richard Sansing, PhD, is Professor of Accounting at the Tuck School of Business at Dartmouth in Hanover, New Hampshire. He has published papers in the nonprofit area concerning the unrelated business income tax and the tax rules that affect private foundations.

Bruce A. Seaman, PhD, is Associate Professor of Economics and affiliated research faculty for the Fiscal Research Center and the Nonprofit Studies Program of the Andrew Young School of Policy Studies at Georgia State University and adjunct faculty at the Georgia Institute of Technology. He is the Past-President of the Association for Cultural Economics, International and member of the editorial board of the *Journal of Cultural Economics* and *Estudios de Economia Aplicada*. He is a consultant on local economic development projects, and commercial/antitrust/civil litigation.

David L. Sjoquist, PhD, is Professor of Economics and holder of the Dan E. Sweat Chair in Educational and Community Policy in the Andrew Young School of Policy Studies at Georgia State University. He has published widely on the areas of public finance, particularly state and local public finance, urban economics, and educational policy.

Rayna Stoycheva is a PhD candidate in Public Policy at Georgia State University, with a concentration in Public Budgeting and Finance. Her current research is focused on pension reform in the public sector.

Daniel Tinkelman, PhD, is a CPA with a Doctorate in Accounting from the Stern School of Business at New York University. He currently lives in Brooklyn, New York, and teaches accounting and auditing at Hofstra University.

Stefan Toepler, PhD, is Associate Professor of Nonprofit Studies in the Department of Public & International Affairs at George Mason University, Fairfax County, Virginia.

Howard P. Tuckman, PhD, is former Dean of the Graduate School of Business Administration at Fordham University, New York, and consultant to corporations, attorneys, and public agencies.

Vladislav Valentinov, PhD, is a Research Associate at the Leibniz Institute of Agricultural Development in Central and Eastern Europe in Halle, Germany. His research interests include the institutional economics of the nonprofit sector and the nonprofit sector's role in rural development.

Robert J. Yetman, PhD, is Associate Professor of Management at the University of California, Davis. His research interests include how nonprofit organizations respond to economic incentives caused by taxes, regulation, and disclosure.

Dennis R. Young, PhD, is Bernard B. and Eugenia A. Ramsey Professor of Private Enterprise in the Andrew Young School of Policy Studies at Georgia State University, where he directs the Nonprofit Studies Program.

Foreword
James Alm

A brief story . . .

Over 30 years ago, my first assignment as a graduate research assistant in economics at the University of Wisconsin–Madison was to work with Burton Weisbrod. At the time, Burt was starting his seminal work on the economics of the nonprofit sector, and he had just acquired from the Internal Revenue Service a sample of (he thought) roughly 500 000 'tax returns' for section 501(c)(3) nonprofit organizations. Burt asked me to determine whether it made sense for him to use the existing mainframe computer in the social science building to analyze these returns, or whether he should purchase his own computer to compile the returns and to conduct the statistical work. Remember that this was prior to – but only just – the creation of the personal computer, so the universal consensus from the Wisconsin computer experts was that it was 'insane' for anyone to even consider purchasing their own mainframe computer. As a result, Burt resigned himself to using the existing computing facilities. Of course, within only a few years, the PC came into widespread use.

What this story illustrates and why this story is, I believe, relevant for this collection of original essays is that it shows that there are people who are ahead of the times, even though this may not be accepted or recognized at the time. Burt's belief that studying the nonprofit sector was important – and important to mainstream economics – was not a view that was then widely shared by economists. Eventually, however, his work, and that of others (including many of the people who are contributors to this volume), has led to the creation of a whole new field within economics, one that largely relies upon the standard tools of economists in its analysis and one that forms – in part – the basis of this collection of essays on nonprofit organizations, their behavior and their effects. It is no exaggeration to say that Burt's work and the work of many of the people writing for this volume have led quite quickly to an explosion of research by economists on the nonprofit sector.

Having said this, what should happen now in the study of nonprofit organizations? Most of the existing work – at least most of the work by economists with which I am most familiar – uses only the tools of economists to analyze the behavior of the nonprofit sector: rational decision making, constrained optimization, marginal analysis and the like. One of the central points of this volume of essays is that the purely economic-based approach of economists to the study of nonprofit organizations is too narrow. There are numerous insights from other fields of work, such as the management studies emphasized here, that can help inform the study of nonprofits and can at the same time also help inform the work of economists.

Of course, the other central point of this volume is that non-economists themselves have too often ignored the insights of economics in their own studies of nonprofit organizations. There is much that the understanding of economics can contribute to the understanding of nonprofits more generally.

Indeed – and to come back to my story – I believe that the editors of this volume,

Bruce Seaman and Dennis Young, as well its contributors, are somewhat ahead of their time when they argue for the broadening of nonprofit studies in order to make it a true interdisciplinary effort. In short, the editors and the contributors to this volume are themselves attempting something path-breaking: interdisciplinary cross-fertilization. As Seaman and Young write in their Introduction (p. 1):

> the literatures on management of nonprofit organizations and the economics of nonprofits do not sufficiently intersect and cross-fertilize. The former is an interdisciplinary collection that draws heavily on business management and public administration research, practitioner experience, sociology of organizations and other social science fields, and diverse methodologies including case studies, surveys, grounded theory and statistical testing based on a variety of behavioral theories, hypotheses and models. The latter, in contrast, is more homogeneous and specialized, based largely on a common theoretical framework . . . and focused on issues that can be understood as manifestations of a desire to make the most efficient use of scarce resources . . . Despite the fact that many economists interested in nonprofit organizations have made extra efforts to write for general audiences and to participate in interdisciplinary forums devoted to nonprofit issues, the full benefits of their thinking have not yet been felt in the general nonprofit management research arena. Nor have economists fully benefited from fresh perspectives on nonprofit decision-making issues that emanate from other disciplines as well as experience in practice.

This is an important insight, and this collection of essays makes a significant contribution to the achievement of this goal of linking these largely separate and disparate literatures.

Many varied topics are addressed in this book. Without being fully exhaustive, these include: the pricing of services, competition, labor compensation, outsourcing, product diversification, asset diversification, franchising, internal organizational architecture, risk management, performance assessment, volunteer labor, crowding out, the behavior of charitable foundations, taxation, public policy decisions (e.g. judicial decisions, school vouchers, government regulations). These topics represent natural areas of intersection between economics and management research. However, as these essays argue, the nonprofit management research literature has not fully benefited from the thinking that economists can bring to the table; similarly, economic analysis is also not sufficient to encompass fully the many nuances arising in the nonprofit arena.

As Seaman and Young conclude (p. 4):

> But if there is a 'bottom line' to all of this, it is that economics . . . has been only modestly applied to date to the critical management and policy questions affecting nonprofit organizations, and in turn the contributions this sector makes to the overall welfare of our society. More than anything else, our authors have described a rich agenda of questions and topics that, if addressed by economists at both the applied and theoretical levels, can further enhance the impact and value of the economists' way of thinking, expand the domain of contributions of the economics profession, and add new sophistication and depth to the tools that nonprofit managers and leaders have at their disposal to effectively guide their organizations in an environment of perennially limited resources.

It is hard to argue with this conclusion. I believe strongly that the cross-fertilization that Seaman, Young and others in this volume advocate – and clearly demonstrate in their work – has the potential for significant advances in the understanding of nonprofits.

Indeed, I think that a good case can be made that this volume will help to stimulate the creative thinking that pushes nonprofit studies to move even further into a true interdisciplinary effort. Put differently, I believe that the potential benefits from cross-fertilization extend well beyond the combination of economics and management in this volume. Let me conclude by listing only a few of these new areas for new interdisciplinary work.

One potentially fruitful area for additional cross-fertilization is the application of experimental economics to the study of nonprofits. At first blush, this may seem simply another attempt by economists to exploit a purely economic approach. However, experimental methods have traditionally been used in many areas of social sciences, and even economists are beginning to recognize that these other social sciences have much to offer in explaining why individuals and groups of individuals behave as they do. The laboratory offers the ability to test hypotheses in a controlled setting that is often not available in the naturally occurring world. In the process, the laboratory also generates data that often could not be generated otherwise. Many of the essays in this volume suggest notions that could fruitfully be examined – and only examined – in the laboratory.

Another obvious area is extending nonprofit studies more fully to the international arena. Non-governmental organizations (NGOs) are in many developing countries often the dominant method for providing social services, but the rigorous, interdisciplinary analysis of NGO motivations and performance is quite limited. Again, this may seem like another attempt at economic colonization. However, a full understanding of NGOs requires an explicit recognition of the institutions and cultures in which these organizations operate, which requires in turn full consideration of, say, sociological and anthropological factors that operate in these countries.

Perhaps the most obvious direction for cross-fertilization is to incorporate much more fully the insights of psychology. This area is now loosely referred to as 'behavioral economics', and its growth within economics in even the last five years is staggering. Behavioral economics can be broadly defined as an approach that uses methods and evidence from other social sciences (especially psychology) to inform the analysis of individual and group decision making. There is much evidence – often derived from laboratory experiments – that, contrary to the standard neoclassical approach to consumer choices used in most economic analyses, individuals are not always purely self-interested, they face limits on their ability to compute (e.g. 'bounded rationality'), they systematically misperceive the true cost of actions (e.g. 'fiscal illusion'), they face limits on their 'self-control', and they are affected by the ways in which choices are 'framed' (e.g. reference points, gains versus losses, loss aversion). There is also much evidence that individuals are influenced by the social context in which decisions are made; that is, individuals are not always the outcome-oriented, egoistic and selfish consumers envisioned by standard economic theory but are affected in predictable ways by the processes by which outcomes are determined and also by notions of fairness, altruism, reciprocity, trust and social norms. There is virtually unlimited scope for deeper application of these methods. Many questions of central importance to nonprofit studies are difficult to examine theoretically or empirically, but can be brought into the laboratory for analysis. Indeed, the laboratory may represent the only avenue by which these questions can be tested.

In short, the contributions to this volume – and the other areas not yet fully incorporated here or elsewhere – have the potential to stimulate entirely new directions of research on nonprofits. In this way, the contributors here are following in a distinguished tradition pioneered in nonprofit studies more than 30 years ago by Burton Weisbrod. This is indeed an exciting time to be working on nonprofits.

Acknowledgments

We would like to express our great appreciation to Lewis Faulk and Mary Clark Grinsfelder for their excellent assistance in assembling this volume, keeping us to task, and attending to the details.

Bruce A. Seaman
Dennis R. Young

Abbreviations

AACRAO	American Association of Collegiate Registrars and Admissions Officers
AAM	American Association of Museums
ACES	Association for Children for Enforcement and Support
ACF	Associated Community Fund
AEA	American Economic Association
AMA	American Medical Association
ASOL	American Symphony Orchestra League
ATC	average total cost
ATUS	American Time-Use Survey
BTT	Big 'T' Theater
CAFA	Community Action to Fight Asthma
CEO	chief executive officer
CES	Coalition of Essential Schools
CICA	Canadian Institute of Chartered Accountants
CNCS	Corporation for National and Community Service
COO	chief operating officer
COPPS	Center on Philanthropy's Panel Study
CPS	Current Population Survey
CWLA	Child Welfare League of America
DA	distributable amount (of qualifying charitable distributions)
DEA	data envelopment analysis
EGTRRA	Economic Growth and Tax Relief Reconciliation Act
EMR	electronic medical record
ERM	enterprise risk management
EVAS	expanded value added statement
FAMF	financial asset management firms
FASB	Financial Accounting Standards Board
FTC	Federal Trade Commission
FTE	full-time equivalent
GAAP	generally accepted accounting principles
GDP	gross domestic product
GSUSA	Girl Scouts of the United States of America
HFH	Habitat for Humanity
HFHI	Habitat for Humanity International
IS	Independent Sector
JBFCS	Jewish Board of Family and Children's Services
LBE	land, building and equipment
L–P	Lakdawalla–Philipson model
LVR	Literacy Volunteers of Rochester, Inc.

MAAD	Mothers Against Drunk Driving
MCBS	McGladrey Contract Business Services
MDI	Minnesota Diversified Industries
MFI	Museum Financial Information
MIH	Ministries for International Health
MINIMIZE	a foundation that barely satisfies the minimum distribution requirement
MM	Modigliani and Miller (model)
NCAA	National Collegiate Athletic Association
NCCS	National Center for Charitable Statistics
NCES	National Center for Education Statistics
NEA	National Endowment for the Arts
NGO	non-governmental organization
NTEE	National Taxonomy of Exempt Entities
NVSQ	*Nonprofit and Voluntary Sector Quarterly*
OANO	Ohio Association of Nonprofit Organizations
OLS	ordinary least squares
OMB	Office of Management and Budget
PAC	political action committee
PILOT	payment in lieu of taxes
POS	purchase of service
PPY	Positive Payoffs for Youth
PRI	program-related investments
PSID	Panel Study of Income Dynamics
PUMS	public-use microdata sample
QD	qualifying charitable distributions
REDF	Roberts Enterprise Development Fund
ROA	return on assets
RRG	risk retention group
RSC	Royal Shakespeare Company
SMO	Social Movement Organization
SOI	statistics of income
SPENDER	a foundation that exceeds the minimum distribution requirement by more than 10 percent
SRO	self-regulatory organization
SROI	social return on investment
SUBMIN	a foundation that violates the minimum distribution requirement
TFA	Teach for America
TIMELYMIN	a foundation that barely satisfies the minimum distribution requirement, but does so a year earlier than is required
UBIT	unrelated business income tax
USAS	United Students Against Sweatshops
VHA	Voluntary Hospitals of America
WACC	weighted average cost of capital
WRC	Worker Rights Consortium
XROA	external return on assets

Dedication

We dedicate this volume to the Andrew Young School of Policy Studies, which has nurtured the growth and development of its Nonprofit Studies Program and provided a supportive environment for teaching, research and service and to the community of scholars who study the nonprofit sector. This volume reflects the unique composition of the school, with its Nonprofit Studies Program enriched by the two main departments of the school – Economics and Public Management and Policy.

Introduction: the frontiers of economics and nonprofit management research
Bruce A. Seaman and Dennis R. Young

While closely related, the literatures on management of nonprofit organizations and the economics of nonprofits do not sufficiently intersect and cross-fertilize. The former is an interdisciplinary collection that draws heavily on business management and public administration research, practitioner experience, sociology of organizations and other social science fields, and diverse methodologies including case studies, surveys, grounded theory and statistical testing based on a variety of behavioral theories, hypotheses and models. The latter, in contrast, is more homogeneous and specialized, based largely on a common theoretical framework, postulates of rational decision making and focused on issues that can be understood as manifestations of a desire to make the most efficient use of scarce resources. To a substantial degree, the economics literature is also less generally accessible, requiring understanding of basic concepts such as marginal analysis and opportunity cost, the mathematics of constrained optimization and the subtleties of econometric modeling. Despite the fact that many economists interested in nonprofit organizations have made extra efforts to write for general audiences and to participate in interdisciplinary forums devoted to nonprofit issues, the full benefits of their thinking have not yet been felt in the general nonprofit management research arena. Nor have economists fully benefited from fresh perspectives on nonprofit decision-making issues that emanate from other disciplines as well as experience in practice.

The foregoing is evident with respect to many of the topics addressed in this book. Issues such as the pricing of services, competition, labor compensation, outsourcing, product diversification, asset diversification, franchising, internal organizational architecture, risk management and performance assessment are natural areas of intersection between economics and management research. In each of these areas, our authors demonstrate that general understanding from the nonprofit management research literature has not fully benefited from the thinking that economists can bring to the table. Yet they also find in every case that economic analysis as applied to traditional areas of market activity is not sufficient to encompass the nuances arising in the nonprofit arena. For example, as Seaman points out in Chapter 10, pricing in the business sector rarely embraces strategies intended to advance a social mission at the sacrifice of additional profits, and as Oster explains in Chapter 13, it is the portfolio of loss-making and profitable initiatives intended to advance a social mission in a nonprofit organization that should underlie its product diversification strategy, not simply the seeking of additional profitable opportunities or the enhancing of market power through monopolistic competition. Similarly, Preston and Sacks demonstrate in Chapter 8 that more than marginal labor productivity is involved in determining nonprofit wages, while Cordes and Coventry, in Chapter 17, introduce the notion of 'mission-related benefits and costs' to

1

adapt traditional cost–benefit analysis to the particular venues of nonprofits focused on social missions less comprehensive than society as a whole.

Alaimo in Chapter 12 notes that outsourcing by nonprofits is not a simple (make-or-buy) decision focused on comparing salient transaction, production and purchasing costs of in-house versus external provision, but rather must account for the more nuanced concerns of trust and identity associated with losing control over, and identifying with, the core mission. Young and Faulk in Chapter 15 demonstrate that franchising in the nonprofit sector is not a straightforward matter of implementing a structure that optimizes the control of the central organization as principal over the branches or franchisees as agents, but rather one of determining who are the principals and who are the agents in the first place, and how the intended direction or directions of unilateral or mutual accountability are best imbedded into a federated structure. Finally, both Brown in Chapter 7 and Irvin in Chapter 6 challenge the traditional notions of competition and monopoly in the economics literature by demonstrating how these issues are qualitatively different in the nonprofit arena, in the first instance by having to understand mixed industries and the circumstances under which nonprofits compete with government and for-profit organizations, and in the second instance by understanding where it makes sense for nonprofits to collaborate rather than to compete with one another.

In all of these instances, our authors bring new perspectives to the decision-making arena of nonprofit management by applying economic concepts, tools and ideas, and by summarizing and extending what is known from research to date. At the same time, they are stretching the domain of the economics discipline itself by applying these principles and tools to territory that is less natural to it, though demonstrably quite fertile.

This book also encompasses a set of chapters that address topics peculiarly nonprofit in character, thus not encountered in traditional economics or business research, yet also highly amenable to economic analysis. In some of these areas the authors build on already substantial literatures, while others are more pristine, hence requiring pioneering effort to map the territory and suggest productive avenues of inquiry. The former category includes Tinkelman's review in Chapter 2 of the phenomenon of 'crowding out' (or potentially 'crowding in') between one source of nonprofit revenue and another – e.g. between government funding and charitable donations. While much work has been done on this subject, it is also true that results to date are neither definitive nor comprehensive. In particular, this research has focused on just a few of the possible combinations of income types and has hardly scratched the interactions of earned and charitable income, or other combinations of investment income, in-kind and volunteer contributions, and government funding.

Similarly, substantial work has been done on the vexing issue of assessing the economic value of volunteer labor, but a full consensus on how this should be done continues to be elusive. Leete reviews this issue in Chapter 16, noting that despite the importance of such labor for the nonprofit sector, only a small share of such organizations place a value on that labor. Her insights on how this might be rectified should prove valuable to nonprofit managers, and enlightening to economists who have not been following this debate. Perhaps the most extensive literature applies to the modeling of the economic behavior of nonprofit organizations – or, in economists' terms, identifying the 'objective function' that substitutes for profit maximization in the nonprofit setting. Hughes and Luksetich comprehensively review these issues in Chapter 9, contributing significantly to our understanding of this complex and often contradictory literature where deriving useful guides to nonprofit management in setting strategy and efficiently deploying unpriced resources is especially challenging. Another challenge for management is addressed by Valentinov in Chapter 14, where he probes the increasingly mature but inconsistently helpful transactions cost literature. The organizational economics tradition of comparing the governance mechanisms of market, hybrids and hierarchy has not yet been adequately incorporated into the economic theory of nonprofit organizations. Valentinov advances this long-overdue integration and assesses how nonprofits can best decide to integrate or separate their internal divisions devoted to mission-impacting versus mission-supporting work. This is a critical area for nonprofit management decision making in any substantial (multi-product) nonprofit operation.

Somewhat less guidance is available from previous research on other nonprofit-specific economic issues. These include the issue of income diversification, as discussed by Chang and Tuckman in Chapter 1, i.e. what can be said to guide management on the best balance of funding from charitable, market, government, investment and in-kind sources? Similar questions apply to the behavior of charitable foundations, as considered by Sansing in Chapter 3 and how these institutions should deploy their assets and spend from their corpuses of endowed funds. He also focuses on the particular regulatory requirements applying to private foundations and how these influence the grant-making behavior of these institutions. How indeed nonprofits should account for their unique capital structures and income and expense flows, taking into consideration the social as well as the market value of their assets and programs, is described by Mook and Handy in Chapter 18.

The market value of assets is much on the mind of Bowman in Chapter 5, who addresses the subject of nonprofit asset diversification. Asset diversification is a subject of intense scrutiny in the economics literature applying to for-profits, featuring some common concerns across the sectors such as risk management and productive efficiency. But the issue takes a different twist in the nonprofit arena, where certain assets such as reputation capital and financial endowments are of more prominent concern, and where other assets such as physical plant can have intrinsic social value (such as cultural and historical significance) superseding the marginal contributions they may make to organizational income or profits. In these various areas, economic thinking and analysis contribute much to conceptual understanding, both building on and stretching the for-profit and generic literatures, and pointing the way to productive avenues of future, management-relevant research. A related area where the academic literature has not kept pace in the nonprofit sector with developments in the for-profit sector is capital structure – the critically important mix of debt, capital gains and internally accumulated funds available to an organization to fund capital investment projects, be they tangible buildings or the accumulation of intangible assets linked to philanthropic ventures. Yetman addresses these issues in Chapter 4, including a discussion of how we might overcome the knowledge gap on this issue as applied to the nonprofit sector. And speaking of knowledge gaps, Grace was given the unenviable task in Chapter 11 of suggesting how the well-developed principles of risk management can be applied to nonprofit organizations, where quantifying the tolerance for risk seems especially difficult. He stresses that risk management is a set of proactive approaches that can strengthen and maintain an organization's reputation and opportunities, even in adverse states of the world, and that it is important to think of risk as a matter of overlapping but distinct categories.

Similar observations apply to another cluster of topics that relate more closely to public policy affecting nonprofits than to daily management decision making. The last section of the book is devoted to such topics, where, again, the richness of previous literature varies considerably. Chapter 21 by Sjoquist and Stoycheva addresses the almost untouched landscape of the economic analysis of the impact of property taxes on nonprofit behavior, setting forth a fresh and important new agenda for research. Similarly, Ortmann and Myslivecek in Chapter 19 creatively address certification and self-regulation as two distinct processes of quality assessment, exploring their differences and similarities and the consequences of such differences for the establishment and enforcement of quality standards in the nonprofit sector, and fundamentally, the very trustworthiness of the entire sector.

The economic research literature is somewhat richer in the area of government funding and tax policy towards nonprofits, especially at the federal level. Rushton in Chapter 20 focuses on the tax side, including important analyses of the unrelated business income tax and tax incentives for charitable giving, while Toepler in Chapter 22 concentrates on governmental expenditures, both delineating what we have learned about the impacts of these policies and how they affect the management and behavior of the nonprofit organizations affected by them.

Not all areas of fertile overlap between economics and management could be incorporated into this volume, including the increasingly vibrant research using experimental design methods and behavioral economics challenges to rational choice modeling orthodoxy, a challenge that generally finds great sympathy among the less rigidly defined scholars in the broader management tradition. But if there is a 'bottom line' to all of this, it is that economics, as the science of understanding how resources are deployed and utilized to produce social value, and which has sharp and probing analytical tools at its disposal, has been only modestly applied to date to the critical management and policy questions affecting nonprofit organizations, and in turn the contributions this sector makes to the overall welfare of our society. More than anything else, our authors have described a rich agenda of questions and topics that, if addressed by economists at both the applied and theoretical levels, can further enhance the impact and value of the economists' way of thinking, expand the domain of contributions of the economics profession, and add new sophistication and depth to the tools that nonprofit managers and leaders have at their disposal to effectively guide their organizations in an environment of perennially limited resources.

1 Income diversification
Cyril F. Chang and Howard P. Tuckman

Introduction

Lane et al. (1994) provide evidence that the current tradition of philanthropy is rich and deep, with up to 70 percent of the population of many Western and developed countries making regular contributions. Where are the roots of this tradition?

Robbins (2006), in an impressive historical summary of traditions of philanthropy in the West, traces this tradition back to ancient Jewish life, and Greek philanthropy as a cultural phenomenon that shaped sociology and politics of 'fractious communities, Roman philanthropy as an obligation of civilized people, and the development of Christianity'. These roots 'profoundly influenced the motives of philanthropists, the formation of voluntary associations and the ethos of self-sacrifice' (p. 19). Robbins' provocative analysis concludes that 'many nonprofits survive . . . because of the compulsions toward external or communal service experienced by private donors and . . . that donor motives are usually . . . plural in nature' (p. 28).

Interestingly, diversification of 'revenue' sources took many forms, even in ancient Israel. Ancient gifts involved alms to the poor, shared meals, gleanings from landowners, special tithes for the poor, leavings from untended fields, and donors putting charitable contributions in secret chambers in the Temple, including money and other assets of value. Similar forms of diverse charitable gifts can be found in other early cultures as well. Monetary funds were important, but so too was diversification, which insured that need for charitable funds would not fall on a single revenue source (Robbins, 2006).

In fact, monetary support is, and has always been, vital to the mission and objective of any enterprise, whether for-profit, nonprofit or a governmental agency. In the nonprofit world, contributions of various types can be important sources of support; many nonprofits depend on in-kind contributions, earnings on assets, sales of contributed items, and donated labor to deliver services and carry out their missions. The involvement of volunteers and use of donated non-monetary resources are a time-honored tradition and a common practice among nonprofits. However, most seek consistent, predictable and unearmarked financial support. Not surprisingly, scholars and practitioners continue to pay close attention to how nonprofit activities are financed, and why their revenues change through time (James, 1983; Tuckman, 1993; Weisbrod, 1998; Young, 2006).

In the last 20 years, an impressive body of nonprofit research has emerged that focuses on issues of revenue choice and how to attain an efficient if not optimal mix of nonprofit revenues. Some researchers identify the major sources of nonprofit revenues and develop theories that explain revenue choice by nonprofit decision makers (Grønbjerg, 1993; Young, 2006). Others explore why some nonprofits rely on a single revenue source while others examine why nonprofits derive revenues from a variety of sources (Chang and Tuckman, 1994; Fischer et al., 2007). Yet others have analyzed the risks and rewards of nonprofits' revenue choices (Frumkin and Keating, 2002), and asked whether diversification of revenue sources is associated with financial stability of nonprofits (Tuckman and Chang, 1991; Chang and Tuckman, 1994; Greenlee and Trussel, 2000; Hager, 2001; Hager and Greenlee, 2004).

The purpose of this chapter is to review the progress in the line of research that focuses on sources of nonprofit revenues and revenue diversification and how these elements affect the financial health of nonprofits. Our goal is to summarize what we think we know, where scholars still disagree, and existing gaps in the current state of knowledge. Ultimately we shall point to new directions for future research on the subject.

Sources of nonprofit revenue

The nonprofit sector of the economy comprises a large number and diverse collection of organizations that pursue different missions and rely on many sources for financial support (Boris and Steuerle, 2006). The study of such revenue-related questions as what are the major sources of nonprofit income, why do some nonprofits prefer or at least systematically rely on certain sources of revenues, and whether diversified or concentrated revenues are best for optimal financial performance has provided a rich source of new information and insights on wide-ranging topics related to nonprofit finance. This section summarizes selected recent literature on the sources of nonprofit revenues while the next section focuses on the development of a theory of nonprofit revenue portfolios emerging from the research literature.

Frequently, a new line of research grows out of the availability of new data that allows researchers to reliably identify the sources of nonprofit revenue. For US nonprofits, the federal income tax return, Form 990, filed by tax-exempt charitable organizations with annual receipt of $25 000 or more with the Internal Revenue Services (IRS) is that source. Grønbjerg (1993) conducted a comprehensive analysis of the relationship between community organizations and funding providers in the USA using national Form 990 data. Grønbjerg noted that while government grants may be a source of reasonably predictable funding, the costs of obtaining and maintaining such grants can be high, and many organizations, particularly smaller ones, may prefer not to apply for funds from this source. Tuckman (1993) distinguished two categories of capital funds: internal sources such as interest and dividends from self-owned investments, and earned incomes from program services; and external sources such as donations received from capital campaigns and designated grants and subsidies from philanthropic foundations or government.

By far the most comprehensive review of the major financial sources of nonprofit organizations is the volume edited by Dennis R. Young (2006). It identifies six major sources of income from which most nonprofit organizations draw financial support: charitable giving, government support, fee and commercial income, membership dues, returns on investment, and in-kind volunteer services 'income'.

Charitable giving

According to *Giving USA 2007*, a publication of the Giving USA Foundation, Americans gave $307.65 billion or 2.2 percent of gross domestic product (GDP) in 2008, setting a new record in absolute and relative terms (Center on Philanthropy at Indiana University, 2009). Rooney (2006) and other researchers have noted that charitable giving is a major component of nonprofit finance in many cases such as the American Red Cross and United Way, for which charitable contributions are the dominant mode of financial support.

Charitable giving tends to be local, with donors providing money and other financial gifts disproportionately to local charities that benefit people who live in the same community. Individual giving is also strongly associated with personal income. While individuals at all income levels donate, high-income donors give a disproportionate share of the total gifts. Rooney (2006) observes that many fundraisers now subscribe to the 90–10 rule (i.e. the top 10 percent of the donors give 90 percent of the total gifts in a campaign).

Government support
Nonprofit organizations receive support from the government in a variety of ways. Many nonprofits receive financial support directly from the government through grants and subsidies. Those organized as charitable nonprofits under section 501(c)(3) of the Internal Revenue Code receive support from the federal, state and local governments indirectly through tax exemption from corporate taxes and the privilege of issuing tax-exempt bonds. Governments also support nonprofits directly by allowing individuals and corporations to deduct gifts to qualified nonprofits from income tax liabilities. Government also contracts with qualified nonprofit organizations that have expertise and experience in the delivery of particular goods and services. In recent years, with the increased popularity of outsourcing as a form of service delivery, many nonprofits, especially those in health care and social service sectors of the nonprofit world, have increasingly relied on governments for funding support (Rushton and Brooks, 2006). Even faith-based organizations, with the encouragement of the George W. Bush Administration, have increased their involvement with government by becoming suppliers of social services, increasing their reliance on government as a source of income. Government revenues usually come with specific objectives in mind and nonprofit decision makers must therefore determine whether these fit their mission while, at the same time, keeping a watchful eye on trends in government funding. Failure to do so can lead to destabilizing and unanticipated falls in revenue.

Fee and commercial incomes
Operating income from fee-for-service activities has historically been an important source of financial support for nonprofits in the USA (James and Young, 2006). Museums, local airport and sports authorities, and other nonprofits offer specific services to residents for a fee. Other nonprofits, such as hospitals, nursing homes and day care centers that coexist and sometimes compete with for-profit businesses in the same market, also offer services on a *quid pro quo* basis. Still others, such as the American Association of Retired Persons and the Farm Bureau, rely primarily on membership dues and/or donations for revenue but they also engage in commercial activities and pay unrelated business income tax (UBIT) (Tuckman and Chang, 2006). Unlike those nonprofits that produce 'pure public goods' used by many at the same time (e.g. public service radio and TV), these nonprofits earn commercial incomes and fees from marketable goods and services. That is, they offer private goods 'rival' in consumption and excludable from nonpaying individuals (Chang and Tuckman, 1996).

Membership dues
Individual members of a nonprofit can provide income in three ways: dues, purchases, and donations (Steinberg, 2006). Members of a professional organization such as the

American Economic Association (AEA) or the American Medical Association (AMA) all pay membership dues. Many of them also buy additional services such as educational seminars or vacation trips offered by their associations; and they may also donate PAC (political action committee) money for political lobbying activities to advance the collective interests of their profession. According to Steinberg (2006), information on the amounts of membership dues earned by nonprofits is sketchy and the structure of membership dues is complicated. Much remains to be explored in this fertile area of research.

Returns on investment
Many section 501(c)(3) organizations own endowment funds and use investment income to help to support their missions and charitable activities. Investment incomes consist of interest, dividends and capital gains (Bowman et al., 2006). Although it is not easy to accumulate a large endowment, once accrued, this financial base offers many distinct advantages unavailable to other nonprofits relying on fee-for-service income or donations. One such benefit is the ability to weather economic hard times and the resulting financial uncertainty. Another advantage is that steady investment incomes from endowed assets can reduce staff needs in fundraising and service delivery. However, the accumulation of an extraordinarily large endowment by nonprofit organizations such as elite universities and colleges and the American Red Cross have led researchers and the general public to raise questions about the appropriateness of such a practice and whether the endowment-owning entities are spending enough of the proceeds from investment on charitable activities. For example, Hansmann (1990) questioned whether the accumulation of endowment in universities and colleges is a better use of resources than spending the money on today's students, and Chang and Tuckman (1990) theorize that nonprofit decisions makers are motivated by a desire to accumulate surplus funds and assets without necessarily planning to use them in direct support of mission (Tuckman and Chang, 1992). Bowman et al. (2006) have urged decision makers in nonprofits that have a large endowment to manage their investment portfolios carefully; they also advocate a more active public debate on whether the lure of a large endowment is short-changing the current needs of many nonprofits. It seems clear that more research is needed on how effectively the investment committees of nonprofits manage their investments, particularly those of small and medium-sized nonprofits that rely on the advice of volunteers.

Volunteer services
According to the Bureau of Labor Statistics, 29 percent of Americans 16 years of age or older, or 64 million individuals, volunteered for a formal organization in 2003/4 (Preston, 2006). The Independent Sector (IS) has estimated that volunteers outnumber paid employees by a factor of 6:1 and the hours of work that they provide are equivalent to the total hours of 1.68 million full-time employees. The total market value of volunteer services exceeded $58.9 billion in 2004 (Preston, 2006, p. 183). Volunteer workers, while providing important benefits to organizations that use them, are usually not professionally trained for the work they perform for free. Their use therefore can involve 'hidden costs' associated with lower productivity compared to professionally trained staff. Organizations that use this 'free' resource must understand the factors behind the

supply and demand for volunteer labor and develop strategies to effectively employ this resource in its highest-valued uses (Preston, 2006).

What we know about revenue diversification
The development of a theoretical understanding of the complex issues surrounding the mix of nonprofit revenue and the factors that influence this mix is relatively recent. Early research on nonprofit revenue diversification focused on nonprofits as voluntary entities that served the general public and relied on donations and volunteered labor for support. Weisbrod (1977) regarded nonprofits as providers of 'public goods' that government and the for-profit sector failed to provide while Hansmann (1990) viewed nonprofits as a remedy for 'contract failure' that, if not corrected, results in an insufficient amount of certain goods and services valued by consumers but handicapped by asymmetric information between consumers and producers. Other researchers such as Becker (1976), Andreoni (1989 and 1990) and Kingma (1997) offered an alternative view of individual support for nonprofits, introducing the concepts of 'impure altruism' and the 'warm glow' factor. In their view, individuals derive satisfaction and a 'warm glow' feeling when they help others through funding the work of nonprofits. Here the focus is on giving and volunteering by individuals and the underlying motivations for these altruistic actions and behaviors.

More recently, researchers have broadened their conception of nonprofit revenues and made major contributions to explaining the complex reasons that motivate the quest for revenue and the resulting mix. Weisbrod and his contributors (1998) hypothesize that nonprofit decision makers choose to produce a combination of public and private goods and services, subject to a nondistribution of profit constraint in order to satisfy their own 'utility' or to promote their organization's mission. Alternatively, Galaskiewicz (1990), Bielefeld (1992) and Galaskiewicz and Bielefeld (1998) suggest that nonprofits broaden their income sources for the specific purpose of increasing community 'buy-in' and organizational legitimacy.

Drawing on the utility maximization model of traditional microeconomic theory, Chang and Tuckman (1990) hypothesize that nonprofit managers are motivated by a desire to increase surplus funds specifically to accumulate wealth and equity. They further suggest that many nonprofit decision makers consciously pursue a diverse revenue mix to manage financial risk and reduce vulnerability to financial hard times and uncertainty, over which they have little control (Chang and Tuckman, 1991). Similar views on why nonprofits prefer a diverse mix of income sources have also been expressed by other researchers such as Hager (2001), Greenlee and Trussel (2000 and 2002) and Trussel and Greenlee (2004).

The view that nonprofits prefer a mix of income sources is by no means universally accepted. A number of researchers point out that not all nonprofits pursue diversification and that revenue concentration, as opposed to revenue diversification, may be better for some nonprofits. For example, Grønbjerg (1992) argues that high-performing nonprofits tend to develop a limited number of stable and reliable revenue sources to achieve continuity and efficiency. In her view, continuity of objectives is highly valued and can be achieved by working closely with a few large and reliable funding entities. A side effect of this strategy is that, over time, a symbiotic relationship is likely to evolve between grantor and grantee, with each serving the other's interests.

Frumkin and Keating (2002) argue that concentration of revenue and not a diversified revenue mix may be more beneficial to nonprofits. They support this argument by identifying a number of benefits from a more concentrated revenue base such as lower administrative and fundraising costs and faster revenue growth that can be accomplished when nonprofit staffers concentrate their focus on just a few major revenue sources.

Kearns (2006) offers still another theory on nonprofit revenue mix. Viewing nonprofits as multi-stakeholder/multi-decision-maker organizations with diverse constituents and complex organizational structure, Kearns argues that revenue mix reflects closely the views and preferences of its diverse constituents on one hand and the internal organizational concerns on the other. These concerns include whether an income source is appropriate and consistent with the mission of the organization, whether the source can generate sufficient revenue in the short term as well as in the long term, the risk of not meeting revenue expectations, the likelihood that one income 'crowds outs' another, and the extent to which use of an income source restricts independence or autonomy. Much can be learned about the revenue choices of these organizations by a deeper understanding of the strategic thinking of nonprofit decision makers and their perceptions of the preferences and wishes of the external funders and supporters.

The above discussion clearly suggests that a mix of income offers many benefits but also involves certain risks and says very little about whether certain types of organizations are likely to diversify while others are less likely to do so. Chang and Tuckman (1994) apply a 'revenue concentration index' based on the Herfindahl–Hirschman index used by economists for measuring the degree of market concentration to a large national sample of Form 990 tax returns. They find that the degree to which a nonprofit diversifies its revenue mix is closely associated with its mission. They further argue that 'commercial nonprofits' (those who engage in fee-for-service activities and compete with for-profit suppliers of similar goods and services) are more likely to display a concentrated income mix than 'donative nonprofits' (those that rely mostly on donations and gifts as financial support), and that a diversified revenue portfolio is associated with a healthier financial position as measured by such indicators as asset size, operating margin and growth of net equity (total assets minus total liabilities).

Extending the works of Kearns (2006), Chang and Tuckman (1994) and others who have contributed to the understanding of nonprofit income portfolios and related issues, Fischer et al. (2007) offer both a formal theory of revenue diversification based on the types of goods that nonprofits produce and six testable hypotheses: (1) nonprofits that produce mixed public/private type services are likely to have a more diversified revenue mix; (2) nonprofits that are affiliated with an umbrella organization are more protected from risk and less likely to diversify their revenues; (3) revenue diversification is associated with healthier financial position; (4) older nonprofits are more likely to diversify than younger ones; (5) the degree of revenue diversification is associated with organizational size as measured by the total revenue of the organization; and (6) diversification is associated with the field of service in which a nonprofit operates. Early results from this line of research seem promising.

Strengths and weakness of current research
An extremely important area that needs to be addressed by both researchers and policy makers is improvement of the national data for nonprofit organizations. This includes

but is not limited to the quality of the data currently collected, better access to these data, the current lack of data specificity, needed improvement in data definition, and improved scope of the data. In addition, we consider the need for better restructuring of the database, and the need for better estimation models to predict the survivability of a nonprofit. Each of these items is discussed in turn.

The quality of the current data
We were among the first users of Form 990 data to provide econometric results (Chang and Tuckman, 1990, 1991 and 1994; Tuckman and Chang, 1991 and 1992). As such, we quickly learned their limitations and ways to overcome them. These data were initially collected for an entirely different legal purpose and hence did not include information on many of the uses to which they are now being put, such as evaluating how well nonprofits are managed, measuring efficiency and providing accountability. The 990 forms tended to be filled out quickly, often without instruction, and frequently with errors. The forms were difficult to trace and hard to track from year to year, and many were unaudited. They also lacked many basic items of information necessary to incorporate economic, environmental, political and social factors for research.

Fortunately, beginning in 1999 the nonprofit organization and program classifications (National Taxonomy of Exempt Entities – NTEE) coding system was constructed and merged with the core codes to provide a system that classifies nonprofit entities. It is used by several providers of nonprofit data, such as GuideStar and the Urban Institute/ National Center for Charitable Statistics. This major innovation made it feasible to disaggregate the data by fields of service, giving rise to interesting insights into how mission affects income and expenditure decisions. Together with more careful auditing of individual nonprofits by the National Center for Charitable Statistics, as well as other compilers of nonprofit data, data reliability has improved, aided by the demand and scrutiny of over 100 academic centers, many nonprofit institutions and think-tanks, and the interest of many foundations.

Substantial improvements in computing power have vastly increased the research community's ability to use the Form 990 data to analyze the nonprofit population and to utilize sophisticated analytic tools. Nonetheless, substantial research is needed to iden- tify general weaknesses in the revenue categories, to recognize specific shortfalls in the types of income over- or underreported, to characterize income from multiple complex sources (such as hospitals and universities) and to be aware of limitations in the exist- ing reporting form. Work is now being done on this by the data-gathering agencies but the interest of academic users in refashioning and improving the collection instruments remains somewhat limited.

Access to the data
A key source of data for research remains the Form 990 database, which is not easy for researchers without funding to access. Technically, the providers of these data have the option to offer them at no cost but the preference is that they at least be reimbursed for processing costs. This restricts use of the data to those researchers with funds and it also limits the number of people who might otherwise offer constructive commentary on how best to improve the information. Moreover, it limits how the national databases are used. For example, providers of national data such as GuideStar target their services

primarily to comparative studies within nonprofit mission categories, size groups or geographic entities, limiting their analysis largely to one or two variable comparisons. While this is undoubtedly useful for individual nonprofits that wish to benchmark against other nonprofits, it limits the ability of researchers to conduct large-scale studies of nonprofit data. Questions involving the historical performance of a sector, impacts of changes in policy, accountability and system optimization are difficult to answer given the limited access to the data. The restrictions also limit the ability to construct longitudinal databases and make it harder to work in a multivariate context. They may also encourage individual data collection efforts that result in a proliferation of databases and a limited set of comparative studies on a national basis. This limited access is unfortunate given the concern voiced by the Senate Finance Committee in its 5 April hearings as to transparency and the sharing of information (OMB Watch, 2005).

Greater data specificity
Serious development is needed on the output side to make the data on nonprofits more useful to users. Specifically, estimates are needed on the number of clients served, the types of services provided, consumer and donor satisfaction, and other measures of effectiveness. On the income side, work is needed on defining the existing income categories with more careful reporting of actual program revenues (e.g. separating government and private fees) and of non-conventional incomes such as gains from barters, trades, and income from auctions and from commercial sales. The need for this specificity will grow as more nonprofits become hybrid nonprofits – that is, organizations that have both nonprofit and for-profit components (Tuckman, 2009).

Data reclassification
Over time, there is a need for periodic review of the data systems used to measure nonprofit performance and accountability. Within the nonprofit sector, this means rethinking existing measurements such as appropriate means for valuation of noncash contributions and in-kind gifts. It also means identification of new sources of revenue such as payments from social entrepreneurs, new forms of earned income, and funds earned from auctions, outsourcing and relationship marketing. It is important to both conceptualize these new sources of concern and to provide better guidelines as to how payments should be classified in national studies.

Data scope
The increase in the number of nonprofits with earned income is considerable, as is the amount of such income that these entities are earning. Because Form 990 is an instrument of tax policy and its purpose is to monitor nonprofits in that capacity, it is not a good research tool for capturing linkages between for-profit and nonprofit business. This is because the commercial revenues of nonprofits are reported separately under business tax laws and, consequently, it is very difficult to identify all of the for-profit activities/enterprises of commercial nonprofits, difficult to identify complementary and substitute activities, hard to reconstruct revenue streams from the two sources of revenue, and very difficult to identify multiple sources of compensation (Tuckman, 2009).

Because hybrid nonprofits exist at the border between the for-profit and nonprofit sectors, society has a strong interest in their activities, particularly since over time the two sets of activities are likely to blur. It is important that linked databases be created and made available to researchers and policy makers to allow these activities to be monitored and understood.

Better structuring of the data base

Modern research studies involve both cross-sectional and longitudinal techniques, which can each answer important questions. An important service of researchers at the academic centers is their ability to combine datasets from different years and to utilize modern econometric techniques that can provide answers not attainable a few years ago. This is especially true of mixed time-series, cross-section analyses that provide a dynamic perspective on the questions raised above. If this capability is to be exploited, at least two things need to be improved. First, the IRS must more carefully track entry and exit from the sector and enter Form 990s in their database in a systematic and traceable fashion. It must also spend more time with users of the information to determine what new data are needed to make feasible multi-year studies of the sector.

Better estimation models for predicting survival

A key applied research question is how to advise at-risk nonprofits trying to survive. Some of the studies reviewed (Greenlee and Trussel, 2000; Hager, 2001; Trussel, 2003; Tuckman and Chang, 2006) construct models that enable nonprofit policy makers to plan based on current financial and other information. This is an area where academic research can contribute by creating predictors of success and failure, and it is important that this work continue. The studies conducted thus far are useful in identifying measures of how well a nonprofit is performing, but they require both refinement and further development. More can be done to identify safe strategies for poorly funded nonprofits and to ascertain factors contributing to failure in different nonprofit subsectors. Analyses are particularly weak on the number of nonprofits that exit the sector, what happens to the assets of these entities, the exit strategies of nonprofits, and the predictive models that explain exit.

Agenda for future research

Much can be gained from additional research on the volatility of revenues, how diversification of revenue streams changes through time, and on understanding the financial stability of the sector. In this section, we suggest research on several broad themes that might give rise to interesting findings. We begin with studies of income and income diversification.

Additional research on sources and kinds of income and income diversification

It would be useful to examine the impact that social entrepreneurs have on the choices of revenue streams by nonprofits. At present, the research is fragmentary and it is unclear whether emphasis on social entrepreneurship has stabilized or destabilized the income flows of the nonprofits affected. A need also exists to identify measures of risk for the sector and to use these to evaluate the growth of nonprofit revenue streams, along with their volatility. Such studies would be both cross-sectional and longitudinal, and designed to increase our knowledge of the most stable revenue sources for nonprofits with different types of mission.

A second set of studies would ideally focus on the role of competition as a source of instability in the marketplace. At present, it is difficult to know how the presence of an additional nonprofit affects the revenue of other nonprofits in the area. Though a difficult study to develop because of the question of how to determine geographic boundaries for a market, as well as to identify potential competitors, such a study would open up new vistas for analysis. Third, we note the importance of studies that focus on identifying successful revenue acquisition strategies. While the statistical models discussed above play an important role, it would also be useful to conduct a meta-study of prior research to create alternative models for predicting when mergers and acquisitions are most likely to succeed. Substantial work has been done on this question in the for-profit sector but data availability has slowed studies of nonprofit activity of this type.

Additional research on the effects of the Internet
The Internet has created dramatic changes in our cultural and social institutions, but the nonprofit sector has moved slowly in response (Tuckman et al., 2004). The growth of third parties who accept outsourced dues collection, as well as the direct use of technology to allow nonprofits to collect their own dues, change the dynamics between fundraiser and donor, and the techniques by which membership and voluntary dues are collected. It is useful to study whether and/or how these changes affect access to new revenues, the stability of existing relationships with major income providers, competition from other nonprofits and strategies for income diversification.

A further area for useful study is the extent to which the Internet has spurred world-wide competition for nonprofit revenues and the consequences. Salamon (1994) labels the remarkable growth of NGOs as the global 'association revolution' (pp. 109–22) and Bhagwati (2004) notes that the 'transition from national to global NGOs is a phenomenon with complex causes . . .' (p. 42). Friedman's (2005) flattening of the world raises serious questions for nonprofits that have not effectively recognized that many needs can be addressed by global nonprofit entities. For example, the need for global environmental sustainability can be met in Brazil, China, India or Russia as well as in the USA, and each has its NGO institutions. The question for donors is which of several global nonprofits can do the best job in meeting this need? For some nonprofits, the powerful reach of the Internet may open up new donors and new revenue streams; for others, it may involve growing global competition. However, Bhagwati (2004) provides two caveats: without adequate transparency, nonprofits might 'produce their own counterparts of the occasional corruptions of some multinationals' (p. 44) and 'NGOs, no matter what universalism they profess, are grounded in national political and cultural contexts' (p. 46).

The Internet has certain advantages and disadvantages (Tuckman and Chang, 2006). It is cheaper and faster to use than a strategy that employs individual fundraisers, but the low barriers to entry mean that a nonprofit might find its appeal lost among many other fund seekers. Internet use requires both the donor and recipient to have the knowledge and confidence to use technology and, when either fails, this can lead to errors and lost donations. The Internet eliminates neither the need for personal contact nor the need to persuade, but may require a nonprofit to understand the legal requirements of the different countries in which its donors reside. Nonetheless, the Internet allows a nonprofit to reach many people quickly and inexpensively. It opens communications with new groups, some of whom have previously unrealized common interests. Moreover, a presence on the Internet can bring worldwide awareness of an organization and its mission.

Similarly, the Internet creates unique opportunities for income diversification and presents outsourcing opportunities not previously considered by researchers. Many of these have not previously been contemplated and a careful study of how the Internet is being used for this purpose would be exceedingly useful. Solicitation over the Internet raises issues of trust, transparency as to how dollars are spent, and accountability. It is clear that additional work is needed in this area if e-donating is to begin to gain the stature of e-shopping.

The effect of third-party dispensers of gifts
In a clever attempt to retain investment assets, a number of financial asset management firms (FAMF) have created programs to provide advice to potential donors. Some have fairly large staffs available to help donors decide how to spend their charitable dollars, and most offer financial advice as to how best to invest them. Designed primarily for wealthy investors, these FAMF manage charitable dollars that might otherwise be put in individual or community foundations, usually at a somewhat higher cost. Typically, they enable donors to put a fixed sum into the fund and to allocate it across multiple missions or purposes, making it unnecessary to transfer stocks or other assets each time a donation is made. The effect of these funds is difficult to study because of the absence of publicly available data, but it is likely that they change the dynamics of giving since they introduce into the relationship another advisor usually well versed in the alternative uses of the funds.

Implications of terrorism for revenue diversification
The fight against terrorism has many impacts on nonprofit revenues, liabilities and obligations. The financial impact on non-9/11 charities is well documented – donors shifted their dollars toward charities that met 9/11 needs and away from those that had other missions. The impact was severe. In the period since 2001, some nonprofits have developed specifically to meet security needs, others proposed and funded projects designed to fill homeland security needs, and still others altered existing programs to fit them within a framework that made them attractive to donors with this interest. In a sense, anti-terrorism became a new source of funds.

An unanticipated impact of 9/11 was the pressures from the government to carefully screen donors. Early information indicated that nonprofit funding may have been used to fund terrorism-related activities and this led to stringent government monitoring of nonprofit funding sources. At the same time, the nonprofits were also told that they are responsible for the actions of employers who engage in terrorist activity, even if they are doing so in activities unrelated to their normal job. At present, few studies have been conducted of the financial implications of these and related actions, but it is clear that the costs of raising revenues have increased and the sector remains vulnerable to financial disruptions due to terrorism. Careful study of the issues, as well as of the actual performance of these nonprofits during 9/11, would be helpful in anticipating the effect of future disasters.

Concluding remarks

Nonprofit organizations have grown in importance globally, both in absolute number and in terms of influence and importance. For example, Salamon (1994) suggested that there might be as many as 275 000 NGOs in the UK alone and about 20 000 in poor countries. The number is almost certainly substantially greater today. Their influence has affected decision making on a variety of vital issues, ranging from the pace of globalization to environmental warming, and from care of migrants to monitoring trends in world slavery, healing the sick and providing quality education of many types. While the missions of nonprofit entities differ widely, they share certain needs. These include stable and predictable sources of revenue that provide sufficient program revenues to enable them to carry out their missions. A critical role of academic research is to provide the critique of data, frameworks for analysis and visions for future needs that will enable these entities to reach their goals. This will become increasingly difficult and important as the world continues to flatten.

References

Andreoni, James (1989), 'Giving with impure altruism: applications to charity and Ricardian equivalence', *Journal of Political Economy*, **97**, 1447–58.

Andreoni, James (1990), 'Impure altruism and donations to public goods: a theory of warm-glow giving', *Economic Journal*, **100**, 467–77.

Becker, Gary S. (1976), *Economics Approach to Human Behavior*, Chicago: University of Chicago Press.

Bhagwati, Jagdish (2004), *In Defense of Globalization*, New York: Oxford University Press, Ch. 4.

Bielefeld, W. (1992), 'Funding uncertainty and nonprofit strategies in the 1980s', *Nonprofit Management and Leadership*, **2**, 381–402.

Boris, Elizabeth T. and C. Eugene Steuerle (2006), 'Scope and dimensions of the nonprofit sector', in Walter Powell and Richard Steinberg (eds), *The Nonprofit Sector: A Research Handbook*. New Haven, CT: Yale University Press, pp. 66–88.

Bowman, Woods, Elizabeth Keating and Mark A. Hager (2006), 'Investment income', in Dennis R. Young (ed.), *Financing Nonprofits: Putting Theory into Practice*, Lanham, MD: AltaMira Press, pp. 157–81.

Center on Philanthropy at Indiana University (2009), *Giving USA 2009: The Annual Report on Philanthropy for the Year 2008*, Indianapolis, IN: Giving USA Foundation.

Chang, Cyril F. and Howard P. Tuckman (1990), 'Why do nonprofit managers accumulate surpluses, and how much do they accumulate?', *Nonprofit Management and Leadership*, **1** (2), 117–35.

Chang, Cyril F. and Howard P. Tuckman (1991), 'Financial vulnerability and attrition as measures of nonprofit performance', *Annals of Public and Cooperative Economics*, **62** (4), 655–72.

Chang, Cyril F. and Howard P. Tuckman (1994), 'Revenue diversification among non-profits', *Voluntas: International Journal of Voluntary and Nonprofit Organizations*, **5** (3), 273–90.

Chang, Cyril F. and Howard P. Tuckman (1996), 'The goods produced by nonprofit organizations', *Public Finance Review*, **24** (1), 25–43.

Fischer, Robert B., Amanda L. Wilsker and Dennis R. Young (2007), 'Exploring the revenue mix of nonprofit organizations – does it relate to publicness?' Andrew Young School of Policy Studies Research Paper Series, Georgia State University, No. 07-32.

Friedman, Thomas L. (2005), *The World is Flat*, New York: Farrar, Straus and Giroux.

Frumkin, Peter and E.K. Keating (2002), 'The risks and rewards of nonprofit revenue concentration and diversification', working paper presented at the Association for Research on Nonprofit Organizations and Voluntary Associations (ARNOVA) Annual Conference, Montreal, Canada, November.

Galaskiewicz, J. (1990), 'Corporate–nonprofit linkages in Minneapolis-St.Paul: Findings from a longitudinal study 1980–1988', Research Report, University of Minnesota, Department of Sociology.

Galaskiewicz, J. and W. Bielefeld (1998), *Nonprofit Organizations in an Age of Uncertainity: A Study of Organizational Change*, New York: de Gruyter.

Greenlee, Janet S. and John M. Trussel (2000), 'Predicting the financial vulnerability of charitable organizations', *Nonprofit Management and Leadership*, **11** (2), 199–210.

Greenlee, Janet S. and John M. Trussel (2002), 'A financial rating system for nonprofit organizations', Working Paper.

Grønbjerg, K.A. (1992), 'Nonprofit human service organizations funding strategies and patterns of adaptation', in Yeheskel Hasenfeld (ed.), *Human Services as Complex Organizations*, Newbury Park, CA: Sage, pp. 73–97.

Grønbjerg, K.A. (1993), *Understanding Nonprofit Funding*, San Francisco, CA: Jossey-Bass.

Hager, Mark A. (2001), 'Financial vulnerability among arts organizations: a test of the Tuckman–Chang measures', *Nonprofit and Voluntary Sector Quarterly*, **30** (2), 376–92.

Hager, Mark and Janet Greenlee (2004), 'How important is a nonprofit's bottom line? the use and abuses of financial data', in Peter Frumkin and Jonathan B. Imber (eds), *In Search of the Nonprofit Sector*, New Brunswick, NJ: Transaction Publishers, pp. 85–96.

Hansmann, H.B. (1990), 'Why do universities have endowments?' *Journal of Legal Studies*, **19** (1), 3–42.

James, Estelle (1983), 'How nonprofits grow: a model', *Journal of Policy Analysis and Management*, **2** (3), 350–66.

James, Estelle and Dennis R. Young (2006), 'Fee income and commercial ventures', in Dennis R. Young (ed.), *Financing Nonprofits: Putting Theory into Practice*, Lanham, MD: AltaMira Press, pp. 93–119.

Kearns, Kevin (2006), 'Income portfolio', in Dennis R. Young (ed.), *Financing Nonprofits: Putting Theory into Practice*, Lanham, MD: AltaMira Press, pp. 291–314.

Kingma, Bruce (1997), 'Public good theories of the non-profit sector: Weisbrod revisited', *Voluntas: International Journal of Voluntary and Nonprofit Organizations*, **8** (2), 135–48.

Lane, Jacqueline, Susan Saxon-Harrold and Nathan Weber (eds) (1994), *International Giving and Volunteering*, London Charities Aid Foundation.

OMB Watch (2005), 'Senate Finance Committee discusses nonprofit accountability', available online: http://www.ombwatch.org/article/articleview/2794/1/337.

Preston, Anne E. (2006), 'Volunteer resources', in Dennis R. Young (ed.), *Financing Nonprofits: Putting Theory into Practice*, Lanham, MD: AltaMira Press, pp. 183–204.

Robbins, Kevin C. (2006), 'The nonprofit sector in historical perspective: traditions of philanthropy in the West', in Walter Powell and Richard Steinberg (eds), *The Nonprofit Sector: A Research Handbook*, New Haven, CT: Yale University Press, pp. 13–31.

Rooney, Patrick (2006), 'Individual giving', in Dennis R. Young (ed.), *Financing Nonprofits: Putting Theory into Practice*, Lanham, MD: AltaMira Press, pp. 23–44.

Rushton, Michael and Arthur C. Brooks (2006), 'Government funding of nonprofit organizations', in Dennis R. Young (ed.), *Financing Nonprofits: Putting Theory into Practice*, Lanham, MD: AltaMira Press, pp. 69–91.

Salamon, Lester (1994), 'The rise of the nonprofit sector', *Foreign Affairs*, **73** (4), 109–22.

Steinberg, Richard (2006), 'Membership income', in Dennis R. Young (ed.), *Financing Nonprofits: Putting Theory into Practice*, Lanham, MD: AltaMira Press, pp. 121–55.

Trussel, John M. (2003), 'Revisiting the prediction of financial vulnerability', *Nonprofit Management and Leadership*, **13** (1), 17–31.

Trussel, John M. and Janet Greenlee (2004), 'A financial rating system for non-profit organizations', *Research in Government and Nonprofit Accounting*, **11**, 105–28.

Tuckman, Howard P. (1993), 'How and why nonprofit organizations obtain capital', in D.C. Hammack and D.R. Young (eds), *Nonprofit Organizations in a Market Economy*, San Francisco, CA: Jossey-Bass, pp. 203–32.

Tuckman, Howard P. (2009), 'The strategic and economic value of hybrid nonprofit structures', in Joseph J. Cordes and C. Eugene Steurle (eds), *Nonprofits and Business: A New World of Innovation and Adaption*, Washington, DC: Urban Institute, pp. 129–53.

Tuckman, Howard P. and Cyril F. Chang (1991), 'A methodology for measuring the financial vulnerability of charitable nonprofit organizations', *Nonprofit and Voluntary Sector Quarterly*, **20** (4), 445–60.

Tuckman, Howard P. and Cyril F. Chang (1992), 'Nonprofit equity: a behavioral model and its implications', *Journal of Policy Analysis and Management*, **11** (1), 76–87.

Tuckman, Howard P. and Cyril F. Chang (2006), 'Commercial activity, technological change, and nonprofit mission', in Walter Powell and Richard Steinberg (eds), *The Nonprofit Sector: A Research Handbook*. New Haven, CT: Yale University Press, pp. 629–44.

Tuckman, Howard P., Patrali Chatterjee and David Muha (2004), 'Nonprofit websites: prevalence, usage, and commercial activity', *Journal of Nonprofit and Public Sector Marketing*, **12** (1), 49–68.

Weisbrod, Burton (1977), *The Voluntary Nonprofit Sector*, Lexington, MA: D.C. Heath.

Weisbrod, Burton (ed.) (1998), *To Profit or Not to Profit*, New York: Cambridge University Press.

Young, Dennis R. (2006), *Financing Nonprofits: Putting Theory into Practice*, Lanham, MD: AltaMira Press.

2 Revenue interactions: crowding out, crowding in, or neither?
Daniel Tinkelman

Introduction

Nonprofit organizations in the USA receive money from a variety of sources. According to Chang and Tuckman (1994), in 1986 fewer than 6 percent of all nonprofit organizations had only one revenue source.

According to the National Center for Charitable Statistics (NCCS) (2008) data on nonprofit filings with the IRS, in 2004 US nonprofit organizations reported receiving more than $1.1 trillion in total revenues. Program revenues comprised 71 percent of the total. Donations and government grants accounted for 23 percent, and such other sources of income as rentals and sales of securities accounted for the remaining 6 percent. Private donations are only a part of the 23 percent figure, which also contains government grants. NCCS data for 1998 to 2000 help us understand the relative importance of private donations and government grants; private donations amounted to 8 percent of total revenues, and government grants represented 11 percent (Horne, 2005). Thus the primary support of the nonprofit sector comes from program revenues. The program revenues include substantial government support for the services provided by nonprofit organizations, through such government programs as scholarships to college students and Medicare and Medicaid payments for health care.

The composition of the nonprofit revenue stream varies widely across types of nonprofit organizations. Horne (2005, p. 28) notes that while government grants and contracts only comprised 1 percent of the revenues of the religion sector, they accounted for 53 percent of those of the crime-related nonprofit organizations. Hospitals in his sample derived less than 1 percent of total revenues from donations, while international affairs organizations' donations accounted for 58 percent of their revenues. Organizations too small to report to the IRS are not included in this sample, and their revenue profile may well differ from the reporting organizations.

This chapter deals with the interactions of the several types of nonprofit revenue stream: private contributions; government funding; program income; and other sources of funds, such as investment income. Some aspects of this topic have been much studied, while others have been relatively neglected. Important questions include the following. If the government increases its funding to solve a particular public need, will the increased funding and publicity also increase private funding in that sector, or will government action crowd out private initiative? If the government cuts back support, will private donations rush in to fill a public need? On an organizational level, will a manager's pursuit of government funds, or of program revenues, have favorable or unfavorable effects on donations? Will obtaining a solid donor base impede the ability to compete for public grants? Do the effects vary by type of nonprofit organization?

The issue is complex, and one chapter is not enough to address all the ramifications.

One reason for the complexity is the number of potential revenue sources, which, mathematically, can be received in a variety of permutations. A second reason for complexity is that the issue needs to be considered on at least three different levels:

1. The 'national charitable impulse' level. Here, one needs to compare total national giving with total government spending on public goods, and totals of other non-profit revenue streams.
2. The national demand for a particular public good, such as health care for the elderly. This is the 'cause' or 'sectoral' level.
3. The organizational level. Here, for example, one might consider whether acceptance of government funds for a youth employment program might impact the organization's program revenues from its adult literacy programs. The impact might be direct, due to direct interactions between the revenue sources, or indirect, caused by strategic managerial reactions to changes in one funding source.

For practical purposes, there is interest in not just knowing whether these revenue sources interact, but understanding enough about the interaction to predict responses to particular stimuli. How do various methods of structuring the grants or revenues affect the interaction? For example, government grants could be made in the form of seed money, matching grants, or simple lump-sum unrestricted payments. They could be publicized at the time of grant, or made quietly. Does the form of grant affect the interaction? Are the interaction effects linear with increasing size of the new revenue source? Are the effects symmetric, i.e. equal in increases and decreases?

The issue of the impact of government funding on the nonprofit sector has been much studied, using a variety of tools: pure theory; empirical tests using broad aggregate data, empirical tests using archival organizational level data; empirical tests using survey data on individuals; and experimental tests on laboratory subjects. This is part of a broader literature on the proper economic role of the government. See Carlson and Spencer (1975), for example, for an early summary of the impact of government spending on the private side of the economy. The impact of an increasing reliance on program funding has also received significant scholarly attention.

Conventionally, the government funding issue is often framed as whether government funding 'crowds out' private funding. I follow this terminology, and use 'crowding out' to refer to situations where increases in one source of revenues induce reductions in others. As discussed below, the term 'crowding in' is used to describe situations where increases in one revenue source induce increases in others. At least one author speaks of situations where the government cuts back funding, and private donations rise to fill the gap, as 'reverse crowding out'. Driessen (1985) has argued that the term 'crowding out' assumes that the government action has forced out private action, while a possible scenario is that donors, in the interest of centralization or efficiency, have elected to have the government provide services. The same empirical results could arise from these two different scenarios, which have very different implications for public policy.

What do we know at the level of the overall national giving impulse?
At this level, the question is how total national aggregates of donations, government spending on the types of programs funded by nonprofit organizations, and other

nonprofit revenues interact. Past empirical evidence on the interaction of government spending and donations has been mixed, but I argue that, in general, donations seem to stay around the same level of GDP in the USA regardless of other factors.

Early work by Abrams and Schmitz and others suggested significant crowding out. Abrams and Schmitz (1978) regressed US charitable giving on disposable income, the marginal cost of giving (considering tax factors) and government transfer payments over the period 1948 to 1972. They estimated a crowding-out effect of about 28 cents in the dollar. There are three issues with this work. First, the data are now old. Second, as they noted, there was a negative time trend in their individual giving data, and 'Consequently, any single variable that has risen fairly smoothly over time would be likely to produce a negative coefficient' (ibid., p. 38) Third, it is unclear that government transfer spending is a full measure of the public goods that charities support. Work by Duncan (1999) using data on 1428 households from the 1974 National Study of Philanthropy found that a $1 increase in local government spending would crowd out 24 cents of contributions. Again, the data are now quite old.

Other studies found differing results. Jones (1983) used aggregate UK time-series data from 1961 to 1979. Jones regressed total charitable donations on a tax price variable, national income, and a government expenditure variable. The coefficient is −1.52. Steinberg (1985) notes that, when evaluated at the mean of the independent variables, the implied crowd-out is only 1.5 cents for each dollar of government spending. Steinberg (1985) re-estimated Jones's UK results, making some econometric refinements, and found very small crowd-out, of about six-tenths of a cent for each dollar of government spending.

Garrett and Rhine (2007) find that a failure to control for non-stationarity in the time trends of donations and government funding will lead to spurious results, which is a problem with prior studies. They find there is an association between donations and government funding, but the causality is the reverse of that predicted in the crowding-out literature: they find that decreases in donations cause more government funding.

On an international level, Brooks (2004) quotes Salamon et al. (1999) as follows:

> Salamon et al. (1999) showed that countries with the most generous government social spending per capita also tend to have the highest levels of private giving: In general, rich countries fund charitable activities both publicly and privately more liberally than do poorer countries. The hypothesis simply ignores the confounding influences of income and wealth.

I argue that, in the USA, giving as a percentage of gross domestic product or disposable personal income has been very stable over a half-century while both government domestic spending and nonprofit program revenues have risen. See Table 2.1.

The figures in Table 2.1 indicate that, over 50 years, giving stayed in a band between 1.7 percent and 2.3 percent of GDP. Clearly, government domestic spending increased faster. The 1960s introduced a number of 'Great Society' programs, including Medicare. The federal spending, as a fraction of GDP, almost doubled, rising from 8.7 percent to 16.7 percent. (State and local governments have been ignored for simplicity.) Kerlin and Pollak (2006), using IRS Statistics of Income data, find commercial revenues rose from 48.1 percent of sectoral revenues in 1982 to 57.6 percent in 2002, ignoring hospitals and higher education. The increase did not hold true for all sectors. The authors attribute

Table 2.1   *Historical federal spending and private giving relative to national economic indicators*

Year	Domestic federal spending as % of GDP	Giving as % of GDP	Individual giving as % of disposable personal income
1955	5.4	1.7	2.4
1960	7.0	1.8	2.6
1966	8.7	2.0	2.1
1970	11.6	2.0	2.2
1975	16.0	1.7	2.0
1980	16.3	1.7	2.0
1985	16.7	1.7	1.8
1990	16.6	1.7	1.9
1995	18.2	1.7	1.8
2000*	16.1	2.3	2.4
2005*	16.7	2.3	2.4

Note: * *Giving USA* suggests that the relatively high level of donations in 2000 reflects the high stock prices in the period, and it notes that 2005 giving includes donations in response to an Asian tsunami and to Hurricanes Katrina and Rita in the USA.

Sources: Data for 1966 onwards come from *Giving USA 2007*, which began reporting giving data in 1966. Data for 1955 and 1960 are based on Abrams and Schmitz (1984), who cite *Giving USA 1982*, and federal GDP and DPI statistics.

the increased commercial share of sector revenue to a rise in commercial revenue, not a reduction in the other streams. See also Boris (1998).

These statistics provide an overall reality check on the question of crowding out at the overall national level. Government spending and program service revenues have both increased faster than GDP, while donations have stayed fairly level. This suggests that donations are more or less independent of the other types of revenues, and that government spending and program revenues are complementary.[1] There simply can't be high crowd-out of donations at this overall level. If each dollar of federal spending drove out 25 cents or more of private giving, donations would have been driven to zero as government spending rose from 8.7 percent to 16.7 percent of GDP. Instead, donations have stayed pretty flat.

I argue that the data indicate that people basically are willing to give a certain proportion of their income, and this overall willingness to give drives the stability in the US national giving statistics. Which causes, organizations and programs they give to are questions dealt with below.

National demand for particular public goods

Introduction
This level of discussion deals with a very important public policy question: how best to address important public problems? Should, for example, health care be financed solely by government funding, solely by payments from those receiving services, solely by the

generosity of private individuals, or through some optimal mix of two or three of these sources? In practice, many services in the USA are now provided through a mix of public and private provision. Saidel (1991) describes a number of ways in which state governments, for example, use contracts with nonprofit organizations as a way of accessing personnel and other resources that extend the scope of programs beyond what government budgets alone would allow.

This is a controversial area in the area of political philosophy. Entrenched interests are involved, as are political philosophies. To cite one example, the National Endowment for the Arts is a vehicle used by the federal government to support a variety of arts programs. Its political viability and budget depend in large part on what its perceived impact is on other arts-funding sources. If it were to be discovered that government funding merely displaced private funding, dollar for dollar, then funding the NEA would be pointless from a public policy perspective: no new art is produced. If, on the other hand, each dollar of NEA funding inspires several dollars of new private funding, then the NEA would seem to be a highly effective way of addressing a national objective of increased production of artistic activity.

Clearly, there are some places where government and private provision totally displace private efforts. One sees no charities formed to provide missile defense to the USA, nor any to manufacture paperclips for law firms. The relevant questions here relate to the space in which donations, government funding and such quasi-private provision as the sale of products by nonprofit organizations overlap. Some historical studies have considered times and places when this space changed, and government's role in a particular area became preeminent. Roberts (1984) cites the British experience from the 1600s, following governmental assumption of poor relief, and US experience with charities that fed the poor during and after the Depression in the 1930s. In the 1930s, as government transfers to the poor rose, private donations fell dramatically, and changed their nature. 'Charitable donations underwent a fundamental transformation during the period. They became less concerned with poverty and more concerned with health and social counseling' (ibid., p. 142). Roberts argues that giving to directly support the poor has never recovered to the pre-1930s levels. 'Private transfers to the poor are simply not very large.'[2] Similarly, Gruber and Hungerman (2007) found that church spending on social services fell around 30 percent during the 1930s, which they attribute to crowd-out from the New Deal programs.

This is also a controversial area in the study of human behavior, as it forces us to examine why people give. Can we find economic reasons for altruism, in terms of people's desire for particular public goods to be produced? Is giving instead motivated by such factors as conformity, a desire to show others one's wealth, a 'warm glow' from the act of giving itself, or other factors?

What do we know, at the sectoral or cause level?
The area of the interaction of personal donations with other sources of funding of the provision of a public good has received a great deal of theoretical attention, and there is a rich body of literature in this area. Some of it deals specifically with the impact of tax-funded government service provision on private willingness to give; other literature deals with the related question of 'free-riding' more generally.

I would summarize what we know as follows: the issue is complex; the strength and direction of revenue interactions vary, depending upon a number of identified factors; the interaction effects are likely to be non-linear at certain points; nonprofit organizations react strategically to changes in their funding streams; and both experimental and statistical research tools for measuring the interactions have to be used carefully.

Complexity   We have a well-developed body of theory that can explain a variety of results. We also have a large body of empirical and experimental research that points to the complexity of the issue, and identifies a number of factors affecting the interactions.

As a baseline, I shall discuss a relatively standard economic model for donations in the presence of government funding. Assumptions include:

- Each person consumes a private good, a public good, or some combination.
- Each person acts rationally, for his/her own self-interest, and gets utility only from the amount of the public good produced, and their own private consumption of other goods.
- The public good is undifferentiated, with known quality.
- The amounts of the public good that can be produced are continuous and differentiable, meaning there are no threshold issues or discontinuities.
- The utility the consumer derives from its production does not depend on whether it is funded by the consumer or by others.
- The cost of producing the public good is constant, and is independent of whether it is funded by private donations or government spending.
- All the taxes come from citizenry. Before government provision begins, all citizens have purchased some of the public good. After government provision begins, no citizen is taxed more than their previous purchase of the good.
- Each person knows about the government production and knows the government production of the public good will be funded by a lump-sum tax.
- Each donor knows what other donors will be doing.
- The model does not posit any role for nonprofit organizations. If they are considered at all, they are treated as passive conduits for funding, not as strategic actors.

Early papers using models of this sort predicted that an increased government subsidy financed by taxes would result in dollar-for-dollar crowd-out of donations until donations were zero. See Bergstrom et al. (1986), Warr (1982) and Roberts (1984). The basic idea is that, in some initial condition, the government is producing as much of the public good as the median voter wants. To finance an increase, it taxes people. After the tax, and the government production, people have less disposable income, and if the public good is a 'normal good', there will be a negative income effect on giving. Since marginal utility is assumed to diminish with the increased supply of the public good, there is also a negative substitution effect.

The idea of crowd-out for charities is related to the 'neutrality theorem' in economics associated with the private provision of a pure public good.

The neutrality theorem indicates that any engineered redistribution of income, say through taxes and government provision, among an unchanged set of contributors will not alter the

Nash-equilibrium public good provision. A set of contributors is unchanged when the redistribution policy does not involve a corner solution in which a previous contributor stops contributing or a new contributor begins contributing voluntarily or involuntarily. If a nonprofit firm provides a pure public good and if the government also provides the same good through taxes levied on the contributors, then government provision would crowd out private provision on a pound-for-pound basis. (Khanna et al., 1995, p. 261)

The issue of the impact of other sources of charitable revenue on giving can be modeled using similar tools, and noting that, unlike government provision, they are not tax-financed. In these cases, the theoretical prediction is not as clear. The additional, autonomously financed supply of the public good will increase the consumer's income (presumably generating an increased willingness to give), but will still produce a negative substitution effect. The net impact depends on the relative size of these two effects. The problem can also be modeled using game theory. Under a variety of situations, the rational actor should free-ride on the giving of others.

The complexity of the issue in practice arises because one or more of the above assumptions may not hold. Steinberg (1987, p. 32) summarizes his model by saying:

I show that the sign and magnitude of the donative response to exogenous changes in government spending are each ambiguous, depending on whether donations are normal or inferior, complementary or substitutable for public expenditures, and on whether provision of the public good by others is higher or lower than the donor's unconstrained optimum. It seems most likely that donations will make up for only a portion of governmental cutbacks (denoted partial simple crowd out) although it is possible that donations would rise by more than the cutback or that donations would fall.

Differing strengths, and directions, of interactions   Every economic theory makes simplifying assumptions, and the test of a theory is usually its explanatory power. Table 2.2 is a summary of 134 results from 46 different published or unpublished empirical studies dealing with the interaction of government funding and donations. Studies are grouped by their primary source of data, and listed in date order. The decisions on how many results to list for a particular paper were somewhat subjective. In compiling the table, I treated separate samples as separate results. I also treated results using very different empirical approaches as separate results, unless the authors were simply reporting robustness tests. I also tended to err towards reporting positive crowd-out rather than reporting insignificance. Thus, if a paper used several versions of an OLS (ordinary least squares) model, and only one had significant results, I reported the results as significant.

The bottom line is that the results vary tremendously, but resemble a bell curve centered on crowd-out slightly above zero. I count seven studies with crowd-out coefficients or elasticities[3] more negative than −0.50; 24 where crowd-out coefficients were between −0.10 and −0.50; 78 where the coefficients were either statistically insignificant or around zero (between +0.10 and −0.10); 14 with crowd-in coefficients between +0.10 and 0.50; and eight with coefficients over 0.50. An additional three studies reported a curvilinear pattern, with crowd-in at low levels of government support and crowd-out at high levels. The picture is similar across the types of data used for the studies.

An extensive body of laboratory 'public-goods' experiments exists. Two useful summaries of this literature can be found in Ledyard (1994) and Vesterlund (2006). Vesterlund claims that experimental studies generally tend to show higher crowding out

Table 2.2   Summary of 46 empirical studies of interaction between government funding and donations, by major finding

Crowd-in>50%	Crowd-in between 10% and 50%	Crowd-in or crowd-out <10% or insignificant	Crowd-out between 10% and 50%	Crowd-out>50%
Studies using organizational-level data, such as Form 990 data				
		Posnett and Sandler (1989) [NUS]	Ehrenberg et al. (1993)	
		Callen (1994) [NUS]		
	Khanna et al. (1995) [NUS] 1×	Khanna et al. (1995) [NUS] 3×		
		Payne (1998) OLS 1×		Payne (1998) 2SLS 1×
		Brooks (1999)		
Hughes and Luksetich (1999) 1×	Hughes and Luksetich (1999) 1×	Hughes and Luksetich (1999) 1×	Hughes and Luksetich (1999) 1×	
		Tinkelman (1999) 3×		
	Okten and Weisbrod (2000) 1×	Okten and Weisbrod (2000) 5×	Okten and Weisbrod (2000) 1×	
	Khanna and Sandler (2000) [NUS]			
Payne (2001) 1×			Payne (2001) 1× Ribar and Wilhelm (2002)	
		Marudas and Jacobs (2004) 3× Yetman and Yetman (2003) 2×	Yetman and Yetman (2003) 2×	
			Hungerman (2005)	Dokko (2005)
Horne (2005) 3× Borgonovi (2006) 1×	Horne (2005) 3×	Horne (2005) 19×	Horne (2005) 1×	Horne (2005) 1×
Smith (2007) 1× Heutel (2007)	Smith (2007) 2×	Smith (2007) 3× Gruber and Hungerman (2007) Tinkelman and Mankaney (2007)5× ‡		Smith (2007) 1×

Table 2.2   (continued)

Crowd-in>50%	Crowd-in between 10% and 50%	Crowd-in or crowd-out <10% or insignificant	Crowd-out between 10% and 50%	Crowd-out>50%
Studies using surveys of giving				
		Reece (1979) Jones (1983)[NUS] Steinberg (1985)[NUS]		
	Schiff (1985) 1×	Schiff (1985) 2×		Schiff (1985) 1×
			Kingma and McClelland (1995) Duncan (1999) 2×	
		Simmons and Emanuele (2004) 2×		
Studies using aggregates of individual tax return data				
			Abrams and Schmitz (1978)	
	Pacqué (1982)[NUS] 2× *		Pacqué (1982)[NUS],* 1× Amos (1982) 2×	Amos (1982) 1×
			Abrams and Schmitz (1984)	
		Clotfelter (1985) Lindsey and Steinberg (1990) * 2×		
	Schiff (1990) 1×		Schiff (1990) 1×	
		Gittell and Tebaldi (2006)		
Studies using other sources of data				
		Seaman (1980) (simultaneous equations) Steinberg (1993) 2× Brooks (2000a) 3×	Seaman (1980) (OLS) Kingma (1989) Brooks (2000a) 1×	

Table 2.2   (continued)

Crowd-in>50%	Crowd-in between 10% and 50%	Crowd-in or crowd-out <10% or insignificant	Crowd-out between 10% and 50%	Crowd-out>50%
		Borgonovi and O'Hare (2004)		Ferris and West (2003)
		Manzoor and Straub (2005)	Manzoor & Straub (2005)	
		Garrett and Rhine (2007) 10×	Garrett and Rhine (2007) 2×	

Notes: Studies are listed in date order within each type of data used. Studies are shown in more than one column if they have more than one major regression, as discussed in the text, that falls into more than one category. Studies may also have multiple tests that fall into the same category. The notation 2× means there were two regressions in the sample with effects that fell into the same category.

   Three studies found a curvilinear function, with crowding out at high levels of government funding, but crowding in at low levels. These studies were Brooks (2000b) 2× and Borgonovi (2006) 1×.

2SLS   indicates two-stage least squares. OLS indicates ordinary least squares.
NUS   indicates non-US data.
*   indicates that the study has been listed based upon information in Steinberg (1991, 1993).
‡   Unpublished empirical results related to published paper.

than the empirical studies using archival data referred to above, although there is substantial variation among studies, and the results are sensitive to how issues are framed. Similarly, Ledyard (1994) concludes that it is possible to design experiments in which 90 percent of subjects will act selfishly, but it is also possible to design experiments in which almost all subjects give. Eckel et al. (2005) find that results are highly dependent on how the situation is framed. When individuals are told that some of their money has already been taxed to support a public good, there is complete crowd-out, but when they are simply told of an identical initial allocation of funds (without being told it results from tax), there was essentially no crowd-out.

   Rather than summarize this variety of empirical results by saying that we don't know the answer, I prefer to say that the answer is 'it depends', and we have begun to identify the factors upon which 'it depends'. Our studies illustrate the impact of relaxing assumptions, both in the 'standard' economic model and in our game-theory situations.

   The 'standard' model in the previous section makes a variety of strong assumptions. If these assumptions are relaxed, or changed, then crowd-in at various levels, crowd-out at various levels, or neither, would be predicted.

   Six examples suffice to illustrate the issues.

   First, what if people derive utility from the act of giving itself, in addition to the utility they derive from the amount of the public good that is produced? Several authors have suggested that there is utility in the act of giving, including Arrow (1972), Andreoni (1989 and 1990), and Schiff (1985). Andreoni in particular spoke of the 'warm glow' produced by giving. A number of sociological or psychological factors that would make people desire to give have been suggested, including reciprocity, conformity, signaling high wealth etc. See for example Glazar and Konrad (1996). In this case, public provision of the good would not be a perfect substitute for privately funded provision, and crowd-out will be less than 100 percent. The 'warm glow' concept is cited by various authors as being compatible with the many studies finding crowd-out at less than the 100 percent level.

Second, what if the public good is in fact differentiated, with public financing producing a different good than does private provision? The goods might be complements, substitutes or neither, with very different effects on crowd-out (Schiff, 1985). Rose-Ackerman (1986) speaks of how public support for unsegregated schools could be seen as a substitute for private support of segregated schools, and notes that in other cases managers

> can change their service mix to complement rather than substitute for publicly subsidized programs. The services provided by the members of the Family Service Association of America, for example, have changed markedly in response to government programs. Over a 50-year period, they moved from providing relief to an emphasis on advocating the rights of poor families before government social welfare agencies [reference omitted]. This strategy has apparently permitted them to maintain high levels of private gifts.

Third, what if individuals lack perfect information?

A lack of information about funding sources is certainly plausible; nonprofit organizations only file reports on Form 990 annually, and probably only a small fraction of donors ever refer to them. Horne et al. (2005) indicate that donors often have very limited, or very inaccurate, perceptions of nonprofit funding sources. In their study of 675 donors, donors did a poor job of estimating the amount of government funds received by organizations, and donors' answers to the question of whether an organization had received government funds at all were only slightly better than chance. Clearly, donors who don't know about other funding sources are unlikely to react to them at all, so crowd-out or crowd-in would be zero. Many studies find crowd-out at low levels, or insignificantly different from zero, compatible with this concept.

Donors may lack information about program quality. Rose-Ackerman (1986) and others have also argued that the presence of government funding, or funding by another sophisticated donor that closely examines the organization or the cause before giving, could serve as a quality signal. See also the literature on 'leadership gifts', including Andreoni (2006) and Vesterlund (2003). In such cases, alternative revenue sources would 'crowd in' donations.

One could extend this argument to the case where a potential donor sees organizational size as a quality indicator, and in such cases higher program revenues might serve to draw in donations, or even to attract government funding. Such a quality signal might help to explain the observed 'crowding-in' effects found by Payne (2001) for government research funding at research universities. The National Endowment for Arts has claimed that its screening process helps its grants serve as a quality indicator, causing a multiplier effect on giving although, as discussed above, this finding is disputed. Borgonovi's (2006) finding of crowd-in at low levels of government giving to theater groups is compatible with this quality signaling explanation, as is the finding by Hughes and Lusetich (1999) of crowd-in for federal grants to art museums.

Benzing and Andrews (2004) extend the issue of lack of information to the case where donors don't know for certain whether they will in fact need the services of the charity, for example future disaster relief from the Red Cross. Subjects who were uncertain whether they would be the donor or charity recipient pledged larger contributions and had lower levels of crowding out.

Fourth, what if the public-good cost function is not linear and continuous? Perhaps there is some high threshold of funding needed to, for example, build and stock a museum, and contributions that fail to meet that threshold will have no impact, while those above will have fruitful results. Then public or leadership funding that helps meet the threshold may have a crowding-in effect. See Andreoni (2006) regarding leadership gifts, and List and Lucking-Reiley (2002) for a related field study involving seed money, and a promise to refund contributions if the threshold was not reached. Rose-Ackerman (1986) suggests that perhaps there are economies of scale, and an initial government grant moves the organization along its cost curve, improving marginal productivity of donated funds, and making donating more attractive than under a linear cost curve. There would be reduced crowding out. Perhaps the government funding is in the form of a matching grant (Rose-Ackerman, 1986), which again would make the marginal productivity associated with private donations higher. Or perhaps private provision is cheaper. This would reduce the crowding-out effect. Lee (2006) argues that government giving to nonprofits involves administrative costs at two levels, while donations require only one level of administration, thus making direct donations cheaper in this sense. See also Ferris and West (2003) and Steinberg (1985) and Bergstrom et al. (1986).

Fifth, what if not everyone in the economy originally contributed to the public good? Bergstrom et al. (1986) note that the neutrality theorem would not hold if the government financed the public good in part by taxing non-contributors. Chan et al. (2002) point out that a simple censoring argument would lead to a prediction that crowding out would be partial. As the minimum that each person must pay is moved from zero (in a no-tax world where there is no government financing of the public good) to some fixed minimum tax that exceeds what some people originally paid voluntarily, the total funds provided to finance the public good would have to increase. The censoring argument could serve as an alternate to a 'warm glow' explanation of the incomplete crowding out observed in experimental models.

This argument suggests that the crowding-out impact of government grants varies across sectors of the nonprofit world, dependent upon the fraction of the population that previously supported each sector.

Sixth, the relation between any two revenue sources is unlikely to be a simple linear relation. Seaman (1980) suggested using a set of simultaneous equations to model the simultaneous interactions of private giving, government spending and charitable expenditure. Others have pointed out that the relation could be asymmetric between increases in funding and decreases in funding (see Benzing and Andrews, 2004). Two studies (Brooks, 2000b and Borgonovi, 2006) found evidence that the relation between government funding and contributions was curvilinear – there was crowding in at low levels of government subsidy, and crowding out at higher levels. Brooks (2000b) suggests that, at low levels, the grants may be a quality signal, but once government grants exceed a certain level, donors see the cause as being purely governmental, and stop giving.

A summary of experimental research on public goods provision by Ledyard (1994) noted a variety of factors that impact upon people's likelihood of 'free-riding' in the laboratory setting. In one-shot experiments, subjects usually provided donations mid-way between the free-riding level and the Pareto-efficient level. However, there are many factors that have been posited, or found, to affect the results. His Table 10 lists 19 factors. Group identification increases the contribution rate, as does the amount of the pay-off from provision of the public good, the existence of thresholds, the provision of rebates if the threshold is not achieved, and face-to-face communication among subjects. One of the most significant effects found is that, in repeated experiments, contributions decline with repetition. Ledyard claims that experiments can be designed in which almost all subjects will become selfish Nash-equilibrium players, and that experiments can be designed in which almost all the subjects will contribute to the group interest.

In sum, we know that there are several factors that, if present, can be expected to affect various revenues in various ways.

What don't we know (and why) at the cause or sectoral level?
As the previous section notes, we have a flexible array of theories that can explain why revenues *might* be found to interact in almost any way possible. What we haven't yet done, with a high degree of confidence, is either to measure the interaction now in effect for a particular cause, or to predict future effects from a change in policy. A large number of studies have attempted the measurement task, but the job is far from finished.

The effectiveness of the National Endowment for the Arts is an example of an unresolved issue, with recent and conflicting studies. Borgonovi and O'Hare (2004) looked at the impact of NEA appropriations on donations in the arts sector, and found the two variables were independent. However, they found that the introduction of the NEA 'appears to have caused a decrease in donations'. They posit that this may have resulted simply from publicity regarding government funding. They note that the NEA itself claims crowding in (or leveraging of private donations) through two mechanisms: matching grants and the quality signal entailed by an NEA grant.

In sharp contrast, Dokko (2005) found high levels of crowd-out. She studied 14 824 NEA grant recipients, focusing on the impact of the Republican victory in 1994 congressional elections, which led to a 40 percent cut in the NEA's appropriation. In the subsequent period, private charitable contributions to arts organizations increased by 60 cents for every dollar decrease in government grants. The results are not significantly different from 100 cents lost in the dollar. She notes her results are larger than other studies, cited in Steinberg (1991). 'One possible conjecture is that the relatively large responses to the NEA funding cuts were due to the visibility of the organizations receiving grants as well as the already highly active private sector in FY 1995 that was funding the arts' (Dokko, 2005, p. 21). So, on this one narrow question, crowd-out, crowd-in and independence are all suggested answers, and both empirical studies suggest that a non-linear impact of publicity might be important.

One issue that arises is that of obtaining adequate data granular enough to allow comparison of, for example, giving for a particular public good with spending for that public good. Many studies use broad aggregates of public spending, such as social service spending, which clearly covers many different types of programs, so measurements of the government side of the equation have been imprecise. Efforts to measure giving for a public good have suffered from the same problem. Studies using tax return data on individual itemized charitable deductions can measure only total giving, not giving to a particular cause. Volunteer time is left out of these data, as are bequests and foundation and corporate gifts.

Total organization-level data, such as the databases of IRS Form 990 data maintained by the National Center for Charitable Statistics, are also not granular enough. Such data aggregate programs at the organizational level. In the case cited by Rose-Ackerman, above, the Family Services Association changed from giving direct relief to the poor to doing advocacy for them. This change in type of program function may very well have not shown up in the total program services it reported. The Form 990 data would also aggregate grants from states, localities and the federal government, which is problematic since a variety of studies find differing impacts of each source of funding, and because there are interactions between the different types of government funding. (See Schiff, 1985, 1990; Steinberg, 1987; Hughes and Luksetich, 1999.)[4] Such government programs as tuition grants and Medicare would likely show up in organizational Form 990s as program service revenue, resulting in an underestimate of government subsidies of particular causes.

In reviewing the empirical studies listed in Table 2.2, I noted that most studies using large datasets of Form 990 data have tended to find low or insignificant levels of interaction between government grants and donations. Such studies include those for large organizations in Tinkelman (1999), five out of seven sectors for Okten and Weisbrod (2000), three sectors for Marudas and Jacobs (2004) and 19 out of 27 results for Horne (2005), as well as unpublished results found while writing Tinkelman and Mankaney (2007). It is likely that, with large sets of data, containing not only a variety of types of government funding but a variety of types of program, a variety of effects are partly offsetting each other. If some types of program exhibit crowd-in, and others crowd-out, then it is not surprising that aggregate sector results (containing many programs even for the simplest sector) could be small or insignificant. An exception to this pattern is Smith (2007), who finds substantial crowding-in and crowding-out effects. He uses Form 990 data, but confines his study to very narrowly defined sectors: music, symphony, and opera are three separate sectors in his study.

Only a few studies have been able to obtain information linking particular donors, the causes and organizations they support, and the type of funding they received. Hungerman (2005) investigated the response of church giving to a particular shock – government cutbacks in welfare for immigrants in 1996. He had data on giving per member for a cross-section of churches in one Christian denomination, data on church spending, and data on cross-sectional control variables related to the need for the church programs. He found that each one dollar in reduced welfare spending led to 20 to 38 cents more in church spending. Kingma (1989) looks at individual contributions to 63 public radio stations, using data on individual donors, and, using instrumental variable techniques to deal with endogeneity, estimates a fall in donations of $1350 associated with a $10000 government grant to a typical station. Manzoor and Straub (2005) replicated Kingma's 1989 study on later data, and found the results were not robust. Kingma and McClelland (1995) had data on individual listeners and donors of public radio stations, along with station-specific revenues. They find that an individual listener's giving decreased moderately as government support decreased, but donations from others did not reduce individual giving.

Data are also a problem in experimental studies, due mainly to cost factors. Ledyard (1994) notes that public-goods experiments appear to be quite sensitive to experimental design factors, and that there are many choices of possible designs. He lists 12 different factors that affect results, and notes that there are 2^{12} possible designs to take those factors alone into account. Thus it is difficult to generate enough studies using any one design to amass a truly convincing set of data.

Experimental studies, of course, tend to have a limited number of subjects. Ribar and Wilhelm (2002) argue that the types of altruistic response that are found in laboratory experiments with low numbers of subjects might not extend to large populations. In their models, some types of utility functions could result in people exhibiting partial crowd-out behavior in small groups, but almost zero in large groups.

Over the 25 or more years that empirical studies have been performed, a number of different approaches, from simple OLS to far more sophisticated techniques, have been employed. It appears clear that simple OLS estimation, as used in many studies, produces problematic results. Seaman (1980) compared a simultaneous equations model to OLS models, and found that OLS tended to overestimate the crowd-out effects.

Endogeneity needs to be controlled for, and studies use a variety of approaches. Very few have tried to model simultaneous equations. Some (e.g. Horne, 2005) used lagged variables, while others (e.g. Kingma, 1989; Brooks, 1999; Hungerman, 2005; Gruber and Hungerman, 2007) use instrumental variable techniques.

There is less research on government reaction to charitable giving. Becker and Lindsay (1994) found that private donations to public colleges tended to crowd out government funding at around a dollar-for-dollar level. Using economic aggregate data for a long time series, Garrett and Rhine's (2007) regression results suggest that 'charitable giving causes government funding', and posit that organizations that experience decreases in donations aggressively pursue government grants.

The vast majority of empirical studies posit either a linear or a log-linear relation between some revenue source and donations. Only a few have allowed for the possibility that the sign of the relation changes. Brooks (2000b) included both a term for government subsidies and a term for the subsidies squared, and found a positive coefficient on the subsidies, but a negative one on the squared term. He interprets this as evidence that low levels of subsidies crowd in donations, while high levels crowd them out. Horne (2005) did not find evidence of this curvilinear structure in his tests, but Borgonovi (2006) studied 82 theaters from 1997 to 2001, and reports that a change from crowding in to crowding out came once government support per performance exceeded around $10 500. Borgonovi (2006, p. 447) also found that both the level of subsidy, and the year-to-year change in subsidy, needed to be considered.

> Ignoring the effect of change leads to an underestimation of the intensity of the crowding in effect at low levels and an overestimation of the intensity of the crowding out effect at high levels of public support. Moreover as there is a series of values for which level and change effect have a contrasting impact on private donations, ignoring the change effect results in the identification of crowding out while crowding in is occurring. In such circumstances omitting the effect of change leads to incorrect estimates of both the direction and intensity of the crowding effect.

In recent years, the interaction of program revenues, donations and government spending has also received significant attention. I discuss this below, in connection with organizational level responses to changing funding streams.

What are promising areas of study at the sectoral level?

To me, the key question is in what circumstances a particular social need for services is likely to be funded through private sales to users, through subsidies from the government, or through subsidies from private donations. It seems clear that a tipping point exists, but what needs to be identified is where that tipping point is. For example, based on Horne's (2005) finding that donations are less than 1 percent of hospital revenues, it is clear that hospital care in the USA is only incidentally supported by private donors. My opinion is that we need good empirical studies describing revenue interactions at the level of very specific program levels.

Important public policy choice areas need this information. I have already referred to the issue of the NEA. Aid to the poor is another area with unclear findings. Ferris and West (2003) studied aggregate national data on per capita private contributions to human services and per capita government spending on human services for 1975–94. While they consider a number of different econometric approaches, they tend to find significant crowd-out. Using the mean values of the variables, on one of their models, a 10 percent increase in (very broadly defined) government aid to the poor is predicted to lead to a 5.87 percent decrease in (very broadly defined) private charitable giving for human services. Schiff (1985), focusing on government programs to aid the poor, found that cash transfers to the poor crowded out private giving, but certain other types of government aid were associated with increased giving. We need to better understand the mechanisms that drive such results in order to design efficient funding of our programs.

A second important set of questions has to do with using studies of interaction to better understand donor behavior. Numerous studies have indicated whether the levels of interaction they have found are consistent with the belief that donors give out of 'pure' or 'impure' altruism. One could extend this line of inference by seeing whether observed interactions are compatible with other theories. For example, if government spending provides a quality signal, do interactions differ in across nonprofit sectors based on the difficulty of services to evaluate? Payne's (2001) study indicating crowd-in caused by government support of scientific research at universities is suggestive. See also Diamond (1999). Since it is hard to argue that 'other income' also provides a quality signal, one could look for differences in interaction effects between government support and other income, as a test of the quality-signal hypothesis.

Why is this issue important?

This area of research is very important at two levels: in terms of overall social policy, and for effective nonprofit management.

First, society must decide how best to organize funding of public goods. This requires establishing systems that combine private donations, private purchase of nonprofit services by users of those services, and government subsidies in an optimal fashion. If interactions are misunderstood or ignored, then inefficient funding mechanisms will be selected. Research can help us understand which areas will benefit most from having multiple funding sources, and, to some extent, how those funding sources should function. For example, in theory, matching grants should suffer less from crowd-out than lump-sum grants, but design features within the grants may affect their stringency.

Second, managers need to understand the implications of research in order to best select among funding alternatives, and in order to optimize fundraising campaigns. Research can help managers select new funding sources that will induce crowd-in, or cause minimal crowd-out, of existing revenue sources. The findings of the experimental economics literature on public-goods provision seem very relevant to how fundraising campaigns often function, implying that fundraisers are at least intuitively aware of these relations. For example, communication among subjects tends to reduce free-riding; the use of special events such as dinners is a common fundraising tool, which happens to allow various donors to see each other.

Interactions at the institutional level

Introduction
The focus here is on how changes in one stream of income to a particular organization interact with other income streams. In the previous section, a key question was: if the government increases funding for food aid to the poor, will donations for food aid to the poor fall? Here, a corresponding question might be: if the organization accepts government food aid for the poor, will private donations to the organization, not just for food aid, but for all of its programs, fall? If they do fall, is the cause the effect of the government funding on donors, or on the actions of the organization's managers? How can we tell these two causes apart?

What do we know?
I would summarize the research in this area by saying we have much left to learn, but the evidence is that: nonprofit organizations actively adapt to changing circumstances; the evidence for high levels of direct displacement of donations by other revenue sources is fairly weak; and there is some evidence that there is endogeneity among the various forms of revenue at this level.

The reasons why donors might directly react to new revenue sources by cutting back their donations include the same ones cited in the previous section. Donors might also disapprove of changes in the organization's emphasis required by new government funding, or changes in its image caused by a pursuit of commercial profits.

Crowding out might also result from strategic managerial reactions to an exogenous increase in one type of funding, such as new government grants, or new opportunities to raise commercial revenues. James (1983), Rose-Ackerman (1987), Weisbrod (1998) and Segal and Weisbrod (1998) all consider nonprofit organizations as multi-product organizations, where managers have preferences to engage in certain pure nonprofit activities, but are willing to engage in other, less-preferred activities that generate excess funds that help subsidize the preferred activities. These activities might be performing programs under government grants, pursuing commercial activities, or soliciting contributions with various donor restrictions. Managers are likely to respond to cutbacks in preferred sources of revenues by pursuing less-preferred areas. Managers obtaining windfalls of new resources might cut back on fundraising efforts. Managers are also likely to respond to exogenous increases in demand for their preferred nonprofit services by increasing their efforts to obtain all available sources of funding. See Froelich (1999) for links to resource dependence theory.

Various recent studies are consistent with the predicted managerial reactions to changing funding streams. Andreoni and Payne (2003) find evidence in a panel of arts and social science organizations that charities receiving federal grants do in fact reduce fundraising efforts. Handy and Webb (2003) suggest that one, perhaps unanticipated, result of government funding is that nonprofit organizations tend to save less. 'This effect is strengthened if government officials view unspent donations as indicative of a lack of need' (ibid., p. 261). Government cutbacks spur the opposite reaction. Leroux (2005) finds that nonprofit organizations in her Detroit area sample that adopted entrepreneurial new strategies in the previous five years were more than three times as likely to have suffered government funding cutbacks than non-adopters, and more than twice as likely to have suffered reductions in private donations. Dokko (2005) found that for every $1 decrease in NEA funding in the 1990s, the organizations in her sample increased their fundraising expenditures by 25 cents. In contrast, Connolly (1997) studied funding of academic research, and found that increases in external funding of research did not crowd out internal funding. Ehrenberg et al. (1993) study data on support for science and engineering doctoral students from 1979 to 1984 for 200 doctorate-producing universities. In their baseline regressions, they find that federal support for 100 students crowds out institutional support for 18. In general, the effect is the same, whether federal support is increasing or decreasing. However, the long-term effect is smaller than the immediate effect, and there was variation by type of program and by degree granted.

Why do I say there is weak evidence for high levels of direct displacement? Table 2.2, discussed in the previous section, contains 22 studies (with 78 equations) that used organizational-level data on government funding. By far the most common finding (47 times) was of near-zero crowd-out (or crowd-in) of donations by government funds, with some studies showing varying levels of crowd-out, and some showing varying levels of crowd-in, and one showing a curvilinear relation. The evidence on displacement of donations by program service revenues is discussed below.

The most comprehensive of these studies is Horne's (2005) dissertation, which tested a government crowding-out model on 26 different sectors, using NCCS data on over 87 000 organizations from 1998 to 2000. He did not find support for the curvilinear pattern suggested by Brooks (2000b). Seventeen of his sectors showed near-zero, or statistically insignificant, interactions, and only two moderate or large crowding-out effects.

However, this evidence should be treated with caution for two reasons. As noted above, large-scale studies may include organizations with offsetting effects. This may obscure real effects. They may also group into one category various funding sources with different characteristics. Another reason for caution is that the econometric approaches of these studies varied, and often did not consider endogeneity of the various revenue streams. Steinberg (1987) has noted interrelationships among state and federal grants, and the econometric problems that can results from ignoring this issue. Gruber and Hungerman (2007, p. 1047) note:

> At the level of the individual non-profit, it is natural to think that government transfers and private contributions are jointly determined. Charities which are particularly successful at fund-raising may be able to garner more funds from both sources; this may bias downwards estimates of crowd-out . . . The contradiction between the large crowd-out predictions of theory and the lack of crowd-out evidence in the empirical literature may be due to identification problems with this literature.

Two studies used simultaneous equations methods to deal with the endogeneity.

Seaman (1980) studies data for arts organizations and museums aggregated for 47 SMSAs. He argues that one must simultaneously estimate donations, government subsidies and charitable expenditures. He argues that one-way OLS estimates are inaccurate. He finds moderately small crowding out of donations by government subsidies, but larger crowd-out of public subsidies by donations.

Hughes and Luksetich (1999) is a study that addressed both issues, and found some significant and complex interaction effects. They obtained data on art and history museums, and used a simultaneous equations model to estimate the interrelations of federal funding, state funding, local funding, private donations and earned income. Note that the three government funding sources are not separated in Form 990 data, upon which a number of the studies in Table 2.2 rely. Their results suggest that the impacts of the three types of government funding are in fact different. Federal support stimulates private giving up to a point, beyond which there is crowding out. On average, each dollar of federal support stimulated $10.88 of private support. In contrast, funding from state sources reduced private giving. Earned income was positively related to private and local support and investment income. They found no evidence that earned income substituted for public funding. Local government funding had a large negative impact on state support. For history museums, they find that government support is greater for those museums that make greater efforts to raise private support.

Becker and Lindsay (1994, p. 278) looked for free-riding by the government on private donations. 'Our empirical findings support the proposition that donations to public colleges and universities result in dollar-for-dollar reductions in government spending on these schools. Crowding-out of government support for private schools appears to be negligible.' More studies in this area are needed.

The empirical studies so far, using large samples of organizational-level data to test program revenue or 'other income', have obtained mixed results. Schiff and Weisbrod (1991) used Tobit regressions on IRS Form 990 data for over 11 000 social service organizations from 1973 to 1976. They found that increases in donations were associated with decreased sales. They also found a negative relation between state spending and commercial revenue. These two results would argue in favor of managers reducing their use of commercial activities when other preferred revenue sources were available. However, other studies using overall program service revenue, which show either statistically insignificant or fairly small crowding out of donations by commercial activities with donations include: Khanna et al. (1995); Tinkelman (1999); Okten and Weisbrod (2000); and Marudas and Jacobs (2004). Segal and Weisbrod (1998) report mixed findings: certain regressions find the expected negative relation between lagged donations and commercial revenues, while others, using the log form of the variables, do not.

One possible reason for these mixed results is that donors may react differently to program service revenues (such as museum admissions) that are directly related to the organization's mission and to ancillary activities that are seen as unseemly diversions from the organization's mission. Studies using overall program service revenue data unavoidably mix these two categories of activities. Studies that look closely at particular types of commercial activity are more likely to find crowd-out. Kingma (1995) found crowding out of up to 90 cents of donations for each dollar of such ancillary activities as swimming lessons in his study of American Red Cross chapters. Toepler and Morgan

(2002) find that gross revenues from museum commercial activities partially crowd out private donations and public subsidies. They studied 15 large museums over 11 years. Owalla (2007) finds very high crowd-out in his study of international aid organizations based in the USA. Yetman and Yetman (2003) had access to a large database of tax return data, including data on unrelated taxable income not usually available in public databases, and were able to separate out taxable revenues from other program revenues. The taxable revenues were likely to be ancillary to the organizational mission. They found significant crowd-out of donations of around 59 cents for each dollar of commercial revenue.

What we don't know, and areas for future research
As discussed above, it's not clear if the lack of widespread crowd-out found in various empirical studies is real, or a result of tests that are not well designed. Experimental studies are unlikely to help us here. Experiments typically deal with a simple world that does not have an organizational structure, and are more helpful at the overall cause level. In the studies that did find effects, we need to understand them better; what is it, for example, that makes donations respond differently to federal than state spending? The authors of the papers cited offer tentative suggestions, but more work in this area is needed.

We need more studies on specific industries, to confirm the types of effects found in Seaman (1980) and Hughes and Luksetich (1999), and to indicate variations in these effects across sectors. One interesting new data source has recently become available. Jalandoni et al. (2005) describe the information contained in the Federal Audit Clearinghouse database. It allows tracking federal grants, including those given to states and localities for re-awarding, by the institutions receiving them. Potentially, this would allow researchers to combine information about particular federal grants with Form 990 data on contributions and commercial revenues.

Concluding remarks
There is no one neat, easy conclusion to this chapter. The nonprofit sector is large and complicated, with several large sources of revenue: program revenues, government funding, donations and others. Theoretically, these revenue sources can interact in a variety of ways.

I would argue that, at the level of overall national giving, the picture is fairly clear. American giving to charity has held steady at roughly 2 percent of GDP for about five decades, while both government support for the sector and commercial revenue have risen. As a result, the nonprofit sector has grown as a fraction of GDP, and donations have become a smaller fraction of sector revenues. Total giving is thus relatively constant, and therefore independent of the growth in other revenue forms. Our statistics for program revenues include a variety of types of government support for the sector, such as tuition grants to students and Medicare and Medicaid coverage of medical bills, so it is not surprising that both overall government grants and program service revenues have risen.

At the level of 'the cause', the picture is less clear. Certainly, there are levels of government funding, or commercial support, which could crowd out all private donations, and history reveals certain functions where government has displaced private nonprofit action. A well-developed 'standard' theoretical model, following standard economic arguments, predicts full crowd-out of private donations by government funding. This model could easily be extended to predict crowd-out of donations by commercial activity as well. However, empirically, complete crowd-out is not often found. By modifying key assumptions of the 'standard' model, incomplete crowd-out or even crowd-in can be explained. Our ability to predict, rather than explain after the fact, the actual impact of government funding in particular areas is not yet good.

Finally, considerable attention has been paid to the interaction of revenue streams at the organizational level. Researchers have suggested that interaction could be due to managerial action, or to donor action.

There is fairly clear evidence that nonprofit managers actively adjust their strategies to respond to changes in funding patterns, or to changes in demand for their organizations' services. Indeed, it would be shocking if this were not the case. Thus, studies have shown that organizations that receive exogenous increases in one form of revenue tend to reduce their efforts to obtain revenue from other sources.

The evidence on donor action in response to changes in organizational funding sources is mixed, with some large studies showing no significant interaction. However, studies that have focused on commercial revenues that are clearly unrelated to the organization's core mission or programs have found negative associations.

Notes

1. Since nonprofit organizations record certain types of government money they receive as program revenues (e.g. Medicare payments at hospitals, or federal scholarship funds at universities), this relation is predictable.
2. Gruber and Hungerman (2007) critique his data, noting that prior to 1933 some federal relief spending was channeled through private agencies, while legislation in the 1930s required federal money to be spent directly through the government, causing a mechanical crowding out.
3. Steinberg (1987) properly notes that the relevant figure is the derivative of the curve at the mean point. I have wherever possible used the information given on the derivatives to characterize the studies. Some studies use linear models, so the coefficient is the derivative, and others use log-linear models. For linear models, the derivative is the regression coefficient β; for log-linear models, the derivative would equal $\beta x^{\beta-1}$ where x is the relevant independent variable. Where β is less than 1, and x is at all sizable, the derivative will tend to be near zero.
4. Schiff (1985) claimed that cash transfers to the needy crowded out charity, while spending on social services appeared to encourage donations. He argued that prior studies, which aggregated the two types of government spending, obscured their different impacts.

References

Abrams, Burton A. and Mark D. Schmitz (1978), 'The "crowding-out" effect of governmental transfers on private charitable contributions', *Public Choice*, **33** (1), 29–39.
Abrams, Burton A. and Mark D. Schmitz (1984), 'The crowding-out effect of governmental transfers on private charitable contributions', in Susan Rose-Ackerman (ed.), *The Economics of Nonprofit Institutions: Studies in Structure and Policy*, New York: Oxford University Press, pp. 303–12.
Amos, Orley M. (1982), 'Empirical analysis of motives underlying individual contributions to charity', *Atlantic Economic Journal*, **10** (4), 45–52.
Andreoni, James (1989), 'Giving with impure altruism: applications to charity and Ricardian equivalence', *Journal of Political Economy*, **97** (6), 1447–58.
Andreoni, James (1990), 'Impure altruism and donations to public goods: a theory of warm-glow giving', *Economic Journal*, **100**, 464–77.
Andreoni, James (2006), 'Leadership giving in charitable fund-raising', *Journal of Public Economic Theory*, **8** (1), 1–22.
Andreoni, James and A. Abigail Payne (2003), 'Do government grants to private charities crowd out giving or fund-raising?' *The American Economic Review*, **93** (3), 792–812.
Arrow, Kenneth J. (1972), 'Gifts and exchanges', *Philosophy and Public Affairs*, **1** (4), 343–62.
Becker, Elizabeth and Cotton Lindsay (1994), 'Does the government free ride?', *Journal of Law and Economics*, **37**, 277–96.

Benzing, Cynthia and Thomas Andrews (2004), 'The effect of tax rates and uncertainty on contributory crowding out', *American Economic Journal*, **32** (3), 200–14.

Bergstrom, Theodore, Lawrence Blume and Hal Varian (1986), 'On the private provision of public goods', *Journal of Public Economics*, **29** (1), 25–49.

Borgonovi, Francesca (2006), 'Do public grants to American theatres crowd-out private donations?' *Public Choice*, **126** (3–4), 429–51.

Borgonovi, Francesca and Michael O'Hare (2004), 'The impact of the national endowment for the arts in the United States: institutional and sectoral effects on private funding', *Journal of Cultural Economics*, **28** (1), 21–36.

Boris, Elizabeth T. (1998), 'Myths about the nonprofit sector', *Charting Civil Society*, No. 4, July, series by the Center on Nonprofits and Philanthropy of the Urban Institute.

Brooks, Arthur. C. (1999). 'Do public subsidies leverage private philanthropy for the arts? Empirical evidence on symphony orchestras', *Nonprofit and Voluntary Sector Quarterly*, **28** (1), 32–45.

Brooks, Arthur C. (2000a), 'Is there a dark side to government support for nonprofits?' *Public Administration Review*, **60** (3), 211–18.

Brooks, Arthur C. (2000b), 'Public subsidies and charitable giving: crowding out, crowding in, or both?', *Journal of Policy Analysis and Management*, **19** (3), 451–64

Brooks, Arthur C. (2004), 'The effects of public policy on private charity', *Administration & Society*, **36** (2), 166–85.

Callen, Jeffrey (1994), 'Money donations, volunteering, and organizational efficiency', *The Journal of Productivity Analysis*, **5** (3), 215–28.

Carlson, Keith M. and Roger W. Spencer (1975), 'Crowding out and its critics', Federal Reserve Bank of St Louis, December, 2–17.

Center on Philanthropy at Indiana University (2007), *Giving USA 2007: The Annual Report on Philanthropy for the Year 2006*, Indianapolis, IN: Giving USA Foundation.

Chan, Kenneth S., Rob Godby, Stuart Mestelman and R. Andrew Muller (2002), 'Crowding-out voluntary contributions to public goods', *Journal of Economic Behavior & Organizations*, **48** (3), 305–17.

Chang, Cyril F. and Howard P. Tuckman (1994), 'Revenue diversification among non-profits', *Voluntas: International Journal of Voluntary and Nonprofit Organizations*, **5** (3), 273–90.

Clotfelter, Charles (1985), *Federal Tax Policy and Charitable Giving*, Chicago, IL: University of Chicago Press.

Connolly, Laura S. (1997), 'Does external funding of academic research crowd out institutional support?', *Journal of Public Economics*, **64** (3), 389–406.

Diamond, Arthur M. (1999), 'Does federal funding "crowd in" private funding of science?' *Contemporary Economic Policy*, **17** (4), 423–32.

Dokko, Jane K. (2005), 'Does the NEA crowd out private charitable contributions to the arts?', Working Paper, University of Michigan.

Driessen, Patrick A. (1985), 'Comment on "the crowding out effect of governmental transfers on private charitable contributions"', *National Tax Journal*, **XXXVIII** (4), 571–73.

Duncan, Brian (1999), 'Modeling charitable contributions of time and money', *Journal of Public Economics*, **72** (2), 213–42.

Eckel, Catherine C., Philip J. Grossman and Rachel M. Johnson (2005), 'An experimental test of the crowding out hypothesis', *Journal of Public Economics*, **89** (8), 1543–60.

Ehrenberg, Ronald G., Daniel I. Rees and Dominic J. Brewer (1993), 'Institutional responses to increased external support for graduate students', *The Review of Economics and Statistics*, **75** (4), 671–82.

Ferris, J. Stephen and Edwin G. West (2003), 'Private versus public charity: reassessing crowding out from the supply side', *Public Choice*, **116** (3–4), 399–417.

Froelich, Karen A. (1999), 'Diversification of revenue strategies: evolving resource dependence in nonprofit organizations', *Nonprofit and Voluntary Sector Quarterly*, **28** (3) 246–68.

Garrett, Thomas A. and Russell M. Rhine (2007), 'Does government spending really crowd out charitable contributions? New time series evidence', Federal Reserve Bank of St Louis Working Paper No. 2007-012A.

Gittell, Ross and Edinaldo Tebaldi (2006), 'Charitable giving: factors influencing giving in U.S. States', *Nonprofit and Voluntary Sector Quarterly*, **35** (4), 721–36.

Glazar, Amihai and Kai I. Konrad (1996), 'A signaling explanation for charity', *The American Economic Review*, **86** (4), 1019–28.

Gruber, Jonathan M. and Daniel M. Hungerman (2007), 'Faith-based charity and crowd-out during the great depression', *Journal of Public Economics*, **91** (5–6), 1043–69.

Handy, Femida, and Natalie J. Webb (2003), 'A theoretical model of the effects of public funding on saving decisions by charitable nonprofit service providers', *Annals of Public and Cooperative Economics*, **74** (2), 261–82.

Heutel, Garth (2007), 'Crowding out and crowding in of private donations and government grants', unpublished Working Paper, Harvard University Kennedy School.

Horne, Christopher S. (2005), *Toward an Understanding of the Revenue of Nonprofit Organizations*, Dissertation. Georgia State University and Georgia Institute of Technology.

Horne, Christopher S., Janet L. Johnson and David M. Van Slyke (2005), 'Do charitable donors know enough – and care enough – about government subsidies to affect private giving to nonprofit organizations?' *Nonprofit and Voluntary Sector Quarterly*, **34** (1), 136–49.

Hughes, Patricia N. and William A. Luksetich (1999), 'The relationship among funding sources for art and history museums', *Nonprofit Management and Leadership*, **10** (1), 21–37.

Hungerman, Daniel M. (2005), 'Are Church and State substitutes? Evidence from the 1996 welfare reform', *Journal of Public Economics*, **89** (11/12), 2245–67.

Hungerman, Daniel M. (2007), 'Diversity and crowd-out: a theory of cold-glow giving', National Bureau of Economic Research Working Paper Series, No. 13348.

Jalandoni, Nadine. T., Claudia Petrescu and Gordon W. Green (2005), 'Government funding and the nonprofit sector: exploring a new Census Bureau data source – the Federal Audit Clearinghouse', *Nonprofit and Voluntary Sector Quarterly*, **34** (2), 260–75.

James, Estelle (1983), 'How nonprofits grow: a model', *Journal of Policy Analysis and Management*, **2** (3), 350–66.

Jones, Philip R. (1983), 'Aid to charities', *International Journal of Social Economics*, **10** (2), 3–11.

Kerlin, Janelle A. and Tom H. Pollak (2006), 'Nonprofit commercial revenue: a replacement for declining government grants and private contributions?' Working Paper presented to the UK Social Enterprise Research Conference, London South Bank University, London, UK, June.

Khanna, Jyoti and Todd Sandler (2000), 'Partners in giving: the crowding-in effects of UK government grants', *European Economic Review*, **44** (8) 1543–56.

Khanna, Jyoti, John Posnett, and Todd Sandler (1995), 'Charitable donations in the UK: new evidence based on panel data', *Journal of Public Economics*, **56**, 257–72.

Kingma, Bruce Robert (1989), 'An accurate measurement of the crowd-out effect, income effect, and price effect for charitable contributions', *Journal of Political Economy*, **97** (5) 1197–207.

Kingma, Bruce Robert (1995), 'Do profits "crowd out" donations, or vice versa? The impact of revenues from sales on donations to local chapters of the American Red Cross', *Nonprofit Management and Leadership*, **6** (1), 21–37.

Kingma, Bruce Robert and Robert McClelland (1995), 'Public radio stations are really, really not public goods: charitable contributions and impure altruism', *Annals of Public and Cooperative Economics*, **66** (1), 65–76.

Ledyard, John O. (1994), 'Public goods, a survey of experimental research', *Social Science Working Paper 861*, California Institute of Technology, Pasadena, CA. Reprinted in *The Handbook of Experimental Economics*, ed. by John H. Kagel and Alvin E. Roth, Princeton, NJ: Princeton University Press, 1995.

Lee, Kangoh (2006), 'Voluntary provision of public goods and administrative costs', *Public Finance Review*, **34** (2), 195–211.

Leroux, Kelly M. (2005), 'What drives nonprofit entrepreneurship? A look at budget trends of metro Detroit social service agencies', *American Review of Public Administration*, **35** (4), 350–62.

Lindsey, Lawrence and Richard Steinberg (1990), 'Joint crowdout: an empirical study of the impact of federal grants on state government expenditures and charitable donations', Working Paper No. 3226, National Bureau of Economic Research.

List, John A. and David Lucking-Reiley (2002), 'The effects of seed money and refunds on charitable giving: experimental evidence from a university capital campaign', *Journal of Political Economy* **110** (1), 215–33.

Manzoor, Sonia H. and John D. Straub (2005), 'The robustness of Kingma's crowd-out estimate: evidence from new data on contributions to public radio', *Public Choice*, **123** (3–4), 463–76.

Marudas, Nicholas P. and Fred A. Jacobs (2004), 'Determinants of charitable donations to large US higher education, hospital, and scientific research', *Voluntas: International Journal of Voluntary and Nonprofit Organizations*, **15** (2), 157–79.

National Center for Charitable Statistics at the Urban Institute (2008), 'The nonprofit sector in brief: facts and figures from the nonprofit Almanac 2007', http://www.urban.org/UploadedPDF/311373_nonprofit_sector.pdf. Accessed 3 January 2008.

National Center for Charitable Statistics (2008), 'Quick facts about nonprofits', http://nccs.urban.org/statistics/quickfacts.cfm. Accessed 3 January 2008.

Okten, Cagla and Burton A. Weisbrod (2000), 'Determinants of donations in private nonprofit markets', *Journal of Public Economics*, **75** (2), 255–72.

Owalla, King Odhiambo (2007), 'Government grants, crowding out theory, and American based international non-governmental organizations', doctoral thesis, Georgia State University.

Pacqué, Karl-Heinz (1982), 'Do public transfers "crowd out" private charitable giving? Some econometric evidence for the Federal Republic of Germany', *Keil Working Paper*, No. 152, August.

Payne, A. Abigail (1998), 'Does the government crowd-out private donations? New evidence from a sample of nonprofit firms', *Journal of Public Economics*, **69** (3), 323–45.

Payne, A. Abigail (2001), 'Measuring the effect of federal research funding on private donations at research universities: is federal research funding more than a substitute for private donations?' *International Tax and Public Finance*, **8** (5–6), 731–51.

Posnett, John and Todd Sandler (1989), 'Demand for charity donations in private non-profit markets: the case of the U.K.', *Journal of Public Economics*, **40**, 187–200.

Reece, William S. (1979), 'Charitable contributions: new evidence on household behavior', *American Economic Review*, **69** (1), 142–51.

Ribar, David C. and Mark O. Wilhelm (2002), 'Altruistic and joy-of giving motivations in charitable behavior', *Journal of Political Economy*, **110** (2), 425–57.

Roberts, Russell D. (1984), 'A positive model of private charity and public transfers', *Journal of Political Economy*, **92** (1), 136–48.

Rose-Ackerman, Susan (1986), 'Do government grants to charity reduce private donations?', in Susan Rose-Ackerman (ed.), *The Economics of Nonprofit Institutions*, New York: Oxford University Press, pp. 313–29.

Rose-Ackerman, Susan (1987), 'Ideals versus dollars: donors, charity managers, and government grants', *Journal of Political Economy*, **95** (4), 810–24.

Saidel, Judith R. (1991), 'Resource interdependence: the relationship between state agencies and nonprofit organizations', *Public Administration Review*, **51** (6), 543–53.

Schiff, Jerald (1985), 'Does government spending crowd out charitable contributions?', *National Tax Journal*, **38** (4), 535–46.

Schiff, Jerald (1990), *Charitable Giving and Government Policy: An Economic Analysis*, New York: Greenwood Press.

Schiff, Jerald and Burton Weisbrod (1991), 'Competition between for-profit and nonprofit organizations in commercial markets', *Annals of Public and Co-operative Economy*, **62** (4), 619–40.

Seaman, Bruce A. (1980), 'Economic models and support for the arts', in William S. Hendon, James L. Shanahan and Alice J. MacDonald (eds), *Economic Policy for the Arts*, Cambridge, MA: Abt Books, pp. 80–95.

Segal, Lewis and Burton Weisbrod (1998), 'Interdependence of commercial and donative revenues', in Burton Weisbrod (ed.), *To Profit or Not to Profit? The Commercial Transformation of the Nonprofit Sector*, Cambridge: Cambridge University Press, pp. 105–27.

Simmons, Walter O. and Rosemarie Emanuele (2004), 'Does government spending crowd out donations of time and money?', *Public Finance Review*, **32** (5), 498–511.

Smith, Thomas More (2007), 'The impact of government funding on private donations to nonprofit performing arts organizations', *Annals of Public and Cooperative Economics*, **78** (1), 137–60.

Steinberg, Richard (1985), 'Empirical relations between government spending and charitable donations', *Nonprofit and Voluntary Sector Quarterly*, **14** (2–3), 54–64.

Steinberg, Richard (1987), 'Voluntary donations & public expenditures in a federalist system', *American Economic Review*, **77** (1), 24–36.

Steinberg, Richard (1991), 'Does government spending crowd out donations? Interpreting the evidence', *Annals of Public and Cooperative Economics*, **62** (4), 591–612.

Steinberg, Richard (1993), 'Does government spending crowd out donations? Interpreting the evidence', in Avner Ben-Ner and Benedetto Gui (eds), *The Nonprofit Sector in the Mixed Economy*, Ann Arbor, MI: University of Michigan Press, pp. 99–125.

Tinkelman, Daniel (1999), 'Factors affecting the relation between donations to not-for-profit organizations and an efficiency ratio', *Research in Government and Nonprofit Accounting*, **10**, 135–61.

Tinkelman, Daniel and Kamini Mankaney (2007), 'When is administrative efficiency associated with charitable donations', *Nonprofit and Voluntary Sector Quarterly*, **36** (1), 41–64.

Toepler, Stefan and Barbara Morgan (2002), 'Crowding and commercialization: the effects of nonprofit commercial revenues on donations', Working Paper.

Vesterlund, Lise (2003), 'The informational value of sequential fundraising', *Journal of Public Economics*, **87** (3–4), 627–57.

Vesterlund, Lise (2006), 'Why do people give?' in Walter W. Powell and Richard Steinberg (eds), *The Non-Profit Sector: A Research Handbook, 2nd edn*, New Haven, CT: Yale University Press, pp. 568–87.

Warr, Peter G. (1982), 'Pareto optimal redistribution and private charity', *Journal of Public Economics*, **19** (1), 131–38.

Weisbrod, Burton (1998), *The Nonprofit Economy*, Cambridge, MA: Harvard University Press.

Yetman, Michelle H. and Robert J. Yetman (2003), 'The effect of nonprofits' taxable activities on the supply of private donations', *National Tax Journal*, **56** (1), 243–58.

3 Distribution policies of private foundations
Richard Sansing

Introduction: overview of the private foundation sector

In 2004, there were over 70000 non-operating (i.e. grant-making) private foundations in the USA that held over \$469 billion in assets and made over \$27 billion in grants to public charities. A public charity is a section 501(c)(3) organization whose financial support is provided by the general public (section 509(a)).[1] In contrast, a private foundation is a section 501(c)(3) organization whose financial support is provided by a small group of people, usually members of the same family.

Private foundations are similar to public charities in that a contribution to a foundation is tax-deductible and endowment income is exempt from the federal income tax. But unlike public charities, most foundations simply make grants instead of engaging in charitable activities directly.[2] These private foundations represent a privately controlled endowment whose assets are held for the benefit of current and future public charities. They act as a conduit that transfers private wealth today to charitable beneficiaries in the future in a way that generates current charitable contribution deductions to donors and future virtually tax-exempt investment returns between the time the assets are transferred to the foundation and the time the assets are transferred from the foundation to a public charity. The assets held by these philanthropic institutions are unusual in that public charities in the aggregate have a claim on the returns on the assets because the tax laws governing nonprofit organizations impose the nondistribution constraint (Hansmann, 1980), which forbids foundation assets from being diverted to private interests. However, no particular charity has any claim on the returns of these assets at all.

Because foundations break the contemporaneous link between the charitable deduction to the donor and the eventual disbursement of funds to a public charity, Congress became concerned that some foundations would excessively accumulate funds instead of making distributions to charities. These concerns led to the enactment of several tax provisions in 1969 designed to ensure that private foundations fulfill a charitable purpose (Troyer, 2000). In particular, Congress imposed the minimum distribution requirement, which requires that foundations spend at least 5 percent of their assets on charitable grants or charitable administrative expenditures each year (section 4942). Steuerle (1977) examines the theoretical foundations of the minimum distribution requirement.

In 1984, Congress made the tax rate on endowment income a function of the level of the foundation's charitable expenditures in an effort to further encouraging charitable expenditures. If a foundation's charitable distributions (as a percentage of assets) during the year exceeds a statutory benchmark that depends on prior years' distributions, the foundation pays a 1 percent tax on its net investment income; otherwise, the tax rate is doubled to 2 percent (section 4940(e)). The minimum distribution requirement and the dual tax rate regime are the two primary tax law provisions that Congress has enacted to regulate the distribution policies of private foundations.

Minimum distribution requirement

The minimum distribution requirement is designed to prevent excessive retention of assets within foundations. Between 1969 and 1981, the 'distributable amount' was based on the greater of a percentage of the fair market value of the foundation's investment assets or the foundation's net income. The percentage varied between 5 and 6 percent, depending on the Treasury Department's determination of market investment yields, usually based on five-year Treasury securities. These rules, which reflected a political compromise between those who believed that private foundations should be able to maintain the real value of their endowment in perpetuity and those who believe that foundations should have a limited life, are described in more detail in Steuerle (1977).

The current definition of the distributable amount, established in 1981, is 5 percent of the fair market value of the foundation's investment assets, less the taxes imposed on the foundation (section 4942(d)). Assets used in carrying out the foundation's exempt purpose (e.g. an office building in which the foundation conducts its operations) are not included in the calculation of the distributable amount (section 4942(e)(1)(A)). This amount, which is calculated in the private foundation's annual tax return (Form 990-PF), must be paid out no later than the end of the next year. Failure to do so triggers a 15 percent tax on the undistributed amount (section 4942(a)). Failure to correct the error within the succeeding year triggers an additional tax equal to 100 percent of the remaining undistributed amount (section 4942(b)). Distributions in excess of the distributable amount decrease the distributable amount in future years (section 4942(g)(2)(D)).

The minimum distribution requirement can be satisfied via either grants to section 501(c)(3) organizations or foundation administrative expenditures (section 4942(g)), which include amounts paid for assets used by the foundation (section 4942(g)(1)(B)). Differences in administrative costs among foundations can reflect different approaches to grant making. These differences manifest themselves in the type of institution that receives grants, the type of project that they fund, and the degree of involvement the foundation has with the grant recipients.

Nielsen (1985) uses the Mellon and Ford foundations to illustrate these differences. The Mellon approach to grant making tends to support established institutions in the areas of education, health and the arts. These grants support elite scholars and scientists who compete for Mellon grants on a competitive basis. Support for the disadvantaged comes in the form of scholarships and fellowships to provide educational opportunities. Mellon's administrative costs are low and Mellon tends not to expend significant amounts on grantee oversight.

The Ford approach differs from Mellon's in several respects. Ford is more likely to support new, inexperienced organizations that are trying to develop new ways to address social problems. Ford often funds economic development projects and neighborhood organizations, advocacy projects and minority leadership development programs. Ford spends more on administrative costs per dollar of grants as it takes an active role in overseeing the projects it funds.

Excise tax on investment income

Private foundations are subject to an excise tax on their net investment income. In general, a private foundation faces a 2 percent tax on its net investment income (section 4940(a)). However, this tax rate is halved to 1 percent for a foundation that makes a sufficiently large 'qualifying distribution'. In general, a qualifying distribution is either a grant made to a public charity or an administrative expenditure related to the foundation's charitable (as opposed to its investment) activities.

To qualify for the reduced tax rate, the ratio of qualifying distributions to investment assets must be at least as large as the sum of the average ratio of qualifying distributions to investment assets over the preceding five years, plus 1 percent of the foundation's net investment income. For example, suppose over the preceding five years the foundation spent on average 6 percent of its investment assets in qualifying distributions. This year the foundation has investment assets of $100 million and net investment income of $8 million. If this year's qualifying distributions are less than $6 080 000, then its tax is $160 000; if qualifying distributions are $6 080 000 or more, then its tax is $80 000.

This system features a severe 'cliff effect' in that a $1 shortfall in qualifying distributions doubles the tax on investment income. For example, in the fiscal year ending 31 August 1999, the Eugene McDermott Foundation fell less than $5000 short of the distribution threshold, which increased its tax by over $150 000.

Adjusted qualifying distributions are defined as qualifying distributions minus the reduction in tax in a year in which a foundation qualifies for the 1 percent tax rate. This adjustment prevents the foundation from having to make a steady increase in its level of qualifying distributions to continue qualifying for the 1 percent tax rate. Continuing the above example, if the private foundation made qualifying distributions of exactly $6 080 000 in the current year, its adjusted qualifying distributions would be $6 000 000 – the qualifying distributions less the $80 000 tax reduction. Therefore, next year's base period ratio of qualifying distributions to investment assets would remain at 6 percent.

Unlike the minimum distribution requirement, the dual tax rate system provides two countervailing incentives for foundations to modify their distribution decisions so as to qualify for the 1 percent tax rate. First, they have an incentive to make current year distributions at least as high as in prior years (as a percentage of investment assets) so as to qualify for the lower tax rate. On the other hand, any current-year distribution increases the base period percentage that will determine whether the foundation will continue to qualify for the lower tax rate in future years. This effect will deter current-year distributions in excess of what is needed to qualify for the 1 percent tax rate.

Next, I review empirical research regarding how private foundations respond to the minimum distribution requirement and the dual tax rate regime. Then I describe gaps in our knowledge of how private foundations operate. Finally, I discuss the policy debates regarding the tax policies that influence the behavior of private foundations, how prior research can help inform this debate, and suggest directions for future research.

Research regarding foundation behavior
The Internal Revenue Service (IRS) regularly compiles tax return information using statistics of income (SOI) data, and summarizes the findings in articles published in the *Statistics of Income Bulletin*. In this section I review four IRS studies on private foundations.

Private foundations in 2003
Ludlum and Stanton (2006) provide a snapshot of the private foundation sector as of 2003. In that year, there were over 70 000 non-operating (grant-making) private founda-

Table 3.1   Descriptive statistics of non-operating private foundations, 2003 (dollar values in millions)

Foundation size	Number of foundations	Assets ($)	Distributable amount ($)	Qualifying Distributions ($)	Grants ($)
Assets < $100K	21 288	588	39	858	759
$100K–$1 mil.	26 320	11 077	489	1 566	1 337
$1 mil.–$10 mil.	17 869	54 748	2 426	5 251	4 803
$10 mil–$50 mil.	3 497	73 930	3 244	5 336	4 805
$50 mil–$100 mil.	522	36 588	1 636	2 560	2 282
Assets > $100 mil.	509	259 367	11 354	14 240	12 131
Total	70 004	436 297	19 188	29 811	26 116

tions with over $436 billion in assets, making nearly $30 billion in qualifying charitable distributions (QD), over $26 billion of which were grants. The distributable amount (DA), the minimum amount that could be distributed without violating the minimum distribution requirement, was about $19 billion. The population is very skewed, with the largest 1 percent of the foundations having over 60 percent of the assets and making over 50 percent of the charitable distributions. Table 3.1 summarizes the sector in terms of number of entities, assets, DA, QD and grants for foundations of various sizes.

There is a widespread belief that foundations adhere closely to the minimum distribution requirement, paying out as little as possible. In fact, in the aggregate, the sector paid out about $1.55 for every dollar required to be distributed; the private foundation sector in the aggregate distributed about 6 percent of their assets as grants in 2003. In addition, not all qualifying distributions are grants (although about $7 out of every $8 of qualifying distributions are grants) and the average foundation's 'distributable amount' is only about 4.4 percent of its assets. The ratio of grants to assets is also extremely skewed; many foundations that are 'small' in terms of assets adopt a 'pass-through' policy, distributing most current donations received as current grants instead of accumulating assets with an 'endowment' policy. By the very nature of this policy, a pass-through foundation will tend to be 'small' (as measured by assets), although this characterization is somewhat misleading. For example, in 2005 the Grant Thornton Foundation held assets of only about $50 000 but received donations of $158 000 and made charitable grants of $145 000.

Although the smaller the foundation, the greater the qualifying distributions in excess of the distributable amount, even foundations with over $100 million of assets make distributions 25 percent higher than the legal minimum. The ratio of qualifying distributions (QD) to distributable amount (DA), decomposed into the expression

$$\frac{QD}{DA} = \frac{5\% \text{ of assets}}{DA} \times \frac{Grants}{5\% \text{ of assets}} \times \frac{QD}{Grants}$$

and broken down by foundation size, is shown in Table 3.2.

Even among foundations of similar size, there is considerable variation regarding foundation distribution policies. Some large foundations make qualifying distributions far in excess of the legal minimum, while many small foundations distributed a far smaller

Table 3.2   Qualifying distributions/distributable amount, 2003

Foundation size	(5% of assets) / DA (%)	Grants/ (5% of assets) (%)	QD/Grants (%)	QD/DA (%)
Assets < $100K	75	2581	113	2200
$100K–$1 mil.	113	241	117	320
$1 mil.–$10 mil.	112	175	109	216
$10 mil–$50 mil.	114	130	111	164
$50 mil–$100 mil.	112	125	112	156
Assets > $100 mil.	114	94	117	125
Total	114	120	114	155

Table 3.3   Qualifying distributions/assets, 2003

	< 5%	5%–6%	6%–10%	> 10%
< $1 mil.	26.5	18.8	12.5	42.1
$1 mil.–$50 mil.	31.6	30.9	20.1	17.4
> $50 mil.	29.1	38.0	21.1	11.8

fraction of their assets. For example, nearly 12 percent of foundations with over $50 million in assets had qualifying distribution of over 10 percent of their assets. On the other hand, over 26 percent of foundations with less than $1 million of assets had qualifying distributions of less than 5 percent of assets. These results are summarized in Table 3.3.

Failure to satisfy the minimum distribution requirement triggers a 15 percent tax on the undistributed amount. In 2003, 1257 foundations paid a section 4942 tax on undistributed income. The tax collected was nearly $3 million. If all of the tax had been imposed at a 15 percent rate (as opposed to the 100 percent tax rate on the failure to satisfy the requirement within a year), then there would have been about a $20 million shortfall in required distributions.

Of the 70 000 non-operating private foundations, about 57 000 paid the excise tax on net investment income. Of those, about half paid at the 1 percent tax rate and half paid at the 2 percent tax rate. Larger foundations were more likely to pay at the lower rate. The foundations paying the tax paid $328 million on net investment income of $24.69 billion, for an average rate of 1.33 percent.

Private foundations from 1993 to 2002
Ludlum (2005) analyzes the private foundation sector over the ten-year period from 1993 to 2002. The number of non-operating foundations grew from 40 166 in 1993 to 67 101 in 2002, for an annualized net growth rate of about 6 percent. This net growth rate represents the difference between the rate at which new foundations are created and old foundations go out of existence. According to the Foundation Center, over 1 percent of private foundations went of out existence in 2005, a rate that has increased in recent years (Beatty, 2007).

Table 3.4   Descriptive statistics of non-operating private foundations, 1993–2002 (dollar values in millions)

	Number of foundations	Assets ($)	Grants ($)	Grants/assets (%)
1993	40 166	174.0	10.9	6.3
1994	41 983	182.5	11.4	6.3
1995	43 966	218.3	11.9	5.5
1996	46 066	262.7	14.2	5.4
1997	50 541	314.4	15.9	5.0
1998	52 460	365.0	19.0	5.2
1999	58 840	426.3	24.4	5.2
2000	61 501	432.7	26.6	6.1
2001	63 650	416.8	26.5	6.4
2002	67 101	377.7	25.5	6.7

The fair market value of assets owned by non-operating private foundations grew at about a 9 percent annual rate, from $174 billion in 1993 to $378 billion in 2002. Grants grew at an 11 percent rate, from about $11 billion in 1993 to about $28 billion in 2002. Grants as a percentage of assets exhibit a strong countercyclical pattern, dropping to about 5 percent during the stock market boom in the late 1990s but growing to 6.7 percent in 2002. The fair market value of foundation assets fell by over 11 percent from 1999 to 2002, while grants rose by over 4 percent during the same time period. Table 3.4 summarizes the assets held and grants made by private foundations between 1993 and 2002.

The median payout rate (qualifying distributions divided by investment assets) between 1993 and 2002 exhibits a pattern similar to the 2003 data, with smaller foundations having generally higher payout rates, but with significant heterogeneity within size classes. Foundations with less than $1 million of assets exhibit a 'barbell' distribution, with a substantial number of foundations with payout rates of less than 6 percent and a substantial number with payout rates greater than 10 percent. A much lower percentage of large foundations has payout rates above 10 percent. The distribution of payout rates over time and across size categories in shown in Table 3.5.

Large private foundations from 1985 to 1997
Whitten (2001) examined a panel of the 100 largest foundations in 1997 that had data available every year between 1985 and 1997. Although they accounted for less than 0.2 percent of all non-operating private foundations in 1997, they held over 37 percent of the assets and made 28 percent of the grants in that year. Grants as a percentage of assets, 3.8 percent, is lower for this group than any other group, although this is at least in part induced by defining the panel in terms of assets held in 1997 instead of 1985.[3] While the percentage was higher in 1993, at 4.5 percent, it was still lower than that of any other size groups. The grant-to-assets ratio was in the 4.0 to 4.5 percent range for every year between 1985 and 1996 for the 100 largest foundations. This ratio by foundation size for 1993 and 1997 is shown in Table 3.6.

Table 3.5   Distribution of payout rates for 1994, 1998 and 2002

	< 6%	6%–10%	> 10%
1994			
< $1 mil.	46.1	16.2	37.7
$1 mil.–$50 mil.	63.7	19.7	16.6
> $50 mil.	75.6	16.7	7.7
1998			
< $1 mil.	52.3	12.5	35.2
$1 mil.–$50 mil.	69.4	16.5	14.1
> $50 mil.	77.1	14.4	8.5
2002			
< $1 mil.	45.4	12.5	42.1
$1 mil.–$50 mil.	62.5	20.1	17.4
> $50 mil.	67.1	21.1	11.8

Table 3.6   Grants/assets, 1993 and 1997 (%)

Foundation size	1993	1997
Largest 100	4.5	3.8
> $100 mil. but not in largest 100	5.8	4.0
$50 mil.–$100 mil.	6.8	4.9
$10 mil.–$50 mil.	6.7	6.1
$1 mil.–$10 mil.	7.7	6.8
$100 000–$1 mil.	13.5	10.2
< $100 000	128.0	131.0

Private foundations from 1975 to 1995

Meckstroth and Arnsberger (1998) provide an overview of the entire nonprofit sector, including private foundations. The number of private foundations grew from 26 889 in 1975 to 47 983 in 1995; assets held by private foundations grew from $25.5 billion to $263.4 billion, about a fourfold increase in inflation-adjusted dollars (compared to 74 percent real GDP growth during the same period).

While there has been substantial growth in both assets held and grants made by private foundations between 1975 and 1995, the ratio of grants to the value of assets has steadily declined over the years, falling from 6.3 percent in 1979 to 4.9 percent in 1995.

The IRS studies summarized earlier provide a wealth of descriptive statistics regarding the foundation sector. However, the only source of cross-sectional variation that those studies examine is size. Two recent academic studies of private foundations have looked more deeply into the issue of how distribution policies vary across foundations.

Evidence for foundation distribution policy homogeneity

Deep and Frumkin (2006) examine a random sample of 169 foundations using data from 1972 to 1996. The population of foundations from which they sampled owned assets of at least $5 million in 1970 and had at least ten years of data. They interviewed foundation trustees, officers and financial managers in an effort to understand not only what distribution policies foundations choose, but why those policies were chosen.

The authors find a striking convergence of payout rates around the minimum distribution requirement, at least since the current rules have been in place (as they have since 1982). The payout rate has little correlation with the foundation's investment returns. In good times and bad, the foundations in their sample deviate very little from the legally required minimum distribution.

The authors offer several possible explanations for the unusual degree of homogeneity in foundation distribution policies. First, a tension exists between hard-to-measure social return on foundation grants versus an easy-to-measure endowment level. Foundation trustees and managers frequently have backgrounds in business rather than in nonprofit operations, and tend to put more weight on activities for which performance is easier to measure.[4] Second, if a foundation manager's compensation depends on the size of the foundation's endowment, foundation managers have an incentive to retain assets instead of making grants. Third, the size of the endowment translates into prestige in the sector, which exacerbates managerial preference for asset retention. Fourth, given the difficulty of making the trade-off between increasing current grants and being able to make more grants in the future, foundation managers and trustees may be engaging in 'herding' behavior in which rational decision makers optimally mimic the behavior of others.[5] Fifth, the dual excise tax structure penalizes an increase in current distributions above the foundation's historical average by making it more difficult to qualify for the 1 percent excise tax rate in future years.

Evidence for foundation distribution policy heterogeneity
Sansing and Yetman (2006) examine a panel of 3779 foundations from 1994 to 2000. Their panel includes all non-operating foundations with assets over $10 million during each year, along with a sample of smaller foundations. They excluded foundations with zero assets, which are pure pass-through organizations.

They characterize foundations in terms of their behavior relative to the minimum distribution requirement. If a foundation violates the minimum distribution requirement, it is a SUBMIN foundation (about 1.6 percent of their sample, which is about the same as the fraction of foundations that paid a section 4942 excise tax in 2003). If a foundation barely satisfies the minimum distribution requirement (exceeding the legal limit by less than 10 percent of the limit), it is a MINIMIZE foundation (about 13 percent of their sample). If a foundation barely satisfies the minimum distribution requirement, but does so a year earlier than is required, it is a TIMELYMIN foundation (about 44 percent of their sample). Finally, a foundation that exceeds the minimum distribution requirement by more than 10 percent is a SPENDER foundation, about 42 percent of their sample.

The figures below illustrate the ratio of foundations' qualified distributions relative to the legal minimum (Figure 3.1) and to the distributable amount (Figure 3.2). Figure 3.1 excludes any foundation that satisfied its legal obligation via a distribution in the prior year. The 'spike' just the right of the value 1.0 in Figure 3.1 contains foundations that pay the absolute legal minimum.

Sansing and Yetman (2006) seek to explain variations in foundation distribution policies in terms of their characteristics other than size. These factors were PAYROLL

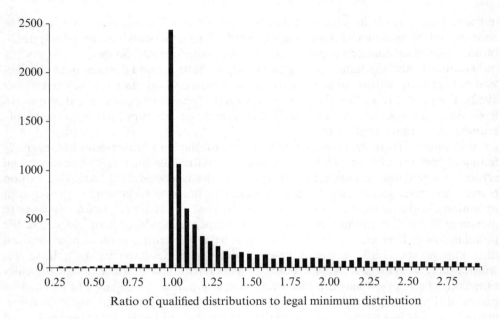

Source: R. Sansing and R. Yetman, 'Governing private foundations using the tax law', *Journal of Accounting and Economics*, **41** (3). © 2006, with permission from Elsevier.

Figure 3.1   *Distribution of foundations relative to the legal minimum*

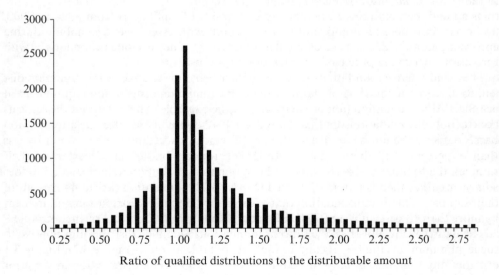

Source: R. Sansing and R. Yetman, 'Governing private foundations using the tax law', *Journal of Accounting and Economics*, **41** (3). © 2006, with permission from Elsevier.

Figure 3.2   *Distribution of foundation payouts relative to the distributable amount* (employee compensation plus professional fees, scaled by assets); BRICKS (value of depreciable property owned and leased, scaled by assets); DONATE (an indicator variable to show if the foundation received any donations during 1994–2000); and GROWTH (rate of growth of foundation assets).They use PAYROLL and BRICKS to distinguish 'active' foundations from 'passive' foundations. They use DONATE and GROWTH to distinguish 'hot' foundations (those receiving donations and with above-average growth) from 'cold' foundations (those no longer receiving donations and with below-average growth). Along with SIZE (natural logarithm of assets), they sort their sample into eight groups based on these three characteristics. Finally, they distinguish firms based on the fraction of investment income (interest, dividends and realized capital gains) that were generated by capital gains (CAPGAIN), and on the fraction of their stock and bond portfolios that were invested in stock (STOCK).

They used these variables to explain variation in foundations' payout behavior as measured by QD/DA and GRANTS/DA. They found that both payout measures were positively associated with DONATE and GROWTH and negatively associated with SIZE and STOCK.

They then used a logit regression to show how foundation characteristics were associated with these four categories. SUBMIN foundations tended to be small, cold and passive. MINIMIZE foundations tended to be large, cold, passive and heavily invested in stock. TIMELYMIN foundations tended to be cold. Finally, SPENDER foundations tended to be active, hot and invested heavily in bonds.

Reconciling the empirical results
The Deep and Frumkin (2006) study portrays a homogeneous sector that adheres closely to the minimum distribution requirement. The Sansing and Yetman (2006) study portrays a heterogeneous sector with some foundations that follow the minimum distribution requirement, and others that distribute substantially more. One explanation for this apparent inconsistency is the nature of the Deep and Frumkin sample selection criteria. First, the foundations in their sample had assets of at least $5 million in 1970, which is over $22 million in 2000 dollars; Sansing and Yetman found that larger foundations tended to have lower payout rates. Second, being able to interview a foundation trustee or officer in the 1990s regarding a foundation that existed in 1970 creates a high likelihood of survival bias in the data; long-lived foundations are more likely to have adopted conservative distribution policies.[6]

Evidence regarding the dual tax rate regime
Sansing and Yetman (2006) also examine how foundations respond to the dual excise tax rate structure. About 52 percent of their sample paid the 2 percent tax rate; 48 percent qualified for the lower tax rate. Foundations paying the 1 percent tax rate tended to be larger and actively managed. They also are more likely to still be receiving donations, suggesting that foundations receiving donations are willing to make the higher level of distributions needed to qualify for the lower tax rate. Low tax rate foundations experience lower GROWTH, suggesting that rapidly growing foundations do not boost qualifying distributions quickly enough to qualify for the lower tax rate. Finally, low tax rate foundations have higher CAPGAIN. In a period with a high level of realized capital gains, foundations appear to strive to qualify for the lower tax rate.

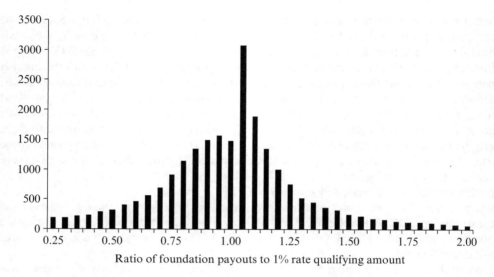

Source: R. Sansing and R. Yetman, 'Governing private foundations using the tax law', *Journal of Accounting and Economics*, **41** (3). © 2006, with permission from Elsevier.

Figure 3.3   *Distribution of foundation payouts relative to the amounts necessary to qualify for the reduced tax on net investment income*

A distinctive feature of the section 4940 excise tax is its 'cliff effect' nature. If qualifying distributions exceed a specific threshold, the foundation qualifies for the 1 percent tax rate; but fall $1 short of that threshold, and the excise tax doubles. Figure 3.3 shows the ratio of foundation qualifying distributions to the threshold to qualify for the 1 percent tax rate. The sharp spike just to the right of 1.0 provides some evidence of the extent to which foundations adjust their qualifying distributions to qualify for the 1 percent tax rate.

Sansing and Yetman (2006) examined the subsample with ratios between 0.9 and 1.1, and saw how foundations that barely qualified for the lower tax rate (SPTAX = 1) differed from those that fell just short (SPTAX = 0). About 19 percent of the observations fell between 1.0 and 1.1; about 11 percent of the observations fell between 0.9 and 1.0. SPTAX =1 foundations were larger, had higher CAPGAIN, and lower STOCK than SPTAX = 0 foundations. This pattern suggests that there are some economies of scale in tax planning and that either foundations time their capital gains realizations to fall in periods in which they face a lower tax rate, or increase their qualifying distributions in periods in which they had high capital gain realizations. SPTAX was also decreasing in STOCK, which suggests it is harder to qualify for the 1 percent tax rate when more of the foundation's portfolio is invested in more volatile assets.

The dual excise tax system compares qualifying distributions to a base amount that reflects distributions made in the previous five years. The authors ask whether foundations that qualified for the lower tax rate had higher qualifying distributions, a lower base, or a combination of both. For the sample as a whole, qualifying distributions (as a percentage of assets) was 30 percent higher for 1 percent tax rate foundations than for

2 percent tax rate foundations; the base amount was 66 percent higher for 2 percent tax rate foundations than for 1 percent tax rate foundations. Foundations with a ratio of qualifying distributions to the threshold amount between 0.9 and 1.1 (SPTAX = 0 and SPTAX = 1) had virtually identical qualifying distributions as a percentage of assets (5.8 percent and 5.7 percent, respectively). The two groups differed in their base amounts. SPTAX = 1 foundations had a base distribution percentage of 5.4 percent; SPTAX = 0 foundations had a base distribution percentage of 6.2 percent, a statistically significant difference. Therefore foundations close to the threshold that qualified for the lower tax rate tended to do so by keeping prior years' distributions low rather than increasing the current year's distributions.

Policy debates and the role of research

The minimum distribution requirement is the focus of an ongoing policy debate between those who believe the minimum should be increased and those who believe it is already too high. The dual tax rate regime has also been criticized. In this section, I review the policy debates over both of these tax law provisions, and describe how prior research can help inform these debates.

Debate over the minimum distribution requirement

The minimum distribution requirement is the subject of considerable controversy, with some advocating an increase in the percentage of assets that must be annually paid out while others defend the current rules. Supporters of the *status quo* argue that an increase would likely deplete the real value of foundation assets, which would in turn cause a decrease in the real level of payout over time (Cambridge Associates, 2000). By avoiding asset depletion, the current rules allow foundations to maintain the real value of their endowment in perpetuity (Craig, 1999). This in turn preserves an endowment for the benefit of the charitable sector, controlled by ostensibly prudent stewards who are not subject to pressures to meet immediate needs at the cost of future unmet needs.

Those advocating an increase in the percentage of assets that must be paid out point to the rapid growth of the private foundation sector, and assert that the field has become 'more concerned with investment banking than with grantmaking' (Mehrling, 1999, p. 1). They reject the idea that perpetuity is a legitimate goal of a charitable foundation. Brody (1997) examines the broader questions of whether the nonprofit sector should even have an endowment, whether this endowment should be controlled by private foundations instead of public charities, and whether private foundations should be allowed to exist in perpetuity. Hansmann (1990) criticizes the accumulation of wealth by universities on grounds of intergenerational equity. Current saving represents a transfer of wealth from the current generation to future generations, which seems inequitable in light of the general increase in economic prosperity over time. Klausner (2003) also examines the trade-off between current and future charity in terms of intergenerational equity. In Chapter 5 of this volume, Bowman reviews the arguments on the accumulation of endowments by nonprofit organizations. Lenkowsky (2002) and Billitteri (2005) review the debate over the minimum distribution requirement.

Deep and Frumkin (2006) list five arguments for a higher minimum distribution requirement and five arguments for a lower minimum distribution requirement. The arguments for a higher required payout rate are: higher current spending increases the chances of solving problems today instead of treating the symptoms of unsolved problems in the future; higher current spending enhances generational equity by better matching the lost tax revenues associated with contributions to private foundations with the generation that benefits from charitable distributions by private foundations; the recent growth in donations to private foundations suggests that the aggregate wealth held by private foundations will not decrease even if current spending increases; and it would help deflect criticism of the foundation sector that could lead to more severe constraints on foundation behavior in the future. The arguments for a lower payout rate are: current problems may get worse in the future, when spending could be more useful; lower spending today protects future charitable beneficiaries from the consequences of a bear market; managers of private foundations may be unable to respond effectively to a regulatory change; lower spending today enables foundations to respond to new and unforeseen future problems; and public charities may not be able to absorb and use effectively a substantial increase in current foundation grants.

A striking feature of the debate over the minimum distribution requirement is how disconnected it is from the facts regarding how foundations actually behave. Both proponents and opponents of increasing the minimum distribution requirement frame their arguments in the context of foundations that distribute the legal minimum each year. Table 3.1 shows that although the distributable amount for private foundations in 2003 was less than $19.2 billion, qualifying distributions exceeded $29.8 billion. This suggests that increasing the minimum distribution requirement would have far less effect on private foundations than its advocates hope or its detractors fear. In particular, naively projecting a 20 percent increase in foundation-qualifying distributions if the minimum distribution requirement is increased from 5 percent to 6 percent grossly overstates the likely effect of such a change. The Sansing and Yetman (2006) paper suggests that the foundations that would be affected by such an increase (SUBMIN, MINIMIZE and TIMELYMIN foundations) tend to be 'cold' in that they received no new donations during the 1994–2000 sample period.

Dual investment income tax rate regime
Although the tax rates on investment income are low relative to those faced by other taxpayers, the marginal effect of distributions around the threshold for the 1 percent tax rate is extremely large. This dual tax rate structure has many disadvantages and essentially no redeeming features. Steuerle and Sullivan (1995) point out the system's many disadvantages. These include costs of tax planning to achieve the lower tax rate, deterring qualifying distributions above a level needed to achieve the lower tax rate, and inducing foundations to smooth their qualifying distributions over time. This peculiar provision arose when a simple proposal to reduce the tax rate from 2 percent to 1 percent was opposed by some who feared that the tax savings would increase the foundation's endowment, and insisted upon a mechanism that would ensure that the tax savings would result in increased charitable distributions. As money is fungible, this demand is hard to comprehend, much less implement.[7]

Recent legislative proposals would replace this two-tiered tax rate with a single flat rate of 1.25 percent (Stokeld, 2000). Unlike the debate over the minimum distribution requirement, the debate over the current excise tax regime is rather one-sided. The research on how private foundations respond to the dual tax rate regime certainly supports changing to a flat rate system. As Figure 3.3 indicates, foundations appear to plan their distributions carefully so as to qualify for the lower tax rate rather than fall just short. Furthermore, the evidence indicates that foundations close to the threshold that qualify for the lower tax rate do so by maintaining a low base level of distributions rather than increasing current-year distributions, as was predicted in Steuerle and Sullivan (1995).

Concluding remarks: directions for future research

Private foundations continue to be an important albeit understudied segment of the non-profit sector. We could learn much from both quantitative studies like the Sansing and Yetman paper and qualitative studies like the Deep and Frumkin paper.

One important limitation to the Sansing and Yetman paper is that it is based on data between 1994 and 2000, during which there was a strong bull market. Given that we know from the IRS studies that the average payout rate for the foundation sector grew from about 5 percent during the bull market of the 1990s to 6.7 percent in 2002, it would be interesting to learn how this increase in payout rate varies cross-sectionally over the private foundation population.

While it is natural to try to classify foundations in terms of the types of public charities to which a foundation makes grants, so many foundations make grants in so many different areas that such a classification would be uninformative (Prewitt, 2006). Because the data on Form 990-PF report the level of grants but not the types of grant recipients or the intended use of the funds (e.g. capital campaign, general support or endowment), little systematic evidence exists on the nature of grant recipients or the types of activities that are funded. However, Margo (1992) provides a detailed breakdown of all foundation distributions in 1988 by expenditure category. He found that 27 percent of grant dollars were for social welfare; 20 percent for health; 19 percent for scientific purposes; 17 percent for education; and 17 percent for cultural and religious purposes. He also analyzed 1988 foundation distributions by type of recipient organization. Educational institutions received 36 percent of grant dollars and direct service organizations received 24 percent. No other type of organization received more than 12 percent of grant dollars.

Qualitative studies that examine the changing role of foundations can yield discoveries that are difficult to glean by examining a foundation's Form 990-PF. Chapter 17 of this volume (by Cordes) explores the ways grant makers evaluate their own performance. Letts et al. (1997) and Lenkowsky (2002) argue that practices developed by venture capitalists are being used by private foundations to add value in the form of expertise as well as cash. To what extent does this occur? Has it been successful? Is it changing the mix of grants and non-grant-qualifying distributions that foundations make?

These questions are suggestive of a larger unanswered question: what is the value added by private foundations to philanthropic activities? Does having half a trillion dollars of financial assets controlled by private foundations somehow increase the quantity or quality of philanthropic activities? It is not enough to argue that the existence of an endowment of financial assets facilitates the work of charitable organizations, because public charities can and do have their own endowments. As Prewitt (2006) points out, if a foundation distributes 5 percent of its assets to public charities, and public charities in turn put those dollars into its own endowment, spending 5 percent on its own activities, the cascading effect causes each dollar of foundation assets to generate one-fourth of a cent of current charitable expenditures.[8] What can the nonprofit sector achieve with grant-making private foundations that it could not achieve if the same assets were held by public charities?

One answer to this question is that when the endowment is held by a private foundation, the donor (or foundation manager) has the flexibility to make grants to the organization that can make the best use of the funds at the time. Unless the organization that can make the best use of the funds (given the preferences of the donor or foundation board) is the same every year, the benefit from retaining flexibility probably outweighs the costs of creating and managing a private foundation. A second answer is that a private foundation may be able to provide guidance and advice in addition to funds to charitable organizations.

Alternatively, does the ability to create a private foundation increase the resources flowing to the philanthropic sector? In other words, without private foundations, an individual could get a tax deduction for a charitable contribution only when wealth is transferred to a public charity. With private foundations, the tax deduction comes when the wealth is transferred to the foundation, irrespective of when it is ultimately transferred to a public charity. Does the possibility of establishing a private foundation affect the total present value of wealth transferred to public charities, or only the timing of these transfers? How would an increase in the minimum distribution requirement affect this decision?

What is lacking in the literature at this point is an economic theory of philanthropic giving. The rate at which the philanthropist discounts future transfers to public charities and the rate of return on financial assets are important elements of such a theory. Cordes and Sansing (2007) show that if the foundation owns assets with a value of V_0, earns a pre-tax rate of return of R, pays a tax rate of τ, distributes the legal minimum of m percent of assets, and uses a discount rate of r to reflect the value of current versus future charitable distributions, then the present value of all future distributions is

$$\frac{V_0(m - R\tau)}{m + r - R}. \tag{3.1}$$

If the discount rate r is equal to the after-tax rate of return $R(1 - \tau)$, (3.1) implies that the minimum distribution requirement has no effect on the present value of future charitable distributions: the lower level of current distributions is exactly offset by the higher level of future distributions. However, a full theory of philanthropic giving would be one in which immediate gifts to public charities, gifts to a private foundation (and subsequent gifts to public charities by the foundation) and testamentary charitable transfers are all possible alternatives to either private consumption or bequests to non-charitable beneficiaries.

Notes

1. All statutory references are to the Internal Revenue Code of 1986, as amended.
2. Private operating foundations engage in charitable activities directly instead of making grants. These foundations face a different set of tax rule restrictions than grant-making foundations. I do not examine private operating foundations in this chapter. Donor-advised funds make grants, but their assets are controlled by a public charity. I do not examine donor-advised funds in this chapter.
3. Suppose 100 foundations are randomly assigned a beginning endowment and a fixed payout rate that is uncorrelated with the endowment. The ending endowment will be negatively correlated with the payout

rate because a foundation with a low payout rate will grow faster than a foundation with a high payout rate.
4. Holmstrom and Milgrom (1987) examine the tensions that arise when an agent has multiple activities, some of which are easy to measure and some of which are difficult to measure.
5. Bikhchandani et al. (1998) review the herding literature.
6. Survival bias is a powerful factor in interpreting results of studies in finance; see Brown et al. (1995).
7. The inability of the Congress to understand the fungibility of money led to a temporary 85 percent reduction in the tax on dividends from foreign subsidiaries, as long as 'the dividend is reinvested in the United States . . . for the purposes of job retention or creation' (IRC section 965(b)(4)).
8. Nevertheless, if future expenditures are discounted at the same 5 percent rate, the present value of future charitable expenditures associated with the one dollar of foundation assets is a full dollar.

References

Beatty, Sally (2007), 'Families wrestle with closing foundations', *Wall Street Journal*, 17 April, D1.
Bikhchandani, Sushil, David Hirshleifer and Ivo Welch (1998), 'Learning from the behavior of others: conformity, fads, and informational cascades', *Journal of Economic Perspectives*, **12** (3), 151–70.
Billitteri, Thomas J. (2005), 'Money, mission, and the payout rule: in search of a strategic approach to foundation spending', Nonprofit Sector Research Fund Working Paper Series, The Aspen Institute.
Brody, E. (1997), 'Charitable endowments and the democratization of a dynasty', *Arizona Law Review*, **39**, 873–948.
Brown, Stephen J., William N. Goetzmann and Stephen A. Ross (1995), 'Survival', *Journal of Finance*, **50** (3), 853–73.
Cambridge Associates (2000), 'Sustainable payout for foundations', Cambridge Associates, Inc., Cambridge, MA.
Cordes, Joseph J. and Richard Sansing (2007), 'Institutional philanthropy', in Dennis R. Young (ed.), *Financing Nonprofits: Putting Theory into Practice*, Lanham, MD: AltaMira Press, pp. 45–68.
Craig, J. (1999), 'In favor of five percent', *Foundation News and Commentary*, **40** (May/June), 23–5.
Deep, Akash and Peter Frumkin (2006), 'The foundation payout puzzle', in William Damon and Susan Verducci (eds), *Taking Philanthropy Seriously*, Bloomington, IN: Indiana University Press, pp. 189–204.
Hansmann, Henry (1980), 'The role of nonprofit enterprise', *Yale Law Journal*, **89**, 835–901.
Hansmann, Henry (1990), 'Why do universities have endowments?', *Journal of Legal Studies*, **19**, 3–42.
Holmstrom, Bengt and Paul Milgrom (1987), 'Aggregation and linearity in the provision of intertemporal incentives', *Econometrica*, **55** (2), 303–28.
Klausner, Michael (2003), 'When time isn't money: foundation payouts and the time value of money', *The Exempt Organization Tax Review*, **41** (3), 421–8.
Lenkowsky, Leslie (2002), 'Foundations and corporate philanthropy', in Lester M. Salmon (ed.), *The State of Nonprofit America*, Washington, DC: Brookings Institution Press, pp. 355–86.
Letts, Christine W., William Ryan and Allen Grossman (1997), 'Virtuous capital: what foundations can learn from venture capitalists', *Harvard Business Review*, **75** (2), 36–44.
Ludlum, Melissa (2005), 'Domestic private foundations, tax years 1993–2002', *Statistics of Income Bulletin*, **25** (2), 162–82.
Ludlum, Melissa and Mark Stanton, (2006), 'Private foundations, tax year 2003', *Statistics of Income Bulletin*, **26** (2), 192–230.
Margo, Robert A. (1992), 'Foundations', in Charles T. Clotfelter (ed.), *Who Benefits from the Nonprofit Sector?*, Chicago, IL: University of Chicago Press, pp. 207–34.
Meckstroth, Alicia and Paul Arnsberger (1998), 'A 20-year review of the nonprofit sector, 1975–1995', *Statistics of Income Bulletin*, **18** (2), 149–71.
Mehrling, P. (1999), 'Spending policies for foundations: the case for increased grants payout', National Network of Grantmakers, San Diego, CA.
Nielsen, Waldemar A. (1985), *The Golden Donors*, New York: Truman Talley Books.
Prewitt, Kenneth (2006), 'Foundations', in Walter W. Powell and Richard Steinberg (eds), *The Non-Profit Sector: A Research Handbook, 2nd edn*, New Haven, CT: Yale University Press, pp. 355–76.
Sansing, Richard and Robert J. Yetman (2006), 'Governing private foundations using the tax law', *Journal of Accounting and Economics*, **41** (3), 363–84.
Steuerle, C. Eugene (1977), 'Pay-out requirements for foundations', in research papers sponsored by the Commission on Private Philanthropy and Public Needs (Filer Commission), 4, 1663-1678. Washington, DC: US Treasury Department.
Steuerle, C. Eugene and Martin A. Sullivan (1995), 'Toward more simple and effective giving: reforming the tax rules for charitable contributions and charitable organizations', *American Journal of Tax Policy*, **12** (2), 399–447.

Stokeld, F. (2000), 'EO proposals target charitable giving, higher education', *Exempt Organization Tax Review*, **27**, 390–94.

Troyer, Thomas A. (2000), 'The 1969 Private Foundation Law: historical perspectives on its origins and under-pinnings', *The Exempt Organization Tax Review*, **27** (1), 52–65.

Whitten, Melissa (2001), 'Large nonoperating private foundations panel study, 1985–1997', *Statistics of Income Bulletin*, **21** (1), 142–51.

4   Capital formation
Robert J. Yetman

Introduction
This chapter discusses capital formation by nonprofit organizations. I define capital as the funds gathered and accumulated for the purpose of spending on what are most frequently relatively large projects. These projects, commonly called 'capital' projects, could be quite tangible, such as buildings to house the nonprofits' operations, additional collections for museums, or repayment of existing debt. Alternatively, many projects are less tangible, such as the array of expenditures necessary for a nonprofit to venture into previously undeveloped charitable activities. Whatever the purpose, the central feature is that current funds are needed to move a project forward, and those funds are needed in relatively large amounts over a relatively short period of time.

Capital providers are typically thought of as either lenders or stockholders. In this sense, a capital provider is one who asks for something back, either a loan repayment or a proportion of future profits. Lenders to nonprofits are legally entitled to repayment of their loans, along with interest. A provider of donations to a nonprofit is not legally able to claim residual profits of the nonprofit and thus nonprofits cannot legally issue stock, although as will be seen there are some circumstances when nonprofits raise capital through quasi-equity. The issue of nonprofit capital formation has been previously discussed in Tuckman (1993), and readers are directed to that excellent paper. My goal here is to expand on Tuckman's analysis with a focus on what we have learned since that study.

Capital can be supplied either externally or internally. The most common form of external capital is debt. Debt and debt-like funding come in many shapes and sizes, including bank loans, mortgage loans, municipal bonds, below-market-rate loans, loan guarantees and linked deposits. Each of these is explored more fully. The second primary source of external capital is program-related investments, which includes quasi-equity or equity equivalents. Program-related investments and equity equivalents are a somewhat new type of funding, but their use has been increasing of late. Finally, internal capital takes the form of accumulated internally generated cash that is sufficient in amount to fund potential capital projects.

When faced with a capital project, a nonprofit must choose among these various sources. The questions of whether to pursue a project, and if so how to fund it, provide a rich and fertile ground for academic research. It is unfortunately a simple task to summarize the existing body of research on nonprofit capital formation and use: we know slightly more than very little. Such is not the case in the for-profit setting where literally hundreds of studies have focused on capital formation and use. The reason for this disparity is not entirely clear, but is likely due to several factors discussed in the chapter. By systematically identifying the state of existing research and highlighting research opportunities, this chapter represents one attempt at sparking research interest into nonprofit capital formation.

The following section starts by examining the state of research, what questions have been asked, and what we have learned from this research. I then explore what questions remain unanswered, followed by the reasons for this situation. I next discuss how existing roadblocks might be overcome, and conclude with an analysis of why it is important to expand our understanding of nonprofit capital formation and use.

What we think we know: areas of general agreement from previous research

Externally supplied capital
Prior to discussing the current state of research, I first outline the existing capital structure theories as they apply to nonprofit firms. Because these theories are 'borrowed' from the for-profit sector, for-profit capital structure theories will be our starting point. In the introduction I defined capital as funds gathered and accumulated for the purpose of spending on what are most frequently relatively large projects. With respect to external capital the two common sources are debt and equity, and a firm's capital structure represents the mixture of debt and equity. In an early paper on the topic, Miller and Modigliani (1961) showed that capital structure has no theoretical effect on firm value. This finding was not in line with current financial thinking and led to a significant body of work attempting to test/overturn their hypothesis.

By means of oversimplification, two competing theories of external capital have arisen in response to the early findings of Miller and Modigliani (1961). Interested readers are directed to the reviews by Harris and Raviv (1990) and Zingales (2000). Briefly, the first theory is known as the 'pecking order' theory and hypothesizes that an organization will have a preference for certain types of financing (i.e. accumulated cash, stock or debt) over others. These choices are based on factors such as the firm's characteristics and manager's knowledge of their own true stock value relative to market prices. The second theory is the static trade-off theory where a firm is hypothesized to trade off the benefits of debt against its costs and arrives at the optimal amount of debt relative to capital stock. The benefits of debt include tax deductions and a reduction of agency costs. Because interest payments on debt are tax-deductible whereas dividend payments to stockholders are not, debt financing effectively lowers a firm's cost of capital relative to stock financing. Unfortunately neither of these two theories directly applies to the nonprofit setting and thus researchers have been required to account for those differences. Nonprofits cannot issue stock and thus the pecking order theory seems to have no place (although nonprofit managers may prefer one type of financing over another for other reasons or capital campaigns can raise funds that in some ways act like stock). However, as pointed out by Wedig (1994, p. 258) donors receive 'dividends-in-kind' in the form of utility gained by seeing the organization's goals advanced. To the extent Wedig's thinking is accurate, donations may act as a form of equity. With respect to the trade-off theory nonprofits do not (in general) pay income taxes and thus there appears to be no tax benefit to debt.

Nonetheless some features of existing theory can be applied to the nonprofit setting. Bankruptcy costs are still present. Although a nonprofit organization cannot be forced into a Chapter 7 involuntary bankruptcy, it may choose to undergo a Chapter 11 reorganization. The managerial disciplining effect of interest payments on debt can apply to nonprofits by forcing managers to consider the cost of their investments. With respect to taxes, municipal bonds can generate a positive net cash flow to the extent a nonprofit has sufficient other cash on hand and invests that cash in taxable investments. If the non-taxable interest earned on the investments exceeds the interest expense on the municipal bonds, the nonprofit can earn a risk-free arbitrage profit on the bonds. For example, if a nonprofit can issue tax-exempt bonds at 3 percent, and invest those proceeds in corporate bonds returning 4 percent, the 1 percent spread is pure profit. This situation is not uncommon as nonprofits do not pay taxes on their investment earnings, yet corporate bonds are taxable to most investors, driving the pre-tax returns upwards. The presence of this investment spread provides an incentive to issue municipal bonds even if the proceeds are not needed (there is a significant and complex body of tax laws aimed at preventing this sort of arbitrage, see Gentry, 2002 for a discussion). Below, I discuss the existing research that has addressed these issues.

Debt
Debt is a financial instrument that permits an organization to use someone else's cash for a period of time. Debt is expected to be repaid in full. Until such time as the debt is repaid, the user of the cash typically pays the owner for the use of the cash. Such a payment is called interest. Interest can be thought of as having two components, the first a result of inflation and the second a result of required real return. If the lender did not charge some interest at least equal to inflation, then upon repayment at some later date the lender would receive less value than they provided to the borrower in real (after inflation) terms. In addition to asking borrowers to protect them from inflation, lenders also ask for a real return on the funds, largely based on their risk.

In one of the first studies on nonprofit capital structure, Wedig et al. (1988) examine nonprofit hospitals (presumably because data were available) and hypothesize that since there is no income tax on nonprofit hospitals (and thus debt has no tax benefit), yet bankruptcy risks remain, nonprofit hospitals would seemingly select an all-equity capital structure. However, empirically, virtually all nonprofit hospitals have debt obligations (Yetman, 2007). In light of this, Wedig et al. (1988) present a capital structure model (and find empirical support for their model) that assumes that nonprofit hospitals maximize the difference between cash inflows and cash outflows, taking into account specific institutional factors of the hospital industry. In a follow-on paper, Wedig et al. (1989) examined a mixture of investor-owned and nonprofit hospitals, finding support for static trade-off theory. Bacon (1992) again examines nonprofit hospitals but in contrast to Wedig et al. (1989) finds support for the pecking order theory. Wedig et al. (1996) again find support for a trade-off theory by finding that nonprofit hospitals appear to have target levels of municipal bonds that decline as the availability of alternative profitable capital projects declines and grows as the level of unused debt capacity (i.e. the ability to borrow and make interest payments) increases. In this paper, Wedig et al. focus on specific characteristics of municipal debt. Bowman (2002) controls for the effects of a nonprofit's investments (endowment assets) and finds additional support for the trade-off theory. Unlike previous studies, Bowman (2002) uses data on nonprofits in general rather than just focusing on hospitals. Gentry (2002) returns to nonprofit hospitals and examines how they use municipal bonds in their capital structure for tax planning purposes. Finally, the most recent published paper on nonprofit capital structure is by Jegers and Verschueren (2006), who examine California nonprofits of all types in a single year (i.e. 1999). Rather than test any specific capital structure theory, Jegers and Verschueren

(2006) take a different approach by attempting to explain nonprofit borrowing levels as a function of three commonly agreed upon costs; equity constraints; agency problems; and borrowing constraints. The authors find mixed support for their hypotheses, and find several results opposite to those hypothesized.

To summarize the somewhat limited empirical research to date on nonprofit capital structure, studies support both the trade-off and pecking-order theories, even though the two theories are not completely compatible with one another. Nonprofits appear to use tax-exempt debt as a tax planning mechanism (by investing the proceeds from municipal bond issuances and investing them in higher-return assets), and the typical costs (such as bankruptcy) one would associate with debt appear to have marginal or no effect.

Program-related investments and equity equivalents
The second category of externally supplied capital is program-related investments (PRIs), or more accurately stated, some types of PRIs. PRIs are sources of capital provided by donors (typically foundations) and given to nonprofit organization in order to fund specific projects or programs. PRI is not new, first appearing in the USA by way of Benjamin Franklin, who dedicated 2000 pounds to establish a revolving fund for young artisans (Cerny, 1999). For two reasons PRIs are typically provided by foundations rather than individual donors. First, to the extent that PRIs meet section 4944 of the IRS Code (i.e. the primary purpose is charitable and not generating income), they can be included as program-related investments and thus count towards foundations' 5 percent payout requirements. Second, foundations have the critical monetary mass to provide funding for capital project grants.

Although PRIs account for a relatively small fraction of total foundation giving, the percentage is increasing. Foundations have three motivations for using PRIs (as opposed to the more traditional grant to nonprofit organizations). First, many PRIs are structured such that the principal amount of the grant is returned to the foundation at some later date. This makes those funds available to other nonprofits at some future time. Second, depending on the structure of the PRIs, they may be able to fill needs that grants could not. For example, a below-market-rate loan (one example of a PRI) can assist a nonprofit with building a credit history, while a direct grant cannot. Finally, it is an empirical fact that most foundations pay out in the form of grants the legally minimum required amount (Sansing and Yetman, 2006). One rationale for this behavior is that paying out additional amounts would deplete the endowment. PRIs that have pay-back clauses are one way in which a foundation can provide funding to nonprofits while minimizing depletion of their endowment capital.

Of the several types of PRIs, the three that do not have equity-like characteristics include below-market-rate loans, loan guarantees and linked deposits. Foundations are commonly in the position to offer loans to nonprofits at rates below those of a commercial lender. Commercial lenders charge high rates when the project being financed is risky, and/or the nonprofit has few assets to pledge. As an alternative, rather than making a direct loan to the nonprofit, a foundation can instead act as a guarantee for a commercial loan made to a nonprofit. In this way the foundation's only financial obligation is to step into the shoes of the nonprofit, to some extent, should the nonprofit default. Finally, foundations can place funds in a depository institution (typically a community development financial institution) in exchange for a commitment from the institution to provide low-interest loans to qualified/specified nonprofit borrowers. In exchange, the foundation accepts a below-market return on its deposits.

One category of PRI can act as quasi-equity, or as equity equivalents. In the traditional sense equity is some fractional ownership of a firm. Equity confers many rights, including the right to proportional earnings of the organization, the right to elect a board of directors, the right to sell equity to others, and the right to recovery of investment in a liquidation (subject to subordination laws). Private inurement laws act to prevent nonprofit organizations from assigning liquidation proceed rights and the right to elect the board of directors. However, in certain circumstances claims to current and future earnings are permitted, such as when the funding is for a specific project or venture. These grants, which are referred to as recoverable grants, are to be repaid to the foundation at some future time, depending on a set of specific conditions. Common examples of projects that are funded with refundable grants include new facilities or new lines of charitable business. One common theme among the projects is that they have the potential to generate sufficient funds to repay the grant. If the project produces sufficient cash flow at some future time, the nonprofit will use those funds to repay the grant. If, however, the project fails to produce sufficient cash flows, the nonprofit is not required to repay the grant. Often the funded projects are 'start-up' ventures, or new charitable activities not currently engaged in by the nonprofit. In this way, the grantor is acting as a quasi-venture capitalist.

Although the terms of recoverable grants vary widely, there are some common elements. Recoverable grants are typically unsecured in that the grantor does not ask the grantee to pledge its assets as it would for a bank loan. Depending on the term of the grant, it could be zero interest, but more commonly a reasonable (and often below-market) interest rate is charged. The projects are expected to be viable, but are relatively high risk and not suitable for financing via a traditional loan. The single feature that distinguishes a recoverable grant from a below-market-rate loan is that loans are always repayable, whether the underlying projects funded pay off or fail. Recoverable grants are forgiven if projects do not pay off as projected.

From the grantor's perspective, the grant is essentially an equity investment in the nonprofit. If the investment 'pays off', the grantor will recover its initial investment plus an additional return. If the investment 'fails', the grantor will essentially consider the investment a normal grant for which it requires no repayment. For accounting purposes, the grantor will carry the grant on its books as an account receivable (and not an 'investment'). When repaid, the receivable will be removed. From the grantee's perspective, the receipt of a recoverable grant is not grant revenue, but rather is a liability until either the funds are repaid (in which case the liability is removed) or the grant is determined to be unpayable, at which time the grantor is notified of intent not to repay the grant (in which case the liability is removed and grant revenue is booked).

To date, there is not a single academic study (i.e. that tests hypotheses using data) that examines PRIs and equity equivalents. There are, however, some excellent descriptive discussions of PRIs, and interested readers are directed there (see Cooch and Kramer, 2007).

Internally supplied capital
In addition to externally supplied capital, nonprofits can also turn to internally generated and/or accumulated funds. In accounting terms, total for-profit organization profits

net of dividends are classified as 'retained earnings'. These retained earnings are not necessarily available in cash, as they could have been already consumed for investment in buildings or equipment, or to repay debt. The amount of capital within a firm that is available for funding projects is more accurately identified by the balances in the cash and investments accounts. The same is true of nonprofit organizations, where the ending fund balance is not a good descriptor of available cash.

In the for-profit setting, investigation of internal capital markets is relatively new, having its genesis about ten years ago. Initial studies in the for-profit setting hypothesized that the role of internal capital markets is to channel limited resources to different uses inside a company (Stein, 1997). If one considers a company as an aggregation of various technologically distinct projects, it is reasonable to presume that these projects compete for resources as they seek funding from corporate headquarters. In this role corporate headquarters functions as a rationing agent supplying capital to its projects (the alternative is to have each project set up as stand-alone company that raises its own external capital). The role of headquarters is to create value by actively reallocating scarce funds across projects. These largely theoretical studies were followed by several empirical papers investigating a broad range of issues such as the efficiency of internal capital markets or their relation to capital structure and officer compensation. The chapter references contain several citations to internal capital market studies. With respect to nonprofit organizations, there is not a single published academic article (i.e. that tests hypotheses using data) on the topic; nor could I find any working papers.

One issue of interest in the nonprofit setting is the utility of donors. When a donor provides funding to a nonprofit, is it the donor's expectation that the funds will be used on some relatively short-term need, or will those funds be accumulated for a rainy day (or a capital project)? If the donor knows what the funds will be used for, does it, and should it, matter? To be sure, some donors are well aware of the anticipated use of the funds, such as when a nonprofit is conducting a fundraising campaign for a specific, perhaps capital, project. But what about general and atomistic donations? When an investor gives a for-profit firm cash, there is the clear intent of getting that cash back, plus more. But what does a donor expect, and how does that expectation map into the nonprofit accumulating those funds for potential future capital project? These and related questions remain unanswered.

Areas of conflicting results and unexplored questions from previous research

External capital markets

Debt   As previously discussed, the issue of debt in the capital structure or nonprofit organizations has seen some work, but for the most part the important questions remain definitively unanswered. Is the pecking-order or the trade-off theory appropriate? Is another, yet unidentified, theory better at predicting nonprofit capital structure behavior? It seems that we have not moved very far in answering the most basic of nonprofit capital structure questions.

Program-related investments and equity equivalents   There is but a single published paper examining equity-like investments in the nonprofit setting (Tuckman and Chang,

1992). Given there is only one paper, it comes as no surprise that there are no conflicting results to report. Hence the potential slate of issues is essentially clean. One obvious place to look for unexplored questions is the existing for-profit literature on equity.

The first research hurdle seems to be defining what nonprofit equity means. Some authors have tried to classify all donations and grants as a form of equity, as the donor requires some amount of utility in return for their gift. While a true donation is not equity in the legal or accounting sense, it could be in the economic sense. This situation is not well explored, although interested readers are referred to the work of James Andreoni as well as that of others (see Andreoni, 2006). If clear economic circumstances in which donations are equity can be drawn, the array of potential nonprofit capital papers literally explodes. For example, what, exactly, do donors require in exchange for their current and continued donations?

Agency problems are another area that seems ripe for additional research. PRIs in general and recoverable grants in particular present a moral hazard situation in which a nonprofit is insured against risky decisions. The effects of moral hazard (such as one's tendency to act recklessly when one's actions are insured against loss) on nonprofits' capital formation is unexplored. It might seem than in a repeated game, the failure to repay one grant might have an effect on the probability of acquiring another recoverable grant, but again this remains unexplored.

Internal capital markets
There is not a single published study (and no working papers could be found) on the topic as it relates to the nonprofit organizational form. As previously, there is no reason to believe that this topic is not equally applicable to the nonprofit form. Nonprofits have various investment opportunities, likely with differing amounts of pay-off (however measured). These projects compete with each other for funding. Managers must decide which activities to pursue and how to finance them. To the extent that external capital is more costly than internal capital, the manager should finance chosen projects with internal capital. The role of management is to allocate internal capital across various projects so as to maximize value, however defined.

To develop a list of unexplored questions in the nonprofit setting for internal capital markets, one need look no further than the extensive body of research questions previously addressed in the for-profit setting. These papers include both theoretical and empirical works, and span US and non-US markets. Rather than include a (rather long) list of potential research topics, I suggest that interested readers consult the list of references at the end of this chapter, including Stein (1997), Shin and Stulz (1998) and so on.

Why there are gaps in our knowledge
Given the significant lack of research on nonprofit capital structure, the obvious question is why such is the case. I see two plausible reasons for the lack of research. First, the types of researchers interested in and qualified to conduct capital structure research are historically not as interested in the nonprofit organizational form as they are the for-profit form. Second, good data are hard to come by. I explore both of these possibilities below.

Historically, capital formation and structure research has been conducted by finance and accounting researchers. In both cases these researchers are brought up in the profit-maximizing paradigm which in turn focuses attention on the for-profit organization. Exacerbating this situation is institutional momentum. The accounting industry is largely focused on the for-profit firm. The Financial Accounting Standards Board, the body responsible for promulgating accounting guidelines, has produced no less than 150 pronouncements, roughly ten of which relate to nonprofit organizations. The New York Stock Exchange contains no listed nonprofit organizations, and thus nonprofits do not command the attention of the bulk of finance practitioners. The academic area of Finance can be broken down into two primary components: investments and corporate finance. The investments area focuses on stocks, and thus pays little or no attention to nonprofits. The corporate finance area is likewise focused on the for-profit firm, but has wandered into the nonprofit realm on occasion. Some accounting and finance researchers have only relatively recently begun to cross over into nonprofit organization research, but they remain the small minority. Clearly this is an area ripe for cross-pollination, and it is likely that more research resources will pour into the nonprofit area from accounting and finance researchers.

With respect to empirical research that relies on data, the roadblocks are many. For example, consider a hypothetical study on nonprofit internal capital markets. In a typical for-profit study in internal capital markets, the data are taken from commercially available databases such as Compustat. In the nonprofit setting similar financial variables are available in the IRS Statistics of Income files available from the National Center for Charitable Statistics at www.nccs.urban.org. However, the Compustat datasets include what are known as 'segment' data. Segment data include financial results of various business segments within a single firm. For example, a conglomerate firm's segments might include tobacco, food products and financial services. This reporting method is required by the Financial Accounting Standards Board. Segment data are useful in internal capital market research as a researcher can observe the amounts of resources devoted to various segments as well as the relative performance of those segments (all of which is included in the Compustat data). Thus segment data provide input measures (the amount of assets devoted to a segment) as well as output measures (the performance of a segment). The Compustat data also contain sufficient information to identify the sources of resources, be they from external (such as issuing debt or stock) or internal (retained earnings) sources. By investigating the relation between inputs from internal versus external sources and relative outputs, a researcher can calibrate differential effects of internal versus external capital markets.

Unfortunately for researchers, the IRS Form 990 contains few if any obvious data on various internal projects, or 'segments' within a single nonprofit. If such data are provided, they are typically only descriptive, with little if any financial information such as resources devoted or expenditures incurred. Thus it is difficult to conduct a study of nonprofit internal capital markets using easily available public information, and this fact likely explains the lack of research on the topic.

This same analysis could be done with respect to PRIs and equity equivalents. There is no easy way to tell if a nonprofit has received a PRI or a refundable grant simply by using publicly available information. This situation does leave ample opportunity, however, for those willing to hand-collect such data. Debt is one area in which some data are available. The IRS Form 990 does break down various types of debt, although the terms of those debt instruments are not disclosed in the same manner as they would be for a publicly traded for-profit firm. The existence of at least some data sources likely explains why this area of nonprofit capital research has seen the most work to date.

What must be done to further our knowledge

Overcoming the seemingly natural reluctance of accounting and finance researchers to engage in nonprofit research is a first step in expanding this area of research. I can speak from experience that this road is not one for the timid. Nonetheless the rewards are possibly quite high in a typical risk–return modeling sense. Once a sufficient number of researchers has been drawn into the area, and journals become accustomed to the type of research, I expect the knowledge gap to shrink quickly thereafter. However, I expect that we are perhaps some time away from nonprofit finance and/or accounting research being considered mainstream. Overcoming the data availability issue will likewise have its own cures. Surveying nonprofits for various types of data that are not publicly available is becoming a more frequent data-gathering technique. Undoubtedly once demand for this type of research rises, supply will follow, and that supply will require data.

Concluding remarks: expanding our knowledge to practitioners, policy makers and scholars

The existing voids in nonprofit capital structure research affect several stakeholder groups. Academics search for new knowledge often for its own sake. By doing so they push the knowledge envelope outwards, and this action is one of many that advances a civilization. But there are more practical implications. Existing practices by industry professionals are to some extent driven by the lessons learned from academic research. With respect to capital structure, it is quite likely that most publicly traded for-profit firms consider some sort of model, either explicitly or implicitly, prior to issuing stock or borrowing. Without similar research in the nonprofit setting, nonprofit managers have little to go on. These issues are very real: how should one finance a capital project? The markets I speak of likewise already exist. Banks give loans to nonprofits. Donors give grants and donations. Foundations give PRIs. The projects I speak of already exist. Nonprofits build buildings. Nonprofits enter into new ventures. What is missing is a body of academic research on how one of these markets maps into the other. This central issue is one in waiting.

References

Andreoni, James (2006), 'Philanthropy', in Serge-Christopher Kolm and Jean Mercier Ythier (eds), *Handbook of the Economics of Giving, Altruism and Reciprocity, Volume 2: Applications*, New York: Elsevier, pp. 1201–65.
Bacon, P.W. (1992), 'Do capital structure theories apply to nonprofit hospitals?' *Journal of the Midwest Finance Association*, **21** (1), 86–90.
Bowman, Woods (2002), 'The uniqueness of nonprofit finance and the decision to borrow', *Nonprofit Management and Leadership*, **12** (3), 293–311.
Cerny, Milton (1999), 'Creative uses of program related investments', *Journal of the International Center for Not-for-Profit Law*, **1** (3), 7–12.
Cooch, Sarah and Mark Kramer (2007), 'Compounding impact: mission investing by US foundations', Report for FSG Social Impact Advisors, Boston, MA.
Gentry, William (2002), 'Debt, investment and endowment accumulation: the case of not-for-profit hospitals', *Journal of Health Economics*, **21** (5), 845–72.
Harris, Milton and Artur Raviv (1990), 'The theory of capital structure', *The Journal of Finance*, **46** (1), 297–355.

Jegers, Marc and Ilse Verschueren (2006), 'On the capital structure of non-profit organisations: an empirical study for California organisations', *Financial Accountability and Management*, **22** (4), 309–29.

Miller, Merton and Franco Modigliani (1961), 'Dividend policy, growth, and the valuation of shares', *Journal of Business*, **34** (4), 411–32.

Sansing, Richard and Robert Yetman (2006), 'Governing private foundations using the tax law', *Journal of Accounting and Economics*, **41**, 363–84.

Shin, Hyun-Han and René M. Stulz (1998), 'Are internal capital markets efficient?', *Quarterly Journal of Economics*, **113** (2), 531–52.

Stein, Jeremy C. (1997), 'Internal capital markets and the competition for corporate resources', *Journal of Finance*, **52** (1), 111–33.

Tuckman, Howard P. (1993), 'How and why nonprofit organizations obtain capital', in David C. Hammack and Dennis R. Young (eds), *Nonprofit Organizations in a Market Economy*, San Francisco, CA: Jossey-Bass, pp. 203–32.

Tuckman, Howard P. and Cyril F. Chang (1992), 'Nonprofit equity: a behavioral model and its policy implications', *Journal of Policy Analysis and Management*, **11** (1), 76–87.

Wedig, Gerard J. (1994), 'Risk, leverage, donations and dividends-in-kind: a theory of nonprofit financial behavior', *International Review of Economics and Finance*, **3** (3), 257–78.

Wedig, Gerard J., Mahmud Hassan and Michael A. Morrisey (1996), 'Tax-exempt debt and the capital structure of nonprofit organizations: an application to hospitals', *Journal of Finance*, **51** (4), 1247–83.

Wedig, Gerard J., Mahmud Hassan and Frank A. Sloan (1989), 'Hospital investment decisions and the cost of capital', *Journal of Business*, **62** (4), 517–37.

Wedig, Gerard J., Frank A. Sloan, Mahmud Hassan and Michael A. Morrisey (1988), 'Capital structure, ownership, and capital payment policy: the case of hospitals', *Journal of Finance*, **43** (1), 21–40.

Yetman, Robert J. (2007), 'Borrowing and debt', in Dennis R. Young (ed.), *Financing Nonprofits: Putting Theory Into Practice*, Lanham, MD: AltaMira Press, pp. 243–68.

Zingales, Luigi (2000), 'In search of new foundations', *Journal of Finance*, **55**, 1623–53.

5 Asset composition
Woods Bowman

Introduction
Assets are resources – factors of production, as economists say. In the for-profit sector, which assets are used and in what proportions are determined by the producer's choice of (1) product, defined to include its level of quality, and (2) the technology used to produce it. Nonprofit status is a legal construct, not a production process. But, in the Coasian view of a firm as a 'nexus of contracts', the legal structure may have a profound effect on the way assets are mobilized in production. The median nonprofit owns \$204 000 in total assets but the range is enormous. Ten percent own less than \$12 500 whereas 10 percent have more than \$4.9 million.[1] Even within industry groups, there is considerable variation in the mix of assets.[2]

What we think we know
Most of what we think we know comes from the literature on business finance and focuses on the classic issue of liquidity. New strands of inquiry are beginning to develop using other ideas from the business literature such as risk control and the closely related concept of asset partitioning.

Liquidity
Current assets help finance day-to-day operations. They consist of cash and cash equivalents or assets that can be converted to cash in less than one year without discount from their fair market value. They include cash, cash equivalents (savings accounts, money market funds) receivables (money owed to the organization), inventory, marketable securities and prepaid expenses. There are significant differences between for-profit businesses and nonprofits in the categories of inventories, receivables and marketable securities.

As far as inventory is concerned, most nonprofits have negligible amounts because they tend to provide services rather than goods. The median inventory for 26 of the 28 major NTEE categories is zero. The exceptions are higher education (\$248 901) and hospitals (\$488 829). More detailed data would probably show that nonprofits that build housing for low-income families have large inventories as a proportion of assets. Further, housing inventories may be difficult to liquidate on satisfactory terms, exacerbating their liquidity problems.

Nearly every seller of goods and services has some accounts receivable as a result of extending credit to buyers. Trade credit is usually payable within 30 days. But a charitable nonprofit,[3] by virtue of its tax-exempt status, has other types of receivables not found in the for-profit sector, namely gifts receivable (pledges) and grants receivable. Nonprofit receivables are often less liquid than receivables of for-profit businesses because: (1) nonprofits may be more tolerant of delinquent accounts,[4] (2) grants receivable and pledges may not convert to cash soon enough to pay an organization's current bills; and (3) state and local governments, which purchase substantial health and human services from nonprofits, are notoriously slow to pay their service providers when they are experiencing budget problems of their own.

For-profit firms outside of the financial services industry hold marketable securities while they are searching for opportunities to grow their business. Nonprofits do this too, of course, but they have other reasons for holding marketable securities. They may hold them as an operating reserve to buffer uncertain gift income. As an endowment or quasi-endowment, marketable securities generate a source of income year after year to subsidize production of goods and services that do not pay their own way.[5] Although nonprofits have more reasons to own marketable securities than for-profit firms, only 19.6 percent of nonprofits report owning them.

While it is reasonable to classify marketable securities owned by for-profit businesses outside of the financial services industry as current assets, marketable securities owned by nonprofits may be long-term assets. Permanently restricted investments in an endowment may not be legally liquidated and expended. Thus individual securities may be highly liquid but, if they are part of an endowment, contribute nothing to the operational liquidity of the nonprofit organization that owns them.[6]

As noted above, temporarily restricted assets tend to be held as cash or invested in very short-term instruments. Consequently, many organizations appear to be highly liquid because they hold much more in cash and savings than they need to finance day-to-day transactions, whereas in reality much of their cash and savings are temporarily restricted. Perhaps this explains why Core et al. (2004) find that the cash position of nonprofits is, on average, substantially larger than that of for-profit firms.

A standard measure of liquidity in both for-profit and nonprofit sectors is the 'quick ratio', which consists of cash, cash equivalents and various receivables divided by current liabilities (mostly payables). Nearly half of nonprofits have no current liabilities. Since the focus of this study is asset allocation, more interesting ratios are quick assets (the numerator of the quick ratio) to total assets and unrestricted quick assets (quick assets minus temporarily restricted net assets) to total assets. See Table 5.1.

In general, liquidity, as measured by the quick ratio, is very high. In nine subgroups this percentage exceeds half of total assets: health (disease-specific), health (research), crime and legal-related, employment-related, international and foreign affairs, civil rights and advocacy, social science, and public and society benefit. However, much of this liquidity is more apparent than real because many of the assets involved are temporarily restricted. An examination of the second column of Table 5.1, which subtracts temporarily restricted net assets from the numerator, reveals only two subgroups with liquid assets exceeding half of total assets.

If we assume that a 'normal' amount of working capital is one month's expenses, we can estimate the median operating reserve by subtracting 8 percent (one-twelfth of a year) from the fourth column (Unrestricted quick assets as a percentage of Total expenses). Religious organizations have hardly any operating reserves. Eleven other subgroups have median operating reserves of 10 percent or less. Only three have median operating reserves exceeding 20 percent: health (research), philanthropy and voluntarism, and public safety and disaster preparedness. It seems reasonable to expect these subgroups to have greater need for operating reserves than others.

Koren and Szeidl (2003) develop a model that predicts that physical assets increase demand for liquid assets. There is evidence that nonprofits conform to this prediction.

Table 5.1   Median asset ratios by NTEE category

		Number	Median ratios			Est. median operating reserve
			QA of TA	UnRQA of TA	UnRQA of Exp.	
	All categories	242 776	27	20	16	8
A	Arts, culture, humanities	26 259	21	13	13	5
B	Education	41 275	20	13	11	3
BH	Higher education	1 833	14	6	11	3
C	Environment	5 305	36	20	20	12
D	Animal-related	4 252	16	11	13	5
E	Health	16 092	42	34	23	15
EH	Hospitals	3 235	25	23	21	13
F	Mental health	6 726	47	40	18	10
G	Health – disease specific	4 732	62	48	24	16
H	Health – research	1 323	59	45	33	25
I	Crime, legal-related	4 638	68	50	18	10
J	Employment-related	3 428	53	48	22	14
K	Food, agriculture, nutrition	2 424	32	24	14	6
L	Housing, shelter	15 274	8	6	18	10
M	Public safety, disaster prep.	3 934	20	18	54	46
N	Recreation, sports	2 553	26	21	12	4
O	Youth development	2 658	27	16	14	6
P	Human services, multi-purpose	3 597	36	28	15	7
Q	International, foreign affairs	4 640	65	42	13	5
R	Civil Rights, advocacy	1 577	74	54	20	12
S	Community improvement	10 060	40	27	22	14
T	Philanthropy, voluntarism	13 079	13	8	34	26
U	Science, technology	1 143	37	26	25	17
V	Social science	452	55	38	24	16
W	Public, society benefit	2 166	61	42	22	14
X	Religion-related	12 918	15	11	8	0
Y	Mutual, membership	600	14	11	25	17

Notes: QA = Quick assets = Cash + Savings + Receivables; TA = Total assets; UnRQA = Unrestricted QA = QA − Temporarily restricted net assets; Exp. = Total expenses.

Based on a sample of nonprofits that have all three kinds of assets (liquid, physical and securities), a double log cross-sectional regression of quick-adjusted assets on the gross value of land, building and equipment (LBE), controlling for holdings of securities, a 1 percent increase in gross LBE increases quick-adjusted assets by 6.6 percent.[7] On the other hand, another regression of the ratio of quick-adjusted assets to total expenses on the log of LBE yields a positive, but statistically insignificant, result.

Risk control
Modern portfolio theory teaches organizations how to minimize risk for a given return or, conversely, how to maximize return for a given risk. Private investors approach the

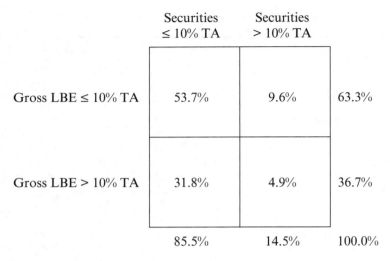

Note: LBE = Land, building and equipment; TA = Total assets.

Figure 5.1   Two-way classification of organizations by size of securities and gross LBE holdings (% of all organizations)

problem first by assessing their 'appetite for risk' and then squeezing as much return on assets (ROA) as possible from their assets within that constraint. Nonprofit organizations should not be motivated by profit, so they should approach the problem from the opposite direction – formally referred to as the dual problem. They should first decide how much ROA is necessary to support their need to replenish their capital stock and to support their aspirations for growth. Within that constraint they should strive to minimize risk, traditionally defined as variation in total ROA.[8] According to modern portfolio theory, asset managers control risk by diversifying their assets.

Organizations with large portfolios of securities hire professional managers and we presume they manage according to modern portfolio theory. However, there is no evidence to suggest that they consider LBE to be part of an organization's portfolio. If they did, (1) organizations with large LBE holdings would have correspondingly large portfolios of securities, and (2) managers would select financial assets that are uncorrelated or negatively correlated with the rate of return (ROA) of the organization they serve. (A necessary condition for diversification to reduce the variance of a portfolio for a given return in that the returns have zero or positive correlations.)

Form 990 does not provide information about the composition of investments in securities, but it does allow us to assess the balance between LBE and securities. Figure 5.1 classifies the sample into four groups: nonprofits with gross LBE above and below 10 percent of total assets cross-tabulated with nonprofits with security portfolios above and below 10 percent of total assets.

For most organizations (53.7 percent), both physical assets and securities are an insignificant fraction of the total assets they own. Organizations clearly specialize in the types of assets they choose to own. For nearly one-third (31.8 percent), LBE is a significant portion of their assets but they have minimal holding of securities. The asset mix of nearly 10 percent (9.6) has substantial holdings of securities, but insignificant amount of physical assets. Only 4.9 percent have significant holding of both physical assets and securities.

Asset partitioning

A more recent strand of the business literature discusses asset partitioning, a topic with immediate applicability to nonprofits. Hansmann and Kraakman (2000, p. 807) argue that organizational law 'plays a crucial role in permitting the formation of a separate pool of assets that can be pledged to bond the contracts of which the firm is the nexus'. They call this function 'asset partitioning':

> The principal rationale for asset partitioning is to reduce the overall cost of credit when dealing with a heterogeneous group of creditors. The reason [it] can reduce costs is that some creditors are better able than other to monitor the value of particular assets, or to extract value from those assets if, upon default by the debtor, the creditor takes possession of them. (Ibid., 810)

On this view, organizational law – the body of law that establishes corporations, nonprofits and even marriages – partitions a group's assets between those pledged to creditors and assets that are available to the firm's owners upon dissolution. (In the case of nonprofits, the latter assets must be transferred to another nonprofit.) However, firms can further partition their assets by forming subsidiaries, as nonprofits do when they enter into limited partnerships with for-profit corporations to obtain access to equity capital without issuing stock in, say, community development and housing ventures. The limited partnership protects their charitable assets from their corporate partner's creditors.

Supporting organizations established pursuant to section 509(a)(3) of the Internal Revenue Code are a form of asset partitioning peculiar to the nonprofit sector. Their purpose is to operate 'exclusively for the benefit of, to perform the functions of, or to carry out the purposes of one or more [public charities]'. Type I supporting organizations are supervised or controlled by the supported organization, Type II are supervised or controlled in connection with the supported organization, and Type III are operated in connection with a supported organization. This wide range of possibilities makes supporting organizations a flexible tool for a variety of financial tasks, although they (particularly Type III) may also serve as a tool for tax evasion.

According to Pollak and Dunford (2005), one in ten public charities manage assets through section 509(a)(3) supporting organizations. Any given supporting organization performs multiple functions: 72 percent pool and manage investments and endowments for supported organizations, 58 percent pay employee- and office-related expenses, 42 percent combine real estate holdings for supported organizations without providing property management, and many provide fundraising support in various forms.

The most common supporting organizations are linked to educational institutions (26 percent), health (19 percent), and human services (17 percent), which are endowed organizations owning substantial real estate and/or doing substantial fundraising (Pollak and Dunford, 2005, p. 2). Although supporting organizations numerically constitute 10 percent of public charities, they control 17 percent of charitable assets (ibid.).

> There are of course countervailing costs [to asset partitioning]. In particular asset partitioning reduces diversification and hence the probability that one of the entities involved will face bankruptcy and its associated transaction costs. Asset partitioning is efficient only when its benefits exceed its costs. (Hansmann and Kraakman, 2000, p. 812)

What we do not know

The theory of nonprofit finance with respect to asset ownership and management is underdeveloped in key several areas. The first is how a nonprofit's capital structure is related to its business model. The second is 'privileged assets', my name for those assets that cannot be sold or substantially altered in form, substance or location for either legal or practical reasons. They create special management problems, because a fundamental right of ownership is the right to alter or sell an asset. Third, a related issue area deals with endowments. Endowments are unique to nonprofit organizations, which may explain why there is no antecedent research in the business literature. Finally, there is the perplexing question of how to reconcile conflicts between the two components of the so-called 'double bottom line' – financial returns and social returns.

Interaction of capital structure and business models

Capital structure is a balance-sheet concept: it is concerned with the mix of assets and liabilities. Business model is an income (activities statement) concept: it is concerned with an organization's revenue mix and how the revenue is created. The mission of for-profit corporations is to make money; they differ only in their choice of business lines. They evaluate each business line in relation to its contribution to the corporation's bottom line. By contrast, the missions of nonprofits are varied. The same business may serve different missions and conversely many different businesses can contribute to a given mission.

Clara Miller (2003) argues that capital structure depends entirely on business model, irrespective of ownership type or mission, and, conversely, different missions are consistent with the same business model.[9] Performing arts organizations, schools and even for-profit airlines are all in the business of selling seats. It is an organization's business – in contrast to its mission – that is the key determinant of its particular asset allocation.

Other research casts doubt on these conclusions. In an exploratory study of universities that spanned two business lines (research and teaching) and three forms of ownership (for-profit corporation, nonprofit organization and government), Bowman (2007) found that ownership type has an impact on capital structure that is independent of business line. But the study looked at representatives of each category and not a stratified sample.

The question of how capital structure and business model interact is a basic one, but, oddly, there is a meager literature. Research on the hospital industry demonstrates that service mix – an essential element of a business model – systematically varies by ownership type (Horwitz, 2005; Friesner and Rosenman, 2004). This pattern is also observed in health plans (Schneider et al., 2004).

Extraneous factors can cause differences in economic performance in hospitals (Eggleston et al., 2006) and schools (Barbetta et al., 2007), so we must assume that they may also have an impact on capital structure. Nonprofit health insurers pay a higher proportion of premium dollars for claims and less for administrative expenses (Barrish, 2004). Surprisingly, they have a stronger capital base than their for-profit counterparts.

Based on the fragmentary research on this topic, it appears that business model and ownership type jointly affect capital structure. Further, ownership type and business model are not independent of each other. Choice of ownership type may depend on prior choice of business model (if you want to be a charity and collect donations, you do not organize as a proprietary firm) and evidence shows that ownership type has a role to play in choice of business model (see discussion of hospital performance above). There is much that we do not know on this topic. It deserves further research.

Restricted and other privileged assets
Ownership of an asset implies a set of well-defined legal rights: (a) the right to use it; (b) the right to benefit from it; and (c) alienation, meaning the right to change its form, substance and location, which includes the right to transfer ownership.[10] Laws place boundaries around an owner's use of his property, which in capitalist economies are expansive. However, laws governing nonprofit ownership are more stringent. The Internal Revenue Code provides for intermediate sanctions that constrain the right to benefit. The Code also requires that upon dissolution, a section 501(c)(3) organization must transfer its remaining assets to another section 501(c)(3) organization, restricting the right to alienate.

Gift restrictions and the mission of a nonprofit organization may further constrict its right to alter 'form, substance, and location' – perhaps dramatically.[11] Trusts that maintain historic sites, museums and libraries exist to preserve cultural assets. Other nonprofits may be so steeped in tradition that it would be unthinkable to alter particular assets – to bulldoze Harvard Yard, to erect a building in MIT's Great Court, or to give Carnegie Hall's acoustically superior auditorium a makeover. I call such assets privileged; they may or may not be restricted in the legal sense.

Not only are privileged assets difficult to alter in form, substance and location, but their economic return may be negative because the cost of protecting them from theft, environmental degradation and ordinary wear may be substantially in excess of their economic return. Kevin Guthrie (1996), describing the chronic financial problems of the New-York Historical Society,[12] writes eloquently about the 'liability of assets'.[13] He points out how its over-broad mission led to indiscriminate acquisition and increased its costs without a commensurate increase in financial resources.

A for-profit business that owned an underperforming asset would sell or discard it. Nonprofits do not have this luxury with many of their most valued assets. Poorly managed nonprofits acquire assets that do not support their mission particularly well and then find they have a difficult time divesting. The New-York Historical Society tried to mitigate its costs and raise some needed cash by selling some of its artifacts that were incidental to its core historical focus – a process that museums call deaccessioning.

The American Association of Museums (AAM) Code of Ethics says that 'in no event shall they [deaccessioning proceeds] be used for anything other than acquisition or direct care of collections' (Weil, 2000, p.152). Guthrie believes AAM's policy is shortsighted. He argues that museums should be able to plow funds from deaccessioning into endowment, pointing out that, if a museum cannot survive on its regular annual income, the alternative is to go out of business and break up its collection. In such cases, it makes more sense to allow it to selectively deaccession and use the proceeds to build its endowment. He makes a good point but the story he tells of the New-York Historical Society spending down its endowment is a perfect cautionary tale.

Privileged assets generally fall into the 'land, building and equipment' (LBE) category on the IRS Form 990. If we assume that most privileged assets are land or buildings and not equipment, we should focus on those organizations that hold some minimal amount of LBE. For purposes of this discussion, I use $500 000 as a threshold. Forty percent of operating public charities own more than $500 000 of LBE as valued at original cost, and 10 percent own more than $2.5 million.[14] Privileged assets are not the same as gross LBE, but they are to be found within this pool of assets.

Privileged assets constitute a special management problem for nonprofits. It would seem that they are likely to increase the demand for liquid assets even more than ordinary LBE, but we do not know.

Endowment and restricted assets
There is a robust literature on how to build an endowment and how to manage one, and if one includes the literature on free-standing endowments – non-operating private foundations – the literature is endless. There is a vigorous debate over whether endowments/foundations should exist permanently or be programmed for extinction, but this is based more on opinion than on research. There is precious little research in the nonprofit literature on how endowments form and how they affect organizational behavior. (See Bowman, 2002; Wedig, 1994; and Wedig et al. 1989 for examples.)

Endowment does double duty as part of a nonprofit's capital structure and as a revenue generator. It is a financing tool that distinguishes the public and nonprofit sectors from the for-profit sector.[15] No for-profit corporation is endowed except as required by law (e.g. cemeteries), not even for-profit universities, hospitals and theaters that coexist and compete with endowed nonprofit universities, hospitals and theaters.

The purpose and function of endowment is antithetical to for-profit publicly traded corporations. As James Tobin, the 1981 Nobel Laureate in Economics, points out, endowment promotes equity over market efficiency and institutional immortality over market opportunism: 'The trustees of an endowed institution are the guardians of the future against the claims of the present. Their task is to preserve *equity* among generations. The trustees of an endowed university . . . assume the institution to be *immortal*' (Tobin, 1974, p. 427; emphasis added).

Tobin's position on intergenerational equity is controversial. Other scholars (Frey, 2002; Brody, 1997; Hansmann, 1990) argue that it short-changes the current generation. Hansmann (1990) observes that the economy is likely to grow and per capita income to increase, concluding that equity requires future generations to subsidize the current generation, and not the other way around, as endowments do. He proposes that universities borrow to the hilt and increase future tuition to repay loans. Fremont-Smith (2002, p. 2) states that:

> If one considers the tax benefits arising from exemptions and charitable deductions as current subsidies, it is a short step to conclude that taxpayers [other than the donors] have an immediate right to a real return on that subsidy.

Other critics simply regard endowment as flagrantly wasteful. Tuckman and Chang (1992, p. 77) state that, 'a nonprofit may seek to accumulate equity without necessarily planning to use it in direct support of its mission'. The 1969 Tax Reform Act requires foundations to spend a minimum amount of their assets each year, although it imposes no such requirement on endowed operating public charities.

Legally, endowment consists of permanently restricted assets. Quasi-endowment is unrestricted assets set aside by a board of directors to be managed jointly with permanently restricted assets for the purpose of generating a steady flow of income. Generally Accepted Accounting Principles (GAAP), however, allow organizations to provide information in the notes that separates endowment investments from other investments. A nonprofit may reject a gift or grant if the restrictions are deemed to be more onerous than they are worth, but if it accepts a restricted gift or grant, it is legally bound to honor the donor's wishes. Conversely, restrictions may only be imposed by donors. Earned income is by definition unrestricted. Boards may designate unrestricted assets for certain specified purposes, but doing so creates no legal obligation; a board may reverse itself at a later date with impunity.

The perplexing double bottom line
In neoclassical economic theory, a firm combines assets such that the marginal contribution of one asset is the same as the marginal contribution of every other asset – that is, return on assets (ROA) is the same for all assets.[16] Nonprofit organizations exist to provide public benefits. Although they are not precluded from selling their services, various laws give them advantages in acquiring non-exchange resources such as gifts, grants and endowment income, which subsidize money-losing activities and acquisition of assets that are costly to own. Analytically, public benefits are positive externalities (non-rival and non-excludable public goods) produced jointly with a good or service that generates income.

Therefore nonprofits have a double bottom line. They have bills to pay and cannot avoid being concerned with making money, even if they are not driven to maximize surplus, but they also have a public-benefit mission. Having two goals introduces ambiguity into decision problems, inviting inconsistent policies. In theory, a nonprofit achieves a socially optimum level of output by equating marginal cost with marginal social benefit, which is the sum of marginal internal benefit and marginal external benefit. The former concept measures the gains to direct beneficiaries of the organization for which the organization is compensated, whereas the latter measures the value of positive externalities in the form of public goods, widely shared throughout society, for which the organization is not compensated. Optimal asset allocation policy requires that the sum of internal ROA[17] and external return on assets (XROA) should be the same for all assets. But in practice it is not this simple.

As a nonprofit begins to acquire an asset (holding other resources constant), the productivity (ROA) of the new asset at first increases. But, as acquisition continues, the principle of diminishing returns predicts that eventually it will reach a point where its productivity (ROA) will diminish. A graph of ROA versus asset utilization is an inverted U. The principle applies to XROA as well, so a graph of XROA versus asset utilization is likewise an inverted U. Ambiguity in a decision problem arises because the asset utilization level that maximizes ROA may not be the same utilization level that maximizes XROA. At the margin ROA and XROA may diverge. See Figure 5.2.

Whenever ROA and XROA rise or fall together (odd-numbered cells), a nonprofit

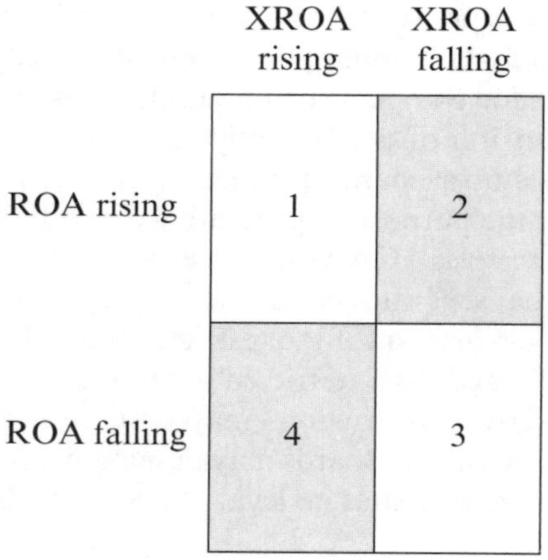

	XROA rising	XROA falling
ROA rising	1	2
ROA falling	4	3

Figure 5.2   Internal return on assets (ROA) versus external return on assets (XROA)

manager receives unambiguous feedback signals on the results of an asset composition decision. However, a rising ROA but falling XROA (even-numbered cells), or vice versa, may flummox her. She will be torn between mission and money. In principle, she knows she should focus on the sum of ROA and XROA, but measuring XROA is fraught with difficulty. It is easier to perceive direction of movement than to know precisely the level of XROA.

The problem disappears if the positive externalities associated with XROA are a monotone function of the jointly produced good or service sold for profit that generates ROA – for example, if XROA is proportional to ROA. Where an asset is dedicated to a particular program, it is reasonable, even likely, that its XROA will be a monotone function of ROA. On the other hand, if an asset is used to produce more than one good or service consumed by different clientele groups, we have no basis for assuming any particular relationship between XROA and ROA *a priori*.

Why there are gaps in our knowledge
The most important explanation for gaps in our knowledge is that much of nonprofit finance is informed by antecedent research on for-profit firms published in the business literature. Issues unique to nonprofits are less well understood because every research project is forced to break new ground. Pioneers always face a tough slog.

Second, there are problems of data availability. The most readily available datasets are based on IRS Form 990. Organizations with less than $25 000 in revenue are not required to file. Churches are not required to file and many church-affiliated organizations do not file, claiming this exemption. Consequently, reporting is uneven – in some cities Catholic Charities file the form, whereas in other cities they do not. The form itself employs a high level of asset aggregation. For example, physical assets are divided into only two categories: investment assets and mission-related assets. Financial assets include several categories of liquid assets, but only a couple of categories of securities: publicly traded and all others. Furthermore, neither GAAP nor IRS Form 990 requires assets in endowment and quasi-endowment to be distinguished from other investments.

Third, there are formidable measurement problems, as the double bottom line illustrates. If we could measure external benefits such that they are commensurate with financial returns, we could add the two together. Then, optimizing firm output would be a straightforward extension of techniques that are well known in the business literature, making the first problem less important.

Fourth, and lastly, there are ideological barriers. Consider the issue of whether wealth accumulation by the nonprofit sector is excessive. On this there is no consensus (Fremont-Smith, 2002, p. 3) and viewpoints are widely divergent. On one side, Nobel Laureate James Tobin, quoted above, supports endowments as a means of preserving intergenerational equity. On the other side, a McKinsey team led by former Senator Bill Bradley estimates that nonprofits 'currently hold about $270 billion in *excess* capital in their endowments', and urge that it be drawn down over 25 years (Bradley et al., 2003, p. 99; emphasis in original).[18] If people believe endowments are wasteful, there are few good reasons to study them.

Or, consider a more fundamental ideological issue: whether nonprofit organizations, with their dazzling diversity of missions and methods, have enough in common to justify attempts to study them *en bloc* and to generalize. (I believe that an organizational mandate to pursue a collective mission coupled with an inability to sell stock are sufficient defining characteristics that, for all the talk of boundary blurring, set nonprofits apart and make them fit objects of serious scholarly attention.) In the end, the ideological barriers may be the most serious because they limit the number of researchers and the scope of their inquiries.

What must be done to further our knowledge
Sherlock Holmes could have been speaking of nonprofit research when he said, 'The temptation to form premature theories upon insufficient data is the bane of our profession' (*Valley of Fear*[19]). Descriptive studies and development of new empirical tools will expand the research horizon and go far toward identifying and framing the salient theoretical questions.

There is a multitude of case studies, and papers using grounded theory, but there is a dearth of cases focusing on finance, addressing issues such as: who owns what kind of assets, in what quantities, and in conjunction with what other kinds of assets? How are capital structure and business model related? How do specific assets contribute to productivity? How is asset acquisition financed? Case studies such as Guthrie's (1996) are invaluable to a better understanding of the interplay between finance and operations, but they are expensive, time-consuming projects. Moreover, the market for such monographs is thin; Guthrie's book has been out of print for some time.[20]

The IRS recently revised its Form 990. It asks for more information, but as one might expect, the questions are driven by tax policy, not by research needs. New questions about income from donor-advised funds are worthwhile and they will probably stimulate further research in this direction, but the asset categories are still too coarse to allow investigation of many interesting questions about capital structure. A simple addition would be to have separate categories for temporarily restricted cash and savings. It would also be desirable to require classification of investments into investments held for income (i.e. endowment and quasi-endowment) and investments for all other purposes.

There are gaps in GAAP, too. It would be helpful to students of endowment if GAAP required what is now optional, namely segmenting investments by purpose. If it were to go in this direction, it would also help to segregate cash along with investments so we can find out how much cash is temporarily restricted and how much is available to meet an organization's liquidity needs.

Even within the constraints of existing financial data, researchers should study how different capital structures affect performance. This may require gathering original data but the stakes are worth it.

Concluding remarks: why it matters and to whom
Filling in the gaps in our knowledge of nonprofit asset composition clearly matters to nonprofit managers. Arguably they have a harder job than their for-profit counterparts. They must operate with a double bottom line. This requires them to measure the external return on their investments, which is seldom simple. They have to juggle competing demands when their financial and external returns move in opposite directions. They face various constraints on their ability to deploy their assets. They have more uncertain sources of income and must maintain larger operating reserves. They are called upon to provide money-losing services, so they must devise internal subsidies, possibly through building an endowment. They need new tools to deal with these new issues.

The New-York Historical Society case study nicely illustrates the issues involved in the complex problem of managing privileged assets with a double bottom line. N-YHS uses the same asset (a building) as a library and a museum. It charges a fee to museum visitors while offering free library access to researchers. Throughout the two centuries of its existence, its XROA, which includes the external value of the library, has been disconnected from its ROA, which is largely attributable to the museum. This has led to inconsistent policies accompanied by recurring financial crises. There are undoubtedly many more organizations in other fields with similar problems, and nonprofit managers need better decision-making tools for dealing with the additional complexity they face.

Creating new knowledge is important for society and therefore of interest to policy makers. There is sufficient similarity among nonprofit organizations (mandate to pursue a collective mission coupled with an inability to sell stock) to justify studying them as a group, but when it comes to making public policy relating to the sector, differences are important. Approximately 10 percent of nonprofit organizations own half of all assets in the nonprofit sector.[21] Policies appropriate for the top 10 percent may be counterproductive for the other 90 percent and vice versa.

Public resources have not kept pace with increasing social needs, prompting policy makers to look around for fresh sources of funding that are more politically palpable than raising taxes. This has fueled concern over accumulation of wealth in the nonprofit sector. The Bradley group estimates the so-called 'excess' to be a quarter of a trillion dollars and has called upon the owners of this wealth to spend it down over the next 25 years. Others have challenged the 5 percent foundation payout requirement as too conservative. Thus far, the debate has been driven by intuition, not research. The stakes could not be higher. Once spent, nonprofit assets are unavailable to future generations, which will have unmet social needs of their own.

Notes
1.   Statistics cited are calculated by the author from data on operating public charities contained in the NCCS digitized data for organizations' fiscal years beginning in 2003. The source document is IRS Form

990, which churches and organizations with less than $25000 in revenue are not obligated to file. The sample used here consists only of filers reporting positive assets and expenses, which is over 95 percent of the NCCS universe.

2. As defined by the 28 categories of the National Taxonomy of Exempt Entities (NTEE).
3. The term 'charitable nonprofit' as used here refers to nonprofits that are tax-exempt under section 501(c)(3) of the US Internal Revenue Code.
4. I do not know of any studies on this point, but I have seen doubtful accounts of charitable nonprofits that reached 98 percent. One wonders why they bother to charge for their goods at all.
5. Unfortunately GAAP do not require nonprofits to separate marketable securities by economic purpose on their balance sheets.
6. Private equity investments are not liquid.
7. My calculations. This result is significant at the $p = 0.001$ level; the $R^2 = 0.83$; $N = 11441$.
8. Total ROA consists of current income (interest and dividends) plus capital gains expressed as a percentage of asset value. Variation is generally measured by the standard deviation of total returns.
9. She finds the capital structures of a performing arts center, a school and an airline to be similar because they are in the same business of selling seats.
10. The ancient Romans identified these rights as *usus*, *usus fructus*, and *abusus*.
11. 'While, in the past, museums often accepted objects with donor-based restrictions, many museums today ask that gifts be given unrestricted. Common donor restrictions include requiring that an object always be exhibited, or that a collection stays together. However, such restrictions can prevent museums from changing their exhibits as scholarship evolves and may introduce conservation issue for delicate objects not suited to continued display.' *Wikipedia*, http://en.wikipedia.org/wiki/Collection_(museum) accessed 16 September.
12. For no apparent reason the Society spells its name with a hyphen.
13. This is a metaphor. The only liability associated with asset ownership in an accounting sense is secured debt.
14. That is, without subtracting accumulated depreciation. I use this metric to capture physical assets that are fully depreciated.
15. An oft-overlooked fact is that some governments have endowments: Alaska's $28 billion Permanent Fund is prominent, and Montana and other states have established permanent trust funds (see Montana Constitution, Article XII). The Chicago Park District is actively fundraising for an endowment to maintain its new Pritzker Music Pavilion. For-profits do not have endowments because stockpiles of financial assets would make a corporation a tempting target for a hostile takeover. A takeover involves the raider getting control through purchasing the target corporation's outstanding shares. Since nonprofits cannot issue stock, corporate raiders are stymied. But, even if they could get control, the IRS would block them from putting the organization's assets into their own pocket.
16. ROA = Change in total net assets / Total assets averaged over the same period.
17. ROA is not the same as internal rate of return (IRR), which assumes a zero net present value of all future returns.
18. They define "excess capital" as the amount by which organizations' investments exceed five years of expected contributions, which they believe to be an 'adequate safety margin against volatility' (Bradley et al., 2003, p. 99).
19. By Arthur Conan Doyle. First published in book form in 1915. Republished by Oxford University Press in 1993.
20. A summary in e-book form, *History Matters: Lessons from the New-York Historical Society's Board Room*, is available from BoardSource at its website, http://www.boardsource.org/Search.asp?search_type=simpleandquery=Guthrieandx=5andy=8.
21. NCCS is the National Center on Charitable Statistics.

References

Barbetta, Gian Paolo, Gilberto Turati and Angelo M. Zago (2007), 'Behavioral Differences between public and private not-for-profit hospitals in the Italian National Health Service', *Health Economics*, **16** (1), 75–96.

Barrish, Susan R. (2004), 'Nonprofit health insurers: the financial story Wall Street doesn't tell', *Health Leaders* (January), available for download at http://www.healthleaders.com/news/wp1.php?contentid=51753and CE_Session=526bd6c2e3b214fbb6bdee85fbd388f1.

Bowman, Woods (2002), 'The uniqueness of nonprofit finance and the decision to borrow', *Nonprofit Management and Leadership*, **12** (3), 293–311.

Bowman, Woods (2007), 'The capital structure of public, nonprofit, and for-profit organizations', unpublished paper presented at the 36th Annual Conference, Association for Research on Nonprofit Organizations and Voluntary Action (ARNOVA) in Atlanta, GA, 16 November.

Bradley, Bill, Paul Jansen and Les Silverman (2003), 'The non-profit sector's $100 billion opportunity', *Harvard Business Review*, **81** (5), 94–103.
Brody, Evelyn (1997), 'Charitable endowments and the democratization of dynasty', *Arizona Law Review*, **9** (3), 873–948.
Core, John E., Wayne R. Guay and Rodrigo S. Verdi (2004), 'Agency problems of excess endowment holdings in not-for-profit firms', *Journal of Accounting and Economics*, **41** (3), 307–33.
Eggleston, Karen, Yu-Chu Shen, Christopher H. Schmid and Jia Chan (2006), 'Hospital ownership and quality of care: what explains the different results?', National Bureau of Economic Research Working Paper No. W12241.
Fremont-Smith, Marion R. (2002), 'Accumulations of wealth by nonprofits', Emerging Issues in Philanthropy Seminar Series, a joint project of the Urban Institute and the Hauser Center, Washington, DC.
Frey, Donald (2002), 'University endowment returns are underspent', *Challenge*, **45** (4), 109–21.
Friesner, Daniel L. and Robert Rosenman (2004), 'Inpatient–outpatient cost shifting in Washington hospitals', *Healthcare Management Science*, **7** (1), 17–26.
Guthrie, Kevin M. (1996), *The New-York Historical Society: Lessons from One Nonprofit's Long Struggle for Survival*, San Francisco, CA: Jossey-Bass.
Hansmann, Henry B. (1990), 'Why do universities have endowments?' *Journal of Legal Studies*, **19** (1), 3–42.
Hansmann, Henry B. and Reinier Kraakman (2000), 'Organizational law and asset partitioning', *European Economic Review*, **44** (4–6), 807–17.
Horwitz, Jill (2005), 'Does corporate ownership matter? Service provision in the hospital industry', National Bureau of Economic Research Working Paper No. W11376.
Koren, Miklos and Adam Szeidl (2003), 'Portfolio choice with illiquid assets', Center for Economic Policy Research Discussion Paper No. 3795.
Miller, Clara (2003), 'Hidden in plain sight: understanding nonprofit capital structure', *The Nonprofit Quarterly*, **10** (1), 16–23.
Pollak, Thomas H. and Jonathan D. Dunford (2005), 'The scope and activities of 501(c)(3) supporting organizations', an Urban Institute report, available at http://www.urban.org/url.cfm?ID=411175.
Schneider, Eric C., Alan M. Zaslavsky and Arnold Epstein (2004), 'Use of high-cost operative procedures by Medicare beneficiaries enrolled in for-profit and not-for-profit health plans', *New England Journal of Medicine*, **350** (2), 143–50.
Tobin, James (1974), 'What is permanent endowment income?' *American Economic Review*, **64** (2), 427–32.
Tuckman, Howard P. and Cyril F. Chang (1992), 'Nonprofit equity: a behavioral model and its implications', *Journal of Policy Analysis and Management*, **11** (1), 76–87.
Wedig, Gerard J. (1994), 'Risk, leverage, donations and dividends-in-kind: a theory of nonprofit financial behavior', *International Review of Economics and Statistics*, **3** (3), 257–78.
Wedig, Gerard J., Frank A. Sloan, Mahmud Hassan and Michael A. Morrisey (1989), 'Capital structure, ownership, and capital payment policy: the case of hospitals', *Journal of Finance*, **43** (1), 21–40.
Weil, S. (2000), *A Deaccession Reader*, Washington, DC: American Association of Museums.

6 Collaboration versus competition in the third sector
Renée A. Irvin

Introduction
The scholarly literature calls for greater collaboration among nonprofit organizations to achieve outcomes that would not be attainable if each organization worked in isolation (Kettl, 2006). Foundations, too, see duplicative effort in the nonprofit sector and often encourage grant seekers to collaborate with other organizations in their community (Golden, 2001). Unfortunately, nonprofit organizations themselves seem reluctant to engage in collaborative efforts, unless motivated to do so with external funding from grant makers (Knickmeyer et al., 2003; National Council on Aging, 2005; Foster and Meinhard, 2002; Schambra, 2004).

To illustrate, the following is a community situation that seems quite dysfunctional. Knickmeyer et al. (2003, p. 13) describe a study of ten urban neighborhood associations in close proximity to one another:

> all ten associations are struggling to address the same community issues with a small number of active members. There is no evidence of joining forces with each other to resolve their common problems . . . even when members of community associations recognize the value of collaboration and express interest in collaborating with others, they have difficulty translating that desire into actual collaborative projects.

Why are they not collaborating? Do the stakeholders in the ten neighborhood associations not see the potential benefits in joining forces? We shall return later to the puzzle with two solutions depending upon the reader's point of view. We shall see that there is little reason for the ten associations to collaborate, yet we shall also point out one potential arena where joint efforts could indeed yield returns for all associations – returns that could exceed the costs of collaborating. Before returning to the neighborhood associations case, however, we outline the theory behind decisions whether or not to collaborate – a task that requires first exploring the nature of competition in the nonprofit sector.

Government agencies, nonprofit organizations and for-profit businesses are all involved in providing solutions to vexing societal problems. In many situations, collaboration within and across sectors can result in solutions that are unattainable by each entity working alone (Irvin, 2007). Even though most nonprofit executive directors will point to their organization's unique ability to serve a societal need, some nonprofits may duplicate each other's missions, which suggests keen competition in the marketplace. However, even if organizations do not have duplicative missions, they still face competition in the fundraising, human resources and media arenas.

Although this chapter will focus on collaboration and competition within the nonprofit sector, note that literature such as Austin (2000), Smith and Lipsky (1993), Smith and Grønbjerg (2006), Galaskiewicz and Colman (2006), and Boris and Steuerle (1999) are excellent resources for studying relationships between nonprofits, governments and businesses.

Collaboration and competition with government entities

Governments rely heavily on nonprofit organizations to carry out programs that benefit the public, from services for disadvantaged populations to civic beautification projects. Although subcontracting can be considered mere 'quasi-collaboration', as it involves formal structures such as contracts, grants, monitoring and reporting of nonprofit outcomes, the transfer of funds from the government to the nonprofit does not entirely negate the collaborative nature of the project. A more obscure topic is nonprofit–government competition. This may occur when a government agency is required to submit a bid in order to obtain tax-supported funding to produce services. In the education field, government schools compete directly with private nonprofit schools for funds if tax revenue for education follows the student. For the most part, however, nonprofit organizations provide complementary services to government services, with nonprofits frequently on the receiving end of collaborative agreements to carry out government initiatives.

Collaboration and competition with for-profit firms

Presumably, the nonprofit and for-profit sectors do not intertwine, as their motivations for formation – profit versus provision of a public good – differ radically. In practice, however, collaboration across the two sectors is commonplace. Businesses benefit from participating in community betterment, whether for marketing purposes, for improving the skills or availability of future employees, or for benefiting and retaining their current employees (Cordes and Steuerle, 2009). Thus businesses are eager partners with non-profit organizations. Businesses also volunteer their facilities, products or services (or provide discounts) for nonprofits, for a wide variety of tasks where professional products and services are needed.

Competition, on the other hand, is also prevalent if the nonprofit organizations and for-profit firms produce similar services. Nonprofit and for-profit health care facilities of all types and fitness-oriented organizations (such as YMCA) come to mind. In these arenas, the for-profit firms protest the granting of tax exemption to nonprofits, while the nonprofits counter by measuring and reporting their uncompensated benefits provided to the community (see Brown's chapter in this volume – Chapter 7 – for a discussion of for-profit and nonprofit coexistence). Note that in past decades, the public policy debate focused on how for-profits compete with nonprofits, but the debate has shifted to a focus on partnerships between the two sectors (Steinberg, 1987; Marmor et al., 1987; Austin, 2000; Cordes and Steuerle, 2009).

Competition in the nonprofit sector

Here, we examine the classical model of profit maximization under conditions of perfect competition and find it to be of limited use – on the surface – yet extraordinarily power-ful if we stretch the definitional boundaries of the model. Profit maximization is a defining feature of the for-profit sector. The first and obvious corollary for the nonprofit sector is when organizations are selling a product for which they can charge a price, such as admission, fees for services, or prices for a tangible product. In addition to the arena of products and services, there are several additional ways in which nonprofits compete – for donated revenues, inputs such as labor, grants and even for media coverage.

Competition for clients when revenue is generated from prices

Three large nonprofit subsectors – health, human services and private education – usually derive the majority of their revenues from sales of a service to clients. Other organizations, such as performing and visual arts organizations, serve audience members who pay for the right to enter a museum or enjoy a performance. In these cases, the quest for operating revenue closely follows the profit maximization model.

Because the product or service can be priced and the price can be charged to a client who is willing to pay, there is no reason to expect that for-profit firms won't also enter the market and produce this product. Accordingly, we see plenty of for-profit health care providers, day care and human services providers. In the broad context of entertainment we see for-profit entities supplying the market with music concerts and movies, both of which compete for audience members with nonprofits. Nonprofit and for-profit cultural institutions, however, tend to self-sort according to the artistic genre of the entertainment.

Oster (Chapter 13 in this volume) notes that even donative nonprofits – those primarily dependent upon donated and not fee-based revenues – also participate in a competitive fee-based product market as a way of cross-subsidizing the core mission product, for which a price may be difficult to charge. Indeed, the complicated revenue mix in the nonprofit sector from donations, grants, endowment income and fee-based products requires a strategic and precarious balance of mission-related goals, crowding-out effects from one revenue source to another, and overall financial viability. Oster's chapter explores product diversification in more depth, but, briefly stated, the existence of for-profit competitors suggests that the predicted long-run market equilibrium for commercial nonprofit organizations or at least organizations with fee-based products is likely to follow the perfect competition model: organizations will compete for clients, innovating and reducing costs wherever possible, arriving at a long-run state where profits are zero (covering only their opportunity costs) and resources are provided at a quantity level that minimizes average costs of production. Furthermore, consumers (clients) enjoy the maximum benefits that this market can possibly offer.

Evidence suggests that the perfect competition model does indeed hold explanatory power for behavior of nonprofit organizations. The well-developed health care literature indicates that increased competition in health care markets is a causal factor in lower prices for health services (Melnick and Zwanziger, 1988). Certainly, we see evidence of nonprofits existing on a razor-thin profit margin over time, but this is not a condition necessarily limited to nonprofits with fee-based revenues. Organizations more reliant on donor funding also exhibit this zero-profit condition in the long run, but for reasons other than direct competition (such as expanding services whenever profit is above normal).

Expanding services whenever a modicum of profit exists implies not profit maximization, but service maximization. Thus a nonprofit may use competitive strategies such as entrepreneurial sorting to maximize outcomes, not profits. A mix of objectives can be utilized to suit the overall mission with a multi-product organization. For example, profits from one service (competition model) might be used to cross-subsidize the production of other services that are not financially viable on their own (service maximization model). In Chapter 9 of this volume, Hughes and Luksetich provide a thorough discussion of nonprofit objectives.

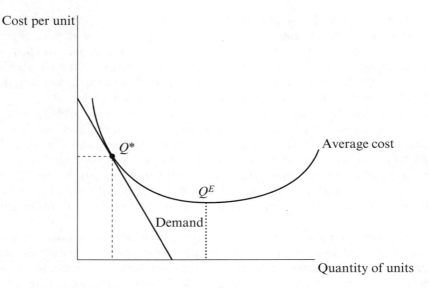

Figure 6.1   Monopolistic competition equilibrium

Competition may come in the form of innovating in order to produce the product or service with lower costs, or differentiating the product in a tangible (changing service attributes) or intangible (advertising) way. Differentiating the product can result in a crowded market, each nonprofit with its own very small market niche or identity. Fortunately, the nonprofit with the unique identity has market demand all to itself – yet a very weak and small market demand. Each organization sees itself as a unique organization with a unique mission. Nonprofits not only vary the features of their product or service to establish their public benefit role, but they can also distinguish themselves by varying the methods by which they accomplish their missions – in essence, the mission itself, the outcomes they produce, and even the production methods they use can be differentiated in order to carve out a unique identity that appeals to funders (Brown and Slivinski, 2006).

Can the demand for nonprofit services be segmented that much and the market still be 'efficient'? Theories of monopolistic competition suggest otherwise. Figure 6.1 illustrates the long-run results of a segmented market – each nonprofit with its own very small market demand and profits, once again, at zero. The difference between price competition and product differentiation in long-run competition, however, is that *product (or mission) differentiation* leads to a long-run equilibrium at output level Q^*, an inefficiently high-cost level of production. *Price competition* without product differentiation, on the other hand, would have led to an equilibrium output level of Q^E, where average costs per item are at their minimum possible level.

Competition for donations
For many nonprofit organizations, it may be impossible to charge a price for the services rendered. The recipient of charity may be unable to pay. Or the nonprofit may be unable to charge a price for the service, no matter how much people are willing to pay (advocacy

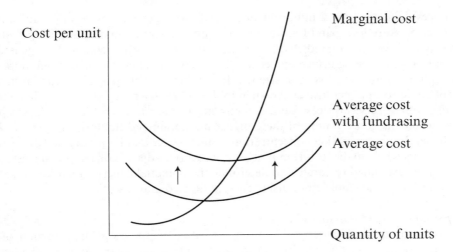

Figure 6.2   Increased average cost of fundraising

organizations come to mind). Donations comprise a vital source of revenue for these types of nonprofits, and competition for donations has grown fiercely over the past few decades. The sharp growth of nonprofit organizations has resulted in an environment of year-round fundraising by trained professionals. One good fundraising idea is copied widely by other nonprofits, as illustrated by the 'what will they think of next' worlds of direct mail and special events.

Borrowing theory from the perfectly competitive fee-based model, and using the assumption that nonprofits will compete by increasing their fundraising efforts, we end up at equilibrium where net revenues from fundraising are competed away for all, with all nonprofits making zero profit in the end. Fundraising costs can be thought of as similar to marketing costs – they add to a nonprofit's fixed costs, yet carry the risk of not resulting in a higher demand for the charitable activity. Figure 6.2 shows average costs before and after a marketing or fundraising campaign (see Seaman, 2004; Brown and Slivinski, 2006). The nonprofit engaging in this costly effort hopes to end up with sub-stantially more demand for the nonprofit's services (which results in more donations), offsetting the increase in costs at each level of output.

There has been little or no discussion of a possible (and potentially testable) implica-tion of this analysis and the relationships exhibited in Figure 6.2 on the structure of the nonprofit sector and the degree of 'market concentration' exhibited by nonprofit organizations. That is, since the addition of a higher fixed cost shifts the average total cost curve but does not affect the marginal cost curve, the minimum point of the shifted average cost curve shown in Figure 6.2 is clearly to the right of the lower average cost curve with lower fundraising costs (the marginal cost curve must intersect both curves at their minimum points). This suggests that the optimal size of the organization has increased with higher fundraising costs. While the argument above suggests that the results of the fundraising will be more demand for the organization's services and higher donations to offset the higher costs, there is also the possibility that prices of services will have to increase to partly offset the higher costs, hence reducing the net quantity of services demanded from nonprofit organizations in general (since all organizations are under pressure to expand fundraising, leading to overall higher fundraising costs in the sector). As would be predicted in the for-profit sector, when competition generates the result of prices being driven higher to offset these higher costs, the combination of a larger optimal representative firm size (as the minimum average costs occurs at higher rates of service output per firm as shown in Figure 6.2) and a reduced quantity demanded overall as those service prices rise (assuming no increase in overall demand, which of course would suggest a failure of these higher marketing and fundraising costs to shift that demand), higher market concentration results (fewer and larger organizations providing a somewhat smaller total amount of services). This discussion simply suggests that one area for expanded research is to determine the potential effects on market or sector concentration of the higher fundraising costs addressed in this section.

Competition for paid staff and volunteers
The nonprofit sector is a service industry, so labor comprises a large portion of its required inputs, from teachers to nature-hike leaders, musicians and counselors, to name a few. A volunteer workforce augments the nonprofit labor pool for lower-skilled work. Nonprofit executive salaries, though nowhere as stratospheric as US salaries for upper-level executives in large firms, have increased sharply over the last decade in the nonprofit sector (Barton et al, 2006), suggesting some upward bidding for leadership talent as a generation of long-time leaders passes the administrative reins to succeeding executive directors (Johnson, 2007). If an organization is constrained to keep salaries modest in order to signal frugality and dedication to the mission, the competition to hire executive talent is that much fiercer, and may play out by compensation via non-monetary perquisites.

Competition for volunteers cannot be salary-based, however, by definition. The mobilizer of human endeavor – the underappreciated volunteer administrator – attracts a dedicated volunteer pool using superior leadership and organizational skills (not to mention an attractive mission). Good volunteers who come regularly, stay with the organization over time and perform valuable services are important and scarce assets for nonprofits. Nonprofits, facing a decline in the number of long-term volunteers, have begun to accommodate 'episodic' volunteers with short-term projects (Macduff, 2005). Thus competition for volunteer labor rests not on salary, but on managerial strategies for luring and retaining valuable volunteers. Hager and Brudney (2004) provide an interesting review of retention strategies used by nonprofits, finding that the strategies most effective in retaining volunteers (volunteer recognition, professional development and training for volunteers etc.) benefit the volunteers themselves, not necessarily the nonprofits, suggesting managerial trade-offs between pleasing the volunteer and benefiting the organization.

Competition for grants and contracts
The struggle to obtain government contracts and grants from foundations is a fascinating researcher's laboratory, yet little theoretical and empirical attention has focused on this revenue strategy. Effort is poured into grant applications for very little return. In the USA, we still see grants for as low as $500, in seeming disregard of the time required to prepare the grant application. We also see nonprofits applying for government contracts

that pay only partial costs – perhaps the nonprofit is just grateful for the subsidy of their services, which they would endeavor to provide even without the government contract. Smith and Lipsky (1993, p. 161) note, 'Many contracts, especially in today's strained budgetary climate, allocate insufficient money for administrative expenses . . . In the worst-case scenario, an agency will obtain a new but substantially underfunded contract . . . and the agency loses money from the day it assumes the contract.' Toepler (Chapter 22 of this volume) notes that inadequate coverage of costs from government grants suggests a private sector subsidy of government objectives.

With insufficient funds to actually complete the project, nonprofits may be treating the underfunded yet successful grant as a first step to obtaining more remunerative funding in the next grant cycle. Some empirical attention by researchers might help the sector achieve somewhat more efficient outcomes with grants and contracts. Nonprofits, competing against many other worthy nonprofits, appear to be in a bidding war, promising much and pricing their services low in an effort to win the grant or contract.

Competition for media coverage
For the nonprofit organizations whose mission involves educating the public on any topic, media coverage of their efforts is critical to their success. Even nonprofits without advocacy-based missions clamor for media coverage to gain legitimacy in the public's mind for their mission and to attract new supporters, donors and volunteers. 'Free' media coverage – such as a laudatory report in the morning newspaper – is not necessarily free, but involves labor costs such as being available for media inquiries, contacting media representatives on a regular basis with press releases, and devising media-friendly angles in special events. Two reasons for nonprofit competition for 'free' media coverage are: the relative lack of spendable income in organizations dependent on donations and grants; and expectations by the public that nonprofits refrain from 'slick' paid advertising (Pallotta, 2009), presumably to appear efficient and frugal stewards of the donated dollar.

The many facets of competition among nonprofit organizations presented here and modeled in Chapter 9 of this volume provide the foundational theory for our main task in this chapter: describing collaborative behavior among nonprofits and determining why organizations are sometimes reluctant to act collaboratively. Knowing how we might design a collaborative project (and circumvent the reluctance to collaborate) might allow us to create public benefit outcomes that would be difficult to achieve with organizations acting alone.

Collaboration in the nonprofit sector
Although it is easy to talk about the importance of collaboration, it is difficult to define exactly what characterizes a 'somewhat' or 'very' collaborative project. Yankey and Willen (2005) provide several examples of collaboration matrices. Confounding the discussion, of course, is the differing nature of collaboration across the nonprofit, business, and government sectors. Table 6.1 shows a continuum of collaboration with common sector participants. Placement of particular arrangements on the continuum may be uncertain. For example, is 'contracting' a simple exchange of funding for services, or is it more like collaboration?

Table 6.1   A sample continuum of collaboration

Degree of partnership	Partners	Description
Minimal	NP, F-P, govt	Contracting, grants for services produced by nonprofits
	NP, F-P	Cause marketing
↓	NP	Non-monetized trading (bartering of services)
	F-P	Sponsorship of nonprofit events
Moderate	NP, govt	Jointly produced events
	NP	Joint purchasing and cost sharing
	NP	Associations of professionals; information and training networks
↓	NP, F-P, govt	Community dialogue, information sharing, advocacy
	NP, F-P, govt	Community initiatives, designing and implementing solutions
Extensive	NP	Integration of operations, merger

Where is the value in collaboration?
Funders may assume that more collaboration in the nonprofit sector automatically implies mutual benefits, plus benefits for external publics as well. However, parsing the value of collaboration into broad categories helps to illuminate the truly important contributions from collaboration that should be pursued by nonprofits and encouraged by funders. Pivotal to this discussion are the relationships among participating nonprofit organizations. Do they compete in the same local market? Or are they peers, producing the same service but in different markets? Do they produce services that are entirely unrelated? Also important are organizational assets and abilities that can be traded with other organizations.

Benefits to sharing information
For peer organizations – nonprofits producing the same good, but for different groups of people or in different geographical locations – mutual benefit can come from associational membership and their concomitant learning opportunities. In fact, these types of associations spring up voluntarily in every field, from museums to health care providers. Gaining knowledge in an association is attractive to the neophytes in the field, but less so for seasoned professionals from well-established organizations. Thus conferences of associated organizations often end up paying or hosting the leaders of the field to serve as instructors for the newcomers.

In addition, certain functional areas common to most nonprofits – such as fundraising or volunteer management – can benefit from associational collaboration. Across local, national and international boundaries, fellow practitioners of fundraising, for example, meet to learn best practices in their field, regardless of their nonprofit subsector. Both of these information-sharing initiatives – among peers in separate geographic markets or among professional peers in unrelated agencies – require little or no stimulus from external funders for collaborative efforts to arise.

Another way to enhance revenue streams is to coordinate with agencies that perform different services, but are in a position to refer clients to each other – such as in social services organizations. A substance abuse counseling agency might benefit from a collegial relationship with a homeless and transitional housing organization. Note that sharing information about client needs and trading best practices tips is easily accomplished among organizations that are not direct competitors for clients, audience members or grants. If the benefits to sharing information are obvious, nonprofits will quickly form associations or networks to do so.

Cost minimization

Nonprofit organizations have ample opportunity to review their use of resources and locate lower-cost solutions by sharing fixed costs with other organizations. Sharing facilities via scheduling differences (one organization uses the facility by day, another at night, for example) can lower facilities costs. Organizations can also share equipment, or personnel such as a front-desk receptionist, payroll clerk or security guard. Variable costs can also be reduced through alliances. Group bulk purchases of supplies and services can reduce the per-unit cost. Fundraising events sometimes involve multiple players if the organizations bring complementary talents to the process, or if the donating public is expected to respond to a joint effort with increased generosity. Group workshops or seminars are key ways to reduce costs of training for employees in new roles (Under One Roof Project, 2004; McLaughlin, 1998).

Trade

Organizations are endowed with different types of assets. Museums and arboreta have beautiful spaces, whereas social service agencies may have human resources in the form of clients who need job-skill training. Thus the local library utilizes teen volunteers from a homeless shelter, and the shelter rents out space in the museum gallery for a fundraising event. Differing assets such as these create potential for trade, as each organization uses its comparative advantage in trading with other organizations (see Irvin, 2007).

Bartering

Nonprofit enterprise is unique in many ways, but the prevalence of bartering is one of its most distinctive collaborative features (Ben-Ner, 1993; Reisman, 1991). Note that the for-profit sector rarely engages in non-monetized trade. Why does this curious practice occur more often in the nonprofit sector? Scarcity of cash is one reason. When a business runs out of cash (i.e. income), the owner shuts it down after a few lean years. When a nonprofit runs out of cash, people pitch in to accomplish the mission anyway, with volunteer labor, homemade tri-fold brochures and jury-rigged equipment. This practice of *production without cash expenditure* extends to partnerships with other organizations. No exchange of income is necessary if the two organizations have a mutually beneficial project in mind. Regarding cost minimization described above, it is possible to envision several ways in which organizations reduce fixed and variable costs via bartering. Each organization produces the product or service for which they have comparative advantage, creating mutual benefits to specialization and trade.

Philosophically, bartering might be viewed as more collaborative than monetized trade, because a cash-based transaction does not imply cooperation. Bartering requires more direct communication between the players. The drawback to bartering is that it requires a double coincidence of wants. Cash allows you to purchase what you need with a form of payment that anyone will accept. Barter, however, requires that you 'pay' for your purchase with an equally desirable product or service. Thus one more dimension is added to the transactions costs of collaboration when bartering.

Ultimately, the question in the back of any nonprofit manager's mind is, does the potential reduction in costs or enhancement of revenue exceed the transactions costs of collaborating? It makes no sense to collaborate if the costs of meeting, working out the details and implementing the project overwhelm the eventual returns to the organization. Collaboration takes time – the nonprofit manager's most precious commodity.

Improving community outcomes
We expect nonprofits to form partnerships with other organizations in order to improve their chances of accomplishing mission-relevant outcomes. Ideally, collaboration may achieve:

- seamless integration of services for disadvantaged clients,
- coordinated response to a community environmental (crime etc.) issue,
- group advocacy to signal a united front for the purpose of influencing policy.

Unfortunately, lacking clear financial signals to each potential partner (revenue growth or reduction of costs), we expect that strategic alliances to improve outcomes will not often self-generate, and may only arise when there is a financial stimulus from an external party in the form of a grant requiring collaboration. Why is there a need for an arranged marriage if the potential outcomes are aligned with each organization's mission? Each party may be unable to see direct benefits to their own organization, relative to the costs of collaborating. Behn (2001, p. 141) asks,

> Who will trade individual accountability for mutual accountability? Who will trade his or her well-understood (and relatively limited) individual accountability . . . for some vague sense of mutual, collective responsibility that will be devised, refined, and revised sometime in the future by people with unknown or even incompatible values? Who has an incentive to cooperate?

Compare three collaborative projects:

1. *Sharing a security guard with a nonprofit next door*   Each organization receives 'security' for half price by splitting the cost with the partner (note the minimal transactions costs). Hiring a security guard has easily measured benefits accruing to both parties. The decision to hire the security guard is expected to be accomplished readily, if both perceive that a half-price guard is a bargain.

2. *Community-wide push to combat crime associated with methamphetamine abuse*   Organizations such as the State Patrol, substance abuse counseling centers, and high school health education instructors are brought together to devise solutions to meth addiction. This collaborative project is more difficult to accomplish. What organization has the spare time to send its executive director or other staff member to meetings? Benefits to the individual organizations are unclear, yet benefits to the broader public are potentially large if the community effort is successful. Even though the organizations'

missions suggest that they should be willing participants, direct benefits to the organizations are not apparent, and participation in the collaboration may depend on whether or not each organization receives funding to participate.

3. *Three local organizations providing shelter for the homeless are urged to collaborate to share information on 'revolving door' clients, streamline costs of operation, and work together on expanding the number of beds in neighborhoods where they are most needed* This case is a hopeful dream for grant makers. If only these organizations would work together! Alas, they are natural competitors, and have strong incentives to protect their territory and gain funding for their own organizations. Each organization is likely to believe it has the better model for providing homeless services. Not only do we expect high transactions for bringing these participants into an alliance, but if grant funding allows the partnership to form, much energy may be required to carefully define the activities and required contributions from each player.

The three scenarios illustrate when collaboration will be somewhat or very difficult to achieve. Much of the academic and trade literature on collaboration focuses on the processes undertaken in collaborative efforts, without noticing that it is the nature of the players that can make the process easy or difficult. Essentially, if the potential collaborators are not direct competitors and the gains to collaboration are obvious and do not involve high transaction costs, then we expect collaboration to occur readily. Conversely, if the potential collaborators are direct competitors (which implies they have similar missions!), we expect spontaneous collaboration to occur only rarely, when benefits to each organization are direct and easily measured. Even with grant funding to stimulate a cooperative project, collaboration among competitors may involve awkward maneuvering over turf and authority.

What about the ten uncooperative neighborhood associations described at the beginning of the chapter? It is no surprise that they lack the desire to cooperate – their identical missions suggest that they are competitors for the same pool of grant funding from the city or from foundations. It is not very realistic to expect the neighborhood associations to collaborate, even though they address the same community issues.

Could we do better? Assume we have a foundation funder that is very committed to collaboration. Considering the problems the neighborhood associations face – drug dealing, trash and vacant housing – we see that some of their most pressing issues could be tackled with better law enforcement practices, more frequent trash collection, strict enforcement of housing code violations and so on. More effective external advocacy is needed – the kind of advocacy that requires a multitude of constituents voicing a common concern and pressing for the same solution. Shaping the external environment, therefore, is the outcome we should target for a grant-funded collaborative effort in this case. That is, strategic grant making in this case should not be broadly defined as any collaborative undertaking, but instead focus on helping the neighborhood organizations advocate as one organization for changes in local housing, trash collection and law enforcement.

Concluding remarks: grant-making policy and practice recommendations
Where organizational benefits to collaboration are obvious, nonprofits will pursue collaborative projects readily. Where collaboration's benefits to the organization are

unclear or indirect, nonprofits may avoid the partnership, as the collaboration is seen as too costly to devote scarce organizational resources to. Foundations, however, provide the external impetus for many collaborative efforts, despite the conflicting incentives or nebulous benefits for the nonprofits themselves. Although Schambra (2004) laments that inducing coordination among separate agencies is costly and futile, perhaps with an awareness of competitive incentives within the nonprofit sectors, grant makers can make some headway. This chapter ends, therefore, with a focus on grant-maker decision making, and a call for more precise evaluation of collaborative projects in a competitive nonprofit environment.

Grant makers must seek out the projects that are most likely to align organizational incentives with intended outcomes. In theory, collaborative grant making to non-competing organizations will have the best chance of success, as the partners are more willing to trade services and combine efforts when they identify as community allies. Grants to groups of competing organizations are far more difficult to design success-fully. Grant makers view the burgeoning number of nonprofits with some dismay, citing the rapid sector growth as evidence of duplication, and hoping that the nonprofits in similar fields can learn to work together for the common good. As Golden (2001, p. 672) notes, 'many grantmakers currently prefer to support collaborative efforts rather than single-organization projects. These funders maintain that collaboration is generally more efficient and more cost effective than single-organization efforts, because costly duplication of effort is avoided.' Unfortunately, precisely where there is 'duplication of effort', we expect collaboration to be least likely to occur, even with financial induce-ment from funders.

Providing grant funding for competing organizations may still yield successful out-comes if the collaborative project is sharply targeted toward activities that benefit the nonprofit participants directly. A good example is the advocacy training grant to the neighborhood associations. The gains to the organizations could be significant if they united their voices and expertly pressure the city to adapt new practices in combating crime or targeting housing vacancy. Pinpointing these advantageous opportunities to bring competitors together is likewise extraordinarily time-consuming, requiring keen analytical skills on the part of the grant maker. Such efforts, however, are likely to yield more definitive outcomes than a grant with hopeful but vague collaborative goals such as 'improve capacity by building networks across neighborhood associations'.

References

Austin, James E. (2000), *The Collaboration Challenge*, San Francisco, CA: Jossey-Bass.
Barton, Noelle, Maria Di Mento and Alvin P. Sanoff (2006), 'Top nonprofit executives see healthy pay raises', *Chronicle of Philanthropy*, 28 September.
Behn, Robert D. (2001), *Rethinking Democratic Accountability*, Washington, DC: Brooking Institution Press.
Ben-Ner, Avner (1993), 'Obtaining resources using barter trade: benefits and drawbacks', in David C. Hammack and Dennis R. Young (eds), *Nonprofit Organizations in a Mixed Economy: Understanding New Roles, Issues and Trends*, San Francisco, CA: Jossey-Bass, pp. 278–93.
Boris, Elizabeth T. and C. Eugene Steuerle (1999), *Nonprofits & Government: Collaboration and Conflict*, Washington, DC: Urban Institute Press.
Brown, Eleanor and Al Slivinski (2006), 'Nonprofit organizations and the market', in Walter W. Powell and Richard Steinberg (eds), *The Nonprofit Sector: A Research Handbook*, 2nd edn, New Haven, CT: Yale University Press, pp. 140–79.
Cordes, Joseph J. and C. Eugene Steuerle (eds) (2009), *Nonprofits and Business*, Washington, DC: Urban Institute Press.

Foster, Mary K. and Agnes G. Meinhard (2002), 'A regression model explaining predisposition to collaborate', *Nonprofit and Voluntary Sector Quarterly*, **31** (4), 549–64.
Galaskiewicz, Joseph and Michelle S. Colman (2006), 'Collaboration between corporations and nonprofit organizations', in Walter W. Powell and Richard Steinberg (eds), *The Nonprofit Sector: A Research Handbook*, 2nd edn, New Haven, CT: Yale University Press, pp. 180–204.
Golden, Susan L. (2001), 'The grant-seeking process', in James M. Greenfield (ed.), *The Nonprofit Handbook: Fundraising*, New York: John Wiley & Sons, pp. 666–91.
Hager, Mark A. and Jeffrey L. Brudney (2004), 'Volunteer management practices and retention of volunteers', an Urban Institute report, available at http://www.urban.org/publications/411005.html.
Irvin, Renée A. (2007), 'Collaboration and barter', in Dennis R. Young (ed.), *Financing Nonprofits: Putting Theory into Practice*, Lanham, MD: AltaMira Press, pp. 207–26.
Johnson, Janet (2007), 'The nonprofit leadership crisis: is the sky falling?', presentation at the 36th Annual Conference, Association for Research on Nonprofit Organizations and Voluntary Action (ARNOVA) in Atlanta, GA, 16 November.
Kettl, Donald F. (2006), 'Managing boundaries in American administration: the collaboration imperative', *Public Administration Review*, **66** (s1), 10–19.
Knickmeyer, Lisa, Karen Hopkins and Megan Meyer (2003), 'Exploring collaboration among urban neighborhood associations', *Journal of Community Practice*, **11** (2), 13–25.
Macduff, Nancy (2005), 'Societal changes and the rise of the episodic volunteer', in *ARNOVA Occasional Paper Series – Emerging Areas of Volunteering*, **1** (2), 49–61.
Marmor, Theodore R., Mark Schlesinger and Richard W. Smithey (1987), 'Nonprofit organizations and health care', in Walter W. Powell (ed.), *The Nonprofit Sector: A Research Handbook*, New Haven, CT: Yale University Press, pp. 221–39.
McLaughlin, Thomas A. (1998), *Nonprofit Mergers and Alliances: A Strategic Guide*, New York: John Wiley & Sons.
Melnick, Glenn A. and Jack Zwanziger (1988), 'Hospital behavior under competition and cost-containment policies. The California experience, 1980 to 1985', *Journal of the American Medical Association*, **260** (18), 2669–75.
National Council on Aging (2005), 'Respect ability web survey executive summary', March, available at: http://www.respectability.org/research/survey.pdf, accessed 6 July 2005.
Pallotta, Dan (2009), *Uncharitable: How Restraints on Nonprofits Undermine Their Potential*, Lebanon, NH: University Press of New England.
Reisman, Arnold (1991), 'Enhancing nonprofit resources through barter', *Nonprofit Management and Leadership*, **1** (Spring), 253–65.
Schambra, William A. (2004), 'Root causes vs. reality', *Philanthropy*, November/December, 25–8.
Seaman, Bruce A. (2004), 'Competition and the non-profit arts: the lost industrial organization agenda', *Journal of Cultural Economics*, **28** (3), 167–93.
Smith, Steven Rathgeb and Kirsten A. Grønbjerg (2006), 'Scope and theory of government–nonprofit relations', in Walter W. Powell and Richard Steinberg (eds), *The Nonprofit Sector: A Research Handbook*, 2nd edn, New Haven, CT: Yale University Press, pp. 221–42.
Smith, Steven Rathgeb and Michael Lipsky (1993), *Nonprofits for Hire: The Welfare State in the Age of Contracting*, Cambridge, MA: Harvard University Press.
Steinberg, Richard (1987), 'Nonprofit organizations and the market', in Walter W. Powell (ed.), *The Nonprofit Sector: A Research Handbook*, New Haven, CT: Yale University Press, pp. 118–38.
Under One Roof Project (2004), 'The Under One Roof Project: benefits and challenges of co-locating nonprofit organizations', website hosted by University of Michigan School of Social Work, www.ssw.umich.edu/underoneroof/.
Yankey, John A. and Carol K. Willen (2005), 'Strategic alliances', in Robert D. Herman & Associates (eds), *The Jossey-Bass Handbook of Nonprofit Leadership & Management*, San Francisco, CA: Jossey-Bass, pp. 257–73.

7 Markets with competition between for-profit and nonprofit firms
Eleanor Brown

Introduction

The competitive advantages of nonprofit firms and for-profit firms are different enough to raise the question of how the two types of firms come to coexist in substantial numbers in significant markets. Nonprofit firms can receive donations and preferential tax treatment; for-profits can raise capital in equity markets. Neither set of advantages seems decisive in any of several markets, including nursing homes, day care, hospitals and hospice care. Credit unions hold their own against banks, while for-profit providers make incursions into microcredit markets and secondary and higher education.

Economic models that address these 'mixed markets' tend to rely on at least one of two generic features, scarcity and heterogeneity, to explain stable coexistence under competitive conditions. The two emphases have different implications for the performance of mixed markets. Other models of mixed markets rely on barriers to entry that limit competition and leave room for both types of firms, or invoke historical evolution with no claim that the present mix of industries is likely to continue.

In this chapter, I provide an overview of economic thinking about the characteristics of markets in which for-profit and nonprofit firms might coexist, and the consequences of that coexistence for market outcomes such as the price, quantity and quality of service provision. In addition to the theoretical work on the extent and performance of mixed markets that is the focus of this chapter, there is a large empirical literature focusing on the behavior of specific mixed markets. This brief overview cannot do justice to these market-specific empirical literatures; happily, these bodies of research have been recently and ably reviewed in various chapters of Powell and Steinberg (2006); see especially the chapter on health care by Schlesinger and Gray (2006).

I begin with a quick review of the basic models economists use to describe the circumstances under which nonprofit firms might be found in a market, paying particular attention to the features of these accounts that might be relevant to the coexistence of nonprofit firms with for-profit ones. I then review the legal environment and how it shapes the universe of markets in which nonprofit firms operate. Next, I look at specific models of coexistence. Summing up, I suggest directions for future research.

Reasons for a nonprofit sector and their implications for competition from for-profit firms

There have been two principal strands of economic thinking about the presence of a nonprofit sector. One view sees the nonprofit sector as 'the third sector', picking up where for-profit and government provision of services leave off (see, e.g., Weisbrod, 1975). If consumers are heterogeneous in their demand for a collective good, government provision of the good will satisfy the median voter (or interest groups, or some other politically favored actors), leaving persons with higher levels of demand underserved. This residual demand can be addressed by the nonprofit sector. For example, government programs such as food stamps designed to provide food for the needy are supplemented by nonprofit soup kitchens and food banks. A second strand of thinking takes the firm to be a nexus of contracts, and considers circumstances under which a nonprofit firm might be an efficient organizational structure given the costs of contracting and decision making under alternative ownership forms; see, e.g., Hansmann (1980). On this view, a hallmark of the nonprofit firm is the nondistribution constraint that formally prohibits those who control the firm from receiving residual profit. For example, prospective donors to a soup kitchen might be reluctant to support a for-profit facility because they cannot verify that their money isn't siphoned away from services in order to increase the profits of owners; the nondistribution constraint on the behavior of nonprofit soup kitchens reduces this concern.

A contracts-based argument holds that nonprofit provision can help to solve incentive problems that arise when contracts between firms and their buyers, workers and donors cannot be written to cover effectively every detail that some party cares about. For example, buyers may lack information about the quality of a firm's output at the time of purchase. The nonprofit firm's requirement that it operate under a nondistribution constraint removes some of the incentive for the firm to cut corners by skimping on costly quality. Between a declared mission other than profit maximization and a reduced reward from skimping on quality, nonprofits have been touted as having an advantage in the provision of such 'trust goods'. Whether there would be room for a for-profit presence in a market for a trust good would depend on the extent to which the nonprofit mission and the nondistribution constraint were effective in constraining opportunistic behavior, and the extent to which at least some customers were satisfied with the low-cost, low-quality goods they would expect from for-profit providers. Children's day care may be an example of such a market, with some parents concerned primarily with verifiable elements of quality such as location (Mocan, 2007).

An extreme version of the trust good is one in which buyers are purchasing goods for distant and anonymous third parties. Donors to, say, international relief funds have little way of seeing what impact their donations have on the delivery of services. The temptation for for-profit firms to direct donations to their shareholders might reasonably dissuade donors from supporting for-profit firms in such an industry. In markets for purely redistributive goods, in which buyer–donors and consumers are distinct groups, the for-profit sector faces daunting challenges in attracting private donations.

It is worth noting the ways in which altruism magnifies the importance of both the third-sector rationale and the contracting-and-trust-goods rationale for the nonprofit sector. Altruism that leads people to care about some common concern, such as the well-being of tsunami victims, creates a collective consumption good where otherwise there is only the private consumption of unfortunate individuals. Collective consumption goods are often publicly provided because of market failures, and government provision leaves unsatisfied demand that gives rise to a nonprofit third sector. At the same time, altruistic concern for distant others creates trust goods where otherwise there would be easy verifiability; I can buy a cookstove for myself and quickly observe its quality, but it is much harder to verify that my contribution to tsunami victims is spent on a cookstove of reliable quality.

Finally, nonprofit provision of services is sometimes an early phase in the life cycle of an industry. A recent example is the pioneering by nonprofit organizations of the provision of microfinancing. After nonprofits demonstrated that it was possible to structure small loans to persons with little collateral and to achieve high repayment rates, the microfinance market has attracted for-profit lenders (McIntosh and Wydick, 2005).

Given these sources of impetus for the creation of nonprofit enterprise, the next necessary step is legal recognition of organizations with nonprofit status. The scope of markets in which nonprofits are allowed to operate, and the restrictions and subsidies that come with nonprofit status, are important in shaping competition between for-profit and nonprofit firms.

Nonprofit incorporation and its advantages
A necessary condition for the coexistence of for-profit and nonprofit firms in a market is the government's willingness to confer nonprofit status on firms participating in that market. The point is obvious, but worth consideration because the boundaries of the nonprofit sector are contested. Certain core missions make firms eligible for nonprofit status: firms seeking status as a section 501(c)(3) organization must be 'organized and operated exclusively for religious, charitable, scientific, testing for public safety, literary, or educational purposes, or to foster national or international amateur sports competition . . . or for the prevention of cruelty to children or animals . . .'. To see that this definition leaves plenty of room for regulatory shaping of the boundaries of the nonprofit sector, consider the issues of nonprofit hospitals and unrelated business income.

In terms of commercial revenue and employment, the hospital industry is the largest nonprofit presence in the USA. And yet what is there in the definition of section 501(c)(3) organizations that allows hospitals to be granted nonprofit status? Health care is not on the list of core missions recognized in the tax code as grounds for tax-exempt status. The modern nonprofit hospital is an anachronism, heir to the tax-exempt status that its nineteenth-century forebears rightly claimed because they were charitable institutions, 'frequently little more than dormitories for those who were too ill or infirm to provide for their own sustenance and who had no wealth or family resources on which to draw for support' (Schmalbeck, 2006, p. 123). Schmalbeck chronicles the series of rulings that have allowed continued nonprofit status for hospitals as their function and clientele evolved. In 1956 it was ruled that a nonprofit hospital 'must be operated to the extent of its financial ability for those not able to pay for the services rendered' (ibid., p. 124) and must not turn away patients who could not afford to pay for medical services. In 1969, the Internal Revenue Service ruled that if a hospital was open to all doctors in a community and its emergency room admitted patients without regard for their ability to pay, that was sufficient charitable care for nonprofit status. Subsequently, the emergency-room requirement was waived for specialty hospitals that did not typically have emergency rooms.

In 1969, the Treasury expanded the notion of charity relevant to the incorporation of nonprofit firms to include a community-benefit standard:

> The promotion of health, like the relief of poverty and the advancement of education and religion, is one of the purposes in the general law of charity that is deemed beneficial to the community as a whole even though the class of beneficiaries eligible to receive a direct benefit from its activities does not include all members of the community, such as indigent members of the community, provided that the class is not so small that its relief is not of benefit to the community. (Quoted in Schmalbeck, 2006, p. 126)

The possible reach of the nonprofit sector was substantially – and ambiguously – extended by this reinterpretation of charitable activity away from a focus on the poor and towards the community at large.

Another regulatory question that affects the reach of the nonprofit sector into markets beyond those directly related to the original core missions is that of unrelated business income. How far can nonprofit firms go in entering markets, such as running parking lots and gift shops, in order to raise income to finance their core mission?

Besides dictating the scope of markets in which nonprofits might choose to operate, regulatory detail both constrains and advantages firms within those markets. First among constraints is the nondistribution constraint, forbidding nonprofits from paying profits to owners of the firm. Nonprofits therefore may not raise financial capital in the stock market, nor can they spur their management to greater effort by paying stock options or similar mechanisms that reward employees for successful effort by sharing profits with them. On the other hand, nonprofits can issue tax-exempt bonds that allow them to borrow at rates lower than those available to their for-profit counterparts. Further, nonprofit firms are exempt from income taxes, and donations to section 501(c)(3) organizations confer tax deductions on their donors. The next section reviews the ways in which economic theory has approached the study of markets in which such differently advantaged firms coexist.

The coexistence of for-profit and nonprofit firms
In markets where nonprofit firms are allowed to operate, when will we find them in competition with for-profit firms? Static models of the coexistence of for-profit and non-profit firms generally rely on one of two features to account for that coexistence. First, there may be a scarce resource whose scarcity limits the size of the otherwise dominant organizational form. Second, there may be heterogeneity in demand that allows each organizational form its niche. In dynamic contexts, a market that is initially the exclusive domain of one organizational form may become hospitable to the other as market conditions, information sets or the regulatory environment change. Finally, there is a growing game-theoretic literature that models markets in which a single nonprofit firm competes with a single profit-maximizing firm; these models take the coexistence of nonprofits and for-profits as a starting point protected by barriers to entry.

One scarce resource that can explain the coexistence of nonprofit and profit-maximizing firms is the supply of agents who are motivated by altruism or other nonre-munerative concerns. Lakdawalla and Philipson (2006) model nonprofit firms as being financed and run by donor–managers who get utility from the output of the firm. This utility can stem from altruism as it is generally understood, or from some other nonpe-cuniary reward (prestige, perhaps) associated with production. This willingness to accept returns to their capital and labor in a nonpecuniary form makes the nondistribution constraint associated with nonprofit incorporation less onerous, so it is these altruists who seek the tax advantages that come with incorporation as a nonprofit. Both the tax breaks and the willingness to substitute nonpecuniary rewards for monetary ones allow the nonprofit firms (dubbed 'profit deviators') in an industry to produce at lower cost than purely profit-driven firms.

On this view, a mixed market in which for-profit and nonprofit firms coexist results from a scarcity of donor–entrepreneurs with nonpecuniary motives. Purely profit-driven firms enter the market to satisfy demand not met by the limited supply of lower-cost nonprofit firms. Because the profit-maximizing firms are always the marginal firms in a mixed industry, the Lakdawalla–Philipson model yields two salient predictions about the behavior of mixed markets. First, entry and exit due to changing market conditions should take place among the profit-maximizing firms. While this prediction of higher entry and exit rates for for-profit firms relative to nonprofits can be generated in other ways – access to equity markets gives for-profits an edge in entering a growing market faster than nonprofits and the need to earn a competitive return on capital makes for-profits exit a declining market sooner than nonprofits – the Lakdawalla–Philipson model suggests additionally that the entry and exit rates of for-profits should vary geographically with the nonprofit share of the market as a larger or smaller for-profit fringe absorbs all the adjustments of the market.

Besley and Ghatak (2005) also see a cost advantage accruing to firms whose managers and workers are motivated by nonpecuniary interests. They view many workers as 'motivated agents' who extract intrinsic benefits from certain kinds of work. The mission of a nonprofit firm can be a source of intrinsic benefits. Besley and Ghatak model a firm as consisting of a manager–owner and a worker. The manager contracts with the worker to undertake a project, and that project may be infused with the manager's mission, which may or may not motivate the worker. The probability that the firm's project is successful depends on the unverifiable level of effort made by the worker. A motivated worker receives nonpecuniary benefit from the successful completion of the project. Besley and Ghatak demonstrate that motivated workers make more effort for any level of performance bonus offered. Once again, the sense of mission that is associated with the nonprofit sector gives a cost advantage to the firms that draw resources (in this case, labor) from persons who get nonpecuniary rewards from the production of the firm.

An implication of the cost advantage accruing to mission-oriented nonprofits is that these firms will dominate a market (assuming that consumers do not observe the mission and find it sufficiently odious) unless the supply of managers and workers (and donors) who receive intrinsic benefit from mission is scarce. In the case of a scarcity of motivated managers and workers, the marginal firms in the market will again be the higher-cost for-profit ones.

For economists interested in studying the performance of markets, life is made easier by models with a limited supply of agents who receive nonpecuniary benefits that translate into lower production costs for a limited number of nonprofit firms. When for-profit firms and nonprofit firms coexist in such markets, it is because demand has pulled into the market all of the altruistically advantaged nonprofit firms and left room for the entrance of higher-cost for-profit producers. In such markets, as long as they remain mixed, all responses to market conditions come from the marginal for-profit firms and, as Lakdawalla and Philipson point out, economists know a great deal more about analyzing the behavior of profit maximizers than of agents receiving nonpecuniary benefits. Empirical support for models in which for-profit firms are the marginal firms can be found in the work of Chakravarty et al. (2006), who find that entry and exit rates in the hospital industry are significantly higher for for-profit hospitals than for nonprofit ones.

When mixed markets respond to changing market conditions as if they were populated entirely by for-profit firms, one policy-relevant consequence is that the benefits of taxpayer subsidies for the nonprofit sector are largely inframarginal and therefore less readily visible to the public eye. This could cause political headaches for advocates of the nonprofit sector. On the other hand, it is the nonprofit part of the market that is predicted by these models to respond to changing conditions that affect the limited supply of altruistic concern for output in the market: events such as national disasters are likely to be occasions on which the public eye sees nonprofit firms as more responsive than their for-profit counterparts.

In models in which altruistically motivated suppliers of resources are central to the conception of the nonprofit sector, the nature of that altruism will have consequences for market structure. One important distinction is whether altruistically motivated agents care only about the quantity or quality of a good produced, or whether their satisfaction comes from their own contribution to the production of that quantity or quality. In the literature on altruism, these orientations have been dubbed 'pure altruism' if it is the overall production that enters the utility function, and 'impure altruism' or 'warm glow' if the individual cares about his or her own contribution towards the production of the good. In the models of Lakdawalla and Philipson and of Besley and Ghatak, altruistically motivated actors see a clear link between the allocation of their resources (capital or labor) and the level of output from which they derive nonpecuniary benefits. The possibility of free-riding does not arise for Besley and Ghatak's workers, for example, because their effort is the sole input into the production of the output they care about.

To illustrate the importance of the type of altruism when free-riding is a possibility, consider the question of wages paid by for-profit and nonprofit firms in the same market. In the contracting model of Francois (2003), workers care about the level of output, but they are pure altruists who are happy to free-ride on the efforts of others. They won't take wage cuts in order to produce the output they care about, preferring that others take the cuts and produce the output. With all workers thinking this way, none takes a cut in pay in order to work in the nonprofit sector. Their concern with output matters, however, as it interacts with the nonprofit employers' nondistribution constraint. By limiting their ability to appropriate profit, the nondistribution constraint limits the motivation of nonprofit manager–owners to step in and take up the slack when a worker shirks. This implies that workers in nonprofit firms shirk less, knowing that their shirking will have a bigger impact on output than would shirking under a manager–owner who would offset more of their shirking by working harder herself in order to enjoy more profit. Worker motivation thus allows nonprofits to elicit effort with a bonus wage that is lower than the bonus wage for-profits would have to offer. Because for-profits cannot competitively elicit effort through a bonus wage structure, those for-profits that find a way to compete must be avoiding shirking another way, presumably by monitoring their employees and threatening serious consequences for anyone caught shirking. The resulting prediction is that wages are higher in the bonus-paying nonprofit sector than in the employee-monitoring for-profit sector, in contrast to Besley and Ghatak's mission-motivated agents whose bonuses are smaller than those paid to workers in profit-maximizing firms.

Just as the nondistribution constraint limits the incentives of nonprofit owner–managers to lend their costly effort to compensate for shirking employees, it limits the incentives for nonprofit owner–managers to shirk in the provision of hard-to-observe quality. Glaeser and Shleifer (2001) propose that the choice of nonprofit form is a commitment device that makes it costly for entrepreneurs to appropriate profits. Consumers care about product quality but cannot contract over it because it cannot be observed and adjudicated by a third party. Owner–managers who choose the nonprofit form do so knowing that they cannot distribute profits to themselves except by converting net revenues into job perquisites, which are not as attractive as cash. The gains from shirking on quality are thereby reduced, and in equilibrium nonprofit firms produce greater quality than for-profit firms.

This association of nonprofit output with high quality is likely to be even stronger when the donor–managers of the nonprofit are also among its customers. One might think of high-end cultural nonprofits, such as symphony orchestras, museums and opera companies as examples of nonprofits whose donors and board members are consumers of the nonprofit's output. The conception of a nonprofit as a membership organization similar to a club suggests that the objective function of the firm might include concern with consumer surplus. Further, these are nonprofits that are often large relative to their markets, which are local, and face only a small number of competitors; models of nonprofits concerned with consumer surplus and competing with for-profit firms tend to place them in markets that are less than perfectly competitive.

Herbst and Prufer (2007) show that the nondistribution constraint can serve to exclude from membership those potential members who have a preference for low-quality output; a donation acts essentially as a membership fee that cannot be returned as profit and therefore serves as a mechanism for exclusion. They model nonprofits as maximizing consumer surplus, and the result is an inefficiently high level of quality. As markets become more competitive and the array of available substitutes reduces demand for the nonprofit's good, the total surplus generated by the nonprofit falls relative to that of for-profit production. Lien (2002) characterizes a nonprofit firm as receiving tax subsidies and having an objective function that maximizes a linear combination of profit and consumer surplus. In a Cournot duopoly with one nonprofit and one profit-maximizing firm, he shows that the positive weight on consumer surplus leads to a prediction that the nonprofit firm will be larger than its profit-maximizing rival and that, as the weight on consumer surplus increases, both the size differential and the size of the overall market grow, leading to a lower equilibrium price. Goering (2007) models the nonprofit firm as the leader in a Stackelberg game with an objective function that includes profit plus the fraction of consumer surplus that accrues to its stakeholders. If the for-profit firm is a lower-cost producer than the nonprofit, the nonprofit's concern with consumer surplus might lead it to cut back its output in order to spur expansion by its low-cost rival.

To illustrate the link between nonprofit motive and market performance, Harrison and Lybecker (2005) model price competition between a nonprofit and a for-profit firm with differentiated products under three alternative specifications of the nonprofit firm's objective function. The nonprofit is assumed to maximize a linear combination of profit and one of three motives commonly ascribed to nonprofits: quantity; the quantity that can be cross-subsidized for charitable provision at no charge; and quality. By varying the importance given to profit in the objective function, the model predicts how price and quantity respond to an increased emphasis on the motive other than profit. When the nonprofit cares about its quantity of output, its price is lower than that charged by its profit-maximizing competitor; as the weight assigned to quantity in the nonprofit's objective function increases, the quantity produced expands and both firms' prices fall. This is in contrast to the case in which the nonprofit cares about the quantity of its good it can provide at no charge: the stronger this motive, the higher the nonprofit's price charged to its paying customers. The for-profit firm takes advantage of this opportunity to increase its price as well. The case of quality shows the two firms' prices moving in opposite directions. As the nonprofit puts more emphasis on quality, it raises its price along with its chosen level of costly quality. This makes it harder for the profit-maximizing firm to compete on quality grounds, and the for-profit competitor adjusts its price and quality downwards.

Harrison and Lybecker model the shift in the nonprofit firm's emphasis on profit maximization as arising exogenously, leaving open the question of what might induce such a change. Increased regulatory scrutiny of the nonprofit sector may push nonprofits to distinguish themselves more blatantly and sympathetically from their profit-maximizing and taxpaying competitors, spurring nonprofits to put more emphasis on their nonpecuniary motives. In the other direction, increased competition from profit-maximizing firms may force nonprofits to behave more like for-profits. McIntosh and Wydick (2005) model explicitly the effects of increasing competition on the extent to which microfinance nonprofits make loans to the poorest of the poor. Increasing competition for the pool of borrowers who can be charged a high rate will reduce the nonprofit's ability to cross-subsidize its poorest borrowers, thereby reducing the distinction between their behavior and that of their profit-maximizing rivals; the effect of an increasingly competitive environment on charitable provision is similar to the effect on charitable provision of an exogenously increased emphasis on profit maximization in the model of Harrison and Lybecker. Steinberg and Weisbrod (2005) model a price-discriminating nonprofit that maximizes a weighted sum of consumer surplus because it cares more about generating surplus for some potential consumers than for others; the firm's ability to price-discriminate and cross-subsidize disappears when a for-profit firm enters the market and competes on price.

Concluding remarks: directions for future research
Building on earlier scholarship on the nature of nonprofit enterprise, recent scholarship has yielded important insights into the functioning of mixed markets under competitive conditions and in markets with a small number of firms. This literature makes contributions in many areas, including the implications of the nondistribution constraint for the ability of nonprofit firms to compete with their profit-maximizing counterparts, the competitive advantage afforded nonprofit firms in the presence of altruistically motivated donors, managers and workers, the differences between for-profit and nonprofit output and pricing decisions in imperfectly competitive markets, and the ability of nonprofits to price their services in order to cross-subsidize service for a targeted set of clients. The approaches taken in this literature suggest several fruitful directions for further research, which I describe briefly in closing.

To what extent do nonprofits have an advantage in motivating agents, and are there markets in which altruistically motivated consumers might be taken into account? For example, do doctors work harder in a nonprofit hospital than in a for-profit one, and do volunteers pay attention to whether the hospital they volunteer in is for-profit, nonprofit or public? When do mission-driven firms have to contend with differently inclined consumers who prefer, say, fair-trade coffee, products made in the USA, or pizza from firms whose owners oppose or protect abortion rights? When is mission neutrality a competitive advantage?

Nonprofits cannot raise funds in equity markets, and they are incorporated with the understanding that they devote themselves 'exclusively' to a restricted list of areas of operation. Do these restrictions translate, respectively, into limitations on the scale and scope of nonprofit firms, and if so are they disadvantaged in competition with profit-maximizing rivals? Empirical work on the relative performance of for-profit and non-profit firms has found that firms that are parts of chains behave differently from firms that are independent; how do we make theoretical sense of these differences?

Nonprofit firms have frequently been modeled as having objective functions that deviate from profit maximization by including concern with the firm's output level or with the amount of consumer surplus generated in the market. Neither of these specifications captures the notion of charity very well, and while it is good to remember that much of the nonprofit sector is not primarily charitable, there is room for further consideration of charitable aims, such as the provision of goods and services to a population with limited ability to pay. Harrison and Lybecker (2005), McIntosh and Wydick (2005) and Steinberg and Weisbrod (2005) provide examples of research in this direction, and there is room for more. For example, in models in which nonprofit firms have a cost advantage, how would market equilibrium change if nonprofits used their cost advantage to support the charitable provision of services? If the size of the targeted population is scarce relative to the supply of altruistic motivation, do altruists compete to serve the needy, or do they attempt to free-ride on others' generosity?

Nonprofit activity in markets often precedes the substantial entry of profit-oriented firms. Sometimes the entry of profit-maximizing firms is a response to changes in the environment due to changes in government policy; see Skloot (2000) for a discussion of health maintenance organizations after changes in federal regulations in the early 1980s and human services after the welfare reforms of the mid-1990s. Is there also a generic imperfect information problem that leads nonprofits to enter a market first, and for profit maximizers under certain circumstances to follow? Is there scope for nonprofits to behave strategically and to forestall entry of profit-seeking rivals? Should we consider predatory altruists pricing services below costs achievable by their higher-cost rivals? Can economists model the circumstances that pull nonprofit firms into markets first, with for-profit firms entering second, if at all?

How does our understanding of mixed markets change as we add government provision to the mix?

More generally, the literature seems poised to look at interactions other than simple competition among firms in mixed markets. One direction is the consideration of strategic contracting between nonprofits and for-profits, as suggested for example by Weisbrod (1997) and O'Regan and Oster (2000). Other interactions include mergers and competition (in fundraising, for example) among nonprofits: do they behave differently in the presence of for-profit firms that can perhaps merge more easily due to an alignment of motives around strict profit maximization? If for-profit and nonprofit firms behave differently when it comes to mergers or if their mergers have differing consequences for welfare (Prufer, 2007), there is reason to rethink antitrust regulation that does not distinguish between profit-maximizing and nonprofit firms (Philipson and Posner, 2006). The economics literature on competition between for-profit and nonprofit firms, once narrowly focused on issues on taxation, now provides a promising foundation for revisiting many canonical topics in industrial organization in which scant attention has been paid to the existence of the nonprofit sector.

References

Besley, Timothy and Maitreesh Ghatak (2005), 'Competition and incentives with motivated agents', *American Economic Review*, **95** (3), 616–36.

Chakravarty, Sujoy, Martin Gaynor, Steven Klepper and William B. Vogt (2006), 'Does the profit motive make Jack nimble? Ownership form and the evolution of the US hospital industry', *Health Economics*, **15** (4), 345–61.

Francois, Patrick (2003), 'Not-for-profit provision of public services', *The Economic Journal*, **113** (486), C53–C61.

Glaeser, Edward and Andrei Shleifer (2001), 'Not-for-profit entrepreneurs', *Journal of Public Economics*, **81** (1), 99–116.

Goering, Gregory E. (2007), 'The strategic use of managerial incentives in a non-profit firm mixed duopoly', *Managerial and Decision Economics*, **28** (2), 83–91.

Hansmann, Henry B. (1980), 'The role of nonprofit enterprise', *Yale Law Journal*, **89** (5), 835–98.

Harrison, Teresa D. and Kristina M. Lybecker (2005), 'The effect of the nonprofit motive on hospital competitive behavior', *The Berkeley Electronic Journal of Economic Analysis & Policy*, **4** (1), Article 3, available at http://www.bepress.com/bejeap/contributions/vol4/iss1/art3

Herbst, Patrick and Jens Prufer (2007), 'Firms, nonprofits, and cooperatives: a theory of organizational choice', CentER Discussion Paper No. 2007–07, Tilburg University.

Lakdawalla, Darius and Tomas Philipson (2006), 'The nonprofit sector and industry performance', *Journal of Public Economics*, **90** (8–9), 1681–98.

Lien, Donald (2002), 'Competition between nonprofit and for-profit firms', *International Journal of Business and Economics*, **1** (3), 193–207.

McIntosh, Craig and Bruce Wydick (2005), 'Competition and microfinance', *Journal of Development Economics*, **78** (2), 271–98.

Mocan, Naci (2007), 'Can consumers detect lemons? An empirical analysis of information asymmetry in the market for child care', *Journal of Population Economics*, **20** (4), 743–80.

O'Regan, Katherine M. and Sharon M. Oster (2000), 'Nonprofit and for-profit partnerships: rationale and challenges of cross-sector contracting', *Nonprofit and Voluntary Sector Quarterly*, **29** (1), 120–40.

Philipson, Tomas J. and Richard A. Posner (2006), 'Antitrust in the not-for-profit sector', National Bureau of Economic Research Working Paper 12132.

Powell, Walter W. and Richard Steinberg (2006), *The Nonprofit Sector: A Research Handbook*, 2nd edn, New Haven, CT: Yale University Press.

Prufer, Jens (2007), 'Competition and mergers among nonprofits', CentER Discussion Paper No. 2007–82, Tilburg University.

Schlesinger, Mark and Bradford H. Gray (2006), 'Nonprofit organizations and health care: some paradoxes of persistent scrutiny', in Walter W. Powell and Richard Steinberg (eds), *The Nonprofit Sector: A Research Handbook*, 2nd edn, New Haven, CT: Yale University Press, pp. 378–414.

Schmalbeck, Richard L. (2006), 'The impact of tax-exempt status: the supply-side subsidies', *Law and Contemporary Problems*, **69**, 121–38.

Skloot, Edward (2000), 'Evolution or extinction: A strategy for nonprofits in the marketplace', *Nonprofit and Voluntary Sector Quarterly*, **29**, 315–24.

Steinberg, Richard and Burton A. Weisbrod (2005), 'Nonprofits with distributional objectives: price discrimination and corner solutions', *Journal of Public Economics*, **89** (11–12), 2205–30.

Weisbrod, Burton A. (1975), 'Toward a theory of the voluntary nonprofit sector in a three-sector economy', in Edmund S. Phelps (ed.), *Altruism, Morality, and Economic Theory*, New York: Russell Sage Foundation, pp. 171–95.

Weisbrod, Burton A. (1997), 'The future of the nonprofit sector: its entwining with private enterprise and government', *Journal of Policy Analysis and Management*, **16** (4), 541–55.

8 Nonprofit wages: theory and evidence
Anne E. Preston and Daniel W. Sacks

Introduction

Compensation in the nonprofit sector has been a source of much thought and research over the last 30 years, with little consensus on whether there are differences in level and type of compensation from that of the for-profit or government sectors. This lack of agreement may seem surprising given how small (8 percent of employees in the US labor market) and homogeneous (predominantly professional, college educated and female) the labor force is. However, the homogeneity of the workers stands in stark contrast to the large variety of firms that employ these individuals.

Characteristics of the nonprofit, for-profit and government labor forces are displayed in Table 8.1. Of the three categories, the nonprofit worker is most highly educated (14.9 average years of education), most likely to be professional (50 percent), most likely to work in a service industry (92 percent), most likely to live in the northeast (27 percent) and most likely to be female (69 percent). A closer look reveals that the typical nonprofit worker looks more similar to her government than her for-profit counterpart in terms of education, occupational and industry location, and sex, and both groups have significantly more experience than their for-profit counterparts. The average wage of the nonprofit worker, however, is significantly lower than the wage earned by government employees and not significantly different than the wage earned by for-profit workers. While nonprofit workers, like government workers, work fewer hours than for-profit employees, the shorter work week should not necessarily affect the hourly wage. Therefore, given the high qualifications of nonprofit employees relative to the general workforce, these wage rates point to low relative levels of compensation.

An organization qualifies for nonprofit status if it fits into one of the categories in section 501(a) of the Internal Revenue Code. This code describes a host of organizations including categories 501(c) 1–27 (excluding 20 and 24), 501(d), (e), (f), (k) and (n), and 521(a). We tend to equate nonprofit with charitable organization, but these include only the section 501(c)(3) organizations, which in 1985 made up less than half the total number of nonprofit organizations.[1] The rest include such diverse organizations as labor unions, farm cooperatives, cemetery companies and mutual insurance companies, to name a few. While all of these organizations are supposed to serve some type of common good, the extent and character of social benefits are quite varied, as seen by a comparison of the output of a country club and a soup kitchen, for example. In addition, only those entities organized for charitable purposes, section 501(c)(3)s, enjoy benefits beyond the corporate income tax exemption, most notably the right to solicit tax-deductible donations and exemption from sales and property taxes.[2]

Any chapter that examines employment and wages of the nonprofit sector must begin with an explanation of the complexities of the establishments and the people who make up the sector. We turn to economic theory, which, even when examining organizations that seem to flaunt a total contempt for the goals set forth in the theory of the firm, can

Table 8.1   Selected characteristics of nonprofit, for-profit and government employees using 2000 US Census data[a]

	Nonprofit	For-profit	Government
Years of education	15.0	13.5	14.7
	(2.4)	(2.2)	(2.4)
Years of potential experience	20.7	18.7	21.6
	(12.1)	(12.2)	(11.4)
Occupation			
% professional	53.6	17.0	43.8
% manager	15.6	14.9	11.7
% clerical or Sales	18.6	31.1	19.5
Industry			
% all services	91.6	31.8	52.6
% educ., health, Social Services	64.6	11.1	48.8
% health services	31.7	8.0	6.2
% female	68.8	45.0	56.0
% living in northeast	26.9	20.5	19.8
% white	83.0	80.0	75.7
Hours	38.6	40.9	39.8
	(12.3)	(11.1)	(10.3)
Wages	18.72*	18.69	19.9
	(56.6)	(41.7)	(76.6)
N	6 588 829	58 130 099	14 104 502

Notes:
[a]   The sample is taken from the 2000 Census 5 percent PUMS and includes 18–70-year-old employed individuals who are not self-employed and who are not employed in the military. All means and percentages are calculated using Census-provided frequency weights.
   All statistics are significantly different across the sectors except where noted.
*   Wages of nonprofit and for-profit works are not significantly different at the 0.1 level.

give guidance on how and when wages of nonprofit workers may diverge from those of their for-profit counterparts.

Economic theory and nonprofit wages

Theoretical explanations of a nonprofit earnings differential must begin with the differing legal treatment of nonprofit organizations. Organizations that incorporate as nonprofit are exempt from the corporate income tax, but in return they must operate under the non-distribution constraint which prohibits the distribution of profits to individuals in control of the organization. The theory of the firm predicts that distribution of profits is necessary in order to ensure that managers provide a profit-maximizing level of effort. Since managerial compensation cannot be tied to profit, boards will design contracts so that managers maximize other objectives (Roomkin and Weisbrod, 1999; Preyra and Pink, 2001). Because the demand for labor is derived from the process in which firms maximize their objective function, alternative objective functions may lead to different wages.

Identifying a reasonable alternative objective requires returning to the implications of the legal treatment. Nelson and Krashinsky (1974) in an article on day care first acknowledged the asymmetry of information between suppliers and consumers of the nonprofit service. Hansmann (1980) later developed this idea for most nonprofit services. Asymmetries can arise because of third-party purchasing, as in day care where parents buy care for their children or in charities where donors buy aid for the needy, or because of the nature of the product where the quality level is difficult to evaluate for a non-expert and/or the response to the service is not immediate and not guaranteed, as in various forms of health care. Arrow (1963) argued that hospitals choose nonprofit status as a response to these information asymmetries. If nonprofits have arisen to deal with this market imperfection as institutions of trust, they can offer high-quality products with no incentive to renege on their promises (Holtmann and Idson, 1993; Handy and Katz, 1998; Glaeser and Shleifer, 2001). Within a given industry nonprofit providers will provide the higher-cost, higher-quality product, and because most nonprofit services are labor intensive,[3] the higher-quality product will require higher-quality workers. If worker and product quality are not fully observed, seemingly similar workers will be paid higher wages in the nonprofit firm. Alternatively, if managers are concerned less with organizational success and more with own utility, they may use excess profits to compensate employees in order to boost worker appreciation (see, e.g., Preston, 1988). Such behavior conforms to the property rights literature, which stresses non-cost-minimizing behavior by managers who cannot lay a claim to profits.[4] These two arguments for higher nonprofit wages are different in that managerial largesse implies a wedge between nonprofit worker productivity and wages while high-quality nonprofit products do not.

The extent to which wages can exceed productivity is limited by two forces. First the more competitive the product market, the more necessary cost minimization will be for survival. Second, charitable nonprofits (section 501(c)(3) organizations) can lose their tax-exempt status, and ability to solicit tax-deductible donations, if the compensation they pay to employees is unreasonable, or above the value that would ordinarily be paid for 'like services by a like enterprise under like circumstances'.[5] However, this regulation applies primarily to the pay of people who are instrumental in the firm's activities, and may not apply to pay levels for the full range of workers.

As Glaeser and Shleifer show, the competitive advantage of nonprofit status in providing services that are hard to evaluate represents one reason that even profit-maximizing entrepreneurs would found a nonprofit. But it is likely that altruistic goals motivate the formation of the majority of nonprofits: unconcerned with profit, the nondistribution constraint is hardly a constraint for altruistic boards of directors. Indeed, section 501(c)(3) organizations by mandate serve a public purpose, such as 'charitable, religious, educational, scientific, literary, testing for public safety, fostering national or international amateur sports competition, and preventing cruelty to children or animals'.[6] If managers also have a taste for altruism in the form of providing public goods, then they will accept lower compensation (in the form of foregone residual profit) in order to provide public goods.[7] Furthermore, in industries where nonprofits and for-profits compete, nonprofit managers, stewarding institutions of trust, might choose, instead of high-quality services, to expand the clientele or the type of service to broaden the social benefits provided. Not only are social benefits, like quality, hard to gauge, but they are also not easily marketable and so might best be purchased with foregone profits. To the extent that managers share their board's goals, their actions will maximize their board's objective function.

The taste for altruism bears on the supply of labor in the nonprofit sector, since products and services provided by these organizations have a higher social-benefit component than those provided by for-profit organizations. There may be workers who find non-profit work more socially rewarding and more interesting than for-profit work and are willing to work for lower wages, as Weisbrod (1983) and Frank (1996) report for lawyers. This compensating differential argument, often called the labor donation hypothesis, implies that as long as the supply of these workers exceeds the number of nonprofit jobs, there will be a negative nonprofit wage differential.

Wages in the nonprofit sector, and therefore the nonprofit wage differential, depend on the supply and demand of labor, each of which is influenced by the nature of the goods and services produced. The IRS definition of the nonprofit firm ensures that the typical nonprofit produces goods and services with a higher public-good component than those produced by the typical for-profit firm. The nondistribution constraint suggests that nonprofits, when competing with for-profits, produce goods of higher quality or greater public benefit. The constraint also suggests that managers may use their lar-gesse to subsidize wages. While nonprofits in industries producing high-quality goods are predicted to have relatively high wages due to unobserved worker quality, nonprofits in industries producing public goods are predicted to have relatively low wages, because of labor donations. We therefore expect the nonprofit differential to be negative in the aggregate but to vary substantially between industries. In the rest of this chapter we shall use our understanding of the link between legal restrictions and wages to make sense of previous estimates of the nonprofit wage differential and to guide new ones.

Literature review

Economy-wide studies
Early literature on the economy-wide nonprofit wage differential suffered from an inabil-ity to identify workers employed at nonprofit firms. Preston (1989), using the Current Population Survey 1979, 1980, applied an industry definition derived by Rudney and Weitzman (1982) from the 1977 Census of Industries and the 1980 Bureau of Labor employment data where a worker is classified as nonprofit if he or she works in an indus-try for which at least two-thirds of privately employed workers work for a nonprofit firm. The overall estimated negative differential of 15 percent for white-collar workers is more severe for managers and professionals than for clerical workers. Starting with the 1990 Census, government surveys added a question designed to identify the employing firm's status. Papers that take advantage of this innovation (Leete, 2001; Ruhm and Borkoski, 2003) estimate economy-wide nonprofit differentials of roughly −11 percent. These estimates are comparable to the earlier estimates, which were based solely on white-collar workers, who tend to experience more severe wage differentials than do blue-collar or service workers. Most recently Salamon and Sokolowski (2005) use IRS records to identify whether an employing firm has tax-exempt (and thus nonprofit) status in the Quarterly Census of Employment and Wages Program. They estimate an 11 percent difference in average weekly wages paid by for-profit and nonprofit firms. The negative economy-wide nonprofit differential of these varied studies using different data over different time periods is not surprising given the earlier theoretical discussion. The typical nonprofit product is likely to be associated much more closely with social benefits than the typical for-product profit when looking at the aggregate economy, and thus the

negative pressure on wages should be strong. Positive forces on wages resulting from a lack of competition coupled with managerial largesse or high-quality products might just as likely arise with for-profit firms once the full economy is examined. Therefore the negative pressure on nonprofit wages is likely to dominate.

Studies that identify the firm's sector have the advantage of estimating the differential with extensive industry controls. Once Leete includes detailed industry (and occupational) controls in her analysis, the nonprofit differential becomes insignificant and close to zero. However, she notes that the insignificant differential is not the result of comparable wages for nonprofit and for-profit employees within the relatively low-paying industries in which nonprofit firms locate, but rather within industry nonprofit wage differentials, which range from significantly positive to significantly negative. Ruhm and Borkoski's estimates mirror those of Leete, and similarly Salamon and Sokolowski find that within the industries of hospitals, education, social services, residential care, nursing care and child care the differences between nonprofit and for-profit average wages are positive or insignificant. But Salamon and Sokolowski are using firm-level rather than worker-level data and do not control for worker characteristics. To conclude, as Salamon and Sokolowski do, that the differential is simply an industry differential is problematic since industry location and nonprofit status are inextricably linked and within-industry nonprofit differentials are not all zero. Furthermore, many of these economy-wide studies which conclude that industry and occupational controls explain the nonprofit differential fail to recognize the variation in the size of the differential by occupation and gender. Generally the differential is most severe for professionals, the majority of nonprofit workers, and men, a minority of nonprofit workers, and as shown later in this chapter, these within-group differentials remain significant even in the face of industry controls.

Industry-based studies
Within-industry studies estimate varying differentials. Weisbrod (1983) estimates a negative nonprofit differential of about 25 percent for public-interest lawyers controlling for experience, quality of education and educational performance using a relatively small sample of lawyers surveyed in 1973. Frank (1996), in a study of a number of different samples and industries, notes that in New York City at the time of his study the prominent law firms were paying starting salaries of $80 000 while the American Civil Liberties Union was paying $25 000. Obviously not derived from a random sample, the statistics do point out the variation one might find across the sectors. Within legal services, the negative nonprofit differential should not be surprising since the kind of services and the clients served are very different across the two sectors, with nonprofit legal services having a much higher social-benefit component. In addition, revenue sources for nonprofit legal work are neither plentiful nor lucrative.

In the hospital industry, nonprofit wage differentials are neither large nor consistent. Roomkin and Weisbrod (1999) find that at the highest executive level nonprofit salaries are higher than for-profit salaries but for-profit firms pay higher bonuses, making total compensation higher. On the other hand, at the level below CEO and COO, nonprofit executives are earning higher compensation than for-profit executives. The insignificant differentials might be explained by further research, which shows that nonprofit and for-profit hospitals provide very similar products in a somewhat competitive market. Duggan (2000) exploited a natural experiment when California introduced a program to provide monetary incentives for hospitals to provide services to indigent clients, and found that nonprofits and for-profits responded similarly. Furthermore, contrary to expectations, the extra revenue going to nonprofit hospitals expanded financial wealth rather than services. Brickley and Van Horn (2002) find that CEO turnover in nonprofit hospitals is highly dependent on return on assets, and that nonprofit boards do not reward altruistic actions, such as higher numbers of nurses per patient or revenue per patient day, through lower turnover or higher salaries.

The higher nonprofit wages for registered nurses in nursing homes and for child care workers may point to the explanation of higher-quality nonprofit products in industries where quality of care is difficult to evaluate and the social-benefit component of the service is similar for nonprofit and for-profit providers. Holtmann and Idson (1993) find that the positive significant nonprofit differential can be explained by selection of high-quality workers into nonprofit nursing homes. Preston (1988) finds that wages of child care workers are higher in federally regulated nonprofit day care centers than in federally regulated for-profit centers. And in a related paper using the same data (Preston, 1993), she finds that in this regulated sector of day care, where minimum social-benefit levels are required, non-profit centers provide higher-quality care, as measured by higher staff-to-child ratios, lower staff turnover and greater employment of specialists, than for-profit centers. In the more competitive unregulated sector of day care, salaries are equivalent across sectors (Preston, 1988) and nonprofit centers separate themselves from for-profit centers with high levels of social benefits (Preston, 1993). Mocan and Tekin (2003) argue that the positive nonprofit wage differentials they estimate in day care are not the result of higher-quality workers but rather of managers' freedom to maximize objective functions other than profits.

Differentials by gender

The variation in wage differentials by gender is first noted by Preston (1989) when she finds that the differential for white males is much larger (and still significantly negative) than the differential estimated for all workers. The implication that the differential for women is not as severe as for men motivates her study on female representation in the nonprofit sector (Preston, 1990b), which finds that in addition to occupational locus, nonprofit female wages draw women to the sector. They are a draw because they are not too different from female wages earned in the for-profit sector and because their similarity to male nonprofit wages creates a high degree of equality within the sector. Leete (2000) finds further evidence of wage equity across occupations in the white-collar occupations and across race throughout the nonprofit sector. Preston (1990a), still using the industry-based definition, charts the nonprofit differential for women over the period from 1973 to 1985 as women were achieving more success in occupations traditionally reserved for men and located in for-profit firms. She finds that the female nonprofit differential for white-collar workers remained negative and significant but doubled in magnitude over the period examined.[8]

New estimates using the 2000 Census

Economy-wide estimates

To explore the current nonprofit differential we turn to the 5 percent public-use micro-data sample (PUMS) from the 2000 Census. Our sample includes non-disabled, working

Table 8.2   Nonprofit and government wage differentials from wage regressions run on 2000 US Census data[a,b]

	Controls include			
	1 None	2 Human capital, race, sex and location	3 Human capital, race, sex, location and occupation	4 Human capital, race, sex, location, occupation and detailed industry
Coefficient on:				
1. Nonprofit	0.038 ***	−0.096***	−0.118***	−0.009***
	(0.001)	(0.001)	(0.001)	(0.001)
2. Government	0.144***	−0.012***	−0.001	0.036***
	(0.001)	(0.001)	(0.001)	(0.001)

Notes:
[a]   Dependent variable is natural logarithm of the hourly wage.
[b]   Sample size is 3 878 504.
*** Significant at the 0.01 level using a two-tailed test.

individuals aged 18–70 who are not in the military or self-employed and who are fluent in English. To explore the nonprofit differential we estimate the following regression:

$$\text{Ln(wage)}_i = a + b(\textbf{SECTOR}_i) + c\textbf{X}_i + d(\textbf{OCC}_i) + f(\textbf{IND}_i) + e_i$$

The dependent variable is the natural logarithm of the hourly wage of employed workers; therefore all coefficients can be interpreted as percentage changes in wages. The vector of sector variables includes two variables representing sector of employing firm: one for nonprofit firms and the other for government. The variables in the **X** vector include controls for human capital (years of education, years of potential experience and years of potential experience squared) and controls for race, region of workplace, whether the workplace is in an urban area, and whether the individual works part time. The vector of occupational controls includes variables representing managerial, professional, service, and clerical and sales occupations. The vector of industry controls includes the full set of 3-digit census industry codes.

Table 8.2 presents the nonprofit and government wage differentials estimated with this regression. Column 1 gives the simple differentials without any controls, and average nonprofit wages are 3.8 percent higher than for-profit wages while government wages are 14.4 percent higher than for-profit wages. Once controls for human capital, part-time status, sex, race and location are included (column 2), the differentials look very different. Comparing individuals who are similar along these dimensions, the nonprofit worker earns almost 10 percent lower wages than the for-profit worker, and the government worker earns 1 percent lower wages. Adding broad occupational controls (column 3) makes the government differential insignificant and reduces the nonprofit differential further to −11.8 percent. These nonprofit estimates for 2000 are similar to the economy-

Table 8.3   Nonprofit wage differentials by gender

	Controls include:	
	1 Human capital, occupation, race and location	2 Human capital, occupation, race, location and detailed industries
Nonprofit differential for:		
1. Men	−0.231*** (0.002)	−0.048*** (0.003)
2. Women	−0.058*** (0.001)	0.014*** (0.002)

Note: *** Significant at the 0.01 level using a two-tailed test.

wide estimates of Leete, Ruhm and Borkoski, and Salamon and Sokolowski. If the sample is constrained to the managerial, professional, and clerical and sales occupations of Preston's early studies, the differential is −0.16 percent, almost identical to the differential she estimated. Once detailed 3-digit industry codes are included in the regressions (column 4), the government differential becomes positive and significant, and the nonprofit differential falls to −0.9 percent, a differential that, while significant, seems small and relatively unimportant.

Table 8.3 presents the results from columns 3 and 4 of Table 8.2 for subsamples of men and women. As predicted, the nonprofit wage differential for men is much more severe; comparing men of the same human capital characteristics, occupation, race and job location, those employed in nonprofits earn 23 percent lower wages than men employed by for-profit firms. Once detailed industry controls are included, the magnitude of the differential falls to just under 5 percent. The nonprofit wage differential for women with similar human capital and occupational locus is much smaller at −6 percent. Controls for occupation cause the female differential to become +1.5 percent. Clearly men experience a more severe wage loss than women if they choose to become nonprofit workers, and within the nonprofit sector male and female wages are more equal than in the for-profit sector.[9]

Table 8.4 presents the differential within broad occupational classifications. Researchers have posited that the labor donation hypotheses will be more pronounced for those employees who have some power over the product. Therefore the negative pressure on wages should be greater for managers and professionals. Because the economy-wide differential may reflect the differences in social benefits between the typical nonprofit and for-profit product, we might expect to see differences in this differential by occupation. Column 1 gives the differentials without detailed industry controls. The differential, which is negative and significant for all occupations, ranges from −0.01 for service workers to −0.19 for professionals and managers. The more influential employees experience the most severe wage loss within the nonprofit sector. Once detailed industry controls are included (column 2), the differentials fall in magnitude. While service workers enjoy a positive differential, managers and professional continue to experience

Table 8.4   Nonprofit wage differentials by occupation

	Controls include:	
	1 Human capital, sex, race and location	2 Human capital, sex, race, location and detailed industries
Nonprofit differential for:		
1. Blue-collar workers	−0.060*** (0.005)	−0.024*** (0.005)
2. Service workers	−0.010*** (0.004)	0.010** (0.004)
3. Clerical and sales workers	−0.072*** (0.002)	−0.004 (0.003)
4. Professional workers	−0.194*** (0.002)	−0.013*** (0.002)
5. Managers	−0.187*** (0.003)	−0.072*** (0.004)

Notes:
*** Significant at the 0.01 level using a two-tailed test.
** Significant at the 0.05 level using a two-tailed test.

significant wages losses at −0.07 and −0.01 respectively. Note that because relatively high-paid employees (i.e. men, professionals and managers) experience the most severe wage loss by working in the nonprofit sector, the sector's wage distribution must be more compressed than the for-profit wage distribution.

What can be learned by looking at the differential within industries?
Tables 8.2, 8.3 and 8.4 clearly reveal that adding industry controls to our wage regressions significantly reduces the magnitude of the estimated negative nonprofit wage differential. Some researchers have used this diminution as evidence against the labor donation hypothesis and a wage differential altogether. However, theoretical arguments all point to the movement of a negative differential towards zero as one looks within industry. First, products and services will be much more similar within industries than across them, so the difference in social benefits will not be so great. In addition, as nonprofit and for-profit firms compete for similar workers, the compensating differential is likely to fall as nonprofit firms work to retain high-quality workers. Finally, and almost always overlooked, the inclusion of industry controls ignores the importance of wages of workers employed in industries that are exclusively nonprofit. There are four such industries: religious services; civic, social, advocacy services and grant-making and -giving services; labor unions; and business, professional, political and similar organizations. These four industries employ 20 percent of the nonprofit employees according to the 2000 Census. Furthermore, including a dummy variable for these industries reveals that workers in these industries earn 28 percent lower wages than their for-profit counterparts, while the other nonprofit employees, those who are employed in industries with

Table 8.5   Nonprofit differentials by selected industries

	Controls include human capital, sex, race, location and occupation
Nonprofit differential for:	
1. Legal services	−0.224***
	(0.019)
2. Day care	0.037***
	(0.007)
3. Hospitals	0.045***
	(0.003)
4. Nursing care	0.023***
	(0.006)

Notes:
*** Significant at the 0.01 level using a two-tailed test.
** Significant at the 0.05 level using a two-tailed test.

for-profit employees, earn only 8 percent lower wages. These low-paying industries are not outliers in the nonprofit sector. In fact most industries in which nonprofits locate are low-paying, and all employees, regardless of sector, work at relatively low wages given their human capital. Therefore many of the for-profit workers in these industries, like journalists on trade magazines or preschool teachers in day care centers, are giving up potential income for the ability to do socially worthwhile work.

Many researchers imply that with the reduction of the overall nonprofit differential in the face of industry controls, nonprofit and for-profit workers earn similar wages within industries. Such an argument masks the big differences in within-industry differentials. With Census data, one can estimate the within-industry nonprofit differential by running the regressions of column 3 in Table 8.2 within each industry where both for-profit and nonprofit employees coexist. For those industries previously most studied, the differentials are presented in Table 8.5. Even though our regressions cannot control for firm-level characteristics, a staple of industry studies, the results look quite similar to earlier studies. The nonprofit differential of −22 percent for legal services is very close to that estimated by Weisbrod (1983). Within nursing care, hospitals and day care, the estimated differentials are small but significantly positive and very similar to those differentials estimated in the industry studies.

Beyond the four industries of Table 8.5, we estimate nonprofit differentials for 100 more industries which have at least 50 nonprofit and 50 for-profit workers. Fifteen of these industries have a positive significant nonprofit differential, 42 have a significant negative nonprofit differential, and the rest have nonprofit differentials not significantly different from zero. Many of the industries that have a negative differential are ones where one can imagine a difference in services or clients between sectors, such as public TV and commercial TV in radio and television broadcasting or university presses and commercial publishers in publishing except newspapers. Others industries are more surprising, such as not specified manufacturing or groceries and related product wholesalers, industries where the nonprofits may be cooperatives that pay relatively low wages but whose workers may share in the benefits. Of the 15 industries with a positive differential, 82.5 percent of the nonprofit workers work in the five health-related industries. These are the types of industries where theorists expect nonprofits to locate on the high end of the quality spectrum.

Given the variety of differentials across industries, we test for significant relationships between the nonprofit wage differential and industry characteristics. Being somewhat limited by the Census data, we regress the estimated industry nonprofit wage differential on the percentage of workers who are nonprofit, the percentage who are government, the percentage who work in professional organizations, a dummy variable for the health sector, and the average wage residual (from the basic log wage regression of column 3 in Table 8.2) for each industry. The percentage nonprofit and percentage government are included since they signal the extent of extrasectoral competition. All else equal, the higher the percentage of nonprofit workers and the lower the percentage of government workers, the less outside competition nonprofits will face. According to the property rights hypothesis, without competition nonprofit managers can indulge in utility-maximizing behaviors, which may include directing foregone profits to worker wages. The percentage professional is included as a proxy for the extent of informational asymmetry. Professional workers have advanced degrees and provide a service closely tied to their training. Therefore it is likely that a non-expert will have difficulty judging the level and quality of service provision. We include a dummy variable equal to one for all industries that are health-related since the argument about nonprofit provision of high-quality products is made most frequently concerning health care industries. Finally we include the average industry wage residual. These residuals determine whether, controlling for worker characteristics, the industry is high-paying or low-paying. A positive residual means the worker is paid a wage higher than predicted by the wage regression. If the average of the residuals for all workers in an industry is positive, the industry is high-paying. We include the residual because, if the labor donation hypothesis holds and contributing to the public good is a normal good, then the nonprofit differential should be lower in higher-wage industries.

Table 8.6 presents the results of this industry regression. The coefficient on the percentage nonprofit variable is negative yet insignificant while the coefficient on government is positive and significant. The signs of the coefficients are telling the same story. As extrasectoral competition falls, so too does the within-industry nonprofit differential. Given that the average nonprofit differential is −0.04 for these 104 industries in the regression, these coefficients imply that with less competition from the for-profit or government sector, nonprofit wages are falling further behind for-profit wages. Such a finding refutes the assumption that with the separation of ownership and management in nonprofit firms, nonprofit wages will exceed worker productivity in non-competitive markets. Rather, as nonprofits face more competition from government and for-profit firms, wages are rising to meet the wages of other sectors.

While the coefficient on percentage of workers who are professional is not significant, the coefficient on the health care industries is large and significant. The nonprofit wage differential is 8 percentage points higher in the health care industries than in other industries, all else equal. With the average nonprofit differential at −0.04, the coefficient on the health care industry increases that differential to 0.04. This positive significant coefficient supports the theoretical argument that nonprofit firms supply high-quality health services.

Table 8.6   Determinants of within-industry nonprofit wage differential[a]

Determinants	Coefficient
1. Percentage of workers who are nonprofit	−0.044
	(0.071)
2. Percentage of workers who are government	0.085**
	(0.043)
3. Percentage of workers who are professional	−0.061
	(0.054)
4. Health-related industry	0.081***
	(0.028)
5. Wage residual	−0.220***
	(0.064)
6. Constant	−0.046***
	(0.011)
7. R^2	0.176

Notes:
[a]   The dependent variable is the estimated industry nonprofit wage differential.
*** Significant at the 0.01 level using a two-tailed test.
**   Significant at the 0.05 level using a two-tailed test.

Finally, the coefficient on the average wage residual is negative and significant, imply-ing that the differential is smaller, probably more negative, in high-wage industries. A one standard deviation increase in the wage residual[10] results in a 3 percentage-point reduction in the nonprofit wage differential. Clearly nonprofit workers earn low wages, and the extent of the relative wage loss is at least partially determined by the market wages in the industry in which the nonprofit worker is employed.

Concluding remarks
The average nonprofit worker, a highly educated, professional woman working in a service industry, looks very similar to a government worker along all dimensions except salary. Instead she earns a salary comparable to the average for-profit worker whose qualifications are appreciably inferior. Comparisons of equally qualified men and women show that in economy-wide studies the average nonprofit worker earns 11–12 percent lower wages than comparable for-profit and government employees. This wage loss is robust over a series of datasets and time periods.

Certain types of workers experience a more severe wage reduction. Men and profes-sional and managerial workers sacrifice wages to a greater extent than women and blue-collar, service, or clerical and retail workers. In addition, the differential is less severe and much more variable when one looks within industry, but wage loss is greatest in high-wage industries and on average positive in health industries.

Theoretical arguments supporting a nonprofit differential explain both why nonprofit wages might be lower and why they might be higher than for-profit wages. The labor donation hypothesis posits that nonprofit workers give up wages for the opportunity to engage in socially beneficial work. Alternatively, if nonprofits are institutions of trust in industries where quality is difficult to judge, nonprofit firms may produce higher-quality products with higher-quality workers, or according to the property rights hypothesis, nonprofit managers, without disciplining owners or the ability to share in profits, will pay higher than market wages. In the research conducted for this study, there is little evidence supporting the property rights hypothesis since nonprofit wages are universally low, industries exclusively nonprofit are very low-paying, and the mixed industries in which nonprofit wages are higher than for-profit wages are primarily health care industries where the argument for higher nonprofit quality is most relevant. The low wages, which are especially striking in the professional and managerial occupations where workers have control over the service provided, support a labor donation hypothesis. In addition, the labor donation (i.e. wage loss) increases with the potential income of the worker since it is most extreme for men, high-paying industries, and high-paying occupations, and is therefore most likely a normal good. A better understanding of the variation of within-industry nonprofit differentials will shed more light on the validity of these competing hypotheses, and to achieve that goal, data measuring social benefits, information flow, level of competition, and quality of service by industry and sector are crucial.

Notes

1. See Appendix Table A9 in Weisbrod (1988). More recent estimates have not been found.
2. Some nonprofit organizations beyond section 501 (c)(3) organizations can set up a charitable fund to which contributions are deductible. The fund must itself meet the requirements of Internal Revenue Code section 501(c)(3) and the related notice requirements of Internal Revenue Code section 508(a).
3. Data from the 2002 Economic Census reveal that the ratio of payroll to total receipts for service industries was 0.43 and for non-service industries 0.12.
4. Early applications of the property rights literature to the theory of the firm attempted to explain the differences in behavior of owner-controlled and manager-controlled firms. For a discussion of these applications see Furobotn and Pejovich (1972).
5. See the discussion on 'Intermediate Sanctions' in 'Tax Information for Charitable Organizations' at www.irs.gov.
6. See 'Tax Information for Charitable Organizations' at www.irs.gov.
7. Alternatively, if managers are risk-averse but do not select into nonprofits, then nonprofits may pay managers less in bonus and stock, but more in salary, so that on average they earn less in the nonprofit sector but are indifferent between sectors in expectation. See Preyra and Pink (2001).
8. While comparisons of older industry-based estimates with new ones based on self-identification of nonprofit status are problematic, estimates using the 2000 Census imply that the negative differential for women was not much different in 2000 (−0.70) than it was in 1985 (−0.72).
9. The female wage differential in the nonprofit sector is −0.10 as compared to −0.27 in the for-profit sector.
10. The mean of the residual is −0.03 with a standard deviation of 0.14.

References

Arrow, Kenneth J. (1963), 'Uncertainty and the welfare economics of healthcare', *American Economic Review*, **53** (5), 940–73.
Brickley, James A. and R. Lawrence Van Horn (2002), 'Managerial incentives in nonprofit organizations: evidence from hospitals', *The Journal of Law and Economics*, **45** (1), 227–49.
Duggan, Mark (2000), Hospital ownership and public medical spending', *Quarterly Journal of Economics*, **115** (4), November, 1343–74.
Frank, Robert H. (1996), 'What price the moral high ground?', *Southern Economic Journal*, **63** (1), 1–17.
Furobotn, Eirik G. and Svetozar Pejovich (1972), 'Property rights and economic theory: a survey of recent literature', *Journal of Economic Literature*, **10** (4), 1137–62.
Glaeser, Edward and Andrei Shleifer (2001), 'Not-for-profit entrepreneurs', *Journal of Public Economics*, **81** (1), 99–116.
Handy, Femida and Eliakim Katz (1998), 'The wage differential between nonprofit institutions and corporations: getting more by paying less?', *Journal of Comparative Economics*, **26** (2), 246–61.
Hansmann, Henry B. (1980), 'The role of nonprofit enterprise', *Yale Law Journal*, **89** (5), 835–98.

Holtmann, Alphonse G. and Todd L. Idson (1993), 'Wage determination of registered nurses in proprietary and nonprofit nursing homes', *Journal of Human Resources*, **28** (1), 55–79.

Leete, Laura (2000), 'Wage equity and employee motivation in nonprofit and for-profit organizations', *Journal of Economic Behavior and Organization*, **43** (4), 423–46.

Leete, Laura (2001), 'Whither the nonprofit wage differential? Estimates from the 1990 Census', *Journal of Labor Economics*, **19** (1), 136–70.

Mocan, H. Naci and Erdal Tekin (2003), 'Nonprofit sector and part-time work: an analysis of employer–employee matched data on child care workers', *Review of Economics and Statistics*, **85** (1), 38–50.

Nelson, Richard R. and Michael Krashinsky (1974), 'Public control and economic organization of day care for young children', *Public Policy*, **22** (1), 53–75.

Preston, Anne E. (1988), 'The effects of property rights on labor costs of nonprofit firms: an application to the day care industry', *Journal of Industrial Economics*, **36** (3), 337–50.

Preston, Anne E. (1989), 'The nonprofit worker in a for-profit world', *Journal of Labor Economics*, **7** (4), 438–63.

Preston, Anne E. (1990a), 'Changing labor market patterns in the nonprofit and for-profit sectors: implications for nonprofit management', *Nonprofit Management and Leadership*, **1** (1), 15–28.

Preston, Anne E. (1990b) 'Women in the white-collar nonprofit sector: the best option or the only option?' *Review of Economics and Statistics*, **72** (4), 560–68.

Preston, Anne E. (1993), 'Efficiency, quality, and social externalities in the provision of day care: comparisons of nonprofit and for-profit firms', *Journal of Productivity Analysis*, **4** (1–2), 165–82.

Preyra, Colin and George Pink (2001), 'Balancing incentives in the compensation contracts of nonprofit hospital CEOs', *Journal of Health Economics*, **20** (4), 509–25.

Roomkin, Myron J. and Burton A. Weisbrod (1999), 'Managerial compensation and incentives in for-profit and nonprofit hospitals', *Journal of Law Economics and Organization*, **15** (3), 750–81.

Rudney, Gabriel and Murray Weitzman (1982), 'Significance of employment and earnings in the philanthropic sector, 1972–1982', Program on Nonprofit Organizations Working Paper No. 77, Yale University, New Haven, CT.

Ruhm, Christopher J. and Carey Borkoski (2003), 'Compensation in the nonprofit sector', *Journal of Human Resources*, **38** (4), 992–1021.

Salamon, Lester M. and S. Wojciech Sokolowski (2005), 'Nonprofit organizations: new from QCEW data', *Monthly Labor Review*, September, 19–26.

Weisbrod, Burton A. (1983), 'Nonprofit and proprietary sector behavior: wage differentials among lawyers', *Journal of Labor Economics*, **1** (3), 246–63.

Weisbrod, Burton A. (1988), *The Nonprofit Economy*, Cambridge, MA: Harvard University Press.

9　Modeling nonprofit behavior
Patricia Hughes and William Luksetich

Introduction
Among William Baumol's many contributions to economic science is a presentation titled 'What can economic theory contribute to managerial economics?' (1961). Baumol draws a clear distinction between biological research and economic research using the life cycle of the fruit fly to illustrate. Recognizing that a clock mechanism exists in many species, biologists can gather substantial amounts of data in controlled experiments to measure the timing of the animal's development. With the aid of a mathematician, they can find a mathematical equation to fit the development of the fruit fly allowing predictions accurate enough to confirm the periodicity observed in this and many other species. The biologist has substantial amounts of data and a good mathematical model, but no analytical explanation of the observed behavior.

The economist, on the other hand, is an expert model builder who lacks data. The economist recognizes the basic structure of a problem by focusing on the main elements and carefully outlines the interrelationships between those components. Economists build models based on ideas and intuition, not on observed data. The general economic models of firm behavior are often abstract and hard to implement, yet they provide insight into human behavior. Every organization may face a unique situation requiring a specific model to highlight it. This is precisely the reason that economic theory is so important to managerial decision making. Economists offer managers a set of tools and approaches to solve a myriad of problems mainly because the rigor of analysis allows them to focus on the essentials of the issue at hand.

In this chapter we are concerned with the modeling of nonprofit behavior. Our starting point will be to present the theoretical issues associated with the choice of organizational form. The initial goals of a nonprofit organization are set by the organization's founders and are often a reaction to some real or perceived market failure. An organization will have leadership in the form of directors, officers, managers and perhaps workers in the form of paid employees and/or volunteers. It is the behavior of those in a leadership position and the accountability to the major stakeholders of the organization that affect the achievement of the goals or the redirection of the organization.

Model specification
An economic model is only as good as the theory behind it. In modeling nonprofit behavior the assumptions that are incorporated into the behavior of nonprofit organizations will significantly influence the predictions and policy implications of the model. Steinberg (1993) focuses on four major areas of model design that are important for estimation and policy analysis in the nonprofit sector. These include the objective function of the organization, the legal definition of the nonprofit industry, the level of competition, and the information structure regarding the good or service being provided.

The objective function of a nonprofit organization depends on the board of directors, the type of good or service, the respective financing, the level of competition, and the current financial condition facing the organization. Various objectives have been postulated in models, including maximization of quantity, quality, social welfare, inputs, budget, equity and even profit. For the model to be specified correctly, the objective must be consistent with the competitive and legal environment, and must be flexible enough to deal with changing financial conditions. If the objective of the organization is inconsistent with minimum average cost (such as quality maximization), a nonprofit would not survive in a highly competitive environment without some long-term financial cushion or other barrier to entry. Even with entry barriers, allowance should be made that as finances change, so too may the goal of the organization.

The second design issue deals with incorporating the legal definition of a nonprofit into the operating constraint. This may involve some sort of output requirement (social welfare), salary restriction (nondistribution constraint) or (balanced) budget restriction. Imposing a very strict interpretation may lead to unrealistic predictions or inconsistency with stated goals.

The third issue focuses on competition and long-run equilibrium. The behavior of a 'monopolist' and a 'competitive' firm differ, but only when there are barriers to entry that protect that position. Likewise a barrier or financial cushion must exist for nonprofits to operate in a distinctly different manner from for-profits for an extended period. Tax exemptions, donative inputs or information asymmetries allow long-run differentials in output and/or price between nonprofit and for-profit organizations.

The fourth point of the analysis deals with information asymmetries and Hansmann's (1980) role for nonprofit organizations in resolving the problem of contract failure. The type of information asymmetry defines the scope of the nonprofit sector and the level of competition from the for-profit competitors. How the information asymmetry is resolved should be consistent with the goals of the organization and the resulting role of the for-profit competitors.

The main point of Steinberg's analysis is that the assumptions of a model significantly influence the predictions and policy implications of the model. The assumptions should be internally consistent and consider the market as a whole when predicting long-term competitive outcomes.

Ortmann (1996) argues that game theory should play an important role in developing a more complete theory of nonprofit behavior. Defining the role of nonprofits based on information asymmetries and contract failure, the motivation of the nonprofit is not explicitly specified. The nondistribution constraint is presumed to limit any self-interested behavior, leaving nonprofits as trustworthy suppliers working for the welfare of their customers. If the nondistribution constraint is unenforceable or a 'reasonable' compensation constraint is unmeasurable, contract failure that undermines the for-profit sector will also impact the nonprofit sector.

Rather than assuming altruistic behavior or relying on increased regulations, Ortmann suggests considering the motivation and incentives of the nonprofit players using a game-theoretic framework. The principal–agent problem highlights the question of trust, and in what circumstances shirking is more likely. While acting in their own self-interest, long-term reputational considerations may give the impression of altruistic, trustworthy behavior. Understanding the motivation, the monitoring, the ability to detect shirking and the reputational enforcement tend to be more effective in modeling and policy design than rigid, inflexible regulations.

Most firms in the high cultural live performing arts – symphony orchestras, opera, theater and ballet – are nonprofits. Hansmann (1981) argues that they choose this form of organization because it allows them to engage in a form of price discrimination that results in average price above average total costs. These organizations tend to have high fixed costs and there is no one price that results in price greater than average total costs. The nonprofit form allows organizations to seek tax-deductible donations from their patrons. The organization will charge a price below its profit-maximizing (loss-minimizing) level, in the inelastic range of the demand curve, to encourage patrons to make a tax-deductible donation. The patron incurs a lower net cost while the organization receives an average revenue above average total cost.

Donative financing plays a major role in determining the goals of the nonprofit organization in the performing arts. Donations come in two forms, those requiring specific activities to be undertaken, and those that do not require specific services, called lump-sum grants. According to Hansmann, how these lump-sum subsidies are allocated helps to determine the goals of the firm. If these funds are spent on activities designed to spread to the widest possible audience, the goal of the firm is output maximization. Spending to enhance the quality of the performance indicates quality maximization, while budget-maximizing activities result in the enhancement of both quality and attendance.

Focusing on unrestricted subsidies, Rose-Ackerman (1987) models the reaction of nonprofit charities to an increase in government grants when nonprofit managers have goals that differ from donors. The model assumes that managers maximize quantity/quality, and that managers prefer a 'different' quality from that of donors. In its simplest form, competitors (other nonprofits) do not respond to changes in the production mix of the manager. Nonprofits balance their budget, equating total (gross) revenue from donations with the sum of solicitation and production costs. Rather than selecting the quality level that maximizes net revenue (donations less solicitation costs), managers pursue a higher quality more consistent with their tastes. The mismatch between donor taste and manager offerings can persist if some barrier restricts for-profit competitors from entering with a more preferred quality option. For instance, if nonprofit managers are willing to accept a lower financial return than for-profit managers, the opportunity provided by this mismatch is not lucrative enough to draw entrants. Given this structure, an increase in unrestricted government grants will tend to further the interests of managers over donors. Managers will increase both the quantity and quality of their service offerings. The increase in quality is unwanted by donors, reducing the marginal return to fundraising. Given the lower return, organizations will reduce the amount of fundraising and hence donations. In this model, quantity will increase, but the increase allowed by the influx of money is dampened by the higher quality and lower fundraising effort and return.

Tuckman and Chang (1992) take a different approach, modeling nonprofit managers as deriving utility from program services and equity (capital). Equity accumulation is defined as total revenue minus total cost, with annual revenue generated from the sale of program services, donations and the return on assets; annual costs are based on program costs, fundraising costs and interest payments on debt. For a given set of prices (program services, fundraising, interest rates), managers select the quantity of program services and equity accumulation such that the marginal utilities per dollar are equal. This simple constrained optimization problem yields demand equations that are then estimated using nonprofit financial data. The demand for equity is a function of the marginal profit from the sale of program services (price minus cost), the interest rate and the annual surplus. The model predicts a positive relationship between marginal profit and equity, a negative relationship between the interest rate and equity, and a positive relationship between equity accumulation and equity. Empirical results indicate a positive and significant relationship between equity accumulation and equity, supporting the hypothesis that growth in equity is deliberate and predictable.

Considering the overall model design, it is a partial equilibrium analysis in that prices are given and are not influenced by the actions of the organization. The managers select the optimal quantity of program service provision and equity accumulation (subject to diminishing marginal value) given the price of services, interest rates and the cost of donations. The organization's behavior does not influence price, in particular the use of donations (equity versus program service) does not affect the cost of acquiring donations. The aspect of long-run competitive forces is not addressed, allowing managers' the discretion of using funds in a manner commonly thought to be at odds with donor intentions.

Steinberg and Weisbrod (2002) characterize the patterns of pricing and rationing (exclusion) when nonprofit organizations are able to utilize price discrimination in service provision, using profits from high-end consumers to subsidize the price (below cost) to low-end consumers, necessarily restricting access to some consumers at any price. Managers seek to maximize a weighted sum of consumer surpluses, with revenue generated primarily by the sale of these services. If the organization values the welfare of all individuals, not necessarily equally (hence the weights), price discrimination is used to set prices below the reservation wages for those individuals allowed access to the good. Those with high demand pay more than cost, those with relatively low demand pay less than cost, but each pays less than their reservation price. Due to budget constraints, some low-end clients are necessarily denied access to consumption. This model provides an example where the profit potential of the nonprofit organization is used to increase social welfare rather than to further the interests of the nonprofit managers. When competition is introduced, a comparable for-profit competitor (also able to price-discriminate) will set a slightly lower price schedule for all profitable customers, eliminating the subsidies for the charitable provision by the nonprofit sector. For nonprofits to offer this charity care some type of barrier to entry is required, one such barrier being the current tax exemptions.

Ben-Ner (1994) makes some interesting policy recommendations for better governance of nonprofit organizations. The motivation for support of the nonprofit sector is again based on the concept of for-profit and government failure in providing certain goods or services, particularly public goods and trust goods. In such cases demanders turn to the nonprofit form to pursue objectives that tend to be undermined by the profit incentive. These demanders are in the best position to define the goals of the nonprofit organization and pursue policies that are consistent with these goals. Unfortunately the free-rider problem may limit the commitment of these stakeholders to actively manage the operations of the nonprofit organization, ceding control to a board and management team monitored by the nondistribution constraint. In this instance, the nondistribution constraint does not tend to align the goals of the nonprofit board with the goals of stake-holders.

The principal–agent problem is also an issue in the for-profit sector, but variation from profit maximization is dealt with internally through stockholder voting rights and externally through hostile takeovers. Ben-Ner suggests a similar structure for nonprofit organizations. First, nonprofits should have very clear and explicit goals in their mission statement. Stakeholders can 'buy' into an organization through purchases or donations (time and money). Managers will run the day-to-day operations of the organization, with stakeholders voting on radical changes in the mission statement or major structural changes in the organization. Internal control is key in resolving problems of market failure. Most of the benefits of the nonprofit sector go to those that financially support the sector. While some redistribution occurs, 'charity is only a *marginal* pursuit of the nonprofit sector in every area in which nonprofit organizations are prominent: health, education, religion, social services, arts and culture, and foundations' (Ben-Ner, 1994, p. 732).

The economic theory of the firm, which assumes profit maximization, has strong empirical support and predicts well in the for-profit sector. Studies of executive compensation show that profits are an important determinant of executive compensation, even in large corporations with diffuse ownership. Nevertheless, statistical studies also show significant behavioral differences between firms that are owner-operated proprietorships and shareholder-owned manager-controlled firms. An agency problem arises in the latter structure whereby the goals of the managers conflict with the goals of the owners. Specifically, the goal of the owner is to maximize profit, while managers may pursue a different set of goals, of which profit is but one aspect. Consequently, managers increase their own compensation or perquisites of their office at the expense of profit.

Similarly, the particular goals of any nonprofit organization are initially set by the founders of the nonprofit. The economic theories of nonprofit behavior have emphasized the choice between quantity and quality of output. It is also possible that decision makers within the organization may pursue activities that are not consistent with the intent of its founders or its patrons. There is the possibility that the nonprofit firm may attempt to maximize its budget. This may lead to greater quantity and quality, or to some sort of expense-preference behavior on the part of the organization's decision makers. Niskanen (1971, p. 83) explains that 'In some cases, a nonprofit organization will act more like a profit-seeking monopoly, spending the difference between revenues and the minimum total costs as perquisites to the managers and employees of the organization.' Managers may pursue goals that diverge from the owners of the organization and, in the case of nonprofits, the founders of and the donors to the organization.

Hansmann's (1980) classification of nonprofit organizations shows the wide variety of types and suggests the possibility of a divergence between those controlling the organization and its stated goals. He classifies nonprofits into categories by sources of funding and the nature of control. Donative nonprofits receive their funds in the form of donations, while commercial nonprofits receive their funds largely from the sale of goods and services. Control rests in the hands of the directors of nonprofits and falls into two categories: mutual and entrepreneurial. Mutual nonprofits are controlled by patrons; entrepreneurial nonprofits are controlled by a self-perpetuating board of directors. Hansmann's classification of nonprofits implies that the greater the control of nonprofits that rests with self-perpetuating boards of directors and with funds that come from commercial ventures, the more likely it is for decision makers to pursue goals that diverge from the original mission of the organization.

Empirical models: nonprofit goals

Virtually all of the empirical models economists have developed to estimate the goals of nonprofit organizations use data from either health-related organizations or from arts and cultural organizations. Data from these types of organizations are more readily available in a systematic manner because they are regulated by government or belong to associations that, sometimes reluctantly, make their data publicly available. Moreover, firms in these industries generally consist of both for-profit and nonprofit firms, and have organizational forms within more general classifications. For example, the nursing home industry contains firms that are for-profit, nonprofit, government owned, independently owned, chain affiliated and religiously affiliated or secular. Obviously, data from this industry provide researchers with a wide variety of issues to analyze.

Modeling/empirical results/hospitals

In his theory of nonprofit institutions, Newhouse (1970) assumes that three parties play a role in determining the goals of the nonprofit hospital: the trustees; the administrators; and the medical staff. To fulfill the nonprofit mission and enhance working conditions all three will have quality and quantity as their dominant goals. In contrast, the profit-maximizing hospital will produce a combination of quantity and quality of services that yield maximum profits, i.e. produce each up to the point where their marginal revenue equals their marginal cost. The nonprofit hospital will expand production beyond this point, using the 'profit' to increase quality and/or quantity. As such, the nonprofit sector will dominate the higher end of the quality spectrum with larger institutions to insure that their patients will be adequately served.

As evidence to support this contention of higher quality, Newhouse offers that the percentage of nonprofit hospitals that are accredited is greater than that of proprietary hospitals. Moreover, the percentage of registered nurses in nonprofit nursing homes is greater than in for-profit homes while the percentage of licensed practical nurses and staff that are not registered or licensed is lower in the nonprofit homes. Finally, the model predicts an over-abundance of sophisticated equipment in nonprofit hospitals. Newhouse documents a large percentage of nonprofit hospitals having equipment for open-heart surgeries but no cases of such surgery being performed, and others having advanced equipment of a different sort with only a few cases of use of that equipment. This evidence is consistent with quality maximization and the concomitant goal of enhancing the prestige of trustees, administrators and medical staff.

The result of this type of performance is a reduction in economic efficiency. Entry motivated by civic-mindedness does not reduce this quality bias. Philanthropy and tax breaks allow higher costs (higher than minimum average total cost – ATC) and greater inefficiency. Tax incentives and subsidies raise the barrier to entry for profit-making hospitals, limiting the benefits of competition. From a policy perspective, a bias against lower-quality offerings is reinforced by tax incentives and subsidies, calling into question their purpose and continued existence.

While the evidence of higher quality in the nonprofit sector is consistent with the model emphasizing managerial objectives, it is also consistent with the model of non-profit hospitals maximizing social welfare. Hirth (1997) points out that much of the previous work focusing on nonprofit objectives considers the effect of ownership type in isolation, without regard to competition from the other sector. He considers the effect of competition between nonprofit and for-profit firms on the performance of each and the provision of socially desirable services. Depending on the level of competition, nonprofit organizations pursuing the socially optimal mix of services may increase the quality of their services, and in doing so increase the standard for all firms in the industry. Pursuing the socially optimal quality may result in a differential between the nonprofit and for-profit firms, although in a highly competitive nonprofit mix the standard may be raised for all organizations eliminating any differential.

In Hirth's framework, nonprofit organizations provide the quality assurance discussed by Arrow (1963) and Hansmann (1980) relating to information asymmetry. Consumers are of two types: informed or uninformed as to the quality of the service received. Firms are of three types: 'honest' nonprofits; 'dishonest' nonprofits (for-profits in disguise); and for-profits. When possible, the for-profits will try to sell low-quality service at a high price, exploiting the uninformed consumer. Fearful of being cheated, the uninformed consumers gravitate to the more trustworthy nonprofit sector, hoping to receive a high-quality product due to the nondistribution constraint. The existence of the dishonest nonprofits depends on the enforcement of the nondistribution constraint, with greater enforcement reducing the existence of the for-profit in disguise.

Given a strongly enforced nondistribution constraint, an increase in the nonprofit market share will lead to an increase in the proportion of informed consumers in the for-profit market, forcing a more honest product offering from the for-profit providers. The model has several implications for the observed service provision based on the level of competition between for-profit and nonprofit providers. First, the level of competition from the nonprofit sector raises the overall quality across both sectors. Second, the existence of a competitive nonprofit sector may increase the overall quality of the for-profit sector, eliminating any quality differences between the two sectors. Third, if there is a quality differential between the two sectors, this may be the result of information asymmetry (nonprofits can offer the quality reassurance) and not necessarily a reflection of the preferences of nonprofit managers. The key to understanding the goal of the nonprofit sector is to see how the level of nonprofit competition affects the for-profit behavior, and how the level of for-profit competition affects the nonprofit behavior. These issues are discussed in Chapter 6 of this volume, dealing with competition in the nonprofit sector, and Chapter 7 dealing with competition in mixed industries.

Hirth considers the competition between for-profit and nonprofit firms in the hospital sector offering private goods and public goods. In the case of the pure public good that produces no direct benefit (profit) to the organization, only nonprofit firms will offer the good. In general, the value of nonprofit ownership will be reflected in the difference between the provision of the public good between for-profit and nonprofit firms. In the case of a public good that provides an indirect (although unprofitable) benefit to the organization, such as charity care providing good public relations and referrals, the effect of nonprofit competition on for-profit behavior may provide a specific measure of the value of nonprofit ownership. If the provision of the public good by the for-profit firm is unaffected by the level of competition from the nonprofit sector, the difference in the provision of the public good between the nonprofit and for-profit firm provides an accurate measure of value of nonprofit ownership. If competition from the nonprofit sector increases the provision of the public good by for-profit firms (to increase their competitive edge), the differential between the two types of organizations will understate the value of the nonprofit organization. If the provision by the nonprofit sector reduces the public-good provision by the for-profit sector (the indirect benefits decreasing as more is offered), the difference between nonprofits and for-profits will overstate the value of the nonprofit organization.

Ideally one would like to observe the behavior of mixed industries with various levels of competition and note both the overall level of performance and the differential in performance between the two types of organizations. The empirical results from previous studies are not designed as such, but still provide evidence as to whether the observed behavior of the hospital sector is consistent with nonprofit organizations maximizing social welfare. Shortell et al. (1986) look at the impact of competition on the provision of 18 unprofitable services offered by nonprofit and for-profit hospitals. They find that, on average, nonprofit hospitals provide more unprofitable care than for-profits. In addition, for-profit hospitals located in competitive markets tended to offer more unprofitable services. While these results are consistent with the nonprofit goal of social welfare, with positive spillover effects on the behavior of the for-profit competitors, the model design is not rigorous enough to provide conclusive evidence. The measure of competitiveness was crude and the ownership of the competitors was not specified, providing consistent but not conclusive evidence as to the value of nonprofit ownership.

Hughes and Luft (1990) provide a direct test of the effect of for-profit competition on nonprofit behavior. Selecting CT scanning as a profitable service, and newborn nurseries as an example of an unprofitable service, they look at the effect of for-profit competition on nonprofit service delivery. Their study indicates that when a for-profit competitor is present, nonprofit hospitals were more likely to have a CT scanner and less likely (statistically not significant) to have a newborn nursery. The competitive pressure may be reducing the ability of the nonprofit to fulfill its community service, redirecting its efforts toward financial needs away from community needs. Unfortunately the study did not consider the effect of nonprofit competition on for-profit behavior.

While nonprofit hospitals perform many services that provide community benefit, the most visible and politically sensitive is charity (uncompensated) care. If nonprofit status and support are based on the amount of charity care relative to rival hospitals, the intersectoral spillover is extremely important in making these comparisons. The empirical evidence on the effects of competition on charity care is mixed. Confounding the results is the location decision of nonprofits and for-profits based on income and need. In areas with a high need for charity care, we are apt to see nonprofit provision and very little competition from for-profit providers. In higher-income areas with lesser need for charity care, we are more apt to see a more competitive for-profit presence. Norton and Staiger (1994) report that nonprofits and for-profits provide similar levels of charity care based on their location, indicating a possible spillover effect. It is also noted that for-profits tend to locate in areas with less need for charity care. Shortell et al. (1986) find that competition lessens the amount of charity care offered by for-profit hospitals, contradicting the positive spillover effect. When the location decision is taken into account, assuming that areas with less need attract greater competition, the possible spillover effect is not contradicted. The point is that in measuring the value of the non-profit sector, simple comparisons can be very misleading. The level of charity care will be based on need, locational choice, the level of competition, the type of competition, indirect benefits, spillover effects, financial constraints and type of ownership. A simple comparison of the level of charity care between for-profit and nonprofit providers will underestimate the value of the nonprofit sector when there are positive spillover effects, and overestimate the value of the nonprofit sector when there is crowding out.

Horwitz and Nichols (2007) consider the effect of hospital ownership type and for-profit market share on service provision and operating margins in an attempt to reconcile the various theories of nonprofit ownership. In particular they focus on four major categories of nonprofit theories (theories I–IV) and the implications for observed service provision and operating margins. The first category is termed firm output maximization, such as Newhouse (1970), where nonprofits maximize some combination of quantity and quality subject to a balanced budget. This model includes an element of cross-subsidization by nonprofits, using profitable activities to subsidize unprofitable activities in their maximand. As the level of competition from for-profits increases, the nonprofits will lose their ability to cross-subsidize, and their behavior will appear more like that of their for-profit counterparts. With the balanced budget constraint, the profit margin is not affected by the proportion of for-profit firms.

In the second category (e.g., Weisbrod, 1988), nonprofits maximize total market output by providing more public goods and quality assurance resulting from market and government failures. As the size of the for-profit sector increases, nonprofits may need to increase the level of all profitable activity to offset cherry-picking by the for-profits. The amount of unprofitable activity may increase if the competitive mix is dominated by for-profits not offering these services. The nonprofit must have a balanced budget on average, but may see more pressure (lower margins) with greater competition from for-profits.

In the third category nonprofits are in fact profit maximizers, posing as for-profits. As such, there should be no discernible difference in the behavior of nonprofits and for-profits as the level of competition from for-profits increases. The profit margin will vary depending on how attractive the nonprofit form is in the market. If there is some advantage to the nonprofit ownership form (i.e. higher profit margin), more firms should choose the nonprofit form. Therefore a higher concentration of for-profit organizations should be associated with a lower profit margin for the nonprofit.

The fourth category is the mixed objectives theory (theory IV – Hirth, 1999), combining both nonprofits maximizing output and nonprofits maximizing profit. Given that this is a hybrid of theories I and III, the predictions are somewhat mixed. In this framework, true nonprofits have a zero profit margin, the for-profits in disguise seek to maximize profits and face their greatest competition from other nonprofits. The presence of the honest nonprofit will limit their ability to increase prices. The greater the proportion of for-profit competitors, the greater the ability of the for-profit in disguise to earn positive profits, causing the average operating margin of the nonprofit sector to increase. If, however, the nonprofit sector is composed almost entirely of for-profits in disguise, the effect would be negative as per theory III. The impact of for-profit concentration on service provision is indeterminate, combining the conflicting results in theories I and III.

Table 9.1 Four theories of nonprofit behavior and predicted nonprofit profit margins

Theory of Nonprofit Behavior	Nonprofit profit margins: predicted impact from increased for-profit competition/concentration
I Own output maximization	Profit margins not affected
II Total market output maximization	Lower profit margins
III Profit maximization	Higher profit margins
IV Mixed objectives	Mixed results:
Dominated by own output max.	Higher profit margins
Dominated by profit max.	Lower profit margins

A summary of the predictions from the four theories of nonprofit behavior is given in Table 9.1.

Horwitz and Nichols (2007) gather annual data for 1988 through 2005 on hospital characteristics, including all non-rural, non-federal general medical and surgical hospitals in the USA. Their model includes 45 individual medical services (categorized as high, low or variable profitability) to test whether offerings differ by the interaction between hospital ownership and market type (high and low for-profit hospital market penetration). The model also tests whether operating margins differ by the interaction of hospital ownership and market type, holding all else equal.

The results confirm that nonprofit hospitals in high for-profit markets are more likely to offer profitable services than those in low for-profit penetration markets. Nonprofit hospitals were systematically less likely to provide unprofitable services in for-profit markets than in other markets. These findings are confirmed by the services with variable profitability. When the services were profitable, nonprofits were more likely to offer these services in the high for-profit markets, and when the services were unprofitable, nonprofits were less likely to offer them in high for-profit markets. The results do not indicate any significant effect of market type on nonprofit hospital margins. There is also no significant difference between nonprofit and for-profit operating margins in high for-profit penetration markets. These results are most consistent with the first general theory of nonprofits (Newhouse) with the goal being own-output maximization, or the fourth model (Hirth) with a mix of own-output-maximizing and profit-maximizing nonprofits. Given the negligible effect of for-profit market share on the operating margin of nonprofits, the evidence suggests that very few nonprofits are operating as for-profits in disguise.

The explanation for the nonprofit hospital tends to be based on contract failure and/or historical factors, with the presence of the for-profit sector based on greater operational efficiency and access to capital. Due to the complexities involved in the hospital sector, the empirical results are mixed regarding the relative efficiency of the for-profit versus the nonprofit hospital. Some of the variation in results is due to the inability to adequately adjust for the scope and scale of the hospitals sampled. The location and level of competition also bear on the efficiency of provision. The regulations and compensation structure will also impact operations. Often the cost differential is attributed to agency and monitoring problems, leaving unclear the appropriate measure to use to compare the relative efficiency of ownership status. Carter et al. (1997) attempt to reconcile the mixed results regarding ownership and operational efficiency by focusing on the discretionary portion of administrative expenses and limiting their study to a more homogeneous mix of hospitals.

For each ownership form, separation of management and ownership leads to a conflict between higher agency costs and higher profit. Managers may pursue higher wages, increased staffing and better equipment to increase the satisfaction they get through their working conditions. Because performance of for-profit firms is more objectively measured, the threat of takeovers in the for-profit sector keeps firms relatively cost-efficient. The lack of ownership in the nonprofit sector eliminates the takeover threat, allowing nonprofit managers more discretion to pursue cost-increasing improvements in working conditions. That nonprofit organizations receive tax exemptions and donations also lessens the need to be cost-conscious.

To test the theory that for-profit hospitals are more cost-efficient than nonprofit hospitals, Carter et al. measure whether organizational form affects hospital expenses and hospital staffing decisions, all else equal. To control for the regulatory and financial climate of hospital administration, the sample consists of data from 1989 including only hospitals in the state of Texas with 50 beds or greater. The model focuses on three types of hospital expenses: administrative expenses (which includes administrative salaries); administrative salaries separately; and operational expenses. It is believed that more discretion exists in the administrative salaries and operational expenses, since the more comprehensive administrative expense category includes many non-negotiable and non-exploitive types of expenses such as personnel support functions related to accounting, purchasing and data processing, overhead expenses, management fees assessed by multi-hospital systems, and interest expenses. The impact of ownership type will be more influential on the discretionary expenses (salaries and operating expenses) than on overall administrative expenses. The results indicate that for-profit hospitals have higher overall administrative expenses, but lower discretionary spending on administrative salaries and operating expenses, and fewer full-time-equivalent employees than nonprofit or government hospitals. The greater the competition between hospitals, the lower the overall administrative expenses regardless of ownership type, although the impact on salaries, operating expenses and staffing is insignificant. Ownership type seems to impact discretionary spending, while competition reduces overall expenses regardless of ownership type.

The mixed results of previous studies stem from the difficulties in controlling for the differences in the scope and scale among hospitals, the quality of service, and the financial and demographic climate. The results here indicate that for-profit hospitals may be more cost-efficient when considering certain aspects of the budget, particularly administrative salaries and operating expenses. The proprietary hospitals also operate with fewer full-time-equivalent employees. If administrative expenses are considered, or quality differentials occur, the for-profits may no longer be considered more cost-efficient.

Modeling/empirical results/day care
In mixed industries, comprising for-profit and nonprofit organizations, the major question involves the difference in product/service offerings arising because of organizational form and the desirability of subsidizing one business form over another. Studies in the child care and nursing home sectors examine these issues and support the proposition that organizational form will influence firm behavior.

Cleveland and Krashinsky's (2004) research on the child care centers in Canada uses regression analysis to determine whether organizational form affects the quality of day care services. They measure quality primarily as the 'developmental potential in the classroom' as measured by the 'You Bet I Care' survey administered in 1998. The raw data show substantial variation in quality in both the commercial and nonprofit sectors, but with the average quality (significantly) higher in the nonprofit centers. Within the commercial centers, sole proprietorships provide the best care relative to partnerships or incorporated businesses.

Recognizing that organizational form may affect client mix and resource availability, regression analysis is used to account for these influences on quality and to isolate the impact of organizational form. Based on mission and goals, nonprofits and commercial centers may also select different input factors with the intention of influencing quality. Comparing these additional factors, nonprofits will have greater access to resources, tend to serve younger children, more special-needs children, more low-income children, and tend to choose better-qualified staff and utilize lower child/staff ratios. All else equal, the nonprofit status alone accounts for a 3.94 percentage-point increase in quality. Through the choice of inputs, and with other unobservable or unmeasured factors, the results confirm that a primary goal of the nonprofit organization is quality enhancement.

While nonprofit day care centers may offer a higher-quality service, Taylor (2006) argues that for-profit centers play an important role in the industry and should not be eliminated. The inclusion of for-profit centers increases the range of choices for families, with many for-profits offering a high quality of care. Restricting the provision to nonprofit providers will restrict access to regulated day care. It is also noted that the for-profit sector responds more quickly to increases in demand, increasing access and choice. The inclusion of the for-profit providers tends to increase competition, making the entire industry more cost-efficient.

Modeling/empirical results/nursing homes
The nursing home sector also represents a mixed industry in which quality and cost may vary by organizational form. Luksetich et al. (2000) investigate whether performance differs across ownership type for Minnesota nursing homes, and provide a model that can be used in any industry where for-profit and nonprofit firms coexist.

The authors use a five-equation simultaneous model to identify behavioral differences between nursing homes based on ownership type and chain affiliation. Minnesota nursing home regulations set rates, preclude entry, and provide an efficiency incentive to encourage savings on expenses other than nursing care. The regulations were designed to assure that resident care did not greatly deviate below the norm. If the regulations work as anticipated, nursing home performance should not be influenced by organizational form or affiliation. However, the allocation of the surplus generated by the efficiency incentive may affect performance and expense ratios, helping to identify organizational goals.

The empirical results indicate persistent spending differences on average nursing care due to both ownership type and chain affiliation. Nonprofit nursing homes spend more on nursing care than for-profit homes. While the gap in spending appears to be decreasing over time for government and secular nonprofits, the religiously affiliated homes tend to consistently spend more to provide higher-quality care. The nonprofits also spend less for general and administrative expenses per resident day and operated with significantly fewer resident days than did the independent for-profit homes. This is similar to the findings by Carter et al. in the hospital sector, which find that the for-profit hospitals had higher administrative expenses but lower administrative salaries. Luksetich et al. also find that nonprofit nursing homes provided greater compensation to their head administrators.

Comparing independent versus chain-affiliated homes, the latter consistently spent less on nursing care than their independent counterparts (religious, secular, for-profit), with the exception of for-profit Minnesota chains. The difference due to chain affiliation appears to be decreasing over time, with the exception of the nonprofit national chains. The gap in spending between the nonprofit national chains and the nonprofit independents appears to be increasing over time.

Turning from patient-related costs to administrative expenses, chain affiliation increases administrative costs, indicative of an agency problem. Owners of homes in chain affiliations have less control over administrators, who then secure a greater share of revenue for themselves. In for-profits the problem occurs with the national chain affiliation. In the nonprofits the expenses were higher with the Minnesota chain affiliation. The differences due to chain affiliation tend to be falling over time, with the exception of the religiously affiliated chains.

How the different types of organizations distribute their surplus is typically a good indication of their respective goals. Most of the surplus of independent for-profit homes goes to the owners of the organizations. For-profit chain-affiliated homes tend to divert more of their surplus into administrative expenses. Secular nonprofits belonging to national chains also divert a considerable amount of their surplus to administrative expenses, reflecting expense-preference behavior or perhaps agency problems.

Overall, in the case of Minnesota nursing homes, organizational form has a significant effect on performance. While for-profits tend to maximize their surplus, nonprofits tend to maximize quality (as measured by spending on care). All nonprofit homes tend to spend more per resident day on nursing care than do the for-profits, although chain membership lessens this difference. Chain-affiliated nonprofit nursing homes behave more like for-profits than their independent cohorts, perhaps uncovering the 'for-profit in disguise'.

Knox et al. (2006) compare the relative performance and quality of nonprofit nursing homes by comparing the relative costs and profitability of individual facilities. They model the differential impact of private versus government, religious versus secular, and independent versus chain affiliation on the cost efficiency, profit maximization and quality of service of Texas nursing homes.

The empirical results indicate a possible difference in technical efficiency between independent and chain facilities, with the cost of chains approximately 0 to 3.5 percent lower than independents. Government facilities have estimated costs 13 percent to 16 percent higher than private secular homes. The costs for religious homes are 1 percent to 6 percent higher than private secular homes. Assuming similar quality, organizational structure implies an efficiency ranking (from best to worst) of private secular, private religious and government.

The results also indicate a significant difference in allocative efficiency between chain members and independents, with chain members 45 percent more profitable than independents. There is not a significant difference between government and private secular profitability, although private religious facilities are significantly less profitable than private secular facilities. The empirical results indicate no significant difference in quality between independents and chains, and no difference between government, private secular and private religious facilities.

The results support the contention that organizational structure is influencing the operating goals of the various nonprofits, possibly reflecting agency costs, lack of property rights, asymmetric information or other contract failures. While all facilities in the current study are nonprofit and no systematic difference in quality among the various structures is indicated, systematic differences exist in the level of technical and allocative efficiency between chains and independents, and between government, private secular and private religious facilities. The article highlights the importance of the organizational governing body in determining goals and the importance of accountability in the agency relationship in fulfilling these goals.

Modeling/empirical results/performing arts
Throsby and Nielson (1980), in their analysis of the goals of nonprofit performing arts firms, also examine the effects of including both the quantity and quality in the objective function of the decision maker. The allocation of lump-sum subsidies (subsidies not requiring specific services be performed, sometimes called unrestricted grants) from private or public sources is used to ascertain the goals of the firm, a point also emphasized by Hansmann (1981). If the subsidy is used to enhance quality, costs may increase or decrease, and demand may increase or decrease depending on audience reaction. Quality affects the decision maker's utility in two ways: first through its direct inclusion in the utility function and second through its indirect effect on the demand for the organization's output. In the case of a lump-sum grant, the choice of what quality change should be undertaken will be the one that yields the greatest expected increase in utility of the organizer.

Rejecting the notion that there is a universal definition of quality, Throsby and Nielson attempt to identify some aspects of quality that are not subject to value judgments and other more subjective measures of quality that enjoy a firm consensus of opinion in the industry. They settle on five criteria, identify characteristics that define each criterion, and assign values to the characteristics. This allows them to obtain a 'grand' total for each of the criteria.

The first of these criteria is the source of the arts organization's repertoire. Sources of repertoire are grouped into four categories: the classics; works by well-known contemporary authors or composers; works by little-known authors or composers, and general entertainment such as revues. Rankings within each of these categories are based on the difficulty of undertaking the performance and ranking of the authors and composers of the works being performed. The second criterion, technical factors, is closely tied to input costs and used as a proxy for quality of the production, although it is recognized that there are numerous examples to the contrary. Benefits to the audience (criterion three) are difficult to measure, although surveys and reviews by critics may be an indicator of quality. The fourth and fifth criteria, the benefit to society and the benefit to the art form, are the remaining factors in their evaluation of quality. Throsby and Nielson argue that these are not likely to affect the judgment of the current audience but may be important to funding groups and firms emphasizing social dimensions in their work.

To test their model, Throsby and Nielson use data from five theater companies in Australia for the years 1974 to 1979, inclusive. The major focus of their empirical work is threefold: (1) to estimate the effect of quality on output (attendance); (2) to estimate the effects of the admission price and quality of performance on the size of the subsidies received each year across the five theater companies; and (3) to determine the goals of the theaters in their sample by ascertaining whether the subsidies are used to enhance output or quality. Given the small size of their sample, they recognize that the results obtained are preliminary and suggestive.

The strongest conclusion was that quality had an important influence on the demand for the performances of the theaters in their sample. In addition, the results clearly indicate that theaters that charged lower prices and offered higher quality received larger subsidies. In general, the subsidies were used to lower prices and increase quality further, which in turn resulted in increased output. In their model, price, quality and subsidy are determined simultaneously and because of the small sample they were unable to adequately account for this problem.

The American Symphony Orchestra League (ASOL) annually collects data from its members on all sources of revenue and all categories of expenditures each year. Using data from 1970, Luksetich et al. (1978) estimated four equations corresponding to attendance, price, number of concerts and quality based on the annual reports submitted to the ASOL by member orchestras. The data contain information on the amount of grants received and whether or not they required specific services to be performed. The disposition of the 'lump-sum' grants, not requiring specific services, is used to infer the goals of the organization. Given their specification, if quality is positively related to the lump-sum grant, the orchestra is a quality maximizer. If attendance is positively related to the lump-sum grant, they are maximizing attendance. If the lump-sum grant affects both quantity and quality, the objective is indeterminate.

ASOL classifies orchestras as major, metropolitan, or urban/community by the size of their budget. For the major and urban/community orchestras, the estimated coefficients on the lump-sum grant are positive and statistically significant in both the attendance and quality equations, leaving the objective indeterminate. These orchestras appear to have both output and quality in their maximand. The coefficient on the lump-sum grant for metropolitan orchestras is statistically significant in only the quality equation leading to the conclusion that these orchestras are dominated by quality-maximizing goals.

When additional ASOL data became available, Luksetich and Lange (1995) were able to estimate the model taking into account the simultaneous nature of symphony orchestra behavior, again drawing heavily on Hansmann's (1981) theory. Their six-equation model includes attendance (cultural experiences), the average price, administrative expenses, orchestra quality (spending on artistic personnel, production, etc.), the number of concerts performed and donations received from individuals as simultaneously determined. These measures are the most likely empirical counterparts associated with the performance measures of output, quality and expenses-preference behavior. Price, quality, expenses and the number of concerts are the management decision variables used to achieve orchestra goals.

A unique aspect of the model is that it takes into account the differential nature of production and consumption: while orchestras produce concerts and other performances, attendees consume cultural experiences. It is not possible to measure production and consumption in the same units. The price may not be the market-clearing price; orchestras may try to induce voluntary price discrimination by holding price below revenue-maximizing levels to induce patrons to give tax-deductible donations. If patrons make such donations, they are akin to lump-sum grants and will influence orchestra behavior.

Orchestras have some local monopoly power in the 'high-culture' performing arts market. Consequently, a supply curve cannot be identified; since attendance maximization may be an orchestra objective, the number of concerts has a bearing on the number of seats available for orchestra services. The four management decision variables (price, quality, expenses and number of concerts) are simultaneously determined in the model. Patron donations affect the budget constraint and are assumed to affect all of these decision variables; none of the four decision variables is assumed to be affected by current attendance. Exogenous variables include population characteristics, income tax rates and past development expenditures. Grants requiring that specific services be performed and lump-sum grants are also included as right-hand-side variables, the relationship between the latter and the decision variables allowing for the determination of orchestra goals.

The model is estimated with ASOL data for the years 1975–84, inclusive. Models are estimated separately for orchestras classified by budget size: major, metropolitan, or urban/community. With respect to the relationship between price and revenues, the authors found that all orchestras set price in the inelastic range of demand, below the revenue-maximizing price level. For major orchestras, the relatively low price increases donations from individuals, supporting Hansmann's argument that the major orchestra can elicit a tax-deductible contribution, thereby achieving voluntary price discrimination. The statistical estimates also indicate that, for the major orchestras, a doubling of ticket prices would maximize ticket revenues; however, an increase in ticket prices of 62 percent would maximize the combined revenue from ticket sales and donations.

Although both the metropolitan orchestras and the urban/community orchestras set prices in the inelastic range of demand, neither saw an increase in donations from individuals in response to these lower prices. The estimates revealed no relation between ticket pricing and donations for the metropolitan orchestras, while in smaller markets, higher prices elicited greater donations. Perhaps the higher prices indicate higher quality and thereby provide an inducement to increase donations. The relatively low pricing by the orchestras is consistent with attendance maximization as part of their maximand.

A more direct method of determining organizational goals is based on the allocation of the lump-sum grants. For metropolitan orchestras, the lump-sum unconditional grants are positively related to concerts per capita, which in turn increase attendance. The smaller market orchestras also have attendance maximization as a primary goal, as evidenced by the positive and significant relationship between lump-sum grants and the number of concerts.

For major orchestras, the unconditional grants have a positive and significant impact on administrative expenses, which in turn are positively and significantly related to quality. This supports the proposition that decision makers have quality in their maximand. These grants are also negatively and significantly related to average ticket prices, which translates into greater attendance. The higher quality, however, leads to higher prices and lower attendance. The latter effect may be indicative of the higher-quality performances having a more limited audience. The results support the presence of quality and expense maximization as goals of these organizations, with output maximization being a secondary goal.

With data from the Royal Shakespeare Company (RSC), Gapinski (1984) models nonprofit performing arts to determine the effect of government patronage on the RSC's activities. With output represented by cultural experiences (attendance), Gapinski estimates production and demand functions for Shakespearian plays. He uses a Cobb–Douglas production function with attendance dependent on labor and capital, a dummy variable to distinguish between the two theaters offering the performances, and a trend measure accounting for technical changes. The demand function that performed best based on statistical criteria is relatively simple. The dependent variable, attendance per capita, is a function of real own-price, real per capita income, and the dummy variable to distinguish between the two theaters. Demand is found to be price-inelastic and highly income-elastic, -0.657 and 1.237 respectively.

During this period, the theaters came to increasingly rely on government subsidies. The ratio of total government patronage to total income was 13.4 percent for the 1965–66 season, and had risen to 41.6 percent by the 1979–80 season. To determine the effect of government patronage on the behavior of the two theaters, Gapinski compares the actual performance in the two venues with what it would have been had the two theaters operated as profit maximizers. As profit maximizers, they would have employed less of both factors of production and charged higher prices than was actually observed. The effect on one theater was to increase output by 14-fold and in the other case by a factor of 2, increasing output far beyond what otherwise would have been without the subsidies.

In a second article, Gapinski (1985) uses the previous model and its empirical results in an effort to determine the objective function of the RSC. The model predicts that the RSC optimizes, but does not pursue revenue maximization, does not satisfice, and quickly adjusts to changing economic conditions. Increases in lump-sum contributions cause increases in output along the expansion path, and changes in factor prices result in changes in factor proportions. Although Gapinski never specifies an objective function for the RSC, he maintains that the results imply that the company produces efficiently, although not at the profit-maximizing level.

Quality of output has often been associated with the nature of the repertoire. Works of the classics, e.g. Shakespeare, Puccini, Verdi, Mozart, are assumed to be more 'quality' orientated than less 'popular' works. Indeed, since the classics are the most popular, it is difficult to determine whether organizations with repertoires heavily biased towards the classics are quality, attendance or budget maximizers. Three recent articles examine the effect of government grants on the repertoire of performing arts organizations and provide some evidence concerning the effects of these subsidies on the behavior of the organizations.

Pierce (2000) explores the effect of culture, politics and government funding on the decisions made by US opera companies regarding the choice of repertoire over the period 1989–94. He develops conventionality indices for 65 opera companies, 32 of which are included in his empirical work. The index for an opera company is the average number of times an opera produced by one company is produced by all companies in the group. For example, if there are three companies in an opera group and they produced 24 operas by three different authors, the conventionality index would be equal to 8, ignoring the fact that one opera might be performed 20 times. Higher values for the index indicate greater degrees of conformity.

Pierce regresses the index for the opera company on its budget, per capita city income, the percentage of revenue from non-federal public sources, the percentage of revenue from the National Endowment for the Arts (NEA), and indices of conservatism and inflexibility for each city in which the opera is performed. While local government funding tends to promote more conventional programming, NEA funding has the opposite effect. Pierce notes that these results are consistent with expectation, arguing that the NEA has a reputation for supporting more controversial and newer artistic productions, and not pressuring recipients to engage in certain types of behavior. Local officials, Pierce argues, are more likely to apply pressure to support programs that appeal to wider audiences, which accounts for the finding that local government funding results in more conventional programming.

Heilbrun (2001) provides evidence of a decline in repertoire diversity in US opera companies. Using data provided by Opera America, Heilbrun constructs conventionality indices and Herfindahl indices for six opera seasons between 1982/83 and 1997/99. He concludes that over the time period examined, opera companies in the USA have been shifting performances toward more popular and less demanding repertory.

O'Hagan and Neligan (2005) examine the effect of public subsidies on the nonprofit theater in England and whether the subsidies affect the composition of the repertoire presented in recipient theaters. They regress the conventionality index for 40 grant-aided English theaters on the size of the subsidy relative to total income, the size of the theater, the theater's location, and the population and average income in the area. Increases in state subsidies result in less conventionality in the English theaters.

Modeling/empirical results/fundraising
Steinberg (1986) proposes a way to infer the objective functions of nonprofit organizations from estimates of the marginal donative product of their fundraising. Rather than assuming a firm's objective function, Steinberg indicates how a firm reveals its objective function by its fundraising behavior. The objective function is modeled as a weighted average of the organization's level of service provision and budget size, the weights equal to β and $(1 - \beta)$ respectively. For organizations that maximize budget size the weights correspond to $\beta = 0$, and for service maximization $\beta = 1$. Maximization of the objective function with respect to fundraising corresponds to

$$\partial \text{Contributions}/\partial \text{Fundraising Expenses} = \beta.$$

To estimate β, Steinberg constructs a model whereby an organization's contributions are based on current and past fundraising and administrative expenditures and organization size. If the sum of the estimates of the coefficients on fundraising expenditures are zero, the organization is assumed to budget-maximize; if the sum is one, service maximization is assumed. Steinberg's results indicate that welfare, education and arts firms act as service maximizers; health firms act as budget maximizers; and the results for research organizations were inconclusive.

Various authors have modeled the impact of fundraising on donations with varying results in terms of fundraising elasticity and the corresponding marginal donative product. Studies by Weisbrod and Dominguez (1986), and Okten and Weisbrod (2000) report fundraising elasticities that are generally not significantly different from zero. Posnett and Sandler (1989), Khanna et al. (1995) and Tinkelman (1996) estimate significant fundraising elasticities between zero and one. As Tinkelman (2004) points out, much of the difference in the reported elasticities is due to errors in data reporting and extreme observations in the data. In another article he reports that 'A recent guide to 35,000 large, publicly supported charities notes that 62 percent report zero fundraising expenses in their latest Form 990 filing' (1999, p. 140). When the elasticities are reported as the mean of the elasticities calculated for each observation, the averages may not be representative of the sample due to the existence of extreme observations. When studies calculate the elasticities based on the mean values of the relevant sample variables (fundraising, donations etc.), the results are much more consistent across studies.

Following Steinberg, Brooks and Ondrich (2007) expand the choice of possible objectives facing the nonprofit arts organizations to include service, quality and budget maximization. A sample of 104 public radio stations over the period of 1990–96 is used to estimate the impact of client base and fundraising on earnings and donations. Based on the observed behavior of organizations as estimated by a two-equation system, the authors reject service maximization as the goal for 30 percent of the stations, reject quality maximization for 49 percent of the stations, and reject budget maximization for 69 percent of the stations. The primary goal of public radio stations would appear to be service-oriented.

Concluding remarks
Theories of nonprofit organizations compare the behavior of firms that maximize quantity, quality, social welfare, budget and/or profit. Theory predicts a bias towards higher-quality provision by nonprofits that are organized for the public benefit and adhere to the nondistribution constraint. The nature of an organization's governance structure can influence the behavioral aspects of the nonprofit. The for-profit theory of the firm allows for an agency problem when there is a separation of ownership (the stockholders) and control (the managers). There is the possibility that the managers will pursue goals other than profit maximization. A similar conflict may exist in the nonprofit organization between stakeholders and board members. Whoever controls the organization can influence behavior and the attainment of organizational goals.

Designing executive compensation plans that align with organizational goals may resolve that conflict. Oster (1998) has noted that it is difficult to find determinants of nonprofit executive compensation in practice because of the absence of good output measures. Hallock (2002) finds that organizational size tends to be the major determinant of nonprofit executive compensation. He finds no evidence of performance evaluation relative to industry averages as a determinant of executive compensation. Carroll et al. (2003) find that while size does matter, the efficiency of spending efforts (the ratio of funds received to the amount spent) also affects executive compensation, and that compensation positively affects executive performance. A properly devised compensation scheme may enhance (encourage) organizational goals.

Hansmann's classification of nonprofits by their source of funding and organizational structure provides further insight into potential agency problems. Donative/mutual nonprofits receive their funds from donors and it is the donors that control the board of directors. At the other extreme, commercial/entrepreneurial nonprofits are those receiving the bulk of their funds from commercial activities and have self-perpetuating boards of directors. The former are more likely to undertake activities akin to the stated purpose of the nonprofit; the latter types are more likely to suffer agency problems resulting in the dreaded for-profit in disguise.

Stakeholders and policy makers can garner information concerning the goals and performance of nonprofits by determining the allocation of funds across the various functional areas. These spending patterns have been shown to be affected by the ownership form, the organizational structure of the firm, and the size of the organization. While it is not possible to definitively determine a firm's goals, research has provided enough information to have confidence in expectations regarding goals and performance. For example, research on the performance of pre-school and health organizations consistently provides evidence that the quality of care is superior in nonprofit versus for-profit institutions. There is also evidence that religiously affiliated nonprofit institutions provide better-quality care than secular nonprofits and that agency problems are more likely to occur in nonprofits with chain affiliations.

Practitioners can benefit from designing managerial compensation schemes to enhance performance as noted above. In addition, data envelopment analysis (DEA) has been developed to measure and evaluate production efficiency. The efficiency of performing a particular task within an organization depends on its ability to transform inputs into outputs. Hughes and Luksetich (1997) provide an example of DEA comparing the relative efficiency of orchestras regarding their revenue generation. The outputs in the analysis are funds received from individuals, businesses, foundations and government. Inputs are measured as the costs of staff, printing and posting, telephone and other development expenses. Relatively inefficient orchestras can compare their scores against their peers' to identify more efficient counterparts to emulate.

More recently, Boyle (2007) used DEA to measure increases in productivity of symphony orchestras in Australia as the orchestras evolved from government control to seemingly private entities. He documented the changes in the relative productivity (attendance) of four orchestras over a five-year period, identifying areas where improvement in efficiency could be attained.

When data have become available, economists have been able to test the various theories of nonprofit behavior. These empirical models are counterparts to the more developed theoretical models of the for-profit organizations. Unfortunately, the data that have been available to estimate these models come from a relatively limited number of areas. It is suspect to use the information drawn from these studies to derive conclusions concerning behavior or policy recommendations for nonprofits in general. The heterogeneity of purpose results in a very mixed industry that will not fit well under one theory of nonprofit behavior. In addition, models of behavior based on different goals may yield very similar predictions in terms of observed behavior. Economists have demonstrated their expertise as model builders, allowing a better understanding of nonprofit behavior but not definitive proof of the underlying goals. If economic theory is to be useful to decision makers in nonprofits, more comprehensive industry data are required.

References

Arrow, Kenneth J. (1963), 'Uncertainty and the welfare economics of medical care', *American Economic Review*, **53** (4), 941–73.

Baumol, William (1961), 'What can economic theory contribute to managerial economics?', *American Economic Review*, **51** (2), 142–6.

Ben-Ner, Avner (1994), 'Review: who benefits from the nonprofit sector? Reforming law and public policy towards nonprofit organizations', *Yale Law Journal*, **104** (3), 731–62.

Boyle, Stephen (2007), 'Ownership, efficiency and identity: the transition of Australia's symphony orchestras from government departments to corporate entities', unpublished PhD dissertation, Macquarie University, Sydney, Australia.

Brooks, Arthur and Jan Ondrich (2007), 'Quality, service level, or empire: which is the objective of the non-profit arts firms?' *Journal of Cultural Economics*, **31** (2), 129–42.

Carroll, Thomas, Patricia Hughes and William Luksetich (2003), 'Managers of nonprofit organizations are rewarded for performance', *Nonprofit Management and Leadership*, **16** (1), 19–42.

Carter, Richard B., Lawrence J. Massa and Mark L. Power (1997), 'An examination of the efficiency of pro-prietary hospital versus non-proprietary hospital ownership structures', *Journal of Accounting and Public Policy*, **16** (1), 63–87.

Cleveland, Gordon and Michael Krashinsky (2004), 'The quality gap: a study of nonprofit and commer-cial child care centers in Canada', Working Paper, University of Toronto at Scarborough, Division of Management, available at http://www.childcarepolicy.net/pdf/NonprofitPaper.pdf.

Gapinski, James (1984), 'The economics of performing Shakespeare', *American Economic Review*, **74** (3), 458–66.

Gapinski, James (1985), 'Do the nonprofits performing arts optimize? The moral from Shakespeare', *Quarterly Review of Economics and Business*, **25** (2), 27–37.

Hallock, Kevin (2002), 'Managerial pay and governance in American nonprofits', *Industrial Relations*, **41** (3), 377–406.

Hansmann, Henry B. (1980), 'The role of nonprofit enterprise', *Yale Law Journal*, **89** (5), 835–901.

Hansmann, Henry B. (1981), 'Nonprofit enterprise in the performing arts', *Bell Journal of Economics*, **12** (2), 341–61.

Heilbrun, James (2001), 'Empirical evidence of a decline in repertory diversity among American opera compa-nies 1982/83 to 1997/98', *Journal of Cultural Economics*, **25** (1), 63–72.

Hirth, Richard (1997), 'Competition between for-profit and nonprofit health care providers: can it help achieve social goals?', *Medical Care Research and Review*, **54** (4), 414–38.

Hirth, Richard (1999), 'Consumer information and competition between nonprofit and for-profit nursing homes', *Journal of Health Economics*, **18** (2), 219–40.

Horwitz, Jill and Austin Nichols (2007), 'What do nonprofits maximize? Nonprofit hospital service provision and market ownership mix', National Bureau of Economic Research Working Paper No. 13246.

Hughes, Patricia and William Luksetich (1997), 'Efficiency of fund-raising activities: an application of data envelopment analysis', *Nonprofit and Voluntary Sector Quarterly*, **26** (1), 73–84.

Hughes, Robert and Harold Luft (1990), 'Keeping up with the Joneses: the influence of public and proprietary neighbours on voluntary hospitals', *Health Services Management Research*, **3** (3), 173–81.

Khanna, Jyoti, John Posnett and Todd Sandler (1995), 'Charity donations in the UK: new evidence based on panel data', *Journal of Public Economics*, **56** (2), 257–72.

Knox, Kris Joseph, Eric C. Blankmeyer and J.R. Stutzman (2006), 'Comparative performance and quality among nonprofit nursing facilities in Texas', *Nonprofit and Voluntary Sector Quarterly*, **35** (4), 631–67.

Luksetich, William and Mark Lange (1995), 'A simultaneous model of symphony orchestra behavior', *Journal of Cultural Economics*, **19** (1), 49–68.

Luksetich, William, Mary Edwards and Thomas Carroll (2000), 'Organizational form and nursing home behavior', *Nonprofit and Voluntary Sector Quarterly*, **29** (2), 255–79.

Luksetich, William, Mark Lange and Philip Jacobs (1978), 'Managerial objectives of symphony orchestras', *Managerial and Decision Economics*, **7** (1), 273–78.

Newhouse, Joseph (1970), 'Toward a theory of nonprofit institutions: an economic model of a hospital', *American Economic Review*, **LX** (1), 64–74.

Niskanen, William (1971), *Bureaucracy and Representative Government*, Chicago, IL: Aldine-Atherton.

Norton, Edward and Douglas Staiger (1994), 'How hospital ownership affects access to care for the uninsured', *RAND Journal of Economics*, **25** (1), 171–85.

O'Hagan, John and Adriana Neligan (2005), 'State subsidies and repertoire conventionality in the nonprofit English theater sector: an econometric analysis', *Journal of Cultural Economics*, **29** (1), 35–57.

Okten, Cagla and Burton A. Weisbrod (2000), 'Determinants of donations in private nonprofit markets', *Journal of Public Economics*, **75** (2), 255–72.

Ortmann, Andreas (1996), 'Modern economic theory and the study of nonprofit organizations: why the twain shall meet', *Nonprofit and Voluntary Sector Quarterly*, **25** (4), 470–84.

Oster, Sharon M. (1998), 'Executive compensation in the nonprofit sector', *Nonprofit Management and Leadership*, **8** (3), 207–21.

Pierce, J. Lamar (2000), 'Programmatic risk-taking by American opera companies', *Journal of Cultural Economics*, **24** (1), 45–63.

Posnett, John and Todd Sandler (1989), 'Demand for charity donations in private nonprofit markets: the case of the UK', *Journal of Public Economics*, **40** (2), 187–200.

Rose-Ackerman, Susan (1987), 'Ideals versus dollars: donors, charity managers, and government grants', *The Journal of Political Economy*, **95** (4), 810–23.

Shortell, Stephen, Ellen Morrison, Susan Hughes, Bernard Friedman, James Coverdill and Lee Berg (1986), 'The effects of hospital ownership on nontraditional services', *Health Affairs*, **5** (4), 97–111.

Steinberg, Richard (1986), 'The revealed objective functions of nonprofit firms', *RAND Journal of Economics*, **17** (4), 508–26.

Steinberg, Richard (1993), 'Public policy and the performance of nonprofit organizations: a general framework', *Nonprofit and Voluntary Sector Quarterly*, **22** (1), 13–31.

Steinberg, Richard and Burton A. Weisbrod (2002), 'Give it away or make them pay? Price discrimination and rationing by nonprofit organizations with distributional objectives', Working Paper, Indiana University at Indianapolis.

Taylor, Peter (2006), 'Child CARE: improving child care services for Canadian families: evidence from Canada and around the world', report prepared for and released by the Association of Day Care Operators of Ontario, Canada, available at http://childcaretoday.ca/files/ADCO20child20care20paper_1.pdf.

Throsby, C.D. and Elizabeth Nielson (1980), 'Product quality decisions in nonprofit performing arts firms', Research Paper No. 215, Macquarie University, School of Economic and Financial Studies, Sydney, Australia.

Tinkelman, Daniel (1996), 'An empirical study of the effect of accounting disclosures upon donations to nonprofit organizations', doctoral dissertation, New York University.

Tinkelman, Daniel (1999), 'Factors affecting the relation between donations to not-for-profit organizations and an efficiency ratio', *Research in Governmental and Nonprofit Accounting*, **10**, 135–61.

Tinkelman, Daniel (2004), 'Using nonprofit organization-level financial data to infer managers' fund-raising strategies', *Journal of Public Economics*, **88** (9–10), 2181–92.

Tuckman, Howard and Cyril Chang (1992), 'Nonprofit equity: a behavioral model and its policy implications', *Journal of Policy Analysis and Management*, **11** (1), 76–87.

Weisbrod, Burton A. (1988), *The Nonprofit Economy*, Cambridge, MA: Harvard University Press.

Weisbrod, Burton A. and Nestor Dominguez (1986), 'Demand for collective goods in private nonprofit markets: can fundraising expenditures help overcome free-rider behavior?', *Journal of Public Economics*, **30** (1), 83–96.

10 Pricing strategies
Bruce A. Seaman

Introduction

While nonprofit organizations have more complex objectives than merely maximizing profit, and rely upon mixed revenue sources beyond earned income, pricing strategies are important for at least significant subsets of such organizations. In particular, nonprofit hospitals, nursing homes and other health care providers, performing arts organizations, nonprofit and academic journal publishers, and colleges and universities price their services and engage in increasingly complex strategies, while museums and social service organizations frequently debate the merits of charging prices of any kind. Some nonprofits, especially those engaged in the delivery of social and emergency services such as the Red Cross, CARE and the Salvation Army would frequently find the charging of positive prices antithetical to their very purpose, although this too depends on the specific products and services, and sometimes the cultural setting, e.g. the American Red Cross charges for blood products from its blood centers (Jacobs and Wilder, 1984), and food banks in Europe charge positive prices while similar institutions in the USA do not.

This chapter explores the pricing strategies employed in these distinctly different segments of the nonprofit sector, with an emphasis on better understanding the roles played by demand, capacity constraints and congestion, cost and cost uncertainty, subsidies, competitive versus market power considerations, complex objective functions, and the forces of tradition versus innovation. How these factors affect prices in the nonprofit versus the for-profit sectors, and whether the adoption of various pricing strategies is fundamentally different in the two sectors, is also addressed briefly, but a full analysis of those differences is beyond the scope of this chapter.

Pricing has not always played a big role in nonprofit research. For example, despite the considerable breadth of the papers in Young (2006), exploring how to improve nonprofit organization decision making when faced with increasing uncertainty and growing financial pressure, there is almost no focus on pricing and fee setting in that particular volume (in contrast to other similar collections of papers discussed below). And Brooks (1997), in an early monograph for the Symphony Orchestra League, uncharacteristically devotes little space to pricing even though he is addressing tactics and strategies for improving orchestral revenues.

In fact, the scope of nonprofit research having pricing as the main focus is notably uneven. The medical care industry, primarily hospitals, receives by far the most attention both in terms of single-firm models not focused on competitive considerations (e.g. Weisbrod, 1965; Feldstein, 1971; Dranove, 1988; Dranove et al., 1991; Ennis et al., 2000), and via the vast and growing literature on the changing effects of competitive pressures on pricing among nonprofit hospitals, including antitrust policy implications (e.g. Melnick et al., 1992; Lynk, 1995; Melnick et al., 1999; Keeler et al., 1999; Dranove and Ludwick, 1999; Young et al., 2000; Irvin, 2000; Greaney, 2006). More limited attention has been paid to other non-hospital segments of the medical industry, including mental health providers (Forder, 2000), blood banks (Cumming et al., 1974; Jacobs and Wilder, 1984) and nursing services (Hendricks and Baume, 1997).

Education receives some attention, with differential (discriminatory) pricing in undergraduate colleges the focus of Yanikoski and Wilson (1984), with Jenny (1968) investigating pricing and the optimum size of a university. The potential antitrust implications of college and university pricing generated an extensive literature with the so-called 'Overlap Group' case in which primarily Ivy League institutions were accused of collusive behavior in the setting of undergraduate financial aid (this literature is vast, but Carlton et al., 1995 provide the essential case supporting the defendant, MIT, the only institution to directly challenge the Justice Department Antitrust Division; Carlson and Shepherd, 1992, provide a comprehensive review of the arguments suggesting that this behavior harmed competition and promoted inefficiencies). As is generally true in all cases except for hospitals, spatial competitive factors have rarely been studied in education or other sectors (see Seaman, 2004 as applied to the performing arts), with the lone education exception being McMillen et al. (2007).

Even ignoring most of the large empirical literature on demand studies (Seaman, 2006), the nonprofit performing arts (e.g. Touchstone, 1980; McCain, 1987; Jenkins and Austen-Smith, 1987; Greffe, 2000; Garber Jr et al., 2000), and museums (e.g. Steiner, 1997; Bailey and Falconer, 1998; Anderson, 1998; Kirchberg, 1998; Goetzmann and Oster, 2003; Prieto-Rodríquez and Fernández-Blanco, 2006), the arts sector rivals hospitals in terms of substantive studies of pricing, including the optimal strategy regarding ticket scalping (see also Courty, 2003, for an analysis not limited to the nonprofit arts). In fact, the performing arts have been a primary focus for much of the work on nonprofit price discrimination and product-bundling strategies, starting with Hansmann's seminal theory of the role played by voluntary price discrimination in rationalizing the nonprofit organizational form itself (1981; but West, 1987 is among the skeptics). Although Hansmann believed that the scope for price discrimination would be limited in the pricing of tickets for performances in contrast to voluntary price discrimination via donations (1981, p. 343), some of this work has focused on the degree of ticket price discrimination itself (Blaug, 1978; Seaman, 1985; Huntington, 1991, 1993; Seaman and Green, 1994). Other papers explore the relationship between earned and unearned income in a price discrimination context (even if the full extent to which organizations can price-discriminate over both revenue sources is limited by our not having data on the 'full combined prices' via ticket purchases and donations paid by specific individual arts patrons; see below). Such studies of multiple revenue source price discrimination in the arts include Kushner and King (1994), O'Hagan and Purdy (1993), and Luksetich and Lange (1995). Kushner and Brooks (2000) provide an intriguing look at purely voluntary price discrimination on a smaller scale in their study of street performance (busking), and Halcoussis and Mathews (2007) provide compelling evidence of the potential for creative price discrimination in the online auctioning of concert ticket prices, a technology that can obviously be exploited by nonprofit as well as for-profit organizations.

Without focusing on any particular nonprofit segment, the theory of nonprofit price discrimination has been greatly enhanced by Ansari et al. (1996), and Steinberg and Weisbrod (2005), while critical foundations for later work on nonprofit pricing of various types were established by Holtmann (1983), James and Rose-Ackerman (1986) and Steinberg and Weisbrod (1998). Bertonazzi et al. (1993) and the related Maloney and McCormick (1989) utilize a unique dataset regarding the relationship between ticket purchases and donations for home season ticket sales to university football games in extending our understanding of how price discrimination strategies can be employed over multiple revenue sources (while also finding evidence for the 'Alchian–Allen theorem' regarding the effects of a common fixed cost in reducing the relative price of a higher-priced, higher-quality good or service compared to a lower-priced, lower-quality good or service).

A smattering of pricing studies has been directed at other types of nonprofit services such as UK social rental housing (Stephens et al., 2003); social service organizations (McCready, 1988); and the charity retail sector in the UK (Parsons and Broadbridge, 2004). Bergstrom (2001) provides strong empirical evidence of much lower prices charged by nonprofit academic journal publishers compared to for-profit publishers, but Rosenbaum and Ye (1997) find that almost all journals (at least in economics) eventually engage in sophisticated price discrimination strategies. Results are more mixed when efforts are made to compare the pricing strategy and performance of managers in nonprofit versus for-profit electric utilities (Peters, 1993).

Some common problems faced by firms in the for-profit sector are studied in the context of nonprofit organizations. For example, capacity constraints and congestion are the focus of Lovelock (1984) and Brown (2002), while the opposite problem of pricing with excess capacity is addressed in a hospital setting by Ennis et al. (2000). And capacity constraints are viewed as a critical motivation for commodity bundling by Cairns (1991). Optimal pricing when faced with cost uncertainty is addressed by Hanchate (1996), and applied to the restoration of art objects in museum laboratories, while the classic analysis of optimal underpricing in theater-type settings when faced with property right failures (i.e. 'seat enforcement problems') was provided by Cheung (1977), with a more general theory of 'intentional mispricing' being provided by Haddock and McChesney (1994, not limited to nonprofit settings).

What we think we know: areas of general agreement from previous research
With several recent overviews of pricing issues in the nonprofit sector, one might suspect that this is familiar ground covering wide areas of knowledge and agreement. This is only partly the case. Oster et al. (2004) quickly remind us that pricing for nonprofit organizations is unusually problematic by dividing the issue into two parts: (1) should nonprofits charge positive prices at all (clearly not a common dilemma facing most firms in the for-profit sector, although whether to price Internet content directly or simply rely upon advertising revenue linked to websites has become one of the great challenges facing many Internet content providers, e.g. Facebook)?; and (2) assuming prices are to be charged, how should they be structured? James and Young (2007) focus special attention on fees charged by nonprofit organizations related to their primary 'social mission' in contrast to fees designed to generate earned income from available commercial ventures designed in large part to subsidize the primary mission.

The main purpose of both of these overviews is to provide usable guidelines to nonprofit managers rather than comprehensively survey the literature on nonprofit pricing. While that orientation is not identical to this chapter, their more pragmatic focus serves to highlight basic principles common to any economic research on pricing regardless of organizational form: (1) the importance of pricing in reducing congestion and rationing (and shifting) usage when capacity is constrained; and (2) the ways in which various differential pricing and product-bundling strategies can generate additional revenues for a given number of units of goods and services sold when compared to simpler single-pricing approaches. There is indeed considerable agreement regarding the role played by capacity constraints in justifying specific pricing approaches as well as the importance (if not all of the mechanics) of price discrimination in the nonprofit sector. These and other topics such as the role that competition plays in determining prices, even in the nonprofit sector, that have received considerable research attention are addressed below.

However, the scope of solid research results becomes much thinner when the focus shifts to pricing considerations of special significance to nonprofit organizations such as: (1) the role that positive prices can play in changing and improving the behavior of specific clients, especially in social service settings; (2) the degree to which independent sources of quality evaluation are available so as to avoid the well-known (if poorly understood) problem of how price reductions can reduce demand when price is a proxy for quality; (3) the scope of situations in which positive prices, even if so low as to be largely 'tokens', can enhance the nonprofit mission by increasing the dignity of the client, including the obvious question 'what level of price serves this dignity enhancing function and how does it vary across nonprofit settings?'; (4) the importance of higher 'standard' prices in creating expectations that can be strategically manipulated into substantial attendance increases via well-designed special discounts, including free admission days for museums, aquariums and performing arts organizations. Oster et al. (2004) provide interesting, but limited, examples of how these considerations have affected the results of pricing strategies in specific nonprofit settings, but the research on these issues is currently quite thin and our understanding understandably limited.

Nevertheless, there are important areas where we seem to know quite a lot:

1. Market power and competitive considerations are important for both profit and nonprofit hospitals (and universities), and while mergers among nonprofit hospitals have at times been subject to less stringent antitrust oversight, the absence of a blanket antitrust exemption linked to nonprofit organizations (including universities) appears fully justified. Concerns about the effects of diminished competition on consumer welfare via both prices and product quality exist in both the nonprofit and for-profit hospital sectors, with most (but not all) of the studies finding that, at least over the past 15–20 years, increasing concentration (largely through merger and consolidation) in the hospital sector has caused prices to be higher without clear benefits of better health service quality.

2. Classic nonprofit theories of the firm, identifying potentially unique price discrimination opportunities for nonprofit organizations, have been subject to increasing empirical testing, especially for performing arts organizations, universities, community organizations providing services very similar to the for-profit sector (such as gym memberships), and to some extent religious organizations. The role of tying sales and product bundling has been a special focus, with results suggesting that nonprofit pricing sophistication is growing. The digital revolution has provided expanded opportunities for price discrimination via online auctions, and even in situations such as academic journal subscription rates, where nonprofit prices have been as low as $0.18 per page (and $0.15 per cite) compared to $0.82 per page (and

$2.40 per cite) via for-profit distribution (Bergstrom, 2001), price discrimination is widespread across organization types (Rosenbaum and Ye, 1997).

3.   Empirical studies frequently find low (inelastic) price elasticity of demand, even at the nonprofit firm (individual-organization) level in contrast to the naturally lower price elasticity at the industry level, although those findings are not as uniform as sometimes thought (especially when available data allow the calculation of price elasticity for more than just the average price and across more refined consumer segments; Seaman, 2006). Where confirmed, such low-elasticity results are often consistent with complex product-bundling strategies, including the conscious sacrifice of earned income to enhance the amounts of contributed income and income from the sale of ancillary services. Hence, such strategies can reflect quite savvy revenue-increasing strategies. But low-price strategies are also consistent with nonprofit managements weighting consumer welfare more heavily than producer welfare (Holtmann, 1983), and in general being very conscious of the role played by lower prices in furthering the unique mission of many nonprofit organizations. Those missions need not be limited to social service organizations providing food, housing and medical supplies to low-income families, but can include firms like electric utilities, where the evidence is that nonprofit utilities have tended to charge prices that on average fall significantly below marginal cost. However, in this case, in contrast to the journal publication pricing cited above, there has been less evidence of significant price discrimination differences between nonprofit and for-profit electric utilities (Peters, 1993).

4.   While the controversy regarding the commercialization of nonprofit service organizations (including the social enterprise concept, see also Chapter 7) does not normally focus on pricing issues *per se*, pricing so as to increase earned revenues from such ancillary commercial goods and services is clearly linked to the pricing of the services keyed to an organization's primary mission, and to the potential for cross-subsidization across commercialized and social mission parts of the organization. Hence nonprofit organization pricing of its primary services cannot be understood without also exploring the commercial pricing strategies of organizations. This capacity for internal cross-subsidization is another explanation for the frequently observed price-inelastic strategies in the performing arts, where there are many commercialized tie-in options that can generate other revenue (gift shops and cafes being the most obvious).

5.   It also seems clear that core economic considerations of either excess capacity or deficient capacity (excess demand at a given price), uncertainty and demand fluctuations can have similar effects on the pricing strategies of both nonprofit and for-profit firms. Some of the policy recommendations (and observed results) are obvious, such as lower medical reimbursement rates in hospitals with excess bed capacity (Ennis et al., 2000), or charging positive congestion prices (including to low-wage clients) in neighborhood social service facilities (Brown, 2002; McCready, 1988). Others can be more obscure and dependent upon more careful economic modeling, such as the Holtmann (1983) result that 'the greater the slope of the demand function facing the profit-making firm, the less the difference between the pricing policies by the profit-making monopolist and a social welfare-maximizing firm when both are facing a random demand' (p. 441).

What we do not know: areas of conflicting results and unexplored questions from previous research

Despite our growing understanding of pricing behavior in various nonprofit subsectors, significant gaps in our understanding persist:

1. The complex interaction between price discrimination in the sale of primary services (e.g. tickets to performing arts performances; tuition for higher education) and price discrimination in the 'sale of status' via donated income is still not fully understood, although it is increasingly recognized that revenue maximization requires the 'optimal' differential generation of revenues from patrons in both their direct customer and donor roles. This is in large part a problem of data availability, since only aggregate data are typically available on levels of donations and amounts spent on tickets and related 'earned income' sources. Admittedly, many organizations will publish lists of donors in various categories, and researchers can make inferences about the level of such donations, but it is quite difficult to match even those rough estimates with the total amounts spent on purchasing tickets (either individually or via season tickets).

2. While suboptimal service pricing (in the inelastic range of primary product demand curves) is consistent with a broader strategy of income maximization (considering donated income and the income from the sale of ancillary services linked to the primary product), it is also consistent with either naïve pricing strategies focused on individual services, or break-even strategies where overall income from combined sources is not being maximized. Our ability to distinguish clearly among these conflicting interpretations of the motives and sophistication of nonprofit managers is still limited.

3. The unique psychological role that pricing may have on the clients of nonprofit organizations (especially social welfare and community service providers) is still not well understood. While it is recognized that charging positive (even if very low almost-token prices) may have unique effects on self-esteem and client respect for such programs that go well beyond the usual rationing, capacity management and earned income motives, the scope of such unique pricing benefits and their implications for optimal pricing are still not fully explored.

4. Despite the similarities in the economic forces facing nonprofit and for-profit hospitals and nursing homes regarding pricing issues, there remains significant controversy as to whether nonprofits in the health care sector are delivering more 'charitable care' via lower prices overall, more charitable care via lower prices (including zero prices) to the indigent, and better overall access to health care than for-profit health care providers. Even where there have been demonstrated differences in the level of prices charged between for-profit and nonprofit firms, such as with electric utilities, some puzzling similarities remain. As noted by Peters (1993), 'although managers at nonprofit electric utilities clearly behave differently, there are either no statistically significant differences between the efficiency of nonprofit and for-profit utilities, or nonprofit utilities outperform for-profit utilities in many measures of cost and efficiency' (p. 599). Since pricing strategies are constrained by underlying cost considerations, a full understanding of how pricing differs between comparable firms in those differing sectors must also account for these puzzling cost and efficiency behaviors.

5. Despite some recent work in the arts sector regarding the relative merits of collusion (including on prices) versus competition, and the seeming economic benefits resulting from collusion in the provision of financial aid (and hence net tuition prices) by Ivy League schools related to the MIT (Overlap) antitrust case, the degree to which competition does and should characterize nonprofit organization pricing remains under-studied. On a related point, the degree to which nonprofit organizations are best modeled as 'mini-monopolists' versus competitive or oligopoly firms remains controversial, although the monopoly model has tended to dominate most of the research in this area (Seaman, 2004).

Why there are gaps in our knowledge: the relative roles of theory, data availability and empirical analysis

Significant progress could be made on resolving these remaining controversies and gaps in our knowledge if we had more publicly available data, or even privately provided data under strict confidentiality agreements or coded so as to retain anonymity. For example, it is very difficult to examine the 'full price' paid by any arts patron since, even if we could trace the prices paid by individuals for tickets, we would need access to information regarding their specific tax-deductible donations. The absence of such data has limited our study of price discrimination via product bundling. Also, the enormous difficulty in obtaining reliable transactions (net of all discounts) data on hospital pricing continues to be a significant problem.

Because there is such well-developed theory of pricing and price discrimination, it is less clear that major progress in our knowledge is being seriously impeded by theoretical limitations alone. However, the next section discusses in considerable detail some of the enigmas that exist in fully understanding and testing various propositions regarding a topic as seemingly basic as price discrimination. In other areas, however, our current modeling limits are likely to be more serious, and will certainly benefit considerably from the expanding research agendas in both experimental and behavioral economics. One example is the specific role played by price as a signal of the inherent value of a particular social service that could justify positive pricing even where no congestion exists. These issues are not well understood at present.

What must be done to further our knowledge: suggestions for extending the literature

While it is common to observe that pricing within nonprofit organizations is often 'highly non-linear' and characterized by considerable price discrimination, our understanding of such pricing strategies remains incomplete. The anomalies that remain are well exhibited by a reconsideration of just what Hansmann (1981) suggested about such pricing as he focused on the performing arts.

Hansmann argued that price discrimination in the pricing of admission tickets is inherently limited in the arts because of problems in identifying individuals and groups with differing demand elasticities, and in making admission tickets non-transferable. Furthermore, some type of additional revenue per performance is critical due to the generally high fixed cost of arts performances, and the inherently limited audience size for such products. If ticket prices are kept close to marginal cost, revenues will certainly not cover all costs; in fact, demand may be so low relative to average total cost that no price level will generate admission revenues sufficient to break even.

Given these problems in generating adequate admission revenue, contributed income becomes especially critical, and Hansmann identifies voluntary donations as the most effective way to price-discriminate since individuals having more inelastic demand for arts services (and hence more consumer surplus at given ticket prices) can be induced to pay more for the services via voluntary donations). Hansmann did not argue that ticket price discrimination was impossible; it was just limited. That is, the charging of higher prices for more desirable seats represents a form of price discrimination, even though the product sold is not strictly identical at all seat locations. This device solves the problem of limiting the resale of tickets that would otherwise doom such price discrimination. Hansmann's statement of this possible strategy and its limitations is worth quoting:

> if those patrons whose demand for a given performance is most inelastic also have the strong-est relative preference for good seats over bad seats, then it may well be possible to establish a price schedule that will channel those with inelastic demand into the good seats at high prices, and those with more elastic demand into the inferior seats at lower prices. This device is limited, however, by the strength of the preference for good seats over bad seats that is exhibited by patrons whose demand for performing arts productions is relatively inelastic. (Hansmann, 1981, p. 857)

Seaman (1985) sought to identify empirical tests of some of Hansmann's observations, in particular the hypothesis that price discrimination (across ticket prices, donations, or both) would be more prevalent where fixed costs were high relative to audience size, *ceteris paribus*. Note that Broadway theater is viable as a for-profit operation since fixed costs can be spread over a larger number of performances per production and over a larger total audience. The essential result of that work was to discover that ticket price discrimination (as measured by the coefficient of variation in ticket prices and other alternative measures) did vary significantly across art forms (symphony, opera, theater and ballet), and that those forms discriminating the most (i.e. opera) had the highest fixed cost per attendee, and those forms discriminating the least (i.e. theater) had the lowest fixed cost per attendee. Furthermore, no significant differences were found in the measured price discrimination across art forms in terms of donation discrimination (as measured by the coefficient of variation in the minimum dollar amount across the posted 'donor brackets' of arts organizations).

Clearly, more detailed evidence regarding ticket price discrimination among such non-profit organizations would be desirable since Seaman (1985) was limited to comparing 'average' measures of price discrimination across art forms and testing for statistically significant differences in the mean price discrimination measures. It would be preferable to use cross-sectional regression analysis (or time-series analysis if the data were avail-able) using individual arts organizations as observations, and extending the list of inde-pendent variables beyond the fixed cost per attendee variable stressed by Hansmann.

One of the problems inherent in any examination of price discrimination is definition and measurement. For example, among the measures used to identify price discrimina-tion in Seaman (1985) was the coefficient of variation in ticket prices to a performance of a particular art form. A skeptic could argue that simply measuring the standard devia-tion relative to the mean of prices does little more than document the known fact that prices do differ by location in a performance hall, and that such differences may not even constitute real price discrimination. The distinction between price differences and price discrimination is, of course, an important one. Furthermore, even if one were to concede, as does Hansmann, that this pricing would constitute a 'form' of price discrimination, it may still be the case that ticket price discrimination is too limited to solve the financial problems of arts firms and that Hansmann's thesis about the primacy of donation discrimination requiring nonprofit organizations may still be valid. The Seaman (1985) finding that ticket price discrimination varied across art form according to fixed cost and audience size, but a similar measure of donation price discrimination (the coefficient of variation in 'donor price categories') did not, is also not determinative, since these measures of price discrimination may be inadequate. Also, even if the measures are adequate, no direct evidence is easily obtained about the 'full' price paid by any individual arts consumer, i.e. the donation plus the ticket prices actually paid.

Some studies have come close to solving this problem, but not entirely. For example, Kushner and King (1994) examined unique data from the Bach Choir of Bethlehem (Pennsylvania) that allowed them to identify over a nine-year period the average number of tickets purchased by donors making 'excess' donations (defined as more than the 'minimum required pledge') and compared that mean to the average number of tickets purchased by donors making only the minimum suggested pledge. Their finding that, for each of these nine years, greater donations were associated with higher numbers of ticket purchases (but not necessarily dollars spent) was interpreted as important evidence of a positive interaction between charitable giving and the direct consumption of performing arts services – an interaction required of a more comprehensive form of price discrimination across both forms of revenue.

In the quite different context of examining booster club fee schedules related to season tickets to Clemson University football games, Maloney and McCormick (1989) found a remarkable pattern of multi-tier prices by which a combination of the ticket price and the required 'donation' (which rose notably as the number of tickets to be purchased in a group increased) yielded 'total block prices' that translated into rising unit prices (i.e. per ticket purchased). For example, people in Level I who bought two tickets paid a combined per-unit price of $150, and those in Level III buying a block of six tickets paid a combined per-unit price of $183, while those in the highest Level VI buying a block of 12 tickets paid the combined per-unit price of $517. They concluded that in order to avoid the problem of big demanders 'hiding themselves' by simply purchasing numerous small blocks of tickets (as with Level I or Level II, where combined prices per unit were notably lower than those for Levels V and VI), they would force such large demanders to reveal themselves by bundling quantity and quality together, i.e. by forcing anyone wanting to have not just ten tickets, but ten tickets for seat locations next to each other to buy them as a package. Hence they had to pay the required $2000 donation (for this Level V package). Of course, the number of buyers fell notably at these higher-priced levels, revealing a standard downward-sloping demand, but this bundling strategy allowed for the opposite of the customary 'second-degree price discrimination' result of declining prices over larger 'blocks' of units consumed. This was an increasing multi-tier price schedule.

An alternative to finding sufficiently disaggregated data to allow for the better matching of individual consumers to a 'full price' that combines donations with ticket expenditures is to further test the premise that ticket-price differences are in fact effective price discrimination by examining, at the firm level, two hypotheses that follow from the standard theory of price discrimination: (1) price discrimination will vary systematically with price-elasticity differences among consumers and the market power of firms, and (2) price discrimination generates more revenue per unit of output than nondiscriminatory pricing. Of course, price discrimination may not be intended to generate more revenue, as was seemingly the case in the 'need-based' rather than 'merit-based' financial aid strategies followed by the so-called 'Overlap' colleges and universities, which were accused by the Antitrust Division of the US Justice Department of collusion based on their information-sharing practices they claimed were designed to avoid 'excess competition' for the most qualified students (Carlton et al., 1995; Carlson and Shepherd, 1992). Social service pricing may also seemingly generate higher prices to lower-price-elasticity, higher-income clients compared to higher-price-elasticity needier clients, consistent with the revenue-maximizing strategies of third-degree price discrimination, but again the purpose of such pricing may be to generate 'fairer' social outcomes rather than higher gross revenues (Young and Steinberg, 1995, discuss such 'mission-based' pricing on pp. 173–6).

However, in testing the two standard price discrimination hypotheses in nonprofit settings where revenue maximization goals are more plausible, Seaman and Green (1994) constructed another database expanding upon the first in Seaman (1985). Individual organizations were again contacted, with requests also made for financial information from annual reports. While results were not invariant to subsample, strong support was found for hypothesis (1): measured ticket price discrimination does vary with proxies for price elasticity of demand variations in a market, and with proxies for the degree of local arts market competition. This hypothesis achieved its strongest support in the theater and opera subsamples, and some support in the full sample and the ballet subsample. Less success was achieved in documenting a causal connection between the ticket price discrimination and the ticket revenues per attendee (or as a percentage of total income) earned by arts firms. Average price level for tickets was a stronger determinant of ticket-price discrimination than the variance in these prices.

As with Seaman (1985), little success was achieved in documenting causal factors determining the measure of donor price discrimination. Not only did the measure of such discrimination not vary significantly on average across art form, but it did not vary significantly at the individual art-firm level with Hansmann's expected fixed-cost variable, or with the price-elasticity proxies that performed fairly well in equations estimating ticket-price discrimination. This failure may or may not shed light on the adequacy of Hansmann's theory regarding the important role played by voluntary donor price discrimination depending on the adequacy of the proxy used to measure that discrimination.

The issue of how to measure price discrimination regarding donations remains a fascinating one. In fact, there are also serious conceptual challenges even in measuring ticket-price discrimination in nonprofit settings such as the performing arts, which would seem to be much simpler than in other areas. For example, one measure could simply be the number of different price locations quoted for subscription package deals. This is normally (but not always) identical to the number quoted for individual ticket sales. In Seaman (1985) and Seaman and Green (1994), to count as a different location, the price had to be different. That is, the labeling of sections A and B as distinct on a seating plan would not count as two sections if the prices were identical. The second measure is the coefficient of variation (standard deviation divided by the mean) of those different price locations. Again, subscription prices were the focal point, and when different subscription series had different values, an average was constructed. A third measure used extensively in both of those studies is the product of the first two measures. That is, if the coefficient of variation is 0.5, and the number of price locations is 5, the value of this measure is simply 2.5. The rationale for this is the necessity of adjusting for the tendency of a greater number of prices to reduce the coefficient of variation (unless the additional price locations have prices that are especially high or low relative to the mean price). Intuitively, a more effective price discriminator has a greater variety of prices (for a given cost, which does not vary per person seated) measured both in terms of a dispersion measure and an absolute number of different prices. This third measure combines these two considerations. Finally, an index number could be constructed to capture the combination of different subscription 'packages' and different seat locations. For example, this last measure would equal 15 if an organization had five different seat locations and quoted three different schedules of prices for them (as in one schedule for weekend matinees, one for Wednesday evenings, and one for weekend evenings). Thus, a person buying, say, a ten-concert subscription package has, in effect, 15 different price options. To the extent that this last measure involves the possible mixture of different products (where a Wednesday evening concert is deemed incomparable to a Saturday evening concert), there may be theoretical grounds for not using it. Yet airline-pricing schemes that involve different prices depending upon day of week traveled are frequently characterized as exploiting price-elasticity differences between business and tourist travelers.

As suggested above, constructing price discrimination measures for voluntary donations is an even harder enterprise, and Steinberg (2007) has more recently confronted some of these problems in the context of membership fee schedules across a much wider variety of nonprofit organizations than just arts organizations. Obviously, the connection between prices charged and prices paid is closer in ticket sales than any comparable measure regarding private, voluntary donations. But there is an intriguing feature of fundraising that can be examined for its (at least, surface) similarity to ticket pricing – the establishment of various donor categories suggested to potential donors. Some organizations identify a complex array of such options, and occasionally separate categories for corporations, small businesses and individuals. Others identify few if any such donation targets. Clearly, there are only so many dollar amounts that could rationally be chosen. No one expects to see a donor category of $13.85 to $47.50, followed by 'super-donor' ranging from $5000 to $25000. But, within the limits of reasonable numbers, the variety is fascinating. Can it really be that so little thought goes into such a structure that systematic study is unlikely to reveal any determinants of such variations? Or can we view such a structure of suggested donations as a 'relative price' structure analogous to that of ticket pricing? Common sense as well as some theoretical analysis (and experimental research) suggests that donors will tend to give at the bottom of any suggested range. Thus, if $50 is the minimum required to be a 'patron', that category should be heavily populated with $50 donations. Thus organizations can influence the size and variety of donations by establishing such relative prices. Just as no one can be forced to pay a particular high price for the box seats, no one can be forced to contribute $20000 just because that is the top-of-the-line donor category. But the mere quotation of such prices is suggestive of organization expectations and efforts to exploit varying degrees of willingness to pay. A complete analysis might also examine the perquisites and benefit packages that accompany these categories. A key issue is to determine the extent to which the setting of different donor prices will be the equivalent of setting different price-to-cost ratios.

Concluding remarks: why it matters and to whom

1. While nonprofit managers have been improving their business expertise, they remain in serious need of savvy regarding the pricing of their services. Unless they operate in unique segments where service pricing would be antithetical to their mission (e.g. the delivery of emergency food and water following natural disasters), or provide largely homogeneous services in highly competitive settings (not the usual market description for such organizations), research advances on the pricing of nonprofit services are critical to practitioners (assuming they can be translated into operational applications).
2. The nonprofit organizational form continues to be a fascinating challenge to economists applying standard constrained maximization models, and finding sufficient flexibility in the rational choice framework to accommodate more complex objectives. Yet the basic principles of tie-in sale contracts and other forms of price discrimination are well enough known that they should be applicable to the nonprofit sector and provide further examples of the robustness of those pricing models.
3. Public sector policy makers and private funding sources also have an interest in knowing whether nonprofit recipients of their largesse are engaging in defensible pricing strategies – defensible from the point of view of both a larger concept of welfare maximization as well as the narrower perspective of being able to use pricing to reduce the revenue shortfalls that plague the nonprofit sector.

References

Anderson, Robert G.W. (1998), 'Is charging economic?', *Journal of Cultural Economics*, **22** (2–3), 179–87.

Ansari, Asim, S. Siddarth and Charles B. Weinberg (1996), 'Pricing a bundle of products or services: the case of nonprofits', *Journal of Marketing Research*, **33** (1), 86–93.

Bailey, Stephen J. and Peter Falconer (1998), 'Charging for admission to museums and galleries: a framework for analysing the impact on access', *Journal of Cultural Economics*, **22** (2–3), 167–77.

Bergstrom, Theodore C. (2001), 'Free labor for costly journals', *Journal of Economic Perspectives*, **15** (4), 183–98.

Bertonazzi, Eric P., Michael T. Maloney and Robert E. Mccormick (1993), 'Some evidence on the Alchian and Allen theorem: the third law of demand?', *Economic Inquiry*, **31** (3), 383–93.

Blaug, Mark (1978), 'Why are Covent Garden prices so high?' *Journal of Cultural Economics*, **2** (1), 1–20.

Brooks, Arthur C. (1997), 'Improving the orchestra's revenue position: practical tactics and general strategies', *Research Studies Series No. 1*, Evanston, IL: Symphony Orchestra Institute.

Brown, H. Shelton (2002), 'Optimal facility placement and discriminatory congestion pricing in neighborhoods with different time costs', *The Annals of Regional Science*, **36**, 181–96.

Cairns, John A. (1991), 'Commodity bundling as a response to capacity constraints', *Journal of Cultural Economics*, **15** (1), 71–84.

Carlson, Donald Robert and George Bobrinskoy Shepherd (1992), 'Cartel on campus: the economics and law of academic institutions' financial aid price-fixing', *Oregon Law Review*, **71**, 563–629.

Carlton, Dennis W., Gustavo E. Bamberger and Roy J. Epstein (1995), 'Antitrust and higher education: was there a conspiracy to restrict financial aid?', *RAND Journal of Economics*, **26** (1), 131–47.

Cheung, Steven N. S. (1977), 'Why Are Better Seats "Underpriced"?', *Economic Inquiry*, **15** (4), 513–22.

Courty, Pascal (2003), 'Some economics of ticket resale', *Journal of Economic Perspectives*, **17** (2), 85–97.

Cumming, Paul D., Edward L. Wallace, Douglas MacN. Surgenor, Barbara D. Mierzwa and Francis A. Smith (1974), 'Public interest pricing of blood services', *Medical Care*, **XII** (9), 743–53.

Dranove, David (1988), 'Pricing by non-profit institutions', *Journal of Health Economics*, **7** (1), 47–57.

Dranove, David and Richard Ludwick (1999), 'Competition and pricing by nonprofit hospitals: a reassessment of Lynk's analysis', *Journal of Health Economics*, **18** (1), 87–98.

Dranove, David, Mark Shanley and William D. White (1991), 'How fast are hospital prices really rising?', *Medical Care*, **29** (8), 690–96.

Ennis, Sean, Michael Schoenbaum and Theodore Keeler (2000), 'Optimal prices and costs for hospitals with excess bed capacity', *Applied Economics*, **32** (9), 1201–12.

Feldstein, Martin S. (1971), 'Hospital cost inflation: a study of nonprofit price dynamics', *The American Economic Review*, **61** (5), 853–72.

Forder, Julien (2000), 'Mental health: market power and governance', *Journal of Health Economics*, **19** (6), 877–905.

Garber, Lawrence L., Jr, Jan G. Muscarella, Paul N. Bloom and Jennifer L. Spiker (2000), 'Consumer based strategic planning in the nonprofit sector: the empirical assessment of a symphony audience', *Journal of Nonprofit & Public Sector Marketing*, **8** (1), 55–86.

Goetzmann, William and Sharon M. Oster (2003), 'The economics of museums', in Edward Glaeser (ed.), *The Governance of Not for Profit Firms*, Cambridge, MA: National Bureau of Economic Research Volume on Nonprofit Organizations.

Greaney, Thomas L. (2006), 'Antitrust and hospital mergers: does the nonprofit form affect competitive substance?', *Journal of Health Politics, Policy and Law*, **31** (3), 511–29.

Greffe, Xavier (2000), 'Pricing the artistic services: from price cultures to price practices', Working Paper, presented at the 10th Biennial Conference of the Association for Cultural Economics, International, Minneapolis, May.

Haddock, David D.and Fred S. McChesney (1994), 'Why do firms contrive shortages? The economics of intentional mispricing', *Economic Inquiry*, **32** (4), 562–81.

Halcoussis, Dennis and Timothy Mathews (2007), 'eBay auctions for Third Eye Blind concert tickets', *Journal of Cultural Economics*, **31** (7), 65–78.

Hanchate, Amresh (1996), 'Nonprofit pricing of services under cost uncertainty', *Journal of Cultural Economics*, **20** (2), 133–44.

Hansmann, Henry B. (1981), 'Nonprofit enterprise in the performing arts', *The Bell Journal of Economics*, **12** (2), 835–901.

Hendricks, Joyce and Pierre Baume (1997), 'The pricing of nursing care', *Journal of Advanced Nursing*, **25** (3), 454–62.

Holtmann, Alphonse G. (1983), 'A theory of non-profit firms', *Economica*, **50** (200), 439–49.

Huntington, Paul A. (1991), 'Buying behavior over a defined product', *Journal of Cultural Economics*, **15** (1), 55–71.

Huntington, Paul A. (1993), 'Ticket pricing policy and box office revenues', *Journal of Cultural Economics*, **17** (1), 71–88.

Irvin, Renée A. (2000), 'Should St. Merciful Hospital become CorpHealth, Inc? Ownership and quality in U.S. health care organizations', *Nonprofit Management & Leadership*, **11** (1), 3–20.

Jacobs, Philip and Ronald P.Wilder (1984), 'Pricing behavior of non-profit agencies: the case of blood products', *Journal of Health Economics*, **3** (1), 49–61.

James, Estelle and Susan Rose-Ackerman (1986), *The Nonprofit Enterprise in Market Economics*, Chur, Switzerland: Harwood Academic Publishers.

James, Estelle and Dennis R. Young (2007), 'Fee income and commercial ventures', in Dennis R.Young (ed.), *Financing Nonprofits: Putting Theory Into Practice*, Lanham, MD and Plymouth, UK: AltaMira Press, pp. 93–120.

Jenkins, Stephen and David Austen-Smith (1987), 'Interdependent decision-making in non-profit industries: a simultaneous equation analysis of English provincial theatre', *International Journal of Industrial Organization*, **5**, 149–74.

Jenny, Hans H. (1968), 'Pricing and optimum size in a nonprofit institution: the university', *The American Economic Review*, **58** (2), 270–83.

Keeler, Emmett B., Glenn Melnick and Jack Zwanziger (1999), 'The changing effects of competition on non-profit and for-profit hospital pricing behavior', *Journal of Health Economics*, **18** (1), 69–86.

Kirchberg, Volker (1998), 'Entrance fees as a subjective barrier to visiting museums', *Journal of Cultural Economics*, **22** (1), 1–13.

Kushner, Roland J. and Arthur C. Brooks (2000), 'The one-man band by the quick lunch stand: modeling audience response to street performance', *Journal of Cultural Economics*, **24** (1), 65–77.

Kushner, Roland J. and Arthur E. King (1994), 'Performing arts as a club good: evidence from a nonprofit organization', *Journal of Cultural Economics*, **18** (1), 15–28.

Lovelock, Christopher H. (1984), 'Strategies for managing demand in capacity-constrained service organizations', *Service Industries Journal*, **5** (November), 12–30.

Luksetich, William A.and Mark D. Lange (1995), 'A simultaneous model of nonprofit symphony orchestra behavior', *Journal of Cultural Economics*, **19** (1), 49–68.

Lynk, William J. (1995), 'Nonprofit hospital mergers and the exercise of market power', *Journal of Law and Economics*, **38** (2), 437–61.

Maloney, Michael T. and Robert E. McCormick (1989), 'Block pricing and the distribution of demand', Working Paper, Clemson University.
McCain, Roger A. (1987), 'Scalping: optimal contingent pricing of performances in the arts and sports', *Journal of Cultural Economics*, **11** (1), 1–21.
McCready, Douglas J. (1988), 'Ramsey pricing: a method for setting fees in social service organizations', *American Journal of Economics and Sociology*, **47** (1), 97–110.
McMillen, Daniel P., Larry D. Singell, Jr and Glen R. Waddell (2007), 'Spatial competition and the price of college', *Economic Inquiry*, **45** (4), 817–33.
Melnick, Glenn A., Emmett Keeler and Jack Zwanziger (1999), 'Market power and hospital pricing: are non-profits different?', *Health Affairs*, **18** (3), 167–73.
Melnick, Glenn A., Jack Zwanziger, Anil Bamezai and Robert Pattison (1992), 'The effects of market structure and bargaining position on hospital prices', *Journal of Health Economics*, **11**, 217–33.
O'Hagan, John W. and Mark Purdy (1993), 'The theory of nonprofit organizations: an application to a performing arts enterprise', *The Economic and Social Review*, **24** (2), 155–67.
Oster, Sharon M., Charles M. Gray and Charles Weinberg (2004), 'Pricing in the nonprofit sector', in Dennis R. Young (ed.), *Effective Economic Decision-Making by Nonprofit Organizations*, New York: The Foundation Center, pp. 27–46.
Parsons, Elizabeth and Adelina Broadbridge (2004), 'Managing change in nonprofit organizations: insights from the UK charity retail sector', *Voluntas: International Journal of Voluntary and Nonprofit Organizations*, **15** (3), 227–42.
Peters, Lon L. (1993), 'Non-profit and for-profit electric utilities in the United States: pricing and efficiency', *Annals of Public and Cooperative Economics*, **64** (4), 575–604.
Prieto-Rodríguez, Juan and Víctor Fernández-Blanco (2006), 'Optimal pricing and grant policies for museums', *Journal of Cultural Economics*, **30** (3), 169–81.
Rosenbaum, D.I. and Meng-Hua Ye (1997), 'Price discrimination and economic journals', *Applied Economics*, **29** (12), 1611–18.
Seaman, Bruce A. (1985), 'Price discrimination in the arts', in Virginia Lee Owen et al. (eds), *Managerial Economics for the Arts*, Akron, OH: University of Akron, pp. 47–60; reprinted in Ruth Towse (ed.) (1997), *Cultural Economics: The Arts, the Heritage and the Media*, Vol. II, Cheltenham, UK and Lyme, US: Edward Elgar, pp. 434–48.
Seaman, Bruce A. (2004), 'Competition and the non-profit arts: the lost industrial organization agenda', *Journal of Cultural Economics*, **28** (3), 167–93.
Seaman, Bruce A. (2006), 'Empirical studies of the demand for the performing arts', in Victor A. Ginsburgh and David Throsby (eds), *Handbook of the Economics of Art and Culture*, Amsterdam: North-Holland, pp. 415–72.
Seaman, Bruce A. and D. Green (1994), 'Price discrimination in the arts: a cross-sectional analysis', Working Paper, presented at the Southern Economics Association Meetings, Orlando, Florida, November.
Steinberg, Richard (2007), 'Membership income', in Dennis R. Young (ed.), *Financing Nonprofits: Putting Theory Into Practice*, Lanham, MD and Plymouth, UK: AltaMira Press, pp. 121–56.
Steinberg, Richard and Burton A. Weisbrod (1998), 'Pricing and rationing by nonprofit organizations with distributional objectives', in Burton A. Weisbrod (ed.), *To Profit or Not to Profit: The Commercial Transformation of the Nonprofit Sector*, Cambridge: Cambridge University Press, pp. 65–82.
Steinberg, Richard and Burton A. Weisbrod (2005), 'Nonprofits with distributional objectives: price discrimination and corner solutions', *Journal of Public Economics*, **89** (11–12), 2205–30.
Steiner, Faye (1997), 'Optimal pricing of museum admission', *Journal of Cultural Economics*, **21** (4), 307–33.
Stephens, Mark, Nicola Burns and Lisa Mackay (2003), 'The limits of housing reforms: British social rented housing in a European context', *Urban Studies*, **40** (4), 767–89.
Touchstone, Susan Kathleen (1980), 'The effects of contributions on price and attendance in the lively arts', *Journal of Cultural Economics*, **4** (1), 33–46.
Weisbrod, Burton A. (1965), 'Some problems of pricing and resource allocation in a non-profit industry – the hospitals', *The Journal of Business*, **38** (1), 18–28.
West, Edwin G. (1987), 'Nonprofit versus profit firms in the performing arts', *Journal of Cultural Economics*, **11** (2), 37–48.
Yanikoski, Richard A. and Richard F. Wilson (1984), 'Differential pricing of undergraduate education', *The Journal of Higher Education*, **55** (6), 735–50.
Young, Dennis R. (ed.) (2006), *Wise Decision-Making in Uncertain Times: Using Nonprofit Resources Effectively*, New York: The Foundation Center.
Young, Dennis R. and Richard Steinberg (1995), *Economics for Nonprofit Managers*, New York: The Foundation Center.
Young, Gary J., Kamal R. Desai and Fred J. Hellinger (2000), 'Community control and pricing patterns of nonprofit hospitals: an antitrust analysis', *Journal of Health Politics, Policy and Law*, **25** (6), 1051–81.

11 Nonprofits and the value of risk management
Martin F. Grace

Introduction

The use of risk management in nonprofits is really about the use of incentives to minimize the risk of loss as much as it is to increase the output potential for nonprofits. Fama and Jensen (1983) discuss various types of nonprofits, showing how agency problems are mitigated by a separation of management from control. In particular, while nonprofits do not have residual claimants, as a traditional corporation might have, they do have monitors who oversee the actions of the managers. In fact, the success of the nonprofit sector is testament to the fact that useful monitoring does exist. Risk management can thus be used to complement monitoring as well as to protect assets that give a nonprofit its comparative advantage. Further, risk management can be used to enhance the opportunity set for nonprofit organizations.

Nonprofits have different missions and may have different objective functions. This is, in part, why individual nonprofits exist. The objectives and risks facing nonprofit hospitals are different from those of the Red Cross. The Red Cross, in turn, has a different risk profile from the local nonprofit performing arts theater or from Scouting. There is no one set of risk management tools that provides a one-size-fits-all method for managing the risks facing nonprofits. This chapter will provide background to the theory underlying risk management, which, in turn, is based upon the underlying theory of corporate finance and provides a starting point for the discussion of value of risk management in general. Second, a brief overview of the risk management process is provided. Finally, the strategic benefits of risk management are discussed. In addition to minimizing the cost of risk, the proper use of risk management can provide new opportunities or preserve opportunities in the event of a serious problem.

Theory of risk management

Risk management is a relatively new term for what many people think is really just insurance. However, it is much broader as it contains elements of the use of technology to reduce risk, the use of self-insurance (savings) for protection, as well as the use of market-based products to reduce risk (Ehrlich and Becker, 1972). These market-based products can range from simple commercial automobile insurance to sophisticated financial risk management products sold to large endowment managers.

Most think of risk management as a way to merely reduce risk; however, risk is a necessary input in the cost of production of the firm and, like all other inputs, its costs must be minimized for profit maximization. Presumably the ability of the firm to bear risk at a lower opportunity cost than other firms creates value, which then attracts investors.

For a nonprofit there is a different objective function guiding the firm's operations. Thus a major difference between the uses of risk management for a for-profit and nonprofit organization with respect to risk management would be what management believes is the objective of the firm. Different objective functions might yield a different set of methods to manage risk.

The theory for the demand for risk management starts with the Friedman and Savage (1948) approach to the demand for insurance. Starting with a neoclassical expected utility function, they derived some important results. The result that we care most about in this chapter is the fact that more risk-averse individuals will be willing to pay a higher risk premium to avoid a risk. The result was more formally treated by Arrow (1963) and Pratt (1964), who derive an explicit measure of this risk premium. Thus the more a nonprofit organization reflects the risk-averse preferences of its managers, the greater the value risk management will have to the organization. This is an important point that will be mentioned again below.

At the other end of the spectrum risk management theory is bounded by the work of Modigliani and Miller (MM) (1958), which provided two important results. The first was the irrelevance of the firm's capital structure (the amount of debt versus equity) to the value of the firm. A similar result is derived, which states that the firm's value is not increased by undertaking risk management activities. MM make a number of assumptions setting up the ideal conditions for the study of corporate finance. In this frictionless world there are many atomistic investors with well-diversified portfolios acting as owners of the firm. In addition, there is perfect information, no agency disputes between managers and stockholders or between stockholders and other potential stakeholders (such as employees or neighbors), no taxes, and no possibility of bankruptcy. Each of these assumptions is of course violated in the real world, and their violations are what help create the value of, and the demand for, risk management.

To see how this works, let us examine a counter-example envisioned by the MM assumptions. Suppose that a firm faces a risk of fire for one of its production facilities. It could buy insurance. Suppose it buys insurance that includes a return to the insurer for its risk transfer services. This implies that the price of insurance will be

$$Price = (1 + \lambda) E[X],$$

where $E[X]$ is the expected value of a fire loss and $(1 + \lambda)$ is the mark-up to the insurer for the risk transfer services.

The shareholder notes that there is a fire risk (from the assumption of perfect information) and would be able to readjust his portfolio to reduce the effect of the fire risk on the overall returns. If he can change his investment portfolio at a lower cost than the insurer can purchase insurance, then risk management creates no value for the firm. MM's initial assumptions were that there were no transactions costs; thus stock trading is free and will always be less expensive than the service fee charged by the insurer. In the event of no transactions costs ($\lambda = 0$), the shareholder would be indifferent between the use of insurance or the reallocation of his portfolio. Managers who employed costly insurance would reduce their profits and shareholders would sell their shares to avoid the lower returns. In equilibrium, managers will adopt the risk preferences of the shareholders and, under MM's assumptions, shareholders are well diversified and therefore appear to be risk-neutral.

Thus traditional theory suggests that there is no value for risk management. However, as mentioned above, each assumption that is violated allows for risk management to create value for the firm. Essentially what happens is that the firm's risk-neutral linear profit function becomes concave to the origin and starts to resemble a risk-averse utility function. Thus, while firms are risk-neutral, violations of the assumptions underlying the MM model alter the firm's incentives and create an incentive to use risk management. The more concave the objective function becomes, the more valuable risk management becomes to the firm.

For example, if income taxes exist, then insurance premiums are deductible from taxable income. This may reduce the after-tax price of insurance below actuarially fair values (e.g. $Price < E[X]$). This would create a demand for insurance where in the absence of taxes there was indifference. Similarly, risk management may reduce bankruptcy costs. This can be seen by the following example. Suppose banks are willing to loan funds to a company, but they are concerned about the risk of bankruptcy. In order to make a loan, the banks will need to receive an additional risk premium to cover the firm's risk of default. However, if the firm could buy insurance or hedge through the financial markets, some of the risk borne by the firm and this hedging activity reduce the bankruptcy risk; then lenders will not demand as high a premium. Thus risk management can add value if its purchase can reduce the cost of external financing. While the firm is still risk-neutral, its profit function is no longer linear in risk because of the costs of bankruptcy. So if the costs of insurance are less than the marginal benefit due from the reduction of bankruptcy costs, the firm should undertake this type of risk management.

For nonprofits there may be a concern about the future viability of the enterprise that is akin to bankruptcy risk. If the future is uncertain, then the ability to obtain future donations might be put at risk. To the extent that risk management can increase the prospects of survival for the nonprofit, it reduces the costs of obtaining future funds. For certain types of nonprofits this may be one of the more important aspects of risk management.

The value of risk management depends solely upon the objective function of the firm under realistic assumptions about market frictions. Other market frictions exist that violate the MM assumptions which may be more applicable to nonprofits. For example, one of the major problems for nonprofits is that they have no shareholders to discipline managers. Fama and Jensen (1983) point out that most nonprofits have boards that oversee the managers of the nonprofit. This board of directors protects against managerial incompetence if the board is interested in the long-run reputation of the nonprofit. However, without the disciplinary power of shareholders or other residual stakeholders, there is no monitoring of the board of directors. This agency problem can cause the nonprofit to deviate from its stated objectives as managers use the nonprofit as a way of maximizing the management's utility. Risk management can thus be employed as an external monitor to monitor the monitors. To the extent that directors' and officers' liability coverage will be offered to nonprofits conditional upon good corporate governance practices and that subsequent renewals will depend upon the use and further development of these practices, then the nonprofit contributors and beneficiaries both benefit.

Further, if the firm has certain property critical to the operation of the nonprofit's activities, insurance might be appropriate to guarantee survival of the organization's mission. This property can be real property such as a building, which provides significant benefits for the organization but which cannot easily be replaced in the event of a loss from future contributions. The use of risk management here is akin to the argument for

Table 11.1   Risk management process

Step	Description of process
1	Risk identification and assessment
2	Risk quantification
3	Risk aggregation into a portfolio
4	Strategic acceptance of risk, risk control and risk financing
5	Return to Step 1

risk management in the for-profit world. While the risk of bankruptcy is quite different in the for-profit arena, a loss of a sufficient magnitude would preclude the nonprofit's future operation.

A third rationale for the use of risk management in nonprofits is that risk management services often come with what Mayers and Smith (1982) call 'real insurance services'. This would be advice about making operating programs safer or advice about protecting employees or volunteers. In addition, it also contains claims services (processing and paying claims to injured parties). Most small (or even large) firms do not have the ability to monitor and manage claims that might be made against it; thus they may employ companies with specific competence to do so. Risk management firms might also provide information about loss mitigation strategies and advice that may come bundled with insurance or can be purchased separately from risk management brokers and consultants.

Deciding on which risks to manage and which risks to avoid presupposes that an organization understands the risks it is facing. This process of understanding its risks is necessary in order for the firm to determine the proper financing or loss avoidance approaches.

Risk management process
The risk management process is relatively simple in concept yet is often difficult to accomplish. This is because it requires attention from members of the board and those involved in the operation of the day-to-day activities. The process is summarized in Table 11.1 and is a generic process for all types of firms, no matter their profit status. The only thing that depends upon individual preferences is the organization's risk appetite or its tolerance for risk.

For a for-profit firm, the board of directors has to determine how much risk the company can withstand. This 'risk appetite' is important as it determines the ultimate strategy concerning how much risk the firm can hold. For example, if the firm can tolerate no risk, it will have to insure or hedge all risks. The demand for risk management will be much greater for such a firm, holding other things constant. Similarly, an organization that tolerates a great deal of risk, say Doctors without Borders, may have a larger need for risk management, holding other things constant. One interesting thing to note is that the board of directors may not explicitly understand its risk appetite at the beginning of the exercise. It often must undertake the risk management process before it understands the types of risks the firm is facing and whether the firm should retain or eliminate the risk.[1] A nonprofit board of directors may bring its own risk preferences to bear in determining what the nonprofit's risk tolerance is. If members of the board derive significant revenue from the operation of the firm, then this would provide an indication of the risk tolerance of the board. In this case risk management has greater value the greater the board's level of risk aversion. In contrast, if the board members have well-diversified portfolios, then they will not have risk-averse attitudes towards the activities of the nonprofit. What one would care about is how important the nonprofit's performance is related to the board's preferences. If the board is highly visible and provides some significant non-pecuniary benefits to members, then this will likely evoke some risk aversion. Ideally, nonprofit board members must have some tie to the nonprofit to ensure that there is alignment with the goals of the nonprofit and the interests of the members of the board.

After understanding the risk tolerance of the board, the first step in the risk management process is the identification of risk facing the firm. For for-profit companies this is often a difficult exercise due to the compartmentalization of organizations. In addition to management hierarchies there are also geographic and product-line divisions. These same problems can exist in a large nonprofit. However, the goal of the exercise is to identify all of the risks facing the firm from the lowest level to the highest level.

Risk can also be categorized into reputational, operational, financial, credit, market environmental, regulatory and strategic.

- Reputational risk is any type of risk that can negatively affect the organization's reputation. Nonprofits are probably not more susceptible to these kinds of risks, but they have made major headlines over the years.[2] In fact, while nonprofits may not be more susceptible to reputational risks, these are likely to be the risks most likely to ruin a nonprofit.
- Operational risks are those the management can directly control. These include employee behaviors, product liabilities, malpractice, as well as risks such as information technology failures. Hospitals are routinely exposed to malpractice risk and the Canadian Red Cross was held liable for harm casued by blood-borne diseases like HIV and Hepatitis C.[3]
- Financial risks, in contrast, are those that are result from changes in interest rates or foreign exchange rates. Nonprofits with significant endowment management concerns would also be likely to be exposed to financial risk. The recent financial market upheaval left several universities unable to access their short-term investment funds placing day-to-day operations at risk.[4] Further, endowments were exposed to significant changes as the broader market fell approximately 55 percent between its October 2007 high and its October 2008 low.
- Credit risk is the risk of the firm being able to obtain credit, or in the case of nonprofits the ability to raise future donations as well. This would likely be overlapping with reputation risk as the future operation of the nonprofit would be impacted by a serious reputational failure. The Archdiocese of Boston had to sell significant properties and had to close a number of churches because of damage claims and the inability to raise funds through normal tithing processes.[5]
- Market risk relates to the risk due to being a competitor in a market. Competitors for nonprofits exist, especially for the arts or hospitals. New products developed by others (whether for profit or nonprofit) will affect the value of the services provided by the nonprofit firm. For some types of nonprofits, this is more a problem than it

is for others, but it is still a risk to be managed. Many nonprofits have significant competitors. In just one market (youth activities) there is Boy and Girl Scouting, Indian Guides, Campfire, Boys and Girls Clubs, YMCA, and various nonprofit and community clubs and leagues for sports. There is also significant competition among nursing homes, universities and hospitals. The competition among these groups with for-profit or state-supported organizations for membership or customers is important for their continued growth and survival.[6]

- Environmental risk relates to the physical environment. Environmental risks include wind, flood and other types of disasters that might interfere with the ability of the firm to provide its services. Certain environmental nonprofits such as the Colorado Trust for Land Restoration are responsible for reclaiming lands that contained mining operations. The environmental liability risks to neighbors or downstream residents due to various poisonous mining byproducts is significant.

- Regulatory risk is the risk of regulators undertaking actions that increase the costs of providing the nonprofits goods or services. Potential actions by the IRS to remove nonprofit status is a good example. Compliance costs will likely rise as a result of increased scrutiny, as organizations will have to document their activities more carefully. Recently, Senator Grassley (R. Iowa), the ranking member of the Senate Finance Committee, issued subpoenas to a number of churches asking them to justify their nonprofit status given various political and commercial activities they may have engaged in. He is also making similar inquiries of universities with large endowment funds and nonprofit community hospitals that are alleged to be shirking their duty to provide uncompensated care for the community.[7]

- Finally, strategic risks are those that have a direct effect on increasing the possibility set of the firm. Examples of strategic risks are the decisions to provide a new product or service or to open a new hospital. Alternatively, one can undertake a service that would operate as a natural hedge to the main mission of the nonprofit so that when one part of the operation does poorly, the other does well and vice versa. This strategic risk will be discussed further below.

Often these categories overlap. For example, if an operational risk (i.e. information technology failure) is great enough, it may negatively influence the firm's reputation. If firms cannot manage their finances, employees, technology or their volunteers, significant reputational injuries often result. In fact, although the above list is not exhaustive, each problem described also had a concomitant reputational risk. A failure in one area lowers reputation, whether it is the YMCA, a church or a hospital.

The second step in the risk management process is risk quantification. This is also difficult for for-profit firms because it requires data collection and analysis. For organizations producing services like those of nonprofits, this process is particularly difficult and requires significant investments of time as the risks to property, employees, the public and volunteers must be understood. While difficult for nonprofits, this is not really any harder than for for-profit firms. However, what might be problematic is the willingness of the board to spend money on understanding and quantifying risks rather than spending money directly related to the mission of the organization. In reality, risk quantification can be as simple as 'low, medium or high' or as complex as sophisticated actuarial models to predict episodes of substandard care that lead to morbidity or mortality in a hospital.

The third step is to aggregate the firm's risks. This is an important part of the risk management process because it is fundamental to the nature of what the firm does. Ideally, a firm will develop a comparative advantage and will use risk management to further this objective. This will be discussed further below. It is important to note, however, that this comparative advantage can be the result of a long history of providing a service at a lower opportunity cost than others, the use of a new technology, specific investments in human capital, or the good fortune of having a certain location. It could also be the ability to bear a risk at a lower opportunity cost than others.

In the aggregate, one examines the activities of a firm and retains those risks that lead to the firm's comparative advantage. For example, service organizations focus on doing what they do best, raising money to support arts initiatives, rather than raising money to support other causes. In the absence of other rationales, cooperatives focus on what they do best rather than setting up for profit subsidiaries to sell to co-op members and the general public.[8] Other risks need not be borne as they are either expensive, detract from the firm's mission, or both. To the extent that risks increase costs without contributing to value, these risks can be eliminated. The elimination can be through subcontracting, insurance or other risk management activity. However, since risk management is costly, the firm might avoid the risk and the cost of managing it through divestment or shutting down a part of the enterprise.

There has been a relatively large number of studies in the insurance industry examining mutuals (owned by policy owners) and stock companies. The mutuals have many characteristics of a nonprofit as their owners are the insurers' policy owners, who do not have the ability to monitor the management in the same way as large groups of shareholders might be able to do in a stock company. As a result, many suggest that mutual insurers should be less efficient and will be driven from the market. Mayers and Smith (1988) describe an organizational theory that would allow mutuals and stocks to coexist. They theorized that due to the inability of owners to monitor, mutuals would evolve to produce relatively simple and transparent products. In contrast, for-profit stock companies would organize to employ sophisticated managers who could manage more complex products. The strategic choice to focus on a particular type of insurance gives the mutual insurer a comparative advantage. In essence, the insurer chose a portfolio of risks to bear and then sold services consistent with that choice. This is exactly the strategic choice the organization has the opportunity to make when it aggregates its risk.

In conjunction with risk aggregation is the financing of those risks that are ultimately retained. Ideally, retained risks are those that complement the production of the activities which are the source of the nonprofit organizations' comparative value. Risk financing can be undertaken in a number of ways. First, Ehrlich and Becker (1972) point to a firm's problem as determining whether to self-insure (save), self-protect (use risk-reducing technologies to mitigate losses), or use market-provided insurance. Ideally, one might save if there were market asymmetries which precluded obtaining insurance at a fair price. This occurs when the cost of separating high-risk entities from low-risk entities is high. Most likely small firms with little or no experience will have difficulty in obtaining certain types of insurance at rates reflecting the firm's own risk. A perfect example is workers' compensation insurance. This insurance is priced based upon the experience of the firm. However, if the firm is new, has no credible loss experience, but believes that its workforce is a low potential risk relative to similar firms, it will still be priced-based on

Table 11.2   Value of risk management

	Low severity	High severity
Low probability	Cash flow	Insurance
High probability	Cash flow	Savings

some type of industry average losses by the private market. It might make sense, then, for the firm to self-insure these losses rather than purchase higher-priced market insurance. An alternative source of 'self-insurance' is to set up a risk retention group (RRG), which is like a mutual insurer for a set of firms within a well-defined industry. The RRG arguably will be more likely to understand a certain sector's business and understand how to underwrite it better.[9]

Self-protection is the purchase of services to reduce the probability of a loss as well as the severity of a loss. A simple example is fire suppression technologies. These do not influence the probability of a fire starting, but they have an effect on the severity of the loss. Other technologies might be used to reduce the likelihood of theft or other types of loss. These technologies might be purchased as substitutes for other types of market risk management services or in conjunction with them. These mitigation activities could also be related to good risk management practices in terms of compliance. For example, good practices for cash management will reduce embezzlement losses, and good practices for workplace safety will reduce employee accidents.[10]

Finally, there is market insurance. Market insurance is based upon expected losses and presumably is purchased for those types of risks that cannot be saved for or mitigated through self-protection in a more efficient manner. Table 11.2 shows the relationship between the likelihood of a loss and the size of the loss and the type of financing that makes most sense. For low-severity events, financing from cash flow makes sense. This is true whether there is a low or a high likelihood of loss. If self-protection is relatively inexpensive, then the low-severity events can be mitigated by controls or oversight reducing, in turn, the effect on cash flow. These low-severity events are a small cost of doing business. However, if there is a potential high-value loss that is also a high-probability event, then insurance markets will not provide coverage. This is because the insurer cannot diversify the risk cross-sectionally across similar risks. The way to finance a loss that is highly likely to occur is through 'savings'. This can be done by the firm or in conjunction with an insurer through a long-term contract that acts like a forced savings plan.[11] Essentially, the insurer and the insured agree to pay a fraction of the loss each year over a period of time of, say, ten years. The actual price will depend on the likelihood of the loss within the ten-year period and contingencies for the event that no loss actually occurs. If the loss occurs in the first year, the insurer will pay for the loss and the insured will continue to make payments for the next nine years.

After financing decisions are made, the final step is to start the process. Over time the nature of the organization changes and the nature of the risks facing the organization also changes. Thus a good risk management process would contain a constant evaluation of risks. For nonprofits that are in stable markets this re-evaluation is not needed as often, but for others it might occur regularly.

After going through this process and using the board's tolerance for risk to direct the risk management for the firm, it is still possible to think about risk in another dimension. As part of the risk aggregation process a portfolio of risks is created. This portfolio can be the basis for some thought about the future of the firm. It can also help the firm understand its comparative advantage as the risks it decides to bear are essentially a strategic choice about the future of the firm.

The strategic use of risk management
The objectives of nonprofits are likely to be based on some form of mission continuation or expansion. These objectives can be accomplished through increasing donations (for a grant-seeking organization), increasing the value of services (for service organizations), or for increasing the membership size or the value of membership (for membership organizations). In addition to these goals there are, of course, the potential agency costs problems from the lack of residual claimants monitoring the firm.[12] As mentioned above, and consistent with the objectives of the firm, there is the need to minimize the cost of risk.

We can focus the value of risk management on how it increases the opportunity set of the firm. Risk management used in this way can be called strategic risk management. Recall that Mayers and Smith's (1988) analysis of stock and mutual companies suggests that organizations can adapt their risk portfolios to complement their business model. It is possible to use risk management to reduce the cost of risk, and if the reduction in costs increases the ability of the firm to offer services, it thus creates new opportunities for the firm.

Suppose we have a stylized nonprofit organization that takes donations and provides volunteer activities in the community. The firm has an objective function N, which depends upon the value of donations and the work of volunteers ($B(D,V)$).[13] Thus the firm benefits from both donations and the work of its volunteers. There is a cost of raising donations (d) and a cost of overseeing volunteers (v). Then N can be written as

$$N(D,V) = B(D,V) - dD - vV. \tag{11.1}$$

Assuming a standard maximization, we would end up with the marginal benefit of raising donations being set equal to the marginal cost of donations, and the marginal benefit of using volunteers being set equal to the marginal cost of monitoring the volunteers.

If we allow for the possibility that the volunteers undertake actions that have a negative effect on donations, then we can rewrite the equation as

$$N(D,V) = B(D,V) - dD - vV - \rho(V). \tag{11.2}$$

Again, the volunteers have a positive effect on the reputation of the firm. However, the additional term $\rho(V)$ represents the cost caused by the volunteers' possible reputation reducing actions that then, in turn, reduce the value of donations to the firm. This reputation-reducing activity can be anything that a volunteer might do that reduces the probability that donors will give money in the future. Now, if we looked at the first-order conditions we would see that the use of volunteers would be lower than under the result in equation (11.1) because of the additional reputational costs of volunteers' behavior.

The net value of the firm ($N(D,V)$) and its output (however it is measured) will also be lower due to the reduced number of volunteers. If the cost of misguided volunteers can be reduced or eliminated by any type of risk management that is less expensive than the cost imposed by the volunteers' activities, then the firm can increase its ability to serve its target audience. So, if the price of risk management (whether market insurance or mitigation) is less than the marginal cost of the reputation reduction, risk management adds value to the nonprofit in terms of ability to provide more services.[14] Thus, given the presence of risk, a wise use of risk management can increase the output of the firm. Thinking about risk management in this way is strategic since it goes directly to the ability of the firm to potentially increase output in its niche.

An alternative way of thinking about this is when an organization makes investments (sets up rules and regulations) that enhance reputation. A nonprofit can treat its reputation as a strategic asset. Firms with better reputations will be more successful and will be able to serve greater numbers of beneficiaries. The Boy Scouts of America undertook a reputation enhancement exercise in response to a number of sexual assaults on youth by volunteers (Potts, 1992). The program, which has been in place since the mid-1980s, requires the training of every adult leader in youth protection, and provides materials for youth and parents. The program on a superficial level seems successful as there are apparently fewer reported cases of inappropriate behavior. The point here is that this has been a costly program to develop and maintain for the last 20 years, but it provides some assurance of concern for the safety of the children in the program, making the program more valuable. Similarly, salary limits, grant-making controls and donor intent controls help enhance the value of charitable giving for organizations like the United Way. These controls reduce the utility of senior managers of the organization, but enhance the member charities' benefits as donors will put more trust in them as they will be better stewards of donations.

A second way to think about the strategic use of risk management is to imagine what would happen to the firm if a certain event occurred such as the death of a key manager or loss of a key piece of property. Risk management allows the firm to have opportunities in averse states of the world. If a key person dies, then a life insurance policy, for example, would provide breathing room for the organization while at the same time providing resources for temporary managers and the time to find a new person to manage the firm. The use of risk management allows the firm to provide value to its constituents, even in bad states of the world.

Concluding remarks: directions for further research
The current stock of applied research in the value of risk management in the for-profit field does not necessarily translate well into the nonprofit arena because it focuses on costs that do not generally arise in the nonprofit organization. If one thinks about the rationale for risk management, it is founded on reduction of agency costs, reduction of tax costs and reduction of bankruptcy costs. Tax costs are almost irrelevant to nonprofits and the reduction of bankruptcy costs may provide small benefits to a nonprofit relative to a for-profit company. This is because there is no shareholder value at stake. Employees, creditors, donors and deprived beneficiaries are the major losers in a nonprofit bankruptcy. The exception might be for those organizations that depend upon raising funds. Any fear of bankruptcy will have a significant effect on the ability to

continue to raise money. In addition, for the most part no one has examined bankruptcy as a risk management tool for nonprofits, although some Catholic dioceses have actually used bankruptcy as a method to allow time to raise money or to allow time for the sale of property to satisfy judgments (Boozang, 2005).

Other types of bankruptcy, by nonprofit hospitals for example, are likely due to reasons other than liability risk, but it would be interesting to examine a number of cases to catalogue the types of firms that use bankruptcy and the types of costs levied on the stakeholders. This potential value of risk management in reducing bankruptcy costs is unknown for nonprofits, but it is knowable. Further, there are certain exemptions in the bankruptcy code that exempt a nonprofit from involuntary bankruptcy. Thus creditors have a reduced ability to impose bankruptcy costs on the firm. The value of risk management is in reducing bankruptcy costs, but the types or the size of cost that risk management can mitigate for nonprofits is not clear.

Thus we are left with reducing agency costs as a major value-enhancing rationale for risk management in nonprofits. Again, this is because there is no set of well-defined shareholders to monitor the firm which can lead to the possibility of significant agency costs. Agency costs arise from insider relationships between boards and officers that reduce the value of the firm's reputation. Agency costs also arise because boards may not have the expertise to monitor the nonprofit organization's managers. Risk management provides value in reducing agency costs in the form of directors' and officers' insurance (where the insurer is a monitor of good corporate governance); cash management controls (where the firm's accountant monitors for certain types of compliance); or through a separation of the board from the officers (where the board monitors the managers). Some organizations are based on volunteers, some are based on raising money to support a particular activity, and some provide services in a competitive market. Each type of organization will probably have a different need for a specific type of risk management. The state of research existing in the for-profit field does not yet address these issues for for-profit companies at a micro level. Thus future research in the nonprofit area would be state of the art. In particular, understanding how the link between a particular type of nonprofit's reason for existence is related to its use of risk management would be a novel contribution to how risk management influences firm value. For example, can risk management really take the place of institutional arrangements and/or is it a substitute for networks of like-minded individuals, the IRS, state attorneys general, or nonprofit rating agencies?

A second area of research based on agency costs would be to see which types of nonprofits benefit from various types of risk management options like those shown in Table 11.2. Are hospitals' risk management needs significantly different than those of universities? Are fundraisers different than arts groups? Is the importance of the firm's objective function the underlying reason for risk management? Determining a for-profit firm's risk tolerance is a non-trivial exercise and determining a nonprofit's would be similarly difficult. What makes nonprofits' problems more problematic is the definition and measurement of success metrics and how to evaluate the trade-off that exists between risk tolerance and success as well as the trade-off between success and the cost of risk.

Another area of analysis would be an analysis of nonprofit performance and how that is related to risk management. This stream of literature is only now occurring in the for-profit arena (see, e.g., Cummins et al., 2006) and does not always suggest that risk management invariably solves agency problems (Hayne, 1998). A related area of potential research concerns the use of nonprofit governance, good practices and the performance of the firm. Nonprofit governance is a complement to risk management, but the value of these activities has never been documented.

The goal of risk management is to reduce the cost of risk rather than eliminate all risk. Nonprofits can create value to their beneficiaries by using risk management. The value can be from reduced losses and from an increased opportunity set for the provision of the nonprofit's services. For risk management to provide value it must be undertaken with a process of risk assessment and risk quantification in mind. In addition, managers must understand the individual nonprofit's aggregate portfolio of risks and how holding risks adds to or subtracts from the firm's comparative advantage. The managers, using their tolerance for risk, must then choose the risks to bear and determine how to finance or eliminate the remaining risks. All types of risk management, whether self-protection, self-insurance or market-based risk management products, have the opportunity to increase the opportunity set of a nonprofit organization given the presence of risk.

Notes

1. See, e.g., Harrington and Neihaus (2004) for more details of this process.
2. There are numerous examples of reputation-harming scandals involving non-profits. For example, the pedophile scandals in the Roman Catholic Church, and the Red Cross's decision to use funds raised on behalf of potential 9/11 victims for other purposes are just two high-profile cases.
3. See, e.g., *Tainted Blood*, CBC News at http://www.cbc.ca/news/background/taintedblood/, viewed on 4 November 2008.
4. 'Colleges, universities frozen out of funds', *Philadelphia Inquirer*, 2 October 2008, p. C1.
5. The *Boston Globe* reported that the 2007 annual appeal by the Archbishop was closer to the level achieved in 2000 after a significant drop-off in the early part of the decade, which was due to the pedophile scandal (10 January 2008, p. B2).
6. There is significant reputational risk in competition. The Atlanta Area Council of the Boy Scouts of America as well as others admitted to overreporting membership figures to obtain funding from area charities ('Boy Scouts Suspected of Inflating Rolls', *Washington Post*, 29 January 2005, p, A1).
7. See, e.g., 'M.D. Anderson submits its record on Charitable Care', *Houston Chronicle,* 9 October 2008, viewed at http://www.chron.com/disp/story.mpl/front/6050254.html, on 5 November 2008.
8. Cobb EMC, an electrical cooperative, set up for-profit activities. Customers successfully sued the co-op because they alleged their rate money was being used in for-profit subsidiary ventures. See 'Cobb EMC agrees to buyout deal', *Atlanta Journal Constitution*, 30 October 2008, viewed at http://www.ajc.com/search/content/business/stories/2008/10/30/cobb_emc_buyout.html, 5 November 2008.
9. See Zinkewicz (2008) for a discussion of the RRG for nonprofits. RRGs can be used to supply liability insurance in the event the private market will not do so. For example, the Roman Catholic dioceses formed a liability RRG to offer protection for future liability claims because the private market appeared to be no longer willing to provide insurance to them.
10. In a seminar presented by Ethics Point, 12 recent nonprofit scandals were mentioned. Most involved improper use of funds, excessive salaries, or theft or embezzlement. See presentation at http://info.ethicspoint.com/files/web_seminars/2007/ACUAQ1/Slides_ACUAQ107.pdf, viewed 5 November 2008. Simple accounting controls would have likely stopped the embezzlements and thefts while a board with a better understanding of its fiduciary role and responsibilities would likely reduce other types of scandals. These are relatively inexpensive methods of self-protection.
11. This is a type of so-called alternative risk transfer, see, e.g., Culp (2002). What is being transferred is timing of the loss risk rather than risk of loss. Thus one could think of this as intertemporal risk transfer rather than cross-sectional risk transfer which is typical of most insurance.
12. See, e.g. Malani et al. (2003) for more discussion of these issues.
13. This objective function is assumed risk-averse in donations, which, in turn, reflects the risk appetite of the board of directors.
14. The converse is also true if the cost of risk management is greater than the cost savings from reducing the risk, when the firm's value is reduced. This is why it is important to understand the risks facing the firm. One can overspend on risk management and reduce value. In the case of a nonprofit a reduced value can be translated into a reduced ability to provide services.

References

Arrow, Kenneth J. (1963), 'Uncertainty and the economics of medical care', *The American Economic Review*, **53** (5), 941–73.

Boozang, Kathleen M. (2005), 'Introduction: bankruptcy in the religious non-profit context', *Seton Hall Legislative Journal*, **29** (2), 341–4.

Culp, Christopher L. (2002), *The ART of Risk Management: Alternative Risk Transfer, capital structure, and the convergence of insurance and capital markets*, New York: John Wiley & Sons, Inc.

Cummins, J. David, Dionne Georges, Robert Gagné and Nouira Abdelhakim (2006), 'Efficiency of insurance firms with endogenous risk management and financial intermediation activities', Centre Interuniversitaire sur le Risque, les Politiques Economiques et l'Emploi, Working Paper 0616, Montreal, Quebec.

Ehrlich, Isaac and Gary S. Becker (1972), 'Market insurance, self-insurance, and self-protection', *The Journal of Political Economy*, **80** (4), 623–48.

Fama, Eugene F. and Michael C. Jensen (1983), 'Separation of ownership and control', *Journal of Law and Economics*, **26** (2), 301–25.

Friedman, Milton and Eugene Savage (1948), 'The utility analysis of choices involving risk', *The Journal of Political Economy*, **56** (4), 279–304.

Harrington, Scott and Gregory R. Niehaus (2004), *Risk Management and Insurance*, New York: Irwin-McGraw Hill.

Hayne, E. Leland (1998), 'Agency costs, risk management, and capital structure', *The Journal of Finance*, **53** (4), 1213–43.

Malani, Anup, Tomas Philipson, Guy David and Edward L. Glaeser (2003), 'Theories of firm behavior in the nonprofit sector: a synthesis and empirical evaluation', in Edward L. Glaeser (ed.), *The Governance of Not-for-Profit Organizations*, Chicago, IL: University of Chicago Press, pp. 181–215.

Mayers, David and Clifford Smith (1982), 'On the corporate demand for insurance', *The Journal of Business*, **55** (2), 281–96.

Mayers, David and Clifford Smith (1988), 'Ownership structure across lines of property-casualty insurance', *The Journal of Law & Economics*, **31** (2), 351–78.

Modigliani, Franco and Merton H. Miller (1958), 'The cost of capital, corporation finance and the theory of investment', *The American Economic Review*, **48** (3), 261–97.

Potts, Lawrence F. (1992), 'The Youth Protection Program of the Boy Scouts of America', *Child Abuse & Neglect*, **16** (3), 441–5.

Pratt, John W. (1964), 'Risk aversion in the large and in the small', *Econometrica*, **32** (1–2), 122–36.

Zinkewicz, Phil (2008), 'Insuring nonprofits', *Roughnotes*, retrieved from http://www.roughnotes.com/rnmagazine/2008/may08/05p096.htm.

12 Contracting out
Salvatore Alaimo

Introduction

Contract management has gained attention and increased in activity in the US nonprofit sector over the past few decades. The devolution of the US government has resulted in an increase in contracting out services to nonprofit organizations, particularly in the area of social services. This activity, along with the challenges nonprofit organizations face in managing government contracts, has been widely studied and researched (Bernstein, 1991; Ferris, 1993; Gann, 2001; Kettner and Martin, 1996; Saidel, 1991; Salamon, 1987; Smith and Grønbjerg, 2006; Smith and Lipsky, 1993; Van Slyke and Roch, 2004; Young, 1999); see also Chapter 22 of this volume. Charitable nonprofit organizations that have IRS section 501(c)(3) tax status also contract out for services and collectively spend an estimated more than $100 billion annually; however this activity has not attracted the same attention from researchers and scholars.[1]

Scholars and practitioners suggest that nonprofits are increasingly hiring independent contractors or outsourcing functions as a means to improve the management of their organizations and remain competitive (Winkler, 2000; Ben-Ner, 2004). There is some evidence of the types of nonprofits contracting for services, the types of services, the costs for those services, the motivations behind contracting and what implications this activity has for nonprofit organizations. One example is technology's influence on the health subsector, such as recent developments in electronic medical record (EMR) software that enables real-time entering of patient data and reduces the outsourcing of billing functions (Lowes, 2003). The Voluntary Hospitals of America 2007 survey reported that 63 percent of their respondents planned to invest in EMR (VHA, 2007). Another example is recent legal proceedings around telemarketing for fundraising conducted by the Illinois Supreme Court, The US Supreme Court and the Federal Trade Commission (FTC), resulting in the amendment of the Telemarketing Sales Rule in 2003 (FTC, 2003). There are other examples of nonprofits contracting for services, some of which will be briefly discussed at the end of the next section.

This chapter serves to broaden our understanding of the characteristics of nonprofit contracting through analyzing the existing research, conducting an exploratory study, and suggesting how researchers and scholars can fill the existing gaps in our knowledge for this topic. 'Contracting' is defined as 'the design and implementation of contractual relationships between purchasers and suppliers' (Domberger, 1998, p. 12). 'Outsourcing' typically refers to contracting out externally for functions that have been typically performed internally; however, these terms are occasionally used interchangeably to reflect their use in the literature and to simplify content for the reader.

What we think we know: areas of general agreement from previous research

Contracting for services has existed in the for-profit and nonprofit sectors for many years, and there are indications that this activity has grown substantially, particularly in the for-profit sector, over the past few decades in the USA. Dun & Bradstreet Information Services reported that there were approximately 146 000 companies that provided outsourced services in 1994, a 65 percent increase from 88 000 and a 24 percent increase in total employees from 1989 (Information Services, 1994). A 1996 survey of 619 CEOs of businesses conducted by the American Management Association revealed that 94 percent of those businesses outsourced at least one activity with an average of nine activities each (AMA Survey in Greaver, 1999). All of the 600 North American members of the International Facility Management Association surveyed in 2000 indicated that they outsourced services that either required skills not internally available or cost effective (Monroe, 2000). The market for outsourcing finance and accounting has increased 45 percent from 2005 to 2007 (Krell, 2007).

A Bureau of Labor Statistics report projected that employment in the professional and business services sector would increase by approximately 4 092 000 jobs from 2006 to 2016. This is the largest projected increase of any industry sector that 'is led by providers of administrative support services and consulting services' (Bureau of Labor Statistics, 2007, p. 34). The second-largest projected growth is in the health care and social assistance sector, which is expected to increase by approximately 4 049 000 jobs. Educational services are projected to increase by approximately 1 412 000 jobs, ranking as the third-largest increase in employment (ibid.). The growth in these three areas is being spurred by specific industries,[2] all of which have implications for nonprofit contracting, particularly in the health and education subsectors.

A nonprofit organization may outsource its functions to a company, hire a direct provider of services, or contract with consultants who may assist with strategic planning; all these are considered 'independent contractors' by the Internal Revenue Service (IRS). The IRS uses this term for Part II of Schedule A on the 990 tax return form in Part II-A, entitled 'Compensation of the Five Highest Paid Independent Contractors for Professional Services' and Part II-B, entitled 'Compensation of the Five Highest Paid Independent Contractors for Other Services'. For both 'professional' and 'other' listings, charitable nonprofits must list the name and address of each contractor, the type of services contracted for, and the compensation for each of the top five contractors that were paid more than $50 000 each. They also must indicate the number of additional contractors beyond the top five compensated for more than $50 000.

Nonprofit organizations' decisions as to whether to contract for services or produce them internally may be driven by a single factor or any combination of multiple factors including price, required capital for infrastructure, issues concerning core functions, industry standards, government regulation, the organization's boundaries, economies of scale, specialization, timing, flexibility, cost reduction and flexible external control. There are costs, risks and benefits involved in the contracting process. If price is a significant factor that influences this activity, we should remember that costs are incurred in determining the price for purchasing goods and/or services and for determining who provides them. There are also costs related to the development, negotiation, completion, monitoring and evaluation of contracts, all of which are known as 'transaction costs' (Williamson, 1996). We can argue that these costs may be necessary precautionary measures to deal with issues driven by the contracting environment. They include information asymmetry, incomplete contracting, bounded rationality, and the potential results of unfulfilled promises and other contracting hazards due to the opportunism and exploitation of these issues by contractors.

Contractors seek to earn a profit while the purchasers of their goods or services desire to receive the best value for their money from the contractual agreement. To the non-profit purchaser's desires we can implicitly add the impact on the organization's work towards their mission, and the pressures to utilize resources efficiently and effectively while held in the public trust as tax-exempt organizations. These objectives, combined with the agency problem of trust, require that contractual relationships be monitored. 'Monitoring costs' become an ongoing concern once a contract is agreed upon between the purchaser and provider of services. Such costs involve observing, measuring and attempting to control the behavior of the contractor with operating rules, budget restrictions and compensation incentives (Jensen and Meckling, 1976). Monitoring externally produced goods or services is typically more challenging than monitoring in-house production. This is especially the case when an organization does not have adequate criteria for monitoring the function when it was performed internally or if the function is new to the organization and no criteria have been established at all, as for a highly specialized function.

One primary issue of trust lies in the contractor's avoidance of fulfilling the contract's components in an attempt to save their costs, and these actions can easily go undetected by the purchaser of their services (Domberger, 1998). Ben-Ner reminds us, however, that 'Contracts can be a fairly good substitute for trust because they provide remedies in the event of breach of the terms of the contract' and he also points out that the 'purchaser and supplier depend on each other to varying degrees' (2004, p. 77). We can conclude that monitoring is important for reducing agency problems, ensuring fulfillment and preventing breach of contract. It is important to remember that a nonprofit's staff time spent monitoring a contract represents an actual cost in terms of their salary or wages, as well as an opportunity cost for how they would normally be using their time.

There are other costs that may be less obvious to the contracting process. A 'loss of skills' can result from an organization contracting out its core functions and along with that can be a 'loss of organizational knowledge' (Domberger, 1998). These costs can have an impact on organizational learning, which some suggest is important for an organization to remain viable and competitive in today's environment (Schwandt and Marquardt, 2000; Senge, 1990). In a highly competitive and rapidly changing environment organizational learning must occur quickly and be sufficient to match or be greater than the change outside the organization (Schwandt and Marquardt, 2000) and in a way that can sustain its mission and purpose (Dym and Hutson, 2005).

Due diligence for contracting involves assessing potential risk, which is an inherent part of any contractual agreement. This process should be a component of a nonprofit organization's overall risk management (see Chapter 11). Three main categories of risk within the contracting context are *operational* for items such as meeting deadlines, responding to changes in service parameters, and support from the organization's leadership; *technological* for the organization's ability to adapt to new technologies; and *relationship*, which includes expectations for service delivery and the impact on staff (Brown and Wilson, 2005). Issues of risk should not be separated from the costs or benefits of contracting and should be part of the decision as to whether to contract for services.

One area of risk that can be overlooked is determining whether a person hired to perform a service is an employee or an independent contractor. The inability to make this distinction may have legal ramifications with one or more agencies, including the IRS, the state's unemployment and workers compensation insurance agencies, the state tax department and the US Department of Labor (Fishman, 1997). Determining the status of the person hired can be difficult due to the ambiguities and inconsistencies of existing laws, and the common law and economic reality tests used to make this determination. Courts have decided on these types of cases inconsistently by choosing different criteria to determine the level of economic dependence on the hiring firm. They have included the skills required to perform the work, the amount of the worker's investment in facilities and equipment, and the duration of the working relationship. In conclusion, this fine line suggests that nonprofit organizations hire an attorney to be better equipped to make this distinction, resulting in another transaction cost that is justified by this risk.

A holistic approach has been suggested to managing risks with outsourcing such as the enterprise risk management (ERM) process (Juras, 2007). The framework for this process includes four categories of risk:

- strategic, which concerns the entity's achievement of its overall mission and goals;
- operational, which addresses the entity's use of people, processes, assets, and technology to achieve its objectives;
- financial/reporting, which emphasizes the reliability of the entity's financial statements and reports; and
- compliance, which focuses on the laws and regulations. (Juras, 2007, p. 45)

This process also looks at the objective, or why an organization is deciding to outsource; what it is deciding to outsource; who are the key stakeholders involved and how they will be impacted; how the outsourcing process will be implemented and measured; where the vendor and the process will take place; and when the process will take place (Juras, 2007). This holistic and strategic approach can help determine the broader impact on the organization and help the organization ensure that outsourcing is 'done in a way that does not harm the trust that its customers and other stakeholders place in it' (Ben-Ner, 2004, p. 81).

There are several benefits an organization can reap from contracting for services. There can be the flexibility of adjusting production and the size of the organization at a lower cost and faster rate (Domberger, 1998; Ben-Ner, 2004). Cost savings can result from eliminating start-up costs, economies of scale, lower administrative costs and other means. Nonprofits can also realize an improved service delivery to their consumers through a contractor's participation in their core functions or through indirect participation which allows them to focus more on, and utilize more resources for, their core functions. Organizational transformation can also be a benefit when contracting for services brings in new technologies, areas of production or service, new innovations or when it opens up new markets (Greaver, 1999).

Examples of nonprofit contracting activity
There are many examples that serve to support the aforementioned reasons why nonprofits contract for services. Some of them represent a specific reason while others contain multiple reasons for contracting. For example, health organizations have been outsourcing billing and collections to reduce costs, avoid the complex bureaucracy of the health insurance environment, improve performance, enhance quality control and

enable more focus on core functions (Simms, 2005); or serve as a stop-gap measure for organizations lacking the infrastructure (Lowes, 2003).

A growing trend in the contracting for financial management services has resulted from nonprofits realizing the similarities between financial statements and accounting procedures in the for-profit and nonprofit sectors as promoted by the Financial Accounting Standards Board (Kahan, 2000). One example is McGladrey Contract Business Services (MCBS), which has handled the day-to-day accounting services for the Girl Scouts of Chicago, YWCA of Metropolitan Chicago, and the Adler Planetarium and Science Museum. Firms such as MCBS can in effect serve in various capacities such as chief financial officer, managing payroll, accounts receivable, accounts payable or the entire accounting department.

Another reason for increased contracting for financial management has been the recent growth of donor-advised funds and venture philanthropy within the world of community foundations, and the increased activity in endowments by colleges and universities (Fremont-Smith, 2004). This has resulted in hiring firms such as Fidelity Investments and Merrill Lynch, especially when boards of nonprofits or investment committees do not have the knowledge or skills to make the best choices for such investments and/or may choose to focus more on oversight (Fremont-Smith, 2004; Galloway, 2005). Relinquishing investment decisions to a contracted investment adviser does not absolve a nonprofit organization from overseeing the legal responsibilities of such investments, acting prudently, and exercising reasonable care when assessing potential investments and their risk according to the Uniform Management of Institutional Funds and Uniform Prudent Investor Acts (Guenthner et al., 2005). There have been cases where investments have not complied with these laws (ibid.); and the Senate Finance Committee has considered requiring organizations to disclose investment information so that their stakeholders are aware where funds are invested and they can determine whether this activity is consistent with the mission.

The emergence of the Sarbanes–Oxley Act and a renewed focus on stewardship and accountability has elevated the importance of auditors. A study conducted by Tate in 2003 of approximately 16 000 nonprofit organizations found that changes in an organization's revenue mix regarding government grants and other contributions influenced an organization's decision to change auditors (Tate, 2004). Management reputation was also a significant factor as nonprofit organizations receiving unfavorable audits were more likely to change auditors. Larger nonprofits were more likely to change auditors, resulting in a reduced auditor fee. Nonprofits contracting with Big Five auditors (Accenture – formerly Arthur Andersen LLP, Deloitte & Touche LLP, Ernst & Young LLP, KPMG LLP and PricewaterhouseCoopers LLP) were less likely to change auditors (Tate, 2004).

The coverage of professional fundraisers, sometimes referred to as consultants, in the nonprofit literature would lead us to believe that fundraising is the most contracted service by nonprofit organizations. Their functions may include running campaigns, conducting feasibility studies, managing special events or other scenarios where the organization lacks the fund development staff or infrastructure. The 1995 Chronicle of Philanthropy study of 1105 of its subscribers indicated that 11.8 percent used professional fundraisers for creative services while 16.1 percent used them for telemarketing and 10.3 percent used them for direct mailing. A 1998 study of IRS Form 990 tax returns of 1540 nonprofit organizations revealed that only 8 percent of all respondents 'contracted with a professional fundraiser the previous year' (Hager et al., 2002, p. 320). The higher the total number of grant dollars raised, the higher percentage of nonprofits contracted with fundraisers.

Outsourcing has been and continues to be a strategic tool that health care executives use in attempting to maintain the quality of patient care while containing costs (Roberts, 2001; Shinkman, 2000). Over the past three decades, one of the most rapidly growing examples has been hospitals contracting for total management services that manage day-to-day operations of their facilities (Alexander and Lewis, 1984; Biggs et al., 1980). In 1994, 14.5 percent of general, nonfederal hospitals were contract managed (Zinn et al., 1997). A 2000 study revealed that approximately 33 percent of 796 nonprofit, multi-business health care firms were classified as 'contractors' (as opposed to core service or mission-based providers) that contracted for non-core activities with physician groups (Inamdar, 2007). Reasons for contracting out that hospitals typically reference include increased management expertise, reduced costs, specialized services, personnel, joint purchasing and capital (Alexander and Lewis, 1984).

Higher education institutions have increasingly engaged in contracting to increase efficiency, reduce costs, improve services and remain competitive (Bekurs, 2007; Ferris, 1991; Moore, 2002; Palm, 2001; Savarese, 2003); and respond to calls for greater accountability (Schibik and Harrington, 2004). Some examples include George Mason University's 50 contracts totaling $30 million including the management of their 10 000-seat arena (Mercer, 1995); the University of Wisconsin–Madison contracting with Reebok for $9.1 million and the University of Michigan contracting with Nike for over $20 million for athletic apparel (Wright et al., 2007); and Salt Lake Community College contracting their IT services to CollegisEduprise for $26.5 million (Olsen, 2002).

A 2000 study by Wertz that looked at outsourcing in approximately 130 higher education institutions indicated that vending, food services, laundry services, bookstores and concessions were the top five most outsourced functions (Wertz in Bekurs, 2007). The American Association of Collegiate Registrars and Admissions Officers' (AACRAO) 2001 survey of 423 nonprofit institutions (52 percent private and 44 percent public) revealed 'extremely or very important' reasons for contracting that included staffing constraints, budget constraints, enhancing service and access to technology. The most frequently cited benefits were efficiency, increased productivity, improved service for students, alleviating the need to purchase new equipment, better use of their budget and allowing more time to be spent with students (AACRAO, 2001).

Colleges and universities have also been contracting out for course instruction for many years through the hiring of part-time or adjunct instructors (Schibik and Harrington, 2004). This activity presents the challenge of less tangible results to monitor, in spite of student and department head evaluations, when we consider that part-time instructors may not have the time or resources to engage in the cutting-edge research of their area of specialty. It is important to also note that certain institutions have regulations for how many part-time faculty they can hire in lieu of their ratio to full-time, tenured faculty. The National Center for Education Statistics (NCES) reported that in 2003, 56.7 percent of instructional faculty and staff in US public and private, not-for-profit Title IV participating, degree-granting institutions were full-time while 43.3 percent were part-time (NCES, 2007).

Several universities in the late 1990s had their students express concerns about their institutions' supply chain management practices with athletic apparel companies engaged in unfair labor practices (Palm, 2001). The United Students Against Sweatshops (USAS) was founded in 1998 by two Duke University students and quickly became a national organization (Wright et al., 2007). Student protests and awareness campaigns resulted in Duke University joining the Worker Rights Consortium (WRC) and Notre Dame University hiring PricewaterhouseCoopers as independent monitors, establishing a code of conduct for its licensees, and overseeing factory work environments and practices. Student pressure influenced similar results at the University of Wisconsin at Madison, University of Michigan and University of Oregon. These experiences served as wake-up calls to institutions that license their products to be more proactive to ensure social responsibility in their supply chain management (Wright et al., 2007) and consider allowing student affairs representatives to have a voice in future decisions (Moore, 2002).

Arts organizations have been the subject of numerous research studies and discussion concerning their economic impact (Americans for the Arts, 2003; Cohen et al., 2003; Penne and Shanahan, 1987; Seaman, 2000; Sterngold, 2004). In spite of the ongoing debate on the accuracy and usefulness of these studies, there has not been much research or discussion around a more direct component of their economic impact when they contract for services. The 2005 Americans for the Arts' Arts & Economic Prosperity III study of 6080 nonprofit arts and culture organizations revealed an average total expense for contract staff of $14 691; average total payment to non-local artists (including taxes and benefits) of $63 562; and average total for contract services of $43 309, however the choices for respondents were limited to 'legal' and 'accounting' (Americans for the Arts, 2005).

The American Association of Museums (AAM) reported that 37 percent of the 806 museums surveyed contracted for flexibility by using seasonal staff (median of six each) to supplement their full-time paid staff and 93 percent used volunteers with a median of 60 for each museum (American Association of Museums, 2003). The Museum Financial Information (MFI) also reported that more than 80 percent of the museums had retail operations such as museum stores, gift stores or bookshops, with 4.8 percent of these museums contracting out for these services. Approximately 25 percent of the museums had on-site food services, of which 68 percent were contracted. The AAM also indicated that, for their 809 museums they had a median security expense of $51 156 and that 14.6 percent (compared to 14 percent in 2003) of them outsourced a median of three security personnel for this function (American Association of Museums, 2007).

What we do not know: areas of conflicting results and unexplored questions from previous research

Some researchers and practitioners indicate that more nonprofit organizations are utilizing outsourcing as a management tool (Billi et al., 2004; Gose, 2005; Kremic et al., 2006; Luman, 2006; Menachemi et al., 2007; Vaughn, 1997); however, documented case studies of nonprofit organizations contracting for services that might confirm this claim are sparse. Interest in the activity of nonprofit organizations contracting out for services prompts several inadequately or unexplored research questions:

- Does the size (total revenue) and subsector (service delivery) of the organization influence this activity in any way?

- In what circumstances do nonprofits contract out for input goods and services rather than produce them in house?
- What factors explain such contracting behavior and what are the implications for the functioning and management of such organizations?
- How does this activity factor into a nonprofit organization's overall accountability?
- Are the issues of trust, agency theory and opportunism as prevalent in the nonprofit sector as the literature might indicate?
- How satisfied are nonprofit purchasers of services with their contractors? How commonly is performance measurement used to assess these services? How often do contractors default on their agreements with nonprofits?
- How often do nonprofits realize and exploit the benefits of contracting?
- Are leaders of nonprofits aware of transaction costs as referenced by the literature, and if so are they tracked?
- Are leaders of nonprofits aware of the risks involved in contracting and are they part of the organization's risk management?
- What role does the board of directors play in their organization's contracting process?
- What role do other volunteers play in the contracting process?
- Are there relationships between nonprofit contracting and nonprofit enterprise? If so, what are the characteristics, dynamics, costs and benefits of such relationships?

Why there are gaps in our knowledge: the relative roles of theory, data availability and empirical analysis
Some scholars and practitioners suggest that the trends for outsourcing in the for-profit sector have impacted such activity in the nonprofit sector (Winkler, 2000; Ben-Ner, 2004). Recent changes to the nonprofit sector have also influenced what appears to be increasing activity in outsourcing, such as the growth of the sector, financial reporting changes, the desire to focus more on mission and the increasing call for accountability. A review of IRS 990 forms indicates there is substantial contracting activity in the nonprofit sector. However, the details necessary to draw definitive conclusions about such activity are lacking.

Subsector umbrella organizations, such as those for the arts, have conducted a limited number of studies and have included only a few types of services. These studies have also been limited to their member organizations, resulting in selection bias. National studies of nonprofit contracting are very sparse as opposed to those conducted by various organizations for for-profit contracting. The results of answering unexplored questions remaining from existing research on nonprofit contracting include, but are not limited to, trend data; national representative samples; accurate dollars spent on those additional contracts over $50 000 and under $50 000 which are not tracked; and segregated data by subsector, geographic location, revenue and other characteristics.

What must be done to further our knowledge: suggestions for extending the literature
The existing literature on this topic provides a foundation for answering these questions. This study seeks to build upon this foundation and provide exploratory, descriptive

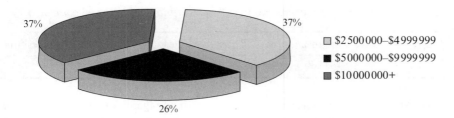

Figure 12.1   Percentage of sample by total revenue (n = 1000)

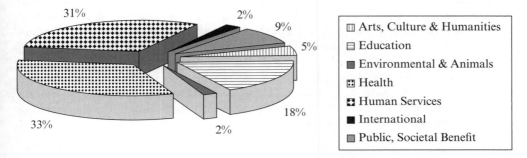

Figure 12.2   Percentage of sample by subsector (n = 1000)

information that can help answer questions, fill knowledge gaps and establish a future research agenda for this topic. A random sample of Form 990 IRS tax returns from 1000 nonprofit organizations, for their fiscal years ending in 2006, was drawn from a population of 36 316 organizations contained in GuideStar's database. This population comprised the total number of organizations represented in the 50 United States and District of Columbia, from the top three total revenue levels[3] and seven subsectors of Arts, Culture and Humanities; Education; Environment and Animals; Health; Human Services; International; and Public, Societal Benefit listed in GuideStar.

The sample was stratified by total revenue and subsector as shown in Figures 12.1 and 12.2. Religious organizations, organizations raising funds for single organizations, those whose 990 forms were unavailable, and those whose only available 990s were from fiscal years ending prior to 2006 were excluded.

Information on each organization's contracting activity is obtained from Schedule A, Part II-A of the 990 tax form, entitled 'Compensation of the Five Highest Paid Independent Contractors for Professional Services' and Part II-B, entitled 'Compensation of the Five Highest Paid Independent Contractors for Other Services'. This section is found on page 2 of Schedule A. The types of goods and services contracted for were largely driven by what the organizations indicated in this section of their 990 tax form. If the types were not specified by the nonprofit organization, the organization contracted with was researched on the Internet to determine the type of goods or services. If the type could not be determined it was placed in the 'Other' category or in the case of consultants, it was placed in the 'Consultant (non-specified)' category. If more than one contract existed for a type of service, those amounts were added and entered as an organization's total amount for that service.

Table 12.1   Calculation of lower- and upper-bound estimates for 'other' contracts

No. of 'other'	Lowest amount in top 5	Lower-bound estimate	Upper-bound estimate
5	$143 560	$50 001 × 5 = $250 005	$143 559 × 5 = $717 795

Some organizations contracted for more than five engagements above $50 000. This number was entered by the organization next to where the form reads 'Total number of contractors receiving more than $50,000 for professional services' or 'Total number of contractors receiving over $50,000 for other services'. This number is used to calculate the lower-bound estimate of additional contractors by multiplying that number by $50 001 and the upper-bound estimate by multiplying the number by the lowest amount contracted for minus one. These calculations are illustrated in Table 12.1.

The second phase of this study comprised interviews with representatives of five nonprofit organizations randomly selected from the sample that were key stakeholders in their organization's contracting process. These were intended to acquire some insight into their organization's contracting process, their motivations for contracting out, and their organizational context for such decisions.

Results – entire sample

The 1000 organizations in this study had an aggregate income of $27.6 billion, expenses of $25.9 billion, and an excess of $1.7 billion for their fiscal years ending in 2006. Approximately 53 percent of the organizations in this sample contracted for at least one engagement worth more than $50 000. The lower-bound estimated averages for the sample were about $1.8 million, comprising 5.6 percent of total expenses while the upper-bound estimated averages were $9.8 million, comprising 7.4 percent of total expenses. The median for both estimates was skewed downward to about $60 000, based on 47 percent not having any reported contracted expenses over $50 000.

Construction led all services in the total amount of dollars spent and the percentage of organizations in the sample contracting for it, as shown in Tables 12.2 and 12.3.

We see, however, in Table 12.4 that construction, which is typically a big-ticket item for nonprofit organizations, ranks sixth in the total average cost per organization for those services. General medical services ranked second in total dollars spent and second in the total average cost per organization (after the outlier of one organization contracting for product development).

Results – by total revenue and subsector

The results of the sample are broken up by total revenue and subsector in Tables 12.5 and 12.6. The lower-bound estimated totals were positively correlated to the total revenue at 0.594 while the upper-bound estimated totals were positively correlated to the levels of income at 0.443 (both significant at the 0.01 level, 2-tailed) using the Pearson correlation.

The subsectors represented in this study are Arts, Culture & Humanities (A,C&H), Education (E), Environment & Animals (E&A), Health (H), Human Services (HS), International (I), and Public, Societal Benefit (P,SB). These abbreviated codes are used

Table 12.2   Top ten services contracted for by total dollars

Rank	Service	Total $ contracted	% of total LB $*
1	Construction	$279 184 064	15.7
2	General medical services	$268 336 961	15.1
3	Food	$101 722 374	5.7
4	Research	$77 663 116	4.4
5	Physicians	$42 067 281	2.4
6	Operations management	$34 148 850	1.9
7	Architects	$33 693 367	1.9
8	Employee Benefits	$32 412 347	1.8
9	Legal counsel	$28 085 801	1.6
10	Publications	$24 146 387	1.4

Note: * Lower bound estimated total for entire sample.

Table 12.3   Top ten most frequent services contracted for by percent of organizations

Rank	Service	% of organizations contracted
1	Construction	10.4
2	Legal counsel	9.3
3	Food	6.4
4	Architects	6.1
5	Facility maintenance / management	5.5
6	Auditing & Physicians (tie)	4.8
7	Temp. staffing & consultants, non-specified (tie)	4.7
8	Accounting	4.2
9	General medical services	4.1
10	Physical therapy / occupational therapy	3.9

to identify them below in Table 12.6. The highest amounts for each criterion within each subsector are in bold.

The high costs of health care can be seen in Table 12.6, as Health had the highest average lower- and upper-bound dollars spent on contracted services. Health's average lower-bound dollar amount was 57 percent higher and its upper-bound average was 123 percent higher than the next-highest subsector, Public, Societal Benefit. This is consistent with general medical services being the second-most expensive service per organization and 43 percent higher than the next service type, the highest difference of any service category in the top ten, with the exception of the outlier for product development.

Table 12.7 indicates that construction, legal counsel, and food were the top three most contracted services for the entire sample. These services tend to be highly specialized and they cut across all subsectors. Fundraising consultants were the third-most contracted service for the Arts, Culture & Humanities and Environment & Animals and, combined, they accounted for one-third of all contracted in the sample. This raises the questions of

Table 12.4   Top ten services contracted for by total average cost per organization

Rank	Service	Total average cost per organization ($)
1	Product development*	18 197 879
2	General medical services	6 544 804
3	Research	4 568 419
4	Dialysis	3 457 485
5	Curriculum/Course development	2 791 574
6	Construction	2 684 462
7	Publications	2 682 932
8	Equipment maintenance	2 517 977
9	Teachers/Faculty	2 324 857
10	Radiation therapy	2 031 219

Notes: * This is an outlier, as one organization contracted for this amount in this category. It is interesting to note that only 31 organizations contracted for fundraising-related services worth more than $50 000 each, accounting for 3.1 percent of the organizations in the sample, with 21 hiring a fundraising consultant, 5 hiring a telemarketer, and 5 hiring a direct mail provider. This might indicate that some of the controversy around hiring professional fundraisers tends to attract more attention and/or that the majority of contracted fundraising services are under $50 000 each.

Table 12.5   Contracting expenses by subsector

Total revenue ($)	No. & % organizations spending > $50 000		LB mean $ & avg. % of total expenses		UB mean $ & avg. % of total expenses	
2 500 000–4 999 999	106	28.7%	$129 367	3.9%	$130 760	4.0%
5 000 000–9 999 999	126	49.6%	386 960	6.0%	409 716	6.1%
10 000 000+	296	78.5%	4 322 778	6.9%	25 655 457	11.6%
All	528	52.8%	$1 775 712	5.6%	$9 824 426	7.4%

Table 12.6   Contracting expenses by subsector

Subsector	No. & % organizations spending > $50 000		LB mean $ & avg. % of total expenses		UB mean $ & avg. % of total expenses	
A,C&H	29	59.2%	$1 011 585	**14.4%**	$1 237 682	**15.4%**
E	86	46.5%	1 614 754	5.3%	9 084 293	7.6%
E&A	14	**66.7%**	693 010	6.4%	742 389	6.6%
H	**207**	62.0%	**3 236 378**	6.6%	**20 994 278**	10.9%
HS	132	43.9%	491 430	3.3%	717 237	4.0%
I	6	28.6%	48 512	0.3%	48 512	0.3%
P,SB	54	60.7%	2 055 861	6.0%	9 422 459	11.3%
All	528	52.8%	$1 775 712	5.6%	$9 824 426	7.4%

Table 12.7   Top three most frequently contracted services (percent of organizations)

Subsector	1 – Service	%	2 – Service	%	3 – Service	%
A,C&H	Architects	24.5	Construction	22.4	Fundraising consultants & Legal counsel (tie)	10.2
E	Construction	16.2	Legal Counsel	11.9	Food	10.3
E&A	Facility mgmt & legal counsel (tie)	19.0	Construction	14.3	Fundraising consultants; Landscaping; Auditing; Printing; Project management (tie)	9.5
H	Physicians	12.9	Construction & General medical services (tie)	9.9	Temporary staffing	9.3
HS	Construction	7.0	Legal counsel	6.6	Accounting; Food; Physical / Occupational therapy; Consultants (non-specific) (tie)	5.0
I	Legal counsel & management consultants (tie)	9.5	Marketing consultants; graphic design; computer services; accounting; auditing; project management; consultants (non-specific) (tie)			4.8
P,SB	Consultants (non-specific) & Legal counsel (tie)	13.5	Auditing	9.0	Facility management & Accounting (tie)	7.9
All	Construction	10.4	Legal counsel	9.3	Food	6.4

whether those subsectors are more likely to contract for those services due to their constituencies or because they are less likely to have fundraising staff.

Results – Interviews
Interviews were conducted January through February of 2008, with representatives of five organizations randomly drawn from the sample. The results are shown in Boxes 12.1 through 12.5. The actual individual and organizational identities remain confidential; however, the characteristics of each organization are discussed so we can get a sense of their influence on the process.

Sheila, Y-Health's Vice President of Fund Development, emphasized the importance of having both parties understand what a contracted relationship is. She prefers contractors

---

BOX 12.1   Y-HEALTH

Respondent:	Sheila, Vice President of Fund Development
History:	Founded in 1940s as part of national organization that has existed for almost 100 years
Subsector:	Health
Finances (2006):	$3.2 million total revenue
	$3.4 million expenses
	−$200 000 (deficit)
Dollars spent on contracting:	$80 000 (2.3 percent of total expenses)
	4–8 contracts below $50 000 (estimated)
Types of services contracted:	Temporary staffing
Contract acquisition:	Established through personal contacts, mostly from the board of directors

Contract management:

- Vetting process – reference and background checks
- Decision process – funneled through operations, executive director and board president with board's final decision
- Performance – monitoring process is informal and decentralized among departments
- Determination for renewal – budget adherence

Costs:

- Transaction costs – minimal due to contracting history and executive director's previous background in HR functions
- Other costs / percentage of total expenses – not tracked

Core functions:	Services to ensure equal learning and employment opportunities for people with disabilities. Contracted for service providers in 2005 to add full-time staff
Motivations:	Flexibility – to accommodate increases and decreases in staffing needs depending on the time of the year

---

that are experienced not just in their field but also in contracting in general. Knowing boundaries between the organization and the contractor is an important part of Y-Health's process. Sheila stated that contracting is a part of Y-Health's overall accountability, as the board and staff are ultimately responsible for the stewardship of resources they acquire from public and private sources. She also felt that the services contracted for directly impact the organization's work towards its mission, and that the organization was satisfied

BOX 12.2   POSITIVE PAYOFFS FOR YOUTH (PPY)

Respondent:	Craig, Executive Director
History:	Founded in 1990s to help children in an urban, predominantly African American community
Subsector:	Human services
Finances (2006):	$21.8 million total revenue
	$20.2 million expenses
	$1.6 million
Dollars spent on contracting:	$770 000 (3.8 percent of total expenses)
	3 contracts below $50 000
Types of services contracted:	Public relations, government relations, management consulting, program evaluation and training
Contract acquisition:	Minority vendors are preferred provided they meet selection criteria and clear the screening process; but no percentage quota. Non-minority contractors are suggested to subcontract with minority firms when feasible. Contracts are awarded depending on the service and potential contractors
Contract management:	

- Vetting process – initial screening by department heads. Proposal terms examined, past clients contacted, samples of past work requested, and PPY's budget examined
- Decision process – Executive Director makes final decision
- Performance – benchmarks tied to deliverables. A 30-day 'out clause' for both parties. Monitoring is decentralized and progress is reported to ED. Exception would be an organizational contract, which ED would monitor
- Determination for renewal – performance benchmarks, meetings with contractors and review of reports

Costs:	Transaction costs – staff time
Core functions:	Grant making and making sure the programs they support are impacting children as intended. ED states PPY would not contract out for those functions
Motivations:	Specialization – evaluation, market research. Cost savings – economies of scale. Objectivity – external evaluator

---

BOX 12.3   ASSOCIATED COMMUNITY FUND (ACF)

Respondent:	Bernie, Executive Director
History:	Founded in 1957 as part of national organization that has existed for approximately 120 years
Subsector:	Public, Societal Benefit
Finances (2006):	$3 million total revenue *$2.4 million expenses* $600 000
Dollars spent on contracting:	$150 000 (estimated) (6.3 percent of total expenses) All contracts below $50 000
Types of services contracted:	Bookkeeping, information technology, web master, video production, portfolio management for an endowment, building lease, copier maintenance
Contract acquisition:	Word-of-mouth referrals from their board, staff, or other local organizations
Contract management:	
	● Vetting process – informal and driven by relationships
	● Decision process – Executive Director makes final decisions except for high-level or long-term contracts which require the approval of ACF's board of directors
	● Performance – investment policy for the endowment; informal monitoring by Executive Director
	● Determination for renewal – satisfaction of contract terms, price
Costs:	Transaction costs – minimal staff time due to low level of activity and mostly short-term contracts
Core functions:	Raises funds through annual campaign and distributes to local nonprofit agencies. Contracting core function is unlikely
Motivations:	Specialization – IT, web master. Infrastructure – lacking capacity for internal production. Opportunity costs – freeing up staff to focus on core functions

---

with the performance of their current contractors. Y-Health tends to contract with people or organizations that understand their mission and/or have been personally impacted by their services. Sheila stated that this enthusiasm 'changes the relationship a little bit and it's not so cut and dry. There is now an element of passion in the relationship.'

BOX 12.4   BIG 'T' THEATER (BTT)

Respondent:	Jim, General Manager
History:	Founded in 1964
Subsector:	Arts, Culture & Humanities
Finances (2006):	$11.1 million total revenue
	$9.9 million expenses
	$1.2 million
Dollars spent on contracting:	$210 000 (estimated) (2.1 percent of total expenses)
	All six (estimated) contracts below $50 000
Types of services contracted:	Existing or touring productions, information technology, office supplies
Contract acquisition:	Networking within the arts community

Contract management:

- Vetting process – informal
- Decision process – initially decided by staff working in areas of contracted services and then finally decided by the general manager. Cost–benefit analyses conducted for make or buy decisions
- Performance – informally evaluated by staff using timeliness of the service delivery, perceived value of the service, ongoing costs, and incremental increases during the contract period as performance criteria
- Determination for renewal – satisfaction of contract terms, price

Costs:	Transaction costs – minimal staff time
Core functions:	Live theatrical entertainment which has been contracted for in the past
Motivations:	Specialization – External expertise. Opportunity costs – freeing up staff to focus on core functions

---

Overall, Craig is satisfied with the services from PPY's current contracts but emphasized they would be continuously be evaluated. He stated that with the changes in philanthropy around the focus on quality of programs, these relationships directly contribute to PPY's work towards their mission. He also believes the contracting process is a part of PPY's overall accountability because they are responsible for ensuring a transparent process. Craig added, 'There is also a responsibility that when we hire these contractors, we have overall improvement in the area where they focus on. So we have a fiscal responsibility and a program responsibility.'

Bernie indicated that contracting out for their core function was a remote possibility,

BOX 12.5   MINISTRIES FOR INTERNATIONAL HEALTH (MIH)

Respondent:	Bob, Director of Operations
History:	Founded in 1987 to support health ministries overseas
Subsector:	International
Finances (2006):	$2.7 million total revenue
	$2.4 million expenses
	$300 000
Dollars spent on contracting:	$800 000 (estimated) (33 percent of total expenses)
	All 32 (estimated) contracts below $50 000
Types of services contracted:	Allocating medical supplies, shipping and transportation
Contract acquisition:	Cooperative relationships and sharing information with 90 other faith-based organizations involving communication through e-mail list serves and at conferences.

Contract management:

- Vetting process – personal relationships and referrals from faith-based co-op organizations
- Decision process – based on specific needs of the health facilities overseas, cost, location of the items and shipping requirements
- Performance – quality of equipment, shipping, repairing, and overall fulfillment of the agreement are monitored
- Determination for renewal – satisfaction of contract terms, price

Costs:	Transaction costs – Bob's labor-intensive time for which MIH is considering charging a management fee
Core functions:	Funding specific projects that their partners overseas operate; collecting and shipping medical supplies and equipment; and recruiting health care providers to serve overseas. Core functions are regularly contracted
Motivations:	Specialization – equipment repair. Core functions – mission and contracting for core functions are linked

'We might do it at a low level . . . we might hire an event planner to do a special event, but we have not done that.' He is satisfied with the current contracted relationships but shared a past example of dissatisfaction. 'We had one web master at one time who we arranged a contract for. They made sure we fulfilled our obligations but then they backed off totally and they weren't responding to us, so we had to fire them.' Now they use their current web master when they need him and they are not locked into a monthly fee.

Bernie feels that ACF's contracted services contribute to the work towards their mission within the context of focusing on core functions, opportunity costs and specialization. 'Everything we have is based on our credibility, so I want to make sure we're doing things right . . . When I bring somebody else in it frees up our staff to dedicate time to doing things more related to our mission, such as a special event instead of dealing with these tax forms that an expert can knock off in an hour.' He also felt that managing the contracting process is a part of ACF's overall accountability because they're accountable to the IRS, those that left bequests for the endowment, campaign donors, member agencies and the community.

The profile information for the Big 'T' Theater (BTT), a Tony Award-winning theatre, is shown in Box 12.4. Their board's role in the contracting process is very limited, usually to only suggesting potential vendors. Jim, their general manager, believes that the contract management process is a part of BTT's overall accountability, especially with regard to relationships and their mission. He explained that without these contracted services performing artists would not have means to make a living and the theatre wouldn't have any performances.

One unusual example of a decision not to outsource a function is BTT's ticketing process. Jim explains that they decided to retain it in house 'because we feel the level of service is not the same, and we have found that is one of our competitive advantages – the level of customer service that people receive – by using our on-site ticketing process rather than a third party where extra fees are tacked on.' Jim added that the service is a big part of the patrons' experience with the theater, and it hasn't impacted accessibility because they can purchase tickets at the theater, over the phone or on line. Retaining control over a function that impacts patrons' relationships and overall experience with the theater drove that decision. Jim indicated that it has enabled BTT to track patrons' preferences and has contributed to return business.

Bob, MIH's Director of Operations, explains the basis for their contracting activity:

> If we're unable to find supplies, we will contact other organizations that are doing the same thing we are, especially with equipment . . . and we would negotiate the handling fees. MIH has received donations of equipment we are unable to handle for repair, so we have taken those items and forwarded them to other organizations, outsourced the refurbishment, have it sent back to us crated and ready to go to our partner overseas. We do that kind of outsourcing often.

If a health facility is looking for a surgical table, Bob's first task is to determine if he can procure one locally. He also determines if they have volunteers who can certify it, repair it, acquire the accessories and ensure it is in a shippable condition. 'For example, if I cannot find a table, I will call up Rick at company xyz, because that's his specialty. That's all he does and he does it well.' There have been instances when price was not the primary factor in the decision process, such as when grants came in from the Danish Mission, the

United Nations, the World Bank or some other donor. One example was the opening of a hospital in Liberia, where the funds were given to MIH so they could work the deals to acquire supplies.

Bob sees his role as an extended employee for the (overseas) hospital by collecting information for them, trying to find the best deal and providing it to the hospital to make the decision as the end user. The overseas hospitals are typically short-staffed, do not have good Internet connections and do not have access to the abundant health supply market in the USA. Bob also sees his role as a broker, negotiator and collaborator. MIH's board also has a role in this process, as they meet three times a year to review projects and shipments, and engage in general oversight. The executive committee meets every month to review requests, and sometimes has to approve some of the larger shipments before Bob is authorized to move forward to complete the transaction.

Bob indicated that MIH has to be a good steward of its donated funds and sees his function in trying to get the best deal as a big part of that stewardship. Bob sees this process as a calling and a core part of the organization's mission. He stated that dealing with firms that stand by their products is an important part of the process. One example he referenced was when a piece of equipment failed at a hospital in Tanzania and the supplier replaced it at no charge.

Limitations of this study
The limitations of this study serve to establish a future research agenda by emphasizing what must be done to contribute to the literature and expand our knowledge on this topic. The statistical analysis in this study was unidimensional. Future studies should incorporate a more comprehensive, multivariate analysis of contracting activity that incorporates total revenue, subsector, specialization-driven behavior and other factors to demonstrate their relationships to decisions for contracting and to each other. The size of the data sample and group of interviews should give caution to generalizing these conclusions about contracting in the nonprofit sector. A larger sample combined with more interviews or case studies would provide a more accurate representation of this activity. This study was limited to IRS Form 990 information available from 30 September 2007 to 16 January 2008. Many large universities' information was not available, indicating Education would have a larger presence.

Information on services contracted for less than $50 000 appears to be unavailable without a formal, primary research inquiry of nonprofit organizations. Further analysis of contracting activity for engagements under $50 000 would provide a broader and more accurate picture of this activity. Both large and small nonprofit organizations have contracts in this range and such an examination might reveal more accurate trends for this activity. We also do not have the exact amounts for the other services contracted beyond the top five, limiting the study to lower- and upper-bound estimates. Vague, generic terms such as 'professional services' used by organizations in the dataset required additional investigation via the Internet and subsequent subjectivity in determining the types of services. Lastly, not all organizations described services in a consistent manner.

We don't have an overall sense of whether contractors' services are meeting the expectations of their nonprofit customers, providing the promised deliverables, resulting in desired outcomes and contributing to the nonprofits' work towards their missions. This raises research questions worth investigating. How do nonprofit organizations typically find potential contractors? What motivated them to purchase services externally in lieu of providing them internally, and how to these factors match up with economic, sociological and psychological theory? Are nonprofit organizations aware of the transaction costs involved in their contracting process? If so, do they factor them into their decision-making process on whether to contract and do they track them over time? Contract management's role in nonprofit management prompts questions concerning performance measurement. What mechanisms, if any, do they have for evaluating their contractors' performance? Have contracted engagements contributed to the improvement of the management and overall performance of the organization? Nonprofit organizations that use their resources to contract for services include contract management as part of their overall accountability and stewardship. However, we are unsure of how many nonprofit organizations view their contracting activity in this regard. Are nonprofits conscious of how much contracting they engage in, what percentage comprises their total expenses, or concerned about resembling a for-profit, resulting from excess activity? Are the nonprofit organization's stakeholders, particularly donors and volunteers, aware that the organization they support contracts out for services? If so, do they care and how does this knowledge affect their relationship with the organization? How do *pro bono* services provided by law firms, health care consultants and other service providers factor into the contracting process? Are these free services managed by nonprofits in the way paid services are, and do they provide the same quality?

These issues collectively present contracting out for services as a valuable prospect for further research. The longitudinal tracking of a database (panel study) would provide helpful information to affirm or refute stated trends in the nonprofit contracting environment. Contract management can be a strategic management tool; however, we are not sure how many managers and leaders view it in this regard. Do they view their contracting efforts as strategic, tactical, stop-gap measures or a combination thereof? Should contract management, or at least a thorough understanding of it, be part of a nonprofit executive's responsibilities? If so, this presents educational opportunities for the 100+ graduate programs in nonprofit studies, as this topic can be included in leadership development and overall nonprofit management curriculums.

Why it matters and to whom: the relative importance of expanding our knowledge to practitioners, policy makers and scholars

The intention of this study is to raise the profile of the topic and help establish a future research agenda. With the proper mix of quantitative and qualitative research, nonprofits and their contractors can both acquire a deeper understanding of how they may work more effectively with each other. If nonprofit organizations are to be able to compete for resources and be accountable to their stakeholders, they must be effective and efficient stewards of resources. The following conclusions help serve as indicators for why this topic is relevant and important for practitioners, policy makers and scholars.

The diversity of the nonprofit sector is reflected in contracting for services   Laundry services, architects, physicians, food catering services, orchestra conductors and others represent a diversity of services contracted for by a diverse group of organizations. Some services, such as construction or auditing, cut across all subsectors while others are influenced by and predominant in a specific subsector.

Infrastructure, leadership and culture influence whether to contract out core functions   The decision to contract out core functions may be driven by economic reasons, the organization's environment and/or a particular business model, as in the case of hospitals contracting for physicians and nurses. Some of the case study interviews demonstrated examples of organizations contracting out their core functions for reasons of staffing, organizational purpose and service delivery. Other examples showed that some organizations would not contract out those functions, reflecting leadership and cultural influences.

Size (total revenue) matters   In the sample of 1000 organizations, there was a positive relationship between the size of the organization with respect to total revenue and the dollars spent on such services. As the total revenue amounts went up, so did the dollars spent on contracted services. This supports the theory that size, bureaucracy and economies of scale are driving factors behind decisions to purchase services externally. These substantial gaps might suggest there are psychological, organizational culture and infrastructure issues behind contracting decisions made by smaller organizations.

The healthcare environment drives Health's large presence in contracting for services   The presence of the Health subsector comprised 33 percent of all organizations with total revenue of $10 million or above, more than any subsector. Their organizations had the highest mean dollars spent on contracted services, 82 percent higher than the mean for all, skewing the entire sample's data upward. Health services typically cost more than those from any other subsector, and hospitals tend to be larger organizations, as 72 percent of the 25 largest organizations in the sample were hospitals, all with an income above $200 million. Hospitals have also adopted a model of contracting services that includes more of what might be considered core services, such as emergency departments, physicians etc., than any other subsector. Of the 126 organizations with a total estimated contracting expense of over $1 million, 50 percent came from Health organizations. This supports some of the literature that discusses the intense competition between hospitals and some that suggests nonprofit hospitals resemble for-profit hospitals in disguise.

Specialization has a role in organizations' decisions to contract for services   Examples of contracting for specialized services not typically performed internally include auditing, advertising, graphic design, radio and television production, legal counsel, architects, computer services, government relations, construction and others. Specialization also has a role in contracting with consultants, as 195 were hired from organizations in the sample, mostly for IT, marketing, fundraising and management consulting. Some examples of specialization were driven by the service delivery of a particular subsector, such as physicians, nurses and anesthesiology within Health; artists/performers within Arts, Culture & Humanities; research, curriculum development and teachers/faculty in Education; psychiatrists and case management in Human Services; and science consultants and environmental engineers in Environment & Animals.

There is substantial contracting activity for engagements less than $50 000   All five organizations interviewed indicated that they had current contracts below the $50 000 amount totaling between 49 and 54, with an average of five contracts each at this level. When we consider the number of these smaller contracts engaged by nonprofit organizations of all sizes, an analysis of these engagements would (1) substantially increase the total dollars spent on contracted services, (2) likely reveal other types of services that typically cost less and (3) provide further insight into the dynamics and trends for this activity.

Relationships play a role in the contracting process   A theme found in some examples in the literature as well as all five interviews was how relationships impacted the contracting process. Some organizations acquired contractors through relationships with board or staff. Some organizations conveyed that their relationship with their clients or customers was an important part of deciding what to contract for and who to contract from. Interorganizational relationships played a part when similar organizations used networking, references and personal recommendations as factors in deciding whom to contract with. Lastly, most of the organizations indicated that the relationships with their contractors were important for their credibility.

The entities nonprofits contract with are an extension of their organization   When nonprofit organizations contract for services, quite often the process is seamless – their stakeholders, especially consumers, are not aware of this relationship. Poor performance and illegal or unethical behavior by a contractor reflects directly on the nonprofit organization that has contracted for their services. The nonprofit organization's brand, reputation and credibility are at stake.

Concluding remarks

The contribution of this work to the field of nonprofit management and the study of philanthropy is the provision of exploratory, descriptive research on nonprofit organizations contracting for services. Contracting for services has performance, legal, social, economic, political and ethical implications for nonprofit organizations. As the call for accountability and competition for resources continue to intensify, nonprofits should be conscious of how they use resources for contracted services. Such activity contributes to their ability to be effective and efficient stewards of their resources, to be accountable to all stakeholders and ultimately to accomplish their goals as they strive to satisfy their missions. Contracting will continue to gain more attention, increase in importance, and to present opportunities for future research to expand our knowledge and impact policy.

Notes

1. Author's note: This estimate has been derived from the sample of 600 nonprofit organizations' Form 990 tax returns for fiscal year 2006 used in this study, which yielded a total lower-bound estimate of $1 424 592 950. Approximately 52 percent of the organizations in this sample contracted for at least $50 000 in their fiscal year ending in 2006, with a lower-bound estimated average of $2 378 285. The 36 316 organizations comprised in the seven subsectors and top three total revenue levels in GuideStar multiplied by this lower-bound average would yield a total of $86 369 768 060. Due to limitations of not knowing the amount of dollars used to hire the other contractors beyond the fifth listed of more than $50 000 each and those hired for less than $50 000 each, this estimate is conservative at best.
2. Bureau of Labor Statistics (2007), p. 37: 'Of the 20 industries projected to gain the most jobs, 8 relate to healthcare, social assistance, and education. These 8 industries are general medical and surgical hospitals; elementary and secondary schools; offices of physicians; colleges, universities, and professional schools; home healthcare services; services for the elderly and persons with disabilities; community care facilities for the elderly; and child daycare services. The employment gains in these industries reflect increasing demand for services from an aging population and rising enrollments in schools.'
3. GuideStar – http://www.guidestar.org.

References

Alexander, Jeffrey and Bonnie L. Lewis (1984), 'The financial characteristics of hospitals under for-profit and nonprofit contract management', *Inquiry*, **21**, 230–42.
American Association of Collegiate Registrars and Admissions Officers (AACRAO) (2001), 'Survey on

outsourcing in higher education', available at http://www.aacrao.org/pro_development/Outsourcing_
    Analysis.pdf.
American Association of Museums (2003), '2003 Museum Financial Information (MFI)', Washington, DC:
    American Association of Museums.
American Association of Museums (2007), '2006 Museum Financial Information (MFI)', Washington, DC:
    American Association of Museums.
Americans for the Arts (2003), 'Arts and economic prosperity: the economic impact of nonprofit arts organiza-
    tions and their audiences', National Report. Washington, DC: Americans for the Arts.
Americans for the Arts (2005), 'Arts & economic prosperity III: the economic impact of nonprofit arts and
    culture organizations and their audiences', available at http://www.americansforthearts.org/pdf/informa
    tion_resources/research_information/services/economic_impact/aepiii/national_report.pdf.
Bekurs, Gray (2007), 'Outsourcing student housing in American community colleges', *Community College
    Journal of Research and Practice*, **31** (8), 621–36.
Ben-Ner, Avner (2004), 'Outsourcing by nonprofit organizations', in Dennis R. Young (ed.), *Effective
    Economic Decision-Making by Nonprofit Organizations*, New York: The Foundation Center, pp. 67–82.
Bernstein, Susan R. (1991), *Managing Contracted Services in the Nonprofit Agency*, Philadelphia, PA: Temple
    University Press.
Bernstein, Susan R. (1991), 'Contracted services: issues for the nonprofit manager', *Nonprofit and Voluntary
    Sector Quarterly*, **20** (4), 429–43.
Biggs, Errol L., John E. Kralewski and Gordon D. Brown (1980), 'A comparison of contract-managed and
    traditionally managed nonprofit hospitals', *Medical Care*, **XVIII** (6), 585–96.
Billi, John E., Chih-Wen Pai and David A. Spahlinger (2004), 'Strategic outsourcing of clinical services:
    a model for volume-stressed academic medical centers', *Health Care Management REVIEW*, **29** (4),
    291–7.
Brown, Douglas and Scott Wilson (2005), *The Black Book of Outsourcing: How to Manage the Changes,
    Challenges, and Opportunities*, Hoboken, NJ: John Wiley & Sons.
Bureau of Labor Statistics (2007), 'Industry employment', *Occupational Outlook Quarterly*, available at http://
    www.bls.gov/opub/ooq/2007/fall/art03.pdf, 30-38.
Cohen, Randy, William Schaffer and Benjamin Davidson (2003), 'Arts and economic prosperity: the economic
    impact of nonprofit arts organizations and their audiences', *The Journal of Arts Management, Law and
    Society*, **33** (1), 17–31.
Domberger, Simon (1998), *The Contracting Organization: A Strategic Guide to Outsourcing*, New York:
    Oxford University Press.
Dym, Barry and Harry Hutson (2005), *Leadership in Nonprofit Organizations*, Thousand Oaks, CA: Sage
    Publications.
Federal Trade Commission (2003), 'Charities and for-profit telemarketers calling on their behalf', *Facts for
    Business: Complying with the Telemarketing Sales Rule*, available at http://www.ftc.gov/bcp/edu/pubs/
    business/telemarketing/bus27.shtm.
Ferris, James (1991), 'Contracting and higher education', *The Journal of Higher Education*, **62** (1), 1–24.
Ferris, James (1993), 'The double-edged sword of social service contracting: public accountability versus non-
    profit autonomy', *Nonprofit Management and Leadership*, **3** (4), 363–76.
Fishman, Stephen (1997), *Hiring Independent Contractors: The Employer's Legal Guide*, Berkeley, CA: Nolo
    Press.
Fremont-Smith, Marion R. (2004), 'Investment and expenditure strategies', in Dennis R. Young (ed.), *Effective
    Economic Decision-Making by Nonprofit Organizations*, New York: The Foundation Center, pp. 101–20.
Galloway, Christine K. (2005), 'The case for outsourcing asset management', *The Chronicle For Philanthropy*,
    17 (20), 4–5, 26–7.
Gann, Nigel (2001), 'Toward a contract culture', in J. Steven Ott (ed.), *Understanding Nonprofit Organizations:
    Governance, Leadership and Management*, Boulder, CO: Westview Press, pp. 247–55.
Gose, Ben (2005), 'The companies that colleges keep', *Chronicle of Higher Education*, **51** (21), B1–B11.
Greaver, Maurice F. (1999), *Strategic Outsourcing, A Structured Approach to Outsourcing Decisions and
    Initiatives*, New York: American Management Association Publications.
Guenthner, Robert L., Kathleen Nilles and Sheldon E. Steinbach (2005), 'Investment policies are not optional',
    Chronicle of Philanthropy, **17** (20), B24–B25.
Hager, Mark, Patrick Rooney and Thomas Pollack (2002), 'How fundraising is carried out in US nonprofit
    organizations', *International Journal of Nonprofit and Voluntary Sector Marketing*, **7** (4), 311–24.
Inamdar, S. Noorein (2007), 'Examining the scope of multibusiness health care firms: implications for strategy
    and financial performance', *Health Services Research*, **42** (4), 1691–717.
Information Services (1994), 'Outsourcing is everywhere', *CFO Magazine*, **10** (12), 23.
Jensen, Michael C. and William H. Meckling (1976), 'Theory of the firm: managerial behavior, agency costs
    and ownership structure,' *Journal of Financial Economics*, **3** (4), 305–60.

Juras, Paul (2007), 'A risk-based approach to identifying the total cost of outsourcing', *Management Accounting Quarterly*, **9** (1), 43–50.

Kahan, Stuart (2000), 'Outsourcing nonprofit's financials', *Practical Accountant*, **33** (5), 53–6.

Kettner, Peter M. and Lawrence L. Martin (1996), 'The impact of declining resources and purchase of service contracts on private, nonprofit agencies', *Administration in Social Work*, **20** (3), 21–38.

Krell, Eric (2007), 'Finance and accounting outsourcing – making an informed decision', *CMA Management*, **81** (7), 38–40.

Kremic, Tibor, Oya Icmeli Tukel and Walter O. Rom (2006), 'Outsourcing decision support: a survey of benefits, risks, and decision factors', *Supply Chain Management: An International Journal*, **11** (6), 467–82.

Lowes, Robert (2003), 'Outsource billing? Here's how', *Medical Economics*, **80** (10), 30–39.

Luman, R. Lyle (2006), 'Developing a strategic contracting strategy in an integrated delivery system', *Journal of Healthcare Management*, **51** (3), 203–10.

Menachemi, Nir, Jeffrey Burkhardt, Richard Shewchuk, Darrell Burke and Robert G. Brooks (2007), 'To outsource or not to outsource: examining the effects of outsourcing IT functions on financial performance in hospitals', *Health Care Management Review*, **32** (1), 46–54.

Mercer, Joye (1995), 'Contracting out: colleges are turning to private vendors for more and more campus services', *Chronicle of Higher Education*, **41** (26), 37–8.

Monroe, Linda (2000), 'Strategic Outsourcing', *Buildings*, March, 8.

Moore, James E. (2002), 'Do corporate outsourcing partnerships add value to student life?' *New Directions for Student Services*, **100**, 39–50.

National Center for Education Statistics (2007), 'Supplemental table update May 2007', available at http://nces.ed.gov/pubs2002/2002163u2.pdf.

Olsen, Florence (2002), 'Fed up with delays, a president pushes to outsource technology operations', *Chronicle of Higher Education*, **48** (23), A41.

Palm, Richard L. (2001), 'Partnering through outsourcing', *New Directions for Student Services*, **96**, 5–11.

Penne, R. Leo and James L. Shanahan (1987), 'The role of arts in state and local economic development', in Anthony J. Radich and Sharon Schwoch (eds), *Economic Impact of the Arts: A Sourcebook*, Washington, DC: National Conference of State Legislatures, pp. 127–58.

Roberts, Velma (2001), 'Managing strategic outsourcing in the healthcare industry', *Journal of Healthcare Management*, **46** (4), 239–49.

Saidel, Judith R. (1991), 'Resource interdependence: the relationship between state agencies and nonprofit organizations', *Public Administration Review*, **51** (6), 543–53.

Salamon, Lester M. (1987), 'Partners in public service: the scope and theory of government-nonprofit relations', in Walter Powell (ed.), *The Nonprofit Sector: A Research Handbook*, New Haven, CT: Yale University Press, pp. 99–117.

Savarese, John (2003), 'To outsource or not to outsource . . .' *University Business*, **6** (1), 38–9.

Schibik, Timothy J. and Charles F. Harrington (2004), 'The outsourcing of classroom instruction in higher education', *Journal of Higher Education Policy and Management*, **26** (3), 393–400.

Schwandt, David R. and Michael J. Marquardt (2000), *Organizational Learning: From World-Class Theories to Global Best Practices*, New York: St Lucie Press.

Seaman, Bruce A. (2000), 'Arts impact studies: a fashionable excess', in Gigi Bradford, Michael Gary and Glenn Wallach (eds), *The Politics of Culture*, New York: New York Press, pp. 266–85.

Senge, Peter M. (1990), *The Fifth Discipline*, New York: Currency Doubleday.

Shinkman, Ron (2000), 'Outsourcing on the upswing', *Modern Healthcare*, **30** (37), 46–51.

Simms, Leigh Ann (2005), 'Outsource to upgrade?' *Medical Group Management Association Connexion*, **5** (8), 23–4.

Smith, Steven Ragbeth and Mark Lipsky (1993), *Nonprofits for Hire: The Welfare State in the Age of Contracting*, Cambridge, MA: Harvard University Press.

Smith, Steven Rathgeb and Kirsten Grønbjerg (2006), 'Scope and theory of government–nonprofit relations', in Walter Powell and Richard Steinberg (eds), *The Nonprofit Sector: A Research Handbook*, 2nd edn, New Haven, CT: Yale University Press, pp. 221–42.

Sterngold, Arthur H. (2004), 'Do economic impact studies misrepresent the benefits of arts and cultural organizations?', *The Journal of Arts Management, Law, and Society*, **34** (3), 166–87.

Tate, Stefanie L. (2004), 'Auditor change and auditor choice in nonprofit organizations', *Auditing: A Journal of Practice & Theory*, **26** (1), 47–70.

Van Slyke, David and Christine Roch (2004), 'What do they know, and whom do they hold accountable? Citizens in the government–nonprofit contracting relationship', *Journal of Public Administration Research and Theory*, **14** (2), 191–209.

Vaughn, Emmett T. (1997), 'Outsourcing in the nonprofit sector: a strategic approach to the challenges of growth and staffing', *Nonprofit World*, **15** (5), 50–53.

Voluntary Hospitals of America (VHA) (2007), '2007 Services Contracting Survey', available at https://www. vha.com/portal/server.pt/gateway/PTARGS_0_186177_0_0_18/scm_wp_LC0180607.pdf.

Williamson, Oliver E. (1996), *The Mechanics of Governance*, New York: Oxford University Press.

Winkler, Dennis (2000), 'Why are non-profit executives moving to outsourcing?' *Fund Raising Management*, **31** (3), 34–5.

Wright, Christine M., Michael E. Smith and Brian G. Wright (2007), 'Hidden costs associated with stakeholders in supply chain management', *Academy of Management Perspectives*, **21** (3), 64–82.

Young, Dennis R. (1999), 'Complementary, supplementary, or adversarial? A theoretical and historical examination of nonprofit–government relations in the United States', in Elizabeth T. Boris and C. Eugene Steuerle (eds), *Nonprofits and Government: Collaboration and Conflict*, Washington, DC: Urban Institute, pp. 31–67.

Zinn, Jacqueline S., Jose Proenca and Michael D. Rosko (1997), 'Organizational and environmental factors in hospital alliance membership and contract management: a resource dependence perspective', *Hospital and Health Services Administration*, **42** (1), 67–86.

13 Product diversification and social enterprise
Sharon M. Oster

Introduction: thinking about multi-product nonprofits

Consider a moderate-sized regional art museum. In addition to its standing collection, the museum likely hosts visiting exhibits. Almost all such museums have at least a small gift shop, many hold classes for students, and most have a café. Some museums run summer programs, while others rent out space. In this sense, the typical museum produces a variety of goods and services, just as do most nonprofit organizations in other sectors. Indeed, in the nonprofit sector, in contrast to the private sector, it is difficult to find a single-product firm, for reasons we shall explore. Given the ubiquity of multiple products in the sector, understanding the way in which the various products and services of the typical nonprofit complement and compete with one another is important. At the end of this chapter, we shall focus on the earned-income venture as a particular category of new product found in many nonprofits.

Before we look at the evolution and management of the multi-product nonprofit, it is helpful to think about some of the more general characteristics of nonprofit production. From the earliest work on the economics of the nonprofit structure, it has been recognized that the core mission product of most nonprofits is at least to some extent a collective or public good (James, 1983 and Schiff and Weisbrod, 1991). One of the features of public or collective goods is that a single unit of such good delivers simultaneous benefits to multiple people. The security advantages of a police force come to all those in a neighborhood, for example, rather than being consumed by any one individual. As a consequence, when we determine the benefits to society of a public good, we add the benefits that accrue to each of the affected individuals. Of course, in measuring the benefits of a strictly private good, we simply attend to the benefits of the single consumer of that good who, if all is well in the market, will be the person with the highest marginal value for that good.

What difference does it make in understanding the economics and management of a nonprofit to recognize the collective nature of its output? Again consider the typical museum, deciding whether or not to pull together a new exhibition on Assyrian pottery. What are the benefits from creating and opening this exhibition, benefits that will eventually be weighed against the costs? First there are the private benefits to the viewing audience, some of which can likely be monetarized via admission fees. Exposing that audience to the Assyrian culture may at the same time confer benefits on a small set of art-loving donors who value the fact that their community is being educated. The record of the exhibition will likely have value to the art historians who now see artifacts in a new way. Perhaps the exhibition stimulates a local teacher to develop a new lesson plan. A key feature of these benefits is that they are at least on the face of it non-rival in consumption. That is, the fact that art visitors derive private enjoyment from the exhibition in no way takes away from the value of that exhibition to donors, teachers or art historians.

Thus, even for a nonprofit that does only one thing – say curate exhibitions – multiple products are nevertheless simultaneously being produced: the exhibition *qua* entertainment; the exhibition *qua* historical record; the exhibition *qua* cultural developer. A nonprofit can potentially sell the same thing over and over again to different audiences attracted to different aspects of the same good or service. Thinking about these virtual multi-products of a nonprofit gives us insight into optimal levels of production of the nonprofit good, the optimal configuration of the good and the optimal financing of that good. We explore this feature of the nonprofit product portfolio in this chapter as well.

Broadening the product portfolio: strategic thinking and opportunistic behavior

The framework
Consider a nonprofit with an established mission and product portfolio. What might drive this organization to broaden the products and services it offers? In thinking about this issue, it is helpful to start with the core product of the nonprofit, focusing on the social value produced by that core product. Just as we return continuously to the question of how a new strategy affects shareholder value for a for-profit, so too we should think of actions in the nonprofit world insofar as they influence delivery of the core mission. Indeed, this is one argument some have made against the development of earned-income ventures of nonprofits – as tending to dilute mission (see Weisbrod, 1998).

How might a new product addition increase the value created by a nonprofit in delivering its core mission? In economic terms, the value of a good or service is the difference between a consumer's willingness to pay for that good or service and the sum of the opportunity costs of its production.[1] As we have already seen, in the case of collective goods produced by the nonprofit, because the good gives rise to multiple streams of benefits to multiple audiences, willingness to pay will be summed across those audiences to create an estimate of total value. Some of the benefits associated with these streams may be hard to measure, and many will be hard to capture, but conceptually value creation in the nonprofit sector is quite like value creation in the for-profit. Most particularly, a guiding principle of nonprofit production should be that unless it creates value, it is not worth doing. That you can create an event or deliver a service at costs greater than your patrons are willing to pay in and of itself entitles you to no largesse from donors or government. Instead, it is the fact that your service or event simultaneously delivers a second, third or fourth stream of benefits to other constituents both present and future that potentially makes the case for incremental support from those groups.

Recognition that value creation comes from the difference between willingness to pay and the sum of opportunity costs leads us directly to an understanding of why a nonprofit might want to introduce a new product or service. New products and services can increase the value created by the nonprofit either by raising the sum of the willingness to pay for the nonprofit's output or by lowering the costs of production. Note, again, the key here is not whether the new willingness to pay can necessarily be easily captured by the organization, to determine social value; we want only to know how much value is created.

In practice, willingness to pay is increased by new programs that more effectively accomplish the organization's mission. One way to do this is to reinvent programs to more closely match social and cultural changes, or take advantage of new technologies. Another way to raise willingness to pay is to develop programs that complement the original program on the demand side. In practice, such changes can have effects on the intensive and the extensive margins, both increasing willingness to pay of existing audiences for goods and services as well as bringing in new audiences.

An alternative way to improve the value an organization brings to the market is by reducing costs. Adding new products or services can reduce costs in situations in which we have economies of scope. Cost economies can occur on either the production or distribution side, and are a common motive for a product extension as organizations look for new ways to use existing fixed assets more effectively.

Notice in this discussion that the logic of the new product or service comes from the central mission product of the nonprofit. New products are introduced either to enhance the mission delivery on the demand side or to reduce the costs of the mission product on the supply side. How do earned-income ventures fit in to this typology, or even the goods that Weisbrod (1998) terms 'nonpreferred private goods', designed solely to generate revenues to help finance the mission good? I would argue that the only way these goods can actually serve their purpose of generating revenues for the mission part of the business is if there are some economies-of-scope and/or willingness-to-pay reasons coming from the core mission area. Absent this, the nonprofit will have no competitive advantage in the new product and will be unlikely to succeed. Thus, in terms of both managerial pragmatism and avoiding mission drift, nonprofits should always come back to the core product in thinking about the merits of product extensions.

Product extensions that raise willingness to pay

Extensions that promote the old mission in a changed world   In the fall of 1990, Lincoln Center added Classic Jazz to its family of arts organizations. In 2002, Benhaven, a leading provider of services to autistic children and their families, added a for-profit venture, the Benhaven Learning Network, to consult with public schools about techniques for mainstreaming children with autism. In 2004, Achievement First added four charter schools in Brooklyn, New York to its collection of New Haven charter schools. Each of these product extensions can be seen as an attempt to increase the willingness to pay of the various constituents of each organization by enhancing the ability of each organization to accomplish its original mission in a changing world.

Consider Lincoln Center. It was founded in 1955 as a performing arts center, managing the space and programs in the Lincoln Center facilities. Its mission is 'to present the highest quality performing arts to the widest possible audience'. Originally this meant the Metropolitan Opera, New York Philharmonic and New York City Ballet. As time progressed, however, the collective cultural definition of high-quality arts expanded to include film and, most recently, jazz. Here we have a clear example of a product expansion creating value by recognizing new dimensions of an old mission. At the same time, this broadening opened up new possible streams of benefits to be counted and, it was hoped, captured.

What about Benhaven? When Benhaven started in 1967, it focused on residential services for children with autism, with ten schools in the New Haven, Connecticut region. By the mid-1980s society's vision of appropriate placement of children with autism had changed, with more interest in returning students to their local public schools. Here too, Benhaven's new venture was a way to accomplish its original mission of helping children with autism and their families in a more modern way. As it happened, Benhaven's expertise allowed it to create value for school systems that faced new challenges and had some resources to allow them to pay for those services.

Finally, Achievement First, which is a network of charter schools begun in New Haven, CT, in 1999. The mission of the organization was to drive public school reform by demonstrating that the achievement gap between inner-city African-American students and more affluent suburban students could be eliminated. Early success in New Haven was met with skepticism about the scalability of the educational ideas. Thus expansion to other areas was necessary to accomplish the broader social mission of the organization. As a result of charter school laws, the new schools had to be set up as independent charters, each with their own boards and by laws, united by a common management service.

The form of the product extensions varies considerably across these three organizations. In the cases of Lincoln Center and Benhaven, the extensions were new services; in the case of Achievement First, we see a geographic extension. For Benhaven, the extension involved the use of an earned-income venture, while Lincoln Center added its new service to the same family, and Achievement First's expansion required a new organizational form. But in all of these examples, the potential value creation from the new product was clear: in all cases the goal was to add product to enhance the willingness to pay of all constituents based on an improved articulation of the mission of the organization.

Production of complementary goods   Most nonprofit organizations produce services, rather than goods, and, as a result, most involve at least some benefit consumption at the point of production. Museum benefits come in part to local visitors to the museum; schools educate children on site; a homeless shelter provides some of its benefits to the otherwise homeless who stay there. Whenever our principal good is consumed on site, there are possibilities to enhance the value of those goods by producing other goods or services that will be simultaneously consumed on the spot. Theaters can increase the value of the movie by offering popcorn for sale. Starbucks can enhance the value of its coffee by offering wireless service. In the same way, a museum café can enable visitors to stay longer at exhibitions; an after-school program can minimize disruption and transport costs to families; a hospital gift shop can improve hospital stays by offering gifts for forgetful visitors. A common type of product extension is into a second product that will be consumed with the first, and for which convenience of offering is one of the main value enhancers of the nonprofit. Some people refer to this basis for a product extension as the advantage of 'preferred access to customers'.

Sometimes this preferred access occurs not because customers are on the spot, ready to consume, but because in the provision of the primary good the organization has identified a set of consumers or clients who are likely to be differentially interested in the new product. When Sears launched its Discover card in 1985, the first people it targeted were Sears customers, who they believed would be especially interested in a no-fee, cashback credit card. In fact, the card take-up among this group was considerably above average.[2] The Metropolitan Museum runs a chamber music concert series using its member base as a marketing advantage. In these instances, the organization can take advantage of selection forces among its core customers to reduce its marketing costs in a new venture.

A more subtle complementary good can be seen in what are commonly called 'social' 'affirmative businesses'. These firms use labor from disabled or disadvantaged individuals to produce goods or services that are sold in the marketplace. For example, Rochester Rehabilitation Center in Rochester NY operates a range of affirmative businesses: its earned-income venture Parrett Paper produces and markets animal greeting cards now sold in a number of zoos and aquaria throughout the country. While the core mission of Rochester Rehabilitation Center is its rehabilitation and support services to individuals with disabilities, its mission also includes 'putting people to work and fostering active living'. As part of this mission, the operation of a venture that produces and markets a product is an important complement to the training provided, enabling the clients of Rochester to enter more fully into the mainstream market economy. Here the greeting card business complements the core nonprofit business.

Minnesota Diversified Industries has taken this model to the extreme. MDI is a $40 million firm operating as a nonprofit in the business of plastics manufacturing for a range of clients. Its nonprofit mission is 'to assist people with disabilities and disadvantages by offering progressive development and job opportunities in a competitive business enterprise. Our business is the engine that provides us with the majority of our funding as well as opportunities for vocational and skill development for our employees' (MDI website). Here too we see that the market business is hypothesized to increase the value of the job-training services offered; the two services are complements.

Economies of scope to create value
We have just explored the several ways in which nonprofits look to product extensions to enhance the value of their core programs through the demand side. Another set of possibilities comes from product extensions that have the capacity to increase value by lowering the costs of the core program, typically by sharing those costs in one way or another. We turn now to this category of product extensions broadly thought of as scope economies.

Economies of scope exist whenever the total costs of producing two goods together are less than the costs of producing each of them separately. More formally, for two goods x and y:

$$TC\,(x, y) < TC\,(x, 0) + TC\,(0, y)$$

In the competitive-strategy literature, economies of scope are often characterized as a firm's potential to leverage its core assets. That is, assets developed in one area can be used to create competitive advantages in a second. As a result, the costs of producing the two goods in one firm will be lower than would be their costs in two different operations.

What are the usual sources of scope economies? On the production side, we see scope economies in all stages of production. At the front end, R&D assets may allow an organization to conceive and develop new products at lower costs than could an organization using its facilities looking for only one new idea. There is a wonderful story of the scientists at 3M developing Post-it-Notes® from an adhesive that failed to stick securely enough. When R&D requires much testing and regulatory review, scope economies are almost inevitable, as the learning from one area spills over into a second, and fixed assets are applicable to both. Innovations in the educational curriculum area may spill over from elementary school to upper level school. Scope economies may also emerge from bargaining power in acquiring raw materials. Wal-Mart surely can use the fact that it carries many different Proctor & Gamble products, in many different stores, to extract better prices for those products. Finally, scope economies may come from the use of fixed assets in production. For example, a factory may be able to use a stamping machine to make a range of different products, and in this way spread the cost of that machine.

Scope economies also occur on the distribution side. A facility that allows a firm to distribute groceries might also provide a handy outlet for financial services, providing a reason to move into that business. A truck carrying apples from upstate New York to the city might find it easy to bring back bagels, tempting the local farmer into the bagel business. Scope economies can also occur on the branding side: in general, firms find that brand name can often be extended to multiple products, affording scope economies in advertising and other brand-building activities.

In the nonprofit world, the two most common sources of scope economies are in the use of fixed assets and in brand extension activities. Perhaps the simplest example of an expansion in the product portfolio precipitated by a quest for scope economies is the use of a nonprofit's facilities in a secondary activity. Consider the proliferation of summer camps run by nonprofit schools. Most schools operate only nine months per year. Even with a month to regenerate the facilities in preparation for a new school year, that leaves most schools with two months of down time. As long as the summer-camp revenues can cover the variable cost of using them (carefully and correctly calculated!), then operating a summer camp will help defray the fixed costs of the physical facilities. Many schools prefer running these programs themselves to renting out the space, both to control timing and damage to the property and as a product side complement to their families. In a similar way, many historical museums find that operating a wedding facility business, again either by themselves or with a partner; helps to defray the often sizable costs of their facilities.

A more difficult type of fixed asset that some nonprofits seek to leverage in their product expansion is the expertise of the executive director and/or staff. An organization that does an excellent job of providing shelter to a population of homeless adults may feel that its expertise in dealing with this population uniquely enables it to develop other programs, say in job training, for this group. In the corporate world, Roll (1986) has argued that managers often overestimate themselves, believing that they bring more to the table in running a soon-to-be acquired business than did the former managers. A similar caution applies to nonprofit executives.

From the early work on the economics of nonprofits, the key role of reputational capital has been recognized (see, e.g., Hansmann, 1980; Easley and O'Hara, 1983; Ben-Ner, 1986). In competing with their for-profit counterparts, as well as with one another, nonprofits have a key asset: the trust placed in them by clients and donors alike. In some ways, the trust due to nonprofits allows them to make use of the multiple streams of benefits we described earlier as being one of the hallmarks of the nonprofit world. My own work describing the prominence of the franchise in the nonprofit world (Oster, 1996) similarly focuses on the role of reputational capital in driving nonprofit organizational form. The fact that a local organization is called Habitat for Humanity surely helps it to attract both volunteers and financial capital over what might be provided to a similar but

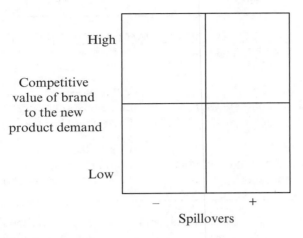

Figure 13.1   Product extension matrix

unbranded operation. When the Yale School of Management opened its doors in 1979, it was clearly better positioned to attract faculty and students than would have been a no-name business school, even one with equivalent resources.

Recent work on global branding in development organizations provides another example of the role of reputational capital. In a survey of Europe and the USA, the power of the nonprofit brand was striking. (See a discussion of the survey and the general topic of global branding in Laidler-Kylander et al., 2007.) In the US survey, Amnesty International ranked 13th, just behind Johnson & Johnson and Proctor & Gamble in terms of brand trust. In the European survey, Amnesty International ranked ahead of Michelin. Clearly, name and reputation are valuable assets.

The value of the nonprofit name, particularly in the case of a large, long-established nonprofit, is a clear lure to expansion of the product portfolio. Having invested in developing a reputation, using that reputation to market, sell or distribute incremental products or services seems like an easy way to spread the costs of an existing program. How should the nonprofit think about leveraging this asset?

Figure 13.1 provides a matrix useful in thinking about this issue. On the vertical axis, we rate the pull of the brand extension: what is the competitive value of the brand in the new product? Looking at this question requires the organization to think hard about both the importance of branding in general in the potential new business and the value of their particular brand in driving demand. On the x-axis, we describe the spillovers of the expansion into the core business of the nonprofit. Is there a spillover, and, if so, is it positive or negative? Clearly the most successful product extensions are ones for which the brand has strong salience and the spillovers are positive.

In looking at the matrix, I have categorized four different products for a hypothetical organization in the family planning business (think Planned Parenthood but hypothetical). In the lower right quadrant, we might put Family Planning condoms; this product is consistent with the mission, and so spillover effects are positive, but the typical young user of a condom is not likely to be attracted to the branding. In the bottom left, we might put a product like Family Planning cigarettes. Again, the brand is not likely to

---

BOX 13.1   SUMMARY OF COMMON NONPROFIT PRODUCT EXTENSIONS

On the demand side:
Old mission done in a new way
Complementary goods

Examples:
Lincoln Center Jazz
Museum café; affirmative business

On the cost side:
Production-based scope economies
Reputation/brand-based

Examples:
Summer camps
Yale School of Management

---

attract the target audience, but now the spillovers are negative, tending to tarnish the brand. This is a lose–lose new product. In the top left corner, one might put a new video that advocates abstinence as the major source of birth control. Coming from the Family Planning organization, this would have strong brand connections, but with a message contrary to the central organization, spillovers are likely to be large and negative. In my recital, the much-desired top right quadrant, the sweet spot of product expansions, has only a question mark. Finding these win–win products is the holy grail of product extensions.

Box 13.1 summarizes the major categories of product extension types that we see in the nonprofit world, along with an example of each type. We turn now to thinking about some of the managerial challenges associated with developing a new product.

Managerial challenges in product extensions
Thus far, we have described the range of motivations for product extensions for a non-profit based on either demand-side enhancement of mission delivery or supply-side cost moves. In moving to multi-product status, the nonprofit potentially faces three types of managerial challenges: getting the costs right; managing multiple benefit streams to reduce conflict; and keeping a focus on the core mission. We consider each issue in turn.

Getting the costs right
As we suggested in the last section, a key driver of product extensions in the nonprofit sector (or in the for-profit sector) is an interest in spreading fixed costs. The fact that some of the fixed costs of an operation can be shared across old and new products potentially creates a number of interesting management challenges.

Let us return to the summer-camp example. If the summer camp were to be run as a stand-alone business, its income statement would list among the costs the rental cost of the facilities. Unless the revenue generated could cover these costs, in addition to the costs of staff and materials, the business could not make it. As a second product line within an existing organization, however, the criterion for success is not the same: now the camp need only cover the incremental costs of its operation. As long as it makes any contribution to the fixed costs of the facilities, the organization as a whole is better off with the camp than without it.

In practice, this focus on incremental costs and contribution is trickier than it may first appear. Principal among the issues is that many costs that appear to be fixed actually have opportunity costs. If the school rents out its facilities were the camp not to be run, then that foregone rental income needs to be weighed against the revenue generated by the camp. If the school has a second idea for using the facilities, then the calculation needs to take that into account. If the use of the camp causes physical depreciation, this too must be considered.

A related issue comes from what Dees (2005) has called the problem of confusing cash flow and accounting profits. Free cash flow is cash produced by a venture that is not needed for reinvestment: it is free to be used by the rest of the operation. New ventures typically require investments in order to reach a level of sustainability. But if the main driver for a new product expansion is to exploit economies of scope via shared costs, then ultimately the test of the success of that venture should be that it creates incremental cash.

Managing multiple benefit streams
As we suggested earlier, one of the challenges of managing a nonprofit is the multiple benefit streams that underlie the revenue portfolio. As nonprofits increase the number of products they produce, the complexity of those multiple streams increases exponentially.

One of the difficult empirical questions in the economics literature is the extent to which there is crowding out among the various revenue sources of the nonprofit. Does an increase in government funding or donations reduce the likelihood that nonprofits will develop more commercial revenue streams? Working the other way, do increases in commercial revenue reduce the incentives of donors to contribute to the organization? Theory is less help here than one might hope. To the extent that donors give for what have been termed 'warm glow effects' (Andreoni, 1993), crowding out of donations is reduced. Indeed, if new revenue sources increase the health of the organization, warm glow may be enhanced. On the other hand, if donors give for instrumental reasons, donations may well be reduced if they now believe the organization has less 'need' of their money.

The empirical evidence in this area is also mixed, complicated by problems of identification and what appears to be heterogeneity across sectors. Steinberg (1993) finds, for example, relatively strong crowding out of donations by government funding. Weisbrod (1998), in a broad sample of nonprofits, finds varying levels of crowd-out both from commercial revenues to donate and vice versa. In a study of university giving, Oster (2003) finds that endowment growth has relatively large crowding-out effects for at least some classes of donors.

In the earlier discussion, we distinguished between product extensions that added to the value of the core mission on the demand side versus those that are principally cost-related. In earlier work, I developed a product portfolio matrix (Figure 13.2) that can be used to help organizations keep track of the underlying motives for setting up new product lines (Oster, 1995). On the y-axis, we track the contribution of the new product to the mission of the organization, while on the x-axis we measure its contribution to the economic vitality of the organization. The sweet spot for an organization is the top right quadrant, in which we have new product lines that both add to the mission and help to

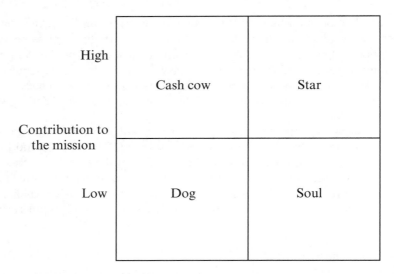

Figure 13.2   Product portfolio matrix

support the basic economics of the operation. In the lower left quadrant we place the dogs – new products that lose on both mission and money grounds. For many nonprofits, the soul of the operation are the programs in the bottom right, contributing strongly to the mission, but requiring incremental funding. Trying to place all of the current and proposed products on this matrix is a helpful group exercise for both staff and boards of a growing nonprofit.

In some cases, the issue appears to be not so much one of crowding out on the part of donor preferences, but of what I have elsewhere called 'abandonment' (Oster, 2003). Managers faced with increased revenues from a new venture may reduce their efforts in the development area. Donations thus fall not due to lack of donor interest, but lack of staff initiative. This leads us into our third managerial challenge, keeping focus.

Keeping managerial focus
One of the striking features of the nonprofit form is the strength of the staff. Indeed, early work in the health care area modeled hospitals as staff cooperatives (Pauly and Redisch, 1973), and that theme has been pursued by a number of other scholars in the field (for a recent model of this form, see Glaeser, 2003). How do the likely preferences of the nonprofit staff fit in with our discussion of nonprofit product extensions?

Here the work of Lakdawalla and Philipson (1998) is useful. In the Lakdawalla–Philipson model, entrepreneurs choose organizational forms. In making that choice, L–P argue that entrepreneurs choose between the benefits of nonprofit status – in particular access to donations – and the value of the for-profit status in permitting the extraction of profits. For entrepreneurs with tastes for high quality and quantity of the service to be produced, the access to donations will be important. Thus the model ends up by sorting those entrepreneurs, with those most interested in higher output and/ or higher quality sorted into the nonprofit sector. These entrepreneurs can be thought of as mission-driven. Similar observations were made about differences in the teacher quality of nonprofit versus for-profit day care centers (Mauser, 1993), as well as by Scott Morton and Podolny (2003) in their paper distinguishing owner-managed versus corporate wineries.

A natural consequence of the staff sorting that we see in the nonprofit sector is to encourage sub-goal pursuits in the multi-product organization, as individual staff members focus on the elements of the product package most aligned with their own mission preferences. In earlier work (Oster, 1995), I explored the workings of a New Haven social service nonprofit, operating in the areas of emergency food, children's recreational services, adult training and a program for mentally challenged adults. The revenue streams meshed nicely in this organization and there were strong economies-of-scope justifications for the multiple products. But there was also considerable managerial tension, particularly around the way in which the fixed costs were allocated. Because all of the staff were mission-committed to their own sub-area, and because they all sought the highest quality for their own programs, the gains of shared costs turned into squabbles over cost allocations. The very strength of the nonprofit – the mission drive of its staff – make such conflicts commonplace.

A special case: the earned-income venture
Earned-income ventures are ventures started by nonprofit organizations with an explicit goal of raising revenues to support the nonprofit operation. While the data do not allow us to distinguish between mission-related programs with fee revenue and strict earned-income ventures, there is a general view in the field that commercial activity is growing. Weisbrod, for example, argues that 'new commercial activities are the major path open to nonprofits to generate additional revenue' (Weisbrod, 1998, p. 9). A business planning competition sponsored by Yale School of Management, Pew Charitable Trust and the Goldman-Sachs Foundation generated applications from over 2500 nonprofits in the course of the three-year competition, all of which were planning to initiate a new earned-income venture.

Given the recent growth in the earned-income venture, it is interesting to look at one of the earliest forms of these commercial ventures. A recent interesting paper by Nelson and Zeckhauser (2003) describes the sale of private chapels by the Catholic Church in Renaissance Florence. The money raised from private individuals by selling these chapels within churches helped to pay for the costs of erecting those churches. Nelson and Zeckhauser argue that the competitive advantage of the Church in the sale of these chapels was its 'monopoly on afterlife benefits', which allowed them to sell their chapels at prices considerably in excess of the construction value.

What shape do the new ventures in the more modern period take and what are the challenges in running them? Some are relatively straightforward: a large chain of day care centers in Washington, DC proposes to use excess capacity in its kitchen to launch a catering business. A women's shelter plans to open a shop to reupholster furniture in rural Virginia. A California nonprofit that provides technical information systems support to other nonprofits opens a reduced-price source for software, using material donated by large players like Microsoft. Notice all of the ventures described here – and indeed all of the successful ventures that I have been able to identify – follow the pattern of successful product extensions described earlier. All rely on leveraging some key asset of the organization, reputation, customer access or fixed facility, to create a new venture that can compete against for-profit vendors.

It is this last point that is sometimes missed in the enthusiasm for the earned-income venture. As a general matter, these ventures will be competing with small businesses run by profit-seeking entrepreneurs. This competitive frame poses a number of challenges as well as some opportunities for the venture in the areas of both economics and organizational culture.

There are a number of differences between nonprofits and for-profits in the way operations are run. Nonprofits are more labor-intensive, run with flatter organizations, use more consensus decision making and more professional reference points. Decisions take longer to make as a result. When a nonprofit competes against a motivated small business person, slower decision making can be problematic. Nonprofits in business may also find themselves the victim of cream skimming by for-profit competitors. Not all customers are created equal; some are harder and more expensive to serve than others. For a for-profit firm, picking the low-hanging fruit is often a good strategy. For a nonprofit, even one with a venture designed to make money, leaving the harder to serve on the wayside may be uncomfortable. Fairness in pricing may sometimes come up against principles based more closely on relative demand elasticities. Using financial incentives to motivate staff is also more problematic in the nonprofit sector, both culturally and legally. Finally, to the extent that an earned-income venture is highly successful, the tax status of the nonprofit may be challenged. While nonprofits can of course earn commercial revenue unrelated to their core mission (as long as they pay the unrelated business income tax), IRS rules suggest that when such activity becomes 'substantial' its tax status may be challenged.

One potential solution to any incompatibilities between the nonprofit organizational structure and culture, and the demands of the competitive marketplace, is to spin off the earned-income venture into a separate for-profit subsidiary. This subsidiary can then both make charitable contributions to the nonprofit and pay dividends to the nonprofit owner. While it can be expensive to establish a subsidiary, doing so would allow the firm to create a culture and structure more in line with the competitive marketplace.

Concluding remarks

In the for-profit sector, while more than half of the firms are single-product firms, more than one-third of the growth in US manufacturing in the last 20 years comes from the addition of new product lines by existing firms (Bernard et al., 2010). There is no reason to think that existing nonprofits are not equally creative in developing new products. But an important difference in the sectors lies in the relative difficulty the typical nonprofit has in abandoning product lines. For for-profit firms, new product adoption is often matched by old product abandonment (Bernard et al., 2010). In the presence of at least some advocates for a nonprofit service, it is hard to make the exit decision. For nonprofits, therefore, a more common pattern is a growing bundle of product and service offerings, with new ones joining a crowded field of the old. Few universities have abandoned study of the classics even as they embrace information technology. As a result, the attention to connections across products of the sort that we have described in this chapter takes on growing importance.

Notes

1. The principle of value creation and its companion value capture have a long history in the field of economics, going back to Ricardo. For a modern explication, see Brandenburger and Nalebuff (1996) or Oster (1995, pp. 228–31).
2. For an interesting discussion of this, see Evans and Schmalensee (2005).

References

Andreoni, James (1993), 'An experimental test of the public goods crowding out hypothesis', *The American Economic Review*, **83** (5), 1317–27.
Ben-Ner, Avner (1986), 'Nonprofit organizations: why do they exist?' in Susan Rose-Ackerman (ed.), *The Economics of Nonprofit Organizations*, Oxford: Oxford University Press, pp. 94–113.
Bernard, Andrew, Peter Schott and Stephen Redding (2010), 'Products and productivity', *American Economic Review*, forthcoming.
Brandenburger, Adam and Barry Nalebuff (1996), 'Value based business strategy', *Journal of Economics & Management Strategy*, **5** (1), 5–24.
Dees, Gregory (2005), 'Putting nonprofit business ventures in perspective', in Sharon M. Oster (ed.), *Generating and Sustaining Nonprofit Earned Income*, San Francisco, CA: Jossey-Bass.
Easley, David and Maureen O'Hara (1983), 'The economic role of the nonprofit', *Bell Journal of Economics*, **14**, 531–8.
Evans, David and Richard Schmalensee (2005), *Paying with Plastic: The Digital Revolution in Buying and Borrowing*, Cambridge, MA: MIT Press.
Glaeser, Edward (2003), 'Introduction', *The Governance of Nonprofit Organizations*, Chicago, IL: University of Chicago Press.
Hansmann, Henry (1980), 'The role of nonprofit enterprise', *Yale Law Journal*, **89** (5), 835–901.
James, Estelle (1983), 'How nonprofits grow: a model', *Journal of Policy Analysis and Management*, **2** (3), 350–65.
Laidler-Kylander, Nathalie, John Quelch and Bernard Simonin (2007), 'Building and valuing global brands in the nonprofit sector', *Nonprofit Management and Leadership*, **17** (3), 253–77.
Lakdawalla, Darius and Tomas Philipson (1998), 'Nonprofit production and competition', National Bureau of Economic Research Working Paper No. 6377.
Mauser, E. (1993), 'The importance of the nonprofit sector in the day-care industry: a look at the motivation of day-care directors and consumer preferences', paper prepared for the Spring Research Forum, Independent Sector, San Antonio, TX.
Nelson, Jonathan Katz and Richard J. Zeckhauser (2003), 'A Renaissance instrument to support nonprofits: the sale of private chapels in Florentine Churches', in E. Glaeser (ed.), *The Governance of Not-for-Profit Organizations*, Chicago, IL: University of Chicago Press, pp. 143–80.
Oster, Sharon M. (1995), *Strategic Management for Nonprofit Organizations: Theory and Cases*, New York: Oxford University Press.
Oster, Sharon M. (1996), 'Nonprofit organizations and their local affiliates: a study in organizational forms', *Journal of Economic Behavior & Organization*, **30** (1), 83–95.
Oster, Sharon M. (2003), 'Is there a dark side to endowment growth?' in F. King Alexander and Ronald G. Ehrenberg (eds), in theme issue 'Maximizing Revenue in Higher Education' for *New Directions for Institutional Research*, No. 119, pp. 81–90.
Pauly, Mark and Michael Redisch (1973), 'The nonprofit hospital as a physician's cooperative', *American Economic Review*, **63** (1), 87–99.
Roll, Richard (1986), 'The hubris hypothesis of corporate takeovers', *Journal of Business*, **59** (2), 197–216.
Schiff, Jerald and Burton A. Weisbrod (1991), 'Competition between for-profit and nonprofit organizations in commercial markets', *Annals of Public and Cooperative Economics*, **62** (4), 619–39.
Scott Morton, Fiona M. and Joel M. Podolny (2003), 'Love or money: effect of ownership on motivations in the California wine industry', *Journal of Industrial Economics*, **50** (4), 431–56.
Steinberg, Richard (1993), 'Does government spending crowd out donations?', in Avner Ben-Ner and Benedetto Gui (eds), *The Nonprofit Sector in the Mixed Economy*, Ann Arbor, MI: University of Michigan Press, pp. 99–125.
Weisbrod, Burton A. (1998), *To Profit or Not to Profit: The Commercial Transformation of the Nonprofit Sector*, Cambridge, UK: Cambridge University Press.

14 Internal organization and governance
Vladislav Valentinov

Introduction

Nonprofit organizations in the USA and worldwide find themselves in an increasingly difficult environment. Governmental funding goes down, competition with for-profit firms and other nonprofits becomes more intensive, while the tasks to be performed by nonprofit organizations continue gaining societal relevance. Nonprofit organizations thus experience a sustained need for organizational adaptation. This chapter argues that understanding the processes of organizational change in the nonprofit sector can be usefully informed by re-examining the relevant literature on the theory of the (for-profit) firm. Two interrelated strands of this literature are particularly relevant: those dealing with the delineation of organizational boundaries and those studying the determination of cost-effective governance mechanisms. This chapter will explore some of this literature's implications for the way the organizational boundaries and the governance mechanisms evolve in the nonprofit sector. Bringing the theory of the for-profit firm to bear on the economics of nonprofit organization will be enabled by the explicit consideration of the fact of nonprofit firms' mission orientation. Nonprofit firms are thereby supposed to engage in activities that may be related or unrelated to their core missions; it is to be expected that the decisions on both organizational boundaries and governance mechanisms are made differently for these two activity types.

The chapter is organized as follows. The next section discusses the way the nonprofit organizational boundaries are affected by transaction cost considerations, paying special attention to the difference between mission-related and mission-unrelated activities. The following sections explore the governance mechanisms used in nonprofit firms by developing the continuum representation of market, hierarchy and nonprofit organization. The complex interactions between the governance mechanisms, boundaries and mission orientation in nonprofit firms are also examined.

Transaction cost determinants of nonprofit organizational boundaries

The transaction cost theory of the for-profit firm analyzes the issue of organizational boundaries mainly in the context of vertical integration, understood as the 'make-or-buy' decision. A key difference between for-profit and nonprofit firms is that the latter's behavior is driven (and constrained) by their substantive missions whereas the for-profit orientation of the former is compatible with a broad range of profit-generating activities. Hence it may be expected that the effect of transaction costs on the governance of mission-unrelated activities will resemble the way this cost influence the boundaries of for-profit firms, while the governance of mission-related activities is less clear. Thus the effect of transaction costs on the governance of mission-related activities is the most unexplored issue and will be the main theme of this section.

The transaction cost theory of the for-profit firm encompasses two major strands, which can be designated as the incentive alignment perspective and the Coasian perspective (Valentinov, 2008). The former perspective places the economic role of the for-profit firm in minimizing opportunistic behavior potentially resulting from information asymmetries. By contrast, the latter perspective assumes economic agents to be equally limited in their capacity to search for, process and communicate information, and locates the economic role of the for-profit firm not in minimizing opportunism, but in minimizing the cost of handling information. In the following, both perspectives will be taken to explore the effect of transaction costs on the delineation of boundaries of nonprofit firms' mission-related activities.

The Coasian perspective
In his seminal 1937 paper, Coase identified two basic ways in which for-profit firms economize on transaction costs understood as the cost of searching for, processing and communicating information. First, these firms reduce the number of contracts that need to be concluded among all cooperating individuals. Each individual needs to conclude a single contract with the firm rather than with all other individuals involved in this firm's activity. Second, for-profit firms allow the replacement of short-term contracts with long-term ones, thus eliminating the need to conclude new contracts to cover every new contingency. Both of these ways are clearly applicable to nonprofit firms. Hence, for both for-profit and nonprofit firms, higher cost of searching for, processing and communicating information implies a greater role for internal organization and thus broadens organizational boundaries.

For for-profit firms, the effect of costliness of information on the drawing of organizational boundaries is little else than that. For nonprofit firms, however, the cost of searching for, processing and communicating information involves a dimension that is not relevant for for-profit firms, and that concerns the cost of identification of individuals supporting a certain nonprofit mission. As this motivational characteristic is not readily observable, mission-driven individuals may need to incur non-trivial costs in identifying like-minded individuals, while the monetary motivation underlying individual involvement in for-profit firms can be safely assumed as universally present. These search costs may therefore exceed the respective costs for for-profit firms and thus exert a constraining effect on the boundaries of nonprofit firms. These costs can be economized by nonprofit firms if they actively inform the general public about their missions, activities and resource requirements (particularly in the form of fundraising campaigns). The information provided to the general public reaches like-minded individuals (such as donors, volunteers, individuals willing to accept relatively low wages), thus enabling them to reduce their costs of individual search. The ability of nonprofit firms to reduce these individual search costs is particularly important when the individuals concerned have only low intensities of preference for specific kinds of nonprofit missions. These individuals would be unlikely to contribute to the activities of nonprofit firms if the search costs they had to accept were substantial. Their participation becomes realistic only when they can avoid the search costs by benefiting from the information freely provided by the existing nonprofit firms.

The incentive alignment perspective
The incentive alignment aspect of the transaction cost-economizing function of for-profit firms lies in these firms' ability to hinder opportunistic behavior. In the area of

mission-unrelated activities, nonprofit firms would evidently enjoy the same advantages. For the mission-related activities, however, the incentive alignment problem acquires a new dimension. The notion of mission-drivenness indicates the presence of intrinsic motivation for pursuing a particular mission (Valentinov, 2007). Intrinsically motivated individuals are, by definition, uninterested in any type of shirking from working to achieve the mission in question. There is no need for any additional aligning of incentives of individuals who are intrinsically motivated to work toward achieving the missions of their nonprofit firms.

To be sure, the irrelevance of opportunism to intrinsically motivated individuals by no means implies that nonprofit firms are free from opportunism. Rather, opportunism can be practiced by those who do not share the relevant intrinsic motivation but pretend that they do. The latter individuals may be attracted to nonprofit firms, in particular, by relaxed hierarchical control and supervision, opening greater space for shirking. In turn, the need for relaxing hierarchical control may stem from the need to avoid the crowding out of intrinsic motivation of those who have it. While ensuring a positive work atmosphere for mission-driven individuals, relaxed hierarchical control may thus entail an unintended consequence of encouraging opportunism, which may endanger the nonprofit firms' survival.

Hence the relevant incentive alignment problem of organization of mission-related activities must consist of hindering the external opportunists in getting engaged in these activities. This may be achieved by the use of screening devices, one of which is the practice of paying lower wages in the nonprofit sector than can be earned elsewhere (e.g. Preston, 1989; Ballou and Weisbrod, 2003; Leete, 2006). However, all screening devices incur costs of their own. Low wages may make employment in the nonprofit sector impossible for individuals who are intrinsically motivated to work for a particular nonprofit mission yet have no alternative sources of income to support their existence. Moreover, to the extent that the screening devices are not effective, the instances of opportunistic behavior in nonprofit firms may reduce the intrinsic motivation of those who have it and thus make them less willing to join these firms. Hence, all in all, the presence of opportunism constrains organizational boundaries of mission-related activities.

Nonprofit governance: an organizational economic perspective
The preceding discussion analyzed the determinants of organizational boundaries of nonprofit firms while abstracting away from the fact that the redefinition of boundaries usually involves a change in the governance mechanisms within and across these. This section will therefore emphasize the importance of governance mechanisms. In the nonprofit literature, governance primarily refers to the operation of the board of directors and the distribution of responsibilities between major stakeholders such as board, management, staff, volunteers etc. (Ostrower and Stone, 2006). However, the organizational economics literature on the theory of the for-profit firm treated the governance concept at a more fundamental level, referring to the governance mechanisms of market, hybrids and hierarchy. Indeed, the very institution of the for-profit firm has been defined by its use of a specific governance mechanism, such as hierarchy (see Williamson, 1991). Moreover, the governance mechanism underlying the institution of the for-profit firm is clearly positioned with respect to its main alternative (market), most obviously in the

form of specific versions of the so-called governance continuums that normally classify market and hierarchy as the polar modes of economic organization.

It seems, however, fair to say that the organizational economics tradition of comparing the governance mechanisms of market, hybrids and hierarchy has so far not been sufficiently integrated into the economic theory of nonprofit organization. As a result, the common contrasting of the nonprofit and for-profit sectors does not take account of the latter sector's institutional diversity embodied in the complex combinations of the above governance mechanisms. At the same time, recognizing that the nonprofit sector fulfills a unique role that cannot be imitated by the for-profit sector implies that the former sector involves forms of governance different from the latter sector's governance mechanisms. Yet comparing nonprofit organization with these governance mechanisms has not so far attracted much scholarly attention. This section will take one of the first steps to fill this gap.

A major challenge in comparing nonprofit organization with market, hierarchy and hybrid governance mechanisms probably lies in the lack of clarity about whether nonprofit organization embodies a distinct governance mechanism comparable to these. Evidently, hierarchical governance is not unused by nonprofit firms, particularly in manager–employee relations and sometimes in board–staff relations. Yet hierarchical governance can hardly be taken to be as essential to nonprofit organization as it is to the for-profit firm, particularly in view of the recognized self-governing nature of the former (Salamon and Anheier, 1992). Nonprofit firms may therefore be thought of as containing a mix of governance mechanisms, some of which may be characteristic of the for-profit sector and some of which must be unique to the nonprofit sector. Comparing nonprofit organization to other governance mechanisms therefore requires clarifying the nature of the nonprofit-specific governance mechanism that is not reproducible within the for-profit sector.

Roger Lohmann (1992) argued for a positive definition of nonprofit organization's identity in terms of collective action aimed at producing the common goods. Indeed, collective action is clearly different from both the buyer–seller interaction within the market governance and from superordinate–subordinate interaction within the hierarchical governance, and thus may underlie the distinct and independent identity of nonprofit organization. This chapter follows Lohmann's argument by considering collective action to be the nonprofit-specific governance mechanism. Empirically, the collective-action governance within nonprofit firms is most characteristically (although not exclusively) embodied in the activity of the boards of directors jointly seeking to realize their nonprofit firms' missions. Based on this insight, the following subsections will explore the possibility of integrating nonprofit organization into the conventional market–hierarchy continuum and analyzing the determinants of institutional choice between market, hierarchy and nonprofit organization.

Governance mechanisms in organizational economics
The governance mechanisms that have been initially investigated and comparatively analyzed by institutional economists are those of markets and hierarchies (Coase, 1937; Williamson, 1996), whose principal characteristics are reliance on price-based and authority-based coordination, respectively. However, since the 1990s, attention has been increasingly focused on organizational arrangements that could be attributed neither to

market nor hierarchical forms of governance, and have been designated as 'hybrid' or 'intermediate' forms (Ménard, 2004, p. 2; Williamson, 1991). The possible examples of hybrid forms include long-term contracts, networks, franchising, collective trademarks, partnerships, cooperatives and alliances (e.g. Ménard, 2004). Similarly to hybrid organizational arrangements, the nonprofit-specific collective-action governance is clearly different from market and hierarchy. Its rejection of hierarchical governance directly follows from its self-governing and voluntary nature. Its rejection of price-based coordination can be established from the fact that nonprofit organization does not involve agents buying and selling from each other, but rather presupposes collective action aimed at achieving common purposes.

The incompatibility of collective action with both market and hierarchical governance naturally gives rise to the question whether it can be considered to represent a hybrid organizational arrangement. This question, in turn, calls for a clarification of the nature of hybrid organization focused on the following fundamental and interrelated issues: how is hybrid organization to be principally understood? And how is it conceptually positioned with respect to markets and hierarchies? The way in which these two issues are addressed in the major studies explicitly dealing with the concept of the continuum of governance mechanisms (Williamson, 1991; Peterson et al., 2001; Ménard, 2004) can be designated as the 'conventional view' of this continuum. According to the 'conventional view', markets, hierarchies and hybrids differ from each other in terms of the following attributes: (1) the type of economic adaptation they support; (2) incentive intensity; and (3) reliance on administrative controls (Williamson, 1991).

Regarding the first attribute, markets are efficient in that kind of adaptation for which 'prices serve as sufficient statistics', i.e. allow rapid responses to changes in relative prices. Hierarchies are efficient for the adaptation involving bilateral dependence of transactors and requiring coordinated action. In terms of the second attribute (incentive intensity), hierarchical governance presupposes a looser connection between effort and remuneration than is characteristic of market governance. Finally, the third attribute – reliance on administrative controls – represents a fundamental characteristic of hierarchy, is in practice not relevant for market, and exhibits intermediate relevance for hybrids. Indeed, with regard to these three attributes, hybrids are located somewhere between markets and hierarchies, as has been argued by theorists proposing the concept of governance continuum (Williamson, 1991; Peterson et al., 2001; Ménard, 2004).

Conventional governance continuum and nonprofit organization
The above review of the nature of hybrid governance implies that the nonprofit-specific collective-action governance is not hybrid because hybrids do not have any independent identity apart from being a mixture of market and hierarchy (Valentinov, 2006). Indeed, whereas market is coordinated by prices and hierarchy – by authority relation – hybrids are supposed to rely on various combinations of these two coordination principles. Hybrids are thus attributed to neither markets nor hierarchies in the sense that they do not represent 'pure' markets or hierarchies, but rather a mixture of these. This view of hybrid organization is evidently relevant, for example, in various forms of vertical coordination that do in various proportions combine the coordinating functions of prices and authority relation. However, it is problematic for collective action. The reason is that collective action can be identified neither as a market nor as a hierarchy not because

it does not represent any of these governance mechanisms in the pure form, but rather because it rejects both of them at the same time.

However, the conventional view of the continuum is not the only possible view. Indeed, the conventional view has been developed to analyze business transactions whereas transactions characteristic of nonprofit organization are of a very different kind, reflected, specifically, in their mission orientation rather than profit orientation. Consequently, the criteria underlying the conventional view of the continuum (type of economic adaptation, incentive intensity, reliance on administrative controls) have been geared to comparison between market and hierarchical governance rather than between market, hierarchical and collective-action governance. That means, in turn, that the possibility of the continuum incorporating all three of these mechanisms depends on whether more relevant criteria can be found. Apart from ensuring the meaningful comparability between the three mechanisms, these criteria should also recognize the existence of the independent identity of collective action rather than treat it as a mixture of markets and hierarchies. Identifying these criteria will be the task of the next section.

Toward an alternative view of the governance continuum
This chapter advocates the view that the criterion whereupon such an extended alternative continuum can be built is the commonness of interests of the participants of respective governance mechanisms (Valentinov and Fritzsch, 2007). The commonness of interests is understood here as the extent to which the objectives of these participants overlap with respect to given transactions. However, in somewhat schematic terms, it can be argued that market, hierarchy and collective-action governance exhibit successively growing reliance on common interests of their respective participants. The commonness of interests is highest for collective action as it is evidently based on sharing an interest that motivates this action. In nonprofit firms, this shared interest evidently relates to realizing these firms' missions. Lesser commonness of interests is to be expected in the case of the hierarchical governance mechanism, as the employees' interests in relation to organizational activities deviate from the respective supervisors' interests due to the familiar principal–agent problems. Arguably, even less coincidence of interests must be characteristic of the market governance mechanism, as the participants of market transactions need not have more than minimal concerns about each other's activities (beyond ensuring the mutual respect of property rights).

Thus the commonness of stakeholder interests may be used as a criterion for representing market, hierarchy and collective action (embodied in nonprofit organization) as elements of an alternative-governance continuum. This continuum is different from the traditional market/hierarchy continuum proposed by Williamson (1991), Peterson et al. (2001), and Ménard (2004) in two respects. First, it does not consider all governance mechanisms other than market and hierarchy as hybrids between these. Second, it is based on the criterion of commonness of stakeholder interests rather than those of incentive intensity and the degree of reliance on administrative controls, as developed by Williamson (1991), for the reason that the latter criteria do not enable a meaningful distinction between collective action, on the one hand, and market and hierarchy, on the other (Valentinov, 2006). Whereas the conventional view of the governance continuum can be described as 'from markets through hybrids to hierarchies', the proposed alternative view implies a different sequence – from markets through hierarchies to collective action embodied in nonprofit organization.

Implications for institutional choice

An advantage of the continuum representation of governance mechanisms lies in enabling a systematic understanding of institutional choice, i.e. choice among these mechanisms. In the traditional continuum of Williamson (1991), the criteria of institutional choice include asset specificity, frequency and uncertainty of transacting. While these criteria are helpful for understanding the choice between market and hierarchy, they are evidently less suited for the choice between market or hierarchy, on the one hand, and collective action, on the other. Rather, a more appropriate criterion for the latter choice must be the extent to which the concerned economic actors perceive their interests in relation to a particular activity to be common. If this extent is substantial, they will choose the collective-action governance, which is structurally embedded in nonprofit organization. If the interests of some actors are perceived as more substantial than those of others, then the hierarchical governance will be chosen, which endows the former actors with more rights than the latter ones. An even greater divergence of interests indicates the choice of market governance, while the zero intersection of interests implies that no governance mechanisms need to be chosen at all.

A central issue in institutional choice concerns the consequences of choosing the wrong governance mechanism. In Williamson's framework, these consequences take the form of increased transaction costs that adversely affect the competitive standing of organizations in question. While this viewpoint is surely correct for the market/hierarchy continuum, the incorporation of collective action into this continuum enables identifying the consequences of two additional types of suboptimal institutional choice. First, collective action may be chosen in cases when market or hierarchy would be optimal, i.e. when the actual commonness of stakeholder interests is less than the perceived one. The second type of suboptimal choice is the opposite of the first type: market or hierarchy may be chosen in cases when collective action would be optimal, i.e. when the actual commonness of stakeholder interests exceeds the perceived one.

The consequences of the first type of suboptimal choice are clearly the increased transaction costs that find expression in enhanced organizational slack and shirking due to the missing market or hierarchical incentives and controls. In contrast, the second type of suboptimal choice would result not (necessarily) in higher transaction costs *per se*, but rather in the missing delivery of nonprofit missions. This choice means, in fact, the substitution of nonprofit organization with for-profit one, and its consequences may therefore be well inferred from economic theories exploring the nonprofit sector's unique functions that cannot be imitated by for-profit firms. Along these lines, the substitution of nonprofit organization with for-profit one may cause, among other things, underprovision of certain collective-consumption goods and trust goods (see, e.g., Steinberg, 2006).

Governance mechanisms, boundaries and mission orientation

While the preceding section explored the nonprofit-specific governance mechanism of collective action, it also admitted that nonprofit firms may have recourse to hierarchical and market governance as well. This section will emphasize that nonprofit firms exhibit a mix of governance mechanisms interacting with each other, and that this interaction affects these firms' structure and behavior in several ways. First, governance mechanisms and boundaries of nonprofit firms are essentially co-evolving, as institutional choice between market, hierarchy and nonprofit organization affects the way the nonprofit boundaries are drawn. Second, the nonprofit-specific governance of collective action affects the utilization of market and hierarchical governance, as participants of market and hierarchical transactions may, to various extents, be committed to the missions of the nonprofit firms concerned. The use of market and hierarchical governance in nonprofit firms may thus be different from that in their for-profit counterparts. Third, the use of market and hierarchical governance may potentially constrain the scope of the nonprofit-specific governance of collective action and thus endanger the nonprofit firms' identity and mission orientation. The following subsections consecutively address these issues in more detail.

Governance mechanisms and organizational boundaries
The relationship between governance mechanisms and organizational boundaries is based on the fact that recourse to market governance involves transferring transactions outside the boundary, while hierarchical and collective action governance both imply intra-organizational activity. Evidently, collective-action governance is utilized by a core of intrinsically motivated internal stakeholders, e.g. represented by a volunteer board of directors. Volunteer directors are evidently neither hierarchically subordinated to each other nor entertain any mutual market transactions, but rather jointly seek ways to fulfill their nonprofit firms' missions. Hierarchical governance may be utilized to govern the relationship between the board and hired staff, as well as internal relationships within this staff (although the next subsection will argue that this hierarchical relationship may be relaxed by the staff's mission orientation). Since collective-action and hierarchical governance encompass intra-organizational activities, their use delineates the overall boundary of nonprofit firms.

According to the model of institutional choice suggested above, the relationship between the organizational boundaries and governance mechanisms in nonprofit firms is such that a higher commonness of stakeholder interests over a particular activity will result in a higher likelihood of this activity being governed within the organizational boundaries. This principle applies most directly to mission-related activities that, by definition, must represent the object of common interests of the intrinsically motivated stakeholders. Hence the mission-related activities cannot be outsourced, by definition. As nonprofit firms also engage in activities that are only indirectly mission-related, the commonness of stakeholder interests over these may be less significant, indicating the use of hierarchical and market governance. This relationship, however, must be understood sufficiently flexibly to account for the fact that there exist no hard-and-fast definitions or indicators of both organizational boundaries and commonness of stakeholder interests. An application of this relationship in practice therefore requires corresponding operationalization of the above contexts, depending on the situational context.

Effects of collective-action governance on market and hierarchical governance
As mentioned above, the nonprofit firms' use of hierarchical and market governance is affected by the fact that the participants of respective transactions may support

these firms' missions. This support makes both markets and hierarchies to some extent similar to collective action. The hierarchical governance within nonprofit firms may be loosened to prevent the crowding out of intrinsic motivation of hierarchically subordinated actors. Most importantly, this applies to the board–staff relations (e.g. Ostrower and Stone, 2006). While managerial staff must in some respects be subordinate to the board (e.g. Carver, 1990), they are often expected to display initiative and commitment reaching beyond the sheer execution of instructions received (e.g. Herman and Heimovics, 1990). Hence, instead of being viewed as strictly hierarchical, the board–staff relationship has often been described as partnership-based (e.g. Drucker, 1990), highly dynamic (e.g. Golensky, 1993), and importantly influenced by a wide range of personal, organizational and environmental variables (see Ostrower and Stone, 2006 for an overview).

The peculiarities of the nonprofit firms' use of market governance may be distinguished for various markets in which these firms act: labor market, market for land and physical capital, and market for donations. In all of these markets, nonprofit decision makers are confronted with trade-offs not characteristic of the for-profit sector. In the labor market, the major difference of nonprofit firms from for-profit ones lies in their access to intrinsically motivated workers offering their services at discounted wages (Brown and Slivinski, 2006), even though the for-profit–nonprofit wage differentials vary widely at the level of particular occupations (Leete, 2006). Through their 'labor donations', employed workers may be considered to participate in collective action with their employers toward achieving their firms' missions. The nonprofit firms' advantage in employing intrinsically motivated workers is however compensated by the potentially high costs of searching for these and distinguishing them from those that are not so motivated (see above).

As noted by Brown and Slivinski (2006, p. 142), 'there is no obvious reason for the existence of a nonprofit mission to affect behavior in the markets for land and physical capital'. Yet, as these authors state further, the behavioral peculiarity of nonprofit firms in these markets arises as a result of their regulatory and tax treatment. The tax exemptions are granted to nonprofit firms in recognition of their missions corresponding to the broader public interest and thus embodying public collective action in the broad understanding of the term. The nonprofit firms' tax exemptions reduce the cost to them of land and physical capital, and thus predict their greater size in comparison with for-profit firms, in terms of the respective assets. The nonprofit firms' cost advantages are however compensated by the for-profit firms' ability to raise capital by selling stock (ibid.).

A further peculiarity of market governance in nonprofit firms consists of the existence of the market for donations, which does not exist in the for-profit sector. Donations reflect the support for the nonprofit missions of actors not affiliated with the concerned nonprofit firms, and create the impression of collective action by these actors and nonprofit firms toward achieving these firms' missions. Competition in the market for donations (at least theoretically) favors those nonprofit firms that have the most appealing missions and the most effective management. The relevant trade-offs in this market stem from the possibility of strategic behavior of both donors and recipient nonprofit managers, each of which must weigh the benefits of entering particular donation transactions against the possible costs. For donors, the costs relate to the possibility of managers not using the funds in the way most preferred by the donors (e.g. Rose-Ackerman, 1987).

For managers, receiving a donation may entail an obligation to engage in activities not necessarily corresponding to their preferences of what their firms should do (ibid.).

Effects of market and hierarchical governance on collective-action governance
The effect of market and hierarchical governance on collective-action governance in nonprofit firms most obviously reveals itself in the first two governance mechanisms displacing and eroding the last one. These processes are often associated with the ongoing nonprofit commercialization induced by the increasing competition and shortage of funds in the nonprofit sector. In terms of the continuum of market, hierarchy and collective-action governance, nonprofit commercialization entails a growing domination of the first two governance mechanisms over the last one in the nonprofit firms concerned. Commercialization has often been perceived as a threat to the preservation of identity of nonprofit firms and as a factor potentially undermining these firms' ability to deliver their missions.

Yet the model of institutional choice between market, hierarchy and collective-action governance suggests that commercialization does not necessarily entail suboptimal institutional choice in the form of using market and hierarchical governance for governing the activity of mission realization. To the extent that these governance mechanisms are used for activities that are not directly mission-related, while collective-action governance regulates the mission-related activities, there seem to be no grounds for questioning the preservation of the nonprofit identity. Evidently, this identity is threatened only when the directly mission-related activities are governed in a way other than through genuine collective action. As shown above, suboptimally replacing collective action with market and hierarchical governance would indeed result in these activities being underprovided. Thus, whether commercialization does erode the nonprofit identity is an empirical question to be answered by exploring the governance of the mission-related activities in specific nonprofit firms.

However, this argument does not exclude the possibility of commercialization actually undermining the mission orientation and therefore the nonprofit identity of nonprofit firms. This may happen, for example, because the increased exposure of nonprofit stakeholders to the use of markets and hierarchies may weaken their commitment to collective action as a governance mechanism for pursuing common interests. Nonprofit stakeholders, however, may be conscious of this possibility and may take measures to protect their nonprofit firms' identity. One way of doing so would be to preserve and strengthen the intrinsic motivation of nonprofit firms' stakeholders, besides ensuring a high degree of transparency and accountability in commercial operations.

Concluding remarks
This chapter identified the key factors that influence managerial decision making on the delineation of organizational boundaries and the use of governance mechanisms in nonprofit organizations. Both of these organizational parameters have been shown to depend critically on the constellations of interests of relevant stakeholders. Arguably, the close embedding of nonprofit missions into the societal institutional fabric makes the stakeholder interest constellations more diverse, more ambivalent and more dynamic than is the case with for-profit firms. Recognizing and being sensitive to these interest constellations is the key challenge that must be faced by nonprofit managers at all levels.

Failure to live up to this challenge results in suboptimal institutional choices that imperil the survival of the concerned nonprofit organizations.

It has been shown that the transaction cost determinants of nonprofit organizational boundaries often have different effects on the boundaries of the mission-related and mission-unrelated activities. In this sense, speaking about the 'overall' nonprofit organizational boundaries may be misleading insofar as it underemphasizes this distinction. Another major result consists of identifying the nonprofit-specific governance mechanism of collective action, which is used by nonprofit firms beside the traditional mechanisms of market and hierarchy. The collective governance differs from market and hierarchy in being based on a high commonness of stakeholder interests and thus underlies the distinct positive institutional identity of nonprofit organization. As the basic modes of for-profit economic organization, market and hierarchy represent suboptimal governance mechanisms for those transactions whose participants' interests coincide to a substantial extent. At the same time, various governance mechanisms utilized by nonprofit firms have been shown to interact with each other and thereby to affect the evolution of these firms' boundaries, structure and behavior. The proposed continuum view of market, hierarchy and nonprofit organization may be regarded as an institutional economics restatement of the old wisdom that nonprofit organization embodies collective action of free individuals seeking to achieve common purposes.

Summing up, this chapter has proposed an open-ended framework that may both support managerial decision making and inform scholarly research on the nonprofit sector. Managers may benefit from the explicit identification of the factors determining nonprofit organizational boundaries and internal as well as external governance mechanisms. The proposed framework, of course, needs further specification and adaptation to individual situational contexts if it is to yield any specific prescriptions for actual managerial behavior. This specification, at the same time, is a task that may be taken up by the scholarly community. The suggested hypothetical relationships between production costs, transaction costs and organizational legitimacy considerations on the volume of mission-related and mission-unrelated activities need to be operationalized and empirically tested. Further developing and testing the relationship between organizational boundaries and the internal and external governance mechanisms presents yet another implication for future research.

References

Ballou, Jeffrey P.and Burton A. Weisbrod (2003), 'Managerial rewards and the behavior of for-profit, governmental, and nonprofit organizations: evidence from the hospital industry', *Journal of Public Economics*, **87** (9), 1895–920.
Brown, Eleanor and Al Slivinski (2006), 'Nonprofit organizations and the market', in Walter Powell and Richard Steinberg (eds), *The Nonprofit Sector: A Research Handbook*, New Haven, CT: Yale University Press, pp. 140–58.
Carver, John (1990), *Boards that Make a Difference*, San Fracisco: Jossey-Bass.
Coase, Ronald H. (1937), 'The nature of the firm', *Economica*, **4** (16), 386–405.
Drucker, Peter F. (1990), 'Lessons for successful nonprofit governance', *Nonprofit Management and Leadership*, **1** (1), 7–13.
Golensky, Martha (1993), 'The board–executive relationship in nonprofit organizations: partnership or power struggle?', *Nonprofit Management and Leadership*, **4** (2), 177–91.
Herman, Robert D. and Richard D. Heimovics (1990), 'The effective nonprofit executive: leader of the board', *Nonprofit Management and Leadership*, **1** (2), 167–80.

Leete, Laura (2006), 'Work in the nonprofit sector', in Walter Powell and Richard Steinberg (eds), *The Nonprofit Sector: A Research Handbook*, New Haven, CT: Yale University Press, pp. 159–79.

Lohmann, Roger A. (1992), 'The commons: a multidisciplinary approach to nonprofit organizations', *Nonprofit and Voluntary Sector Quarterly*, **21** (3), 309–24.

Ménard, Claude (2004), 'The economics of hybrid organizations', *Journal of Institutional and Theoretical Economics*, **160**, 1–32.

Ostrower, Francie and Melissa M. Stone (2006), 'Governance: research trends, gaps, and future prospects', in Walter Powell and Richard Steinberg (eds), *The Nonprofit Sector: A Research Handbook*, New Haven, CT: Yale University Press, pp. 612–28.

Peterson, H. Christopher, Allen Wysocki and Stephen B. Harsh (2001), 'Strategic choice along the vertical coordination continuum', *International Food and Agribusiness Management Review*, **4** (2), 149–66.

Preston, Anne E. (1989), 'The nonprofit worker in a for-profit world', *Journal of Labor Economics*, **7** (4), 38–63.

Rose-Ackerman, Susan (1987), 'Ideals versus dollars: donors, charity managers, and government grants', *Journal of Political Economy*, **95** (4), 810–23.

Salamon, Lester M. and Helmut K. Anheier (1992), 'In search of the nonprofit sector. I: the question of definitions', *Voluntas: International Journal of Voluntary and Nonprofit Organizations*, **3** (2), 125–51.

Steinberg, Richard (2006), 'Economic theories of nonprofit organization', in Walter Powell and Richard Steinberg (eds), *The Nonprofit Sector: A Research Handbook*, New Haven, CT: Yale University Press, pp. 117–39.

Valentinov, Vladislav (2006), 'The logic of the nonprofit sector: an organizational economics perspective', *Zeitschrift für öffentliche und gemeinwirtschaftliche Unternehmen*, **29** (2), 214–26.

Valentinov, Vladislav (2007), 'The property rights approach to nonprofit organization: the role of intrinsic motivation', *Public Organization Review*, **7** (1), 41–55.

Valentinov, Vladislav (2008), 'The transaction cost theory of the nonprofit firm: beyond opportunism', *Nonprofit and Voluntary Sector Quarterly*, **37** (1), 5–18.

Valentinov, Vladislav and Jana Fritzsch (2007), 'Are cooperatives hybrid organizations? An alternative viewpoint', *Journal of Rural Cooperation*, **35** (2), 141–55.

Williamson, Oliver E. (1991), 'Comparative economic organization: the analysis of discrete structural alternatives', *Administrative Science Quarterly*, **36** (2), 269–96.

Williamson, Oliver E. (1996), *The Mechanisms of Governance*, New York: Oxford University Press.

15 Franchises and federations: the economics of multi-site nonprofit organizations
Dennis R. Young and Lewis Faulk

Introduction
The purpose of this chapter is to consider the various economic factors that may explain the formation and structure of multi-part, multi-site nonprofit organizations that operate on a regional, national or global scale. We are particularly interested in how federations are related to nonprofits' capacities to achieve efficient scale in promulgating their missions and services.

Following Selsky (1998), we define federations simply as 'associations in which the affiliates [members] are organizations rather than individuals' (p. 286). This is a more inclusive definition than others. For example, O'Flanagan and Taliente (2004) define a federation as 'a network of local affiliates that share a mission, a brand, and a program model but are legally independent of one another and of the national office'. This is one type of widely recognized nonprofit federation, akin, as we shall discuss below, to a franchise system. Here, however, we shall take a wider view that includes several other variants.

Indeed, nonprofit federations exist in a wide variety of forms and can be described by various terms including federations, franchises, membership associations, systems, leagues, councils and decentralized corporations. Some are aggregations of organizational units of very similar function and structure, all of which consider themselves to be part of the same overall system or umbrella, such as YMCAs or chapters of the March of Dimes. Others are aggregations of more distinct and varied organizations in the same industry or field of service, such as the Child Welfare League of America or the American Symphony Orchestra League. Still others are aggregations of differentiated organizations in a broad field of service that consider themselves part of the same system, such as a regional Catholic Charities or Jewish Federation. Yet others are aggregations of diverse nonprofit organizations that affiliate with one another for a specific purpose such as collaborative fundraising, policy advocacy or capacity building, such as a regional United Way or a statewide association of nonprofit organizations like the Ohio Association of Nonprofit Organizations (OANO).

While these alternative manifestations are quite varied in nature, they are all 'federated' in some way, i.e. they all feature some sharing of authority and control between their participating units (affiliates) and a central office. However, these federations form in several different ways and for different reasons. Some develop through the aggregation of various pre-existing organizations while others manifest themselves through expansion of a nuclear organization into multi-unit entities. Moreover, federations evolve under alternative internal logics involving a number of different economic considerations including transaction costs among organizational units, economies of scale and scope, internalization of externalities and principal–agent problems.

In this chapter we first review research from the nonprofit, economics and management literatures to give us a sense of what we currently know about the structure and economics of nonprofit federations. However, since nonprofit federations are not precisely defined in any uniform way, we then describe multiple varieties of them and identify what distinguishes one type from another. We further characterize alternative scenarios through which different types of federations are likely to form and the underlying economic rationales that appear to drive these scenarios. This brings us to questions thus far unresolved or unexplored in previous research, particularly the issue of 'going to scale' in the nonprofit sector. A concluding section considers why this all matters in the broad context of nonprofit management, policy and research.

What do we know?
Early papers by Young (1989) and Oster (1992, 1996) sketched out taxonomies of nonprofit federated organizations. Young divided these organizations into three categories – corporate organizations in which authority and control were centralized, federations in which there was a balance between central authority and that of local affiliates, and trade associations in which sovereignty resided in organizational members. Subsequently, Oster claimed that most nonprofit organizations in the USA were part of overall national systems that could be divided into two categories – corporations with branch offices, and franchises in which rules and incentives ensured substantial autonomy for local affiliates. Franchise systems have been described in the business literature as a hybrid form of organization, between a hierarchy and a market, 'requiring a nationally recognized brand name and efficient back-office operations, with customer service occurring locally' (Baucus et al., 1996, p. 374). Oster (1996) argued that, for various reasons, including access to capital, performance incentives and mobilizing and motivating volunteers, the franchise form was preferred for the majority of national nonprofit organizations that she examined. These arguments are generally consistent with those in the for-profit literature on franchising, which identify shirking behavior, risk sharing and free-rider problems as factors that influence companies when they decide to franchise out or wholly own retail units (Brickley and Dark, 1987).

What don't we know?
The literature on nonprofit federations is fragmentary and piecemeal. Thus an important contribution to knowledge would be to classify and categorize nonprofit federations and begin to explore the factors that have led to different forms. Federations vary along several dimensions including size, as indicated by memberships, revenues or expenditures, or other economic measures; geographic scope; fields of service; governance structures; religious affiliations; sources of income and so on. Two important generic variables on which we focus here are (a) the nature of the relationship between a central body and the affiliated organizational units, and (b) the degree of homogeneity among the affiliated units. In combination, these two variables describe a wide spectrum of federations and also correlate with different economic rationales and scenarios under which federations develop. They are also key decision variables, as leaders of federations must make strategic and negotiated choices about memberships, governance and the degrees to which authority and control are distributed between affiliates and a central authority.

Nature of affiliates

Federations can consist of affiliates that are highly homogeneous, highly heterogeneous, or distinct but complementary in some important way. For example, the affiliated councils of the Girl Scouts of the USA or the Boy Scouts of America are highly homogeneous. While they are separately incorporated, they all take the same form, follow the same rules, use the same symbols and materials, earn their revenue in similar fashion and operate in pretty much the same manner. The same is true of many health charities, such as the American Cancer Society or the March of Dimes.

In contrast, member organizations of a local United Way are highly heterogeneous, consisting of different kinds of health and social service organizations whose common thread is to serve the needs of a local community while receiving some fraction of their support from a shared community fundraising campaign. Similarly, the Child Welfare League of America (CWLA) encompasses diverse social service organizations that address the needs of children in some way. Its members have a variety of missions and programs, including day care, foster care and education, and separate names, logos and incorporated status, and are likely to belong to other federations within their communities or particular fields of service as well. They join CWLA for its educational resources, conferences, policy advocacy on behalf of children and other common needs and interests, paying with membership dues.

Another category of federation features organizational affiliates that relate to one another as a 'system' and/or part of a larger religious or ethnic community. Catholic Charities, Jewish Philanthropies and Lutheran Services fit this description. They consist of various social service organizations, schools and health care organizations that are interconnected through systems of referral, resource allocation and fundraising, shared values and policy setting by a central (regional) federation body. While these affiliate organizations have highly diverse missions, they are complementary to one another so that as a whole they can address the needs of clients or communities with multiple issues and challenges.

Central–affiliate relations

Relations between a federation's central office and its affiliated organizations also encompass a wide spectrum of possibilities. These range from tight control through a corporate governing structure that limits affiliate autonomy, to a balanced system in which central and affiliate units share authority, to highly decentralized arrangements in which affiliates are autonomous and the central office is substantially confined to a limited support role. Here a distinction is made between control and decentralization. A large federation may delegate administrative authority to its affiliates for efficiency purposes but still retain authority or control through various mechanisms of accountability, such as issuing and revoking charters. In this sense, some nonprofit federations operate like franchises, setting rules and often narrow limits on affiliates' discretion, while eschewing direct control. Other federations operate essentially as unified corporations, with their affiliates more tightly controlled and better characterized as 'branch offices' (Oster, 1996). Alternatively, in highly decentralized federations, autonomous members may choose to follow guidelines or policies defined by the central body but retain discretion to deviate from those policies. Bradach (2003) reasons that federations whose programs are more highly standardized or that do not strongly depend on

Table 15.1 Structural variety of nonprofit federations and nature of affiliates

Control/diversity	Homogeneous	Diverse	Complementary
Centralized	Chapters	Branches	Divisions
Balanced	Franchisees	Affiliates	Partners
Decentralized	Affiliates	Members	Associates

replicating a particular organizational culture can employ looser, more decentralized structures, while those that are less standardized or more highly dependent on a particular organizational culture must necessarily be tighter and more centralized. He cites STRIVE, a job-training organization, as an example of the former, and City Year, an organization that engages young people for a year of urban community service, as an illustration of the latter.

Health charities such as the American Cancer Society or March of Dimes tend to be more centralized, corporate-type federations (Standley, 2001). Social service federations such as Volunteers of America or Catholic Charities tend to balance central authority with local autonomy and discretion, setting rules and guidelines for operations but also allowing programmatic choice at the local level. Finally, federations that have coalesced around a common set of issues or interests are likely to be highly decentralized, operating essentially as membership associations. The Southeastern Council of Foundations, the National Council of Nonprofits, Independent Sector, or the Nonprofit Academic Centers Council are examples of such association-type federations whose central offices' authority derives essentially from the consensus they can develop among their member organizations.

Clearly both the homogeneity of affiliates and the degree of central control are continuous rather than dichotomous variables. Moreover, many multi-part nonprofits involve a mixture of forms – for example, having both branches and franchised units, as also found in for-profit companies (e.g., see Brickley and Dark, 1987). For purposes of explication Table 15.1 may be helpful in developing a language and taxonomy of nonprofit federations, recognizing that the borders in the table are necessarily porous. The names for local units suggested in this table are common and descriptive, but by no means uniformly employed.

Note that Oster's pioneering work addresses only two of the nine varieties of federated organizations charted in Table 15.1. Her analysis applies basically to organizations all of whose affiliates do essentially the same thing, sometimes as chapters or branches controlled directly by central headquarters and sometimes as franchisees influenced through a combination of controls and incentives. O'Flanagan and Taliente (2004) focus solely on the latter category. Young's (1989) classification stretches a little further to cover decentralized organizations better characterized as organizational membership associations, as well as organizations whose affiliates perform diverse functions as part of a federal organization or as members of an association. Neither the early works of Oster nor of Young address federated systems that combine diverse but complementary affiliates in a coordinated system. The analysis here attempts to broaden the discussion by examining the scenarios through which these various kinds of nonprofit federations form and the underlying economic considerations that drive them.

Scenarios of nonprofit agglomeration and growth

One can think of any complex organization as having started with a single (or a few) self-contained organizational units, much as biological creatures begin as single cells. In the nonprofit sector, a nuclear organization may come into being in a number of ways. In particular, it could be established from 'whole cloth' by an entrepreneur or entrepreneurial team that successfully attracts resource support from interested donors and clients. Or it could be spun off from an established organization that determines that it, and its spin-off, would be better off operating separately. In the latter case, some affiliation between the new organization and its parent may be retained, perhaps through a federation. For example, a church might decide to spin off its soup kitchen or used-clothing distribution center, but continue to support it financially and with client referrals. New organizations may also be established by multiple parent organizations, such as a coalition to revive a downtown area, which parent organizations may support through financial assistance. A variant of this scenario involves the engagement of a funding organization that supports the coalition and provides leverage for a central organization to take root, exert control over coalition members, and perhaps replicate itself elsewhere. In these latter scenarios, the new organizations already contain the seeds of multi-part federated arrangements.

The centrality of entrepreneurship and growth in the development of federations mirrors the logic of franchises in the business sector. Baucus et al. (1996) argue that franchises grow in part because entrepreneurs are anxious to exploit the benefits of a franchise system in order to gain a competitive advantage over rivals in starting or expanding local businesses. Similarly, case studies of start-ups as well as program innovations and expansions in the nonprofit sector often reveal entrepreneurial choices to leverage the advantages of federations and the difficulties of undertaking such initiatives independently (Young, 1985). As a nuclear organization grows and develops, its structural form becomes a more important issue. Various growth (and non-growth) scenarios are possible. The organization could fail and disappear, or it could find an equilibrium state without further growth. And if it grows, it may do so in a number of ways:

1. Expand as a single entity, establishing internal divisions and branch offices as needed to manage efficiently. Thus the March of Dimes was established as a single organization and grew through the establishment of tightly controlled chapters throughout the country.
2. Replicate itself through franchise arrangements that allow it to retain control over the character of its affiliates as they spread and grow, establishing a central office to oversee franchised units. Once the system is established, independent local nonprofit entrepreneurs could decide to buy into it, establishing local franchises and agreeing to abide by the rules of the system. Breakthrough Collaborative is one contemporary example (www.breakthroughcollaborative.org). McCarthy (2002) provides several examples from the social movement field – the Anti-Saloon League, the Southern Farmers' Alliance, Mothers Against Drunk Driving (MADD) and the Association for Children for Enforcement and Support (ACES) – whose evolution varies considerably in terms of the level of control exerted, initially or ultimately, by the central organization and its sharing or delegation of authority and responsibility with affiliates.
3. The organization could be imitated by other groups or entrepreneurs who adapt its concept to other venues. In this process, the original organization could be passive,

possibly hostile, or it might actively assist its imitators, perhaps licensing or selling its programs or products (Taylor et al., 2002). Eventually, the original organization and its imitators may decide to collaborate by establishing an umbrella organization to assist with common challenges, support further growth, and possibly police the parameters of operation. The United Way of America and Boys and Girls Clubs of America illustrate this mode of development. The Committee for a SANE Nuclear Policy appears to be another, albeit somewhat ragged, example in which many chapters emerged simultaneously, requiring a national organization that could regulate and weed out affiliates (McCarthy, 2002).

4.   The organization could expand its concept, diversifying the kinds of goods and services it offers, and the clients and donors it attracts. For example, a social service organization emphasizing treatment of a particular target group may find that it can do a better job by adding preventive or education services to its program portfolio. The Jewish Board of Family and Children's Services (JBFCS) in New York grew in this way, partly through mergers with other local social service organizations, and under the purview of an umbrella federation that encouraged its diversification and expansion (Young, 1985). Project HOPE, a poverty fighting organization in Detroit, began as a food distribution program, later extending to job training and education but remaining local in its operation, an approach that Taylor et al. (2002) call 'scaling deep'.

5.   The organization could decide to remain narrowly focused in its services but increase effectiveness by expanding its affiliations with other organizations that provide complementary services. This may lead ultimately to a federated system of diverse, related organizations such as Lutheran Social Services or Jewish Philanthropies. Local nonprofit entrepreneurs, e.g executives of existing, perhaps fledgling, independent organizations, might choose to negotiate entree into such a federation.

6.   Organizations growing (or struggling) through all of the above scenarios may identify areas of common interest with other organizations, leading them to form associations of diverse members that pursue mutual goals. The American Association of Museums and the Child Welfare League of America illustrate this mode of development. Taylor et al. (2002) cite the establishment of the Coalition of Essential Schools (CES), a network of member schools and educational centers that share ten essential principles of school restructuring and redesign. More broadly, even more diverse sets of nonprofit organizations may form federations such as state associations of nonprofit organizations (e.g., see Selsky, 1998), in order to pursue common interests in policy advocacy, and educational and technical assistance services.

Gaps in our knowledge

Much additional research on nonprofit federations is needed, including more systematic data collection, empirical modeling and analysis. All this depends, however, on better theory, which in turn requires probing of the underlying economic factors behind the alternative structures and growth scenarios. These factors include economies of scale, economies of scope, transaction costs, inter-organizational externalities and principal–agent issues.

Economies of scale

A nuclear organization may find that it can address its mission more efficiently by expanding the scale at which its services, or certain of its activities or functions, are carried out. Given competitive or other pressures to become more efficient or effective, several strategic avenues may lead nonprofits to increase the scale of operations. One obvious strategy is internal expansion or possibly merger, but depending on the nature of the scale economies there are other strategies as well. For example, if savings from expanding scale stem from more efficient purchasing, marketing or fund development, such support functions can be retained by a central office while smaller-scale field operations may be accomplished through branching or franchising. Indeed, for franchise-like federations whose members provide very similar services, O'Flanagan and Taliente (2004) argue that economies of scale in the areas of brand management, back-office services, fundraising and performance management constitute the essential justification for federation. Similarly, Bradach (2003) and Taylor et al. (2002) argue that having a national umbrella allows nonprofits to exploit scale economies in quality management, organizational and programmatic learning, as well as administrative support services. This mirrors observations that economies of scale in franchise operations in the business sector manifest themselves in such functions as 'regional and national advertising, quality control and product standardization' (Brown, 1998, p. 322). Alternatively, if the nuclear organization chooses not to expand internally (or finds that attaining sufficient scale to reap savings is beyond its grasp), it may choose to join with imitators or organizations of similar interest in forming umbrella organizations, or join industry associations that perform the support functions at an efficient scale under an appropriate fee structure. Similarly, an organization choosing to join a system of complementary organizations may also take advantage of that system's scale to achieve support function economies.

Risk management is another area where economies of scale may apply (Taylor et al., 2002). A federated system may be viewed as a portfolio of (semi-) autonomous enterprises each with its own probabilities of success and failure. By differentiating its organizational 'holdings' through federation, a growing nonprofit organization may reduce the volatility of its overall performance or maximize performance within chosen parameters of risk tolerance. The effectiveness of this approach in managing risk necessarily grows with scale since expansion enables diversification. Expansion also permits greater organizational learning, helping members of the organization to avoid poor practices and learn about less risky ones. Alternatively, when organizations band together into a federation, they can exploit economies of scale to insure themselves against risk. In effect, the federation serves as a safety net for any one of its affiliates.

Finally, a flip side to risk management is innovation, which can also benefit from economies of scale. In particular, federations serve the purpose of bringing together many local units that can (systematically or randomly) experiment with different programmatic approaches while the central organization collects, analyzes and disseminates these experiences to the benefit of the entire set of affiliates.

One particular nonprofit federation that illustrates economies of scale as a driver is Teach for America (TFA), a national nonprofit organization whose purpose is to build a teacher corps of young college graduates and place these individuals into inner-city and rural schools where students lack the resources for a good education. Since 1989, TFA has grown impressively into a national organization with more than 500 full-time staff, some 3500 members (volunteers), an annual budget of $70 million, operations in 26 regions of the USA, and a strong central headquarters office.

TFA can be characterized as a unified corporation with a single governing board and multiple branch offices. This structure seems efficient in view of important functions of the central office that are subject to economies of scale. Headquarters is organized into national 'teams' that address admissions of new corps members, alumni affairs, growth strategy and development, finance and fiscal control, marketing and communications, program design, recruitment, research and public policy, human resource development, technology and teacher preparation. These are all functions that can be centrally managed more efficiently at larger scale, especially because TFA has developed a particular brand and makes its mark with a distinctive (uniform) program design.

Economies of scope
Often the mission of a nonprofit organization is more effectively addressed if its services are offered in tandem or combination with other, complementary services. For example, the effectiveness of an occupational rehabilitation or work-training organization may be enhanced if convenient child day care services are easily accessible to its clients. A social service organization addressing the needs of children with behavior problems may be able to accomplish its goals more easily if it can coordinate its services with a family counseling program. A nonprofit devoted to improving conditions in a low-income community engages a variety of service providers, in areas such as housing, social services, health care and youth recreation. As with scale economies, there is a variety of approaches to exploiting economies of scope. A nonprofit can expand laterally to encompass multiple service divisions under one organizational roof. Or it can form contractual relationships with other complementary nonprofits. If economies of scope are sufficiently compelling in such contractual relationships, the parties may find it in their mutual interests to knit themselves together into an integrated system with its own separate central coordinating body. Alternatively, if the original nonprofit were set up by a parent body such as a community-based religious or fraternal organization, the latter might see the merits of spinning off other such complementary nonprofits and serving as the coordinating mechanism, such as Catholic Charities has done.

If economies of scope are present but relatively weak, a loose affiliation among complementary nonprofits such as a community council structure may suffice to exploit them. Stronger economies of scope may call for a local federated arrangement such as Catholic Charities. Economies of scope that are stronger still might call for the development of a single, comprehensive nonprofit or the legal merger of complementary nonprofits such as the JBFCS. Economies of scope may also play a role in the development of nonprofits with relatively more homogeneous service models. In these cases, it may be advantageous for the nonprofits involved to be members of multiple federated structures. For example, a Girl Scout Council would be a franchisee of the Girl Scouts of the USA but it might also be a member of the Child Welfare League of America and a member of its local United Way planning council. The latter affiliations would help the council exploit economies of scope by connecting with other services and organizations helpful to its own programming for girls.

Economies of scope play an important role in Community Action to Fight Asthma (CAFA), a complex network of organizations that can be described as a loose federation of local coalitions supported by a statewide organization in California with regional centers in various parts of the state. The purpose of CAFA is to address the indoor and outdoor environmental hazards that trigger asthma in school-age children in California

(CAFA, 2005). CAFA formally stems from an initiative of the California Endowment, a private, statewide health foundation that was formed in 1996 as a result of Blue Cross of California's creation of WellPoint Health Networks, a for-profit corporation. The California Endowment's mission is to expand access to affordable, quality health care for underserved individuals and communities, and to promote fundamental improvements in the health status of all Californians. However, the CAFA initiative built upon and focused the work of local coalitions of diverse organizations with an interest in asthma, including hospitals, health plans, health clinics, community-based organizations, local chapters of the American Lung Association and public health departments. CAFA engages 12 such coalitions around the state, which coordinate with CAFA through three regional centers, which in turn report to the CAFA State Coordinating Office. The origins of the 12 local coalitions are diverse. Most pre-existed CAFA and were initiated by leaders of local organizations concerned with air quality and local health issues. Other coalitions were stimulated by the CAFA initiative itself, which offered grant funding to organize the coalitions and develop programs to address environmental hazards triggering asthma. In all cases, CAFA funding and technical support have strengthened the local coalitions and focused their priorities on environmental causes of asthma in children.

Economies of scope are clearly important to CAFA's growth and development. The local coalitions form largely as a result of the varied contributions that different kinds of health care and community organizations can make to the overall solution of asthma-related environmental problems. As a coordinated group, hospitals, clinics and other community organizations are able to be more effective in addressing the overall problem than they could be as individual actors. Similarly, partnering organizations with the state coordinating office combine their expertise in research, policy and media utilization.

Transaction costs
All structural arrangements involve transaction costs, i.e. the costs of doing business associated with economic exchanges, including the gathering and assessment of information, and the monitoring and evaluation of processes and results. Ronald H. Coase (1937) recognized that the growth and size of a firm, and the boundaries between the firm and the open market, were intimately related to the nature of transaction costs. Coase hypothesized that a firm would continue to expand until the cost of the marginal transaction of doing business inside the firm exceeded the cost of performing that same transaction through a contractual arrangement in the marketplace. An application of this idea is developed by Brown (1998), who argued that the costs of motivating employees through an internal system of merit promotion rise as the ratio of subordinates to supervisors increases. At some level, therefore, firms choose to accommodate additional growth through franchises. This substitutes performance-based financial incentives for promotional opportunities and leads to a mixture of internally owned and franchised retail outlets.

This basic idea is powerful for understanding how many nonprofit federations develop. A nuclear nonprofit may grow through internal expansion until it becomes too costly to conduct all business through a central hierarchy – at which point alternatives may be considered, including the establishment of branches, chapters or divisions on the one hand, or franchises or affiliates on the other. This decision may hinge on the relative costs of carrying out transactions under these different arrangements. In the former cases, the transaction costs center on internal administrative, budgeting and control systems, while in the latter cases, transaction costs involve more arm's-length mechanisms of negotiation, monitoring and resource exchange through contracts. Transaction costs considerations apply to all three types of program combinations provided by nonprofit federated organizations. For homogeneous services, transaction costs may determine the point at which a nonprofit organization decides to franchise itself rather than grow internally as well as what combination of franchised and internally controlled branches it chooses to operate as it continues to grow. At very large scale, a further decision may be required to compare the transaction costs of franchising versus even more decentralized membership arrangements. For example, within the USA, the Girl Scouts of the USA may be understood as a franchised operation with strong central authority, whereas internationally the Girl Scout movement is organized more loosely as a membership association among national Girl Scout federations.

Similarly, for nonprofits offering diverse but related services (e.g. variations on child recreation programs), growth may require deciding on expansion through the creation of internal divisions (as a local Jewish Community Center might do) versus establishing similar affiliates meeting stipulated guidelines (such as Boys and Girls Clubs of America) versus looser affiliation among diverse organizations through a membership association structure (such as the Child Welfare League of America). These various arrangements involve different combinations of internal versus market-based transactions, the relative magnitudes of which change with the scale and scope of the organization. Thus the observation that franchises in the business sector represent a hybrid form between hierarchies and markets applies to nonprofit federations as well (Baucus et al., 1996).

Similar arguments apply to federations involving complementary services. A nonprofit child day care organization that needs a counseling component must decide whether to set up a new internal division, establish a separate, more autonomous affiliate governed by an overall social service system, or form contractual arrangements with autonomous providers, perhaps through a looser associational arrangement.

Overall, it is clear that the nature of transaction costs varies among different kinds of structural arrangements and types of services. For nonprofits offering a singular mode of service, the costs of monitoring the expansion of operations may be relatively modest through franchise operations compared to internal expansion, for example. Uniform rules, standards and procedures can be clearly delineated and monitored from afar, allowing efficient administration over larger and more widely dispersed operations. Such transaction costs become more substantial if expansion entails the engagement of more diverse modes of provision. Either tighter controls are needed through the development of integrated systems or lower degrees of control must be accepted.

The Cleveland Orchestra and the American Symphony Orchestra League (ASOL) illustrate the role of transaction costs in organizational growth and the development of a federation structure. The Cleveland Orchestra (Rosenberg, 2000) is a very successful, locally based ensemble that has achieved worldwide recognition among classical orchestras. It has grown as an organization in several ways. It tours and sells its music worldwide, it includes a chorus and youth orchestra, and it operates a summer entertainment venue. The orchestra belongs to ASOL, the national association of major symphony orchestras. As such, it is highly autonomous part of a loose nonprofit federation. Orchestras are essentially local organizations with few compelling reasons to affiliate closely with other orchestras, except to bolster the appeal of classical music in general. There are few economies of scale in orchestra playing. And while there are economies of scope associated with joint operation of choruses, youth orchestras, gift shops and summer entertainment venues, these do not generally extend beyond the locality (Cleveland). Nor is the welfare of the Cleveland Orchestra much harmed if the Los Angeles Symphony declines, nor is it helped if the latter improves. Moreover, the argument that federations help assure the consumer of quality control through uniformity does not apply in this field; indeed, the classical music consumer may look explicitly for a variety of styles or approaches from different orchestras. Only to the extent that classical orchestra music as a field suffers or rises in reputation or popularity is the Cleveland Orchestra affected indirectly by the triumphs or tribulations of other orchestras.

Given the localized nature of the orchestra business, transaction costs fail to drive the Cleveland Orchestra towards any form of strong federation. While there are certainly many cases of orchestra conductors with multiple orchestra appointments, none are the result of organizational consolidation or coordination. At best, these conductors negotiate separately with each of their employers and must try to accommodate different tastes and capacities. Thus transaction costs across ensembles are very high except in pursuing common industry issues – leading only to loose association among orchestras and little incentive for any one orchestra, no matter how good, to replicate itself or expand outside its own venue. The ASOL serves to accommodate these minimal transaction costs through a very loose form of association.

Principal–agent considerations

Principal–agent theory deals with the problems of carrying out the intent of a decision maker or an 'owner' when the task is delegated to a manager, subordinate or contractor (see Barney and Hesterly, 2006). Delegation or contracting inevitably involves some loss of control that must be addressed through a combination of incentives and oversight. In the for-profit literature various factors are cited as affecting the ability of managers to control their operations, including geographical dispersion of operations, costs and effectiveness of alternative reward systems, and ability to measure performance (Brown, 1998).

In the context of nonprofit federations, alternative structural arrangements offer differing degrees of oversight, control and alignment between principal and agent, and may be more or less effective for the different variants of service embraced by a federation. In particular, the measurement of performance in some service areas is more difficult than in others, and some services are delivered in more geographically dispersed patterns than in others. There are some special characteristics of nonprofit service that appear to complicate decisions to engage various structural forms. For example, the dearth of unambiguous quantitative measures of performance (such as profit) may enhance the attractiveness of federated arrangements that allow for benchmarking of some units against others, using whatever quantitative and qualitative indicators may be available. The more easily such internal comparative measurements can be developed, the more the principal–agent problem can be ameliorated, assuming that the measures themselves are not too costly to collect or too distorting in the incentives they may introduce.

Interestingly, the principal–agent problem in the for-profit sector is usually viewed as a 'top-down' issue. In the nonprofit sector a more fundamental question is raised by the alternative federated arrangements and modes of nonprofit expansion – namely who exactly is the agent and who is the principal in any given case? The three kinds of arrangements in Table 15.1 yield different answers. For centralized federations, the central organization is the presumed principal and the divisions or branches are the agents for carrying out its intent. Alternatively, for decentralized federations, sovereignty for the members is implied and the central organization or federation may be considered an agent of the members. For balanced federations, the situation is more complex: the balanced model suggests that the central organization and its affiliates are each both principals and agents, with each level having some degree of autonomy and accountability to the other.

The scenario through which a nonprofit federation grows provides clues as to the direction in which the principal–agent relationships flow. Nuclear nonprofit organizations that grow into federations through establishment of branches, differentiated divisions, franchises or licensed affiliates clearly intend to remain in control of their systemic agendas, seeking to work through the various kinds of subordinate units or local agents. Alternatively, federations that are established by several autonomous nonprofit organizations seeking advantages of scale or scope are based on affiliate sovereignty, which is not lightly surrendered. Here, the affiliates are the principals and the central office of the federation is the agent for carrying out their common purposes. Finally, it must be recognized that as federations evolve through these various scenarios, circumstances change. For example, franchisees or affiliates may negotiate or otherwise acquire greater autonomy as they develop. Alternatively, members of negotiated federations may surrender considerable autonomy to the central office, yielding situations where principal and agent roles must be parsed for different areas of responsibility as in a federal constitutional system. Thus the evolution of a federation may involve a sorting-out process in which authority for different issues, especially new ones, is allocated to different levels, and checks and balances may be instituted between levels of authority. Bradach (2003) cites such evolutionary developments in the structures of STRIVE and City Year.

Habitat for Humanity (HFH) provides another interesting example of the role of principal–agent issues in federation growth and development. Habitat is a loose federation of 1600 local affiliates in the USA and 2300 in total worldwide (Bridgespan Group, 2007). The original HFH model was launched by Millard and Linda Fuller in 1968 in Southern Georgia and subsequently implemented by the Fullers in Zaire (now Democratic Republic of Congo) in the mid-1970s. Habitat for Humanity International (HFHI), which became the central organization in a federation, was established in 1976. Over the 1976–84 period, HFHI expanded its operations in the USA and created its affiliate network. The organization grew rapidly through the 1980s and 1990s powered by a strong 'brand' recognition reinforced by celebrity participation, most notably former President Jimmy Carter. However, affiliates were independently incorporated, rooted in their particular communities and encouraged to be innovative and individualized in their approaches to building low-income housing in their communities. Under Mr Fuller, HFHI's CEO until 2005, expanding the number of affiliates while maintaining local discretion was an explicit growth strategy. Fuller's idea was that the more affiliates there were, the more affordable housing would be built.

Recently, however, under the new leadership of Jonathan Reckford, HFHI has put the brakes on this strategy and begun to exert more central control – enforcing a 10 percent tithe on local affiliates, disaffiliating several US affiliates that had been relatively inactive or in arrears, and proposing a comprehensive new agreement between HFHI and its affiliates which includes a quality assurance checklist, specifies conditions for disaffiliation and gives HFHI additional controls and rights to affiliate assets in the case of dissolution (Strom, 2007; Foundation Center, 2007). The proposed agreement would replace a two-page covenant of principles and guidelines. There is mixed support among affiliates for signing this agreement. Principal–agent issues are salient at the present stage of HFHI's evolution. Until recently, it has been clear that the organization has been one of shared responsibility and control between autonomous affiliates and headquarters, with sovereignty residing largely with the affiliates. The proposed new agreement would cede substantial control and monitoring responsibility to headquarters.

Inter-organizational externalities
Inter-organizational externalities are the indirect economic impacts that one organization has on another, outside the realm of direct market transactions. Business sector research-ers recognize this phenomenon in the context of franchises where, for example, poor performance by renegade outlets or lack of consensus among franchisees and franchisors on overall goals or strategies can reduce performance of all franchisees (Baucus et al., 1996). In the case of nonprofit federations, as in business, such effects are closely bound to issues of reputation. For example, Taylor et al. (2002) warn against the harm that can be done by 'renegade' affiliates. Organizations sharing the same or similar names, or to a lesser degree, organizations operating in the same industry or realm of service, can affect each other by their actions because consumers, donors or the general public may associ-ate such 'related' organizations with one another in their own minds, and paint them all with the same brush when it comes to allocating resources, choosing service providers or advocating for changes in policy. Thus, all United Ways were badly hurt by scandals in the central office or in isolated local United Ways in the 1990s. All Catholic parishes were hurt by the pedophile problems of certain highly visible dioceses. And, perhaps to a lesser degree, all foster care agencies are hurt by stories of abuse in some foster homes, just as all universities are hurt by corruption scandals involving student loan officers in some institutions. The recent decision by Harvard, for example, to provide deeply discounted tuition to students of middle-class families is having a strong ripple effect among other private universities (Glaton, 2007).

Inter-organizational externalities are made all the more salient by the role of trust in the nonprofit sector. Trust is one of the theoretical pillars on which the presence of nonprofit organizations in a market economy is understood (Steinberg, 2006). In situa-tions where consumers or donors are disadvantaged by asymmetry of information, the nonprofit form serves as a signal of honesty and integrity, based on the incentives and governing arrangements that differentiate nonprofits from for-profit firms. Issues of trust cut both ways for nonprofit federations. Nonprofit organizational units that are part of a federation can be hurt by such affiliation if one of its members behaves badly. Alternatively, nonprofit organizations are helped by belonging to federations that enjoy name recognition and trust, and which encourage or enforce appropriate behavior. Bradach (2003) calls this 'ensuring the brand'.

This phenomenon is most obvious for federations that operate as franchise systems, especially in an age of easy transportation and communication when people are more mobile and less deeply rooted in their own communities than they used to be (Putnam, 2000). Thus nonprofit franchise systems confer the same trust to a Girls and Boys Club in Ohio as in Georgia or New York. A nuclear nonprofit seeking to expand from a location where it is well known to other locales where it is not, may be well served by establishing a national brand name that is widely accepted, or by qualifying for affiliation with a pre-established franchise that already enjoys such recognition and trust. It is also important for a franchised system to protect its name by resisting infringement by imitators using similar names. While there may be just one American Cancer Society, for example, there are numerous charities with 'Cancer' in their title.

Inter-organizational externalities also affect other federated structures, though perhaps not as strongly. Members of a federated system of complementary nonprofits will all be affected by reputational problems associated with individual parts of the system (e.g. Jewish Philanthropies or Catholic Charities) but they also retain some organizational distance because they offer different products or services. Correspondingly, they will benefit somewhat less from such affiliation; even if the system maintains an overall reputation for quality and honesty, they must also prove their reputations individually so as to compete with hospitals, social service agencies or schools outside the system. Similarly it will help nonprofits to belong to looser federations or associations, especially if those associations offer some form of 'seal of approval' by virtue of their qualification standards or codes of behavior, although this protection may be relatively modest. At the same time, such nonprofit members are less likely to be severely damaged by problems associated with any given member of such an association.

Overall, then, inter-organizational externalities play an important role in the growth and development scenarios of federations. Nuclear nonprofits seeking to grow must often extend their trustworthy reputations, either by establishing their own and projecting them through systematic franchise or affiliate arrangements, and/or by joining other federations and associations from whose reputation-enhancing mechanisms they can benefit. And federations must guard the reputations of their members through appropriate standards and guidelines governing membership, oversight and use of organizational symbols.

The Girl Scouts of the USA offers an interesting illustration. Girl Scouts USA is a tightly knit federation consisting of some 300 local, semi-autonomous councils. GSUSA formed originally through a process that is perhaps best described as franchising. The Girl Scout 'movement' began in 1912 when its entrepreneurial founder Juliet Low established the first 'troop' in Savannah, Georgia, patterned on the Boy Scouts and Girl Guides in the UK. Thereafter, the organization encouraged the development of separately incorporated Girl Scout councils in other parts of the country, each with its own governing board, eventually reaching a total of more than 300 councils serving more than 2.7 million girls and engaging 925 000 volunteers (Rodriguez, 2007). Nonetheless, GSUSA exerts a substantial degree of central control over the councils, having the authority to issue and revoke local council charters and influence the appointment of council executive directors through its system-wide personnel system. While the size of local councils varies widely, the programs and operational procedures of each council are based on the same model and they all consider themselves part of one overall organization.

Currently GSUSA is engaged in a consolidation initiative, intending to merge local councils and reduce their number to 109. Thus, while the growth and evolution of GSUSA over the twentieth century was based on considerations of system-wide economies of scale in fund development and marketing, and the control of inter-organizational externalities, the recent initiative recognizes that competitive pressures leading to declines in membership since 1990 require greater scale economies at the local level. The current effort seeks to achieve more uniformity in the size of councils, as well as greater consistency in council programming and higher levels of inter-council collaboration. Thus inter-organizational externalities continue to play an important role in GSUSA's growth and development strategy. The consolidation in the number of councils will offer easier monitoring of the councils by the national organization as well as lower risk that smaller, less sophisticated or comprehensive councils would negatively reflect on other councils or the federation as a whole.

All five economic factors discussed here play important roles in the growth and development of nonprofit federations. Transaction costs and principal–agent issues are pervasive, while economies of scale and scope determine the transition points when an organization or federation must determine whether to adopt a new structure to accommodate its development. Finally, inter-organizational externalities come into play when a centralized internal structure gives way to a federated arrangement or when the organization participates in an industry or field where it must protect itself against the transgressions of other similar or related organizations.

What needs to be done to extend our knowledge?
A driving force behind the various modes of nonprofit growth and agglomeration into alternative patterns of federation is the drive for nonprofits to become more effective and efficient through greater scale and coordination of nonprofit resources. Hence a future research agenda can be framed by a definitive clarification of what 'scaling up' means, where such a thrust is appropriate, and how it should manifest itself in different circumstances. First, general theoretical principles need to be woven into a comprehensive theory of nonprofit federation. Second, a substantial and systematic database of nonprofit organizational experiences must be assembled and analyzed in order to create models that nonprofit organizations can use to guide their development. There is substantial current interest in the issue of taking new ideas and programs in the nonprofit sector and applying them on a larger scale so that they generate maximal impact and social benefits (Bradach, 2003; Taylor et al., 2002). Questionable assumptions behind this preoccupation include the notions that nonprofit entrepreneurs may lack the motivation or business acumen to expand their ventures much beyond their original designs and that there is no strong market mechanism (e.g. potential corporate takeover specialists who might wrest control) pushing them to do so. Studies of social and nonprofit entrepreneurship, however, reveal substantial evidence of entrepreneurial energy and motivation (Kerlin, 2006; Young, 1983). Moreover, it often goes unappreciated that 'going to scale' has long been a part of the logic of nonprofit organizational development. Although reliable data are notoriously hard to obtain, it is variously estimated that something like a quarter of local nonprofits are affiliated with a national structure in the USA (McCarthy, 2002), so that the nonprofit sector is less dominated by 'cottage enterprises' than one might suspect (Bradach, 2003). It is also not fully appreciated that 'logics' of expansion

are different, perhaps more complex in the nonprofit sector, and that these logics must be understood before expansion strategies can be properly formulated. For example, in considering how social movement organizations (SMOs) determine how many local affiliates they should have and where they should be located, McCarthy (2002) identifies three different sets of considerations – the extent to which an SMO depends on local members for financial support, the extent to which the affiliates are interdependent in terms of legal liability, and the degree to which an SMO's core technology depends on volunteers, citizen mobilization, advocacy or lobbying. Similarly, Bradach (2003) emphasizes the importance for a nonprofit to fully understand its 'theory of change' (what its essential elements are and how they work) before it can easily replicate its programs elsewhere. While Taylor et al. (2002) define going to scale rather narrowly as 'creating new service sites in other geographic locations that operate under a common name, use common approaches, and are either branches of the same parent organization or very closely tied affiliates of a parent organization' (p. 236), these authors also recognize that scaling up 'is not for everyone' (p. 235); indeed, they describe alternative strategies including internal expansion and selling or licensing of programs to other providers.

While 'going to scale' remains an important concern looking forward in this era of social entrepreneurship, it is instructive to learn from the past experience of nonprofit organizations that have addressed the question in different ways. Such a view reinforces several points made here. First, scaling up is not something new in the nonprofit sector, but rather a common and traditional issue of nonprofit organizational development. Second, there is indeed a variety of legitimate responses to this issue, including decisions not to grow, as well as the various forms through which scaling up can be manifested. Third, reviewing the history of organizations that have chosen different paths ought to help disentangle the various economic factors that have led different nonprofit organizations to take alternative paths to scaling up.

One factor that appears to distinguish the different paths taken by nonprofit organizations is the field of service in which they operate. A casual comparison of alternative nonprofit subsectors suggests that organizations in different fields of service tend to follow different development scenarios. That is, the variations within subsectors appear to be smaller than those among subsectors when it comes to strategies for growth of successful organizations and promulgation of new and successful ideas or program models.

Concluding remarks: why does this all matter?
Research on nonprofit federations promises potential benefits at several levels. Clearly, these organizational forms offer a broad field of inquiry for economists and organizational theorists to ponder the rationales and behaviors associated with almost a full spectrum of organizational structures – and to bring together multiple strands of theory for a more comprehensive understanding of how particular theoretical rationales interplay with one another to produce different results under alternative conditions. With the possible exceptions of fully decentralized networks or partnerships, or ephemeral short-term associations, nonprofit federations offer a provocative glimpse into the functioning of a very wide and important set of organizational issues and forms. And, as traditional formal organizational structures break down under the weight of new technologies, a study of the experiences of nonprofit federations and the primal forces underlying their evolution may suggest new ways of organizing over time.

Certainly, research on nonprofit federations will be of interest to leaders and managers of nonprofit organizations themselves. These individuals are on the front lines of service and advocacy, maintaining the organizations responsible for these critical functions in our society and ensuring that they use scarce resources as effectively as possible. As our analysis here indicates, federation structure makes a difference to the efficiency and effectiveness with which nonprofit organizations can achieve their missions. Thus managers' and leaders' decisions to affiliate with a federation, scale up into a federation structure, stick with the *status quo*, or vary the character of federations in which they are involved, may ultimately be more important than the immediate resource allocation decisions that they make from day to day.

Finally, research on nonprofit federations has potentially important implications for policy makers. The degree to which nonprofits are granted tax and other privileges depends on both the character of the work they do and the effectiveness with which they do it. Policy makers looking for choices of vehicles to fund and deliver public services should be interested in how systems of nonprofits operate and how well they can use government resources and meet the obligations of their tax privileges. In particular, policy makers will be interested in the roles of federations in maintaining accountability and performance of their members. Reciprocally, nonprofits themselves will need to communicate and articulate effectively with policy makers so as to shape policy in ways that best serve the public. This function too will be affected by the federation forms through which nonprofit leaders manifest their voices.

References

Barney, Jay B. and William Hesterly (2006), 'Organizational economics: understanding the relationship between organizations and economic analysis', in Stewart R. Clegg, Cythia Hardy, Thomas B. Lawrence and Walter R. Nord (eds), *The Sage Handbook of Organizational Studies*, 2nd edn, Thousand Oaks, CA: Sage Publications, pp. 111–48.
Baucus, David A., Melissa S. Baucus and Sherrie E. Human (1996), 'Consensus in franchise organizations: a cooperative arrangement among entrepreneurs', *Journal of Business Venturing*, **11** (5), 359–78.
Bradach, Jeffrey L. (2003), 'Going to Scale', *Stanford Social Innovation Review*, Spring, available at http://www.ssireview.org/site/printer/going_to_scale/.
Brickley, James A. and Frederick H. Dark (1987), 'The choice of organizational form: the case of franchising', *Journal of Financial Economics*, **18**, 401–20.
Bridgespan Group (2007), 'Habitat for Humanity: funding growth', February.
Brown, William O., Jr (1998), 'Transaction costs, corporate hierarchies, and the theory of franchising', *Journal of Economic Behavior & Organization*, **36** (3), 319–29.
The California Community Action to Fight Asthma (2005), *Asthma and Environmental Advocacy in California: The Role of Health Coalitions – Lessons Learned 2002–2005*.
Coase, Ronald H. (1937), 'The nature of the firm', *Economica*, **4** (16), 386–405.
Foundation Center (2007), 'Habitat for Humanity ousts some affiliates', *Philanthropy News Digest*, 18 October retrieved through http://foundationcenter.org/pnd/.
Glaton, Jonathan D. (2007), 'Feeling pressure from Harvard on college cost', *New York Times*, 29 December, pp. A1, A11.
Kerlin, Janelle (2006), 'Social enterprise in the United States and abroad: learning from our differences', in Rachel Mosher-Williams (ed.), *Research on Social Entrepreneurship*, ARNOVA Occasional Paper Series, **1** (3), 105–25.
McCarthy, John D. (2002), 'Franchising social change: logics of expansion among national social movement organizations with local chapters', draft presented to the Conference on Social Movements and Organization, University of Michigan, 1 May.
O'Flanagan, Maisie and Lynn K. Taliente (2004), 'Nonprofits: ensuring that bigger is better', *McKinsey Quarterly*, May, 2.
Oster, Sharon M. (1992), 'Nonprofit organizations as franchise operations', *Nonprofit Management and Leadership*, **2** (3), 223–38.

Oster, Sharon M. (1996), 'Nonprofit organizations and their local affiliates: a study in organizational forms', *Journal of Economic Behavior & Organization*, **30** (1), 83–95.

Putnam, Robert D. (2000), *Bowling Alone: The Collapse and Revival of American Community*, New York: Simon & Schuster.

Rodriguez, Lissette (2007), 'The Girl Scouts: uncharted territory', *The Nonprofit Quarterly*, Fall, 16–22.

Rosenberg, Donald (2000), *The Cleveland Orchestra Story: Second to None*, Cleveland, OH: Gray & Company.

Selsky, John W. (1998), 'Developmental dynamics in nonprofit federations', *Voluntas*, **9** (3), 283–303.

Standley, Anne (2001), 'Reinventing a large nonprofit: lessons from four voluntary health associations', *Nonprofit Management and Leadership*, **11** (3), 305–20.

Steinberg, Richard (2006), 'Economic theories of nonprofit organizations', in Walter W. Powell and Richard Steinberg (eds), *The Nonprofit Sector: A Research Handbook*, 2nd edn, New Haven, CT: Yale University Press, pp. 117–39.

Strom, Stephanie (2007), 'Some worry home charity is shedding grass roots', *New York Times*, 18 July, retrieved through http://www.nytimes.com.

Taylor, Melissa A., J. Gregory Dees and Jed Emerson (2002), 'The question of scale: finding an appropriate strategy for building on your success', in J. Gregory Dees, Jed Emerson and Peter Economy (eds), *Strategic Tools for Social Entrepreneurs*, New York: John Wiley & Sons, pp. 235–66.

Young, Dennis R. (1983), *If Not for Profit, for What?* Lexington, MA: D.C. Heath and Company.

Young, Dennis R. (1985), *Casebook of Management for Nonprofit Organizations: Entrepreneurship and Organizational Change in the Human Services*, New York: Haworth Press.

Young, Dennis R. (1989), 'Local autonomy in a franchise age', *Nonprofit and Voluntary Sector Quarterly*, **18** (2), 101–17.

Websites

www.breakthroughcollaborative.org
www.teachforamerica.org
www.guidestar.org
www.girlscouts.org.

16 The valuation of volunteer labor
Laura Leete

Introduction

Volunteer labor is a significant input to nonprofit organizations and a defining characteristic of the nonprofit sector. Its valuation, however, remains problematic for those who research or work in the nonprofit sector. While the value of monetary gifts is often proudly reported by donors and recipients alike, and tracked for the purposes of claiming tax deductions, the value produced by volunteers for nonprofit organizations can be virtually invisible. According to *Merriam-Webster*, 'valuation' has three primary meanings: 'the act or process of valuing'; the 'estimated or determined market value of a thing'; and 'the judgment or appreciation of worth or character'. Understanding the nature of what is produced by volunteer labor can be complex along all three lines; there is no clear consensus regarding the process by which we value volunteer work, how to determine its market value nor how to judge its overall worth or character in a broader context. These difficulties in part stem from the fact that, by definition, volunteer labor has a market price of zero; thus economists' usual methods of inferring value from market prices are not applicable here. This is further complicated by the fact that nonprofit organizations themselves are often engaged in producing goods or services that are not traded in the market. Furthermore, the definition of volunteerism is both contested and multidimensioned, and the uses of volunteer labor are at least as diverse as the nonprofit sector itself. Finally, researchers have recently come to recognize that the nature of the value produced by volunteers can be direct (meeting the direct needs of the organization's clients), indirect (providing benefit more broadly to the community as a whole) and personal (accruing to the volunteer themselves).

These factors conspire to make the issue of the valuation of volunteers a complex one. The aim of this chapter is to bring some clarification to this complexity. First, I discuss the significance of these issues for policy makers, nonprofit organizations and researchers. I then summarize the existing literature relating to the valuation of volunteer labor, discussing the empirical strategies that have been taken and connecting those to underlying concepts of value. Finally, I review the questions that remain unanswered and the kinds of future work that will likely be fruitful in moving forward the research agenda in this area.

Why does the valuation of volunteer labor matter?

Volunteerism has long been recognized as central to a democratic and civil society (Tocqueville, 1988) and as being a key to community building and to the formation of social capital (e.g. Putnam, 1995). And yet, because accurate estimates of the amount of volunteer labor used and of the value produced have been elusive, the value produced by volunteers has been invisible from national accounts, organizational bookkeeping and research agendas. This invisibility has implications at both macro- and microeconomic levels and these implications relate to economic policy, organizational strategy and the ability of researchers to contribute to the knowledge base in both these areas.

At the macroeconomic level, failure to account for the value produced by volunteers implies a gross underestimation of the scale of economic activity in the national accounts of any country with a significant level of volunteerism and of the share of that activity attributable to the nonprofit (or 'third') sector. Because much of volunteerism is located within the service sector of the economy, especially in social, educational and cultural services, the scale of these activities is discounted as well. Furthermore, to the extent that volunteerism either reflects or builds social capital, the valuation of social capital is significantly hampered by the invisibility of volunteerism (Narraway and Cordery, 2006). While numerous issues are involved in estimating the number of hours worked by volunteers and placing a value on those hours (discussed below), by any account the scale of these contributions is not insignificant. Hamdad et al. (2004) estimate that accounting for the value of volunteer work in Canada increases the portion of Canadian GDP attributable to the nonprofit sector by 25 percent. In the USA, the Urban Institute estimates that in 2006, 61.2 million persons volunteered a total of 12.9 billion hours (Wing et al., 2008). Valuing this work based on an average (private sector, nonfarm) US wage would imply the addition of 1.6 percent to recorded GDP in that year.[1] In the first large-scale project to establish comparable numbers for the nonprofit sector internationally, Salamon et al. (1999) estimate that in 22 countries where paid employment in the third sector accounts for 5 percent or more of total nonagricultural employment, the recording of volunteer work would add 3.5 percent to GDP.

A consequence of the invisibility of volunteer work is that we fail to grasp the relationship between economic policies (e.g. taxes, subsidies, government expenditures), the value produced by volunteers and the actual level of production in the affected sectors. Our ability to understand specific nonprofit sector issues, such as the relative importance of donations of time and money, and how the value of those donations is influenced by policy, is also hampered.

The value of volunteer production can be similarly invisible even at the organizational level. While some organizations do record the number of volunteer hours contributed to their organization, Mook et al. (2005) report that only one-third (37 percent) of organizations say that they do so. And Mook et al. (2005) and Narraway and Cordery (2006) both note that only a small share of nonprofit organizations take the next step to estimate any measure of the value produced by their volunteers. They cite, among other things, a lack of requirement to do so, as well as a shortage of resources to complete the task, and the lack of reliability of the measures themselves. In the USA, for the purposes of public reporting on the IRS Form 990 and for meeting the accounting standards for nonprofits put forth by the Financial Accounting Standards Board (FASB), the value of volunteer services may only be recorded on financial statements (including statements for internal and external purposes, grant proposals and annual reports) if those services increase the value of physical capital owned by the organization, or if a volunteer is performing a specialized skill for a nonprofit and the organization would have purchased the services if they had not been donated (FASB, 1993). In Canada, the Canadian Institute of Chartered Accountants (CICA) promotes comparable standards.

This lack of record of volunteer production has implications at the organizational level as well. Just as economic theory suggests that profit-maximizing organizations should shut down (in the long run) if their profits drop below zero, the application of social welfare theory to nonprofit organizations suggests that such organizations should only operate (in the long run) if they produce benefits that exceed the cost of producing those benefits. Organizations often will have ways of measuring the benefit they produce, and they may be able to account accurately for organizational expenses associated with using volunteers (e.g. costs of using paid staff to manage and train volunteers, or costs of volunteer appreciation events). But not otherwise accounting for the value of the volunteer labor input in terms of its alternative (foregone) uses implies that its value is zero, thus leading to an underestimate of the costs of producing any benefits. While assigning a zero cost to volunteers may be accurate in a bookkeeping sense, it is not valid in a broader social sense if we care about the opportunity cost of any activity, including volunteerism. Furthermore, if the benefits to the individual volunteer are not counted, then benefits of any volunteer activity are similarly underestimated.

Additional measurement issues arise if organizational output is measured by (or defined as) the sum of the inputs to the process, as is often the case in social service settings. For instance, an hour of care giving may have no monetizable value other than as the dollar cost of an hour of care. If the care giving is provided on a volunteer basis, establishing the cost, and thus the value, of that care is problematic. Thus the valuation of volunteer time can be critical to understanding both the cost and benefit sides of an organization's operations.

Furthermore, following economic theory, nonprofit and for-profit organizations alike should choose a mix of inputs such that the marginal product per dollar spent on each input is equal. While organizations might measure the out-of-pocket costs associated with using volunteers (e.g. supplies, supervision), if an organization can not measure the cost of volunteer time, then neither can it evaluate the optimal mix of volunteer and paid labor (and other inputs).

Thus accounting not only for the hours spent by volunteers in nonprofit organizations but also for the value of that time is critical to both organizational decision-making processes and to measuring the costs and benefits generated by the organization, by the nonprofit sector and by the economy as a whole. The strategic, policy and research implications are numerous. Although these issues have been relatively unexplored in the related professional and academic literature until recently, there is now a growing literature on this topic. And while there has been considerable advancement in a number of areas, some issues remain poorly understood. In the remainder of this chapter, I present an overview of the progress that has been made and discuss issues that will require further research and clarification.

The valuation of volunteer effort
Any notion of the value of volunteer labor used has two underlying components: the hours of volunteer work and the value of those hours. While still posing a number of definitional and methodological issues, the first of these two concepts, hours volunteered, is the more straightforward one to measure. The valuation of those hours is a more difficult exercise, with multiple approaches and less-than-complete agreement on what value should be captured. In the end, one might conclude that the best approach to take depends not only on the purposes for which the value is being calculated, but also on the resources at hand. I shall first discuss efforts to measure the aggregate hours of volunteer labor and then the details of how one might place a value on those hours.

Counting volunteer hours
In the USA and most other countries, because nonprofit organizations are generally not required to report on the amount or type of contributions of time they receive, there is no official source of data on volunteering. Instead, researchers rely on any number of privately and publicly commissioned and financed surveys. Two methodologies are typically used – retrospective surveys and time-use studies. Among retrospective surveys in the USA, there are currently two key sources of information – annual supplements to the US Current Population Survey (CPS) and a biennial supplement to the longitudinal Panel Study of Income Dynamics (PSID). Since 2002, the supplement to the CPS has been fielded in September of each year to the outgoing rotation group. The survey asks individuals to recall how many hours they volunteered in the past year and what type of organizations they volunteered for. The supplement to the PSID, designed and commissioned by the Center on Philanthropy at Indiana University-Purdue University-Indianapolis (IUPUI) and known as the Center on Philanthropy's Panel Study (COPPS), was administered to over 7500 households in the PSID in 2001, 2003 and 2005. It will continue to be administered on a biennial basis as funding allows. The COPPS data constitute the first nationally representative survey to collect longitudinal data on volunteering behavior, since the same households are interviewed during each wave.

Historical survey data on volunteering include a long-running effort conducted by Gallup polls for the Independent Sector (IS). This random survey of the US population was conducted biennially from 1988 to 2002 (see, e.g., Weitzman et al., 2002). CPS supplements on volunteering were also fielded in May 1965, 1974 and 1989. In addition, Goss (1999) reports on proprietary data collected annually since 1975 as part of a national survey commissioned by an advertising firm.

An alternative to the survey approach is to measure voluntary activity via time-use studies. Because this method of recording activity does not suffer from the same recall bias as retrospective surveys, it is often considered to be a more accurate accounting of time (Juster and Stafford, 1991). The American Time-use Survey (ATUS), administered by the Bureau of Labor Statistics annually since 2003, provides time-use accounts that include volunteer activity. Respondents are contacted by telephone and interviewed about their activities for that one particular day. Time-use data have the advantage that they can be disaggregated by type of activity (e.g. attending meetings versus participating in performance and cultural activities) but they do not explicitly identify the type of organization volunteered for. Historical time diary data can also be obtained from the Michigan and Maryland Time-Use Studies surveys conducted in 1965, 1975–76, 1981, 1985, 1992–94, 1998 and 2001.[2]

Results from these different efforts vary in several respects. First, different efforts have included different populations when counting volunteer hours. For instance, the ATUS covers individuals aged 15 and over, the CPS covers those aged 16 and up, while the COPPS data describe volunteering behavior among household heads and their wives. Historically, the Gallup/IS data covered Americans over the age of 18 or 21, depending on the implementation. Second, different surveys use different methods to inquire about an individual's recent history of volunteering, for example referencing the past year, or the past week, or asking about a typical week. In the case of time-use studies, individuals are asked about that day's activities. In a survey measuring volunteerism in Indiana, Steinberg et al. (2002) demonstrate that the longer and more detailed the survey module used, the higher the reported incidence and hours of volunteerism. Researchers have also long been concerned with recall bias causing individuals to provide misleading answers to questions when referencing past time periods. Thus different approaches are unlikely to yield the same answers.

Third, while number of hours of volunteer work would seem to be a straightforward concept, there is some ambiguity as to its definition. In the academic literature, some have defined a volunteer as a person offering themselves for service without obligation to do so, willingly and without pay (e.g. Shure, 1991), while others limit the idea of volunteering to service that is done for formal organizations (e.g. National Association of Counties, 1990). Others still have expanded the definition to include informal help provided to friends, family or neighbors (e.g. Wilson, 2000).[3] These differences are reflected in the definition of volunteerism implicit in different data collection efforts. The current ATUS and CPS both define volunteer activity as unpaid activity or work that occurs under the auspices of a formal institution.[4] Historically, CPS supplements only inquired about unpaid work for 'hospitals, churches, civic, political and other organizations', and the Gallup/IS surveys included informal volunteering (not performed on behalf of any organization or institution).

Differences in survey methodology can result in considerably different estimates of the scope of volunteering. For example, the 1989 CPS and the 1990 Gallup/IS survey for the same year yielded substantially different estimates of the percentage of US adults who volunteered in a year. The CPS reported that 20 percent of the population aged 16 and over had volunteered in the last year; the Gallup/IS poll reported that 54 percent of those aged 18 and over had (Hayghe, 1991; Freeman, 1997): as noted above, the Gallup/IS poll included informal volunteering while the CPS focused on volunteering for specific types of organizations. The introduction of time-diary data does not entirely clarify the picture either. Tiehen (2000) reported an estimate of 28.4 billion hours annually for aggregate volunteer involvement among adults in the USA in 1993; the Independent Sector figure for that year was 19.5 billion hours. While these examples are drawn from historical data, they illustrate that differing methodologies can generate considerably different pictures of volunteering.

Placing a value on volunteer hours
While methodological problems remain in producing accurate estimates of the amount of time worked by volunteers, even more difficult questions revolve around placing a value on the time worked. First it must be recognized that there are multiple aspects to valuing volunteer labor. Costs and benefits of volunteering accrue to the volunteer herself, to the organization (and its clients) and potentially to society more generally. Thus any effort at valuing volunteer efforts needs to first establish which of these types of values one is seeking to measure.

To date, researchers, policy analysts and practitioners have typically pursued one of three approaches to this issue: (1) opportunity cost; (2) replacement cost; and (3) organizational value. These approaches vary in both what they measure and the ease with which they can be applied. I shall discuss the implications of each in turn.

Opportunity cost   A number of researchers have discussed opportunity cost as the basis for valuing volunteer hours (e.g. Brown, 1999), capturing the value of the opportunity foregone by the use of the volunteer labor. There are two ways to approach this metric. If one considers volunteer contributions of time to be a form of work, a volunteer's opportunity cost might be valued at the market wage (including the value of benefits) that individual would earn if they worked an hour for pay instead of as a volunteer. On the other hand, if one considers volunteer time as a form of leisure (Henderson, 1981, 1984), then the opportunity cost is the value of the leisure foregone.

The ease of applying this concept varies depending on which approach is taken. For individuals who currently work (or have worked recently) in the paid labor market, their market wage (plus benefits) is relatively easy to establish or estimate (see the discussion below pertaining to the estimation of 'replacement costs'). Wolfe et al. (1993) asked volunteers what they would have received if they had worked additional hours for pay. Volunteers who were not in the labor force were asked 'what they believed they could earn if they decided to seek paid employment' (p. 31).

Establishing the value of leisure time is more problematic. For a variety of reasons, including diminishing marginal utility, different individuals will value their leisure in dramatically different ways. One person's invaluable stolen moment of peace and quiet is another's stretch of pointless boredom. The value of leisure can be established either directly or indirectly, and in aggregated or disaggregated ways. A direct approach would be to survey individuals, asking how they value their leisure time (e.g. 'what would you pay for one hour of free time?'). The literature on leisure time yields some insights along these lines. Alternatively, indirect approaches infer the value of leisure time through observation of actual behavior. For instance, since individuals working in the paid labor market give up an hour of leisure for each hour they work, one could presume that their market wage is a ceiling on the value of their leisure time. Similarly, the literature on travel times and the economic trade-offs people make in order to shorten their commute also provides insight into how individuals value their free time. Of course, this brings us back to the use of the market wage as a measure of the opportunity cost of one's time.

An opportunity cost approach to the valuation of volunteer effort carries with it information about what the individual (and thus society) has given up in return for the fruits of the volunteer endeavor. However, this measure does not include any costs borne by the organization when they use volunteers (such as insurance, recruiting, training and supervising), although it is still an important input to measuring the cost of the nonprofit enterprise (either at the organizational level or in aggregate) for the purposes of calculating its costs and benefits (and net benefit) from a social welfare perspective. Beyond this, however, the interpretation of opportunity cost is problematic. As Brown (1999) notes, if a volunteer is concerned only with the value of the production for the nonprofit organization, then their working one hour should either produce a value equal to their hourly market compensation (their opportunity cost) or else they should substitute an hour of their own paid labor for volunteering and donate their pay. Brown (1999) argues that if the value of volunteer production falls short of the volunteer's opportunity cost, then this gap must be accounted for by the additional value that that volunteer obtains from the act of volunteering. Thus the opportunity cost measure may potentially capture both the amount produced for the organization and the value that accrues to the volunteer. If one's goal is to measure a narrower concept of value produced by volunteers, consistent with the value measured in national accounts and measures such as gross domestic product (GDP), then an alternate approach is indicated. To that end we consider the replacement cost approach.

Replacement cost   The second empirical approach to assigning value to volunteer labor is one that assigns a value to each hour of volunteer work according to the cost of replacing that volunteer with a paid employee doing the same work. This is conceptually and empirically straightforward as long as there is a clear market alternative to the work the volunteer performs and the value that the volunteer creates for the organization. This approach has been widely applied and is the one taken in the social accounting approach to assessing the contributions of nonprofits (e.g. Quarter et al., 2003). Unlike the opportunity cost measure discussed above, however, this approach excludes any value that separately accrues to either the volunteer (as discussed above) or value to the organization that springs exclusively from the act of volunteering (as distinct from benefits that accrue from employing paid workers). This additional value might include tangible benefits from volunteers that do not arise from paid workers (e.g. cash or in-kind donations made by volunteers in conjunction their volunteering) and/or intangible benefits (e.g. increased trust by clients or goodwill in the community). As Handy et al. (2006, p. 33) put it, the intangibles might include 'goodwill generated by their presence, their service as ambassadors to the public and enhancement of community relations'.

Questions regarding the application of this approach generally revolve around the specifics of what measure to use. At the most general level, both researchers and practitioners have used an economy- or sector-wide average hourly wage, sometimes constructed specifically for this purpose. For instance, Independent Sector annually constructs a measure compiled from US Bureau of Labor Statistics payroll data. These constructs are narrowed so as to be more specific to the type of work most likely done by volunteers. The measure they put forth is the average hourly earnings of all production and non-supervisory workers on private nonfarm payrolls in the USA, increased by 12 percent to account for the expected value of benefits.[5] The national value for 2007 was $19.51;[6] they also construct a comparable measure for each state. Hamdad et al. (2006) have produced a similar figure for selected years. Alternatively, analysts have achieved more specificity by valuing volunteer labor at market wages that are more closely aligned, either by sector, industry, occupation or geographic location, to the volunteer work being proxied (e.g. Brudney, 1990; Gaskin, 1999). Obviously, the more specific the match between the replacement cost estimate used and the work actually performed, the more accurate is any valuation of volunteer labor.

Even a highly specific wage match, however, may not provide a precise measure of a volunteer's productive value. As Brown (1999) points out, organizations allocating work between paid and volunteer staff are likely to use paid labor to do tasks that require more firm-specific training and knowledge and that are more sensitive to disruptions related to absenteeism and turnover, while allocating other tasks to volunteers. Thus it would probably be difficult to truly match the tasks of volunteer workers to those of paid workers. On the other hand, as Brown (1999) also notes, volunteers bring a different level of general skill to the organization than the average worker – individuals who volunteer are more highly educated than those who do not. A final difference between volunteer productivity and a replacement wage may arise from the fact that market wages are set in a competitive market dominated by for-profit firms that (in theory, at least) use workers and other inputs in an optimal mix. Given that nonprofits face a lower (below-market) cost for volunteers (the cost of using volunteers is not zero, but includes recruitment, training and supervision), it is likely that they use volunteers in less optimal ways. Thus the replacement wage may overstate the true productivity of volunteers in the nonprofit organization in this regard as well.

An alternative approach to establishing the replacement value of volunteers would be to ask managers (in a survey or otherwise) to estimate the cost of replacing their volunteer labor with paid workers. Hager (2004) and Handy and Srinivasan (2004) both take this approach. For the reasons noted above, this approach is more likely to match true volunteer productivity than a replacement wage approach based on actual market data. It will also achieve more location, firm or industry specificity than an approach relying on more aggregate national statistics. In either case, however, a replacement wage approach provides a clearer conceptual match between this method of valuation and the production attributable to paid labor embodied in existing national account statistics in the USA and most countries.

Organizational value A third approach to constructing the value of volunteer efforts centers on how those efforts are valued by the organization itself. This measure captures both the replacement cost value of labor performed as well as any value to the organization that results from volunteerism *per se* (net of any differential in costs to the organization resulting from using volunteers as compared with using paid workers). As discussed above, additional value to the organization resulting directly from using volunteers (as compared with paid workers) might include tangible and/or intangible benefits. This measure of organizational value does not capture any value that accrues to volunteers themselves (a concept embedded in the opportunity cost measure).

Handy et al. (2006) take this approach in a large survey of Canadian nonprofit organizations. When nonprofit managers were asked about the size of a monetary donation they would accept in lieu of one hour of volunteer time, the average value reported was $35.33 (Canadian). While this approach is nicely aligned with the underlying concept of measuring all aspects of what a volunteer brings to the organization, Handy et al. (2006) note that this question was difficult for many managers to answer, and nearly a quarter of respondents answered that they would not accept cash in lieu of volunteer time.

Summary
It is clear that each of the three approaches to valuing an hour of volunteer work measures a different concept and each is associated with different methodological difficulties. The replacement cost measure is the simplest to employ and can be based on existing national data, but it measures only the narrowest concept of value – the value of a market transaction void of volunteers. The key to accuracy in applying the concept is the specificity of the match between the replacement wage used and the work actually performed by the volunteer. The correlation with national accounts statistics is a strength – it is comparable to important economic benchmarks – but is also a weakness – it is void of the broader social value that many analysts would like to see captured when the nonprofit sector is considered. Furthermore, replacement cost measures do not capture any value (tangible or intangible) accruing to the organization that is unique to volunteers. By comparison, the organizational value measure can capture both replacement cost

and any unique value that a volunteer may bring to the organization by virtue of being a volunteer. Collecting this measure, however, is problematic in that it relies on managerial assessment. This assessment is difficult for managers, and its validity and reliability have not been explored. Finally, opportunity cost is a somewhat different concept. It alone measures the value of volunteer work to the volunteer, but does not necessarily reflect any value that accrues to the organization. Importantly, however, opportunity cost is the single measure that represents the cost of volunteering to society (exclusive of the costs incurred by the organization).

Concluding remarks: what we don't know and avenues for future research
Considerable methodological challenges remain in understanding how we should value volunteer labor. As noted above, there are multiple aspects to valuing volunteer labor: costs accrue to both the organization and the volunteer; benefits accrue to the organization, to the volunteer and possibly to society more generally. Depending on the purpose of the valuation, one may want to capture one or more of these concepts. In any case, any effort at valuing volunteer efforts needs to first establish which of these types of values one is seeking to measure.

Beyond the question of exactly what value we should attempt to capture when measuring volunteerism, there are practical issues regarding measurement efforts of any kind. In defining how to measure the hours volunteered, there is no clear agreement on what volunteerism is and how broadly or loosely to define it. While recent survey methodologies have more or less settled on limiting volunteerism to work done through formal institutions, differences in wording can result in measures that capture different ranges of activity. Furthermore, there has been no comprehensive assessment of differences in methodologies for counting the hours volunteered. Each of the major retrospective surveys takes a different approach to how they collect historical information from individuals about their volunteering habits; the time-use surveys represent yet another tactic. To date, researchers have not clearly documented which methodologies are likely to over- or underestimate, or which approach is likely to yield the most accurate estimates.

Furthermore, research that directly measures either the replacement value or the organizational value of volunteers through managerial self-reporting is in its infancy. As with the measurement of volunteer hours, the measurement of the value of the volunteer to the organization raises numerous methodological questions. These include the time frame over which information is collected (volunteers who have worked for the organization in the past year or those who are working today), how the types of volunteers are defined, and how managers are asked to think about either their replacement cost or their overall value to the organization. There has been no systematic study of the implications of using alternate survey wording and methodology or of other approaches to gathering such information.

Considerable progress has been made in recent decades in advancing our understanding of the role and value of the volunteer to nonprofit organizations. This work has progressed rapidly on both theoretical and empirical fronts. Scholarship regarding the valuation of volunteer labor is now much more precise than it was even a decade ago. Future research along theoretical, empirical and methodological lines, particularly as suggested here, will bring additional clarity and consensus to this topic.

Notes

1. Figures from Wing et al. (2008) and US Government Printing Office (2008).
2. The American Heritage Time Use Study (AHTUS) is an attempt to manipulate the data from these older time-use studies to make them consistent with the ATUS.
3. Some authors have imposed requirements relating to the underlying motivations of volunteers. For example, Smith (1982) notes that volunteers should expect to receive psychic benefits, and Ellis and Noyes (1990, p. 4) suggest that volunteering be done 'in recognition of a need, with an attitude of social responsibility . . . going beyond one's basic obligations'. In contrast, Freeman (1997) suggests that perhaps much volunteerism is not voluntary at all, but something that individuals do out of perceived social obligation when asked.
4. The ATUS also collects data on caring for and helping adults and children who are not members of one's household (as well as those who are), but this activity is not coded as volunteer activity.
5. Brown (1999) makes the point that volunteers work primarily in services and not in the production of goods. Thus it may be sensible to further limit the replacement wage to a service sector average, which is considerably below the national average.
6. http://www.independentsector.org/programs/research/volunteer_time.html (last accessed 18 July 2008).

References

Brown, Eleanor (1999), 'Assessing the value of volunteer activity', *Nonprofit and Voluntary Sector Quarterly*, **28** (1): 3–17.
Brudney, Jeffrey (1990), *Fostering Volunteer Programs in the Public Sector*, San Francisco, CA: Jossey-Bass.
Ellis, Susan J. and Katherine H. Noyes (1990), *By the People: A History of Americans as Volunteers*, San Francisco, CA: Jossey-Bass.
Financial Accounting Standards Board (1993), *Statement of Financial Accounting Standards No. 116: Accounting for Contributions Received and Contributions Made*.
Freeman, Richard B. (1997), 'Working for nothing: the supply of volunteer labor', *Journal of Labor Economics*, **15** (1), s140–s166.
Gaskin, Katharine (1999), 'Valuing volunteers in Europe: a comparative study of the Voluntary Investment and Value Audit (VIVA)', *Voluntary Action: The Journal of Active Volunteering Research*, **2** (1), 35–48.
Goss, Kristin (1999), 'Volunteering and the long civic generation', *Nonprofit and Voluntary Sector Quarterly*, **28** (4), 378–415.
Hager, Mark A. (2004), *Volunteer Management: Capacity in America's Charities and Congregations*, Washington, DC: The Urban Institute.
Hamdad, Malika, Sophie Joyal and Catherine van Rompaey (2004), *Satellite Account of Nonprofit Institutions and Volunteering, 1997 to 1999*, Catalogue No. 13-015-XIE, Ottawa, ON: Statistics Canada.
Hamdad, Malika, Matthew Hoffarth and Sophie Joyal (2006), *Satellite Account of Nonprofit Institutions and Volunteering, 1999–2003*, Catalogue No. 13-015-XIE, Ottawa, ON: Statistics Canada.
Handy, Femida and Narasimhan Srinivasan (2004), 'Valuing volunteers: an economic evaluation of the net benefits of hospital volunteers', *Nonprofit and Voluntary Sector Quarterly*, **33** (1), 28–54.
Handy, Femida, Laurie Mook and Jack Quarter (2006), 'Organisational perspectives on the value of volunteer labour', *Australian Journal of Volunteering*, **11** (1), 28–36.
Hayghe, Howard V. (1991), 'Volunteers in the U.S.: who donates the time?' *Monthly Labor Review*, **114** (2), 17–23.
Henderson, Karla A. (1981), 'Motivations and perceptions of volunteerism as a leisure activity', *Journal of Leisure Research*, **13** (3), 208–18.
Henderson, Karla A. (1984), 'Volunteerism as leisure', *Journal of Voluntary Action Research*, **13** (1), 55–63.
Juster, F. Thomas and Frank P. Stafford (1991), 'The allocation of time: empirical findings, behavioral models and problems of measurement', *Journal of Economic Literature*, **29**, 471–522.
Mook, Laurie, Jorge Sousa, Susan Elgie and Jack Quarter (2005), 'Accounting for the value of volunteer contributions', *Nonprofit Management and Leadership*, **15** (4), 401–15.
Narraway, Gwynn and Carolyn Cordery (2006), 'The perception gap – (ac)counting invisible volunteers', paper submitted to Accounting & Finance Association of Australia and New Zealand (AFAANZ), Wellington Conference, July.
National Association of Counties (1990), *The Volunteer Tool-Box: Visions for Improving the Service of America's Counties*, Washington, DC: NACO.
Putnam, Robert D. (1995), 'Tuning in, tuning out: the strange disappearance of social capital in America', *PS: Political Science and Politics*, **28** (4), 664–83.
Quarter, Jack, Laurie Mook and Betty Jane Richmond (2003), *What Counts: Social Accounting for Nonprofits and Cooperatives*, Upper Saddle River, NJ: Prentice Hall.

Salamon, Lester M. et al. (1999), *Global Civil Society: Dimensions of the Nonprofit Sector*, Baltimore, MD: Johns Hopkins Center for Civil Society Studies.
Shure, Richard S. (1991), 'Volunteering: continuing expansion of the definition and a practical application of altruistic motivation', *Journal of Volunteer Administration*, **9** (4), 36–41.
Smith, David H. (1982), 'Altruism, volunteers, and volunteerism', in John D. Harman (ed.), *Volunteerism in the Eighties: Fundamental Issues in Voluntary Action*, Washington DC: University Press of America, pp. 23–44.
Steinberg, Kathryn S., Patrick M. Rooney and William Chin (2002), 'Measurement of volunteering: a methodological study using Indiana as a test case', *Nonprofit and Voluntary Sector Quarterly*, **31** (4) 484–501.
Tiehen, Laura (2000), 'Has working caused more married women to volunteer less? Evidence from time diary data, 1965 to 1993', *Nonprofit and Voluntary Sector Quarterly*, **29** (4), 505–29.
Tocqueville, Alexis de (1988), *Democracy in America*, New York: Harper & Row.
US Government Printing Office (2008), *Economic Report of the President 2008*, Washington, DC.
Weitzman, Murray S., Nadine T. Jalandoni, Linda M. Lampkin and Thomas H. Pollak (2002), *The New Nonprofit Almanac and Desk Reference: The Essential Facts and Figures for Managers, Researchers, and Volunteers*, New York: Jossey-Bass.
Wilson, John (2000), 'Volunteering', *Annual Review of Sociology*, **26** (1), 215–40.
Wing, Kennard T., Thomas H. Pollak and Amy Blackwood (2008), *Nonprofit Almanac 2008*, Washington, DC: Urban Institute Press.
Wolfe, Nancy, Burton A. Weisbrod and Edward Bird (1993), 'The supply of volunteer labor: the case of hospitals', *Nonprofit Management and Leadership*, **4** (1), 23–45.

17 Assessing nonprofit performance
Joseph J. Cordes and Katherine Coventry

Introduction

A changing external environment that demands greater accountability from 'public' (or quasi-public) institutions and changing attitudes among nonprofit staff have resulted in greater openness in the nonprofit sector to being judged on performance. In addition, there is greater receptiveness towards using systematic approaches to guide deployment of scarce resources among activities and organizations. As noted in a recent report on foundation effectiveness (Ostrower, 2004), a sizable percentage of independent foundations undertake some systematic efforts to evaluate the effectiveness of grants made:

- Slightly more than 50 percent of the foundations responding to an Urban Institute survey indicated that they 'often' or 'always' required grantees to collect information on outcomes of their work.
- Just over 40 percent of the foundations surveyed indicated that they undertook formal evaluations of the work funded.

Assessing the effectiveness of the myriad of services provided and activities undertaken by nonprofit organizations is, however, a daunting task. It is frequently argued that measuring nonprofit performance poses a challenge because of the difficulty of constructing 'bottom-line' measures such as profit and return on investment, the widely accepted assessment tools in the for-profit sector. But recently, under the broad rubrics of 'social impact analysis' and 'double-bottom-line investing', some analysts have suggested that it is possible to develop bottom-line measures of the 'social profitability' of nonprofit performance.

This chapter examines several approaches for developing such 'bottom-line' measures of nonprofit performance. These include efforts to estimate what has been called the social return on investment (SROI) in nonprofit organizations as well as cost–benefit analysis (CBA) and cost-effectiveness analysis (CEA). We examine ways in which these approaches can be used to develop quantitative measures of nonprofit performance and guide the allocation of resources both by foundations and by operating nonprofit organizations. We also discuss issues relating to the practical implementation of such measures. The following chapter in this volume by Mook and Handy (Chapter 18) provides additional insights into the social valuation challenge from a primarily accounting perspective.

Social return on investment (SROI)

An important attempt to develop monetary measures of nonprofit performance is the effort by REDF (formerly the Roberts Enterprise Development Fund) to estimate the 'social return on investment (SROI)' of social enterprises in the early 2000s (Roberts Enterprise Development Fund, 2001; REDF, 2001). The SROI was intended to provide a metric for calculating the economic and social return derived from private and public investments in the nonprofit sector (REDF, 2001). For example, calculating the SROI of a nonprofit halfway house for drug addicts might involve estimating the reduced social costs attributable to the successful rehabilitation of addicts and comparing these to the costs of operating the halfway house.

Broadly speaking, the SROI attempted to measure the economic value of two different aspects of a social enterprise: its business value and its social value. It involved several measures of economic and socioeconomic value that were then combined to estimate an organization's SROI. To measure the economic value of an enterprise's business operations, REDF calculated an enterprise value using several steps. First business cash flows derived from selling the enterprise's product or services were projected over a ten-year time horizon using past and current cash flows. Where enterprises experienced difficulty making projections beyond five years, a marginal growth rate was used to extrapolate the experience of the first five years. These cash flows were then discounted to the present using a weighted average discount rate or weighted average cost of capital (WACC). This involved using industry-specific information to calculate the cost of equity and the cost of debt to construct a debt–equity ratio.[1] A terminal value for all values beyond ten years was computed using a perpetuity formula. The present value of the discounted cash flows for the ten-year horizon plus the terminal value were summed to produce the enterprise value.

REDF also attempted to value outputs and/or outcomes of social enterprises that, though not traded in the marketplace, were clearly of value to society, by calculating the social value of an enterprise in addition to its enterprise value. The general procedure was the same as that used for calculating enterprise value, except that social purpose value was the present value of the discounted social purpose cash flows.

For example, consider how one would calculate the social purpose cash flows for a social enterprise intended to help drug addicts by offering them productive employment. First the number of target employees would be projected over the ten-year time horizon. Next the average social cost savings per target employee would be calculated, based on reduced expenditures from public assistance programs, social service programs and criminal convictions.[2] Third, REDF projected the increased income taxes that would result from target employees' employment with the enterprise, assuming a tax rate of 15 percent and an annual 1.5 percent wage growth rate. Lastly, REDF projected social operating expenses of the enterprise. It discounted the social purpose cash flows using the municipal bond rate in 2000 (6.65 percent) as a proxy for the cost of capital for nonprofit organizations. REDF noted that each social enterprise should choose an appropriate discount rate depending on its own circumstances.

The blended value of the social enterprise was computed by adding the enterprise value and the social purpose value and subtracting the long-term debt of the enterprise. Three indices of return were formed by taking the ratios of the three computed values – enterprise value, social purpose value and blended value – to the investment in the enterprise.

In attempting to measure the performance of social enterprises, REDF also cautioned that social purpose enterprises should not necessarily be compared solely on their index of return because the social purpose value would only include measurable items of social value generated by an enterprise. REDF offered additional contextual information

Table 17.1   Social return analysis of Ashbury Images

		Index of return
Enterprise value	$444 560	0.40
Social purpose value	$974 011	0.89
Blended value	$1 418 571	1.29
Investment to date	$1 098 165	

beyond their metrics so that investors could determine for themselves whether a particular investment was worthwhile and whether various enterprises could be appropriately compared using the index of return metric.

Table 17.1 presents the results of an SROI analysis undertaken for Ashbury Images, a social enterprise that employed drug addicts in the production of silk screens and offered them a range of drug treatment services. The enterprise value in Table 17.1 is an estimate of the present value of the revenue generated by the social enterprise from its sale of services. The social purpose value is the present value of the benefits attributed to treatment provided to addicts; and the blended value is the sum of the enterprise and the social value. The numbers indicate that if Ashbury Images were to be judged strictly on the basis of a 'market test', it would be found wanting because the estimated enterprise value is less than the resources invested in the enterprise. The social purpose value, however, is estimated to be large enough so that the blended value exceeds the amount invested. The implications of the analysis are that: (a) absent a substantial subsidy from the government and/or private donors, the enterprise would not succeed in the marketplace, and (b) subsidizing the enterprise created an activity whose total value – taking into account social as well as market benefits – added more to social value on the benefit side than it took from social value on the cost side.

Cost–benefit analysis
Cost–benefit Analysis (CBA) and the closely related methodology of cost-effectiveness analysis (CEA) have become increasingly common means of assessing the consequences of a wide range of government regulations and public spending in a number of areas including public works and education. Someone who is familiar with CBA as it is applied to the evaluation of public programs cannot help but be struck by the similarity between the outcomes that CBA is intended to measure and those that are involved in SROI analysis,[3] which suggests that CBA may provide a useful framework for assessing nonprofit performance.

The objective of undertaking a CBA is to gauge the effect of a particular public policy or program on social surplus. Does the policy or program being evaluated produce outcomes with social benefits that equal or exceed what it costs society to achieve the outcomes? CEA is somewhat less ambitious in scope in that it eschews attaching monetary values to program benefits. Instead it seeks to answer a somewhat narrower, though still important, question: among alternative ways of achieving a policy objective, which alternative achieves the stated objective at the least social cost? Or for a given expenditure, which alternative achieves greater effectiveness?

As Sunstein (2002) has noted, the advantage of evaluating public programs through the CBA or CEA lens is not only, or even primarily, that these approaches result in 'bottom-line' metrics of net social surplus or 'bang per buck' (effectiveness per dollar spent). Rather it is that the accepted economic framework for arriving at these bottom-line measures involves systematically applying a social accounting framework for identifying, classifying and measuring the effects of public programs that is both coherent and comprehensive. This framework is coherent because it draws on a consistent set of economic principles for defining social benefits and costs. It is comprehensive because its objective is to arrive at a 'bottom line' based on the concept of social benefit and cost that is considerably broader than private revenue and cost normally used to assess the performance of profit-making enterprises.[4]

The process of arriving at that bottom line is at least as, if not more valuable than, the bottom line itself, chiefly because careful application of the CBA framework requires the analyst to clearly specify essential features of the policy being analyzed and to account fully for its effects on all stakeholders. This process provides both measures of program effects and valuable insights about ways to improve the program by reducing the costs of attaining particular objective, increasing the potential benefits (positive outcomes) that can be attained for a given outlay of scarce resources, or both.[5]

Cost–benefit analysis and assessing social efficiency

The general approach, as well as the potentially applicability of this framework to measuring nonprofit outcomes, can best be illustrated by reviewing the steps that would be involved in undertaking a CBA of a program that took homeless families off the street and placed them in housing in residential neighborhoods, while also offering them a range of counseling services.

Identifying program impacts

A key first step in undertaking a CBA of such a program would be to identify and classify program impacts. One distinctive feature of CBA as a social accounting framework is the attempt to account for three broad types of program outcome: (1) social benefits, the features of a program that add to social value; (2) social costs, the features of a program that take from social value; and (3) transfers, any program outcomes that neither take from nor add to aggregate social value, but instead shift existing social value from one segment of society (such as taxpayers) to others (such as transfer recipients). In the case of a program providing shelter and services to the homeless, focusing on these three types of effects would require measuring the program's impact along several dimensions, including: (1) how many homeless persons or families received housing and counseling services as a result of the program; (2) the program's impacts on the ability of the homeless to function in society; (3) the main benefits accruing both to homeless persons and to society at large from providing shelter and counseling services; and (4) the resources needed to provide the housing and services.

Monetizing social benefits and social costs

Careful identification and measurement of program outcomes is not unique to CBA, but CBA is different from other program evaluation approaches because it attempts to translate both outcomes and inputs into monetary values to permit a 'bottom-line' comparison between what the program adds to and takes from social value.

An important advantage of pushing the analysis toward monetization is that different programs can be compared against a common benchmark. The main criticism of monetizing inputs and outcomes of social programs is that doing so inappropriately applies 'business-like' thinking to evaluating public programs. On the one hand, it is true that attempting to estimate the social surplus garnered by a public program bears at least a surface similarity to attempting to estimate its 'social profit'. Yet, as noted above, social surplus is much broader than traditional measures of profit because it imputes values to outcomes without regard to whether such outcomes are directly valued in the marketplace. Put slightly differently, the concept of social value recognizes that a positive (negative) program outcome can add to (reduce) social value whether or not it is 'bought and sold' in the private marketplace.

Accounting for program benefits and costs
Programs create social benefits by adding to social value in several ways. Almost all programs that are candidates for evaluation by CBA produce outcomes that are 'goods' with positive value to some stakeholders. For example, the safe shelter provided by programs for the homeless would be an outcome with positive value to homeless families, and perhaps to members of the wider society. Many programs also enhance social value by saving costs for society. Providing shelter for the homeless might, for example, lower public costs such as policing and sanitation.

The process of achieving social benefits, however, also entails costs to society. Implementing and operating public programs requires using scarce resources that have alternative uses. For instance, the illustrative program described above would use staff time, facilities and housing that could be devoted to addressing other social needs.

The analytical benchmarks for attaching monetary values to such social benefits and social costs are provided by two important conceptual measures that reflect two broad ways in which public actions either add to or reduce social surplus. One is the concept of willingness to pay; the other is the concept of social opportunity cost.

Willingness to pay
In the case of goods and services provided by a public program, the social value of such outcomes is defined as the aggregate sum of what individual members of society would be willing to pay for those goods and services. Individual willingness to pay, in turn, is defined conceptually as the sum of money that would need to be taken from a program beneficiary after the program was put in place in order to leave that person as well off after the program was implemented as before, independently of whether the individual actually made such a payment.

Measuring willingness to pay: revealed versus stated preferences
The concept of willingness to pay provides a conceptual benchmark for defining what ought to be measured. The challenge in implementing many cost–benefit analyses is the estimation of willingness to pay in practice.

There are two broad approaches to estimating willingness to pay: revealed preference and stated preference. Economists prefer revealed preference measures, valuations that are revealed through choices the individuals or businesses make in the marketplace. Economists strongly prefer revealed preference measures because they are based on actual behavior rather than on what people say they would be willing to pay in response to hypothetical survey questions. In the case of housing services for the homeless, the revealed preference measure of what a homeless family would willingly pay for the housing would be measured conceptually by consumer surplus, which equals the value of housing services consumed minus the cost of the services, without regard to whether the homeless family actually had the ability to pay, or was required to pay for the services.

Using revealed preference measures requires that policies have effects that can be evaluated either explicitly or implicitly from behavior in markets. There are, however, cases in which program outcomes are not easily evaluated in the marketplace. Fewer homeless people on the street may provide an 'esthetic benefit' to area residents and businesses. This esthetic benefit has value, but no market data exist to estimate it. In such cases, stated preference measures may be used. These measures estimate willingness to pay based on what people state in survey responses. This alternative has gained some acceptance in economics, but remains controversial because it provides information about 'what people say they would be willing to pay' rather than what they actually would have to pay in the market. Since the situation is hypothetical, there seems to be a tendency for people to overlook their budget constraints and overstate their willingness to pay.

Social opportunity cost
Social opportunity cost measures the economic value of what society must forego in order to pursue a particular activity. Or, if the activity results in a saving of resources, social opportunity cost measures the economic value to society of the resources saved. Because the opportunity cost of an input (such as labor) or an activity (such as 'rent-free' use of space in a building) is the value in its best alternative use, opportunity cost can differ from budgetary cost. A basic methodological principle of CBA is that the proper benchmark for determining both program costs and program benefits is to value program inputs and any cost-saving outcomes in terms of social opportunity cost.

To see how the concept of social opportunity cost would guide the estimation of social costs and benefits of the program for the homeless, consider the general approach that would be taken for estimating the value of the scarce resources used to provide the program. The measurement 'default' would be to rely as much as possible on either budgetary or market data to estimate the value of these resources. However, the modifier 'social' that is placed before opportunity cost is meant to denote the fact that, while the value of what society must forego to implement a policy or program is often the same as what people would typically regard to be a financial cost or budgetary outlay, it need not be, because the concept of social opportunity cost is broader.

The social opportunity cost would be the same as a budgeted outlay in the case of payments made from a government grant or contract to cover program staff salaries. As a rule, salaries would be regarded as representing the value of the staff time in its next-best use, such as providing services to clients other than the government, and hence a good estimate of social opportunity cost.

Suppose, however, that operating the homeless program involves shifting existing staff and facilities from another set of activities instead of spending more budgetary resources. In this case, the observed budgetary cost would not correspond to social opportunity cost. Resources shifted from other uses would not show up as budgetary costs but would nonetheless entail a social opportunity cost equal to the value of shifted staff and facilities in what would have been their next 'best' uses.

Dealing with income transfers

Some program outcomes neither add to nor reduce social value but instead redistribute income between stakeholders. A program for homeless individuals might enable participants to apply for and claim social welfare benefits. CBA accounts for outcomes of this sort by treating welfare benefits received as a gain to homeless households be offset by an equal cost to taxpayers who must finance the benefits. Treating transfers in this manner recognizes correctly that such outcomes neither increase nor reduce social value in the aggregate because in a CBA the net impact on social surplus of outcomes that are transfers is always zero. At the same time, it recognizes that enabling homeless persons to receive social welfare benefits that society intends for them would nonetheless be a positive program outcome. In effect, CBA recognizes the dual character of such program outcomes by treating them as benefits to some stakeholders while recognizing that the benefits are financed by others.

The CBA bottom line: social efficiency

Having identified and measured as many effects of the program as possible, one would first determine the estimated annual benefits received and costs incurred by each stakeholder group in order to display the estimated impact of the program or project on the various segments of society that are affected by it. These amounts would then be aggregated, discounting for future benefits and costs when appropriate, to determine the annual net social benefit of the program. From the standpoint of social efficiency, the question would then be whether the policy adds more to social value in the form of social benefits than it takes from social value in the form of scarce resources. A positive bottom line with social benefits exceeding social costs would indicate that the outcome of the program is valued more highly than the costs of achieving the outcome, but of course does not itself reveal whether other programs rank higher in generating net positive social benefits.

Using CBA in the nonprofit sector

The broad character of the social accounting framework in CBA makes it a potentially valuable decision-making tool in the philanthropic and nonprofit sectors. Because nonprofit organizations have an expressly social mission and often provide goods and/or services that substitute for or complement public outputs, there is a certain logic to using evaluation and performance assessment tools used in the public sector to aid foundation staff in the tasks of evaluating nonprofit performance and with allocating scarce financial resources.

CBA can serve as a useful measure of nonprofit performance for many of the same reasons that it is useful in evaluating public programs. It provides agreed-upon protocols for estimating benefits and costs of activities that incorporate social as well as private evaluations of outcomes. Thus the framework is broad enough to be applied to a wide range of activities. At the same time, the requirement that all outcomes be translated into common monetary measures of social opportunity cost and/or willingness to pay provides a consistent framework that, in principle, makes it possible for different programs to be assessed against common benchmarks.

Social versus mission-related benefits and costs

A potential limitation to the use of CBA for measuring nonprofit performance is that the social accounting framework of CBA may not always correspond to what might be termed the mission-oriented accounting framework that might be most relevant to a typical nonprofit organization. But this limitation may be more perception than reality. First, as noted above, there are likely to be many situations in which the mission of the nonprofit may correspond quite closely to an implicit definition of the public interest that seeks to maximize the 'social surplus' garnered from the pursuit of particular public objectives. When the mission of a grant maker or nonprofit can be readily translated into these terms, then the 'public policy' accounting framework of CBA can be transferred fairly directly to aid in evaluating funding priorities and/or performance.

In other cases, however, a grant maker's or nonprofit's mission may reflect specific conceptions of the 'public good' that is to be served. In such instances, the methodology of CBA is still relevant because of its usefulness in measuring benefits and costs that go beyond conventional market value. The principal modification would be the substitution of mission-related benefits and costs for social benefits and costs.

The distinction between mission-related and social benefits and costs may also have implications for how individual grant makers and/or nonprofit organizations treat external benefits or costs. As explained above, when CBA is used in public policy analysis, the methodological guidance is clear: count all social benefits and costs, both direct and external, and weigh them equally in arriving at the 'social bottom line'.

There may, however, be instances in which the grant maker or nonprofit organization gives less weight to certain external benefits and costs because these are not centrally related to its core mission. This may have consequences for how programs are evaluated. For example, a grant maker that saw providing services to the homeless as its primary mission might view a program with, say, $100 000 of benefits comprising $80 000 of direct benefits to clients, and $20 000 of external benefit differently than a program that also had $100 000 of total benefit, comprising $50 000 of direct benefit, and $50 000 of external benefit.

Accounting for distributional effects

As noted above, CBA is primarily intended to measure whether programs enhance economic efficiency. Nonetheless, the data compiled for a CBA also can be used to assess income distributional effects.

In the case of programs with explicit income distributional goals, two different approaches for incorporating distributional objectives in CBA have been proposed. One is to estimate and weigh benefits and costs of different groups to reflect distributional outcomes. In essence, this approach assigns more 'credit' to projects whose benefits flow to lower income groups, and a greater penalty to costs that fall on these groups. This approach has not been much used in practice, however, because of difficulty in coming up with agreed-upon distributional weights.

Another approach for incorporating distributional objectives is the 'distributional needs approach' suggested by Arnold Harberger (1980). This approach is intended to be used when the main outcome of a program is to enable low-income individuals to meet what society deems to be a basic need (such as food, shelter, health or education). In such cases, Harberger proposes that one estimate and compare the social costs per dollar of basic need met through the program with the social cost of alternative means of meeting the basic need. For example, in the illustrative case of the homeless shelter, if the principal benefit was to provide housing to homeless persons, the social cost of providing housing by a nonprofit organization would be estimated and this cost would then be compared with the cost of providing comparable resources to the recipients through alternative means (e.g. housing vouchers, cash social assistance). This approach has strong similarities to cost-effectiveness analysis (CEA), described above.

Estimation of social benefits and costs in practice
An important question is how to undertake a CBA in the face of typical constraints on time and on available data that are likely to face foundation and/or nonprofit organization staff and funding sources. Fortunately, the experience of implementing CBA to evaluate a variety of public sector programs offers many lessons in how this might be done.

Obtaining data to estimate benefits and costs
The data requirements for undertaking cost–benefit analyses can often be substantial, and the timeline for conducting such studies more often than not may preclude undertaking much, if any, original research to value costs or benefits of interest. Often, however, it may be possible to draw on secondary sources for such estimates. One such source is administrative data. For example, savings in policing and sanitation costs from providing shelter to the homeless could be inferred from local budgets.

In other cases, it may be possible to obtain plausible estimates of benefits or costs by drawing on secondary sources, such as administrative data and, where appropriate, the results of previous research. This process is known as benefit or cost transfer.

For example, a program in another city similar to one being evaluated resulted in a 10 percent reduction in recidivism. Studies on the economic costs of crime may have established a range of values for the costs of a typical petty theft incident. In that case, a plausible inference could be made about the benefits in the form of crime reduction provided by the program that was being evaluated.

An obvious difficulty with simply 'borrowing' estimates from elsewhere, of course, is that the estimates of unit costs or benefits may not be comparable due to differences in the affected populations and differences in study methodologies. According to the Office of Management and Budget, 'the extent of these problems and the degree of uncertainty depend on the divergence between the policy situation being studied and the basic scenario providing the benefits transfer estimate' (2003, p. 5502). Nonetheless, if used carefully, existing estimates of benefits and costs can often be 'transferred' with appropriate care from one study to another, reducing the time and effort required to obtain needed quantitative magnitudes of program effects.

Dealing with incomplete and uncertain estimates
Two further issues that must be dealt with in the implementation of CBA and SROI analysis are (a) the existence of real, though often intangible, effects of the activities of nonprofit organizations, and (b) the fact that even estimates of tangible benefits and/or costs are often uncertain. Although these limitations are unavoidable, careful use of the social accounting framework, especially in CBA, can help to bound the uncertainty

about ultimate program impact resulting from these limitations.[6] For example, sensitivity analysis, showing how the bottom line changes if different assumptions are made about either missing or highly uncertain benefits or costs, can provide insight about which benefits or costs 'matter most' in the overall assessment of the program.

Comparing SROI and CBA

SROI analysis and CBA share the feature of striving to measure nonprofit performance in terms of a monetary benchmark. There are, however, a number of differences between the implicit accounting frameworks that underlie CBA and SROI, as it has been applied by REDF.

These differences are illustrated by comparing the SROI results in Table 17.1 with Table 17.2, which takes operating data from Ashbury Images for one year and recasts those data in terms of the accounting framework used for CBA.[7] Applying a CBA framework to the REDF data provides the following perspectives on the various impacts of Ashbury Images.

Participants

The estimates shown in the column labeled 'Participants' indicate the measurable effects of the Ashbury program on drug addicts who participate. These effects include: increased labor market productivity of addicts leading to increased earnings, estimated by REDF to equal $150 060; a reduction in the receipt of some social welfare benefits of $90 390, offset by an increase in receipt of other benefits of $42 120 amounting to a net reduction in social welfare benefits received of $48 270; and payment of increased taxes on Asbury earnings equal to $22 150. When added together, these amounts represent an increase in spendable cash income of participants equal to $79 640. In addition to the extent that employment at Ashbury Images enhanced the future employability of participants and their self-esteem, such effects would be registered as 'intangible benefits' that are difficult to measure, but nonetheless worth recognizing with a '+'.

Nonprofit organization

The column labeled 'Nonprofit organization' shows the effects of the program on Ashbury Images and its volunteers. The results show that Ashbury Images incurred more than $670 000 in costs, and earned more than $608 000 in revenue from product sales. In addition, the social enterprise received an additional $121 000 in revenue in the form of social subsidies for the services it provided to the addicts. Counting social subsidies received, the organization garnered a net financial benefit of just under $60 000. Not counting social subsidies, the enterprise operated at a loss in the marketplace of just over $61 000.

Donors and volunteers

The columns labeled 'Donors' and 'Volunteers' are meant to account for any benefits or costs incurred by private supporters of Ashbury Images and by those who volunteer their services. The donor column is left blank because the REDF data did not provide specific information about donor contributions. However, a typical entry in this column for a nonprofit organization might be the cost to private donors of providing a portion of the social subsidy to the nonprofit organization.

Table 17.2   Asbury Images: benefits and costs ($)

	Participants	Nonprofit organization	Donors	Volunteers	Other citizens	All society
Costs						
Total operating cost		(615 449)				(615 449)
Social operating cost		(54 862)				(54 862)
Total enterprise		(670 311)				(670 311)
Opportunity cost of volunteer time				'−'		'−'
Benefits						
Gross revenue		608 389				608 389
Social operating subsidies		121 000			(121 000)	
Increased participant income	150 060					150 060
Participant employability	'+'					'+'
Volunteer satisfaction				'+'		'+'
Social costs avoided						
Crime					'+'	'+'
Health					'+'	'+'
Transfers and taxes						
Participant tax payments	(22 150)				22 150	
Net change in participant use of transfer/ support payments	(48 270)				48 270	
Decrease	(90 390)				90 390	
Increase	42 120				(42 120)	
Total benefits						758 449
Total costs						(670 311)
Total measurable net benefits	79 640	(61 922)			70 420	88 138

The REDF data also did not provide information on volunteers. However, the entries reflect that fact that in a cost–benefit analysis, the net value of volunteer time would equal the difference between the personal benefits that volunteers derive from time spent volunteering less the value to them of time spent in their highest-valued alternative activity. Because the decision to work as a volunteer is a voluntary choice, it is reasonable to assume that the economic value of the '+' entry in this column would be at least as great as the '−' entry.

If a nonprofit organization wished to explicitly value the participation of volunteers as part of its overall impact, it would have several options for assigning monetary values to volunteer time, as discussed in the chapter by Leete in this volume (see Chapter 16). On the cost side, one option would be to take the average market wage of its volunteers multiplied by the number of hours to estimate the social opportunity cost of volunteer time. On the benefit side, as noted, an extremely plausible assumption is that volunteers should value the personal satisfaction received from volunteering at least as highly as the alternative value of their time. Thus a default assumption might be that the personal benefits from volunteering equaled the opportunity cost of time in which case volunteer time would 'net out' in the bottom-line assessment of the net change in social value attributable to the nonprofit. The implication of making specific assumptions about how volunteers value the personal satisfaction from volunteering relative to the opportunity cost could then be explored if desired.

Other citizens
The column labeled 'Other citizens' shows the effects of the nonprofit organization on other members of society. Other members of society benefit from the activities of Ashbury Images in the form of increased tax revenues and reduced payments of some social transfers to program participants, as well as certain intangible benefits. Other members of society also bear increased financial costs in the form of increases in some social transfers to participants, as well as some $121 000 in social subsidies paid to the nonprofit. Overall, other citizens bear net costs in the process of providing support both to Ashbury Images as an organization, and to employees of Ashbury Images.

Society
The final column, labeled 'All society', aggregates the various benefits and costs experienced by different stakeholders into a social bottom line. Overall, based on the data provided by REDF, Ashbury Images is estimated to increase (tangible) net social value annually by roughly $88 000.

Concluding remarks
We conclude with an assessment of the potential role of the SROI and the CBA frameworks for assessing the performance of nonprofit organizations. Both frameworks are useful for arriving at quantitative measures of nonprofit performance. Attempts to calculate the SROI for specific nonprofit programs demonstrate, for example, that it is possible to estimate the economic value to society of a number of different mission-related activities.

One pay-off from performing either an SROI analysis or a CBA is that monetizing outcomes produces a single money metric that can facilitate comparisons among different program impacts. This feature of SROI analysis and CBA, however, is also controversial; and both practical and conceptual objections have been raised to the monetization of nonprofit outcomes. In practice, while it is difficult enough to devise quantitative measures of the outcomes of programs and activities undertaken by nonprofits, it is even more challenging to translate such outcomes into dollars and cents. For some outcomes, this may not be feasible, and considerable disagreement can arise about how the outcomes can, or even should, be translated into dollar equivalents. While economists have made inroads into some of these determinations, inevitably the decisions on monetization can be very controversial.

A related concern is that, because of difficulties in monetization, attempting to quantify nonprofit performance with either SROI analysis or CBA will tend to favor activities with outcomes that are readily translated into dollars, and/or create incentives for nonprofits to focus more on those activities that can be monetized. This latter concern has been expressed specifically by Gair (2002, pp. 11–12) with regard to SROI analysis, but is of equal applicability to CBA:

> None of the REDF Portfolio nonprofit organizations have the mission of saving taxpayer dollars spent on public services. By using public sector dollars saved as a measure of success, SROI measures an area in which few nonprofits would consider a primary area of achievement . . . Emphasis on public savings in our SROI approach could have an unintended long term effect: it could encourage social purpose enterprises to focus hiring on individuals currently receiving public assistance, and away from those who are not, and who may have greater needs.

A further important practical consideration is the staff time and effort required to perform a CBA or SROI analysis. As noted in Clark et al. (2004), implementing measures such as SROI is relatively feasible when information on program outcomes, cost and revenue is already being collected by an organization. The same general observation applies to CBA. On one hand, the current move to require more systematic outcome assessment provides the 'raw material' for undertaking formal cost–benefit evaluations. On the other hand, converting outcome assessments into CBA requires additional staff time and money, so that having outcome measures is but the first step in making a CBA.

On balance, however, the results obtained from cost–benefit analyses have been shown to be useful inputs into public sector decision making, which suggests that CBA and SROI analysis have great potential for improving the evaluation and, thus, the performance of nonprofit organizations.

Notes

1. In calculations of the SROI presented on the REDF website, the overall discount rate is 12.08 percent.
2. In order to accurately estimate the cost savings, REDF developed OASIS, a 'social outcome tracking system' that includes a range of data on target employees who were tracked for 24 months after being first employed by the enterprise.
3. REDF recognizes this point and describe SROI as a 'retrospective cost benefit analysis' (Gair, 2002, p. 1).
4. See Boardman et al. (2006), chs 1 and 2; and Layard and Glaister (1994). Sunstein (2002) makes a compelling argument that because of its broad scope, when properly used, CBA ensures that the interests of all relevant stakeholders are represented in the analysis.
5. For a useful overview of the various roles of CBA in the policy process, see Boardman et al. (2006).
6. An excellent example may be found in Weisbrod (1981).
7. See Young and Steinberg (1995).

References

Boardman, Anthony, David H. Greenberg, Aidan R. Vining and David L. Weimer (2006), *Cost–Benefit Analysis: Concepts and Practice*, Upper Saddle River, NJ: Prentice Hall.

Clark, Catherine, William Rosenzweig, David Long and Sara Olsen (2004), 'Double bottom-line project report: assessing social impacts in double bottom-line ventures', prepared for the Rockefeller Foundation, New York, pp. 1–70.

Gair, Cynthia (2002), 'A report from the good ship SROI', San Francisco, CA: REDF, pp. 1–15, available at http://www.redf.org/learn-from-redf/publications/119.

Harberger, Arnold C. (1980), 'On the use of distributional weights in social cost–benefit analysis: reply to Layard and Squire', *The Journal of Political Economy*, **88** (5), 1050–52.

Layard, G., P. Richard and Stephen Glaister ([1972] 1994), 'Introduction', in P. Richard, G. Layard and Stephen Glaister (eds), *Cost–Benefit Analysis*, Cambridge, UK and New York: Cambridge University Press, pp. 1–56.

Office of Management and Budget (OMB) (2003), 'Draft 2003 report to Congress on the costs and benefits of federal regulation, Part VII', *Federal Register*, **68** (22), 5492–527.

Ostrower, Francie (2004), 'Foundation effectiveness: definitions and challenges', Washington, DC: The Urban Institute, pp. 1–10.

REDF (2001), 'SROI methodology: analyzing the value of social purpose enterprise within a social return on investment framework', in http://www.redf.org/learn-from-redf/publications/119.

Roberts Enterprise Development Fund (2001), 'Social return on investment collection', http://www.redf.org/learn-from-redf/publications/119.

Sunstein, Cass R. (2002), *Risk and Reason: Safety, Law and the Environment*, Cambridge, MA: Harvard University Press.

Weisbrod, Burton A. (1981), 'Benefit–cost analysis of a controlled experiment: treating the mentally ill', *Journal of Human Resources*, **16** (4), 523–48.

Young, Dennis R. and Richard Steinberg (1995), *Economics for Nonprofit Managers*, Washington, DC: The Foundation Center.

18 Social accounting for value creation in nonprofits
Laurie Mook and Femida Handy

Introduction

Nonprofit organizations are different from business enterprises in some very significant ways. They operate for purposes other than to earn a profit: their efficiency and effectiveness cannot be solely determined through information in financial statements only. Furthermore, their revenue sources are multiple and may be only indirectly related to what they produce: they may receive large amounts of resources from donors or government, who do not expect monetary benefits in return (Razek et al., 2000). Nonprofit organizations are also different from for-profit organizations in that they acknowledge the contribution of multiple stakeholders such as funders, clients, the community and volunteers; as well as having both social and economic goals.

To capture the value created by nonprofit organizations and to understand the contribution of their multiple stakeholders, some scholars have recently turned to social accounting, which addresses some of the difficulties in applying accounting models developed for business enterprises to nonprofit organizations. In particular, the expanded value added statement (EVAS) developed by Mook (Mook et al., 2007b), recognizes this uniqueness by focusing on both economic and social impacts, instead of just the 'bottom line' of financial surpluses or deficits. The EVAS is able to identify key aspects of an organization's functioning that are not apparent from conventional financial statements alone. These key aspects include the impact of unpaid labor/volunteers, the role of the organization in providing employment, skills development and personal growth for its members, and the contribution of the organization to society through service provision, employment and tax payment.

This chapter looks at the EVAS, which focuses on economic and social impacts, instead of the traditional 'bottom line' of surpluses or deficits, and how this alternative model can be applied to accounting for nonprofit organizations. To do this we explore how accounting statements can include the 'unaccountable' aspects of nonprofits, how they can account for the contribution of and return to multiple stakeholders, and how they can assess their social and economic value added. We also discuss some of the obstacles that have precluded the adoption of alternative models by the accounting profession. Finally, we look at why it matters and to whom: practitioners, policy makers, scholars and society in general.

Context

Throughout most of the twentieth century, accounting theory and accounting standards have largely concentrated on profit-making organizations (Skinner, 1987). The predominant trend in accounting has been to extend the statements of profit-oriented businesses to nonprofit organizations. One of the earlier critics of this trend (Henke, 1972, p. 53) argued that 'the financial statements for most not-for-profit organizations show little more than where dollars came from, for what they were expended and the extent to which the acquisitions and expenditures were consistent with the budgetary plan'. Income statements used by nonprofits, which were created for profit-oriented businesses, indicate the net gain or net loss for the accounting period. This information is of benefit to the owners of for-profit enterprises because they are able to see the return on their investment; but for nonprofit organizations that do not have shareholders in the same sense as profit-oriented businesses, an income statement has a more limited role. They also miss an important feature – nonprofits are organizations with a social mission and, as such, their social impact on multiple stakeholders is a vital part of their performance story.

The limitations of conventional accounting are particularly problematic for the subset of nonprofits that rely heavily on either grants or donations from such external sources as government and from individuals, corporations and foundations. For organizations of this sort, conventional accounting documents their costs without assessing their benefits (Anthony and Young, 1988; Henke, 1989). These organizations are portrayed as users of resources rather than as creators of value to society. Their financial accounts are therefore one-sided and lack information upon which to base decisions affecting the organizations and the communities they serve.

In addition, nonprofits rely in varying degrees on volunteers to provide labor, an essential input into the production of goods and services. Yet ironically the value of volunteer labor is often excluded from accounting statements. Indeed this resource, as a vital input, is documented by Salamon and his colleagues for 36 countries to be the equivalent of 20.2 million full-time-equivalent jobs, with a value added of $316 billion (Salamon et al., 2004). In the USA in 2006, 61.2 million volunteers contributed 8.1 billion hours of volunteer service, or the equivalent of 3.9 million full-time-equivalent positions (CNCS, 2007). This represents an invaluable and sustaining contribution to local communities, but neither this contribution nor any additional social impact finds its way into conventional accounting statements.

The American Institute of Certified Public Accountants (1978) attempted to address the thorny issue of the circumstances under which volunteer contributions ('donated services') could be monetized and included within financial statements (Gross and Warshauer, 1979). They suggested four criteria for inclusion: the volunteer labor is measurable; the organization manages the volunteers much like its employees; the services are part of the organization's normal work program and would be paid for otherwise; and the services of the organization are for the public rather than for its members. These criteria were quite restrictive and excluded the services that members donated to nonprofit mutual associations such as religious organizations, clubs, professional and trade associations, labor unions, political parties and fraternal societies. Nevertheless, the criteria did provide some recognition that volunteer labor had a market value that ought to be included in financial statements. In 1993, update No. 116 by the Financial Accounting Standards Board (FASB) had the same restrictive character: 'Contributions of services are recognized only if the services received (a) create or enhance non-financial assets or (b) require specialized skills, are provided by individuals possessing those skills, and would typically need to be purchased if not provided by donation' (Financial Accounting Standards Board, 1993, p. 1).

However, for a variety of reasons, most volunteer contributions still go unreported in financial statements or, at best, are included as a footnote (Canadian Institute of

Chartered Accountants, 1980; Cornell University Cooperative Extension, 1995; Mook et al., 2007a).

Critique of traditional accounting

The traditional approach to accounting is reflected in teaching and professional development, which tends to focus on technique acquisition (Gray et al., 1994; Gray, 1995; Roslender and Dillard, 2003). Overall, accounting education treats the discipline as a neutral, technical and value-free activity (Hopwood, 1990; Lewis et al., 1992). Students are taught that accounting decisions in businesses are made in order to maximize shareholder wealth (Ferguson et al., 2005, 2006). This exclusive focus on economic returns by the accounting profession has played an important role in defining organizations, and in what constitutes 'success'.

Indeed, in the 1960s scholars began to question the assumptions underlying traditional accounting, arguing that accounting practices are neither objective, neutral nor value-free, and that they create, sustain and change social reality (Cooper and Neu, 1997; Craig and Amernic, 2004; Gray, 2002; Hines, 1988; Hopper et al., 1987; Llewellyn, 1994; Lodh and Gaffikin, 1997; Mathews, 1997; Morgan, 1988; Tinker, 1985). For instance, accountants argue that, by the very act of counting certain things and excluding others, accounting shapes a particular interpretation of social reality. This interpretation, which corresponds to particular assumptions about how society functions and should function, has implications for decision making and policy (Hines, 1988; Tinker et al., 1982). Social accounting comes out of this critique, and provides a practical and working framework that takes into consideration a broader range of factors and actors in the accounting process. Social accounting is a broad term that includes a variety of alternative accounting models, including expanded value added accounting, environmental accounting and sustainability accounting. Social accounting is defined as: 'A systematic analysis of the effects of an organization on its communities of interest or stakeholders, with stakeholder input as part of the data that are analyzed for the accounting statement' (Quarter et al., 2003, p. xix).

Examples of alternative accountings for social organizations

Experimentation with integrated social accounting for organizations outside of the for-profit sector is a fairly recent occurrence. For nonprofits, Land (2002) developed a social impact statement that distinguished between three components: output, outcome and side-effect indicators. He used the example of a 'Meals-on-Wheels' program to show how these indicators could be measured. For instance, output indicators included the number of meals delivered and people served; outcome indicators focused on the client satisfaction; and side-effect indicators looked at the impact of the delivery of meals on the client's nutritional or health status.

Based on this framework, Richmond (1999) created the 'community social return on investment' model to look at how social organizations create value from the perspective of the community. Using a case study of a community-based employment training agency serving persons with disabilities and other barriers to employment, the model analyzed the organization's primary, secondary and tertiary outputs in order to reflect the organization's social return on investment. To do so, a comparative economic value for social outputs was included, as well as a value for volunteer contributions.

In 1999, Mook first introduced the EVAS and applied it to a student housing cooperative (Richmond and Mook, 2001). In this model, member contributions and other non-financial items were included in the statement by estimating a comparative market value for them. The model was subsequently applied to volunteer programs in nonprofit organizations (Quarter et al., 2003; Mook et al., 2007b). The remainder of this chapter will outline this model and present a case study looking at the volunteer contributions to a nonprofit organization called Literacy Volunteers of Rochester, Inc.

The EVAS
The EVAS builds on the progressive (although still marginal) practice of mainstream accounting called the value added statement. As Burchell et al. (1985, p. 388) state:

> Value added has the property of revealing (or representing) something about the social character of production, something which is occluded by traditional profit and loss accounting. Value added reveals that the wealth created in production is the consequence of the combined effort of a number of agents who together form the co-operating team.

The value added statement was first proposed in 1954 as a supplemental report, which analyses 'the value added in production and its source or distribution among the organization participants' (Suojanen, 1954, p. 396). The format of the statement is shown in Table 18.1, and is similar to the one used today.

For example, the value added created by a furniture-making company is calculated by taking the difference between the price the furniture was sold for, and the cost of the materials that went into making the furniture (wood, screws, glue etc.). So if a table sold for $300, and the wood and materials cost $100, the value added would be $300 minus $100, or $200. That value added, $200, is then distributed to the stakeholders of the company – its employees, creditors, government (taxes) and shareholders.

The assumption of the value added statement is that an enterprise is responsible to all participants and not only to its stockholders, and that the concept of income,

Table 18.1   The value added statement

Goods produced, at selling price	$1 000 000
Less: purchases of external goods and services	200 000
Total value added by production	$800 000
Source of value added:	
Wages and salaries	$400 000
Taxes	100 000
Interest	20 000
Depreciation	180 000
Profit	100 000
Total value added	$800 000

as it appears on traditional income statements, is deficient as it assumes the organization exists to provide income to its owners. Through the value added statement the conceptual basis of accounting could be shifted from accounting for profit to the wider representation of value added. In this new frame of reference, it is recognized that the organization's primary focus is its viability, not the rights of its shareholders.

Calculation of value added

Value added is the wealth that an organization creates by its own and its employees' efforts (ASSC, 1975). Whereas sales revenue includes the value of work done outside the firm, value added excludes it (Meek and Gray, 1988). Value added is typically measured by the difference between the market value of the goods or services produced, and the cost of goods and services purchased from other producers (Ruggles and Ruggles, 1965). The value added statement shows both the wealth created and how that wealth is used to pay those who created it. It can be expressed as an equation (Riahi-Belkaoui, 1992):

$$S - B = W + I + DP + D + T + R$$

where

S = Sales revenue
B = Bought-in materials and services
W = Wages and benefits
I = Interest
DP = Depreciation
D = Dividends
T = Taxes
R = Retained earnings

However, one limitation of the value added statement is that it focuses only on financial items and pays no attention to intangibles and items that do not pass through the market and hence have no direct market value (price). Organizations have social and environmental impacts as well as economic ones. The impacts may be intended or unintended, and may occur in the short term (up to three years), medium term (four to six years) and long term (seven years or more). In the EVAS we consider all impacts that have occurred as a result of turning those externally purchased goods and materials into something else. In other words, the EVAS incorporates economic, social and environmental value added (or subtracted) by an organization.

To do this, the EVAS takes the value added statement and adapts it. It has four main influences: the progressive practices of mainstream accounting (value added statement); the lens of critical accounting, the principles of sustainability; and the contributions of integrated social accounting (Figure 18.1).

First, the development of the model begins with the value added statement as it focuses on the wider implications of an organization's activities beyond profits/losses or surpluses/deficits. Additionally, at a practical level, the value added statement is straightforward and easy to comprehend (Meek and Gray, 1988). Second, the EVAS uses a critical accounting perspective by recognizing that accounting is not neutral, and that it can be a

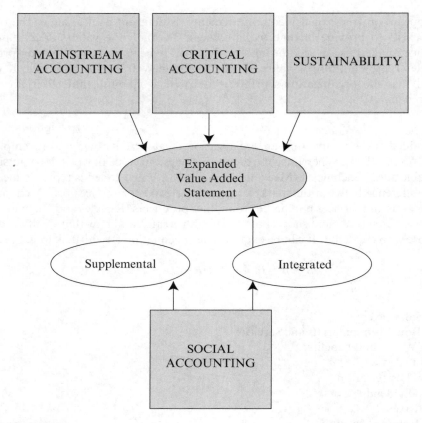

Source: Mook (2007).

Figure 18.1   EVAS

driver of behavior. Third, it is guided by the concept of sustainability in making explicit the economic, social and environmental impacts in allocating resources. So in addition to analyzing performance in terms of efficiency (doing more with less), the EVAS also seeks to promote effective behaviors (doing the right thing in terms of economic, social and environmental impacts). Finally, integrated social accounting informs the EVAS by providing working models that synthesize economic, social and environmental factors into one statement and by developing methodologies to estimate a monetary value for non-monetary activities.

The EVAS is not intended to replace existing financial statements but rather to be presented alongside them. By synthesizing traditional financial data with social and environmental data, the EVAS is another mechanism for understanding the dynamics of an organization and one that shows great potential for focusing attention on value creation and use. As such, it generates an additional set of questions that can be used for decision making. It challenges us to think about organizations in a different way – as creators or destroyers of value to a wide group of stakeholders.

Creating an EVAS

There are two parts to an EVAS: (1) the calculation of value added by an organization, and (2) its distribution to stakeholders. Compared to the traditional value added statement, in the EVAS the value added is broadened from including only financial transactions (that are part of the financial statements) to including non-monetized social contributions such as those of volunteers.

One challenge to creating an EVAS for nonprofit organizations is determining the market value for the outputs. For a for-profit firm, this is relatively straightforward – it is simply the amount of revenues received through sales, or in other words, the amount people have paid for those goods or services in the market. However, for some, nonprofit organization revenues are seen as inputs[1] and the term outputs is generally used to mean the direct products of its activities; for example, the services it provides, such as 'free' counseling for 50 clients. However, determining the market value for the outputs of a nonprofit organization presents unique challenges because its goods and services may not involve market transactions, and non-financial items such as contributions of volunteer labor are generally ignored. In order to assign a comparative market value (a reasonable rate if it were exchanged in the market) to the volunteers of nonprofit organizations, we look to the market to find a comparative market value for similar activities.

Case study: Literacy Volunteers of Rochester

To illustrate the use of social accounting and the EVAS in particular, we examine Literacy Volunteers of Rochester Inc. (LVR), a professional volunteer-based organization that provides assistance to functionally literate adults and others who lack English-language skills.

In addition to economic benefits, studies have found important social and personal benefits from literacy programs: they reduce the sense of isolation felt by illiterate adults and the embarrassment of not knowing how to read in a society that places a high premium on education (Parikh et al., 1996); they help adults get off welfare (Edin and Lein, 1997); and the effect of parents' increased literacy improves their children's performance in school thereby increasing the chances for high-school completion by 30 percent, and reducing the chance of being held back a grade, to drop out, or to be arrested (National Institute for Literacy, 2001). Literate adults were also found to be more likely to engage in responsible family planning and bear healthier children, and to have a positive self-image as well as to exercise their rights (e.g. voting) as citizens. Indeed research has indicated that the single most significant predictor of children's literacy is their mother's literacy level. The more literate the parents become, the more value they perceive in education and the more they support their children's learning, and the more they become involved in their children's schools (US Department of Education, 1999). Recent studies have also found extensive evidence that low literacy, poor health and early death are linked, with health status improving with literacy gains (Hohn, 1998; Rudd et al., 1999). This list of benefits of literacy training is by no means exhaustive and the report by ProLiteracy Worldwide (2003) gives an excellent review on positive outcomes achieved by literacy programs and the people they serve.

Literacy Volunteers of Rochester offers its literacy services free of charge to residents in the Rochester (New York) area. By engaging volunteers to provide one-to-one or small-group tutoring to functionally illiterate adults and to others lacking English-language skills, it is dedicated to fostering literacy in the greater Rochester, NY. It also supplements this person-to-person tutoring with computer-based instruction to further enhance reading and computer skills among its students. Completely run by volunteers, LVR hired its first staff person in 1987. As of its fortieth anniversary in 2004, LVR, including 5000 volunteers, had served over 8000 students. Currently LVR has five paid staff, and 354 volunteers who logged in over 20000 hours and taught 481 students in its last fiscal year. Tutors and students meet at mutually convenient locations throughout the area such as convenient libraries, churches, schools, community centers and other public buildings.

The program was begun by Church Women United in 1964 as a project for migrant workers, adopting the Literacy Volunteers of America model. It separated from Church Women United and incorporated in 1971 as a sector 501(c)(3) nonprofit organization, which implies it is registered with the US IRS as a *bona fide* charitable organization that can receive tax-exempt donations.

LVR has been very successful in teaching basic reading and writing English-language skills to adults, and has been accredited by ProLiteracy America, which is designed to recognize literacy organizations that are distinguished by superior professional leadership, effective programs, committed governing boards and outstanding volunteer support. Accreditation not only gives them greater credibility among the community and funders, but also allows LVR to share in the best practices that ProLiteracy shares with affiliates, increasing its value added in its own community.

Many LVR students have learning disabilities and it is not surprising to find that in some years about 60 percent of the students in the basic literacy program were at the third-grade level or below. Helping such students is a benefit not only to the students themselves, but also to the community, in which literate adults are a great asset.

The value to the community of LVR's services also increases as its forms collaborations with other groups and reaches out to other populations hitherto ignored in terms of literacy skills. For example, LVR collaborates with Step By Step, a group that serves women who are or have been in jail. Through a grant from the Junior League of Rochester, the two groups work together to bring literacy tutoring to inmates.

In addition to volunteering as tutors, volunteers staff the LVR office, help out in the in-house library, interview incoming students, update computer files, conduct tutor preview sessions, teach training workshops and serve on committees. They also, in addition to contributions of time and talent, make monetary contributions to LVR. Recently LVR has been approved for AmeriCorps, which recruits additional volunteers to meet the high demand and reduce the student wait list as well as raise awareness about LVR.

The contribution that LVR makes to the lives of people by offering them literacy skills cannot be totally captured in EVAS, despite the scope of the measures and their sophistication to reflect and capture the value added by the organization. There are certain externalities in the production of literacy that are not captured or measured, and that arise from the self-esteem and confidence gained by the hitherto illiterate becoming literate on a human and social dimension. However, the aspects that can be measured, such as volunteer and community contributions, when included in the EVAS, provide a very different picture of the value added created by the organization than traditional accounting statements alone. The utility of doing so will now be illustrated for LVR.

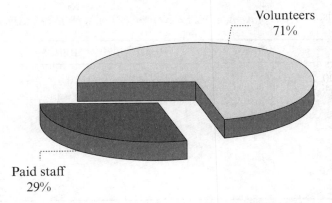

Figure 18.2   Proportion of total activity hours by volunteers and staff of LVR

LVR volunteer contributions
One way of looking at the significance of volunteer contributions is to examine the proportion that volunteers contribute to the overall human resources of the organization. Volunteer activities account for 71 percent of the LVR's human resources (Figure 18.2). Based on the estimate of 20416 volunteer hours and a workweek of 40 hours (2080 per year), volunteers contributed almost ten full-time-equivalent (FTE) positions for the fiscal year ending 30 June 2007. This means that, including volunteer contributions, LVR has the equivalent of a total workforce FTE of 14, more than tripling its paid staff FTE of four. In other words, more than three times the labor is required in the production of LVR's goods and services than is shown by traditional accounting statements.

Estimating the value added by volunteers   To estimate the monetary value of the unpaid services contributed by volunteers, two values were used: (1) an hourly rate based on the Independent Sector calculation for volunteer contribution for New York State; and (2) an hourly rate based on occupation and skill using values based on the US Bureau of Labor Statistics National Compensation Survey. These two values assume a replacement value methodology, where unpaid labor is valued at what it would cost the organization to replace its volunteers with paid staff and continue the services currently provided by volunteers.[2]
The first replacement cost method uses the value of volunteer time based on the average hourly earnings of all production and non-supervisory workers on private nonfarm payrolls (as determined by the Bureau of Labor Statistics). This figure is then increased by 12 percent to account for fringe benefits. For 2006 (the latest available data), the rate reported for the state of New York was $26.18/hour.[3] Taking the total hours contributed by volunteers to LVR (20415.75) multiplied by this rate ($26.18) gives us a value of $534484.
The second method uses an hourly rate based on occupation and skill level, as in the US Bureau of Labor Statistics National Compensation Survey. In this method, volunteer hours need to be collected according to job classifications. For example, in

Table 18.2   Estimated replacement cost of volunteer hours by job classification[a]

Position	Activity	Hours	Rate ($)	Total ($)
Board & Committees	Meetings	803.25	67.56	39 691.50
Board & Committees	Preparations	299.75	67.56	20 251.11
Tutors	Tutoring	8765.00	20.61	180 646.65
Tutors	Preparations	4382.50	20.61	90 323.33
Office		6381.00	14.18	90 482.58
		20 415.75		421 395.17
12% for benefits				50 567.42
Total			22.98	471 962.58

Note: [a]The number of volunteer hours and breakdown by task were provided by LVR. The Board & Committee hours are conservative as the exact number of hours contributed by these volunteers was based on actual meeting times and limited preparation hours for those meetings. This underestimates especially the contributions of officers (President, Vice-President, Treasurer and Secretary).

the case of LVR, volunteer positions could be categorized as 11-1011 Chief Executives (Board of Directors and Committees), 25-3011 Adult Literacy, Remedial Education, and GED Teachers and Instructors (tutors), and 43-0000 Office and Administrative Support Occupations (office volunteers). The corresponding mean hourly rates for these positions for Rochester, New York[4] for May 2006 (the latest available data) were $67.56, $20.61 and $14.18 respectively. As shown in Table 18.2, the replacement cost value of these hours, including 12 percent for benefits as suggested by the Independent Sector, would be $471 963. For the purposes of the case here, we shall use this more conservative value.

When considering the financial and non-financial resources of the organization, volunteer hours account for 59 percent of the total (Figure 18.3). This figure shows that volunteer contributions provide the organization with a significant resource that should be counted in its overall performance. Not recognizing these volunteer contributions as is done in conventional accounting, gives a very different picture of the resources of the organization.

LVR community contributions
Tutoring happens in public places, including libraries, churches, schools and community centers. These organizations in the community provide resources in the form of space for these interactions. In the fiscal year represented by this case, tutors met with learners over 4300 times for a total of 8765 hours. If LVR had to rent space for these interactions, using a very conservative rate of $5.00 per hour, they would have to spend additional financial resources of $43 825. However, this is provided at no charge by these community organizations.

Putting together the EVAS
Using the subtractive method described above, traditional value added is calculated by adding together the amounts for wages and benefits, interest paid on long-term debt,

(a) Not including volunteers

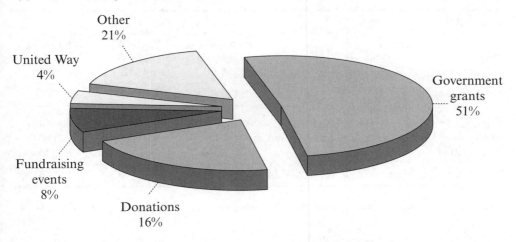

(b) Including volunteers

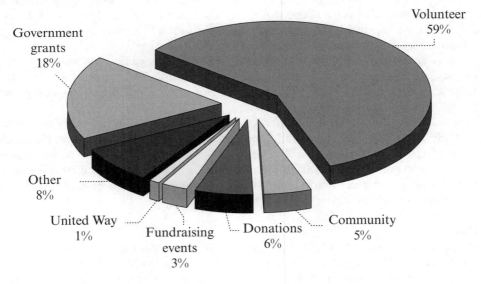

Figure 18.3   Resources of LVR

depreciation, taxes and retained earnings. In the case of nonprofits, the comparative market value of wages and benefits for volunteer hours must also be added in, these amounts added together are what we call expanded value added.[5]

In the case of LVR, the amount paid for employee wages and benefits ($183 146), depreciation ($3556), and the estimated comparative market value of volunteer hours ($471 963) are added together to come up with a total for expanded value added of

Table 18.3   LVR: expanded value added statement (partial[a])

1 July 2006 to 30 June 2007

		Financial ($)	Social ($)	Combined ($)
Outputs		263 003	515 788	778 791
Less external goods & services		76 301	43 825	120 126
Total value added		186 702	471 963	658 665
Employees	Wages & benefits	183 146		183 146
Society	Volunteer contributions		471 963	471 963
Organization	Depreciation	3 556		3 556
Value added distributed		186 702	471 963	658 665

Note: [a] The statement is partial in that not all of the impacts/outputs of the organization are reflected here.

$658 665 (see Table 18.3, column labeled 'Combined'). Externally purchased goods and services are calculated by taking the total amount of expenses for the period, and subtracting the amounts for wages and benefits and depreciation. Using the figures derived for expanded value added ($778 791) and externally acquired goods and services ($120 126), we can then get a value for the organization's outputs by adding these two amounts together to equal $658 665 (shown in the 'Combined' column).

As is shown in Table 18.3, traditional accounting significantly underreports the resources going into the organization and the value added it creates. In the EVAS, the value added reported is $658 665, an increase of almost 252 percent as compared to $186 702 using traditional methods.

In addition, the EVAS highlights that there are many more resources contributing to LVR's activities than financial. Traditional financial statements would only show financial resources totaling $263 003. The EVAS also includes volunteer contributions of $471 963 and community contributions of $43 825. Percentage-wise, financial contributions are only 34 percent of total resources, while volunteers contributed 61 percent, and the community 6 percent.

Discussion

Using the case study of LVR, this chapter has shown the usefulness of the EVAS in understanding the impact of a nonprofit on its community. Social goods and services, those not given a monetary value, are often a large part of a nonprofit organization's operations. Only by taking these goods and services into account do we get a clear picture of either a nonprofit's performance or the contributions made by its members. The EVAS helps various stakeholders, particularly volunteers, to see what value they have added to LVR – in this case, over 70 percent of the value added. In making this more visible, it also helps stakeholders to understand the value created by the organization and to appreciate the substantial volunteer contributions without which LVR could not provide the same level of service at current funding levels.

Some of the limitations of the EVAS are imposed by the selection of items included and by the methods available to put a monetary value on them. In this regard, the challenges faced by the EVAS are shared by other forms of alternative accounting and economics, namely identifying, measuring, quantifying and placing a value on key social and environmental indicators that could encourage and measure sustainable performance (Ranganathan, 1999; White and Zinkl, 1999). Additionally, while it is relatively easy to capture the equivalent market value of non-market inputs, it is more difficult to capture the outcomes.

Although nonprofits are ubiquitous, policy makers in general pay less attention to them, as they look to make policies that have high financial impact. As much of the work done by the nonprofits is not easily monetized, their impact on GDP or other financial indicators is relatively insignificant as compared to their true value added. Social accounting methods, the EVAS in particular, makes visible some of this and allows policy makers and funders to see a clearer return on their investment in nonprofits.

The narrower focus of most policy makers on the more easily understood effect of organizations (both for-profit and nonprofit), structures (e.g. new performing arts centers and sports stadiums), and events (e.g. arts festivals and sports tournaments) on regional or national GDP, employment, personal income and tax revenues also explains the popularity of economic impact studies that focus on largely short-run regional spending flows in contrast to broader measures of economic contribution. This tension between primarily 'instrumental' economic impacts and more 'intrinsic' economic rewards (see, e.g., McCarthy et al., 2004) has been at the heart of the long-simmering debate among economists as to how to properly measure the concept of regional economic impact. In the arts and culture segment of the nonprofit sector, the advantages and disadvantages of the competing approaches of qualitative/historical (including the emerging concept of 'cultural capital' – Throsby, 2001), economic impact, willingness to pay, and choice experiment studies are thoroughly reviewed by Snowball (2008), and distinctions among consumption (both use and non-use) economic impacts, long-run economic development impacts, and short-run spending flow economic impacts have been important to that debate (see, e.g., Seaman, 2003). While economists attempt to adapt their own tools to adequately measure the economic impact of nonprofit organizations that provide significant positive 'externalities' and 'public-good' benefits, social accounting methods such as the EVAS can be viewed as the accounting profession's attempt to confront the similar limitations of its own traditional framework in evaluating the performance of nonprofit organizations.

Concluding remarks: next steps

The application of the EVAS is not restricted to nonprofits; indeed, it can be applied to any type of organization or program. Some examples of cases where this has done include cooperatives, sustainable building, economically targeted investments, social enterprises and corporate volunteering programs (Mook, 2007; Mook et al., 2008). These cases demonstrate the possibility of including social and environmental items alongside economic ones.

Indeed, the framework of social accounting opens up new avenues of inquiry, both in terms of the impacts of organizations, and the impact of accounting models themselves. One of the challenges of social accounting is to shift the paradigm of accounting from focusing on profits for owners and shareholders to focusing on wealth for a larger group of stakeholders. The value added approach is useful in this regard, as it asks us to look at the value added or subtracted in the transformation of externally purchased goods and services by labor and capital, and to whom the value accrues. This provides a way of focusing on the question: what difference do our actions make in economic, social and environmental terms, and to whom? This is in sharp contrast to the question asked by traditional accounting, how can we maximize profit for our owners?

To illustrate how asking the first question leads to new thinking, consider the process of assigning a value to volunteer labor. Theoretically, most services produced by volunteer labor could be done by paid labor at a replacement value. However, the end results are not necessarily the same.

To explore differences between paid and volunteer labor, we asked respondents in another study how much of a monetary donation they would be willing to trade off for an hour of volunteer time (Handy et al., 2006). As organizations could have substituted volunteer labor (with paid labor or other inputs) using the money donation received, the amount indicated by the respondent, we argued, is a reasonable proxy for how they valued the productivity of their volunteer labor. In general, we found that given the choice, respondents are not willing to substitute volunteers with paid labor as they see positive benefits of volunteers over and above the direct tasks they performed. Indeed, we found the average value of a trade-off for an hour of volunteer time to be $35, an amount well above replacement or other valuations of volunteer time used in the literature.

If the value of volunteer labor to the organization is higher than its replacement value, this suggests that there are some positive externalities produced by volunteer labor that are absent when the service is produced by paid labor. This could be due to the attitudes and values volunteers bring to their work, the goodwill they generate for the organization in the community, often also contributing financially in ways that might not be expected of paid labor. We can therefore infer the value of the output of a volunteer hour to an organization by examining the trade-offs made between an hour of a volunteer's time and a dollar amount, assuming that the costs of recruiting the donations of time and money are equal. With traditional accounting, the focus on cost restricts recognition and analysis of social value. The EVAS, on the other hand, takes another view. It looks at organization as creating or destroying value through the use of labor and capital. This value has economic, social and environmental implications, and if we are to move forward towards sustainability, these implications need to be explicit and documented.

The adoption of new accounting models is a complex process that takes time and effort, and needs to consider the realities of accounting policy and education. In terms of policy, the main challenge to social accounting relates to the narrow scope of frameworks and tools that focus almost exclusively on a financial bottom line and ignore important aspects of organizational activities. Hence it is recommended that the current accounting principles and standards be reviewed and revised to reflect the realities and complexities of socially minded organization as well the social and environmental externalities of economic activities.

In terms of accounting education, there are several challenges to be addressed. One has to do with the low exposure of accounting students to alternative accounting models. Additionally, accountants, financial officers and other organizational leaders have few spaces to get together and discuss these issues (Albrecht and Sack, 2000; Amernic and

Craig, 2004; Mook et al., 2005). These networks are crucial for policy development. In fact, the lack of networks has been blamed for the failure of accountants to create change in the policy arena (Neu et al., 2001).

To address these challenges, it is important to encourage the formation of networks and spaces to discuss and learn about these issues, develop curricula and propose policy. It is recommended that critical and social accounting content be introduced in undergraduate and graduate accounting courses. Such content should pay attention to externalities, to the social construction of accounting models and practices, and to the development of rigorous yet flexible accounting models that reflect the realities of for-profit, nonprofit and public organizations. At the same time, workshops and mentoring circles should be developed for practicing accountants to provide support and resources for the adoption and use of alternative accounting practices.

Notes

1. The characterization of revenues as inputs might not apply to nonprofits that earn their revenues from the market.
2. Another method that could be used is an hourly rate based on the hourly opportunity costs incurred by volunteers. For a wider discussion of estimating a value for volunteer contributions, see Chapter 16, by Laura Leete, in this volume.
3. http://www.independentsector.org/programs/research/volunteer_time.html.
4. http://www.bls.gov/oes/current/oes_40380.htm.
5. This particular case, however, is referred to as partial expanded value added, as we consider only volunteer contributions, and do not attempt an extensive analysis of all the outputs of the organization, such as increasing knowledge and building community, which is beyond the scope of this chapter.

References

Accounting Standards Steering Committee (ASSC) (1975), 'The Corporate Report', London: ASSC.

Albrecht, W. Steve and Robert J. Sack (2000), 'Accounting education: charting the course through a perilous future', *Accounting Education Series*, vol. 16, American Accounting Association. Sarasota, FL.

American Institute of Certified Public Accountants (Accounting Principles Board) (1978), 'Statement of position no. 78–10: accounting principles and reporting practices for certain nonprofit organizations', New York: American Institute of Certified Public Accountants.

Amernic, Joel and Russell Craig (2004), 'Reform of accounting education in the post-Enron era: moving accounting "out of the shadows"', *Abacus*, **40** (3), 342–78.

Anthony, Robert N. and David W. Young (1988), *Management Control in Nonprofit Organizations*, 2nd edn, Burr Ridge, IL: Irwin.

Burchell, Stuart, Colin Clubb and Anthony G. Hopwood (1985), 'Accounting in its social context: towards a history of value added in the United Kingdom', *Accounting, Organizations and Society*, **10** (4), 381–413.

Canadian Institute of Chartered Accountants (CICA) (1980), *Financial Reporting for Non-Profit Organizations*, Toronto: Canadian Institute of Chartered Accountants.

Cooper, David J. and Dean Neu (1997), 'Accounting interventions', paper retrieved from University of Manchester, Fifth Interdisciplinary Perspectives on Accounting Conference website: http://les.man.ac.uk/ipa97/papers/neu14.pd.

Cornell University Cooperative Extension (1995), 'Financial operations resource manual (FORM)', Code 817, available at www.cce.cornell.edu/admin/fhar/form/code0800/817.htm (10 June 2002).

Corporation for National and Community Service, Office of Research and Policy Development (CNCS) (2007), 'Volunteering in America: 2007 state trends and rankings in civic life', Washington, DC.

Craig, Russell and Joel Amernic (2004), 'The deployment of accounting-related rhetoric in the prelude to a privatization', *Accounting, Auditing & Accountability Journal*, **17** (1), 41–58.

Edin, Kathryn and Laura Lein (1997), *Making Ends Meet: How Single Mothers Survive Welfare and Low-Wage Work*, New York: Russell Sage Foundation.

Ferguson, John, David Collison, David Power and Lorna Stevenson (2005), 'What are recommended textbooks teaching students about corporate stakeholders?', *British Accounting Review*, **37** (1), 23–46.

Ferguson, John, David Collison, David Power and Lorna Stevenson (2006), 'Accounting textbooks: exploring the production of a cultural and political artifact', *Accounting Education*, **15** (3), 243–60.

Financial Accounting Standards Board (FASB) (1993), 'Statement of financial accounting standards no. 116: accounting for contributions received and contributions made', www.fasb.org/st/summary/stsum116.shtml (5 June 2002).

Gray, Robert (1995), 'Briefing: social and environmental accounting research', Retrieved http://www.st-andrews.ac.uk/~csearweb/intromaterials/esrc.html, retrieved 14 June 2005.

Gray, Robert (2002), 'The social accounting project and accounting organizations and society privileging engagement, imaginings, new accountings and pragmatism over critique?' *Accounting, Organizations and Society*, **27** (7), 687–708.

Gray, Rob, Jan Bebbington, and Ken McPhail (1994), 'Teaching ethics and the ethics of teaching: educating for immorality and a possible case for social and environmental accounting', *Accounting Education*, **3** (1), 51–75.

Gross, Malvern J., Jr and William Warshauer, Jr (1979), *Financial and Accounting Guide for Nonprofit Organizations*, New York: John Wiley & Sons.

Handy, Femida, Laurie Mook and Jack Quarter (2006), 'Organizational perspectives on the value of volunteer labour', *Australian Journal of Volunteering*, **11** (1), 28–37.

Henke, Emerson O. (1972), 'Performance evaluation for not-for-profit organizations', *The Journal of Accountancy*, **133**, 51–5.

Henke, Emerson O. (1989), *Accounting for Nonprofit Organizations*, 2nd edn, Boston, MA: Kent Publishing Co.

Hines, Ruth D. (1988), 'Financial accounting: in communicating reality, we construct reality', *Accounting, Organizations and Society*, **13** (3), 251–61.

Hohn, Marcia Drew (1998), *Empowerment Health Education in Adult Literacy: A Guide for Public Health and Adult Literacy Practioners, Policy Makers and Funders*, Lawrence, MA: System for Adult Basic Education Support.

Hopper, Trevor, John Storey and Hugh Willmott (1987). 'Accounting for accounting: towards the development of a dialectical view', *Accounting, Organizations and Society*, **12** (5), 437–56.

Hopwood, Anthony G. (1990), 'Ambiguity, knowledge and territorial claims: some observations on the doctrine of substance over form: a review essay', *British Accounting Review*, **22** (1), 79–88.

Land, Kenneth C. (2002), 'Social indicators for assessing the impact of the independent, not-for-profit sector on society', in Patrice Flynn and Virginia A. Hodgkinson (eds), *Measuring the Impact of the Nonprofit Sector*, London: Kluwer, pp. 59–76.

Lewis, Linda, Christopher Humphrey and David Owen (1992), 'Accounting and the social: a pedagogic perspective', *British Accounting Review*, **24** (3), 219–33.

Llewellyn, Sue (1994), 'Managing the boundary: how accounting is implicated in maintaining the organization', *Accounting, Auditing & Accountability*, **7** (4), 4–23.

Lodh, Sudhir C. and Michael J.R. Gaffikin (1997), 'Critical studies in accounting research, rationality and Habermas: a methodological reflection', *Critical Perspectives on Accounting*, **8** (5), 433–74.

Mathews, M.R. (1997), 'Twenty-five years of social and environmental accounting research: is there a silver jubilee to celebrate?' *Accounting, Auditing & Accountability Journal*, **10** (4), 481–531.

McCarthy, Kevin F., Elizabeth H. Ondaatje, Laura Zakaras and Arthur Brooks (2004), *Gifts of the Muse*, Santa America, CA: Rand Corporation.

Meek, Gary K. and Sidney J. Gray (1988), 'The value-added statement: an innovation for U.S. companies?' *Accounting Horizons*, **2** (2), 73–81.

Mook, Laurie (2007), 'Social and environmental accounting: the Expanded Value Added Statement', unpublished doctoral dissertation, Toronto: University of Toronto.

Mook, Laurie, Jorge Sousa, Susan Elgie and Jack Quarter (2005), 'Accounting for the value of volunteer contributions', *Nonprofit Management & Leadership*, **15** (4), 401–15.

Mook, Laurie, Femida Handy and Jack Quarter (2007a), 'Reporting volunteer labor at the organizational level: a study of Canadian non-profits', *Voluntas: The International Journal of Voluntary and Nonprofit Organizations*, **18** (1), 55–71.

Mook, Laurie, Jack Quarter and Betty Jane Richmond (2007b), *What Counts: Social Accounting for Nonprofits and Cooperatives*, 2nd edn, London: Sigel Press.

Mook, Laurie, James Cha, Natalie Ambler and Joanna Ranieri (2008), 'Developing and operationalizing a social accounting system for social enterprises', presentation at the North American Congress for Social and Environmental Accounting Research, Montreal, 7–9 July 2008.

Morgan, Gareth (1988), 'Accounting as reality construction: towards a new epistemology for accounting practice', *Accounting, Organizatons and Society*, **13** (5), 477–85.

National Institute for Literacy (2001), 'Fact sheet: corrections education', Washington, DC: National Institute for Literacy.

Neu, Dean, David J. Cooper and Jeff Everett (2001), 'Critical accounting interventions', *Critical Perspectives on Education*, **12** (6), 735–62.

Parikh, Nina S., Ruth M. Parker, Joanne R. Nurss, David W. Baker and Mark V. Williams (1996), 'Shame and health literacy: the unspoken connection', *Patient Education and Counseling*, **27** (1), 33–39.
ProLiteracy Worldwide, US Programs Division (2003), 'U.S. adult literacy programs: making a difference. A review of research on positive outcomes achieved by literacy programs and the people they serve', http://www.lvari.org/about/proliteracy_report.pdf, accessed 14 March 2008.
Quarter, Jack, Laurie Mook and Betty Jane Richmond (2003), *What Counts: Social Accounting for Nonprofits and Cooperatives*, Upper Saddle River, NJ: Prentice Hall.
Ranganathan, Janet (1999), 'Signs of sustainability: measuring corporate environmental and social performance', in Martin Bennett and Peter James (eds), *Sustainable Measures: Evaluation and Reporting of Environmental and Social Performance*, Sheffield, UK: Greenleaf Publishing, pp. 475–495.
Razek, Joseph R., Gordon A. Hosch and Martin Ives (2000), *Introduction to Governmental and Not-For-Profit Accounting*, 4th edn, Upper Saddle River, NJ: Prentice Hall.
Riahi-Belkaoui, Ahmed (1992), *Value Added Reporting: Lessons for the United States*, New York: Quorum Books.
Richmond, Betty Jane (1999), 'Counting on each other: a social audit model to assess the impact of nonprofit organizations', unpublished doctoral dissertation, University of Toronto.
Richmond, Betty Jane and Laurie Mook (2001), 'Social audit for Waterloo Cooperative Residence Incorporated (WCRI)', report to WCRI, Toronto.
Roslender, Robin and Jesse F. Dillard (2003), 'Reflections on the Interdisciplinary Perspectives on Accounting Project', *Critical Perspectives on Accounting*, **14** (3), 325–51.
Rudd, Rima E., Barbara A. Moeykens and Tayla C. Colton (1999), 'Health and literacy: a review of medical and public health literature', in John Comings, Barbara Garner and Cristine Smith (eds), *The Annual Review of Adult Learning and Literacy, Vol. 1*, Cambridge, MA: National Center for the Study of Adult Learning and Literacy, pp. 158–99.
Ruggles, Richard and Nancy D. Ruggles (1965), *National Income Accounts and Income Analysis*, 2nd edn, New York: McGraw-Hill.
Salamon, Lester M., S. Wojciech Sokolowski and Regina List (2004), 'Global civil society: an overview', in Lester M. Salamon, S. Wojciech Sokolowski and Associates (eds), *Global Civil Society: Dimensions of the Nonprofit Sector, Volume Two*, Bloomfield, CT: Kumarin Press, Inc., pp. 3–60.
Seaman, Bruce A. (2003), 'Economic impact of the arts', in Ruth Towse (ed.), *A Handbook of Cultural Economics*, Cheltenham, UK and Northampton, MA, USA: Edward Elgar, pp. 224–31.
Skinner, Ross M. (1987), *Accounting Standards in Evolution*, Toronto: Holt, Rinehart and Winston.
Snowball, Jeannette D. (2008), *Measuring the Value of Culture: Methods and Examples in Cultural Economics*, Berlin: Springer-Verlag.
Suojanen, Waino W. (1954), 'Accounting theory and the large corporation', *The Accounting Review*, **29** (3), 391–8.
Throsby, David (2001(, *Economics and Culture*, Cambridge: Cambridge University Press.
Tinker, Anthony M. (1985), *Paper Prophets: A Social Critique of Accounting*, New York: Praeger.
Tinker, Anthony M., Barbara D. Merino and Marilyn Dale Neimark (1982), 'The normative origins of positive theories: ideology and accounting thought', *Accounting, Organizations and Society*, **7** (2), 167–200.
US Department of Education (1999), 'America reads: start early, finish strong, raising readers: the tremendous potential of families', Washington, DC.
White, Allen L. and Diana Zinkl (1999), 'Standardisation: the next chapter in corporate environmental performance evaluation and reporting', in Martin Bennett & Peter James (eds), *Sustainable Measures: Evaluation and Reporting of Environmental and Social Performance*, Sheffield, UK: Greenleaf Publishing, pp. 117–31.

19 Certification and self-regulation of nonprofits, and the institutional choice between them

Andreas Ortmann and Jan Myslivecek

Introduction

Quality assurance of the services of nonprofits has been a long-standing problem for which various institutional solutions (such as regulation or reputation) have been proposed in the literature. The two institutional solutions that we are interested in here, certification and self-regulation of nonprofits, have been of some interest to researchers and practitioners in Europe but recently also in the USA.

Certification is a process of quality assessment by an external firm that, for a fee, investigates the operations of an applicant (school, hospital, charity etc.). If the quality meets the required exogenously determined standard, the applicant is then allowed to use the certificate for a certain period of time, after which a re-evaluation is conducted. This re-evaluation is often simplified but does not prevent the certifier from investigating the certified organization if circumstances warrant it, as illustrated in a recent high-profile case in Germany involving German certifier Institute for Social Questions, DZI (www. dzi.de), and the German branch of UNICEF.

In contrast, self-regulation is a process of quality assessment established by a voluntary organization, or club, that imposes an endogenously determined standard on its members and – ideally – monitors (and punishes) those who do not meet the standards. The utmost punishment is the expulsion from the self-regulatory organization (SRO). Membership in an SRO is supposed to have effects very similar to a certificate: an outward shift of the demand schedule for the firm's services. (We'll say more about the evidence in favor of this proposition below.)

Indeed, certification and self-regulation have important commonalities – third parties of sorts that address a severe information asymmetry through a signal of quality – and are strikingly similar on the surface. Thus it is not surprising that one can find one or the other as a quality assurance mechanism around the world. Yet surprisingly little is known (both theoretically and empirically) about how, and under what circumstances, these two mechanisms differ and what the consequences are of these differences for quality standards, enforcement of standards, susceptibility to capture and ultimately the trustworthiness of the nonprofit sector as such.

Interestingly, in many European countries one finds certification of charities by a (sole) third party (Guet, 2002; Bekkers, 2003, 2006; Ortmann and Svitkova, 2007; Wilke, 2005), though that is not the case in European transition economies, where one tends to find SROs (if any attempts at quality assurance at all). It is not well understood why that is and whether this state of affairs is transitional and/or desirable in the long run. Theoretical work (e.g., Nunez, 2001, 2007), about which more will be said below, suggests that it is not. Also, rather surprisingly, in the USA the BBB Wise Giving Alliance (since 2003; www.give.org) and the Maryland Association of Nonprofit Organizations (since 1998; www.marylandnonprofits.org; see also www.standardsforexcellenceinstitute.org) only recently moved into the business of accreditation/certification.[1]

It is noteworthy that the extant certification agencies differ significantly in key design features. Indeed, it is questionable (e.g., Wilke, 2005; Ortmann and Svitkova, 2007) whether some so-called certification agencies (such as the Maryland Nonprofits) deserve the label that they lay claim to. Plus, some certification agencies have failed.[2] More research into the reasons for the differences in design and outcomes, and into what constitutes designs most likely to lead to desirable outcomes seems warranted.

It is the purpose of this chapter to establish what we think we know, what we do not know, what must be done to further our knowledge, and why it matters to practitioners, policy makers and scholars, not necessarily in that order.

What we think we know (areas of general agreement from previous research)

There seems to be agreement that both certification and self-regulation are particularly appropriate when reputation does not work.[3] A common scenario in which certification and self-regulation are likely to thrive is the presence of industries with low concentration ratios, significant heterogeneity and/or products that have credence-good characteristics: in other words, industries which to understand would require a significant effort on the part of the consumer. Such industries – because of the resultant severe information asymmetries – might benefit from some organizational entity that is able to observe quality, albeit at a significant cost brought about by the detection technology necessary to overcome the information asymmetry. Fundraising charities, in particular those that have national ambitions, are a prime example. Bio-agricultural producers are another good example. To some extent, schools and hospitals are good examples, too.[4]

An interesting commonality of certification and self-regulation is that severe information asymmetries are being addressed by an organizational entity that can overcome the information asymmetry at a cost.[5]

This entity, while fulfilling a similar (signaling) function in both cases, differs in that the monitoring is done in one case by an external firm and in the other case by a voluntary organization (club) or its delegate.

Another interesting commonality is that the quality assurance is typically provided by the authentication of an 'acceptable' (or desirable) minimum standard rather than rankings. This standard, offering an economizing summary statistic of sorts, differs however in the way it comes about (exogenously determined or endogenously determined) and is likely to differ in its level. The difference in levels is a consequence of the way it comes about.

Yet another commonality is that the authenticator itself must have credibility. In essence, the authenticator provides a substitute or indirect reputation in situations where reputations are unlikely to emerge directly because of characteristics of the product and the market structure. That an authenticator must have credibility is as widely acknowledged as it is assumed rather than shown (see Biglaiser, 1993; Biglaiser and Friedman, 1994; Lizzeri, 1999; Strausz, 2005; Svitkova and Ortmann, 2006 for certification and Shaked and Sutton, 1981 for self-regulation; but see also Nunez, 2001, 2007).

Further complicating the analysis of the institutional choice between certification and self-regulation is the organizational form that the agent takes: will it be a for-profit or a nonprofit entity? The latter complicates the analysis significantly, as nonprofits have multiple objectives (e.g., Steinberg, 1986; Brhlikova, 2007). Almost by construction, SROs are nonprofits whose major task it is to maximize the profit of their members. But what if these members are nonprofits themselves? What then is the objective? Similarly, certifiers are configured as for-profits and nonprofits and, in fact, are often subsidized because in some circumstances they are argued to produce public goods (such as trustworthiness) in a sector. A good example is the European bio-agricultural industries, whose producers are certified in some countries by nonprofits and in others by for-profits and in yet other countries by both (e.g., in the Czech Republic). In the European charitable donations industry, in contrast, all certifiers are nonprofits, but some (e.g. the German DZI, www.dzi.de and the Dutch CBF, www.cbf.nl) are substantially funded by state money in various guises while others (e.g., the Swiss ZEWO, www.zewo.ch, or the Austrian OSGS, http://www.osgs.at) are not; for details see Ortmann and Svitkova (2007).

Since the basic structure of the quality assurance problem of nonprofits (especially commercial nonprofits) is very similar to the problem of quality assurance of for-profits, and since indeed for-profits and nonprofits coexist in some of the industries of interest here (e.g. education and health), and are often regulated by similar governance mechanisms (e.g. the US education's system of accreditation), it is useful to recall at the outset some of the findings of the relevant literature.

We note that, to the best of our knowledge, nothing has yet been published that directly compares the institutional choice between certification and self-regulation. The relevant theoretical or empirical literature looks either at certification or at self-regulation. We start with the former and then move to the latter.

Lizzeri (1999) rationalizes a puzzling observation: a certifier gains information about a certified organization that he does not reveal except for a summary statistic ('pass', or 'pass/fail' a standard). In Lizzeri's model, a monopolistic profit-maximizing certifier is able to commit to a (any) disclosure rule, D, and a price of certification, P. Depending on D and P, a seller – who sells his product to two buyers through an auction – decides whether to apply for a certificate. If these sellers produce a quality that may be negative, a profit-maximizing certifier will set standards to zero and issue certificates to those who meet them. If the expected value of quality is negative, this equilibrium is unique. Thus it is optimal for a certifier who has acquired perfect information about certified organizations to reveal only 'pass/fail' information to the consumers, in equilibrium. This result is derived within the strictures of a one-shot strategic interaction and under the assumption of a monopolistic profit-maximizing certifier: it is easy to intuit – and it is indeed shown by Lizzeri – that competition among certifiers shifts welfare to consumers (lest there are economies of scale) and it is also easy to see that a nonprofit certifier might have different pricing (and disclosure?) rules (for a more formal argument, see Svitkova and Ortmann, 2006).

Strausz (2005) constructs an infinite-period model of certification to show that honest certification requires high prices that may even exceed the static monopoly price. In his model, a single, long-lived profit-maximizing certifier tests a newly born producer every period and reveals his (exogenously given) quality. The temptation of a certifier to accept a bribe from a producer can be resisted only if the price of certification is high enough. (This is essentially the Klein and Leffler 1981 argument that firms trade off the gains from being honest and the gains from cheating.) Competition between certifiers (modeled by Strausz as presence of several certifiers in different periods, thus without actual competition) further increases this price. Thus certification is easiest to sustain in the case of a monopoly certifier. In this model, the certifier reveals full information about the quality. (This result contrasts with other theoretical papers as well as empirical evidence that certification is often of the 'pass' or 'pass/fail' form: Lizzeri, 1999; Ortmann and Svitkova, 2007.)

Biglaiser (1993) and Biglaiser and Friedman (1994) assume a different structure of certification. Instead of mere inspection and evaluation, the external organization takes a role of a profit-maximizing middleman who purchases goods from the producers and sells them to the customers. The middleman may (in the 1993 paper) or may not (in the 1994 paper) possess a technology that allows him to observe the true quality of goods. Even without such a technology, middlemen may be welfare improving. This requires reputation losses resulting from a single defection to exceed the bribes to be had from defection. In the 1993 paper, the middleman tests some of the products and thus achieves separation. In the 1994 paper, the middleman sells more than one product; therefore his potential loss in reputation is larger than that of a producer and thus he is more trustworthy. This explains why a middleman who 'aggregates' sales is more reliable than a single producer, and why certification favors concentration, a result similar to what Strausz (2005) finds. In all cases studied by Biglaiser and Friedman, the certifiers (middlemen) fully reveal the quality of product.

Shapiro (1986) analyzes the impact of licensing and certification on quality in situations where reputation exists, but works imperfectly. He assumes that there are two levels of quality (high and low). By making a larger investment, a producer may reduce his marginal costs of producing (high) quality. Quality is unobservable in the first t of T periods of production and trade. In the remaining periods, reputation is assumed to work and quality is assumed to be observable. Licensing is modeled as a minimal investment for all producers. It is binding only for low-quality producers and it therefore raises the price of low-quality products and shrinks the low-quality market, which harms consumers who have low valuations of quality, but benefits consumers who have high valuations of quality. Certification is modeled as a mechanism that reveals investment into quality, but does not impose any restrictions on it. Depending on the costs, certification may lead to 'perfect information allocation' but also to overinvestment by sellers of high quality (who need to distinguish themselves from sellers of low quality). If both certification and licensing are imposed, low sellers also overinvest into quality.

Ortmann and Svitkova (2007) review commonalities of, and differences between, several examples of certification mechanisms for nonprofits in Europe and the USA. Surprisingly, in this sector certification is more widely used in Europe than in the USA, where secular certification programs are new (for example, Better Business Bureau, Maryland Nonprofits) and evolving, and the incentive compatibility of their design and implementation is in question (Wilke, 2005; Ortmann and Svitkova, 2007). In contrast, certification in Switzerland has a 70-year tradition (60 years in Norway and Sweden). Ortmann and Svitkova also review an example of unsuccessful attempts to establish a certification system in England in 1996 that failed because of the failure to bring some of the key players on board. This failure is interesting in that it reminds us that standards are not easily imposed by an external force but have to be communicated persuasively to a critical mass of target firms.

Building on the stylized facts that Ortmann and Svitkova (2007) provide, Svitkova and

Ortmann (2006) attempt to build a model of certification of charities. Their main ingredients are imperfect and costly detection technology and donors' inability to observe quality. The authors use this model to analyze the impact of alternative objective functions. The numerical results they obtain (analytical results seem not obtainable) suggest that the nonprofit status of the certifier is, relative to both no certification and profit-maximizing certification, beneficial and leads to higher quality standards.

An important question is whether certification does indeed induce the kind of trust, and trustworthiness, that might induce a demand shift for the services of individual organizations and, for that matter, the whole sector. To the best of our knowledge, there is little hard evidence available on this issue although intuition suggests an affirmative answer. There are two references of particular empirical interest in this context.

Bekkers (2003) provides evidence of how a newly established certification system in the Netherlands became known, especially among those who donate to charitable causes. The system was developed to change lack of trust in charities. Interestingly, the general public perceives philanthropic organizations as significantly less efficient than they actually are (43 percent versus 14 percent cost-to-income ratios). Further results suggest that those who trust other people ('social trust') and are aware of the certificates donate significantly more than those who do not. However, this result does not imply causality and does not provide an estimate of how much donations increase due to the certificate.

Bekkers (2006) attempts to document exactly that – how much donations increase after an individual becomes aware of the certificate. Using two surveys in 2001 and 2003, Bekker shows that those who already knew about a certificate in 2001, or those who did not become aware of it even in 2003, did not significantly increase their contributions. In contrast, those who become aware of it during 2001–03 increased their donations from €208 to €260. This would be about a 25 percent effect, but the amounts are not deflated. The analysis of the impact of certificates on fundraising income suffers from the same problem: income from 1994 to 2004 is not deflated. The result suggests a positive impact of about 7 percent in the first year, with the effect declining over time. Furthermore, the results seem to be stronger for medium-sized organizations than for small or large organizations.

Turning to self-regulation, Shaked and Sutton (1981) show that a self-regulated profession restricts supply of its services in order to increase its income. Interestingly, this result does not depend on the objective function of the SRO. However, Shaked and Sutton assume that (potential) quality of production of each producer is fixed. Thus there is no hidden action problem and the SRO does not need to enforce the quality (see Nunez, 2001, 2007). In fact, the self-regulated profession can increase its average quality only by restricting supply, which also increases prices. Whether the SRO has sufficient incentives to enforce standards is not analyzed.

While Shaked and Sutton (1981) are interested in understanding how self-regulation can be used to limit competition, and authors such as Stefanidis (2003) and Maxwell et al. (2000) study self-regulation as an attempt to undermine the perceived need for regulation, Nunez (2001, 2007) analyzes the incentives of an SRO to monitor its members and to reveal (imperfectly) observed fraud. Within the strictures of a dynamic game of incomplete information, Nunez (2007) recaptures the special case he analyzed in Nunez (2001) by assuming that the SRO is not corruptible. For this corruption-free benchmark he shows that there is always an equilibrium in which the SRO does not invest in monitoring and does not reveal any fraud. This is the case when there is no reputational gain to be had from exposing fraud. While Nunez identifies other equilibria, he concludes that there are scant incentives to monitor quality and expose fraud for self-regulated industries. While there are situations where vigilance, fraud deterrence and fraud exposure might occur, it is not clear how significant these situations are. The same problem exists when he adds the possibility of corruptibility of the SRO. Nunez concludes that 'a significant amount of fraud may in practice go undetected or may be concealed in self-regulated activities' (Nunez, 2007, p. 229). How significant an amount of fraud would require some calibration of the model – one of the big challenges for microeconomists.

In Nunez (2001, 2007), the SRO is an external organization that is not 'interested' in its members (their profits, size, quality etc.) in any way, but focuses on its own reputation. This overlooks the fact that the SRO is formed and governed by its members and thus its objective should somehow reflect the preference of its members.

Kleiner (2006) reviews the literature on regulation of professions with focus on quality and profits. He distinguishes four 'levels' of regulation – no regulation, registration, 'certification' and licensing. Registration is a requirement to submit basic information to the regulator to ensure minimal quality (e.g. no criminal record, permanent address). 'Certification' is a form of 'name' regulation – to use a certain name of the profession (such as 'fortune-teller'), one has to satisfy certain requirements (education etc.), but one may offer the same services without using the name of the profession and thus without any regulation. The strictest form of regulation is licensing, when one may offer such services only when certain conditions are satisfied (tests, education, but also required length of residence in a given state etc.). These conditions are often established by an SRO, even though not necessarily – few professions are licensed by the government. The author finds that most professions are becoming more regulated over time and for almost no professions is there a move in the opposite direction. He finds that stricter regulation almost always results in price increases, but the effect on quality is weak (if any, e.g. in the case of teachers), may be only temporary and often benefits consumers who value quality highly at the expense of other consumers.

Wilke (2005), in a fact-filled article that is unfortunately available in German only, reviews the monitoring of charitable (and fundraising) organizations in the USA, the UK and Germany, discussing regulatory guidelines in these three countries as well as attempts at self-regulation and accreditation/certification and related activities by 'watch-dogs'. Apart from having written the institutionally most comprehensive and precise article currently in circulation – no surprise there, as the author is the head of the German certification agency for charitable (and fundraising) organizations, DZI, and also the Secretary General of the International Committee on Fundraising Organizations (ICFO) – Wilke identifies several cases of questionable mislabeling (e.g. whether the Maryland Nonprofits organization deserves its label as a certifier).

There seems to be some agreement about what we do not know. Ortmann and Svitkova (2007) end their article with a list of 'important questions – indeed questions that have to be answered by any real-life version of a certification system – [that] are not answered in a completely satisfactory manner by economic theory' (p. 113). Relatedly, the articles by Nunez pose intriguing theoretical questions about what it takes to make self-regulation work. Unfortunately, the real-life evidence on self-regulation that would allow us to answer these questions is very limited.

What we do not know (areas of conflicting results and unexplored questions from previous research)
Among the open questions that Ortmann and Svitkova (2007) identified (after lengthy discussions with practitioners from the German, Dutch, Austrian, Swiss and English certification agencies for charities) are these:

1. What exactly is the trade-off between the scope, and hence cost, of certification and the welfare benefits that can be captured through certification?
2. How strong is the demand shift, for individual organizations as well as the whole sector, that trustworthiness buys?
3. Does trustworthiness always pay off?
4. To what extent should a certification agency be financed from public funds?
5. How crucial is it that certification be done 'in-house'?
6. Who monitors the monitor? (Can reputation do the trick?)
7. What is the critical mass of key members of targeted industries that one needs to get on board to launch a certification agency with a reasonable degree of confidence?
8. Can self-regulation ever be a viable alternative to certification? (Ortmann and Svitkova, 2007, p. 113, numbering inserted for easier reference)

Some of these (e.g. the first three and number 6) pertain also to self-regulatory systems. Almost by definition, the fourth does not (although it might be worth considering whether it should).

The fifth addresses an important issue that goes to the heart of the quality of the assessment process of the detection technology. 'In-house' describes the choice of the certifier of whether to use its own assessors or whether to use essentially 'hired hands' that are available. (The importance of this distinction is discussed in Ortmann and Svitkova, 2007, pp. 105–07, by way of a comparison of the German and Austrian certification system.)

We conjecture that the independence of the assessors, and the assessing agency, for that matter, is of crucial importance. Indeed, independence of the assessing agency is one of the three fundamental criteria for good certification systems identified by the Institut fuer Oekologische Wirtschaftsforschung (www.ioew.de), the other two being objectivity of the criteria (the degree to which the criteria go beyond legal or regulatory requirements, and transparent development of the criteria) and the thoroughness with which the evaluations are conducted. But the issue is poorly understood and institutional solutions are rather diverse (see Ortmann and Svitkova, 2007, pp. 105–07) and do not give much guidance. It seems that SROs, almost by definition, rely on dependent assessors although the possibility of the independence of assessors in the SRO context seems an interesting issue to pursue.

As regards the seventh question, it is one thing to establish desirable (acceptable, minimum) standards and another thing altogether whether these standards are accepted by the firms in the target industry (see Ortmann and Svitkova, 2007, p. 107 for an example). An important consequence is that the distinction between exogenously and endogenously determined standards is to some extent a fiction. A related consequence is that self-regulation attempts that are not subject to external pressure are likely to lead to guidelines and procedures that have little bite, as also argued by Nunez (2001, 2007) on theoretical grounds. Again, little is known empirically, for example, about the impact of the latent threat of regulation, although outside options are known both theoretically and empirically to be of relevance in many bargaining contexts, and it strikes us as a very interesting topic that might be worth studying experimentally.

As regards the eighth question, it is one thing to establish the potential benefits of certification and/or self-regulation, but another one altogether to quantify the internal costs of certification (which may be large, if not in monetary terms, then in time and effort of employees) and self-regulation. Financial support of these systems may reduce direct financial costs but is unlikely to reduce internal costs. In the end the decision for or against one authentication system is, apart from the various tricky other issues, also a question of the comparison of the internal and external (monetary) costs of certification and self-regulation.

Additional questions

9. Can certification, self-regulation, or some other form of 'market-based' regulation replace governmental regulation or are these complements (as suggested to some extent in Nunez, 2001)?
10. Would the non-profit sector benefit from some form of obligatory certification/self-regulation or should such regulation be merely voluntary?

While, as we have documented, there is published theoretical and empirical research on certification and self-regulation, there is, to the best of our knowledge, none that deals directly with the comparative properties of these two mechanisms. (It was, however, the dissertation project of one of the present authors.)

Why there are gaps in our knowledge (the relative roles of theory, data availability and empirical analysis)?
While anecdotes concerning the effects of certification are plentiful, they are often provided by not completely disinterested parties. We are not, with the exception of Bekkers (2003, 2006), aware of empirical analyses of the effects of quality assurance on the non-profit sector and its financing (donations, sponsorship). We are also not aware of any empirical studies that bear out the dire predictions of Nunez's (2001, 2007) models. The lack of data also does not allow us to answer with any confidence the question of institutional choice empirically. (In fact, we suspect that an answer to this question, and the testing of the design and implementation of appropriate authentication systems, could benefit from good experimental work that as of now could not draw on readily available modeling efforts.)

Likewise, what little there is in theoretical analysis is rarely disciplined by stylized facts. Also, models that incorporate incomplete information quickly get very complicated, as can be seen in Svitkova and Ortmann (2006) for certification and Nunez (2001, 2007) for self-regulation.

An additional problem is that these models are likely to produce multiple equilibria whose occurrence is a function of parameterization, which, to the extent that it can be used for policy advice, requires calibration. Unfortunately, calibration of micro- or industrial organization contexts is much harder than calibration in macro contexts.

Moreover, signaling models that capture the essence of one of the authentication systems quickly become rather complicated. Signaling models that try to capture the essence of certification and self-regulation in a unified manner become rather complicated even more quickly.

Concluding remarks

We believe we have shown that there are significant gaps in our knowledge of the relative merits of certification and self-regulation, both theoretically and empirically. To begin with, since most of the theoretical research focuses on for-profit firms, theorizing attempts that might deepen our understanding of nonprofit certification (of both nonprofit and for-profit producers, although this latter scenario seems unlikely) seem welcome. We have also argued that there are many institutional 'details' that seem to be important for quality assurance, but whose impact is not yet fully understood (e.g. should certification be done 'in house' or can it be farmed out, how does competition between certifiers affect their performance, what happens in those seemingly rare cases where certification and self-regulation compete etc.). It seems very desirable for theorists to take a close look at examples of both successful and failed attempts to establish new certification/self-regulatory systems and explain what caused them to succeed or fail. We hope that this chapter has provided some guidance for theorists. The optimal extent of governmental involvement also remains an open and challenging issue. Public support of voluntary certification systems might help to establish high-quality standards without raising costs for small, local nonprofits that could rely on reputation and would be hurt by legally enforced higher standards. Moreover, the government might want to consider supporting certification and self-regulation systems by offering easier access to public funds to certified/self-regulated charities. The government might even want to consider requiring certification or self-regulation for the nonprofit status of (large) organizations. If the reputation of the certifier and/or SRO is not sufficient to sustain honesty (as some of the theoretical research suggests), the government may find it cheaper and more efficient to supervise (just) the certifier instead of directly supervising all nonprofits.

Even if theoretical research might be able to give answers on some of these questions, empirical, and possibly experimental, studies on these issues seem highly desirable. Empirical testing, however, requires large datasets that are currently not available. Empirical testing would be particularly helpful for a better understanding of complex structures that are too complicated to be modeled theoretically. For example, in contrast to the theoretical literature, where quality almost always is a one-dimensional variable, the quality of nonprofits is multidimensional, and some aspects matter more than others. Needless to say, this complicates data collection and analysis.

The general issue of credible information transmission (e.g. from nonprofits to their prospective supporters), which is the essence of the quality assurance problem, and institutional attempts to solve it, is difficult and poses many theoretically interesting questions. We are convinced that, using theoretical knowledge (even what little we currently have), government and policy makers may find it easier to design more efficient and cheaper systems that may supplement, or even substitute, ineffective public regulation and costly supervision.

Arguably the most pressing challenge is to document clearly, and unequivocally, the benefits that certified organizations enjoy due to their certificates. This may not only increase the number of certified organizations, but also induce some organizations to improve their quality standards in order to become eligible. Thus certification would not only improve the efficiency of the distribution of resources from low-quality to high-quality nonprofits, but also improve the 'average' quality of nonprofits by providing additional motivation for lower-quality nonprofits to improve their operations.

Notes

1. A well-established certification agency – the ECFA (Evangelical Council for Financial Accountability, www.ecfa.org), whose *modus operandi* resembles the way the European certification agencies operate – has provided certification in the USA for more than 25 years. As Ortmann and Svitkova (2007) note: it is puzzling that there were no earlier attempts in the USA to start secular certification programs.
2. An example is reviewed in Ortmann and Svitkova (2007), pp. 107–08.
3. These conditions are discussed in Tirole (1996, 2006) or Ortmann (2001). Briefly, for reputation to work reasonably strong information flows are required: high concentration ratios (i.e. few firms need to be observed), homogeneity of the firms that populate the industry, and characteristics of the good (i.e. they ought to be experience goods rather than credence goods).
4. Schools are a particularly interesting example because the process of accreditation adopts elements of certification (the accreditation agency and the fairly intense periodic on-site assessment process) and of self-regulation (the accreditation teams typically involve faculty members from other schools and therefore the standards seem more endogenously determined than exogenously imposed). Because accreditation systems involve quality control of hundreds, or even thousands, of institutions, and possibly dozens of certifiers (as in the USA), the issue of who certifies the certifiers gains prominence (and invites contention). In the USA, the Education Department is charged with accreditation of accreditation agencies (= certifiers) (http://www.ed.gov/admins/finaid/accred/index.html; see also http://en.wikipedia.org/wiki/School_accreditation): '[a]n agency seeking national recognition by the Secretary must meet the Secretary's procedures and criteria for the recognition of accrediting agencies, as published in the *Federal Register* . . . The Secretary, after considering the Committee's [Education but also review by the National Advisory Committee on Institutional Quality and Integrity's] recommendation, makes the final determination regarding recognition.' The Education Department thus acts as a certifier of certifiers, so to speak. An alternative solution is advocated by the Council for Higher Education Accreditation (CHEA, www.chea.org/default.asp?link=4), a nonprofit organization of colleges and universities that serves as 'a national advocate and institutional voice for self-regulation of academic quality through accreditation' (retrieved 26 February 2008), and indeed supports the accrediting agencies organizationally in various ways. While the government is not directly involved in the accreditation process, it does exert a significant, and ever-increasing, indirect influence through the federal recognition criteria. In effect, it constrains the endogenous determination of the self-regulatory process that accreditation of (higher) education resembles at first sight.
5. It is an interesting theoretical, empirical and policy issue (that bears on the question to what extent certification agencies ought to be subsidized, and maybe even SROs) how much that cost should be, as it takes a credible signal to engineer separation of bad and good types.

References

Bekkers, René (2003), 'Trust, accreditation, and philanthropy in the Netherlands', *Nonprofit and Voluntary Sector Quarterly*, **32** (4), 596–615.
Bekkers, René (2006), 'The benefits of accreditation for fundraising nonprofits', http://www.cbf.nl/Downloads/Bestanden/Algemeen/benefits%20of%20accreditation%20artikel%20Rene%20Bekkers.pdf.
Biglaiser, Gary (1993), 'Middlemen as experts', *RAND Journal of Economics*, **24** (2), 212–23.
Biglaiser, Gary and James W. Friedman (1994), 'Middlemen as guarantors of quality', *International Journal of Industrial Organization*, **12** (4), 509–31.
Brhlikova, Petra (2007), 'Essays on competition and entrepreneurial choice between nonprofit and for-profit firms', CERGE EI Dissertation, http://www.cerge-ei.cz/publications/dissertations/brhlikova_dissertation.asp.
Guet, Ingrid-Hélène (2002), *Monitoring Fundraising: A Comparative Survey of ICFO Members and their Countries*, Berlin: ICFO.
Klein, Benjamin and Keith B. Leffler (1981), 'The role of market forces in assuring contractual performance', *Journal of Political Economy*, **89** (4), 615–41.
Kleiner, Morris M. (2006), *Licensing Occupations: Ensuring Quality or Restricting Competition?*, Kalamazoo, MI: W.E. Upjohn Institute for Employment Research.
Lizzeri, Alessandro (1999), 'Information revelation and certification intermediaries', *RAND Journal of Economics*, **30** (2), 214–31.
Maxwell, John W., Thomas P. Lyon and Steven C. Hackett (2000), 'Self-regulation and social welfare: the political economy of corporate environmentalism', *Journal of Law and Economics*, **43** (2), 583–617.
Nunez, Javier (2001), 'A model of self-regulation', *Economics Letters*, **74** (1), 91–7.
Nunez, Javier (2007), 'Can self regulation work?: a story of corruption, impunity and cover-up', *Journal of Regulatory Economics*, **31** (2), 209–33.

Ortmann, Andreas (2001), 'Capital romance: why Wall Street fell in love with higher education', *Education Economics*, **9** (3), 293–311.

Ortmann, Andreas and Katarina Svitkova (2007), 'Certification as a viable quality assurance mechanism in transition countries: evidence, theory, and open questions', *Prague Economic Papers*, **16**, 99–115.

Shaked, Avner and John Sutton (1981), 'The self-regulating profession', *The Review of Economic Studies*, **48** (2), 217–34.

Shapiro, Carl (1986), 'Investment, moral hazard, and occupational licensing', *The Review of Economic Studies*, **53** (5), 843–62.

Stefanidis, Christodoulos (2003), 'Self-regulation, innovation, and the financial industry', *Journal of Regulatory Economics*, **23** (1), 5–25.

Steinberg, Richard S. (1986), 'The revealed objective functions of nonprofit firms', *RAND Journal of Economics*, **17** (4), 508–26.

Strausz, Roland (2005), 'Honest certification and the threat of capture', *International Journal of Industrial Organization*, **23** (1–2), 45–62.

Svitkova, Katarina and Andreas Ortmann (2006), 'Certification as a viable quality assurance mechanism: theory and suggestive evidence', CERGE-EI Working Paper No. 288.

Tirole, Jean (1996), 'A theory of collective reputations (with applications to the persistence of corruption and to firm quality)', *The Review of Economic Studies*, **63** (1), 1–22.

Tirole, Jean (2006), *The Theory of Corporate Finance*, Princeton, NJ: Princeton University Press.

Wilke, B. (2005), 'Transparenz im Spendenwesen: Siegel, Selbstregulierung, Watchdogs. Ein Vergleich USA, Grossbritannien und Deutschland', in W.R. Walz, H. Koetz, P. Rawert and K. Schmidt (eds), *Non Profit Law Yearbook 2004*, Cologne, Germany: Carl Heymans Verlag, pp. 181–206.

20 Federal tax policy
Michael Rushton

Introduction

This chapter is concerned with the state of recent economic research on the impacts of the tax policy of the US federal government on nonprofit organizations. For comprehensive surveys of the laws governing tax exemption readers are directed to Fishman and Schwarz (2003) and Simon et al. (2006).

The chapter will cover three significant aspects of tax policy: the exemption for nonprofits from the corporate income tax, with the exception of those net revenues subject to the unrelated business income tax (UBIT); the deduction of charitable donations from the base of the personal income tax; and the deduction of charitable gifts from the base of the estate tax. Of these three topics, the first deals with the tax treatment of earnings of nonprofits, and the second and third deal with the effects on donations to nonprofits.

What do we know? What remains to be studied?

Nonprofit organizations in the USA with section 501(c)(3) status do not pay corporate income taxes on their net revenues. The tax exemption is granted when the nonprofit can establish that it is for a charitable purpose, which is defined by the Internal Revenue Code to include 'religious, charitable, scientific, testing for public safety, literary or educational purposes, or to foster national or international amateur sports competition (but only if no part of its activities involve the provision of athletic facilities or equipment), or for the prevention of cruelty to children or animals', and also that the nonprofit abides by the provision that net revenues shall not be distributed to anyone with a controlling interest in the organization, but instead shall be reinvested for mission-related purposes, in other words the 'non-distribution constraint' (Hansmann, 1980).

The exemption from the corporate income tax has been in place since the introduction of the tax in the USA in 1913. Various rationales for the exemption have been put forth: because nonprofits do not have access to equity finance, they need to rely on retained earnings for capital (Hansmann, 1981); because nonprofits are limited in the types of services that are considered charitable, they cannot diversify their portfolios in the way that for-profit corporations can, and so warrant a subsidy (Crimm, 1998); the exemption is a subsidy by the state for the provision of services in the public interest, where the fact that nonprofits receive charitable donations can be taken as evidence of the public interest (Hall and Colombo, 1991; Colombo, 2002); the exemption is a subsidy to a nonprofit sector that generates useful non-proprietary knowledge and innovation regarding the delivery of services (Steinberg, 1991); the exemption serves as a statement of values by the government that the nonprofit sector is worthy of support, to encourage private donations and volunteering (Atkinson, 1990, 1997); and the corporate income tax exists only because the government wants to ensure that individuals do not evade income taxes by hiding income behind a corporate veil, and since nonprofits have no individuals as owners there is no need to tax their net revenues (Rushton, 2007). These various rationales are not all mutually exclusive.

The unrelated business income tax (UBIT) was introduced in 1950 and is levied much like the corporate income tax on net revenues earned from commercial activities unrelated to the charitable mission of the organization (although the purpose of earning the commercial revenues in the first place is obviously to be able to transfer funds to mission-related activities). If there are so many reasons to exempt mission-related net earnings from the corporate income tax (see above), why tax nonprofits' 'unrelated' earnings? Economists reason that it is inefficient for the tax system to distort the choice of organizational form between for-profit and nonprofit, and in the absence of the UBIT, given the corporate income tax in practice imposes a significant effective tax rate even on the marginal dollar of profit, some entrepreneurs would have an incentive to choose the nonprofit form of organization purely for tax-based reasons. In other words, the UBIT prevents the allocation of economic activity across sectors from being tilted in favor of nonprofits (Hansmann, 1989), and ensures that a nonprofit will only have incentive to engage in commercial activity where firm performance will be at least as efficient as in competing for-profit firms (Sansing, 1998).

The application of the UBIT, like any other part of the tax system, is subject to lobbying by particular interests, and for-profit firms facing competition by nonprofits will demand the UBIT be applied so that there is a 'level playing field'; indeed the UBIT was introduced in the first place because of such pressure (Knoll, 2007; Stone, 2005). Consider my local nonprofit hospital, Bloomington General, which pays UBIT for only one source of net revenue, its reference laboratory for diagnostic testing, which provides services not only for the hospital itself, but through outreach to health organizations in the six counties around Bloomington. Testing blood samples is obviously related to the hospital's health services mission, so why are net revenues subject to UBIT? The answer lies in the felt need to tax the net revenues of the nonprofit provider of diagnostic testing at the same rate as applied to the various for-profit competing providers of the same services.

Two kinds of change in federal corporate income tax policy would affect nonprofits. The first lies in the way for-profit corporations are taxed: if the effective tax rate on for-profits falls, any effects on resource allocation arising from the nonprofit tax exemption are diminished. The second involves direct changes to the tax treatment of nonprofits: how are 'mission-related' revenues defined; should mission-related revenues always be tax-exempt or subject to certain conditions; and in turn should more sources of nonprofit revenue be subject to UBIT? For each of these sorts of policy issue, it is not difficult to predict the directions of the shifts in economic activity. However, there is not enough research to be able to discuss with confidence the magnitude of the shifts.

Consider first the effects on nonprofits from a falling corporate income tax rate. Although a tax on 'pure profit' can be quite efficient, in practice in the USA the corporate tax applies at a high rate even to marginal investments, and so generates a significant amount of 'deadweight loss' (the amount by which the losses to the economy from the imposition of the tax exceed the revenue collected by government). One way the efficiency losses manifest themselves is by for-profit entrepreneurs choosing not to incorporate, but rather to conduct business as either limited liability companies or as 'S-corporations', neither of which is taxed through the corporate income tax (Mackie-Mason and Gordon,

1997; Goolsbee, 2004), and these trends have contributed to a decline in corporate tax revenues (Cornia et al., 2005). This choice of organizational form is inefficient because it is driven by tax considerations rather than by what would be the most efficient structure of ownership and management.

Do higher corporate income tax rates also lead to entrepreneurs being more likely to opt for nonprofit status? Corporate tax rates are not the only factor guiding the choice of organizational form between for-profit and nonprofit; as mentioned above, a business can be for-profit without incorporation, and in addition there are entrepreneurs with a strong preference for providing services with high non-contractible levels of quality, and who do not mind enjoying the success of their business through the perquisites that the nonprofit form permits rather than as cash income (Glaeser and Shleifer, 2001). But tax rates will be a factor for at least some entrepreneurs at the margin. An early study by Hansmann (1987), using state-level data, found that in sectors where nonprofits and for-profits compete, higher corporate tax rates had a significant positive effect on the market share by nonprofit firms (he also found that corporate tax rates had more impact than property or sales tax exemptions). Gulley and Santerre (1993) find confirming evidence in the hospital sector; higher state corporate tax rates lead to higher market share by non-profit hospitals. While the direction of the effects of higher state corporate taxes is what we would expect, we remain highly uncertain about the magnitudes of effects, especially when we consider federal tax policy. Working at the state level provides us with a rich set of data, but we do not have much precision in considering the effects of federal corporate tax rates on the choice of organizational form where nonprofits and for-profits compete.

The second key set of questions regarding corporate tax policy involves the treatment of nonprofit organizations directly. What net revenues should be considered tax exempt and what net revenues should be subject to UBIT?

First, note that nonprofits only have incentives to pursue revenue-producing enterprises where the expected return is at least as high as could be earned through passive investments; nonprofits in the health and education sectors are most likely to have such opportunities, through multiple uses of facilities and specialized human capital (Yetman, 2003). For tax year 2003 tax-exempt nonprofits claimed $8.4 billion of gross income from taxable, unrelated business activities (under 4 percent of all nonprofits actually declared unrelated business income), but after deductions unrelated business taxable income was just $23.2 million (Riley, 2007).

Second, nonprofits can exploit tax avoidance possibilities by ensuring that any class of net revenues that is subject to UBIT has as much of the nonprofit's total operating costs as possible allocated to the taxable activity; for this reason the UBIT is a remarkably small source of revenue for the federal government (Cordes and Weisbrod, 1998; Hines, 1999; Yetman, 2001). Because of the ability to reduce tax liabilities through cost shifting, a move by the federal government to shift the classification of net revenues at the margin away from exemption and towards being subject to UBIT might not generate much additional tax revenue at all (Congressional Budget Office, 2005). In addition, the UBIT might induce nonprofits that own assets capable of generating net revenues to license the use of the assets to an unrelated for-profit firm, in exchange for royalty payments that would be exempt from tax as the payments would represent 'passive' investment income for the nonprofit. Sansing (2001) examines the conditions under which this is an optimal strategy for nonprofit organizations.

We can illustrate the policy issues through a recent policy debate: the tax treatment of high-revenue college sports.

Universities, public as well as private nonprofit (tax law makes no distinction), are subject to UBIT. For universities, 'unrelated business income' does not include net revenues from sources that are either directly related to the educational mission, or that provide goods and services for the convenience of students, faculty and staff such as food services, books, clothing, stationery or laundry. As a rule of thumb, UBIT applies to sales by the university to non-university users. Corporate sponsorships are treated as exempt income for the university when the corporate donor receives no return benefit other than the use or acknowledgment of the corporation's name, but are taxable when the sponsorship has a significant degree of advertising; for a recent overview of the tax exemption for universities see Joint Committee on Taxation (2006). Indiana University (IU) is illustrative: it pays UBIT on net revenues from its RTVS transmitter tower and advertising revenues from its University Press, and on a portion of the revenues (that portion not provided as a convenience to students, faculty and staff) from IU athletics outfitters, some parking at its urban Indianapolis campus, and the golf course. In practice, although some of these activities on their own earn positive net revenues after all expenses (the transmitter tower, advertising, Indianapolis parking), the negative net revenues from IU-licensed clothing and the golf course lead overall to a negative UBIT liability.

Recent debate centers on whether high-revenue college sports – football and men's basketball – are mission-related activities of the university. Revenues are indeed high: it was recently reported that the athletics budget for Ohio State University is $109 million, over $100 000 per athlete per year in its 36 varsity teams (Weinbach, 2007). Operating athletic spending is between 3 and 4 percent of total higher education spending for Division I-A schools (Litan et al., 2003), and the share has been rising, sometimes attributed to an 'arms race' between universities that seek to hire the best coaches (many of whom are paid in excess of $1 million annually) and recruit the top prospective athletes. In 2006 the Ways and Means Committee of the US House of Representatives, as part of its wider review of the tax-exempt sector, wrote to the National Collegiate Athletic Association (NCAA) President Myles Brand asking pointed questions regarding whether high-revenue sports are essentially professional operations, especially where athletes have few links with ordinary students and classes, and as such are not qualified for exemption under the language of section 501(c)(3) either in terms of 'educational purposes' or in terms of 'amateur sport' (Thomas, 2006). Brand responded by asserting that 'college sports makes a significant contribution to the university experience for all students and provides educational values to those specific students who participate' (Brand, 2006, pp. 1–2).

There are two interesting issues regarding the federal tax treatment of nonprofits that are brought to light by the dispute. The first is whether, if college athletics were indeed to be declared taxable under the UBIT, any tax revenue would actually be collected. There are two ways that university officials can avoid UBIT. One is to ensure that as far as possible general operating expenses of the university as a whole are attributed to the budgets of the athletics department; this is the familiar technique of cost shifting that already serves to keep aggregate UBIT revenues to the federal government relatively low.

The second avoidance mechanism comes from realizing the ability of semi-autonomous divisions within a large, complex nonprofit organization to ensure that gross revenues remain within the unit and are not used as net revenue sources for other divisions within the organization. In other words, what is generated by athletics stays in athletics, to be used to subsidize non-revenue producing sports, and to provide as high a quality of facilities, amenities and human resources as the budget will permit. Indeed, one recent report found that 'institutional funding provides 27 percent of the revenue for [Division] I-A athletics programs at private universities and 17 percent . . . at public universities' (Syracuse University, 2006, p. iv). For all the high revenue, especially from television rights, generated by football and men's basketball, most athletic departments at large universities are actually subsidized by the central university budget.

But if there is little chance of UBIT revenues actually being generated by removing the tax exemption for university athletics, why would politicians be formally asking for justification of the tax exemption? As stated above, one economic rationale of the UBIT is to prevent a misallocation of activities between the for-profit and nonprofit sectors. But that rationale cannot be seen as a driving force in this case; big-time college sports are so entrenched as part of American culture that it is unlikely that a change in tax treatment would lead to a 'correction', with increased resources devoted to avowedly professional leagues. And so the second interesting issue raised by this recent case relates to how we view the UBIT. One way to view the congressional questioning of the NCAA is that it is really not about tax policy at all, but instead results from an increasing concern that athletics has become a corrupting force in universities (although the golden age of purity in student athletics is mythical: Zimbalist 1999), with a win-at-all-costs mindset, commonplace violations of rules regarding recruitment and compensation of athletes, and special treatment for athletes to ensure academic eligibility. In other words, there is a second role of the UBIT, beyond ensuring economic efficiency. The UBIT becomes a tool for the federal government in the regulation of tax-exempt nonprofits where it would not otherwise have jurisdiction. Hence the UBIT becomes a means of encouraging universities to clean up practices in their athletic departments. It is entirely possible also that some federal politicians see that their threatening changes to rules defining tax-exempt net revenues is a means of providing incentives in other sectors, for example to health care providers. Are requirements that hospitals provide charitable care to the uninsured to be eligible for tax-exempt status a way for the federal government to deal, partially, with the health insurance crisis?

Deduction of charitable donations from the personal income tax is a subject that has been intensively studied: a recent meta-analysis of the research on the response of charitable giving to changes in marginal tax rates (i.e. to changes in the tax price of giving) can be found in Peloza and Steel (2005). The basic analysis is straightforward. Changes in the personal income tax rate structure affect the income and the 'tax price' of giving for a potential donor. 'Across-the-board' decreases in marginal tax rates could cause charitable donations to fall because of the increase in the tax price of giving, but at the same time could cause donations to rise because of the rise in after-tax income – that is, substitution effects and income effects work in opposite directions.

The main econometric problems are as follows: only a proportion of individuals actually itemize their tax deductions, and so take advantage of a tax price of giving less than one; only a proportion of individuals donate at all, so the distribution of donations is truncated on the left; marginal tax rates are dependent on individual or family circumstances and so are not transparently observable; and the marginal tax rate and income are jointly determined, requiring a simultaneous equations estimation. That being said, there is some consistency to estimates. In a survey of the literature, Clotfelter (1985) found a range for the elasticity of charitable giving relative to changes in the tax price of giving of between −1.1 and −1.3. More recently, Peloza and Steel (2005) found that when they remove estimates that are more than three standard deviations from the mean, the weighted average of estimates of the elasticity of giving with respect to the tax price is −1.11, within Clotfelter's range.

From a public policy perspective, does the estimated elasticity matter? Roberts (1987) shows that only if the tax price elasticity of donations is greater than one does the increase in donations generated by the tax deduction exceed the foregone tax revenues. This leads to the conclusion that only if the elasticity is greater than one is the tax deduction 'efficient'. Brooks (2007) applies this notion of efficiency when he estimates the tax price elasticity of giving for different charitable sectors. Using the Panel Study of Income Dynamics from 2001, and the National Bureau of Economic Research's TAXSIM calculator to generate marginal tax rates for individuals, Brooks finds a high elasticity of donations of −2.7. But there is great variation in the elasticity of giving to different sectors; for health organizations the elasticity is just −0.58, while the highest elasticity is in giving to 'combination charities', at −2.68. Following Roberts, Brooks's findings suggest that the tax deduction for donations to health organizations is inefficient: i.e. health care funding can be financed at less cost by direct taxation and government finance than through the tax deduction and subsequent donations from private individuals. That said, a fundamental difference between charitable giving and government finance is who gets to make the allocation decision.

Does the impact of tax policy on giving depend on the motivations for giving? The standard model of charitable donations postulates individual utility as a function of donations, disposable income after taxes and donations, and demographic characteristics, and the solution to optimal giving sets the marginal rate of substitution between giving and private consumption equal to the relevant price ratio. However, this basic model of optimizing behavior takes no account of how the subsidy to charitable giving is implemented.

Suppose that instead of a tax deduction for donations, the government promised a matching grant to any nonprofit organization receiving a donation. For example, suppose under regime X charitable donations are tax-deductible, and the marginal income tax rate is 1/3. I can make a $1 donation to my favorite charity, and it will cost me 67 cents. Under regime Y there is no charitable tax deduction, but the government makes a grant to any charity to which I donate, in an amount equal to 1/2 of whatever I donate. I can give 67 cents to my favorite charity, and the government will give it 33 cents. In the standard way of setting the utility maximization problem, regimes X and Y are equivalent. But are they the same in practice?

The first thing to note is that many people are confused by the use of percentages, and might believe that a matching grant of 50 percent must be larger than a rebate of 33 percent because 50 is a bigger number than 33. So while researchers in experimental settings might make efforts to ensure clarity for the participants, in the real world there is likely to be at least some confusion. Eckel and Grossman (2006) find that individuals tend to give more under a matching system than under a tax-deduction-like rebate system. For rebates, they find the tax price elasticity of giving is about −1.2, in line with the research cited above that uses data from the tax system. But they find a much higher elasticity, −2.6, with respect to matching funds. In a randomized field experiment involving charitable donations to be matched by a 'leadership donor', Karlan and List (2007) find that the existence of a match increases the revenue per solicitation (by 19 percent) and the likelihood of donating (by 22 percent), but they find that the size of the match does not matter. This finding is reminiscent of the 'embedding effect' in contingent valuation studies, where individuals choose an amount they would be willing to give that is independent of the magnitude of the good that the donation is meant to achieve (Diamond and Hausman, 1994). But lest we conclude that a state promise to match donated funds might induce more donations that the extant rebate system, Meier (2007) finds that while matching grants initially induce higher donations, when the matching stops donations fall back to a level below their initial pre-matching grant amounts; this is a reminder of the potential negative effects of incentives on giving, dampening our personal motives for generosity (Frey, 1997; Bénabou and Tirole, 2006).

The federal estate tax applies to the net value of estates after deducting from the gross value any debts, interspousal transfers, some administrative costs involving the estate, and, most important for our purposes, charitable gifts. Unlike the personal income tax deduction for charitable gifts, there is no maximum amount for the estate tax deduction for charitable gifts. Gifts to individuals made while alive, and exceeding $10 000 per year per recipient, are also added to the gross tax base of the estate tax (thus one does not avoid taxes by making gifts before rather than after death). There is a high threshold level for the value of the net estate, below which there is no effective tax. The tax rates are progressive as applied to the net value of the estate. Since 2001, with the Economic Growth and Tax Relief Reconciliation Act (EGTRRA), the threshold net value of the estate above which the estate tax becomes effective gradually rises over time, and the tax rates fall over time, such that the estate tax is fully repealed in 2010. But the Act has a sunset clause, such that without further action by government the estate tax would revert to its 2001 structure in the year 2011. During the presidential election campaign of 2008 candidates took differing positions on whether to make the EGTRRA tax cuts 'permanent', in which case the estate tax would be repealed for good.

The estate tax applies to only a small proportion of households, and a large share of tax revenue comes from a very small number of estates. At the 2001 (and scheduled for 2011) rates, the exemption on the net value of the estate after all deductions is $1 million, and the top statutory rate is 55 percent. As of 2008 the exemption is at $2 million, and the top marginal tax rate is 45 percent. Estates in the form of family farms and small businesses receive special favorable treatment under the estate tax so long as the heirs do not quickly sell the estate to a non-relative. Estimates for 2002, when the exemption was still $1 million, are that 'less than 3 percent of decedents had to file and less than 1.5 percent owed any estate tax . . . Almost 99 percent of the tax falls upon the top 5 percent [of tax units] and over one-third is paid by the richest 1 in 1,000' (Burman et al., 2005, p. 2).

There are two interesting research questions here: first, what are the effects of the estate tax and its possible repeal on charitable giving; and second; what would be the effects of changing the structure of the tax?

An estate tax lowers the incentive to accumulate wealth by the individual, since some of its value will be taxed at death, but on the other hand it increases the incentive to work for potential heirs, since their wealth from anticipated inheritance is reduced. For a given amount of accumulated wealth at death, there is a 'wealth effect' on charitable giving – the higher the value of the estate, the more will be given to charity – and a 'tax price effect' – the lower the after-tax price of giving, the more will be given to charity. The estate tax lowers wealth, in that there is less to be bequeathed to heirs after the tax has been applied, and it lowers the tax price of giving. In general, estimates hold that the tax price effect is greater than the wealth effect, such that the estate tax overall encourages charitable bequests (Bakija and Gale, 2003; Joulfaian, 2000; Wojciech and Slemrod, 2003). This is not surprising when we consider the sharply progressive rate structure of the tax. Consider the 2008 rate structure, where the first $2 million of the net value of the estate is exempt and a 45 percent marginal tax rate applies above that threshold. Then an estate with a net value of $2.5 million has a marginal tax rate of 45 percent but an average tax rate of just 9 percent. Changes in the estate tax – for example, repeal of the tax – thus has a much bigger 'tax price' impact, which depends upon the effective marginal tax rate, than 'wealth' impact, which depends upon the average tax rate (Bakija and Gale, 2003).

Also note that the estate tax has effects on charitable giving during life. A criticism levied by opponents of the estate tax is that it represents 'double taxation': income is taxed when it is earned and taxed again on death. By the same token this means that charitable donations enjoy a 'double deduction', reducing income tax during life and a smaller estate to be taxed upon death.

How large would be the effects of the repeal of the estate tax on charitable giving? Consider three empirical studies that give insight into the magnitudes as well as the challenges involved in making estimates. Joulfaian (2000) uses data from estate tax filings of decedents from 1992. Using a simple model where one's will is written to maximize a utility function that includes charitable bequests and non-charitable bequests as arguments, the reduced-form equation for estimation has $P \cdot C / W$ as the dependent variable, where P is the 'tax price' of giving – i.e. 1 minus the tax rate – C is charitable bequests and W is after-tax wealth, and the independent variables are the logs of P and W, plus a vector of control variables. Evaluated at mean values of his dataset, Joulfaian estimates a wealth elasticity of charitable bequests of 1.2, higher than others have found (Joulfaian, 2000). Estimation of the after-tax price of charitable giving is difficult because while the 'first-dollar' price is exogenous, the 'last-dollar' price is not, since the marginal tax rate applying to the last dollar of charitable donation depends on the amount of the donation. Joulfaian finds tax price elasticity of charitable bequests of −2.5 when the tax price is treated as exogenous, which is within the range of previous estimates. But when the size of charitable bequests and the tax price are estimated simultaneously – i.e. the tax price is modeled as endogenous – the estimated elasticity is reduced to −1.7. Combining the wealth and the (endogenous) tax price elasticities Joulfaian calculates that repeal of the estate tax would lead to a reduction of 12 percent in charitable bequests.

Bakija et al. (2003) use the same model of bequests, and hence the same reduced form for estimation, as Joulfaian (2000). But the dataset includes selected periods since the 1920s, and makes use of variations in state-level estate taxes. When fixed effects for states, years and wealth classes are included in the estimation, they derive a tax price elasticity of −2.1 and a wealth elasticity of 1.6 with respect to the estate tax; both the tax price elasticity and the wealth elasticity are larger than obtained by Joulfaian (2000). Bakija and Gale (2003) use the Bakija et al. (2003) elasticities to arrive at the result that repeal of the estate tax would reduce charitable bequests by 37 percent. Why do slightly higher elasticities from Bakija and his collaborators lead to such large effects by the estate tax on charitable giving relative to that found by Joulfaian (2000)? Bakija and Gale (2003) suggest that Joulfaian (2000) underestimates the effects of estate tax repeal on charitable donations because

> Joulfaian calculates the average estate tax rate by (effectively) weighting observations by wealth, but calculates the marginal tax rate as a simple unweighted average. A more consistent approach would calculate a wealth-weighted marginal tax rate. This measure would be significantly higher than the unweighted marginal tax rate, because high-wealth households face higher marginal tax rates. Using the weighted marginal estate tax rate would imply that repeal would generate a bigger increase in the price of giving than Joulfaian calculates, and therefore a bigger decline in charitable bequests. (Bakija and Gale, 2003, p. 7)

McClelland (2004) attempts to reconcile the different estimates of the effects of the estate tax on charitable donations. First, he applies the two estimation methods to a common dataset from 1999 and 2000. Using Joulfaian's (2000) method with the more recent dataset, and by applying sampling weights, McClelland gets a smaller wealth elasticity, at 1.1 rather than Joulfaian's 1.2, and a larger price elasticity, at −2.0 for 1999 and −2.1 for 2000, compared to Joulfaian's estimate of −1.7 with 1992 data. This leads to an estimated decline in charitable donations in bequests from repeal of the estate tax of 26 percent and 30 percent for 1999 and 2000 data, respectively, significantly higher than Joulfaian's estimate of a 12 percent decline. Turning to Bakija and Gale (2003), McClelland suggests that there is a problem in how they have defined charitable bequests as a share of after-tax wealth. Specifically, McClelland suggests that the way we ought to measure the share of wealth allocated to charitable bequests, call it S, which is the dependent variable in both Joulfaian (2000) and Bakija and Gale (2003), is

$$S = P \cdot C / [W - T],$$

where P is the applicable tax price of giving, i.e. one minus the applicable marginal tax rate, C is the dollar amount bequeathed to charity, W is pre-tax net wealth, and T is what the amount of estate tax would have been in the absence of bequests. In other words, the denominator is the maximum amount that could have been bequeathed to heirs rather than to charity, and the numerator is the charitable bequest discounted by the tax price. McClelland's criticism of Bakija and Gale is twofold: to calculate P, Bakija and Gale use the marginal tax rate that would have applied in the absence of any bequests, rather than the marginal tax rate the donor actually faces; and to calculate T, they use actual estate taxes paid, rather than what estate taxes would have been in the absence of bequests. If we make the adjustment as per McClelland's corrections, the decline in charitable bequests resulting from permanent repeal of the estate tax using Bakija and Gale's method falls from 37 percent to just 22 percent, which is close to the estimated effects from Joulfaian's method of between 26 and 30 percent.

As the above discussion illustrates, the impact of estate tax repeal is significant for nonprofits: best estimates suggest that charitable bequests would fall by at least 20 percent, plus additional effects of the expected decline in giving during lifetime.

What are the alternatives to the repeal of the estate tax, or letting it revert in 2011 to its 2001 structure? Steuerle (2005) holds that the unlimited charitable deduction in the estate tax involves something more than simply setting a 'tax price' of giving, but also amounts to a declaration by the state on behalf of the American public that 'the successful have strong obligations back to the democratic society that made possible their success' (Steuerle, 2005, p. 343). His suggested method for enhancing the recognition of those of the super-wealthy who donate to charity in their estates is to replace the charitable deduction with a tax credit that applies at a rate above the marginal estate tax rate. To illustrate, he provides an example where the marginal estate tax rate is 50 percent, but a nonrefundable tax credit is given for 75 percent of charitable donations. Someone with a $1 billion estate could give $750 million to charity and $250 million to heirs and owe no estate tax, or as an alternative pay $500 million in estate tax and leave $500 million to heirs. Such a scheme serves the purpose of continuing to encourage charitable donations rather than leaving all one's estate to heirs, and in fact should appeal to the super-rich, since under the current system of estate tax someone who left $750 million to charity could only leave $125 million to heirs, with $125 million in tax liability. Steuerle makes additional suggestions, including making it easier for heirs to donate their inheritance to charity without tax penalty when their predecessor failed to do so, and, as a more radical possibility, replace the estate tax with an inheritance tax.

Batchelder (2007) further develops the rationale for moving to an inheritance tax. She proposes a sharply progressive inheritance tax, in which 'heirs would not be taxed on lifetime inheritances of less than $2.3 million. Inheritances above this amount would be taxed at the income tax rate plus 15 percentage points . . . The proposal is estimated to be revenue neutral relative to 2009 law' (Batchelder, 2007, p. 5). The claimed advantages of this reform would be that it would reduce the complexity of wealth tax transfer planning, it would be more efficient, and, most importantly, it would be more equitable, placing the burden of the tax on the most well-off beneficiaries. The switch to an inheritance tax might increase donations to section 501(c)(4)s since they would not be subject to the inheritance tax, but donations to them are not always deductible under the estate or income taxes (ibid., p. 41). Otherwise it is difficult to gauge the effects on donations, since it depends upon the change in the distribution of wealth between decedents and inheritors, even though under Batchelder's plan aggregate net wealth should be close to the same under each alternative, since she is considering revenue-neutral tax changes.

Concluding remarks
Active research is under way on the effects on the nonprofit sector of the structure of corporate taxes and exemptions, and on the effects on charitable donations of the structure of the personal income tax and the estate tax. There is a movement in many areas of applied microeconomics for greater use of natural and field experiments in estimating magnitudes. This suggests that over the next decade we will see greater consensus on various elasticities, which should contribute to well-informed tax policy, and better understanding of tax policy issues by nonprofit leaders.

References
Atkinson, Robert (1990), 'Altruism in nonprofit organizations', *Boston College Law Review*, **31** (3), 501–639.
Atkinson, Robert (1997), 'Theories of the federal income tax exemption for charities: thesis, antithesis, and synthesis', *Stetson Law Review*, **27**, 395–431.

Bakija, Jon M. and William G. Gale (2003), 'Effects of estate tax reform on charitable giving', *Tax Policy Issues and Options*, No. 6, Washington, DC: Urban-Brookings Tax Policy Center.

Bakija, Jon M., William G. Gale and Joel Shemrod (2003), 'Charitable bequests and taxes on inheritances: aggregate evidence from across states and time', *American Economic Review*, **93** (2), 366–70.

Batchelder, Lily L. (2007), 'Taxing privilege more effectively: replacing the estate tax with an inheritance tax', Law & Economics Research Paper Series, No. 07-25, New York: New York University School of Law.

Bénabou, Roland and Jean Tirole (2006), 'Incentives and prosocial behavior', *American Economic Review*, **96** (5), 1652–78.

Brand, Myles (2006), 'Letter to William Thomas, Chairman, Committee on Ways and Means, US House of Representatives from Miles Brand, President, National Collegiate Athletic Association', 13 November.

Brooks, Arthur C. (2007), 'Income tax policy and charitable giving', *Journal of Policy Analysis and Management*, **26** (3), 599–612.

Burman, Leonard E., William G. Gale and Jeffrey Rohaly (2005), 'Options to reform the estate tax', *Tax Policy Issues and Options*, No. 10, Washington, DC: Urban-Brookings Tax Policy Center.

Clotfelter, Charles (1985), *Federal Tax Policy and Charitable Giving*, Chicago, IL: University of Chicago Press.

Colombo, John D. (2002), 'Commercial activity and the charitable tax-exemption', *William and Mary Law Review*, **44**, 487–567.

Congressional Budget Office (2005), 'Taxing the untaxed business sector', background paper.

Cordes, Joseph J. and Burton A. Weisbrod (1998), 'Differential taxation of nonprofits and the commercialization of nonprofit revenues', in Burton A. Weisbrod (ed.), *To Profit or Not to Profit*, New York, Cambridge University Press, pp. 81–114.

Cornia, Gary, Kelly D. Edmiston, David L. Sjoquist and Sally Wallace (2005), 'The disappearing state corporate income tax', *National Tax Journal*, **58** (1), 115–38.

Crimm, Nina J. (1998), 'An explanation of the federal tax exemption for charitable organizations: a theory of risk compensation', *Florida Law Review*, **50** (3), 419–62.

Diamond, Peter A. and Jerry A. Hausman (1994), 'Contingent valuation: is some number better than no number?' *Journal of Economic Perspectives*, **8** (4), 45–64.

Eckel, Catherine C. and Philip J. Grossman (2006), 'Subsidizing charitable giving with rebates or matching: further laboratory evidence', *Southern Economic Journal*, **72** (4), 794–807.

Fishman, James J. and Stephen Schwarz (2003), *Taxation of Nonprofit Organizations*, New York: Foundation Press.

Frey, Bruno S. (1997), *Not Just for the Money: An Economic Theory of Personal Motivation*, Cheltenham, UK and Lyme, USA: Edward Elgar.

Glaeser, Edward L. and Andrei Shleifer (2001), 'Not-for-profit entrepreneurs', *Journal of Public Economics*, **81** (1), 99–115.

Goolsbee, Austan D. (2004), 'The impact and efficiency of the corporate income tax: evidence from state organizational form data', *Journal of Public Economics*, **88** (11), 2283–99.

Gulley, O. David and Rexford E. Santerre (1993), 'The effect of tax exemption on market share of nonprofit hospitals', *National Tax Journal*, **46** (4), 477–86.

Hall, M.A. and John D. Colombo (1991), 'The charitable status of nonprofit hospitals: towards a donative theory of tax exemption', *Washington Law Review*, **66**, 307–411.

Hansmann, Henry B. (1980), 'The role of nonprofit enterprise', *Yale Law Journal*, **89** (5), 835–901.

Hansmann, Henry B. (1981), 'The rationale for exempting nonprofit organizations from corporate income taxation', *Yale Law Journal*, **91** (1), 54–100.

Hansmann, Henry B. (1987), 'The effect of tax exemption and other factors on the market share of nonprofit versus for-profit firms', *National Tax Journal*, **40** (1), 71–82.

Hansmann, Henry B. (1989), 'Unfair competition and the unrelated business income tax', *Virginia Law Review*, **75** (3), 605–35.

Hines, James, Jr (1999), 'Non-profit business activity and the unrelated business income tax', *Tax Policy and the Economy*, **13**, 54–84.

Joint Committee on Taxation (2006), 'Present law and background relating to tax exemptions and incentives for higher education', JCX-49-06, 4 December.

Joulfaian, David (2000), 'Estate taxes and charitable bequests by the wealthy', *National Tax Journal*, **53** (3), 743–63.

Karlan, Dean and John A. List (2007), 'Does price matter in charitable giving? evidence from a large-scale natural field experiment', *American Economic Review*, **97** (5), 1774–93.

Knoll, Michael S. (2007), 'The UBIT: leveling an uneven playing field or tilting a level one?' *Fordham Law Review*, **76**, 857–92.

Litan, Robert E., Jonathan M. Orszag and Peter R. Orszag (2003), 'The empirical effects of collegiate athletics: an interim report', prepared by Sebago Associates for the National Collegiate Athletic Association.

Mackie-Mason, Jeffrey K. and Roger H. Gordon (1997), 'How much do taxes discourage incorporation?', *Journal of Finance*, **52** (2), 477–505.

McClelland, Robert (2004), 'Charitable bequests and the repeal of the estate tax', Congressional Budget Office, Tax Analysis Division, Technical Paper Series No. 2004-8.

Meier, Stephen (2007), 'Do subsidies increase charitable giving in the long run? Matching donations in a field experiment', *Journal of the European Economic Association*, **5** (6), 1203–22.

Peloza, John and Piers Steel (2005), 'The price elasticities of charitable contributions: a meta-analysis', *Journal of Public Policy and Marketing*, **24** (2), 260–72.

Riley, Margaret (2007), 'Unrelated business income tax returns, 2003: financial highlights and a special analysis of nonprofit charitable organizations' revenue and taxable income', *Internal Revenue Service Statistics of Income Bulletin*, Winter, 88–115.

Roberts, Russell D. (1987), 'Financing public goods', *Journal of Political Economy*, **95** (2), 420–37.

Rushton, Michael (2007), 'Why are nonprofits exempt from the corporate income tax?', *Nonprofit and Voluntary Sector Quarterly*, **36** (4), 662–75.

Sansing, Richard (1998), 'The unrelated business income tax, cost allocation, and productive efficiency', *National Tax Journal*, **51** (2), 291–302.

Sansing, Richard (2001), 'In search of profits: measuring income from the unrelated commercial use of a tax-exempt organization's assets', *Accounting Review*, **76** (2), 245–62.

Simon, John, Harvey Dale and Laura Chisholm (2006), 'The federal tax treatment of charitable organizations', in Walter W. Powell and Richard Steinberg (eds), *The Nonprofit Sector: A Research Handbook*, 2nd edn, New Haven, CT: Yale University Press, pp. 267–306.

Steinberg, Richard (1991), '"Unfair" competition by nonprofits and tax policy', *National Tax Journal*, **44** (3), 351–64.

Steuerle, Gene (2005), 'Estate tax reform – a third option', *Tax Notes* (18 July), 343–4.

Stone, Ethan (2005), 'Adhering to the old line: uncovering the history and political function of the unrelated business income tax', *Emory Law Journal*, **54**, 1475–555.

Syracuse University (2006), 'Major effects of the athletics program at Syracuse University: an ad hoc committee report to the Syracuse University Senate', Syracuse, NY.

Thomas, Bill (2006), 'Letter to Miles Brand, President, National Collegiate Athletic Association from Bill Thomas, Chairman, Committee on Ways and Means, US House of Representatives', 2 October.

Weinbach, Jon (2007), 'Inside college sports' biggest money machine', *Wall Street Journal*, 19 October, p. W1.

Wojciech, Kopczuk and Joel Slemrod (2003), 'Tax consequences on wealth accumulation and transfers of the rich', in Alicia H. Munnell and Annika Sundén (eds), *Death and Dollars: The Role of Gifts and Bequests in America*, Washington, DC: Brookings Institution Press, pp. 213–49.

Yetman, Robert J. (2001), 'Tax-motivated expense allocations by nonprofit organizations', *Accounting Review*, **76** (3), 297–311.

Yetman, Robert J. (2003), 'Nonprofit taxable activities, production complementarities, and joint cost allocations', *National Tax Journal*, **56** (4), 789–99.

Zimbalist, Andrew (1999), *Unpaid Professionals: Commercialism and Conflict in Big-Time College Sports*, Princeton, NJ: Princeton University Press.

21 The property tax exemption for nonprofits
David L. Sjoquist and Rayna Stoycheva

Introduction
The special tax treatment of nonprofits has been the subject of a substantial amount of writing. Empirical research on the effect of the tax treatment of contributions appears to far exceed the research on the analysis of the property tax exemption and the federal and state corporate income tax exemption. In this chapter we explore what we know and don't know about the property tax exemption. In summary, we know very little. There is very little theoretical work and even less empirical analysis of hypotheses regarding the effects of the property tax exemption.

In 1988, Weisbrod (1988, p. 122) wrote, 'Only a little is known about the quantitative importance of the various [tax] subsidies that are provided to nonprofits.' While he was referring to the effect of tax subsidies on the size of the nonprofit sector, the statement was true for a broader range of issues. Twenty years later it does not appear that we know much more than we did then.

Much of what has been written about property tax exemptions focuses on the justification for the exemption. (See Chapter 20 in this volume for a discussion of the arguments for the exemption of nonprofits from corporate income taxes, the deduction of charitable donations from the personal income tax, and deduction of charitable gifts from the base of the estate tax.) Historically, nonprofit organizations have been exempt because they provided public services together with or in place of the government. Brody (2002) refers to this as the 'sovereignty' justification for nonprofit exemption. In colonial times there was no explicit distinction between public and private provision of services as there is today, and the tax exemption of nonprofits was analogous to the tax treatment of other levels of government.

Another justification for tax exemption is based on the 'subsidy theory'. Hansmann (1987), for example, suggests that tax exemptions might be justified if there is a public policy reason to favor nonprofit firms, or if some market failure is addressed. This justification is the most economically compelling, but at the same time the approach to deliver the subsidy is questioned. There are no clear requirements about what is expected in return for this subsidy, just a general understanding that the exemption encourages activities that benefit the community. Also, this form of subsidy benefits organizations that own property, while smaller organizations and those that are more labor-intensive are excluded. Furthermore, the burden of the property tax exemption falls on the local government, while the community benefits may be of much broader scope. These criticisms have been at the base of the current challenges to the property tax exemption.

A third justification examines the property tax exemption within a tax base framework. The main argument is that nonprofit property and income do not belong in the tax base. Nonprofit income is used to produce public goods and services, and therefore it should not be treated as taxable income. The property tax exemption is harder to justify using the tax base approach because individual property not used for profit is also taxed.

However, if the property tax is viewed as a proxy for an income tax on the imputed rental value of owner-occupied housing, then nonprofit property does not belong in the tax base (Heller, 1979, cited in Brody, 2002).

The question of whether the tax exemption does result in organizational behavior, such as providing services free or at reduced cost to low-income households, that would justify the tax exemption is certainly of importance. However, that topic is beyond the scope of our inquiry.

We start our discussion of the property tax exemption with a discussion of what we know about how the eligibility criteria for the property tax exemption differ across states and what we know about the magnitude of the tax benefit to nonprofits. We then turn to a discussion of the potential effects of the property tax exemption on the behavior of nonprofit providers and on the market competition between for-profits and nonprofit firms. In the final sections we consider efforts to remove the exemptions through legal action and through PILOTs (payments in lieu of taxes). We also include a somewhat related discussion of the growing trend for local governments to provide additional subsidies to nonprofit firms in order to encourage them to locate within the jurisdiction.

In essence, much of the research regarding differences in behavior between for-profits and nonprofits treats the tax exemption as a zero–one dummy variable. This research simply compares the behavior or performance of nonprofit and for-profit firms. The difference in organizational form reflects the fact that nonprofits have tax exemptions. Our focus is not on the literature that simply compares for-profit and nonprofit firms. Rather, it is on how differences in the size of the tax exemptions affect behavior. Since property taxes and corporate income taxes are both taxes on capital (the property tax is a tax on the value of capital while the corporate income tax is a tax on the return to capital), we also consider research that addresses the effect of the corporate income tax exemption (but see Rushton, Chapter 20 of this volume, for a more complete discussion of the deduction from the corporate income tax).

Eligibility criteria for property tax exemption

States differ in the conditions that must be satisfied in order for a nonprofit organization to qualify for a property tax exemption. Bowman (2002) provides the most recent survey of these conditions, which are summarized in Table 21.1. These results synthesize provisions available in state constitutions and survey responses of state officials where the constitutions are not explicit about the particular criteria. Many of these criteria continue to undergo changes as exemptions are challenged by local governments and the courts develop more precise definitions and criteria for granting a property tax exemption.

Bowman finds that both ownership and use are necessary conditions for receiving a property tax exemption. Thirty-nine states grant a property tax exemption to property that is both owned by a nonprofit and used for a charitable purpose. Only 11 states accept charitable use by itself as a sufficient condition for exemption, and no state would grant exemption just for nonprofit ownership. The original condition for charitable use specified that the property should be used 'exclusively' for the exempt purposes (Bowman, 2002). However, this has changed over time to accommodate practices to lease some of the property to for-profit organizations, such as child care centers in churches, gift shops in hospitals and others. In 31 states nonprofit and for-profit use is assessed separately, and taxes are paid only on the leased portion of the property used for profit. Sixteen

Table 21.1   Criteria for property tax exemption of nonprofit organizations

Ownership versus use		
Nonprofit ownership only	No states	
Exempt use only	11 states	AR, CT, GA, IA, MS, NV, NH, NM, OH, OK, WV
Nonprofit ownership and exempt use	39 states	All except the states identified above
Property leased to a nonprofit is exempt	17 states	AK, AR, HI, IA, ID, LA, MA, MD, MN, MT, NM, NV, OK, OR, RI, SC, UT
Property leased to a nonprofit is not exempt	31 states	AL, AZ, CA, CO, CT, DE, FL, GA, IL, KS, KY, ME, MI, MS, MO, NE, NH, NJ, NY, NC, ND, OH, PA, SD, TX, VT, VA, WA, WV, WI, WY
Nonprofit property leased to a for-profit organization is assessed separately	31 states	AK, AR, CO, CT, DE, FL, HI, IA, IN, KY, LA, MA, ME, MI, MO, MT, NC, ND, NE, NJ, NH, NM, NY, OR, PA, SC, SD, TX, UT, VA, WI
Property is not split, assessment varies by states	16 states	AL, AR, CA, GA, ID, KS, MD, MS, NV, OH, OK, TN, VT, WA, WV, WY

Definition of charity used to grant exemption status	
Organized as nonprofit corporation	Yes: 36 states No: 7 states
Pursue charitable purpose	Yes: 45 states No: 1 state
Relieve government of burden	Yes: 19 states No: 21 states
Derive most of its income from donations	Yes: 14 states No: 23 states
Provide public benefit	Yes: 38 states No: 7 states
Donate a substantial portion of its services	Yes: 15 states No: 22 states
Provide services to all	Yes: 24 states No: 13 states

Source: Bowman (2002).

states do not have rules for separate assessment, and practices vary in the extent to which the nonprofit pays property taxes. On the other hand, few nonprofits are exempt from property taxes when they rent space belonging to a for-profit entity. Only 17 states exempt such property.

The definitions of nonprofit and charity used to determine eligibility for the property tax exemption vary widely across states and localities. The survey by Bowman reveals that 36 states require that the organization should be incorporated as a nonprofit (501(c) (3)). However, nonprofit status is not a sufficient condition for property tax exemption. Forty-five states expect that the nonprofit organization would serve a charitable purpose. Charitable purpose is formally defined in only few states and the statutes provide diverse definitions about what constitutes charitable activity. The main criteria identified by Bowman from those statutes are public benefit, relieving government of a burden, relief of poverty, and income from donations. Using these criteria in his survey, Bowman finds that states use different combinations of these criteria as a way of identifying charitable purpose, as illustrated in the bottom half of Table 21.1.

Given the variety of statutes and practices, Bowman's study provides a good synthesis of the criteria used to determine eligibility for the property tax exemption. Another formidable task that remains is to understand how these criteria are applied in practice due to their vague definitions. Generally, broadly defined eligibility criteria are interpreted in favor of nonprofits, particularly when exemption challenges are taken to the courts. But there is no information about any patterns across states or different nonprofit organizations.

Second, as tax exemptions are challenged, there has been a move toward creating more specific requirements for each of the criteria, for example, defining charity care as a certain percentage spent on uncompensated care and community services by hospitals. Brody (2007) observes that lawsuits and legislation assert tighter definitions for exemption, establishing a widespread use of a *quid pro quo* rationale for granting exemption. Nonprofits are under pressure to quantify even the value of the intangible benefits they claim to provide that have been used to justify the property tax exemption. Again, much of this information is based on prominent cases, such as *Utah County v. Intermountain Health Care Inc.*, and the 1997 Institutions of Purely Public Charity Act in Pennsylvania, both setting very specific requirements to be met for tax exemption purposes (Gallagher, 2002). The most comprehensive examination of legislative decisions on different challenges is presented in Brody (2007).

Further research is necessary to document these modifications in the exemption criteria in order to improve our understanding of their implementation, as well as implications about the future of the property tax exemption. Another line of potential research would focus on explaining the variations in eligibility across states. In addition, it would be of interest to determine how variations in eligibility criteria affect the number or magnitude of nonprofits that are eligible for a property tax exemption.

Magnitude of the revenue loss from the exemption
One can consider the property tax exemption as an implicit subsidy, or a tax expenditure, to nonprofits. Instead of a property tax exemption, local governments could, at least in theory, provide direct subsidies to nonprofit organizations.[1] Such direct subsidies would be determined through the budget process, and thus local governments would decide whether the size of the expenditure and the allocation across nonprofits were appropriate. For this reason, it would be desirable to know the value of this tax expenditure.

Given that nonprofits are not uniformly distributed across jurisdictions, a second policy issue that arises is how the 'cost' of the implicit subsidy is distributed across jurisdictions. For example, universities benefit the entire state as well as out-of-state students, and some hospitals may benefit populations beyond the immediate locality, but the tax exemptions directly impact the local community. Krueckeberg (2004) discusses the unequal distribution of the property tax burden in New Jersey, and finds that the majority of tax exempt property is concentrated in ten municipalities characterized by low income, high exemptions, and high effective property taxes.

No source provides information about the value of the property tax exemption across all local governments. Nor is there a source that provides an annual report of the value of the exemptions for each state. Several factors peculiar to the nature of the property tax impede the estimation of the value of the exemption. First, exempt property is not necessarily assessed on a regular basis or with the care given to other property because tax assessors do not have any incentive to put effort into regular assessment of property that will not be paying taxes. Lipman (2006a) reports that New York, Los Angeles and San Diego spend equal effort on assessing taxable and exempt property, but that other big cities such as Chicago, Detroit and San Antonio do not have sufficient staff to appraise exempt property. Other cities fall somewhere in between. Second, even if there were current property values for exempt nonprofits, it would still be necessary to apply property tax rates for each of the jurisdictions that would in the absence of the exemption levy a property tax on the property. While this is feasible for the area in which the researcher lives, gathering such information across a wide range of jurisdictions would be difficult.

There are periodic efforts to determine for specific jurisdictions the value of the property that is exempt. Many of those efforts are concentrated on a single city, region, or less frequently a state. For example, Lipman (2006b) reports the value of the property tax exemption for some of the biggest metropolitan areas. New York loses $605 million annually and Boston $258 million from the property tax exemption of nonprofit organizations. On the other hand, he estimates that Los Angeles loses only $81 million and San Francisco $42 million.

Cordes et al. (2002) provide estimates of the value of the property tax exemption for eight states that collect such data. The nonprofits in these states constitute about one-third of all nonprofits in the USA, and the total value of the exemption is estimated to be slightly higher than $3 billion (Cordes et al., 2002, p. 91). They also find that charities nationally, excluding houses of worship, held about $500 billion worth of property in 1997. With an average effective tax rate between 1.6 and 2.5 percent, they estimate that the value of the property tax exemption nationally falls between $8 and $13 billion for 1997 (p. 89).

Gentry and Penrod (2000) estimate the magnitude of the benefit of exemptions from capital taxes for nonprofit hospitals. They find that the aggregate value of the property tax exemption in 1995 for nonprofit hospitals was $1.7 billion. The value of the property tax exemption constituted 27 percent of total capital tax exemptions for nonprofit hospitals at all levels of government. Other estimates that we have come across are less informative because they consider only one local jurisdiction or only the value of property that can be subject to PILOTs.

In summary, little is known about the value of the property tax exemption and how the values of the exemption vary across jurisdictions. The absence of such measures is due to the absence of data, and in particular because actual tax rates and assessed values are not available for many local governments. First, collecting assessment data from each assessor is very time-consuming. Further, if assessments are not available, it is necessary to develop a methodology to measure the real-estate value of tax exempt organizations. Second, any estimation of the foregone revenue will require a national database of effective tax rates.

If such data limitations are overcome, scholars can look at the value of the tax exemption and how it compares to the benefits that nonprofit organizations provide. Data about the foregone revenues from the property tax exemption can also be used by local governments to negotiate PILOTs with nonprofit organizations. And such data are necessary to study the effect of the property tax exemption on property ownership by nonprofits.

Economic effects of the property tax exemption

There are many possible economic effects that the property tax exemption might have on the behavior of nonprofits and on the 'market' for the services provided by nonprofits. In this section, we consider several economic decisions or market outcomes that might be affected by the property tax exemption.

Economic models of behavior assume purposeful behavior related to some goals such as profit or utility maximization. The challenges in modeling nonprofit behavior are related to the specification of the goals of nonprofits and the availability of data to test hypotheses derived from the models. There is not general agreement on what goals nonprofits seek or on how the nonprofit market achieves equilibrium. (For a detailed discussion of nonprofit models, see Chapter 9 in this volume.) Furthermore, with a few exceptions tax exemptions have not been explicitly incorporated in the models of nonprofit behavior. We discuss extensions of the models that include the tax exemption, but they are based on economic assumptions about organizational behavior borrowed from for-profit organizations, and are subject to empirical verification.

Use of the financial benefits of the exemption

One of the issues regarding capital tax exemptions concerns how nonprofits use this cost advantage. Steinberg (1991) lists three ways that nonprofits could apply the tax advantage. His discussion was in the context of nonprofits competing with for-profit firms, but the points apply to markets in which there are no for-profit firms, a situation that could be the result of the tax advantages enjoyed by nonprofits. Nonprofits could provide additional or higher-quality goods and services or increase the quality of existing services. They could use the funds from the tax exemption to subsidize the price, and thus increase the quantity demanded. Second, nonprofits could use the tax exemption to provide goods that generate positive externalities. For example, Steinberg suggests that a nonprofit could provide excess capacity, for example more beds in a hospital, or provide price subsidies to low-income households. Third, nonprofits could use the benefits from the tax exemption to enable the nonprofit to use higher-cost production techniques, for example through managerial inattention or employee benefits.

It appears that some efforts have been made to compare the costs of and the nature of the services provided by nonprofits to those of for-profit firms, particularly for hospitals (see, e.g., Hassett and Hubbard, 2000; Norton and Staiger, 1994; Sloan et al., 2001; Kessler and McClellan, 2002; Rose-Ackerman, 1996). But these studies focus on the effects of organizational form, i.e. nonprofit versus for-profit. We could identify no efforts to determine whether the magnitude of the tax exemption affects the cost structure or the nature of the services provided by nonprofits. No one has attempted to determine, for example, whether the differences between for-profit and nonprofit organizations in their cost structures, the nature of services they provide, or the types of clients they serve are smaller in communities with very low property tax rates or states with no corporate income tax. Or, as Colombo (2006) asks in reviewing the Federal Trade Commission and Department of Justice 2004 report on competition in health care, 'Is tax exemption, for example,"buying" charity care for the poor, and would withdrawal of exemption negatively impact health care for the uninsured poor?'

Decision to own versus rent
In most states, property is exempted from property taxes only if it is owned by the nonprofit and is used for purposes that make it eligible for a property tax exemption. Given that the property tax exemption reduces the cost of owning a building, it would be expected that the exemption would influence a nonprofit's decision to own versus rent space, assuming that nonprofits made such a decision based on economic grounds, i.e. a desire to minimize costs. Cordes et al. (2002) present the theory behind such a decision. The rental or user cost per dollar for a for-profit landlord is given by the following equation

$$c/q = r + \delta(1 - t\alpha)/(1 - t) + \tau,$$

where c is the gross market rent charged per dollar invested, q is the value of the property, r is the before-tax cost of capital, δ is the economic depreciation rate, t is the tax rate, α is the percentage of depreciation that can be claimed for income tax purposes, and τ is the property tax rate.

If the nonprofit owned the building, then

$$c^*/q = r + \delta.$$

It would be better to own than rent if $c/q - c^*/q > 0$, or if

$$\tau - \delta t(\alpha - 1)/(1 - t) > 0.$$

If $\alpha = 1$, i.e. tax depreciation is equal to economic depreciation, then the nonprofit saves by owning. But as α increases, the second term gets larger. Thus, if for-profit firms are allowed significantly accelerated depreciation, i.e. if α is very large, then the nonprofit would be better off renting. When α is very large, the depreciation allowance provides a substantial tax subsidy to the for-profit landlord. When the federal government in the early 1980s adopted accelerated depreciation for buildings, there were examples of nonprofit organizations selling buildings to for-profit firms and then leasing the buildings back.

As best we can determine, no papers have investigated whether the size of the property tax exemption increased the likelihood that a nonprofit would own rather than rent. There are challenges to conducting such a study. First, the decision of a nonprofit to own may be driven by considerations other than cost minimization. For example, it may be feasible to successfully conduct a capital drive to build or buy a building, while generating contribution to cover overhead such as rent may be more difficult. Thus a nonprofit may decide to own even when it is not consistent with cost minimization. Second, to conduct such a study requires consideration of nonprofits that face different tax rates, i.e. the sample must contain nonprofits from multiple jurisdictions. Third, it would be necessary to gather data to control for other factors that might affect the decision to own rather than to rent.

Location decision
The property tax exemption should eliminate the property tax as a consideration in the location decision of nonprofit organizations that own their own building. Thus, for example, the property tax exemption would make the location in downtown areas more affordable for nonprofits that own property. On the other hand, nonprofit organizations that rent face the same rental rates as for-profit organizations, unless there is a different assessment of property leased to nonprofit organizations.

Nonprofit location theory has not considered the property tax exemption, but has focused on other factors that determine the location choice of nonprofit organizations. For example, Wolpert et al. (2001) study the spatial patterns of nonprofit location in New York. Among those nonprofits, the type and scale of services provided by the organization require that some nonprofits are located in a central location, such as museums and arts organizations, while hospitals and day care centers may be more dispersed. Also, nonprofits that benefit particular populations, such as homeless shelters, soup kitchens and job training centers, would be located close to them to ensure proper service access. Other nonprofit organizations may prefer to be located together with other similar organizations to benefit from economies of agglomeration and a common pool of skilled labor force. Habitat for Humanity moved its headquarters to Atlanta for similar reasons. Finally, nonprofit organizations that have been established for a long time tend to be located in the central parts of the city. In that respect, the property tax exemption is keeping their current location more affordable regardless of changes in property values, at least in terms of out-of-pocket costs; nonprofits would still face the opportunity cost of owning expensive land. But perhaps nonprofits do not consider such opportunity costs in making these location decisions.

Bielefeld and Murdoch (2004) compare the location patterns of nonprofit and for-profit providers of education and human services in six metropolitan areas. They find that similar nonprofits were clustered and their location was best explained by the needs and resources of the community. Additionally, some nonprofits were located in proximity to similar nonprofits or similar for-profits, indicating agglomeration factors.

In addition to the intra-metropolitan location decision, nonprofits also make inter-metropolitan or inter-state location decisions. There are substantial differences in the number of nonprofits per capita across the country (Weisbrod, 1988). Nonprofits are usually concentrated in major cities, but some smaller cities may also have a disproportionate number of nonprofit organizations relative to their tax bases. Gentry and Penrod (2000) find that the distribution of nonprofit hospitals varies widely across the USA. Nonprofit hospitals dominate in the Northeast, where there are almost no for-profit hospitals. About half of the for-profit hospitals are concentrated in three states: Texas, Florida and California. But neither they nor anyone else that we could determine have considered the extent to which the location pattern is due to differences in property and state corporate income tax exemptions, or even if the spatial pattern is a result of location decisions rather than a decision regarding organization form, nonprofit versus for-profit.

There is a literature that considers the optimal location of public service sites (see, e.g., White, 1979). This literature might be the basis for a theory of the optimal location of nonprofit sites in the presence of property tax exemptions. Such a theory would be necessary in order to specify any empirical work other than some *ad hoc* empirical model of location.

Capital–labor ratio, capital–land ratio, and the size of operation

For for-profit firms, it would be expected that exemption from taxes on capital, such as the federal and state corporate income taxes and property taxes, would increase the ratio of capital to labor used in production because the cost of capital would be reduced, and would increase the level of output since average costs would be lower. But we have not found any theoretical models of nonprofit behavior that consider these issues. Whether we would find such an effect for a nonprofit organization would likely depend on the organization's behavioral objectives. For example, consider Newhouse's (1970) economic model of a hospital. In his model the decision maker maximizes utility, which is a function of the quantity of services provided and the quality of those services. Such a hospital could choose to provide higher-quality services than would a for-profit hospital. If higher quality is associated with higher labor per unit of output, then the nonprofit hospital will have a lower capital–labor ratio and less output than a for-profit hospital.

Various authors have compared the size of for-profit hospitals to the size of nonprofit hospitals. Gentry and Penrod (2000), for example, report that in 1995, while 59 percent of short-term hospitals were nonprofit, they accounted for 70 percent of the beds. In part, this is because nonprofits include some very large teaching hospitals.

Gentry and Penrod also provide data on the capital intensity of hospitals. They report that at the median of their distributions nonprofit hospitals have higher total wages relative to fixed assets and lower capital costs relative to total cost than do for-profit hospitals. This suggests that nonprofit hospitals are less capital-intensive than for-profit hospitals. This is consistent with the simple extension of Newhouse's model presented above. However, this result could also be due to the mix of the particular services provided by nonprofit hospitals as compared to for-profit hospitals. Gentry and Penrod did not conduct an empirical investigation of the relationship between capital tax exemptions and capital intensity.

David (2005) examines the dynamics of hospital convergence in size over time between nonprofit and for-profit hospitals. In 1960, nonprofit hospitals maintained on average three times as many beds per hospital as for-profit hospitals. By 2000, the average nonprofit hospital was only 30 percent larger than a for-profit hospital. The main sources of convergence are: (1) different growth in scale by for-profit (5 percent) and nonprofit (2.3 percent) hospitals up to 1980s, and (2) negative growth by nonprofit hospitals due to the introduction of the prospective payment system (fixed reimbursement on the basis of the number of patients, not on reported costs) combined with positive (modest) growth of for-profit hospitals.

David (2005) models the factors that affect the ratio of nonprofit to for-profit hospitals and their size. The decision to select one organizational form over the other depends on the cost advantages of nonprofit status (tax exemptions), and the non-distribution constraint (profits should be invested in the charitable mission of the organization). With the advantage of tax exemptions, nonprofit hospitals are expected to have higher output. However, assuming that nonprofit owners can convert some of their cost advantage into perks, and that they have the same utility from perks as for-profit owners from profits, the output will depend on the ability of nonprofits to convert their cost advantage into perks. The convergence in size depends on demographic factors, changes in cost advantages and availability of government beds. Nonprofit and for-profit hospitals converge in size when the cost advantages of nonprofit hospitals decrease, when government beds decrease, and when demand for services increases (David, 2005, pp. 23–4).

We were unable to find any study that considered the capital intensity of nonprofit organizations in non-hospital markets or any studies that investigated the effect of the tax exemption on the size of the organization. To conduct good empirical research, it is necessary to have a theory of how the exemption from capital taxes will affect the capital–labor ratio and agency size. In addition, obtaining adequate data is a challenge.

Since the property tax applies to both land and capital, a property tax exemption should not affect the capital–land ratio. But we could not identify any study of the effect on the capital–land ratio. Casual empiricism suggests that there are nonprofits such as some private colleges and universities and churches that have very large land holdings, contrary to the expectation of economic theory that the property tax exemption should not affect capital–land ratio. It could be that the nonprofits are able to hold these lands because the property tax exemption eliminates any cash flow payment, or that for these nonprofits, land is a more important input than for other organizations.

Nonprofit share of the market
The property tax exemption is an implicit subsidy to nonprofit organizations that could increase the size of the nonprofit sector over what it would be in the absence of the exemption. We are unaware of any research that has studied this effect. However, in those markets that contain both nonprofit and for-profit organizations, the property tax exemption could be a factor that explains the nonprofit market share of that industry. We have identified three papers that consider the effect of property taxes on nonprofit market share and three papers that consider the change in the form of organization over time.

Hansmann (1987) considered four markets: short-term hospitals, nursing homes, post-secondary vocational education and primary and secondary education. Using 1975 data for the 50 states, he finds that the statewide weighted average effective property tax rate is positive for all four markets, but statistically significant at the 10 percent level or better only for post-secondary vocational education. He also uses data for the largest city in each state, but obtains no statistically significant coefficients. Nonprofit market share is measured as the number of beds for hospitals and nursing homes, enrollment for vocational schools, and number of nonprofit firms (excluding religious schools) for primary and secondary education. He also includes the state corporate income tax rates. Since both the property tax and the corporate income tax are taxes on capital, one should expect similar effects for the two taxes. However, the coefficients on the corporate tax rate are positive and, unlike the coefficients on the property tax rate, the coefficients on the state corporate income tax are generally significant.

Chang and Tuckman (1990) consider hospitals in Tennessee, using county-level data for 1982–85. Chang and Tuckman note that many counties have no hospital or only one hospital. They investigate whether the nonprofit share of the hospital market, as measured by patient days, increases with the effective property tax, but contrary to expectations, the coefficient is negative and significant. They do find, as expected, that higher property tax rate increases the probability that a county has only one hospital.

Gulley and Santerre (1993) use a five-year increment panel (1967–87) for all 50 states plus DC to consider the effect of higher property taxes on the nonprofit market share of hospitals, measured by the number of beds. Unlike Hansmann, and Chang and Tuckman, Gulley and Santerre consider government hospitals as well. The other two papers treat government hospitals as fixed in supply, while Gulley and Santerre assume the government share is endogenous. Thus they estimate three equations, with the dependent variables being the shares for the nonprofit, for-profit and government hospitals, incorporating the condition that the share must sum to one. They find that the weighted statewide average effective property tax rate and the state corporate income tax rate have positive and statistically significant effects on the nonprofit market share. The coefficients for the for-profit share equation are negative, as expected, but statistically significant only for the corporate income tax. The elasticity of nonprofit market share with respect to the property tax rate is 0.041, which seems rather small.

We identified two papers that consider the effect of just the corporate income tax on nonprofit market share of hospitals. Mullner and Hadley (1984) find that changes in state corporate income tax rates between 1972 and 1983 had no statistically significant effect on the change in for-profit market share. Hu (2006) considers both national 35-year time-series data and longitudinal data (all 50 states plus DC for 1975–2000) to investigate the effect of the corporate income tax exemption on nonprofit share of the hospital market, measured separately by beds and admissions. He finds that the larger the corporate income tax rate, the larger the nonprofit market share of the hospital market.

Related to market share is the effect of the tax exemptions on the magnitude of the commercial activities of nonprofit organizations (see Chapter 20 for a discussion of unrelated business income tax). Cordes and Weisbrod (1998) consider how the property tax and corporate income tax exemptions affect commercial activities. As dependent variables they use commercial share measured as program service revenue as a share of total revenue and whether the nonprofit filed an unrelated business income tax (UBIT) return. The UBIT is a tax on revenues earned from activities not directly related to the charitable mission of the organization. They created two dummy variables, one for whether a state had high property taxes and one for whether the state had high corporate income taxes. Using the 1992 public use sample of IRS Form 990 returns, they find that higher property taxes and higher corporate income taxes are associated with higher commercial share. The probability of filing a UBIT return is positively related with higher corporate income taxes.

The share of the market held by nonprofits will depend on entry into and exit from the industry by nonprofit and for-profit firms, i.e. it will depend on market equilibrium. Suppose that the market is competitive and nonprofit and for-profit firms take the price as given and pick the quantity to provide. Since nonprofit firms have a cost advantage because of the tax exemption, their share of the market will increase, perhaps to 100 percent. One can envision that market structures other than perfect competition and alternative nonprofit behavioral objectives would yield alternative market equilibria.

Additional empirical research on market share should be conducted, particularly for non-hospital markets. However, attempting to measure market share for other services is a challenge. Additional theoretical work is needed to explain market dynamics. Furthermore, the empirical work has focused on explaining existing market share, but empirical research also needs to consider the entry/exit process and how the magnitude of the tax exemption affects that process.

Choice between for-profit and nonprofit status
Clearly related to the nonprofit share of an industry is the effect of the property tax exemption on the decision to organize as a for-profit or a nonprofit firm. There are some theoretical discussions of this choice. Glaeser and Shleifer (2001) develop a model in which an entrepreneur chooses a nonprofit status as a means of committing to soft incentives. They argue that tax exemptions are not relevant to this decision. On the other hand, Lakdawalla and Philipson (2006) develop a model of organizational choice and derive equilibrium conditions, where the marginal firm determines how the industry is split between for-profit and nonprofit firms. Within their model they show that an increase in the tax advantage of nonprofits (i.e. a reduction in the production cost of nonprofits) will increase the share of nonprofits in the industry.

Property value
The property tax exemption, combined with the fact that nonprofits use land within a jurisdiction, means that local governments obtain less revenue than they would from other uses of the property. Does this loss of government revenue get capitalized into the value of property within the jurisdiction?

Theoretically, the effect of nonprofits on housing values is ambiguous. On the one hand, more nonprofits would reduce the property tax base for the local government and it would have to increase taxes for residents, which would lower property values. On the other hand, the presence and services of a nonprofit organization may increase the appeal of the area, thereby raising property values.

A number of studies have investigated the effect that specific nonprofits or types of nonprofits have on housing prices in the area surrounding the nonprofit. For example, Bielefeld et al. (2006) used a hedonic equation to determine the effect on housing prices of a nonprofit that was located within one mile of the house. Dummy variables for the number of different types of nonprofits in one-mile radius are used to capture the effect of their presence on housing prices. Overall, the presence of a nonprofit within a one-mile radius increases the house sale price. However, the effect varies by the type of nonprofit and the number of nonprofit organizations. Arts, animal and environmental nonprofits have initially negative and then positive effect as the number of organizations increases. Health, religion and education nonprofits have a positive effect. Human services nonprofits have a negative effect at any number of organizations.

The findings by Bielefeld are in line with earlier studies. Ottensmann (2000) examined the effect of church proximity on housing values and rent and found a significant positive effect. Ellen and Voicu (2006) find that housing redevelopment by both nonprofit and for-profit organizations increased the value of neighboring houses. Nonprofits invested in more distressed areas and their impact remained stable over time, lending support to the idea that nonprofits are more committed to social services characterized by externalities than for-profits.

However, these studies consider the effect on housing prices within one jurisdiction; for example Bielefeld et al. (2006) used housing data for Indianapolis, Indiana. Using data for one jurisdiction does not allow for variations in property tax rates due to differences in the importance of nonprofits. To conduct a study to determine whether the property tax exemption was capitalized into house values would require a dataset that would be very hard to construct. In particular, it would be necessary to quantify for several jurisdictions the magnitude of the property tax revenue that would have to be replaced and thus the necessary increase in the property tax rate.

PILOTs and efforts to revoke tax-exempt status

The property tax provides a substantial portion of local government revenues. However, its visibility has made it the most unpopular tax among taxpayers. A tax revolt starting with Proposition 13 in California has brought significant restrictions on the revenues that can be raised through property taxes. Furthermore, local governments are facing other fiscal pressures such as cyclical variations in transfers from the federal and state government, and structural constraints due to rising wage and benefits obligations. Therefore cash-strapped cities have looked for other revenue options. An option that has been subject to much media attention is payments in lieu of taxes, or PILOTs. These are agreements between the local government and major nonprofit organizations on payments to compensate the local government for services provided to nonprofit organizations. The tension associated with this practice is illustrated by the fact that governments refer to PILOTs as voluntary agreements, while nonprofits consider them essentially blackmail backed up by threats to revoke their property tax exemption.

Arrangements for PILOTs have existed for many years but have been concentrated among a few cities with large universities such as Harvard, MIT and Boston College. However, the recent fiscal pressures have forced other governments to consider PILOTs, particularly for educational institutions and hospitals with sizable endowments and property. A study conducted for North Carolina nonprofits identifies the main factors increasing the probability for challenges to the tax exempt status of nonprofits (Anderson et al., 2003). The first set of factors is related to the fiscal environment of the local government. Large and frequent budget shortfalls, as well as a considerable concentration of nonprofit organizations within a locality are more likely to lead to challenges of the nonprofit tax exemption. The second set of factors is related to the characteristics of the nonprofit organizations. Nonprofits with large assets and land are more likely to be scrutinized for their exemption, as well as those competing with for-profit companies and generating a significant amount of their revenues through service fees. Barniv et al. (2005) also consider the loss of property tax exemptions among nonprofit hospitals. They find that the larger the tax base of a nonprofit hospital, the greater the likelihood of revoking the tax-exempt status.

The most comprehensive study of the use of PILOTs so far is by Leland (2002), who surveyed the largest cities in the USA. Only seven of the 51 large cities surveyed report that they collect PILOTs from nonprofit organizations, ranging from as low as $260 000 in Minneapolis to $19 400 000 in Boston (Leland, 2002, p. 202). As a percentage of the annual city budget, these revenues range between 0.03 percent and 1.4 percent respectively. While these findings indicate that among large cities PILOTs are not a significant revenue choice, there is no such comprehensive information about the extent of PILOT programs in smaller cities. Leland also finds that the main factors contributing to the introduction of PILOT programs are municipal revenue needs, nonprofit competition with for-profits, and large revenues from services. Brody (2007) also reports that PILOTs are sought from organizations that generate revenues from services and they can be interpreted as attempts to tax non-local beneficiaries of the services.

We do not know whether and how challenges to the tax exemptions and PILOTs influence service levels, financial performance, or the location decisions of nonprofits. Nonprofits argue that any payments to local governments would divert much-needed resources from the pursuit of their missions or would require additional fundraising to compensate for the lost resources. The extent of these impacts has not been established empirically.

However, PILOTs have many disadvantages. They generate some much-needed revenue for local governments, but considering their *ad hoc* and short-term nature, as well as the conflict associated with any arrangement, they do not appear to hold the key to resolving long-term issues. Another more transparent and predictable tool for compensation for provided services is fees for services. There has been a general increase in the use of fees by local governments. However, the extent to which nonprofits contribute to some of these fees is not clear.

Future research on PILOTs should focus on understanding the extent of their use, the stability of the revenue generated from such arrangements, the costs to local governments of implementing them, and the cost to nonprofit organizations in terms of revenue that can be used for community services. Another interesting question is whether nonprofit organizations can shift the cost of PILOTs or fees to their customers, and therefore distribute across localities the burden of the tax exemption. The main obstacle in the current research has been the availability of data, particularly data beyond the case studies frequently discussed in reports.

Direct subsidies by local governments
In addition to the implicit subsidy provided by the property tax exemption, local governments have provided discretionary subsidies to nonprofit organizations in order to influence their location decision. There is no systematic account of the extent of those subsidies, but they are illustrated by several relocation examples from the media. Bixler (2006) reports that the City of Atlanta provided some financial incentives to Habitat for Humanity for its move of part of its headquarter operation from Plains, Georgia to Atlanta. The American Cancer Society was provided with incentive financed by a local foundation to locate in downtown Atlanta (Saporta and Woods, 2006). In 2006, Orlando, Florida won a bid to attract a nonprofit medical research institute with a $310 million incentive package (Hundley, 2006). A similar incentive package, including donated land, was put together for a medical research center affiliated with Ohio State University in Columbus, Ohio (Pramik, 2005). And Orlando provided 165 acres of land, for free, to the Campus Crusade for Christ in exchange for establishing its World Center for Discipleship and Evangelism in Orlando (Allman, 2007). Government incentives include land donations, infrastructure improvements around new developments, and packages to cover relocation costs.

These examples appear to contradict the story that has been told so far, one of tension between local government and nonprofit organizations over the foregone revenues from property taxes. However, they highlight the nature of the issues underlying the property tax exemption – that nonprofit organizations benefit the community with their activity, and exemption and subsidies are necessary to sustain such activity. Future research might attempt to catalogue instances of local governments providing economic incentives to nonprofits to locate in the jurisdiction. It would also be of interest to determine what factors are associated with a decision to provide an incentive; for example, whether local governments that offer such direct subsidies have different revenue patterns than those challenging nonprofit exemptions.

Concluding remarks: why it matters and to whom – the relative importance of expanding our knowledge to practitioners, policy makers and scholars

The property tax is a significant revenue source for local governments that over time has been gradually eroded by popular tax revolts. At the same time, the nonprofit sector has become key in the provision of public goods and services, and tax exemptions are defended as appropriate subsidies for these activities. However, the link between the beneficiaries of the services and their location has become less obvious as technological advances have reduced the importance of physical distance. As a result of all these changes, the property tax exemption has been an issue of interest to local governments, nonprofit organizations and scholars for quite some time and will continue to be an important policy issue.

There are significant theoretical and empirical gaps to be addressed by future research. Policy makers need to know more about the revenues foregone from the exemption, about the advantages and disadvantages of PILOTs and other solutions for distributing more evenly the burden of the property tax exemption. Scholars need to improve their understanding of the economic effects of the property tax exemption by examining further the behavior of nonprofit organizations, both theoretically and empirically. It is not clear to what extent differences in property taxes determine the mix of for-profit and nonprofit organizations, and the quantity and quality of services produced by nonprofit organizations. Furthermore, broadly defined exemption criteria may result in different treatment of otherwise similar organizations, but the extent of this has not been documented yet.

Note

1.   Local governments may not have legal authority to provide direct subsidies to nonprofit organizations. In some cases, such subsidies could be considered gifts or gratuities.

References

Allman, T.D. (2007), 'The theme-parking, megachurching, franchising, exurbing, mcmansioning of America: how Walt Disney changed everything', *National Geographic*, **211** (3), 97–115.
Anderson, Dave, Joel Dunn, Megan Fotheringham, Eva Gao, Tim Greeff and Sandra Johnson (2003), 'The status of nonprofit property tax exemption in the State of North Carolina', report of the Terry Sanford Institute of Public Policy, Duke University, http://www.pubpol.duke.edu/research/students/spring2003-01.pdf.
Barniv, Ran, Dreag Danvers and Joanne P. Healy-Burress (2005), 'An empirical examination of state and local revocations of tax-exempt status for non-profit hospitals', *Journal of the American Taxation Association*, **27** (1), 1–25.
Bielefeld, Wolfgang and James C. Murdoch (2004), 'The locations of nonprofit organizations and their for-profit counterparts: an exploratory analysis', *Nonprofit and Voluntary Sector Quarterly*, **33** (2), 221–46
Bielefeld, Wolfgang, Seth Payton, John Ottensmann, Wendy McLaughlin and Joyce Man (2006), *The Location*

of Nonprofit Organizations Influences Residential Housing Prices: A Study in Marion County, Indiana, Indianapolis, IN: Center for Urban Policy and the Environment, School of Public and Environmental Affairs, Indiana University–Purdue University Indianapolis.

Bixler, Mark (2006), 'Habitat for Humanity moves to Atlanta', *Atlanta Journal-Constitution*, 20 April p. 1D

Bowman, Woods (2002), 'The institutional property tax exemption', paper prepared for the Lincoln Institute of Land Policy and presented at the 2002 Conference of the Association for Research on Nonprofit Organizations and Voluntary Action, Montreal, Quebec.

Brody, Evelyn (2002), 'Legal theories of tax exemption: a sovereignty perspective', in Evelyn Brody (ed.), *Property-Tax Exemptions for Charities*, Washington, DC: The Urban Institute Press, pp. 145–72.

Brody, Evelyn (2007), 'The States' growing use of a quid-pro-quo rationale for the charity property tax exemption', *The Exempt Organization Tax Review*, June, 269.

Chang, Cyril F. and Howard P. Tuckman (1990), 'Do higher property tax rates increase the market share of nonprofit hospitals?', *National Tax Journal*, **43** (2), 175–87.

Colombo, John D. (2006), 'The role of tax exemption in a competitive health care market', *Journal of Health Politics, Policy and Law*, **31** (3), 623–42.

Cordes, Joseph J. and Burton A. Weisbrod (1998), 'Differential taxation of nonprofits and the commercialization of nonprofit revenues', *Journal of Public Analysis and Management*, **17** (2), 195–214.

Cordes, Joseph J., Marie Gantz and Thomas Pollak (2002), 'What is the property-tax exemption worth?', in Evelyn Brody (ed.), *Property-Tax Exemptions for Charities*, Washington, DC: The Urban Institute Press, pp. 81–112.

David, Guy (2005), 'The convergence between for-profit and nonprofit hospitals in the United States', paper presented at the 2006 American Economic Association Meeting. http://www.aeaweb.org/annual_mtg_papers/2006/0106_0800_0204.pdf.

Ellen, Ingrid Gould and Ioan Voicu (2006), 'Nonprofit housing and neighborhood spillovers', *Journal of Policy Analysis and Management*, **25** (1), 31–52.

Gallagher, Janne (2002), 'The legal structure of property tax exemption', in Evelyn Brody (ed.), *Property-Tax Exemptions for Charities*, Washington, DC: The Urban Institute Press, pp. 3–22.

Gentry, William M. and John R. Penrod (2000), 'The tax benefits of not-for-profit hospitals', in David M. Culter (ed.), *The Changing Hospital Industry: Comparing Not-for-Profit and For-Profit Institutions*, Chicago, IL: University of Chicago Press, pp. 285–324.

Glaeser, Edward L. and Andrei Shleifer (2001), 'Not-for-profit entrepreneurs', *Journal of Public Economics*, **81** (1), 99–115.

Gulley, David O. and Rexford E. Santerre (1993), 'The effect of tax exemption on the market share of nonprofit hospitals', *National Tax Journal*, **46** (4), 477–86.

Hansmann, Henry B. (1987), 'The effect of tax exemption and other factors on the market share of nonprofit versus for-profit firms', *National Tax Journal*, **40** (1), 71–82.

Hassett, Kevin A. and R. Glenn Hubbard (2000), 'Noncontractible quality and organization form in the U.S. hospital industry', mimeo.

Hu, Zhenhua (2006), *Two Essays on Corporate Income Taxes and Organizational Forms in the United States*, PhD Dissertation, Georgia State University and Georgia Institute of Technology.

Hundley, Kris (2006), 'Orlando wins biotech plum', *St Petersburg Times*, 24 August, 1D.

Kessler, Daniel P. and Mark B. McClellan (2002), 'The effects of hospital ownership on medical productivity', *RAND Journal of Economics*, **33** (3), 488–506.

Krueckeberg, Donald A. (2004), 'Free New Jersey: the burden of property tax exemptions', report available at http://www.njleg.state.nj.us/PropertyTaxSession/OPI/free_new_jersey.pdf.

Lakdawalla, Darius and Tomas Philipson (2006), 'The nonprofit sector and industry performance', *Journal of Public Economics*, **90** (9), 1681–98.

Leland, Pamela (2002), 'PILOTs: the large-city experience', in Evelyn Brody (ed.), *Property-Tax Exemptions for Charities*, Washington, DC: The Urban Institute Press, pp 193–210.

Lipman, Harvey (2006a), 'Cities take many approaches to valuing tax-exempt property', *Chronicle of Philanthropy*, **19** (4), 14.

Lipman, Harvey (2006b), 'The value of a tax break', *Chronicle of Philanthropy*, **19** (4), 13.

Mullner, Ross and Jack Hadley (1984), 'Interstate variations in the growth of chain-owned proprietary hospitals, 1973–1982', *Inquiry* (Summer), 144–51.

Newhouse, Joseph P. (1970), 'Toward a theory of nonprofit institutions: an economic model of a hospital', *American Economic Review*, **60** (1), 64–74.

Norton, Edward C. and Douglas O. Staiger (1994), 'How hospital ownership affects access to care for the uninsured', *RAND Journal of Economics*, **25**, 171–85.

Ottensmann, John R. (2000), *Catholic Diocese of Cleveland: Economic Value of Selected Activities*, Indianapolis, IN: Indiana University–Pardue University Indianapolis, School of Public and Environmental Affairs, Center for Urban Policy and the Environment.

Pramik, Mike (2005), 'OSU likes dublin site for medical enterprise', *The Columbus Dispatch*, 9 September, 1E.
Rose-Ackerman, Susan (1996), 'Altruism, Nonprofits, and Economic Theory', *Journal of Economic Literature*, **34** (2), 701–28.
Saporta, Maria and Walter Woods (2006), 'Cancer society to relocate', *Atlanta Journal-Constitution*, 9 August, 1B.
Sloan, Frank A., Gabriel A. Picone, Donald H. Taylor, Jr and Shin-Yi Chou (2001), 'Hospital ownership and cost and quality of care: is there a dime's worth of difference', *Journal of Health Economics*, **20** (1), 1–21.
Steinberg, Richard (1991), '"Unfair" competition by nonprofits and tax policy', *National Tax Journal*, **44** (3), 351–64.
Weisbrod, Burton A. (1988), *The Nonprofit Economy*, Cambridge, MA: Harvard University Press.
White, Andrew N. (1979), 'Accessibility and public facility location', *Economic Geography*, **55** (1), 18–35.
Wolpert, Julian, Zvia Naphtali and John Seley (2001), 'The location of nonprofit facilities in urban areas', Lincoln Institute of Land Policy Working Paper, http://www.lincolninst.edu/pubs/dl/111_WolpertNaphtaliSeley01.pdf.

22 Government funding policies[1]
Stefan Toepler

Introduction

Other than for regulation (including fiscal regulation, such as tax exemption rules), government funding policies are the most direct embodiment of the relationship between government and the nonprofit sector. Government–nonprofit relations in turn are arguably the single most important concern across the world for nonprofit advocates and analysts alike. Whether in industrialized or developing nations, philanthropic resources are generally very limited, whereas earned income strategies are either perceived as dubious or hampered by the lack of requisite institutions, such as functioning markets. For nonprofits the choices are thus either to pursue their missions incrementally on a relatively small scale or to look for alternative financial resources to help build up operations and yield results at higher levels. For much of the second half of the twentieth century, nonprofits everywhere have opted to explore and utilize various forms of direct government support to scale up operations and reach additional clients, users or audiences for their work.

Accepting government monies is nevertheless perceived as somewhat of a double-edged sword, leading to a bifurcation of the debate. Two contrary strands of evaluating the role of government support emerged relatively early within the nonprofit literature. One strand portrays the government–nonprofit relationship as largely positive, arguing that the postwar influx of government monies enabled a significant scaling up of nonprofit activity that catapulted the sector to its current position of prominence. The other strand of the literature focuses more on the potentially negative effects of accepting government support for the culture, structure and behavior of nonprofit organizations.

While this debate has been a mainstay of nonprofit research since the early 1980s, it remains far from being settled. Indeed, the introduction of charitable choice in 1996's welfare reform legislation and the subsequent establishment of the White House's faith-based initiative in 2001 relaunched a broad debate about the fundamental issues of helping to scale up small religious and community initiatives: while proponents of the initiative lauded the intention of 'leveling the playing field', opponents – other than those objecting on grounds of the separation of church and state – feared an inevitable corrupting influence.

In this chapter, I shall first discuss what the literature so far largely agrees on, namely that a significant rise in government funding for nonprofits has taken place in the post-World War II period and that this rise has contributed to changing the sector from a small cottage industry into a significant economic force. The prevailing theory of the government–nonprofit relation- or partnership is likewise largely uncontested. There is somewhat less consensus on whether or not this partnership has turned out to be a good thing for nonprofits. Thus, after reviewing the main charges against government support, I shall conclude with a general assessment of the evidence and suggestions for additional conceptual considerations to come into play to help shape the debate going into the future.

Table 22.1 *Government grants and payments to public charities, total revenues, and percentage share, sector total and selected fields, 2005, in billions of dollars*

	Government grants and payments ($)	Total revenues ($)	%
Arts	2.83	22.67	12
Education	23.03	189.79	12
Health care	245.51	672.50	37
Human svcs	52.05	143.29	36
International	3.95	19.84	20
Total	351.01	1196.04	29

Source: Wing et al. (2008), p. 134.

The theory of government–nonprofit partnerships

The issue that goes virtually undisputed is the sheer extent of nonprofit entanglement with government funding. In developed countries, various forms of government support average just under half of all nonprofit sector income, with high marks set with about three-quarters in Ireland and Belgium and slightly under two-thirds in countries such as Germany and Israel (Salamon, 2006).

As of 2005 in the USA, government grants and payments of some $350 billion accounted for nearly 30 percent of the $1.2 trillion in revenues of public charities. Government support is heavily concentrated: payments to hospitals and other health care providers comprising 70 percent of the total (Wing et al., 2008, p. 134). Health care is not the only field where government support is important. Government grants and payments are of similar importance in the human services, where their revenue share of 36 percent equals that of health care (37 percent). In other fields, such as international activities (20 percent), and arts and education (12 percent each), the share of government financing is much smaller, but far from insignificant (Table 22.1).

In addition to this direct support, nonprofits also benefit from indirect subsidies in the form of tax exemptions and assorted fee reductions (such as free use of government facilities or reduced postage rates). The value of these indirect subsidies is hard to establish. Yet a few broad estimates exist. Brody and Cordes (2006) place the value of the corporate income tax exemption at $10 billion. Although not all nonprofits own real estate and not all of those that do are exempt, the value of the property tax exemption is of a similar magnitude, with estimates ranging from $8 to $13 billion (Brody and Cordes, 2006) and $9 to $15 billion (Bowman and Fremont-Smith, 2006). Indirect subsidies are thus substantial, but direct support has been a main factor driving nonprofit growth over the past six decades or so.

This came to pass in several ways. On the one hand, nonprofits benefited from large-scale, provider-neutral policies that neither favored nor disfavored them particularly over public or commercial providers, such as the GI Bill, research funding by the National Science Foundation or the National Institutes of Health, as well as Medicaid and Medicare funding for hospitals and health care providers. On the other hand, some federal programs were specifically targeted towards nonprofit providers, such as the grantmaking programs of the National Endowment for the Arts or the community development and social services grants, benefiting existing nonprofit organizations and stimulating the emergence of new ones (e.g., community action agencies). In sum, the post-World War II entry of the federal government into the nonprofit funding picture changed the sector from a small cottage industry of some 12 500 charities that were registered with the IRS in the 1940s (Hall, 2004) to the economic behemoth that it is today.

None of this is easily explained by the prevailing economic theories about the emergence and roles of the nonprofit sector (see Chapter 9 in this volume by Luksetich and Hughes), but the heavy reliance on third parties to implement (federal) government programs nevertheless constitutes one of the most characteristic general features of public policy making in the USA. Such third-party government arrangements, which predominantly rely on private institutions to carry out public purposes, have allowed the growth of government programs without actually increasing the size of the public sector since the 1960s (Salamon, 1995). Nonprofits are arguably important actors within the third-party-government regime, because they exhibit certain comparative advantages over public agencies (and to some extent over commercial enterprises).

Kramer (1981) in particular identified four special functions or roles that set nonprofits apart from the other sectors and give them an edge and distinctive position in the collective delivery of goods and services. Specifically, nonprofits innovate by experimenting with and pioneering new approaches, processes or programs in service delivery ('vanguard role'); foster and help express diverse values in a way that neither government nor the market can ('value guardian role'); give voice to minority and particularistic interests in the political process and help shape policy ('advocacy role'); and complement or supplement the service delivery of the other sectors ('service provider role'). These distinctive roles are, however, accompanied by a set of characteristic drawbacks that Salamon (1995) referred to as voluntary failures. The original four voluntary failures were 'philanthropic insufficiency' (inability to garner sufficient resources); 'particularism' (tendency of nonprofits and donors to focus on particular groups of clients to the exclusion of others); 'paternalism' (those in need may not have any say in the design of programs and the use of resources); and finally, amateurism (lack of professionalism in volunteer-driven organizations).

On the other hand, government brings its own comparative advantages to the equation that can cancel out these voluntary failures, such as its coercive powers including the power to tax (to overcome free-ridership and philanthropic insufficiency), concern for equity and entitlements (countering particularism), democratic decision-making procedures (countering paternalism), and the ability to set quality standards and demand certifications to combat amateurism and to issue regulations to address accountability problems. As a 'salutary' consequence, in the words of Laurence Lynn Jr (2002, p. 59), 'governmental influence, for example in child welfare, has arguably reduced discrimination, overuse of institutionalization, religious intolerance, and indifference to permanence. In welfare-related services, governmental influence tends toward the promotion of equity and service based on need and disadvantages'.

The organizational impacts of government support
While there is therefore a strong conceptual case for the mutual beneficiality of government–nonprofit partnership as embodied in public funding policies, the issue has raised

concerns. Significantly, while there may be improvements in the quality and availability of services, the relationship does not necessarily mean that nonprofit service providers will also be better off at the organizational level. On one side, government funding will allow organizations to grow and expand (i.e., scaling up), provide a measure of financial stability, and increase an organization's legitimacy and credibility in the community.

On the other side, concerns abound about dependence and loss of autonomy resulting from the uneven partnership. Financial dependence can force organizations to become more commercial when public funds dry up; contribute to the crowding out of private funds; and increase red tape and professionalism while reducing advocacy and lobbying efforts. Government funding can lead to conflicting accountabilities, encourage mission drift and change the nature of nonprofit boards and governance. Finally, in the 'contracting regime' (Smith and Lipsky, 1993), nonprofits succumb to vendorism – a term used to here to describe the specific problems resulting from contracts. In either case, the underlying concern is that such side effects of government funding policies erode the distinctive roles and functions of nonprofits. This is particularly problematic where the democratic functions of citizen associations in a Tocquevillean view are preferred over service-focused, economic-utilitarian concepts of the nonprofit sector (Lipsky and Smith, 1989/90; Smith and Lipsky, 1993; Smith and Grønbjerg, 2006).

Scale, stability and legitimacy
On the positive side of the ledger is the availability of significant resources that allow nonprofits to increase their reach by expanding service to more of their core clients or by reaching out to new clienteles, to develop and scale up innovative programs, and to replicate successful programs in new locales. Due to the philanthropic insufficiency problem, garnering government support holds the strongest possibility for nonprofits to be able to scale up their programs and operations. This has been a perennial issue for NGOs in particular (Edwards and Fowler, 2002). Although rarely explicitly touched on in the broader literature, it applies just as well elsewhere.

What is more, public support also provides a measure of relief from the vagaries and volatility of private funding and the distractions from mission activities that stem from constant fundraising needs and demands (Kramer, 1981). Indeed, the increasing fundraising demands on executive directors are among the main reasons that nonprofit executives require additional managerial training in addition to professional degrees in social work, art history or education that previously were sufficient qualification for the job.

Significant government support can thus contribute to the managerial and financial stability of agencies, providing a measure of financial predictability (Grønbjerg, 1993). Relatedly, Handy and Webb (2003) theorize that nonprofits with higher levels of government funding will exhibit lower savings rates. While this could of course indicate that nonprofits with government support are more likely to use up reserves to cover cash flow problems or underfunded service commitments, it could also indicate that nonprofits with long-term funding arrangements or presumed secure future public support prospects feel more secure and less in need of maintaining rainy-day funds.

Another factor contributing to stability is the legitimacy or recognition and positive reputational effects that come with the receipt of government funding (Jung and Moon, 2007; Austin, 2003). In this sense, public support can have a signaling function, assuring private donors that the agency is worthy of support and subject to oversight by the government, which may in turn reduce a donor's own perceived monitoring needs and costs. Examples of such a signaling function are the role that the National Endowment of the Arts has played in the past by essentially conferring a 'good housekeeping seal of approval' to its grantees (Wyszomirski and Mulcahy, 1995). Likewise, in the sciences, government grants from agencies such as the National Science Foundation or the National Institutes of Health are frequently seen as the ultimate validation of research projects (Toepler and Feldman, 2004).

Effects of retrenchment: commercialization
While the ready availability of government support thus contributed significantly to the scaling up of the sector until the 1970s, the flipside became evident beginning in the 1980s. Reductions in federal programs sharply reduced overall support early in the decade, while social needs and demand for nonprofit services increased (Salamon, 1995). Increases in private philanthropy did not compensate for losses in public support (Abramson et al., 2006). The resulting relative decline of public and private donative support thus forced nonprofits to rely increasingly on fees for services and other market-based revenues (Salamon, 2002a). As a result, an impending 'commercial transformation' of the nonprofit sector gave rise to significant concerns (Weisbrod, 1998). This trend has encompssed an overall shift in the forms of government support towards more indirect forms, such as vouchers, tax credits and other end-user subsidies (Salamon, 2002a; Smith, 2002). This in turn forces nonprofits to compete more directly with each other as well as for-profit outfits, fostering further commercialism.

Mission drift and accountability
Goal displacement and mission drift can of course not only result from increased commercialism among nonprofit managers, but also from government funding, as 'providing contracted services . . . may not address current community needs or the agency's historical mission' (Austin, 2003, p. 103). The government's need for accountability 'shift[s] the organizational norms of nonprofit agencies from their historical emphasis on being responsive to the individual to focusing more on treating all clients alike, an orientation that bears resemblance to that of government service agencies' (Lipsky and Smith, 1989/90, p. 626). Mission drift thus takes place when the focus of nonprofit managers is directed away from original core clientele. In the NGO literature, the resulting problem is often discussed in terms of upward versus downward accountability: NGOs taking international aid monies will shift their attention from serving the needs of beneficiaries, staff and local partner organizations towards servicing funders' reporting and evaluation demands (Ebrahim, 2003; Edwards and Hulme, 1996). In the case of faith-based organizations, this may take the form of a secularization effect on service delivery (Sherman, 1995; Glenn, 2000). This in turn involves a trade-off between mission fidelity and range: 'agencies eschewing secular funding tend to be small [which] suggests that fully autonomous religious agencies reflect faith in many ways, but they often have modest impact on the world' (Smith and Sosin, 2001, p. 661). Fear of losing the spiritual aspects of their work is among the main reasons that faith-based organizations have abstained from charitable choice (Kennedy and Bielefeld, 2006; Pipes and Ebaugh, 2002).

Dependence and autonomy concerns

Among the most frequently cited concerns about government funding are that non-profit organizations become dependent and lose their autonomy. In some sense, the prospect of dependence and loss of autonomy is a generalized concern that either encompasses, or has as its consequences, most other more specific pathologies associated with government support. Yet neither dependence nor autonomy is usually satisfactorily defined or sufficiently empirically specified. Dependence is most commonly understood as financial dependence, which gives rise to control of the organization by external actors (such as governments) in command of critical financial resource flows (Pfeffer and Salancik, 1978). Autonomy is likewise frequently understood as financial autonomy and as such largely synonymous with dependence (e.g. Horch, 1994). However, autonomy can also refer to an organization's ability to set its own mission and goals; and mission drift and goal displacement are a reflection of loss of autonomy in this regard. Third, autonomy can refer to an agency's ability to determine its own programmatic choices.

Jung and Moon (2007) thus suggest that nonprofit autonomy is threatened where government support results in constraints in goal setting, resource allocations and program choices. In their study of Korean cultural organizations, they find that managers perceive lower levels of autonomy in these three areas as a result of government funding, but the actual mechanisms of how this happens remain unclear. Anheier et al. (1997) did not ask managers directly about dependence perceptions, but tried to solicit assessments and strategic reactions to crisis scenarios. They find that managers whose organizations appear financially dependent on government (e.g., more than 50 percent of revenues) typically prefer state-oriented strategies, such as appealing to government first to cover short-term financial losses.

That said, there are of course occasions of direct interference by government administrators that compromise organizational, and particularly programmatic, autonomy. In the arts, attempts to censor (i.e., defund) controversial art perceived by some as indecent or pornographic sparked a political firestorm that led to reduced federal funding and a total restructuring of the National Endowment for the Arts during the 1990s (Zeigler, 1994); and religiously controversial art led the mayor of New York City to try to cut city subsidies to the Brooklyn Museum of Art in 1999 (Rothfield, 2001). In the international aid arena, a prominent example is the so-called global gag rule or Mexico City Policy, which was announced by President Reagan in 1984. The rule essentially prohibited all NGOs – US or foreign – that receive USAID funds from providing any abortion-related services, even with private funds (Crane and Dusenberry, 2004; Dietrich, 2007). As the examples suggest, such interference appears likely where nonprofit services involve contentious public values.

A corollary of the financial dependence argument is the crowding-out phenomenon, which suggests, *inter alia*, that nonprofits receiving significant amounts of public funding may lose private support as a result (see Chapter 2 in this volume by Daniel Tinkelman).

Consequences of dependence: bureaucratization and less political activity

Bureaucratization can also be understood as a side effect of dependence. As Anheier et al. (1997, p. 190) summarize the German case:

> Dependent on government funds, closely tied to public sector policies and often required to adopt state accounting and reporting procedures, nonprofit organizations have come to function as an important vehicle for the 'transfer of bureaucracy' from government to society at large [ultimately] losing whatever distinct characteristics and qualities they once had.

Bureaucratization derives from the administrative demands associated with managing public funds as well as certain preconditions for receiving such funds. Among the latter are requirements concerning certifications and other staff qualifications that lead to the professionalization of agencies (Kramer, 1981; Smith and Lipsky, 1993). While professionals can generally increase the quality of services, they also tend to follow professional blueprints rather than customized solutions for clients. In addition, credentialing requirements sometimes prevent or limit alternative service approaches, such as employing former clients as direct service providers (Sherman, 1995). To manage government funding administratively, nonprofits also require greater managerial professionalism outside direct service provision. Adding support staff, such as accountants or human resource specialists, leads to functional differentiation and more complex organizational structures. In other words, in order to be able to compete for government support, nonprofits need to ramp up their organizational capacity. Accordingly, the need for capacity building among small providers has been among the core issues of the faith-based initiative (Kennedy and Bielefeld, 2006).

Another consequence of dependence relates to the level of political activity. Nonprofit organizations that are dependent on government funding are said to feel more constraint in their ability to do lobbying and advocacy, not wanting 'to bite the hand that feeds'. The fear of losing funds, unclear legal restrictions, or the redirection of organizational activities from political activities to grantwriting and management are among the potential impediments to increased advocacy (Chaves et al., 2004). A recent survey found many organizations unaware of their legal rights and some fearing retribution even if they engaged in legal activities (Bass et al., 2007). While nonprofits that receive significant direct federal support are subject to additional oversight by the Office of Management and Budget and may thus be even less likely to engage in lobbying and advocacy, the general level of political activity among nonprofits is exceedingly low, with only about 2 percent of organizations reporting any lobbying expenditures to the IRS (Reid, 2007). On the other hand, in their study of religious and other nonprofits in St Paul and Minneapolis, Chaves et al. (2004) find little evidence that government funding has reduced political activity. Similarly, analyzing a small sample of US and British NGOs involved in food aid and agricultural issues, McMillan (2006) finds organizational size to be a better predictor of advocacy than the level of government support.

Governance
Another consequence of government support is that nonprofits with high levels of government funding have different boards than nonprofits that do not. Smith and Lipsky (1993) suggest that boards were traditionally large and broadly representative of the organization's community and directors selected 'on the basis of their allegiance to the ideas and values embodied in the organization's character, history, and current practices' (ibid., p. 74). Government contracting, by contrast, leads to smaller and more technocratic boards. This effect is empirically well supported. Stone et al. (2001, p. 286) find that nonprofits with high degrees of government funding in their sample do have smaller

boards, 'because larger numbers of board members are not needed for fundraising purposes or for their linkages to multiple constituencies and donors'. Guo (2007) finds less community representation. Hodge and Piccolo (2005, p. 184) suggest that 'funding source is significantly related to the use of board involvement techniques, as CEOs of privately funded agencies use more board involvement techniques than CEOs of government and commercially funded agencies'. This corresponds with O'Regan and Oster's (2002) finding of more passive and less well-performing boards in government-funded nonprofit organizations. Importantly, they also find that with increasing levels of government funding, fundraising activities as well as individual giving by board members decrease. Overall, they conclude that 'boards with high degrees of government funding do not behave identically to other boards. Boards of these organizations tend to focus less on some of the traditional functions – like fund-raising – and more on fiduciary and boundary spanning kinds of activities' (O'Regan and Oster, 2002, p. 374).

Vendorism or contracting problems

Vendorism is defined by Kramer as 'selling social services to government for an agreed-upon price, usually on a unit-cost basis' (Kramer, 1981, p. 153). In doing this, nonprofits may face several problems: reimbursements below actual costs can lead to deficits that have to be made up elsewhere and essentially constitute a private subsidy for the government; reimbursements that allow for some degree of surplus (or 'profit margin') may attract for-profit competitors into the field; or a lack of cost advantages to government may lead to a 're-publicization' of services by bringing them back into direct government provision. Additional consequences of vendorism include payment delays, future funding uncertainties, increased administrative demands, and potential loss of board member and volunteer interest (ibid., pp. 153–6).

Kramer's litany of problems resulting from vendorism tracks closely the standard set of concerns about contracting (Smith and Lipsky, 1993; Smith, 2004, 2006). Smith (2004) summarizes these as cash flow management issues on the one hand, and the problem of the 'contract renewal dance' on the other. Cash flow problems derive from nonprofits being generally undercapitalized and not having sufficient financial slack to absorb sudden cash flow changes. Such changes can be due to payment delays, initial underestimation of the actual costs of the contracted work or unanticipated rising costs or unexpected expenditures. This may force nonprofits to engage in different stop-gap measures, such as delaying payments to their own vendors, furloughing staff, instituting hiring freezes or launching emergency fundraising appeals. The difficulties that nonprofit face in dealing with these problems is one of the main reasons that for-profit competition has taken hold in areas traditionally dominated by nonprofits, as for-profits can more easily mobilize capital and credit with less concern for contract payment delays.

Although public funding can have generally stabilizing effects, the contract renewal process is a source of uncertainty and unpredictability. While most contracts are renewed eventually, delays frequently occur due to legislative politicking, meaning that contracts sometimes cannot be renewed until agency budgets are settled due to turnover among contract administrators, or to deliberate delays aimed at forcing compliance of nonprofit vendors if they prove resistant, for example, to accepting or negotiating changes to the original contract (Smith, 2004). In addition, the more recent focus of government agencies on performance-based contracts further undercuts the relatively stability of contract-based funding, as these contracts are less likely to be renewed automatically when performance targets are not met.

Concluding remarks and outlook

The foundational works of the government-nonprofit relations literature by Kramer (1981), Smith and Lipsky (1993), Grønbjerg (1993), and Salamon (1995) still appear to have covered the ground fairly comprehensively. Even in the current faith-based debate, there is hardly any concern about government funding that has not been discussed at length in these early works.[2] Newer reviews tend to add to our general theoretical understanding of the relationship (Smith and Grønbjerg, 2006; Young, 2006) and its international patterns (Salamon, 2006); but not too much recent work has focused on how government funding affects organizational behavior and managerial strategies. In particular, there seems to be a rather disappointing near-dearth of empirical work testing the assumptions of the pathological effects of government support. 'The concern is real, but the facts are not certain,' wrote Wedel (1976), noting a lack of systematic research. Salamon (1995) came to a similar conclusion around the early 1990s. As surprising as this may sound considering the importance of the government–nonprofit relationship, it seems hard not to argue that their assessment still stands. This in turn gives rise to a number of observations.

First, the empirical bases for most of what we know about the problems with government funding are interviews with relatively small sets of agency officials. While this has been an effective way of developing grounded theory in this area, it nevertheless leaves the literature open to potential fallacies. For instance, we cannot – at the moment – determine with certainty that government funding is the sole cause of many observed pathologies. The organizational theory literature has firmly established that age and size are typical determinants of bureaucratization, and indeed it seems more likely that larger faith-based organizations explore government contracts than smaller ones (Smith and Sosin, 2001). In the social services, Kramer and Grossman (1987, p. 45) observed much earlier: 'Larger agencies with "track records" tended to receive contracts, both new and renewals, more frequently.' That government administrators may prefer to fund larger organizations that already have bureaucratic capacity rather than small ones that do not has been among the reasons why the faith-based initiative was thought to be needed to help 'level the playing field'.

Second, the literature seems somewhat lacking in efforts to marshal counterfactual conditionals. Looking for the counterfactual would lead to interesting, though largely unasked questions, such as whether, *ceteris paribus*, nonprofits that are not dependent exhibit the same pathologies as the ones that are dependent; and whether there are government-dependent organizations that avoid these pathologies.[3] Pursuing the counterfactual as an explicit research strategy would significantly improve our knowledge of how to structure the government–nonprofit relationship to avoid the common problems.

Third, one exception to these general empirical woes of the literature is the work on board size, composition and performance, where the use of survey data (rather than case studies) actually does allow a comparison of government and privately funded agencies. Yet, even here, we cannot say unequivocally whether the observed differences are a good thing or a bad thing. Consider the finding that boards of government-funded organizations are more closely attuned to fiduciary responsibilities than boards of privately funded organizations. In the current accountability climate, it is hard to view this as negative. Likewise, the evidence seems consistent that boards do less fundraising with rising levels of government support. Taken together with Andreoni and Payne's (2003) suggestion that government funding generally crowds out fundraising efforts, the finding sounds ominous. But there are different ways to look at the issue: as Kramer (1981) has argued, the constant need to raise funds can also be a source of mission deflection. Government support then offers less distraction and more time to concentrate on mission.

Fourth, one can also not avoid an acknowledgment that resource dependence is an issue for public as well as private funding. After all, much of Pfeffer's early work that led to resource dependence theory (Pfeffer and Salancik, 1978) was based on studying nonprofits, such as hospitals. Yet acknowledging that nonprofits may become dependent on government is not sufficient by itself. The more helpful questions here are whether there is a 'magic number' (as a percentage of revenues) at which an organization becomes dependent and at exactly what levels of government funding do which pathologies occur. Kramer observed in this context that

> there is no agreement on the proportion of an agency's budget that can come from a single source without dominating the organization. Although some voluntary agency executives believe that an agency should not depend on any one source for more than 50 percent of its income, there is no evidence that this or any other percentage is an effective guideline for the acceptance of public funds or the preservation of autonomy. (Kramer. 1981, p. 169)

Sadly, this insight remains as fresh as it was a quarter-century ago.

In addition, more work on the remedies for dependence, that is strategies that nonprofit managers could usefully employ, would also be of considerable practical use. Pfeffer and Salancik (1978) offered a range of suggestions back in the 1970s, such as interlocking directorates, the formation of alliances or movement of staff within the given industry, that find not enough reflection in the current literature. The most commonplace suggestion is to diversify revenues. There is a small literature that seeks to measure revenue concentration as part of financial vulnerability indices and suggests a positive relationship between diversity and financial health (see Keating et al., 2005; Chapter 1 in this volume by Chang and Tuckman). However, considerably more work in this area is needed.

Another consideration that merits more attention is whether the pathologies associated with public funding are worse than pathologies associated with private funding (Froelich, 1999). The issue of 'coercive philanthropy' (Brustein, 2000), for example, has earned scant attention by comparison, as have frequent reports of attempted interference by large donors on programmatic decisions by cultural and higher educational institutions. In this respect, a valid question is whether there are indeed any pathologies that are in fact specific to government funding rather than just being the natural results of general resource dependence. Of course, government funders tend to have larger checkbooks and as such hold more power than most private funders and donors. But when controlling for the size of the funder's purse, this may remain an open question.

The one area where there is little doubt that the observed problems are government-specific is vendorism, where there is a preponderance of evidence that the specific problems associated with purchase of service (POS) contracting are real and causally related to the nature of contracting.[4] In this context, it is important to make two important observations: first, the literature on drawbacks of government funding essentially originated with observations of the emerging postwar contracting regime (Wedel, 1976; Kramer, 1966). Second, it originated in the social services field and, with few exceptions such as international aid, has largely remained there. Government dependence seems less of a concern in most other fields, including arts and culture (where government support is limited), higher education (where it is significant particularly in research universities) or health (where it is dominant). This is not to say that there are no problems with government funding in these fields (e.g. censorship attempts in the arts as noted above), but only that the arts, education and health literatures exhibit a lack of comparable concern.

Among the likely reasons for this is that government funding is rarely contract-based in these fields, where grants (arts and education) or fee reimbursements (health) are more common. This then begs the question of whether the drawbacks associated with government funding are mainly associated with one form of support (POS contracting) in a few fields rather than being a pervasive, sector-wide and field-spanning phenomenon.

POS contracting is inherently problematic for nonprofits and at the same time different from all other forms of government support: all else being equal, the purpose of contracts is not to support nonprofits *per se*. Contracts are not typically about fostering the development of innovative approaches to service delivery or the expression of values. Rather their purpose is to enable delivery of specific, government-defined services. Trying to look at contracts as government support in the sense of supporting the work that nonprofits do is thus problematic. There is of course always the possibility that the targeted clients and service approaches of nonprofits show some overlap with the intended clients and desired service approaches of government contracts, but fundamentally the relevance of the nonprofit's mission is limited to being a positive factor in the contract application review. Contracts are intended to support the fulfillment of government needs, not the needs of nonprofits; and nonprofits need to understand what they get into when they consider contracting rather than doing so based on wrongful notions that contracts are a valid option to alleviate their fiscal constraints.

What this suggests is that future work on the effects of government funding policies could usefully employ the tools of government framework suggested by Salamon (2002b) in efforts to parse more finely the specific effects of different funding tools. Although much of the literature speaks of 'grants and contracts' as if they were much the same thing, the grants tool differs principally from the POS contract tool in that it is intended to fund work proposed by the grantee rather than determined by the grantor.[5] Other tools either indeed intend to support nonprofits and their mission-related work (tax expenditures/exemptions, grants) or provide indirect consumer subsidies (vouchers, reimbursements, tax credits, loans). In each case, the effects will likely differ substantially based on the tools choice.

Using some of the tools (Salamon 2002b) that typically benefit nonprofits, Table 22.2 attempts a first, tentative characterization of how the relative strength of the main government funding pathologies varies among different tools. Commercialization will be strongly fostered by tools incorporating market incentives, such as vouchers or social insurance reimbursements. Dependence and autonomy concerns should be most strongly pronounced with contracts, less so with grants (recipients can come to view

Table 22.2 *Hypothesized relationships between tools of government action and pathologies typically associated with government funding*

Pathologies / Tools	Commercial-ization	Dependence/ autonomy	Mission drift	Bureaucra-tization	Loss of political activity	Governance changes	Crowding out	Vendorism
Contracts	Weak	Strong	Strong	Strong	Strong	Strong	Strong	Strong
Grants	Weak	Weak/ moderate	Moderate/ weak	Moderate/ strong	Moderate	Moderate	Strong	Weak
Vouchers	Strong	Weak	Weak	Moderate	Weak	Weak/ moderate	Weak	None
Reimbursements	Strong	None	Weak	Strong	Weak	Strong	Weak	None
Indirect subsidies	None	None	None	Weak	Weak	Weak	None	None
Tax credits/loans	Weak	Weak	None	Weak	Weak	Weak/ moderate	Weak	None

some grant programs as entitlements though) and largely non-existent with indirect forms of support. The same applies to mission drift, which is a core issue with contracts, but can also occur with grants in the form of grantsmanship (Kramer, 1981). The recent tendency of social service agencies to offer health-related programs to tap into Medicare and Medicaid (Smith, 2002) is an example of mission drift caused by reimbursement schemes.

High levels of bureaucratization are required to be able to compete for contracts, but increasingly also for the administration of grant agreements. This is also the case with reimbursements and some voucher schemes, because provider eligibility require-ments are typically involved as well as administrative capability needed to manage the collection of third-party payments. Indirect subsidies, i.e., tax exemptions, by contrast demand only a minimum of formalization to handle reporting requirements. Reduced advocacy and lobbying should be expected most by organizations receiving contracts and grants, as they may have the closest working relationships with their governmental sponsors. Governance changes – the tendency towards smaller boards that are more attuned to fiduciary oversight than fundraising – should be expected as much in organi-zations relying on government reimbursements, such as hospitals, as in those relying on contracts.

Insofar as donors refrain from supporting publicly funded organizations, crowding out should be largely restricted to grants and contracts, because these are the most visible forms of government support. If crowding out results from managerial behavior (e.g., fewer fundraising efforts), it could also be induced by tools employing market mecha-nisms. Vendorism is *ex definitionem* a contracting-related problem. However well these hypotheses turn out, taken together the combination of tools and funding pathologies allows for a rich menu of empirical questions that future research could usefully explore across a wide range of industries.

Notes

1. This chapter benefited greatly from Jan Sacharko's excellent research assistance.
2. The one exception here is the constitutional issues deriving from the separation of church and state, which are peculiar to religion.
3. Sherman (1995) provides some anecdotal evidence that such a thing is possible after all.
4. Then again, it is not impossible that private contracts, such as corporations contracting with nonprofits for child care, are prone to similar issues.
5. There is a tendency, though, for government grant agreements to become so complex that they increasingly resemble contracts.

References

Abramson, Alan, Lester M. Salamon and C. Eugene Steuerle (2006), 'Federal spending and tax policies: their implications for the nonprofit sector', in Elizabeth T. Boris and C. Eugene Steuerle (eds), *Nonprofits and Government: Collaboration and Conflict*, Washington, DC: Urban Institute Press, pp. 107–40.
Andreoni, James and A. Abigail Payne (2003), 'Do government grants to private charities crowd out giving or fund-raising?' *The American Economic Review*, **93** (3), 792–812.
Anheier, Helmut K., Stefan Toepler and S. Wojciech Sokolowski (1997), 'The implications of govern-ment funding for non-profit organizations: three propositions', *International Journal of Public Sector Management*, **10** (3), 190–213.
Austin, Michael J. (2003), 'The changing relationship between nonprofit organizations and public social service agencies in the era of welfare reform', *Nonprofit and Voluntary Sector Quarterly*, **32** (1), 97–114.
Bass, Gary D., Kay Guinane, David F. Arons and Matthew F. Carter (2007), *Seen but not Heard: Strengthening Nonprofit Advocacy*, Washington, DC: Aspen Institute.

Bowman, Woods and Marion Fremont-Smith (2006), 'Nonprofit and state and local governments', in Elizabeth T. Boris and C. Eugene Steuerle (eds), *Nonprofits and Government: Collaboration and Conflict*, Washington, DC: Urban Institute Press, pp. 181–213.

Brody, Evelyn and Joseph Cordes (2006), 'Tax treatment of nonprofit organizations: a two-edged sword?', in Elizabeth T. Boris and C. Eugene Steuerle (eds), *Nonprofits and Government: Collaboration and Conflict*, Washington, DC: Urban Institute Press, pp. 141–80.

Brustein, Robert (2000), 'Coercive philanthropy', in Gigi Bradford, Michael Gary and Glenn Wallach (eds), *The Politics of Culture: Policy Perspectives for Individuals, Institutions, and Communities*, New York: The New Press, pp. 218–24.

Chaves, Mark, Laura Stephens and Joseph Galaskiewicz (2004), 'Does government funding suppress nonprofits' political activity?', *American Sociological Review*, **69** (2), 292–316.

Crane, Barbara B. and Jennifer Dusenberry (2004), 'Power and politics in international funding for reproductive health: the US global gag rule', *Reproductive Health Matters*, **12** (24), 128–37.

Dietrich, John (2007), 'The politics of PEPFAR. The President's emergency plan for AIDS relief', *Ethics & International Affairs*, **21** (3), 277–92.

Ebrahim, Alnoor (2003), 'Accountability in practice: mechanisms for NGOs', *World Development*, **31** (5), 813–29.

Edwards, Michael and Alan Fowler (eds) (2002), *The Earthscan Reader on NGO Management*, London and Sterling, VA: Earthscan.

Edwards, Michael and David Hulme (1996), 'Too close for comfort? The impact of official aid on nongovernmental organizations', *World Development*, **24** (6), 961–73.

Froelich, Karen (1999), 'Diversification of revenue strategies: evolving resource dependence in nonprofit organizations', *Nonprofit and Voluntary Sector Quarterly*, **28** (3), 246–68.

Glenn, Charles (2000), *The Ambiguous Embrace: Government and Faith-based Schools and Social Agencies*, Princeton, NJ: Princeton University Press.

Grønbjerg, Kirsten (1993), *Understanding Nonprofit Funding*, San Francisco, CA: Jossey-Bass.

Guo, Chao (2007), 'When government becomes the principal philanthropist: the effects of public funding on patterns of nonprofit governance', *Public Administration Review*, **67** (3), 458–73.

Hall, Peter Dobkin (2004), 'Historical perspectives on nonprofit organizations in the United States', in Robert Herman (ed.), *Jossey-Bass Handbook of Nonprofit Leadership and Management*, San Francisco, CA: Jossey-Bass, pp. 3–38.

Handy, Femida and Natalie J. Webb (2003), 'A theoretical model of the effects of public funding on saving decisions by charitable nonprofit service providers', *Annals of Public and Cooperative Economics*, **74** (2), 261–82.

Hodge, Matthew M. and Ronald F. Piccolo (2005), 'Funding source, board involvement techniques, and financial vulnerability in nonprofit organizations: a test of resource dependence', *Nonprofit Management & Leadership*, **16** (2), 171–90.

Horch, Heinz-Dieter (1994), 'Does government financing have a detrimental effect on the autonomy of voluntary associations? Evidence from German sports clubs', *International Review for the Sociology of Sport*, **29** (3), 269–85.

Jung, Kwangho and M. Jae Moon (2007), 'The double-edged sword of public-resource dependence: the impact of public resources on autonomy and legitimacy in Korean cultural nonprofit organizations', *The Policy Studies Journal*, **35** (2), 205–26.

Keating, Elizabeth, Mary Fischer, Teresa Gordon and Janet Greenlee (2005), 'Assessing financial vulnerability in the nonprofit sector', KSG Working Paper No. RWP05-002, Cambridge, MA: Harvard University.

Kennedy, Sheila and Wolfgang Bielefeld (2006), *Charitable Choice at Work: Evaluating Faith-based Job Programs in the States*, Washington, DC: Georgetown University Press.

Kramer, Ralph M. (1966), 'Voluntary agencies and the use of public funds: some policy issues', Social Service Review, **40**, 15–26.

Kramer, Ralph M. (1981), *Voluntary Agencies in the Welfare State*, Berkeley, CA: University of California Press.

Kramer, Ralph M. and Bart Grossman (1987), 'Contracting for social services: process management and resource dependencies', *Social Service Review*, **61** (1), 32–55.

Lipsky, Michael and Steven R. Smith (1989/90), 'Nonprofit organizations, government, and the welfare state', *Political Science Quarterly*, **104** (4), 625–48.

Lynn, Laurence E., Jr (2002), 'Social services and the state: the public appropriation of private charity', *Social Service Review*, **76** (1), 58–82.

McMillan, Samuel (2006), 'Fueling funding dependency? Northern governments, NGOs and food aid', paper presented at Annual Meeting of the International Studies Association, Town & Country Resort and Convention Center, San Diego, March 2006, http://www.allacademic.com/meta/p98056_index.html (retrieved 24 February 2008).

O'Regan, Katherine and Sharon M. Oster (2002), 'Does government funding alter nonprofit governance? Evidence from New York City Nonprofit Contractors', *Journal of Policy Analysis and Management*, **21** (3), 359–79.

Pfeffer, Jeffrey and Gerald R. Salancik (1978), *The External Control of Organizations: A Resource Dependence Perspective*, New York: Harper & Row.

Pipes, Paula F. and Helen Rose Ebaugh (2002), 'Faith-based coalitions, social services, and government funding', *Sociology of Religion*, **63** (1), 49–68.

Reid, Elizabeth J. (2007), 'Advocacy and the challenges it presents for nonprofits', in Dennis R. Young (ed.), *Financing Nonprofits: Putting Theory into Practice*, Lanham, MD: National Center on Nonprofit Enterprise & Altamira Press, pp. 343–71.

Rothfield, Larry (ed.) (2001), *Unsettling 'Sensation': Arts-policy Lessons from the Brooklyn Museum of Art Controversy*, New Brunswick, NJ: Rutgers University Press.

Salamon, Lester M. (1995), *Partners in Public Service: Government–Nonprofit Relations in the Modern Welfare State*, Baltimore, MD: Johns Hopkins University Press.

Salamon, Lester M. (2002a), 'The resilient sector: the state of nonprofit America', in Lester M. Salamon (ed.), *The State of Nonprofit America*, Washington, DC: Brookings Institution Press, pp. 3–65.

Salamon, Lester M. (ed.) (2002b), *The Tools of Government: A Guide to the New Governance*, New York: Oxford University Press.

Salamon, Lester M. (2006), 'Government–nonprofit relations from an international perspective', in Elizabeth T. Boris and C. Eugene Steuerle (eds), *Nonprofits and Government: Collaboration and Conflict*, Washington, DC: Urban Institute Press, pp. 399–435.

Sherman, Amy L. (1995), 'Cross purposes: will conservative welfare reform corrupt religious charities?', *Policy Review*, (74), 58–63.

Smith, Steven R. (2002), 'Social services', in Lester M. Salamon (ed.), *The State of Nonprofit America*, Washington, DC: Brookings Institution Press, pp. 149–86.

Smith, Steven Rathgeb (2004), 'Managing the Challenges of Government Contracts', in Robert Herman (ed.), *Jossey-Bass Handbook of Nonprofit Leadership and Management*, San Francisco, CA: Jossey-Bass, pp. 371–90.

Smith, Steven Rathgeb (2006), 'Government financing of nonprofit activity', in Elizabeth T. Boris and C. Eugene Steuerle (eds), *Nonprofits and Government: Collaboration and Conflict*, Washington, DC: Urban Institute Press, pp. 219–56.

Smith, Steven Rathgeb and Kirsten Grønbjerg (2006), 'Scope and theory of government-nonprofit relations', in Walter Powell and Richard Steinberg (eds), *The Nonprofit Sector: A Research Handbook*, 2nd edn, New Haven, CT: Yale University Press, pp. 221–42.

Smith, Steven Rathgeb and Michael Lipsky (1993), *Nonprofits for Hire: The Welfare State in the Age of Contracting*, Cambridge, MA: Harvard University Press.

Smith, Steven Rathgeb and Michael R. Sosin (2001), 'The varieties of faith-related agencies', *Public Administration Review*, **61** (6), 651–70.

Stone, Melissa Middleton, Mark A. Hager and Jennifer J. Griffin (2001), 'Organizational characteristics and funding environments: a study of a population of United way-affiliated nonprofits', *Public Administration Review*, **61** (3), 276–89.

Toepler, Stefan and Maryann Feldman (2004), 'Philanthropic foundations and the innovation function: evidence from a survey of university researchers', paper presented at the 33rd Annual ARNOVA Conference, Omni Los Angeles Hotel, Los Angeles, 18–20 November.

Wedel, Kenneth (1976), 'Government contracting for purchase of service', *Social Work*, **21** (2), 101–05.

Weisbrod, Burton A. (ed.) (1998), *To Profit or Not to Profit? The Commercial Transformation of the Nonprofit Sector*, Cambridge and New York: Cambridge University Press.

Wing, Kennard, Thomas Pollak and Amy Blackwood (2008), *The Nonprofit Almanac 2008*, Washington, DC: Urban Institute Press.

Wyszomirski, Margaret J. and Kevin Mulcahy (1995), 'The organization of public support for the arts', in Kevin Mulcahy and Margaret J. Wyszomirski (eds), *America's Commitment to Culture: Government and the Arts*, Boulder, CO: Westview Press, pp. 121–43.

Young, Dennis R. (2006), 'Complementary, supplementary, or adversarial? Government–nonprofit relations', in Elizabeth T. Boris and C. Eugene Steuerle (eds), *Nonprofits and Government: Collaboration and Conflict*, Washington, DC: Urban Institute Press, pp. 37–79.

Zeigler, Joseph Wesley (1994), *Arts in Crisis: the National Endowment for the Arts versus America*, Pennington, NJ: A Cappella Books.

Index

abandonment 204
abortion 325
Abrams, B.A. 20, 21, 26
Abramson, A. 324
academic journals 144, 145–6
accountability 120, 133, 173, 191, 217, 222, 249, 324
accounting, *see* social accounting; traditional accounting
accounting profits 203
Accounting Standards Steering Committee (ASSC) 267
accounts receivable 69–70
Achievement First 197, 198
adjusted qualifying distribution 44
administrative expenditures 29, 42, 43, 44, 130, 132, 135–6, 172
administrative salaries 130, 132
advocacy 326, 332
affirmative businesses 199
agency problems 121, 124, 132, 138–9, 156, 158, 166, 171, 230–32, 234
agglomeration economies 310
airline pricing 152
Albrecht, W.S. 276
Alchian–Allen theorem 144
Alexander, J. 174
Allman, T.D. 316
allocative efficiency 132–3
alternative risk transfer 167
altruism 9, 22, 32, 33, 97, 99–101, 103, 104, 108–9
American Association of Collegiate Registrars and Admissions Officers (AACRAO) 174
American Association of Museums (AAM) 75, 175, 225
American Association of Retired Persons 7
American Cancer Society 222, 223, 233, 316
American Civil Liberties Union 110
American Economic Association (AEA) 8
American Institute of Certified Public Accountants 264
American Management Association 170
American Medical Association (AMA) 8
American Red Cross 6, 8, 29, 36, 142, 156
American Symphony Orchestra League (ASOL) 134, 135, 220, 229, 230
American Time-use Survey (ATUS) 241, 242

Americans for the Arts 175
AmeriCorps 270
Amernic, J. 265, 276
Amnesty International 201
Amos, O.M. 26
ancillary activities 36–7, 38, 144, 146
Anderson, D. 315
Anderson, R.G.W. 143
Andreoni, J. 9, 27, 28, 29, 35, 65, 203, 329
Andrews, J. 28–9
Anheier, H.K. 211, 325–6
Ansari, A. 143
Anthony, R.N. 264
antitrust regulation 104, 142, 143, 145, 151
Arnsberger, P. 48
Arrow, K.J. 27, 108, 126, 157
arts, culture and humanities sector
   contracting out by 180–81, 185, 187
   measuring regional economic impact in 275
   see also arts organizations; arts programs
arts organizations
   contracting out by 175, 176
   location of 310
arts programs
   funding of 22, 28, 30, 33, 35, 36, 321, 322, 324, 325
   see also performing arts
Ashbury Images 251, 258–60
asset allocation 69–81
   asset partitioning 73–4
   double bottom line 77–8, 79, 80
   endowment and restricted assets 76–7
   expanding research on 79–80
   interaction of capital structure and business models 74–5
   liquidity 69–71
   reasons for gaps in knowledge concerning 78–9
   restricted and other privileged assets 75–6
   risk control 71–3
asset partitioning 73–4
asthma 227–8
asymmetric information 9, 107–8, 116, 121, 126, 133, 170, 209, 232, 280, 281
Atkinson, R. 291
Atlanta 310, 316
attendance maximization 134, 135, 136
auditing 173, 179, 181, 189, 190